China's Economic Culture

China's spectacular rise challenges established economic moulds, both at the national level, with the concept of 'state capitalism', and at the firm level, with the notion of indigenous 'Chinese management practices'. However, both Chinese and Western observers emphasize the transitional nature of the reforms, thereby leaving open the question as to whether China's reform process is really a fast catch-up process, with ultimate convergence to global standards, or something different. This book, by a leading economist and sinologist, argues that 'culture' is an exceptionally useful tool to help understand fully the current picture of the Chinese economy. Drawing on a range of disciplines including social psychology, cognitive sciences, institutional economics and Chinese studies, the book examines long-run path dependencies and cultural legacies, and shows how these contribute crucially to the current cultural construction of economic systems, business organizations and patterns of embedding the economy in society and politics.

Carsten Herrmann-Pillath is Permanent Fellow of the Max Weber Centre for Advanced Cultural and Social Studies, Erfurt University, Germany, Research Professor of Economics and Evolutionary Sciences, Witten/Herdecke University, Germany, and a Distinguished Visiting Professor of Schwarzman Scholars at Tsinghua University, China.

Routledge Studies in the Growth Economies of Asia

121 **Intellectual Property Valuation and Innovation**
Towards global harmonisation
Edited by Ruth Taplin

122 **Marketing and Consumption in Modern Japan**
Kazuo Usui

123 **Economic Growth and Employment in Vietnam**
David Lim

124 **Asian Financial Integration**
Impacts of the global crisis and options for regional policies
Edited by Yiping Huang and Shiro Armstrong

125 **Informal Labour in Urban India**
Three cities, three journeys
Tom Barnes

126 **Business Leadership Development in China**
Shuang Ren, Robert Wood and Ying Zhu

127 **Women, Labour and the Economy in India**
From migrant menservants to uprooted girl children maids
Deepita Chakravarty and Ishita Chakravarty

128 **Negotiating Financial Agreement in East Asia**
Surviving the turbulence
Kaewkamol Karen Pitakdumrongkit

129 **Managing Cyber Risk in the Financial Sector**
Lessons from Asia, Europe and the USA
Edited by Ruth Taplin

130 **Chinese Economic Diplomacy**
Shuxiu Zhang

131 **China's Iron Ore Boom**
Luke W.L. Hurst

132 **Economic Change In Asia**
Implication for corporate strategy and social responsibility
Edited by M. Bruna Zolin, Bernadette Andreosso-O'Callaghan and Jacques Jaussaud

133 **China's Economic Culture**
The ritual order of state and markets
Carsten Herrmann-Pillath

This book is an outstanding piece of work that combines profound knowledge of China's economic history with methodological creativity to establish a new paradigm, *China's ritual economy*. Drawing on an impressive amount of sources and tackling brilliantly the complex relationship between cultural tradition and economic behaviour, Herrmann-Pillath may have come up with the ultimate explanation of what Chinese capitalism in modern times is all about. A must-read!

Gunter Schubert, *Professor of Greater China Studies, University of Tübingen, Germany*

Rituals are fundamental institutions, but often ignored by people. Apart from researching on rituals as classics, most scholars know little about them. In this book, Professor Herrmann-Pillath gives us a key to understanding China's business culture, which is to regard rituals or customs as the behavior patterns which still exist fundamentally and universally in modern society. To understand rituals or customs is more important than to understand written laws, if one would like successful commercial cooperation in China. Meanwhile, this analysis develops a new, correct research approach academically.

Sheng Hong, *Unirule Institute of Economics, Beijing, China*

This is a very thought provoking and important book. It takes a big step towards a more systematic understanding of Chinese economy and society by unfolding the bold hypotheses of understanding the process of modernization in China in terms of ritual. It is unusual by its interdisciplinary approach combining anthropology and philosophy with economics. It puts China's present into the context of China's past and thus transgresses the border between those who focus on modern China and those who strive to understand ancient China.

Susanne Weigelin-Schwiedrzik, *Professor of Sinology, University of Vienna, Austria*

This work is an exemplary study in the tradition of Max Weber and Karl Polanyi yet going beyond these 'Old Masters' in its theoretical ambition and analytical scope. Carsten Herrmann-Pillath demonstrates beyond any doubt that no one can understand China's economy (everything from family firms to state-owned enterprises to macroeconomic policies) without investigating the entire cultural-institutional package that comes with it. In China economic practices are not simply *embedded in culture*; they are the culture. The economist can do no worse than embracing theoretical insights from anthropology, sociology and cultural history, and as a result better grasp the *style* of any particular economic culture. This book provides the methodological roadmap for this kind of genuinely multi-disciplinary work. Highly recommended for students of China, economists as well as intellectually-oriented executives.

Adam Yuet Chau, *University Senior Lecturer in the Anthropology of Modern China, University of Cambridge, UK*

China's Economic Culture

The ritual order of state and markets

Carsten Herrmann-Pillath

Routledge
Taylor & Francis Group
LONDON AND NEW YORK

First published 2017 by Routledge

2 Park Square, Milton Park, Abingdon, Oxfordshire OX14 4RN
711 Third Avenue, New York, NY 10017

Routledge is an imprint of the Taylor & Francis Group, an informa business

First issued in paperback 2018

British Library Cataloguing-in-Publication Data
A catalogue record for this book is available from the British Library

Library of Congress Cataloging in Publication Data
Names: Herrmann-Pillath, Carsten, author.
Title: China's economic culture : the ritual order of state and markets / Carsten Herrmann-Pillath.
Description: Abingdon, Oxon ; New York, NY : Routledge, 2017. |
Series: Routledge studies in the growth economies of Asia ; 133 |
Includes bibliographical references and index.
Identifiers: LCCN 2016017515| ISBN 9780415711272 (hardback) |
ISBN 9781315884653 (ebook)
Subjects: LCSH: Economic development–China. | Economics–China. |
Economics–Sociological aspects. | China–Economic conditions. |
China–Civilization.
Classification: LCC HC427 .H473 2017 | DDC 306.30951–dc23
LC record available at https://lccn.loc.gov/2016017515

ISBN: 978-0-415-71127-2 (hbk)
ISBN: 978-1-138-58808-0 (pbk)

Typeset in Baskerville
by Wearset Ltd, Boldon, Tyne and Wear

Dedicated to the memory of
Professor Masahiko Aoki
and
Dr Werner Jackstädt

The printing of this book has been supported by a Deutsche Forschungsgemeinschaft DFG grant.

Contents

Figures

Preface

This book has had a very long gestation period, being actually the successor volume to my book *Institutional Change, Power and Inflation in China: Approaching the Political Economy of Transition from the Perspective of the Theory of Order* ('Institutioneller Wandel, Macht und Inflation in China: Ordnungstheoretische Analysen der Politischen Ökonomie eines Transformationsprozesses') published in 1991. In this book, I unfolded a panorama of the Chinese economy and politics focusing on the genesis of the events of 1989, venturing to unearth the economic, institutional and cultural deep structures that underlay the interaction between macroeconomic dynamics and political events. As I do in my new book, I went back to distinct theories in German-speaking economics of the first half of the twentieth century, which opened up the vista for the pivotal role of the interplay between state building and market transition, and which I combined with new theoretical notions that, at that time, had just been introduced into the study of China's recent history, namely 'economic involution' and 'state involution', coined by Philip Huang and Prasenjit Duara, respectively, which I connected with detailed accounts of the ideational history of reforms in the 1980s.

My new book is written in the same spirit, but against the backdrop of 25 years of historically unprecedented economic growth and social change, combined with the resilience of Communist Party rule. In 1991, many observers, including myself, envisaged China as approaching a trap of stalled economic and social change, facing high risks of instability and, given the events in the Soviet Union, even the possibility of collapse. Nothing could be further from what really happened. Thus, throughout these 25 years, I pondered the simple question, 'Why'? As an economist, philosopher and sinologist I was convinced that the answer to this question cannot simply rely on historical accidence, such as the lucky conjunction of internal economic reforms and the newly emerging patterns of globalization. Further, I believed that the central hypothesis in my 1991 book, namely that the interaction between state building and marketization is a key to understanding the dynamics of Chinese development, would still remain valid. Meanwhile, I continued to invest much effort in developing theoretical and conceptual foundations for institutional and evolutionary analysis in economics, ranging from international economics to behavioural theory. This work provides the background for deploying the core concept in this book with which I have been concerned since my time as a student of economics: the concept of 'economic culture'.

German-speaking economics has a long tradition of explicitly including culture into economic analysis that goes back to Germany's experience as a 'latecomer' in development, and the corresponding intellectual needs to ground the notion of autonomous paths of development in theorizing about history, beginning with seminal contributions such as List's. There is a deep affinity with current Chinese developments, as Germany's catch-up happened in the context of an authoritarian political system, yet undergirded by distinct forms of liberal thought, such as Hegel's emphasizing both state and market as fundamental aspects of social order. These intellectual traditions nurtured approaches to economic analysis that differed substantially from what was eventually established as 'economics' in the twentieth century, and which were cross-disciplinary in nature. This included intellectual giants who today are not even perceived as contributing to the development of economics proper; above all, Max Weber. I think that this is very unfortunate, because the sheer complexity of cases such as the Chinese one forbids deploying single-disciplinary approaches, and calls for methodological pluralism.

This book builds on another antecedent volume published in German most recently: *Growth, Power and Order: Approaching China from the Viewpoint of Economic Philosophy* ('Wachstum, Macht und Ordnung: Eine wirtschaftsphilosophische Auseinandersetzung mit China') in which I concentrate on these theoretical and methodological underpinnings, though it is also based on thorough and detailed empirical analysis. The fundamental difference between the two books results from the fact that I now explore the central idea that emerged from the previous book, only incipiently visible, namely taking the notion of 'ritual' as the unifying distinct marker of China's economic culture. Thus, I joke that the German book is a 'working paper' in preparation for the basis of this book.

I try to present a condensed analytical picture of the Chinese economic system as embedded into larger social, cultural and political contexts, and I ground these analyses on very detailed pictures of empirical realities, as expounded in what is an astonishingly broad and penetrating body of China research accumulated over past decades, integrating different disciplinary resources, in particular economics, anthropology, sociology or political science. This extremely large literature has created the literal risk of 'seeing the trees, but not the forest', also inducing the danger of being increasingly driven by academic fads and fashions in today's hypercompetitive academia. The argument in my book is deliberately, even provocatively simple, yet claiming comprehensive reach. In order to make my points as clearly as possible, the book actually consists of two parts: the main text and the chapter endnotes. The endnotes play an essential role, as I have included in them most of the academic discussion and empirical details, including all the references, whereas in the main text I present my argument in an almost apodictic way, for clarity, but also out of personal commitment.

I am grateful to many people who accompanied me on my intellectual journey during the 25 years following the publication of my first attempt at integration and synthesis in studying the Chinese economy: too many to pay tribute to all of them here (I give more details in the Preface of the 2015 German book). In the context of the present book, I want to mention just a few who played a crucial role in its gestation, also in representing all the others (and with apologies to the latter). These are, of course, my Chinese intellectual friends with whom I have collaborated, who were my Ph.D. students initially, and are now respected scholars in Chinese academia, namely Feng Xingyuan and Hu Biliang. One of my recent Ph.D. students, Guo Man, played an important role in envisaging the theoretical importance of the notion of 'ritual', since I had first proposed this idea to him, and he explored its ramifications and potential in his own thesis independently (recently published as *Rituals, Performativity of Economics and Chinese Management* in Chinese). I was lucky to be able to pick up many suggestions and remarks made by other colleagues: Gunter Schubert read the entire manuscript and allowed me to share his immense knowledge on China, and the title of the book is based on a suggestion by Adam Chau. My old friends at the Unirule Institute, Beijing, in particular Sheng Hong and Yao Zhongqiu, were always a source of inspiration.

This book is dedicated to two individuals who were essential to my personal development during the past decade. Dr Werner Jackstädt was an entrepreneur who established a foundation in Wuppertal (the Dr Werner Jackstädt Foundation), which has supported my work on China since 2004, and who regarded China as pivotal also for Germany in the future; I was lucky to meet him before he passed away, receiving one of the last grant approvals that was decided by himself in person. In particular, the Foundation supported the establishment of the East West Centre of Business Studies and Cultural Science (now defunct) where I was able to assemble a wonderful China team (Genia Kostka, Alexander Libman, my Ph.D. students, Yu Xiaofan, Philipp Boeing, Ke Xing). from which I learned a great deal. I combined this with financial support from the Federal Ministry of Education and Research in the context of the research network 'KomPost' on Post-socialist evolutions: I am grateful for many inspiring conversations with my project partner Joachim Zweynert. Most recently, additional fieldwork support came from the Hermann und Marianne Straniak Foundation, Vienna.

The Jackstädt Foundation also supported a two-year stint at Witten/ Herdecke University in order to complete this book, where I enjoyed strong personal and institutional support from Birger Priddat. I was extremely lucky to combine this with a long-term Fellowship at the Max Weber Centre for Advanced Cultural and Social Studies at Erfurt University, where Bettina Hollstein and Jörg Rüpke have always encouraged my work. During that time, I joined the DFG (Deutsche Forschungsgemeinschaft) international research group on religious individualization and received much inspiration for developing my ideas on individualism and popular religion in China, which play an important role in my thoughts on economic style. Moreover, the group supported the publication of this voluminous book with a generous subsidy.

Masahiko Aoki is the other person to whom I dedicate this book. When I was a Ph.D. student, his book on the Japanese economy was an essential reading experience in my intellectual growth. In the past decade, he supported my work in many ways, and his influence is highly visible in the theoretical chapter of this book (Chapter 1). Before he recently passed away, he dedicated much effort to the study of China, especially emphasizing the long-term historical perspective. Unfortunately, he was not able to complete this work, and he did not see the final version of my book manuscript. His legacy will grow forever.

This book was completed during difficult times for me and my family. Without the spiritual and emotional help of my beloved wife Sigrun and the immense joy (to be frank, including lots of nerve-racking distractions) of our children, it would not have been possible to fulfil the numerous challenges that I encountered.

Introduction

This book is the result of 30 years of scholarly effort in understanding the Chinese economy. Throughout this long period, observers trained as economists often expressed the expectation that China will eventually fail to achieve her goals of rapid modernization and economic prosperity unless she adopts the institutions of what is commonly called 'Western modernity'. Whereas other social sciences have been discussing the relevance of this benchmark for many years, economics remains stubbornly attached to the belief that it is possible to define a set of institutions that are most advanced in terms of performance, and hence represent 'modernity'. Take, for example, the fast and strong impact of the so-called 'legal origin' theory of economic institutions, which even presented the most explicit claim that common law institutions perform better than civil law institutions in shaping financial markets and corporate governance. In contrast, Chinese institutions always appeared as deviant, so ultimately they must fail. After arriving at the position of the second largest economy in the world, the most recent version of this attitude is the writing on the wall invoking the threat of the 'middle-income trap'. However, none of these doomsday scenarios ever materialized, which had included the fragmentation of China following the USSR example in the early 1990s. I think that this will remain true, although no one can claim to be able to predict history, even in the medium term.

The pessimistic stance towards China is mostly based on the analysis of Chinese institutions, combining with theoretical analysis and empirical information about the past performance of advanced industrialized countries. This reference has been shifting in recent years. Whereas the 1980s and 1990s were shaped by concepts of the 'Washington Consensus' enshrining the so-called 'neoliberal' turn in thinking about economic policy, in the 2000s a more pragmatic approach held sway, in particular following the financial crisis of 2008. Now, what in the past appeared to be heterodox measures of the Chinese approach, such as industrial policy and capital account controls, is becoming part of a pragmatic mainstream. The Chinese experience certainly contributed to this shift. However, following Dani Rodrik's famous dictum of 'one economics, many recipes', this shift still remains within the confines of standard economic theory. This is salient in one of the most comprehensive 'indigenous' attempts at distilling general conclusions for economic theory from the Chinese experience, namely Justin Lin's 'new structural economics', which is a merging of neoclassical theories of comparative advantage with a descriptive account of developmental stages in the context of globalization.

Thus, the core question in analysing China's economy is the role of institutions, and structural or macroeconomic characteristics come second. In this area we observe a very lively debate between different schools of thought in economics, with some explicitly defining an alternative vision to whatever might be regarded as mainstream in economics today. Yet, today, institutions are also the focus of core research interests of the mainstream, and this is often driven by the normative concern for identifying the sources of the 'wealth of nations', the ingredients of the 'European miracle', and the causes of 'why nations fail'. One conspicuous observation about this literature is the neglect or very superficial treatment of China, both past and present. Most of these accounts retell the familiar Whiggish story about institutional progress towards what is basically the Anglo-Saxon model of capitalism, and they argue in stark dualisms, such as 'autocracy' versus 'democracy', or 'limited access orders' versus 'open access orders', and so forth. These dualisms appear to be substitutes for the earlier dualism of 'market economy' versus 'planned economy', which is, of course, also the stage on which the Chinese 'transition' is seen to be unfolding.

This is a highly significant observation because to a certain extent the debate about current Chinese developments matches the literature on China's economic and social history. The latter is often also caught in the dualism between China and 'the West', since a major and still unresolved question is why China failed to give birth to an industrial revolution in spite of having been far more advanced than Europe in the Middle Ages. Many explanations blame institutions and therefore contribute to the mainstream opinion that Western-style institutions are a necessary factor in achieving sustainable growth of per-capita incomes. Thus, current predictions of the eventual failure of Chinese reforms would converge with those analytical approaches to Chinese economic history: China's failure in the past predicts China's failure in the future unless Western modernity is adopted. This belief is certainly undergirded by the observation that almost all intellectual and political leaders of China in the twentieth century also upheld this view, with the slight variation that Marxism had been introduced to China as the most advanced Western theory, thus apparently allowing even for overtaking the West in terms of modernization. Modernization was also the clarion call for Chinese reforms after 1978. Against this backdrop, the paradox of combining a socialist system with a capitalist economy is partly resolved by recognizing that upholding socialism as the ideological beacon may still be seen as a reference to the more fundamental claim on becoming a vanguard of modernity. The relationship between the Chinese present and China's past, however, remains an unresolved issue in this view.

Interpreting recent Chinese history as a story about failed modernization is by no means settled truth. In the past two decades, revisionist historical research has emerged that matches with critical views on the mainstream accounts of Western history. This not only touches upon empirical issues of historical accuracy but also relates to foundational issues in the theory of institutions. The revisionist literature on China basically asserts that Chinese institutions were defining a 'Smithian' economy, thus securing and maintaining the efficient functioning of markets. This view is based on the recognition of certain facts, such as the pivotal role of contracts in arranging economic transactions since the Song dynasty, and on acknowledging functional equivalences such as the correspondence between the European notion of the 'corporation' with traditional social entities such as lineage trusts. This literature implies that the institutions of markets may be necessary but by no means sufficient conditions for modern economic growth and capitalism. In the Chinese case, some contributions would even make the stronger point that the efficient functioning of markets impeded the emergence of capitalist technology and corresponding social formations. Against this backdrop there are two major alternative explanations of the Chinese failure to modernize. The first points towards ecological and geophysical conditions for the cost-effectiveness of new technologies harnessing new sources of energy; the second emphasizes the weakness of government in fulfilling the role as a provider of infrastructure, both material and institutional.

The second explanation apparently leads back to the institutional analysis, albeit with an important shift of perspective. Taking liberal or even libertarian concepts of the market economy as a benchmark, the Chinese empire after the Ming dynasty was an institutional regime that factually left much more freedom for a market-based self-organization of society than most European countries on the eve of industrialization. This is most saliently manifested in the very low tax burden per capita which was partly the result of intentional political decisions of the Qing emperors. In comparison, England had emerged as a highly centralized state capable of imposing very high tax burdens on society. The Whiggish interpretation of this is that increasing political participation in England and emerging legal constraints upon abuse of governmental power led towards stabilizing this institutional regime because of higher legitimacy and acceptance on the part of those social groups which were actually pushing industrialization forward. However, in these arguments the historical record about the performance of other catching-up economies is presented in a seriously distorted fashion. For example, Germany relied on a model of authoritarian market liberalization that contradicts such generalizations of Whiggish history. Therefore, taking both records together, we may conclude that modern capitalism is not necessarily based on constrained government in a general sense, but, in the opposite extreme, on certain formations of strong institutions of government and markets that may be even historically unique in every country case.

Obviously, this argument is highly relevant for China today. The current leadership is pursuing a policy that simultaneously enhances the scope of markets and further strengthens the government, especially in the sense of the central government. China, like Prussia in the nineteenth century, represents the case of authoritarian liberalization, which may sound like an oxymoron to many liberal economists. This position would partly revive similar debates about developmental authoritarianism or even dictatorship in the context of the earlier 'East Asian miracles'. However, a closer look at this would lead analysis astray, at least as an explanation of the Chinese performance thus far.

One of the central arguments in this book is that market transition in China is concomitant to the effort of concluding the unfinished process of state building in China following the collapse of the Empire. More succinctly and provocatively, I claim that markets (and capitalism) after 1978 evolved in the niches created by the ongoing transformation of an empire into a modern state. State building is mainly taking place in two arenas. The first is the dynamics of the relationship between the central government and the local states of China, a fact which is recognized in recent characterizations of the Chinese political economy as 'regionally decentralized authoritarianism'. The second is the institutional and cultural dualism between the rural and urban areas and its impact upon administrative and bureaucratic integration of the Chinese state. This thesis of the primacy of state building for market transition in China may appear less surprising if one considers the fact that Maoism left a legacy of institutional disruption and chaos in the trajectory of state building which had been launched in Republican China, leading towards the verge of dissolving the Chinese nation under the tensions of civil war and Japanese aggression.

If we look at these historical changes in more detail, we cannot avoid the issue of the role of culture in understanding China. The question of how culture and institutions interplay in China's development is the central topic of this book. Since Max Weber, many explanations of the Chinese failure to modernize refer to culture, and in this respect also emphasize the relationship between culture and the nature of the Chinese Imperial state. Thus, I believe that investigating the issue of state building leads us to explore culture in its relationship to economics. This question has been the beacon towards which my own research on China has been directed in the past three decades.

Culture receives much attention in current mainstream economics, after it had been neglected for many years. Many economists seem to agree today that culture is an essential mediating factor between institutions and economic performance, and a major factor channelling institutional change in a certain direction. This view would correspond to the aforementioned approaches to Chinese history. But there is a fundamental methodological difficulty in these arguments.

When economists refer to culture, they largely treat it as an exogenous determinant of economic processes, typically in terms of positing a causal pattern between past variables and current observations, such as historical facts about migration and current values held by a population. This view is very different from modern approaches in anthropology that treat culture as a creative activity. In fact, the economic approach violates fundamental tenets of methodological individualism, whereas the anthropological view sees an active role for individuals, though not necessarily conceived along the lines of rational choice models. The picture of culture that emerges here is a far cry from the view that culture is a legacy of the past which people cannot discharge easily. On the contrary, all cultural activity is innovation, resulting into cultural syntheses, creolism, as well as the revival of tradition. What is a legacy of the past, in this view, is the whole range of symbols, ideas, values, norms or institutions that make up a semiotic repertoire which is handled by cultural activity in the present. Evidently, this may also create continuities between past and present, but these are endogenous to the process of cultural change driven by creative action. Reviving tradition always means creating a new tradition.

This is the perspective on culture that I adopt in this book. If we look at the uses of culture in studies of the Chinese economy, we often meet sweeping simplifications, the most influential one being the notion of 'Confucian capitalism' that was created in dealing with the phenomenal success of Overseas Chinese business in the rise of the Asia Pacific as an economic region. The image of Confucianism as the defining feature of Chinese culture is widespread in economics and management studies, even in terms of introducing a specific set of so-called Confucian values in universal sets of values, or in denoting the entire East Asian region as 'Confucian'. I present a very different approach in this book. If one treats culture as an activity, the culture of the contemporary Chinese economy would emerge as a bricolage of many different elements, traditions, Maoist legacies, imported ideas and norms, and so forth, without any pre-fixed borderline between the 'cultural' and the 'non-cultural'. Chinese culture today is a complex synthesis of which Confucianism may be a part, but probably not a defining one. Again, we recognize similarities between China's past and present. If Confucianism is seen as an important element in traditional Chinese culture, then it is only in the sense of one element in an array of many others, often even staying in tension.

But, after all, this kind of definitional openness would render the term 'culture' almost without precise meaning and reference, so I will offer another radical methodological proposition; namely that culture is always a construct of the observer, and by no means an 'objective' fact of social life. In other words, if culture is a creative activity of the subjects which are the object of inquiry, the observer is also creating culture when she presents her research results. Thus, a book about economic culture like this one is also a cultural activity, even in the sense of co-creating Chinese culture. This is a conceptual conundrum that has been well known to anthropologists for a long time, but that has almost never been recognized in economics. I claim that we need to deploy an economic approach which starts out from this fundamental insight. Thus, this book is not only a contribution to the study of China, but also a contribution to economic methodology.

There is one intellectual precursor in economics, which is the German language literature on 'Wirtschaftsstile' (economic styles) which emerged out of the methodological debates about Weber's distinction between real types and ideal types, and his view that economic analysis would only obtain empirical meaning once it is embedded in cultural analysis ('Kulturwissenschaft'). An economic style is akin to a style in the history of arts. There are certain features of artworks which make them similar, and which are recognized by contemporaries as defining characteristics of this group of artefacts. The art historian, however, may also be able to recognize larger patterns through time ex post, and therefore may be able to detect some boundaries and distinctions of which contemporaries were not fully aware. But this does not imply that the perspective of the art historian turns into an 'objective' view. After all, what matters for the dynamics of the history of styles is what contemporaries perceive, what they receive, and what they create out of that. Philosophically, the concept of style is an instance of what Wittgenstein has called 'family resemblances' among games, in this sense 'forms of life'. Thus, detecting and describing family resemblances diachronically and synchronically is the major task of the researcher on economic styles. 'Diachronically' means pinpointing family resemblances between past and present; 'synchronically' means doing the same for a wide range of contemporary case studies with thick descriptions, across industries, sectors or regions. Indeed, this is what contemporary Chinese studies have accomplished in past decades, namely accumulating an extremely rich collection of detailed case studies on social, political and economic change.

It is important to emphasize that applying the 'economic style' concept results in an entirely different approach to the taxonomy of economic systems than the prevailing one. The established approach classifies economic systems according to fundamental properties of mechanisms of allocation (plan versus market) or ownership (private versus public) or finance (banking vs. capital market based) and so on. These properties are seen as being amenable to 'objective' analysis, including also propositions about the causal relationship between those features and economic performance. In contrast, the concept of economic style follows the principles of biological taxonomy. In other words, categories such as 'species' are certain emerging units in a historical trajectory of evolving forms, which are defined according to certain shared characteristics, and which are located in particular geographical areas. In a similar vein, an economic style is a unit that is defined as belonging to a certain economy at a certain place and in a certain period, which relates historically to certain precursors, and which also stays in relationship with other economies from which it differs. Further, this unit is itself defined in fractal terms. This means that if we talk of 'the economy', this is in fact a complex system of interacting smaller units such as regional economies, industries or even households. These units, amenable to case studies, also manifest family resemblances in their evolution through time, which in the aggregate define the economic style. If we take these two aspects together, we realize that the concept of style has the same properties as the concept of culture. An economic style is a complex set of properties which stay in a certain systematic relationship with each other and which connect with other properties through time and space. Thus, for example, we cannot simply say that there is an 'economic system of China' today which may relate to an economic system of China in earlier times, but we have to ask whether there are certain properties of economic interactions and structures in China today which tie up with other properties in the past, and which manifest peculiar interactions with properties of other economic systems. For example, we might ask how intellectual property rights in China today relate to similar concepts in the past and to similar constructs in the USA. We may further ask how they relate to similar concepts such as land-use rights in China and so forth. Once we have collected a sufficiently large number of observations of this kind, we are able to construct a coherent and distinctive concept of 'style'.

If this idea emerged in German-speaking economics, it is no wonder that it has been revived in the work of a German-speaking economist. Indeed, the economic system in Germany today is characterized as the 'Social Market Economy'. This term was originally introduced as a peculiar 'economic style' by the German economist Alfred Müller-Armack. Clearly, Germany is classified as a 'capitalist' or 'market economy', but this does not echo the distinct features that become visible when considering the tensions between different member countries of the European Union over issues of economic policy, or between the USA and Germany as a member of the EU when negotiating trade agreements. The social market economy is an economic style in combining a number of very distinct features of economic organization into one coherent whole, as diverse as the social security system, the system of savings banks or the role of family business. This characterization can by no means be established as an objective fact, since it is the object of continuous debates and reflections in Germany about what are the constitutive elements of this model. However, at the same time the majority of participants in this debate agree that the social market economy is a defining feature of the German economy after the Second World War, and, historians would add, probably since the time of Bismarck's social reforms, in incipient form.

As this observation on Germany shows, the essential step in constructing an economic style is to identify a concept that may be used as a unifying idea in order to systematize the observations. In the German case, this is the notion of 'social'. Clearly, this is almost meaningless if considered in isolation, but it becomes an extremely powerful idea in the ongoing process of constructing the economic style, both on the part of the participant actors and the scientific observer.

In this book, I propose that the notion of 'ritual' plays a similar role in the Chinese case. 'Ritual', 'li' (礼), has been the central term in defining social order in Chinese civilization since its emergence. Twentieth-century modernization was also defined as a radical attempt at overcoming this social order, hence also transforming and even abolishing ritual. Yet, I claim that China's economic style is the 'ritual economy'. Tellingly, this term has been coined by anthropologists working on China, but it is still rarely used, and is confined to much more narrow meanings. In one of the seminal contributions by Mayfair Yang, the important point is made that ritual is a defining feature of rural society, but that this rural society is also a driver of the ongoing changes in the modern Chinese economy. This would suggest that transformations of ritual also impact upon economic modernization. I generalize on these ideas in trying to show that ritual is also essential in the 'modern' part of the trajectory, because, to begin with, modernization itself is interpreted in the same way as a ritual. In the indigenous Chinese discourse, ritual does not show up explicitly as a term designating current views on the foundations of social order, yet the notion of 'harmony' is intrinsically linked to ritual as a means of establishing harmony (even to the extent that the Confucian 'he wei gui' expression is used). In the current political discourse, the Western notion of a modern social order is apparently applied in emphasizing the 'law' as the alternative principle. Yet reference to ritual is often made when Chinese scholars discuss indigenous perspectives on social relations and values, especially, again, when referring to rural society.

That being said, I use the term 'ritual' in a deliberately ambiguous way. I treat it both as a generic theoretical term and as a term specific to China studies. I argue that this ambiguity renders the term especially powerful in analysing the Chinese economic style. Regarding the generic use, I follow the seminal contribution by Michael Chwe who introduced 'ritual' as a term into the game theoretic analysis of social interaction. Here, ritual encompasses all social actions that create common knowledge. Common knowledge is a central notion in game theory that catches reflexive knowledge; in other words, what people know that other people know that they know, and so forth. In this sense, common knowledge is evidently also part and parcel of what we normally refer to as 'culture', especially in the sense of shared features that go without saying, and are the preconditions for successful interaction. We may also say that ritual includes features that people know how to enact, but not necessarily knowing that they enact them ('knowing how', but not 'knowing that'). In other words, common knowledge engendered by ritual includes a fair amount of tacit knowledge. What the notion of ritual adds to the game theoretic uses of the term 'common knowledge' is that ritual is externalized behaviour involving artefacts, and not just a state of mind as is normally assumed in game theory. This renders common knowledge partly observable, although we clearly need to distinguish between ritual as such and the states of knowledge that ritual instigates. Since we cannot directly access those states of mind, however, observing ritual is a major point of access for understanding culture, and requires interpretive approaches. This is certainly all too familiar to the anthropologist but has rarely been included in economic analysis.

Considering this general notion of ritual, we now notice an important observation about ritual in Chinese society. Ritual is a central category in Chinese tradition. Many scholars have approached ritual as the essential difference between traditional Chinese culture and 'Western' culture in terms of the dichotomy between ritual and law. Interestingly, a related dichotomy also holds in Chinese tradition, namely the distinction between Confucian ritual and legalist law; and, most ominously, in current debates about law in contemporary China, Western 'rule of law' is often compared to Chinese 'rule by law', which certainly has a distinctly legalist flavour in the midst of what is often seen as a revival of Confucianism, both at grass-roots level and in relation to political leadership. Thus, the question arises whether the role of law in contemporary China is shaped by its interaction with ritual, as in Imperial times.

This book presents the hypothesis that 'ritual' can serve as a unifying idea for constructing the economic style of China, both in the generic sense and the culturally specific use of the term. As I outlined previously, this is not a hypothesis based on empirically tested theory, but a cultural construction by myself as the author of this book. Methodologically, 'ritual' serves as an intermediate theoretical term that is not universal, but only applies for a certain slice of time and space. However, I think that there are certain generic theoretical arguments as to why this hypothesis could be powerful in empirical work. One alternative generic approach to the issues at hand is distinguishing between formal and informal institutions and arguing that these two can stay in a diverse relationship with each other. Interestingly, this almost matches with the treatment of ritual vs. law by the foremost Chinese anthropologist of the twentieth century, Fei Xiaotong. In a nutshell, Fei argued that rituals are the informal institutions of traditional rural society, and that the modernization of China requires the transition to formal institutions enshrined by written law, which is the institutional framework of large-scale urban societies. However, this opposition suffers from overlooking the fact that ritual in traditional China was partly a formal institution, that shaping ritual intentionally was the central element in the Confucian way of governing China, and that ritual also held sway in the large cities of Imperial China. For example, traditional lineage organization in the rural areas was certainly a formal institution, and the Imperial state invested huge effort in shaping local practices even by means of the law. Therefore, if we connect these observations with the notion of state building, we cannot simply say that modernization is tantamount to the transition from informal to formal institutions, or from ritual to law. Vice versa, this opens up horizons in order to ponder the relevance of ritual today, based on the generic term of ritual expounded in the context of game theory.

If we move back and forth between this China-specific view on ritual and the generic view, we realize that the blind spot in Western thought has a deeper meaning. In my own philosophical work while writing on China, I became aware of the crucial moment in intellectual history when ritual was blanked out and law became the dominant idea in the context of economics and related political philosophy. Tellingly, this directly relates to modern Chinese history. This historical crossroads was the separation of the Marxist line of thinking from the liberal one in the mid-nineteenth century, and the resulting oblivion of Hegel in Western liberal economic and political thought. For sure, Hegel was the intellectual founder of central liberal notions on civil society and the rule of law. This thinking was grounded in the analytical distinction between law as a formal institution and the 'ethical life' ('Sittlichkeit') in which the law must be embedded. Hegel saw ethical life as an expression of lifeworlds of concrete societies in historical contexts, thus eschewing any kind of abstract legal universalism along Kantian lines. Evidently, the Hegelian view comes close to the Chinese dichotomy of ritual and law, with ritual basically seen as a system of ethics that defines Chinese civilization. So, I think that pondering the Chinese case also makes us aware of the neglect of ethics in modern economic thinking about institutions. By implication, I argue elsewhere that Hegelian philosophy can offer a systematic conceptual framework for approaching the relationship between ritual and law both generically and in the case of China, but I largely refrain from these philosophical considerations in this book. Suffice it to say that the separation of law and ritual and the ensuing neglect of the latter is a Western cultural stance that emerged rather late in modern intellectual history. After all, the founder of modern economics, Adam Smith, was a moral philosopher who also saw a close relation between law as an institution and morality in concrete human societies.

As I have already pointed out, the intriguing fact about my 'ritual economy' notion is certainly that in contemporary China few people would use the term 'ritual' in order to describe their society, although in certain contexts related terms may show up, such as in describing local social interactions according to certain norms of proper behaviour (ritual as politeness and decency). My use of the term is mainly based on the analysis of a large number of empirical observations about institutions and practices, and I posit that the term 'ritual' makes sense of them, in the first place, and add the point that in the light of this interpretation, family resemblances with Imperial China are straightforward to establish. For instance, empirically, ritual refers to the role of status distinctions in governing social interactions, or to the emphasis on expressive behaviour manifest in certain routines as opposed to content. Status distinctions pervade the entire Chinese economy, such as between rural and urban society, between private and state-owned businesses, or between cadres and farmers. Status is expressed in a habitus of modernity, such as modern patterns of consumption activities. All these observations can be arranged into a coherent view once we start out from the notion of ritual. This is the task that I accomplish in this book. My use of the term 'ritual' also allows for connecting the China studies meaning with the generic meaning, because, for example, perceived status differences may be seen as being constitutive of common knowledge that constitutes frames for interactions, thus influencing certain economic processes, such as patterns of finance in rural private business.

If I apply 'ritual' as a unifying idea that refers to an indigenous notion of describing social order and interactions, a supporting argument is to recognize that there are other concepts specific to China studies that relate to this term and prove to be especially useful in establishing family resemblances between past and present. These are not necessarily indigenous terms, but have been developed in China studies to catch certain aspects in the descriptions of China which apparently do not lend themselves easily to direct equivalences with 'Western' institutions and practices. These concepts include, for example, 'orthopraxy', 'culturalism', the 'local state' or 'guanxi'. My argument will organize these concepts in the larger semantic field of ritual in order to achieve coherence and consistency. If we then reflect upon the relationship between ritual and modernity again, we realize what results to be the core idea of the book: modernization proper is conceived and socially performed as a ritual in China. Modernization does not overcome ritual, but is embedded in creative cultural constructions that are strongly shaped by ritual, and which in turn transform ritual. These cultural constructions result in what I define as the distinctively Chinese economic style.

Let me now summarize the chapters included in this book. Chapter 1 develops the theoretical framework of analysing the relationship between culture and economy. I relate the notion of 'culture' with the creative activity of individuals in fixing and expressing their shared identities in interactions. The fundamental methodological challenge to cultural analysis is the 'mirror of culture', which means that all conceptualizations of culture take place in a web of mutual interactions among different observers with different roles and standpoints, especially participant and external observers. Culture is not simply an 'object' in this web, but is continuously being created and re-created by those ongoing observations, communications and interactions. Thus, research on culture cannot rely on an 'objective' measure of culture, but is mainly a higher level reflection on what happens in the mirror of culture, which, however, is also fed back into these processes. I show how this puts standard economic approaches to culture into perspective, such as the use of value surveys in measuring and objectifying culture.

In terms of research methodology, my conclusion is that cultural analysis is proceeding as the triangulation of a variety of different disciplinary approaches, especially combining emic and etic methods into one coherent argument. Emic methods are provided, for example, by sinology as the study of China mediated via explicit consideration of Chinese language materials, written or oral; etic methods are represented by cognitive sciences or social psychology, among other disciplines. In order to coordinate these cross-disciplinary interactions a unifying idea is necessary, which bridges emics and etics. I propose that in the Chinese context this idea is 'ritual'.

The chapter presents a number of more specific analytical tools for cultural analysis, which build on existing approaches in the economic analysis of institutions. If culture is the activity of creating shared identities, we need to dissect this activity into its different aspects and stages. This means making the mechanisms explicit that enable and manifest this activity, which I define as the mechanisms of 'performativity', of performing culture. I propose that Aoki's economic model of institutions is very powerful in this regard, since it allows us to arrange observations on different levels of aggregation to each other, and explicitly includes the role of external artefacts in linking institutions and individual behaviour. Aoki's model is an equilibrium notion in the sense that an institution is regarded as the manifestation of a flow of interactions that results in their recurrent reproduction, embodied in external and public representations. I present a more detailed interpretation of the model that divides this flow into four stages, which form a closed loop with recurrent feedbacks. I call this the 'network approach to culture': actions, individuals, artefacts relate to each other in a causal web. This approach is a disaggregate analysis of social mechanisms which refers to certain objects of interactions with interpretive activities, resulting in certain states, such as social structure and economic outcomes, which feed back on the interactions through framing them. As a result, the notion of 'path dependencies' looms large in applying this approach. Path dependencies are essential for understanding the historicity of the processes, which does not simply mean that history impacts upon the present, but that path dependencies create empirical patterns that allow establishing family resemblances between past and present.

The network approach to culture is parsimonious in adding further analytical concepts. The most important ones are status or status orders and social capital. Status is an essential category in the analysis of ritual as understood in generic terms. Status is also a defining feature of individual identity and a criterion for establishing shared identities, and thus is a core category in cultural analysis. Status relates to interactions in establishing certain capabilities for action. The entire set of capabilities for network interactions is social capital. Thus, in this view, ritual may also be approached as a way of contextualizing the generic notion of social capital, which has also emerged as an important analytical category in economics for understanding markets and economic development.

Finally, I condense my approach into the suggestion that in the context of the economy the interaction between ritual, institutions and economic processes defines the 'economic style'. Describing the economic style of China today is the task of the subsequent five chapters, based on the continuous reflection of the generic notion of ritual and its meaning in China studies, which is embedded in the mirror of culture.

Chapter 2 establishes the reference point for identifying family resemblances between past and present in outlining a concise analytical view on the ritual economy of Late Imperial China. This means presenting stylized facts, based on a particular vantage point which is itself open to debate. I construct this point by building on Fei Xiaotong's theory of Western vs. Chinese society, which centres on the notion of ritual and the fundamental distinction between two different modes of network formation and forming groups with shared identities. Taking into consideration the caveats that I have already mentioned, this helps create a coherent idea of the ritual economy in the past. This approach makes use of many insights of recent historical research that have presented the picture of a 'Smithian' market-based society in which contracts, property rights and corporate organization were ordered by ritual frameworks that produced functional equivalences to 'Western' institutions, such as lineage estates as corporate organizations. At the core of this Smithian economy was the symbiosis of family and market, resulting in a peculiar pattern of economic development which has been labelled 'commercial capitalism'. In this pattern, economic disincentives worked against the transition to industrialization and more complex capitalist corporate organization. In other words, contrary to many earlier explanations also still prevailing until today, we cannot blame culture and institutions for the lack of transformational potential. On the contrary, the traditional Chinese economy was adaptively efficient. In modifying an important concept introduced by Philip Huang; I refer to this pattern as 'market involution'. One essential question in understanding the modern Chinese economy is whether and how forces of market involution still work towards the reproduction of forms of commercial capitalism.

The symbiosis of family and markets was mediated via the market systems that have been elevated to a paradigmatic model in China studies by Skinner. In these local systems, ritual and markets were mutually constitutive, such that we can also conceive of markets as being part and parcel of traditional culture. This perspective emerges from the rich recent historical research on the role of contracts and different forms of associational structures, both kin-related and transcending kinship, in organizing markets; on the other hand, markets emerged as the arena in which social and economic forces shaped the patterns of interactions and their embodiment in social artefacts, such as the geographic distribution of settlements or the spatial organization of popular religion. This peculiar cultural pattern may be grasped conceptually by Foucault's notion of 'governmentality'. Thus, the market as an organizing principle of local society is embedded in the larger context of Imperial rule, which has been characterized by another term specific to China studies: 'culturalism'. Culturalism is a particular form of local governance in the larger institutional context of the Empire which actively relies on and shapes ritual. In this form, the duality of local vs. central state was established as a fundamental pattern of the historicity of the Chinese body politic up until recent times. Modifying another central notion in modern China studies introduced by Prasenjit Duara, the modernization effort of the twentieth century focused mainly on transforming this culturalist model of governance into a modern state conceived along the lines of Western national states, albeit resulting in the phenomenon of 'government involution'.

In the traditional ritual economy, ritual was the bedrock of both market organization and Imperial governance of local society. Hence, most modernizers in the twentieth century waged the battle against ritual, thus viewing economic transformation as being part and parcel of cultural transformation. At the same time, cultural transformation was only feasible as being part and parcel of building a modern state, conceived of as a powerful central state, both internally and externally. These interdependencies created patterns of historicity that are defining elements of the modern Chinese economic style.

The analysis of Imperial governance provides the backdrop of Chapter 3, which starts with exploring the meaning of the concept of modernization for the evolution of economic institutions in China after 1949. More specifically, I introduce the term 'modernism' as a core aspect of ritual in modern China. In the context of the economy, modernism has undergirded a particular growth model that centres on the institutional differentiation between different sectors of the economy, especially rural and urban. I show that this growth model has been a constant since 1949, bridging the apparent transition to reforms in 1978, and is only subject to transformative policies at present, albeit without any substantial changes thus far. In spite of many institutional innovations, the growth model persists and reflects the ritual economy in contemporary China, epitomized in the dualism of the informal and formal economy. Ritual is manifest in cultural conceptions of identity, in particular the qualities of modernity that different groups in society have achieved. In this context, economic growth is not only material progress but a civilizational transformation which is measured against ritualistic concepts, embodied in consumption norms, architectural design and other artefacts. In this way, the emerging modern consumer society is part and parcel of modernist governmentality, thus also establishing a modernist transformation of the market as an element of ritualistic governance.

In this pattern, path dependencies create linkages between past and present, even in contexts such as the massive changes in demography resulting from modernist population policy, which create complex causal interactions among government interventions, social values and resulting behavioural patterns, as reflected in data such as the distorted sex ratio at birth. Aggregate macroeconomic features of the economy such as the extremely high savings rates are shaped by these path dependencies, reflecting, for instance, the norms governing the marriage market in both rural and urban contexts which causally connect status consumption and savings behaviour.

In rural society, path dependencies loom especially large. For understanding economic processes, the legacy of cellularization resulting from Maoist collectivization is highly significant. Especially in South China, radical collectivist policies actually reinforced traditional identities rooted in extended kinship, and group identities have been accentuated by political struggle. This has resulted in patterns of landownership even persisting in modernized urban settlements where kinship groups and village communities control land-use rights and struggle with modernist urban bureaucracies. Although this is a regionally circumscribed path dependency, we can observe interactions between traditional ritual and economic behaviour in many forms across China, epitomized, for instance, in the role of religious activities in creating social capital, as reflected in differential local performances in the production of public goods such as infrastructure or social services.

These developments in rural society have to be seen against the backdrop of one fundamental ritual feature of modernism, namely the institutionalized dualism between rural and urban society enforced by the *hukou* system. Today, in spite of a gradual relaxation of *hukou* controls and a massive influx of migrants into the cities over more than two decades, this formal institution has translated into a differential distribution of social capital across the Chinese population, defining a status order that is also embodied in other institutions such as the educational system, or material structures such as suburban settlements.

Another important interaction between formal institutions and ritual may be observed in the ownership regime. This is an example of modernist forms of ritual which are genuine novelties in the ritual economy. The status order of ownership reflects the administrative hierarchy of government, beginning with the dualism between rural and urban forms of ownership, and continuing with differential status of owners also in the urban domain. It is a determinant of one of the most conspicuous features of economic growth in China, 'localism', as manifest in diverse and even divergent regional patterns of economic development. Therefore, in Chapter 4 I turn to the analysis of government and its role and manifestations of economic policy in the ritual economy.

The pivotal concept in this context is the distinction between the central and the local state, which is empirically most salient in analysing fiscal administration: I suggest that the formal structures of fiscal power are core economic manifestations of governmentality; hence mainly expressions of deeper causal mechanisms in institutional change. One of the glaring family resemblances between past and present is the major role of informal institutions in funding government services at the local level, in particular in rural society. The slow advance of formal fiscal administration beyond the county level is a major indicator of state building in terms of the growing scope of bureaucracy and law, understood along Weberian lines. State building continues to struggle with the forces of government involution, manifest in the intrusion of market-type relations into the public domain, such as education or healthcare, resulting in an astonishinly large variance of local patterns of governance, reaching from 'hollowing out' of the public domain to the resilience of collectivist organizations.

Status distinctions between the rural and the urban, enshrined in both habitus and formal institutions, are driving a major phenomenon in the recent pattern of growth, namely the transformation of rural land into urban areas, which directly feeds into the financing of the local state. Thus, in China's ritual economy the local state stays at the centre of the pattern of localism in economic development, expressed in different types of local states, predatory, developmental, entrepreneurial, and other variants. Local states compete for economic resources and developmental opportunities; hence market competition and government competition are closely intertwined phenomena. Initially, the resulting dynamics triggered the rapid erosion of central fiscal power, thus exposing the forces of government involution; accordingly, the ensuing pattern of reforms, such as the privatization of rural industries and the restructuring of the state-owned sector, has been mainly driven by the reinstatement of central fiscal power, as implemented via tax reforms and related institutional changes. This reveals the pivotal role of the political status order in determining the dynamics of the ritual economy.

However, localism is balanced by the role of the Communist Party as a tightly integrated national institution. In order to understand its role, ritual is, again, essential. We can interpret the CCP as an institutionally embodied status order that encompasses all societal domains, and makes status commensurable across those domains. One particularly significant status distinction separates the local state at the county level from the upper level governments. The ritual function of the CCP is essentially expressed in the distinction between the functions of leadership and administration or implementation. Following the precepts of modernism, the CCP claims the leadership function in all social domains, representing the modernist avant-garde, which is personified in the position of the Party secretary, on all levels of government or organizations in general. This is institutionally embodied in the practices and symbols of the pervasive nomenclature system, which makes status commensurable. This phenomenon also frames developments such as the emergence and growth of civil society.

As is well recognized in the economic literature on China, the competition for rank in the CCP is a driving force of economic growth via the mediation of the formal cadre evaluation system. Up until today, success in terms of fostering local development is a major criterion for promotions on every level of the nomenclature hierarchy. In this particular sense, growth has a ritual meaning, which is also manifest in how statistics and data are handled as public representations of economic performance. There are broader aspects of ritual which are often perceived as ideology but are reaching beyond, since many elements of modern knowledge about technologies of governing are part and parcel of CCP work today. This is reflected in the educational process that accompanies careers as Communist cadres and that is managed in the system of party schools.

If we look at the consequences of these phenomena for economic policy in the narrower sense, the central fact is experimentalism. There is a distinct Chinese policy process that allows for large local variations and systematically creates recurrent interactions among local experiments and central policy design and legislation. Therefore, planning has also assumed a particular shape in China, akin to an educational (*jiaohua*) process managed and supervised by central-level agencies, and mainly implemented via the cadre evaluation system. This process is imbued with modernist aspirations which drive industrial policies, and which define and enforce status orders of industrial sectors, types of companies and qualities of economic actions. As a result, the conventional institutional distinction between plan and market evaporates in the Chinese setting, since markets are embedded in the modernist ritual order, and patterns of status differences pervade the allocation of resources such as financial means to particular economic agents. I argue that modernist ritual is the institutional framework for territorial competition among different government entities, in particular the local states, leading towards the distinct form of 'competitive industrial policy' by the central government. One conceptual approach to this peculiar form of interaction between state and market is 'state corporatism', though modified by the pivotal role of the duality between local states and central government.

In Chapter 5, I take a closer look at markets in terms of a web of social interactions. Here, the notions of networks and social capital are of particular significance, seen against the backdrop of the concept of 'market governmentality' that has emerged from the previous chapters. The chapter starts out from analysing the 'Chineseness' of networks in terms of *guanxi*, relating this to insights from psychology and cognitive sciences, triangulating them with indigenous conceptualizations and Fei Xiaotong's theory. I highlight the field dependence of network boundaries, the instrumentalism of emotional commitments, and long-term reciprocity as stabilizer. This analysis relates to one foundational issue in understanding Chinese culture, namely the issue of 'individualism' vs. 'collectivism'. In the course of the chapter I argue that Chinese networks build on a strong foundation of individualism embedded in active social relations, hence relational collectivism, and structured by status orders, hence vertical orientation, thus basically confirming Fei Xiaotong's theory about Chinese vs. Western society. Accordingly, *guanxi* needs to be interpreted as an element in the larger canvas of ritual in Chinese society.

In the context of markets in relation to government and formal institutions, most economists point towards trust in institutions as a major determinant of market efficiency, which can be disturbed by high levels of corruption that result from deviant informal networks, thus creating the moral ambiguity of *guanxi*. China appears to be a special case, as high levels of corruption are not reflected in low levels of general trust, as indicated by the data in the most recent 2014 World Value Survey. I explain this phenomenon in terms of the particular properties of *guanxi* networks, in the context of changing institutional conditions in different phases of market transition. Both corruption and *guanxi* in general are therefore expressions of ritual in the economic context. Ritualized corruption is based on long-term reciprocity of exchange of favours, which strengthens mutual bonding and therefore does not erode trust in those local contexts. Multipolar *guanxi* networks create flexibility and even possibilities for efficient solutions. Further, levels of confidence in society are also deeply shaped by the patterns of governmentality, especially relative to the dualism of local vs. central state. Thus, while corruption may be largely seen as a local though widespread phenomenon, central power can maintain legitimacy if it assumes the role of moral leadership.

The chapter continues with looking in some more detail into the value basis of market behaviour, such as attitudes towards inequality and opportunity. I try to pull all the strands of the argument together in analysing the general phenomenon of the performativity of markets in the Chinese context. In other words, I look at markets as patterns or institutional equilibria in the Aoki sense that reflect the complex interaction between determinants such as entrepreneurship, government intervention and regulation, or social networks. This works together with the modernist notion of 'market instrumentality', hence approaching markets as a social technology to achieve growth and modernization. Market instrumentality is deeply shaped by prevailing forms of governmentality, thus resulting in distinct forms of market dynamics, such as modularization as conjunctions of firms and markets, tying rural families into supplier structures designed by lead companies, or the *Shanzhai* pattern of informal exploitation of technological knowledge (implying rampant violations of intellectual property rights) in flexible and nimble networks of family firms. Similarly, the status order of ownership is a major determinant of financial structures in the economy, thus explaining financial repression of the private sector as a manifestation of the ritual economy.

Market performativity is partly a reflection of corporate organization. Therefore, Chapter 6 looks at the role of firms in the ritual economy. I present the general argument that in Chinese ritual, 'corporations' are weak in terms of autonomous sites of agency, and that therefore firms are 'enterprises' that manifest the underlying networks of entrepreneurial activity. The Chinese enterprise is a network organization of which corporations are external and even ephemeral expressions. This establishes an important family resemblance between past and present, since the absence of modern corporations was a conspicuous feature of the Chinese economy until 1949, which was actually maintained by enforcing socialist institutions until 1978. Today, the ritual economy of Chinese firms is a continuum of variants between the poles of private business and state-owned companies, with a significant share of hybrid forms. Hybrid forms have played an important role in past decades, such as the Township and Village enterprises that were directly embedded in the local state. Today, the two poles are also a reflection of the dualism of local and central state, with the central state claiming control of the state-owned sector as a modernist avant-garde, and the local state evolving into the domain of the market and private business, with a variety of regional patterns reflecting localism. Thus, the spectrum of companies in China and their ownership regimes is a manifestation of the ritual economy.

In more detail, the Chinese enterprise as a network organization is embedded in the broader pattern of commercial capitalism in which markets, networks and firms are arranged in a mutual relationship. Over past decades, this has coincided with the expansion of global supply chains, where the network principle is also pursued as a modern management approach, thus exploiting convergences between modern management and the ritual economy. Thus, Chinese family business remains an important determinant of Chinese competitiveness in attracting investors. Global supply chains and commercial capitalism of the ritual economy are two sides of the same coin. With reference to this pattern, deviant forms in terms of formal institutions are therefore also manifestations of the ritual economy, such as the *Shanzhai* production systems in South China.

Therefore, Chinese family business deserves further scrutiny. This is a central element of the influential conceptual model of 'Confucian capitalism' that has been created in the context of Overseas Chinese business. Independent from its validity, in Mainland China today this model is under severe pressure given the demographic constraints resulting from the one-child policy. On the other hand, the family is also a general model for designing enterprise organization independent from kinship, as reflected in paternalistic management approaches. In this model of management, authoritarian leadership, care and informal organization work together. I argue that these aspects were also a defining feature of Communist enterprise organization along the lines of the 'danwei' model. Thus, we may regard both to be expressions of the ritual economy, with many functional equivalences to modern aspects of management, such as skill development and education. There are many examples of modern Chinese companies which therefore draw upon the paternalistic model in designing even innovative approaches to corporate organization and management.

The major difference between private business and the state-owned sector resides in the underlying network structures. State-owned companies are the essential element of state capitalism as a modernist insertion into commercial capitalism. I define 'state capitalism' as being shaped by a stakeholder structure which mainly involves representatives of government-related organizations, behind which the CCP provides the encompassing network structure with its inherent status order. This stakeholder structure is also the framework in which ongoing reforms are implemented that aim at a hybrid ownership regime. Broadening the stakeholder structure is a major aspect of political change in China, in the sense of including a budding civil society in ritualistic governance schemes, such as in labour–management relations and wage-bargaining processes or in consumer protection and environmental concerns.

The chapter concludes with an analysis of corporate culture in general. Corporate culture is understood as a framework for the explicit design of firm identities, and is an influential topic in China today. I concentrate on the role of traditional ideas in shaping entrepreneurial approaches to corporate culture, which may be distinguished from direct references to socialist ideology or the import of managerial models and practices from abroad. One important observation is that there is a tension between humanistic and legalist management methods, and that the choice between the two is driven by status distinctions. In particular, legalist management methods, largely characterized as 'militaristic', are often applied in units that employ huge numbers of migrant workers. One neglected issue in understanding corporate culture in China is the role of Daoism, which is an important background to popular religion and practices. Interestingly, Daoist notions inspire the adoption of management approaches that combine organization and market also internally, thus undergirding the resilience of modular network organization as an organizational principle of commercial capitalism. In this respect, China's ritual economy is turning towards creating management innovations that may contribute to the evolution of global standards, since these forms of organization appear to converge with new models emerging in the context of the digital economy.

In summary, these five chapters present a concise view of the 'style' of the Chinese economy. I claim that this picture is much richer than competing labels such as 'state capitalism'. The main drawback of these labels is that they cover a larger number of countries with very different institutional structures and performance (such as Brazil and Russia). The conceptual richness of the notion of economic style is necessary to achieve complete causal explanations for what we observe in China today. Thus, in spite of the fact that I highlight the singularity of the Chinese economic style, I also claim that only this allows for empirically valid causal explanations that in turn build on general hypotheses. In making this particular methodological claim, my approach stands in the intellectual tradition of Max Weber and his notion of 'Kulturwissenschaft'. In order to achieve empirically valid insights into complex historical realities of economic systems, we have to recognize the complexity and contextuality of the single case, while drawing on theoretical resources that are offered by economics. Economics cannot directly explain these realities, but needs to be embedded methodologically in an analysis of culture that is informed by the humanities and the other social sciences.

1 Culture, ritual and economic style

The complexity of culture: culture as sense-making

The topic of this book is China's economic culture. This term is ambiguous. We can either read it as 'the culture of China's economy' or as 'China's culture is economic'. This ambiguity tells us something very essential about culture and economy: We cannot unequivocally separate the two concepts in the sense of referring them to two distinct social domains. As I will demonstrate in this theoretical chapter, this is not unique to the case of China, but applies for cultural analysis in economics generally. Yet, in the Chinese case this insight has a distinct slant. As we will see, in many respects specific aspects of Chinese culture such as particular values and beliefs indeed relate to economic activity implicitly or explicitly, such that we can say that China's culture is 'economic'. Just think of the ubiquity of the 'God of Wealth' in popular religion, which is a far cry from religious attitudes that distance themselves from the pursuit of profit. This observation goes back to the fact that Chinese society in Late Imperial times was a market society in structural and institutional terms, and that these traditional patterns have seen a revival in the recent period of 'reforms and opening up', which is reflected in the cultural framework. It also means that this cultural framework is essential in determining the nature of the Chinese economic system past and present. Thus, this book makes the special claim of a peculiar 'fit' between economy and culture in China. Chapter 2 will lay the historical foundations for this claim.

I argue that this relationship between economy and culture is constituted via the role of the state in mediating this relationship. This relates the ongoing process of 'economic reforms' (i.e. the transition to the market economy) to the secular process of building a modern state in China, which started in the second half of the nineteenth century as a response to the challenge of Western imperialist nation states. In this process, the linkage between the past and present is constituted by what Foucault calls a particular form of 'governmentality' in his analysis of the evolution of the state and structures of power in Western European history. With this term, Foucault encapsulates the fact that systems of ruling large societies encompass much more than legal institutions or mechanisms of enforcement of power, but include, for instance, hegemonial structures of knowledge or, in particular, internalized systems of disciplining the self. Therefore, in his view, modern market economies based on liberal doctrines are part and parcel of modern states and their systems of governing large-scale complex societies.[1] In China studies, this idea has been very influential in recent attempts to grasp the paradoxical 'neoliberal' nature of emerging Chinese capitalism combined with a socialist state. Indeed, what appears as a paradox to many Western observers, namely the combination of authoritarian one-party rule with rampant capitalist practices, may be understood as a specific form of governmentality: the market is part and parcel of the system of rule in China. Thus, understanding the *longue durée* of evolving Chinese governmentality can start out from considering the role of markets in Chinese society and culture, past and present.[2] In this book I will develop the idea that this linkage may be best understood in using the analytical lens of a particular term that played a central role in the traditional form of governmentality in the Chinese Empire, namely 'ritual'. This term, I claim, encapsulates a particular form of governmentality that manifests many family resemblances with forms of governing and governance in contemporary China which centre on the relationship between state, market and society.

However, on the theoretical level I also pursue the idea that all economic activity is cultural. This differs fundamentally from the current approach to culture in economics. After a long time of neglect, in the past three decades of research culture has been rediscovered by economists. However, in this research the explicit assumption is made that the two domains of culture and economy are separable, which is methodologically reflected in the standard econometric approaches which treat certain cultural data as exogenous parameters. This exogeneity also follows from the general idea that 'culture' refers to a legacy of the past, which by definition cannot be changed by activities taking place in the present. In these approaches, culture often become devoid of any specific content, because it is defined only in terms of past identities of certain culturally demarcated populations. This means, for example, that economists show that third-generation immigrants still manifest differences in values and beliefs in the present compared to other groups, which is then explained in terms of a peculiar cultural heritage.[3]

These approaches stay in astonishing tension with methodological standards that are normally upheld by economists, in particular methodological individualism and rationality. In a hard-nosed economic approach, cultural phenomena in the present would have to be explained by rational choices of individuals facing certain contextual data, such that culture would appear to be strictly endogenous, thus eschewing any idea of an immutable legacy of the past.[4] In fact, the economic interest in culture could even go back to the observation that cultural explanations therefore enhance and fruitfully modify these standard economic explanations without questioning their fundamental validity.

Indeed, if we look at the approaches to culture in the disciplines that originally deal with these phenomena, we meet the entirely different view that, to a certain extent, comes surprisingly close to the standard economic approach in emphasizing the endogeneity of culture and the role of the individual. This view posits that culture is not an external determinant of human action rooted in the past, but an activity of individuals interacting with other individuals. In this sense, cultural analysis always starts out from the individual, thus apparently coming close to methodological individualism in economics. The major difference lies in the notion of rationality, which ties up with other important notions such as 'equilibrium', and which is confronted with the idea of cultural creativity which would appear to be a non-equilibrium force by definition. In a first approximation, I therefore introduce culture as the 'activity of sense-making by individuals staying in recurrent interaction with others'. The difference between the two views is then straightforward: for example, economics treats preferences as givens and irreducibly subjective, whereas cultural analysis asks how individuals create their preferences when interacting with others. This also implies, however, that there is no fundamental contradiction between economic notions of rationality and cultural analysis, even though rationality itself is seen as a procedure that is subject to creativity and hence as not universally binding.[5]

In this book about China I cannot explore these theoretical and methodological issues in great detail. Thus, I just posit my own position and elaborate on those methodological aspects that are necessary for deploying my empirical approach to China's economic culture. As is well known, the definitions of 'culture' are multifarious. Thus, I pick out the one that is most directly related to my idea of culture as sense-making. This is the definition proposed by Beugelsdijk and Maseland: 'we loosely define culture as those behavioral and ideational structures that are deemed essential to the constructed identity of a community.' This definition introduces a new term, 'identity', which I regard as fundamental.[6]

The definition is remarkable in several respects. The first is that no reference is made to the past. Culture relates to 'behavioral and ideational structures' which can be inherited from past activities, but not necessarily are. The term 'structure' suggests that culture relates to phenomena which manifest a certain stability through time, which implies that there is a link between past and present. Yet, what counts is the activity of 'constructing an identity' which takes place in the present. Thus, for example, Confucianism may be regarded as an 'ideational structure' which we can identify via texts and speeches of individuals who activate these ideas in identifying themselves as 'Chinese'. However, if we reflect upon this example, we immediately recognize the immense complexity of this notion of culture. To begin with, how can we demarcate the 'community' independent from the process of constructing its identity? This is done largely in a rather naive way, namely by referring to the borders of nation states today (such as the PRC), or to some historical link to populations of origin (such as the ancestors of contemporary Chinese immigrants in the USA). But if we proceed along this line, can we then assert that 'Confucianism' is a necessary element of the identity of these groups? What is the condition here? Do we need to show that people actually read Confucian classics? Would that imply that people who do not rely on Confucianism in identifying themselves as 'Chinese' are actually not Chinese? These are by no means moot issues, as is evident from the conceptual difficulties in demarcating 'national minorities' from the Han Chinese majority population in China today.[7]

Things become ever more complicated if we distinguish between behaviour and ideas. Can we approach 'Confucianism' exclusively in terms of behaviour? In other words, we would consider the possibility that certain individuals behave according to certain standards which we as observers identify as 'Confucian', without implying that these individuals 'make sense' of their behaviour in terms of Confucian ideas. For example, people may take special care of their parents without invoking the Confucian notion of 'filial piety', 'xiao' (孝). Yet we would not speak of a cultural phenomenon if these behaviours are not activated in the context of identifying themselves as a member of a 'Chinese' community (for example, in arguing that 'the Chinese' pay particular attention to their parents as compared to other ethnic groups). This means that we introduce a fundamental methodological distinction between two positions of observers – external and internal – which relates to the two methodological positions of emics and etics.[8] The external observer may identify certain behaviours as being distinctive for a certain population, but whether these are 'cultural' phenomena can only be decided if we move to the position of the internal observer, and hence to that of the members of the supposed community, and show that those observers refer to that behaviour as an element in constructing their identity. This has important consequences for assessing the relevance of one of the most important areas in established research on culture, namely value surveys. Alleged differences in values across different populations can only count as 'cultural' if they are perceived by internal observers as being constitutive for distinguishing themselves from other communities.

This insight leads us to ponder another intricacy of culture. If there were only Chinese in the world there would be no 'Chinese culture', and, indeed, in ancient times 'culture' was perceived as being tantamount to 'civilization' that separates humans from mere 'barbarians'. For example, the early Confucian thinkers considered the Chinese ritual as being the defining difference between human beings and animals. Thus, our definition of culture relates essentially to the mutual recognition of cultural differences in cross-cultural interactions. In this sense, we cannot approach culture as a property of a certain community which exists independently from cross-cultural encounters. Indeed, this would lead us into the trap of cultural essentialism, which, in my view, has happened to recent economic research on culture. On the contrary, culture is by definition a cross-cultural phenomenon and therefore a property of both external and internal observers in cases where they interact. We can even say that without this interaction culture does not exist as a phenomenon.[9]

This important observation has two methodological consequences. The first is that culture relates directly to the nested structure of communities. Thus, if as external observers we refer to 'China' as a certain geographical area and its inhabitants, we need to recognize the fact that this area is covered by a large number of different communities that have different identities, which, however, overlap and criss-cross in a complex fashion. Thus, there are Hakka communities within the 'Chinese' area, or there are cohorts of individuals who identify themselves referring to a shared experience, such as the 'sent-down youths' of the 1970s, and so forth. All culture is an agglomerate and mosaic of subcultures. Facing this bewildering complexity of culture, how can we extract a core meaning of 'Chineseness' that is shared among all observers, both internal and external? Anything that is not universally shared, in fact, identifies another community than 'the Chinese'. Thus, when investigating Chinese culture in the sense of looking at cultural phenomena in the geographical territory of China, we need to recognize the diversity of Chinese culture as a basic fact. This is also a necessity in historical terms, as China throughout her history was a multi-ethnic state and was shaped by the experience of frontier societies during the centuries of migration and expansion. In this sense, Chinese culture has always been the culture of an empire, and one peculiar feature of the modern Chinese nation state is its fragile or even defunct grounding in a concept of national culture.[10]

The second consequence of treating culture as a cross-cultural phenomenon is that writing about culture becomes a part of the culture that is being analysed. There is no detached position which allows one to fix an 'objective' content of culture. Thus, in writing this book about China's economic culture I am not simply doing empirical, descriptive or explanatory work. As a 'German', I take part in the activity of constructing the identity of 'the Chinese'. This consideration applies to all levels of the nested hierarchies of culture, so that, for example, Hakka culture is nothing that is a given which is independent from who else in China observes Hakka culture and comments on it, and which foreigners observe Hakka and non-Hakka and perceive these differences relative to their own position. This also implies that there is no certainty as to whether 'culture' is perceived in the same way by different kinds of observers of culture. In fact, culture will look different from each of those different perspectives, and there is no presumption that behind this kaleidoscope of culture there is an immutable fixed point.

In the context of anthropology, this problem has been labelled the 'orientalism' phenomenon which describes the special effect that can emerge if Western observers construct an image of Asian societies and culture which also partly reflects their own context and cultural problematics. Orientalism gives rise to another phenomenon, namely 'reverse orientalism'. This happens if Asian people start to describe themselves along the lines of the Western perceptions, which in turn feeds back on the Western discourse. These issues are not merely theoretical ones, but have been popping up in the context of studies of Chinese business and economy on several occasions, in particular following the rise of the 'tigers' in the Asia-Pacific. When, on the part of Western researchers images of 'Chinese capitalism' had been produced, many actors in the Chinese cultural domain began to perceive their own practices and beliefs in terms of the cultural constructions which were undergirded by cross-cultural settings especially in Southeast Asia, where the business success of the Chinese diaspora was also seen as a social issue. Thus, the 'Chineseness' of Chinese business became a narrative that was also told by Chinese entrepreneurs themselves, and who might not even be aware of the larger academic setting. As a result, Western perceptions of 'Chineseness' may be readily confirmed by the authentic actors. Critical observers pointed out, on the contrary, that Chinese business practices reflect nothing but the specific historical and structural circumstances of the dynamics of capitalist development in the Asia-Pacific, and that therefore the discourse on culture can actually be appropriated by attempts at giving legitimacy to what appear to be mere expressions of economic forces and social structures of dominance and power, reflected in the organization of Chinese entrepreneurship and business.[11]

So, we need a methodological framework that allows for the analytical recognition of these interactions and the resulting complexity of culture. The challenge is to establish a systematic relationship between etic and emic approaches to culture, and to navigate between the Scylla of cultural essentialism and the Charybdis of the postmodern arbitrariness of culture. This is the principal task of this chapter.

Triangulating 'culture' in the mirror of culture

My approach to reconciling emics and etics starts out from the 'mirror of culture' (Figure 1.1).[12] The 'mirror of culture' encapsulates the fact that 'culture' as an object is something that is essentially embedded in processes of mutual observations and discourses about these observations among observers with different perspectives. Ideal typically, I distinguish between two roles of observers, namely 'reflecting observers' and 'participating observers', which can coincide for particular individuals, such as managers who write about their experiences for a business magazine. Observers may be 'internal' or 'external' to the culture being constructed

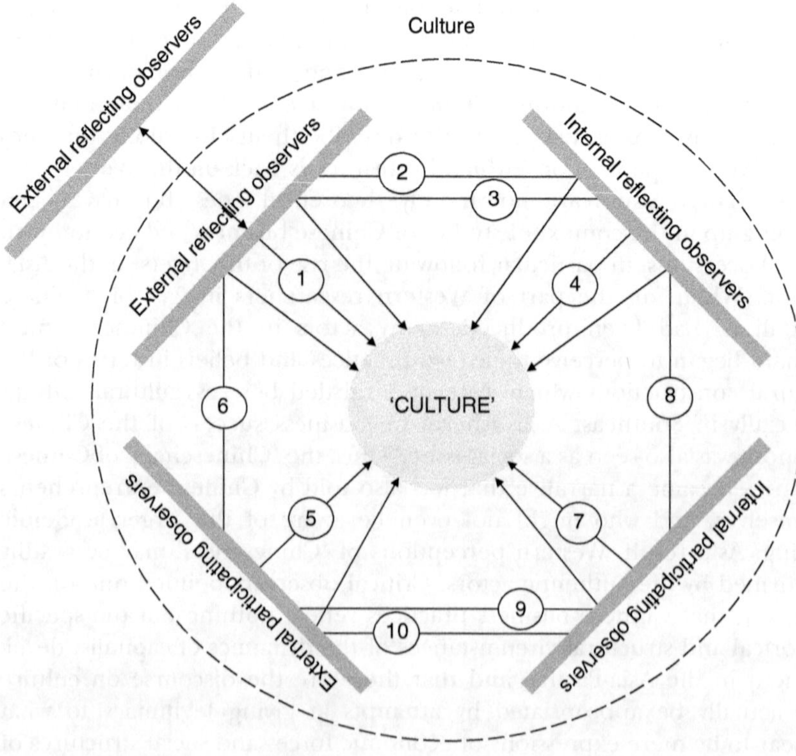

Figure 1.1 The mirror of culture.

in the process, and they communicate with each other. So, for example, a Chinese manager, an internal participating observer, may directly form perceptions about her culture in the context of an international joint venture (7). At the same time, she communicates with external participating observers; that is, Western managers who also form perceptions (5), such that the Chinese manager also starts to form perceptions that are mediated by Western observations (10). In order to adopt a professional approach, the Chinese manager may read academic work about cross-cultural issues which also impacts upon her view of Chinese culture (8). These academic works result from direct reflections about Chinese culture (4) which in a similar fashion are being shaped by mutual mediations (2, 3) which result from the academic discourse with Western researchers who study Chinese culture, partly by reading indigenous texts reflecting on Chinese culture. The Western literature may in turn impact upon the Western managers (6), for example, when they participate in cross-cultural management courses. Finally, external reflecting observers may move to a second-order observation if they reflect methodologically on their own approaches to culture, as in the discourse over 'orientalism'.

So, I conclude that culture as CULTURE is nothing that we can observe directly, which would only be the 'CULTURE' at the centre of the mirror, but is only what we can perceive as emerging from that mirror; that is, culture is what is going on in the mirror, involving all different roles of observers. By implication, CULTURE as an emergent property of the entire web of interactions will always reveal blind spots in its representations from the perspective of one of the interacting positions. Therefore, every single contribution to cultural analysis is itself a part of the cultural dynamics that it may be claiming to describe and analyse 'objectively'. This conclusion questions any attempts to clearly distinguish between 'etic' and 'emic' approaches to culture and to suggest the possibility of identifying a purely etic description of culture. In fact, research can only achieve a methodological view on culture, in the sense that the second-order reflection strives to produce an image of the mirror of culture *in toto.* In other words, that culture is a philosophical category in the broadest sense and not an 'object' out there. That may appear to be an elusive, even obscurantist approach. However, the methodological view on culture has a very specific and analytically and empirically tractable meaning. This is that culture can only be identified in using multidisciplinary approaches and aiming at a conceptual integration, and that maintaining a continuous discourse between different perspectives is a methodological imperative. Such an integration is a methodological achievement, and in this particular sense 'culture' is a philosophical notion, not a descriptive one.

In this book, I draw upon many different methods to construct China's economic culture. These methods may be roughly classified as either 'etic' or 'emic'. If I concentrate on those methods that play the most important role in my work, etic approaches are, first, psychological and cognitive science approaches that build on experimental methods, and which are increasingly supplemented by experimental research in economics. The other major etic method is the wide range of value studies, in which questionnaires are used that are applied universally; that is, the same set of questions is used across cultures and therefore serves as an objective benchmark for assessing cultural differences. In contrast, emic approaches include all methods that directly aim at accessing the self-perceptions of Chinese as reflected in oral or written accounts. These include literary studies in the broadest sense, such as trying to relate Chinese philosophy to business practices, which can be done by both participating and reflecting observers, and all kinds of participating observations which include direct interaction with Chinese. Emic approaches always include an interpretive and appreciative dimension. Theoretically, this interpretive dimension would not play a substantial role in etic approaches.

My discussion about the mirror of culture questions this sharp methodological separation of emic and etic. This is of immense importance for economic research on culture. Typically, economic research relies on results of other disciplines when looking for indicators and proxies of cultural differences. Take, for example, economic research on 'trust', which is at the same time a core topic of emic reconstructions and also self-descriptions of Chinese culture, especially with regard to Confucianism. Mostly, economic research uses the so-called 'general trust' question of the World Value Survey (WVS). If we look at the results for China, China emerges as a 'high-trust' country which comes close to the values of Scandinavian countries. These results stay directly in tension with common descriptions of Chinese culture in general and with current perceptions of the Chinese and the 'crisis of trust' in their country. Thus, we confront a serious problem if we realize that in comparative economic research the WVS results on China are just one value in a large sample that may be used to assess the relative role of trust in social capital impacting upon economic growth applying econometric techniques. That may be captured in realizing the role of China as an 'outlier', but given the significance of China for understanding global economic growth, this only begs the more serious methodological questions.[13]

One way to resolve the issue is to switch to other questions in the WVS, such as the question whether people trust others whom they meet for the first time. Here, the results fit preconceived ideas, with China scoring low. However, if we reflect upon this result, we will obviously need to find an explanation why the two questions produce such different pictures for the Chinese case. These explanations lead us towards adopting an interpretive stance. For example, we may ponder whether the general trust question evokes very different pictures of what 'generally' means in everyday life. We might suggest that Western participants may have in mind society at large, so also considering the daily presence of strangers, whereas Chinese might envisage their local contexts, in which they may rarely interact with strangers. But this is a mere hypothesis. We can only check this hypothesis by directly investigating the perceptions of people, which means shifting towards an emic approach.

The deep dilemmas of all values surveys become salient in considering the most widely used cultural classification in the management sciences: the Hofstede cultural repository. Hofstede presents an etic approach in claiming to be able to describe all cultures along the lines of only five or six dimensions, depending on the version to which we refer. The ascriptions of cultures to the dimensions are based on questionnaires that are akin to values surveys, but mostly concentrate on professional and work contexts, as in his seminal study of IBM. The Hofstede data are widely used in the management sciences as an input for other comparative research on culture, and they have exerted an enormous impact upon education in cross-cultural management.

The methodological deficiencies of the Hofstede approach have been extensively documented in the literature. One problem is that the statistical clustering techniques always have to be accompanied by some interpretive fine-tuning of responses to single questions. This means, on the one hand, that the dimensions of culture have been extracted from applying factor analysis on the original data. But when it comes to the classification of single cultures, responses may be directly assigned to particular dimensions, or are sometimes neglected outright if they appear to contradict some previous understanding of the significance of certain dimensions for particular cultures. At the same time, the entire set of dimensions is obviously biased towards highlighting what may be conceived of as typical 'Western' culture, since some dimensions cover a very large number of countries, whereas others cover a much smaller number. One essential example in our context is the juxtaposition of 'individualism' versus 'collectivism'. There is a large number of collectivist countries and a small number of individualistic countries. This highlights the 'separateness' of Western values and blurs cultural diversity between 'collectivist' countries; the same applies for 'power distance'. Thus, in the end, the Hofstede approach cements the common narrative about the distinctiveness of Western society.[14]

This kind of distinctiveness has also been ascribed to so-called 'Confucian' countries in the course of amending and enhancing the explanatory power of the Hofstede dimensions. This occurred when other values studies happened to identify an allegedly peculiar dimension in which East Asian societies appear to be distinct, and which was then added to the Hofstede dimensions: the 'long-term orientation'. Here, Western countries, in particular Anglo-Saxon ones, score low, and East Asia scores very high, this time probably affirming cultural clichés held by East Asians about themselves. It turned out that this new dimension was unstable, even immanent to Hofstede's methodology, since in the most recent versions of the Hofstede scales of culture the dimension has been split into two: 'long-term orientation vs. short-term normative orientation' and 'indulgence vs. restraint'.[15]

Beyond the stability of certain etic categorizations, there is one aspect in which interpretive aspects loom large directly within the methodological foundations of these approaches. This follows from the fundamental ambiguity of all questions about values: a 'value' can reflect a current state of society, such as accepted standards of behaviour and valuations, or it can reflect what people desire and aspire to, while recognizing that the current state is deficient with regard to those values. This is of the utmost importance, because in the latter case it is impossible to compare scores across cultures, as we would also always need to compare the diverse reference points for those marginal valuations. In other words, if we ask people about 'collectivist values' this may end up with a high score because people appreciate collectivist orientations and follow these convictions in their actual practices, or, to the contrary, they may recognize a strong individualism in current conditions but deplore that and express their appreciation of a stronger collectivist orientation. This means that without adding substantial contextual information we are not able to evaluate and compare single scores across cultures. This, however, implies that the claims of an etic methodology are undermined, since those contextual comparisons cannot be done without taking the perspective of the participant observers into consideration which are part and parcel of the context.[16]

As we see, there are some fundamental issues with value surveys with regard to cross-cultural comparisons. These difficulties also affect what appears to be an ideal etic methodology, namely the experimental approach in economics and psychology, since typically experimental data on behaviour need to be checked econometrically in order to test alternative explanations of the results. Experimentalists normally recur on values surveys and use common standardized questions to extract data on values that might explain the observations. This is not necessary in the approaches that are most distant from the need to involve interpretive perspectives, such as in experiments of cognitive sciences. In this case we have pure observational data on certain cognitive performances, which may reveal systematic differences across groups that differ in fundamental demographic characteristics which are normally covered by simple assignments to different criteria of ethnicity, such as 'American Caucasian' versus 'Mainland Chinese'. As a result, we sometimes get very pronounced variations across different groups, such as in experiments using the 'rod and frame test' which is a simple cognitive task in assessing locations and shapes of objects in changing graphical contexts. However, these results, though clearly etic in nature, need substantial enrichment in terms of their explanation. In these explanations we are back with all the difficulties I have discussed thus far.[17]

So, in fact we cannot escape the mirror of culture. I think that this result is one manifestation of a fundamental impossibility theorem in epistemology, namely Quine's 'indeterminacy of translation'. If we deal with culture, we always need to refer to linguistic or quasi-linguistic, hence symbolic, structures, in the most general sense. These structures need to be interpreted; they are meaningful. However, we can never translate perfectly those meanings into other linguistic structures, because we can never fully prove the equivalence without taking into consideration the entire framework of the symbolic structures. This means that if, for example, we consider single values in a values survey, we cannot conclusively assess their meaning without a full understanding of the entire universe of meanings in the complete set of values in question. This evidently leads us into a serious, even unsolvable, methodological dilemma, because our empirical claim has been to reconstruct the cultural universe by looking at its elements. So we have to accept the fact that we will never be able to fully understand and explicate what the defining features of a culture are in comparison with others.[18]

This may appear to be a negative result at first sight, but it also allows for a positive methodological conclusion. It means that we opt for a triangulation methodology (Figure 1.2). Then, we use the results of etic research in order to fit it with other results gained from different methodologies. In particular we can match etic research, which we describe as being done by external reflecting observers, with the results of emic research, in particular reflections by indigenous scholars, which we need to access via translations. This does not imply that we ultimately achieve a position that is free from the fundamental epistemological dilemma of the 'indeterminacy of translation', but we can build our construction on different data and sets of information which are independent from each other, thus adding validity to each other if they appear to converge on certain aspects of culture.

In disciplinary terms, this means that research on culture needs to build on both Chinese studies in the narrow sense, in particular in terms of 'sinology', and on the social sciences and the sciences, if we assign cognitive science and psychology to the latter. Sinology is important for two reasons. First, as we have seen, sinology allows access to emic views in enabling translations of indigenous descriptions of perceptions of culture. Second, if we want to grasp the persistence and stability of culture through time we need the input of historical research, which is to a large degree concerned with the interpretation of written sources. This is indeed what is largely done when considering culture in the context of economics. However, as we will see, triangulation also implies that we refer contemporary research on psychology back to historical conditions if we can present compelling

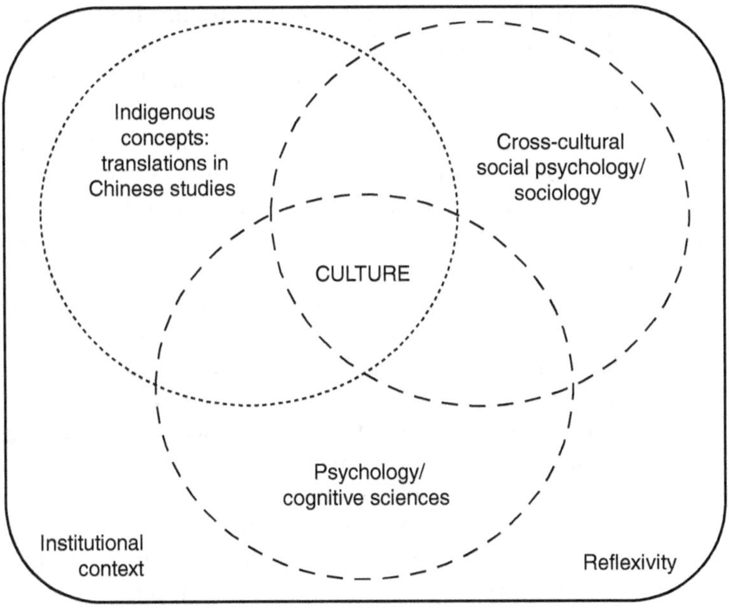

Figure 1.2 Triangulating culture.

reasons why psychological features may be stable through time. This is how the different disciplinary perspectives actually tie up. When psychologists today venture a hypothesis that modern psychological features may be traced to certain exogenous determinants that have been stable throughout most of Chinese history, then we may not simply treat this as an impact of past developments upon the current situation, but would also posit that those features also apply to the past. Then, as we will see, modern cognitive science is also relevant for historical analysis, especially if we identify emic categories by which we can further relate historical observations to contemporary research.

Further, triangulation always has to consider reflexivity in the 'mirror of culture'. That is, the results of triangulation have to be fed back into the discourses that take place in the mirror, possibly engendering new rounds of triangulation. Finally, concern for culture should never blank out the independent role of the institutional context, which I will discuss in detail below.

Thus, triangulation is a complex procedure. In order to achieve unification of results, I introduce another term inspired by the philosophy of language, which is Wittgenstein's notion of 'family resemblances'.[19] One way to construct an external observer's view of culture is to identify family resemblances between China's past and present. This does not imply that there are any direct impacts of past culture upon present culture, but only reflects the external observer's interpretive stance. Once family resemblances are posited, however, an important question for research may be to demonstrate how specific historical chains of causality lead towards similarities of constituent phenomena that give rise to the family resemblances. So, in this book, I use a historical reconstruction of culture and economy in Late Imperial China to identify family resemblances with contemporary China. However, this construction can only claim to be insightful if it is accompanied by the triangulation exercise, hence combining it with results from the other disciplines. Thus, one feature of this book is the recurrent switch between different disciplinary accounts of culture, independent from the actual time of reference.

In other words, in spite of the fact that the reconstruction of 'culture' ultimately remains a creative interpretive act of the observer, she can use a lot of qualitatively different materials in order to build an image of culture which ultimately succeeds empirically. What is the ultimate measure of success? I propose that this is, in the end, the convergence of views among the different observers, and therefore communicative success in terms of the sustainability of discourses about culture, both on the level of participant observers and of reflecting observers. So, empirical validation is only possible as a reflexive action in the mirror of culture. Triangulation does not result in an 'objective' fact of culture, but in a reflexive process in which culture is undergoing continuous transformations. This means, finally, that supposed 'external' observers always will and need to participate actively in creating and sustaining culture in their cross-cultural interactions. Thus, for example, if in this book I introduce 'ritual' as a core notion to approach Chinese economic culture, this on the one hand receives a traditional notion of Chinese culture as perceived in a long tradition of reflecting on Chinese culture, but at the same time I explicitly submit a proposal how to reconstruct and further develop Chinese culture. In this sense the book is part and parcel of the evolving Chinese culture, and not just the product of a detached scientific observer.

In this endeavour, the most difficult issue is to distinguish between 'culture' and the institutional context. I turn to this question next.

The ecological approach to culture and performativity

One of the most dangerous fallacies of cultural research is misplaced essentialism and internalism. This is, again, most obvious in values studies, and in Hofstede's approach in particular, though it is by no means necessary. By this 'essentialist internalism' I refer to the belief that 'culture' refers to some deeper level properties of individuals, such as certain values, which determine the observed behaviours and interaction patterns with others. At first sight this also seems inherent to the Beugelsdijk and Maseland definition of culture. However, in this definition we have the explicit reference to group identities. This raises the intricate issue of how far group-level phenomena actually determine identities, such that what we perceive as being an 'internal value' would in fact emerge as an ecological phenomenon in terms of being based on interactions between the individual and the group level. In more detail, the question is how far the individual-level properties are actually individual embodiments or manifestations of group-level phenomena. Typically, this may be referred to as 'internalization'. Internalization means that group-level phenomena, such as behavioural standards that are enforced by institutions, become internal properties in terms of individual beliefs or values. However, this does not mean that those internal properties become fixed properties of the individuals, as in fact we can only access them via behavioural or linguistic expressions which themselves occur in institutionalized contexts. Evidently, this notion of internalization provides a systematic foundation for the concept of governmentality that I introduced in the first section.[20]

Even if we use the term 'internalization', this leaves open how far those internalized properties are stable beyond the ongoing interactions in the group. This is, for example, assumed in Hofstede's notion of 'mental programming', and has apparently been recently confirmed by a growing number of economic inquiries which show, as I have already alluded to earlier, lasting effects of country-of-origin on the behaviour or values of immigrant populations in the USA, even in the third and fourth generation. However, this research begs the question how far those communities also maintain long-term stability of interaction patterns in the respective groups, which could be the actual carriers of the resilience of the observed phenomena. It is very difficult to prove how far current internalization only depends on repercussions of past socialization, resting on the argument that, after all, at least the parents remain a primordial group in which current internalization takes place.

This ambiguity certainly inheres to the notion of 'culture', which is definitively seen by all cultural theories as a property of a group in terms of being shared by individuals. Thus, if economists now use the term 'culture', they stay in tension with the proclaimed 'methodological individualism' that they normally hold up as a methodological beacon. In this view, conventionally the assumption of a generic general purpose rationality will hold, such that 'culture' cannot be a property of individuals (which are basically seen as 'identical' along certain anthropological constants), but should reflect certain patterns of incentivization that hold for the group of which they are members. Typically, certain behaviours can be reconstructed as equilibria in games that are used to model those interactions in the group. In this sense, an economic approach to culture would be an externalist one. Of course, this may in turn raise the question of where the group-level patterns emerge from, but I leave this additional question aside in the current context. Obviously, if economists begin to treat culture as something that persists through time in spite of changing contexts, they violate their own traditional methodology. In fact, the economic use of 'culture' is a methodological paradox. The ultimate empirical proof of 'culture' would be to show that there are behaviours that cannot be explained by any contextual causal factor in the present that directly impacts upon the rational choice of individuals. Yet, this would mean that the only explanation can be systematic differences between preferences, which are by definition excluded from the explanatory domain of standard economics.[21]

I have already argued that modern anthropological research in fact comes close to the economic methodology, albeit without accepting the assumption of a generic general purpose rationality, when it approaches culture as an individual creative activity. We will try to define a mutually compatible perspective in considering the following:

- Cultural creativity builds on existing repertoires of sense-making. This means, on the one hand, that there are certain artefacts, patterns or interpretive narratives which can be directly activated and manipulated in cultural creativity. On the other hand, the creative aspect also looms large in the bricolage of items which are not 'cultural' in the first place, but can become part and parcel of sense-making and the construction of identities. However, in all these cases individual cultural creativity needs to be balanced and mediated via group-level processes of communication and establishing shared understandings of those cultural actions.

- Further, cultural creativity operates under constraints. Constraints may be seen as representing incentive structures in the dynamic perspective; that is, patterns of behaviour result from incentives under which individuals act, and which channel cultural creativity. However, creativity also means that constraints can be changed via creative agency. Again, constraints are manifest in group-level dynamics.

I call this approach 'ecological' in the sense that the environment plays an essential role in shaping culture, as opposed to internal properties of individuals.[22] More basically, this is an externalist perspective, clearly opposing any sort of cultural internalism. The ecological approach, however, does not fully eschew partial internalist explanations, for two reasons. The first is that we take account of internalization, which for practical matters means that we ask for the role of cultural socialization in explaining certain observed behaviours; however, internalization means that certain beliefs about the contexts are shared among individuals who exchange signals and cues about their beliefs. The second is that there can be generic aspects of cognition that impact upon the more specific behavioural phenomena. This comes to the fore when we consider the question how far incentives are mediated by the way in which individuals perceive them, which can be a cultural phenomenon in turn, because all perception is also interpretation. One of the most general descriptions, hence not exclusively, is the characterization of 'field dependency' of East Asians. Field dependency of perception would imply that the Chinese have a particularly strong tendency to perceive and respond to group-level signals and cues in order to adapt their behaviour. This is clearly different from an internalist approach that would ascribe 'group orientation' as a value directly to the individuals. Thus, this is an ecological explanation of pertinent experimental research. Yet we also include an internalist perspective in assigning this property of field dependence to the individuals. Then, the next question is to explain this property, which leads back to the externalist position if it is seen as the result of socialization in certain group contexts. In other words, internalist explanations can be reduced to externalist explanations that explicitly introduce the time dimension, both ontogenetically and historically or even evolutionarily.[23]

I resolve this possible tension between internalist and externalist approaches to culture through the notion of 'performativity'. Culture is a performance of individuals in groups, and it responds to a generic anthropological need, the search for and maintenance of individual identity. The notion of performativity is borrowed from the philosophy of language and refers to a certain kind of action by which social facts are created, the existence of which depends on the recognition within a certain group of individuals in which those actions are performed. Thus, for example, if a priest declares a couple to be married, this creates a social fact. The status of a fact is reflected by the causal powers that the fact obtains through the performative action.[24]

Corresponding to the Beugelsdik and Maseland definition, I approach culture as an individual performance of identity, mediated by ascriptions to groups. Identity is always referring to group-level phenomena: even if I consciously and explicitly aim at expressing my individual identity, this always results in defining lines of demarcation from other individuals in a reference group. The important consequence of this is that we cannot delineate a certain domain of 'culture' as being different from other domains, such as 'politics', and then ask how 'culture' affects 'politics'. The notion of performativity means that all possible phenomena can become activated as means to perform culture, and thus to express and maintain the individual identity in a group context. There is only one constraint, which relates to the ease as to how far a certain phenomenon is prone to diffuse indiscriminately across different groups and populations.[25] Evidently, if a certain artefact, such as a mobile phone, diffuses easily for reasons of expediency and practicality, this technology as such cannot be of any use to express individual identities. Thus, in this example, design features that do not express generic ergonomic aspects of usage could serve as a vehicle for expressing individual identity. So, for example, the countless variants of mobile phone designs in China's so-called *Shanzhai* industries may be interpreted as a cultural phenomenon sui generis, beyond the simple interpretation as a way to undermine the constraints of patents and copyright in trying to exploit cost advantages of Chinese producers of mobile phones. The vast repertoire of design features that go far beyond what mainstream producers can and want to offer are media of expressing the individual users' identities.

Why do people pursue identities? This is not the place to delve into the vast relevant literature, but I want to point to the following explanations which are important for my reasoning.

- First, and contrary to the standard assumptions in economics, individuals are not perfectly informed about the range of behavioural options they face and the corresponding valuations. Even more so, they are not even fully informed about their own preferences, but they learn about them via the experiences they have through their own choices, contextualized in their social settings. Forming an identity is a means to resolve these information asymmetries and deficiencies through what we will call a 'mimetic performance', referring both to one's own actions in the past and the observed actions of others.[26]
- Second, identities respond to a generic human need of belonging to a certain group, thus reflecting fundamental human sociality and the universal tendency to distinguish between in-group and out-group. This has important implications if we consider the fact that therefore any impacts upon identities that do not result from individual action may have direct effects on the satisfaction individuals receive from having an identity. This gives rise to externalities in social interactions,

if individuals who deviate from accepted understandings of identities thereby do not only affect their own identity but also the identities of others. A manifold of effects follows that result in the maintenance of cultural phenomena, such as by-standing third-party enforcement of norms and values.[27]

- Third, identities help overcome dilemmas of social interaction because they identify, in the language of game theory, types of players, and thereby alleviate another kind of information asymmetry. Simultaneously, ostracism becomes a very powerful means to incentivize cooperation even in what is structurally a one-spot interaction because identities are by definition creating sequential games in the sense of establishing cross-connections among different games, since reputation effects transfer among them.[28]

Thus, identity is the crucial causal mediator between external group-level phenomena and individual actions. Culture is not a property on the group level, but is a notion that refers to regularities which observers can identify in the pertinent performative actions of individuals. One extremely important consequence of this approach is that the culture of individuals becomes context-dependent on the environments in which their identity is maintained and communicated. In other words, a Chinese visiting in a foreign country will manifest different cultural patterns than the same Chinese as a Hakka in a Chinese environment, since the reference for identity is different. Identity should never be misunderstood in terms of essentialist internalism, namely as a property that is carried on by individuals independent from context. In fact, individuals combine many identities into their set-up as a person, such as the identity of a Chinese, of a Hakka, of a member of a profession or as a member of their family. This corresponds to the previous observation that culture is in fact multifaceted, depending on different groups as references.[29]

In the context of economic behaviour, there are different domains where cultural analysis of identities may be applied fruitfully. One is consumer behaviour, for example, when we ask how far consumption activities also express individual identities with reference to certain groups. For example, Chinese consumers often choose foreign brands in order to define themselves relative to other groups in society, but this choice can become problematic in defining themselves as 'Chinese' relative to world society; correspondingly, even though foreign brands permeate Chinese society today, brand management in China is facing complex issues related to culture.[30] Another is, of course, management, which is not necessarily only referring to cross-cultural management, but, for example, to in-group/out-group boundaries across different social groups, such as migrant workers vs. locals, where local culture operates as a marker that excludes migrants from social networks.[31] Still another is the interaction between informal institutions and formal institutions, such as in the context of corruption, where certain mechanisms to create trust within social groups might interfere with the enforcement of formal laws. For example, gift-giving among business partners can become a contested issue in creating shared corporate cultures in foreign-invested companies.[32]

As all of these examples show, we cannot reduce 'culture' to a monolithic version of 'Chinese culture', even though we clearly discern patterns that appear to distinguish Chinese from others. In all of these cases, recurrent interactions among individuals create contexts where individual behaviour is channelled into stable patterns of behaviour which are then interpreted as cultural norms expressing the identities of people, consumers, migrants, managers and so on. So, in a nutshell, what we observe is a process that is embodied and realized via a number of distinct mechanisms. Thus, I argue that the ecological approach to culture ties in with the recent literature on mechanisms in sociology.[33]

In considering this literature, the surprising result is that culture can be analysed in terms of causal mechanisms; that is, in a naturalistic way broadly interpreted. This differs from common views that would approach cultural analysis as a hermeneutical task in the first place. However, the mechanism approach allows one to conjoin the different perspectives and is therefore a way to render triangulation methodologically operational. The central features of the mechanism approach are the following.

- A mechanism is a process that links causes with effects that can be traced empirically. The causal analysis is not based on regularities, especially of a statistical kind, but on the identification of certain constitutive structures that enable the mechanisms to work out their effects. Therefore, mechanisms are a variant of causal explanations. In a nutshell, mechanism research focuses on 'how' questions in the first place, and only secondarily on 'why' questions.[34]
- Mechanisms are local and plural. Mechanism research eschews large-scale structural explanations on the macro level, which would include notions such as 'culture' in the sense of an aggregate property of populations. Instead, mechanisms are seen as being embodied in local contexts and structures, and thus require corresponding empirical approaches. At the same time, there are no global and omnipotent mechanisms; this means that, in explaining certain regular patterns in empirical observations, the interactions among a number of mechanisms need to be considered explicitly.[35]
- Mechanism research leads towards the formulation of medium-range theories which only apply for certain places and periods. Such theories identify the constitutional structures which relate a set of mechanisms to each other. A medium-range theory connects a set of local studies and claims a constrained universality within the scope of place and period.[36]

- Mechanism analysis is multi-level, and thus eschews simple micro–macro dualisms. This means, first, that mechanisms on a certain level can often be decomposed into mechanisms on a lower level; and second, mechanisms of different reach and scope can interact, such as economic mechanisms on a regional level and on a local level, or mechanisms related to institutions with different reach and scope of enforcement and so on.[37]
- Mechanisms may be of different quality and hence with different disciplinary references. In the context of analysing culture, it is of particular importance to distinguish between cognitive mechanisms and other mechanisms, such as economic ones that directly involve causal factors such as resource scarcity. Cognitive mechanisms refer to the perception and interpretation of external facts by cognitive agents and include the symbolic domain, hence allowing for the integration of emic and etic analysis.[38]

In the following sections, I will develop a mechanism-based approach to culture that will guide my empirical work on China. For this, the relationship between culture and institutions is essential. Given my definition of culture, there is a clear distinction between institutions in general. I posit that institutions are actually an important part of the constitutive settings in which mechanisms are deployed. Then, we can approach institutions partly as embodiments of mechanisms, and partly as representations of mechanisms mediated via symbolic media.

Culture, institutions and ritual: the basic analytical model

The focus on institutions is congenial with economic analysis. My topic is China's economic culture, and therefore the natural focus is on the economic system and its institutions. The previously outlined approach to culture has a close affinity with institutional analysis, because institutions in general define contexts in which individual behaviour is geared towards stable patterns via incentivization and information. These patterns are realized by mechanisms. Further, the notion of culture bears a close relationship with the notion of 'informal institutions'. I have developed general theoretical categories and approaches elsewhere, so here I wish only to emphasize that my concept of institutions is a broad one including both formal and informal institutions as well as social norms and conventions, and treating institutions as a fundamental and generic feature of human social interaction. Elsewhere, I have coined this 'institutionally guided behavioural patterns' (IGBP). This captures an idea that is very common in the economic literature on institutions since Veblen's seminal contributions and matches with the aforementioned notion of internalization in general and governmentality more specifically. Institutions are not simply external mechanisms enforcing certain behaviours by means of various incentive mechanisms, but they are also partly internalized.[39] In other words, with regard to institutions, we face a similar methodological problem as with culture, which I am going to resolve in analysing institutions as also performative, and dissecting their workings into mechanisms on different levels. However, what clearly distinguishes institutions from culture is that the latter focuses on identity, whereas the former focuses on power as a more encompassing and general aspect of behaviour and behavioural coordination.

In the past, the role of power in institutions has been largely emphasized by sociology and political science, whereas economics tended to keep power out of its analytical concerns, highlighting criteria of efficiency instead. However, a growing number of economists have recently proposed power-based analytics in a positive theory of institutions.[40] I follow this line of thinking for two reasons. One is that considering formal institutions in their differences of habits, conventions and other related phenomena, the distinctive feature of the former is certainly the fact that formal institutions are enforced by formal and informal means. Enforcement is always rooted in asymmetries of power, which enables enforcing actions by one party onto another. Further, economic institutions may be seen as social mechanisms which tend to alleviate tensions or conflicts that arise from the struggle over scarce resources. The second reason is that in the Chinese context the issue of power looms especially large, as one of the core issues in understanding the Chinese economy today is the relationship between the political system and economic institutions.

The conceptual link between cultural and institutional analysis is straightforward to establish if we consider the question how IGBP can also be a defining part of individual identities, and how individual identities feedback on IGBP. Generally, the notion of institutions is far broader than the notion of culture that I submit in this book, since we include all institutions which cause behavioural regularities without necessarily being also constitutive of individual identities. For example, the institutions of a stock market may be treated as generic and universal, and may be analysed based on the blueprints of the legal norms that apply. However, the way in which they affect real-world behaviour might be mediated via the identities which relevant groups adopt in this particular context, such as lawyers, corporate directors, supervisors, etc. Their identities may play a role in the enforcement process and hence add a cultural dimension to what are generic formal institutions in the first place. Yet, analysis has to be very careful here, as those identities are also impregnated by power relationships, such as between the legal professions and the Communist Party.[41]

One question that can only be decided by methodological choices is how the scope of the notion of institutions is defined. I go for a very broad scope, which may be contested terrain. This also allows one to subsume certain aspects of individual economic behaviour under the rubric of institutions, such as consumer behaviour. If someone prefers salty dishes to sweet ones this may be purely idiosyncratic behaviour, and hence a habit. If this preference is regarded as a special aspect of regional food cultures in China, and is reflected in institutionalized forms of behaviour, such as established recipes for dishes, then we can also label this individual behaviour as IGBP, and ask how far this also relates to cultural phenomena. However, this still needs to distinguish neatly between institutionalized consumption patterns in general and those patterns that demarcate identities. Thus, a taste that is shared among members of a group may be entirely neutral regarding group boundaries, but it can assume the role of a boundary marker in the context of network formation, which involves creating in-group/out-group distinctions.

I adopt the general model of institutions developed by Masahiko Aoki in his program of Comparative Institutional Analysis (Figure 1.3). This approach matches my methodology because it emphasizes the role of institutions in the information architecture and information flows in the economy, and because it is externalist. In Aoki's view, institutions are sustainable patterns of social interaction in a population of actors which are mediated by public representations, or, more generally and in my parlance, by signs. The signs play an essential role in enabling the function of 'information compression' in the face of the overwhelming complexity of social interactions, especially in large populations. Single signs can only be fully interpreted in the context of sign systems. In other words, I introduce the perspective of semiotics into institutional analysis.[42] The resulting model is a general framework for analysing institutional mechanisms. On the one hand, it describes a causal circuit that is closed and manifests

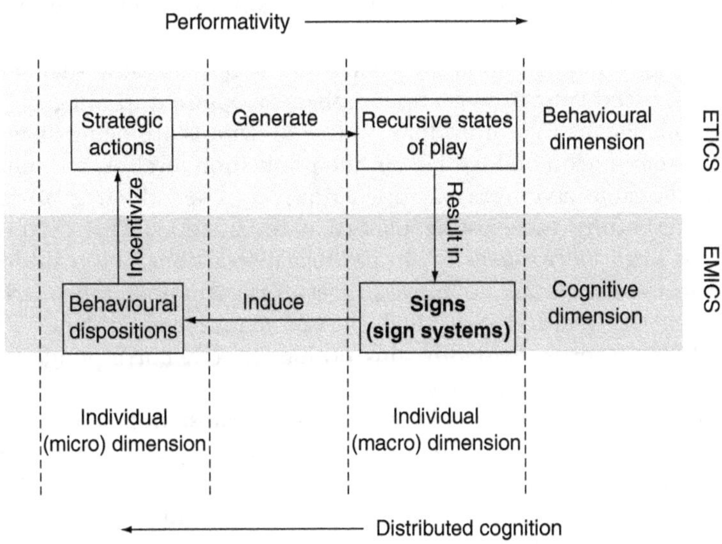

Figure 1.3 The revised Aoki model of institutions.

self-reinforcing effects; on the other hand, the concrete workings require dissection into a large number of mechanisms on different levels, such as the population level and the individual or even sub-individual level.

The feedback loop of an institution connects two different dimensions of analysis: one is the individual level versus the population level; the other is the behavioural level versus the cognitive level.

On the individual level, we observe the generation of certain actions expressing behavioural dispositions by means of cognitive mechanisms. A behavioural disposition can be measured, for example, by values surveys, thus connecting with an important strand of cultural analysis in social psychology. Since institutions by definition cover social interactions, we can apply general methods of game theory to understand the causality between the resulting individual actions and the emerging patterns of behaviour on the population level, in the sense of 'recursive states of play' as equilibria. This is another kind of mechanism typically examined by economics. One aspect of those states is the generation of certain signs. For example, in social interactions across in-group actors and out-group actors a certain habitus (in Bourdieu's sense) may be essential, such as wearing particular clothes or adopting particular styles of speech, actions which manifest the identities of actors and hence reduce the need for information. This is the information-compressing function of signs. This presupposes that signs are not idiosyncratic but are shared among the members of a population, so that we can say that individual cognitive performance is determined by population-level processes. This is called the 'distributed cognition' function of institutions which is well recognized in institutional economics in general. The underlying mechanisms are semiotic in nature and connect up with cognitive mechanisms, which closes the model.

Thus, the signs impact upon the behavioural dispositions, such as expressing enhanced trust in in-group members as opposed to out-group individuals. This means that individual choices of actions are being channelled via the semiotic embeddedness on the population level. As a result, the range of possible actions is narrowed down to a set which is more probable in sustaining the existing pattern of interaction. This corresponds to what I call 'performativity'. In performative actions, the realized social patterns induce certain cognitive processes via semiotic embeddedness, such that the realized individual choices manifest a tendency to reproduce these patterns. Evidently, this notion directly corresponds to Yamagishi's ecological approach to culture.[43]

This is a generic theoretical model, which can be substantiated empirically if we look at the persistent interaction patterns as such. This is the upper part of the diagram, which is the level on which we can typically apply economic analytical tools, such as those taken from game theory. Therefore, we adopt the etic perspective here. For example, we describe a certain institution as the outcome of interactions among rational actors who perceive and obtain certain pay-offs in their interactions, and who have therefore performed actions that stabilize the population-level pattern of actions. However, since these equilibria can only be maintained relative to a certain informational set, we have to move on to the cognitive dimension. Here, we meet an intricate analytical issue because, on the one hand, the signs that mediate between institutional equilibria and individual actions are population-level phenomena and therefore cannot be changed at whim by the individuals. Thus, they obtain a quasi-objective status relative to the individuals. Yet, on the other hand, signs are always being interpreted by individuals, which introduces a thoroughly subjectivist dimension. In institutional economics, this transition has been somewhat disguised, but also recognized, through the notion of 'shared mental models'. In our context, we argue that what is being shared is the same repertoire of signs, but these signs are not necessarily interpreted in the same way by all participants. So, there are forces of convergence and divergence. This is necessary in being able to explain why and how institutions change: the interpretive actions on the part of individuals, which result in certain dispositions to take action, introduce the necessary variety and diversity to trigger evolutionary changes.[44]

Thus, in my approach, the 'institution' is the entire feedback loop described in the model, and it is accessible in four ways. First, we can observe and evaluate individual actions; second, we can analyse patterns of actions on the population level; third, we relate these patterns to signs; and fourth, we can try to reconstruct the interpretive processes that connect signs, dispositions and actions. So, this approach combines etics and emics, and hence the model matches triangulation as an empirical approach. Methodologically, this analysis requires dissection into mechanisms on different levels, and to arrange them into one constitutive explanation. In this explanation, the institution is not a causal factor in explaining certain behaviours as is normally assumed by economists, but is itself an architecture of mechanisms in which the observed behaviour is one element.

We can now substantiate in more detail what cultural analysis means in the context of institutional analysis. For this, I introduce the central term in this book: 'ritual'. By 'ritual', I mean all institutionalized activities that serve to maintain a given set of signs and their interpretations that create, confirm and sustain the identities of actors in a population that shares these ritual practices. In the context of game theory, rituals are those activities that create common knowledge among the members of a population. Common knowledge reflects a particular cognitive structure which is reflexive; that is, the members of a population know that other members know that they have this knowledge, and that this is centred on the same sorts of facts. Knowledge of this kind is essential to stabilize behavioural patterns in institutional equilibria. Thus, ritual is an externalist notion that explains the coordination of behaviour by means of practices and not by internal cognitive states as the prime causal factor, which is conventionally the economic view. Further, I claim that shared identities are a most important means to create and stabilize common knowledge; and, vice versa, common knowledge defines identities. Hence, we can refer ritual to culture in the sense that culture, as the semiotic repertoire of creating and maintaining identities, is produced and reproduced by rituals. Finally, via rituals, the performative function of culture is realized; hence rituals generate culture as a social fact. In other words, we can now conjoin central terms in the analysis thus far, namely culture, institutions and ritual, in a simple definition of ritual: ritual is the institutions of culture as being embodied in social practices.[45]

I refer to this part of the mechanism of institutions as the 'distributed cognition' function which covers another idea that has been around in economics for many decades, such as in Hayek's view on institutions that emerge from 'human action, but not human design'.[46] This is a necessary correlate of the information-compressing function of institutions: By implication, individuals are never aware of all functions, causes and effects of institutions, because that would eventually erode the informational advantages from following an institution. In fact, for example, the high costs of maintaining a judicial system reveal the high investment that is necessary to make the full information transparent that is embodied in certain institutional practices, and often even these costly efforts remain contestable.

Common knowledge is constitutive of individual identities, because identities are mutually recognized by those individuals. Thus, we may conclude that identities and institutions are deeply enmeshed with each other in the sense that all institutions are also shaped by culture. Identities create a commitment mechanism because following an institution also means expressing and asserting a particular identity. On the other hand, as institutions are not directly a manifestation of culture, we can think of situations where institutions are established and enforced by political means, but which do not relate to the identities of actors, such that tensions emerge.

Let me give one Chinese example for the mechanisms that I have outlined thus far. During rural collectivization in the 1950s and 1960s, new organizational units were created: the People's Communes and the subordinate units, brigades and teams (for a detailed treatment and references, see Chapter 3). This introduced an entirely new set of signs (political symbols, slogans, etc.), bolstered by intensive ideological campaigns, which I regard as a form of ritual. However, these efforts partly failed to change the identities of actors, which were defined in terms of the traditional rituals of kinship in their daily interactions at the grassroots level. Thus, we clearly recognize that the social transformation that was triggered politically can only be properly understood by considering local mechanisms that involve complex interactions across levels and domains.

In this situation, the newly established signs were often interpreted in terms of the traditional ritual, which means, for example, that the assignment of farmers to collective units replicated the traditional kinship structure in the villages, thus preserving the material context of their individual identities (such as settlement patterns). Hence, collectivization resulted in a peculiar institutional equilibrium which was not simply the socialist collective property regime, but retained traditional notions of lineage property in the actual patterns of behaviour of farmers. In this sense, we can say that the socialist institutions, though being enforced by political means, remained embedded in culture. Since they also affected the identities of farmers, this process entailed serious tensions and conflicts in the villages, which often were not political in nature but were deeply shaped by the personal relations rooted in traditional understandings of kinship and relationships, hence traditional ritual.

To summarize: the Aoki model is a basic analytical structure that allows one to analyse the mechanisms that undergird the functioning of institutions in society, with the core mechanism being a semiotic one that enables the information-compressing function of institutions. This mechanism deeply connects institutional and cultural analysis. Both institutions and culture are performative, and institutions have a cultural dimension insofar as IGBPs can be constitutive of individual identities. This is an essential part of common knowledge in a society that underlies and enables the generation of stable equilibria in recurrent interactions. I have labelled the open set of societal practices that produce and reproduce this common knowledge as 'ritual'. At a closer look, we need to add the observation that ritual as such is also a kind of institution, namely all institutions that maintain and even enforce certain rituals producing common knowledge. Examples of institutions of this kind are religions, educational systems or political parties that enforce certain ideological positions among their members.

The emphasis on ritual is the core idea of this book, and it emerges from the mirror of culture. Although I introduce the term as a generic one, it also stays at the centre of all attempts to define distinctive features of Chinese culture as compared to Western culture. This applies for both Western scholars and Chinese indigenous approaches. The notion is always used in the context of Imperial China, but I will claim that, based on my generic model of institutions, we can also use it with reference to contemporary China. The foundational status of ritual in understanding traditional China has been largely established in comparing this concept with 'law', as in the work of Fei Xiaotong which I consider in Chapter 2. Fei argues that Western social theory distinguishes between the 'rule of law', 'fa zhi' (法治) and 'rule by men', 'ren zhi' (人治), thus overlooking a third alternative, 'rule by ritual', 'li zhi' (礼治). Here, Fei not only has the Chinese case in mind, but also makes a general point: Chinese ritual is seen as a special case of ritual order in general. Indeed, economic research on institutions focuses mainly on formal aspects of law, and certainly highlights the 'rule of law' as the distinct feature of Western modernity. In the indigenous Chinese reference, however, 'ritual' has a similar status to 'law' and has always been presented as an alternative way of creating social order, especially in Confucian thinking. In subsequent chapters, I will try to show that with the help of the generic notion of ritual we can also develop a more precise grasp of the Chinese meaning of 'ritual' and its relevance for understanding contemporary Chinese culture.

However, this convergence of Chinese uses and the theoretical concept of ritual has to be interpreted also in the sense that the one-sided emphasis on law is, in turn, a cultural notion. In other words, I do not simply assert that ritual is more important than law in China compared to the West. On the contrary, in the mirror of culture both notions seem to be entangled in cycles of orientalism and reverse orientalism. Ritual as a generic category in analysing social order is as important in the West as in China; however, Western self-perceptions tend to shift ritual into a blind spot, such that it has rarely achieved a central status in Western theories about social order. The Chinese emphasis on ritual, as a cultural concept, leads us also to re-appreciate the universal significance of ritual in understanding economic institutions. In other words, if we approach China in terms of ritual, we should avoid falling into the analytical trap that this also means that law is a less significant notion. After all, in traditional China ritual was also enshrined in legal institutions. On the other hand, when taking 'the West' as a comparative benchmark, we should move out of the blind spot in which we blank out the importance of ritual as a generic form of creating and maintaining social order.[47]

There is another aspect of this comparison which looms large also at the theoretical level. A fundamental difference between the Western notion of 'law' and the Chinese notion of 'ritual' is that both posit different normative claims. 'Law' appears to be tied to the idea of equality before the law, in the sense of being abstract rules that do not refer to particular properties of actors, whereas Chinese 'ritual' regards the inequality of individuals as a basic assumption. However, if we use 'ritual' as a generic theoretical term, we can draw upon a substantial literature also in economics that emphasizes the role of status differences in imposing order upon market transactions and their institutional context. We can then approach ritual as complementary to law even in the Chinese meaning, applied in the cross-cultural context and even at the generic theoretical level. In these generic uses of the related notion of 'status', status differences have the function of signalling quality and hence overcoming information asymmetries in any kind of social interaction, including economic ones; further, and evidently, status is a medium through which decentralized and self-organizing mechanisms of enforcing institutions can operate.[48]

In this view, status is an essential analytical category in understanding culture, since status is a defining aspect of individual identity in terms of relating to reference groups and in defining in-group (sharing the same status) and out-group (with a different status). Thus, cultural action is often deeply enmeshed with signalling status distinctions among different groups. This is an aspect of culture that is largely highlighted in the field of 'cultural studies', which also emphasize the role of status differences in maintaining structures of power in given societies.[49]

Therefore, we can close our conceptual framework at this point in relating the notion of ritual to the concept of governmentality that I highlighted at the beginning of this chapter: As in Foucault's original thought, ritual as common knowledge is a way of socially organizing knowledge in society, especially with reference to what Foucault calls 'les savoirs assujeti'. Chinese ritual was essential in maintaining social order in terms of social hierarchies. Yet, this is only a special example of the generic function of ritual across all human societies. We can now say that governmentality therefore relates to all ritual means by which status differences in societies are maintained that impact upon the enforcement of institutions, which in turn make up the body politic in terms of regulating all kinds of conflicts over resources and power. In this sense, governmentality closely relates to the term 'governance', but goes far beyond 'government'. Institutions define governance regimes in societies, and governmentality determines the resilience and stability of institutions, rooted in status orders that are maintained by ritual.

To summarize this central section in the deployment of my theoretical approach, I present the following definition of ritual:

> Ritual is the open set of institutionalized social practices that involve semiotic repertoires and related communicative actions by which the culture of a certain population of actors is produced and reproduced; thereby, ritual maintains status orders in a population which are constitutive for individual identities of actors. Status orders undergird the enforcement of institutions, a part of which also maintain ritual, and hence are an essential element of governmentality in a particular society sharing ritual practices.

Expanding the analytical toolbox: path dependencies in networks of culture

I will now introduce a conceptual structure that helps render my abstract theoretical framework operational for empirical analysis. The Aoki model describes evolutionary institutional equilibria. The pivotal phenomena are the signs, which, as we have seen, are reproduced by rituals that are part and parcel of the entire institutional set-up. Now, we need to recognize that there is no limitation to the kinds of phenomena that can obtain the status of a sign, because this is the expression of the creativity of the cultural process. Therefore, I introduce the more general term 'element'.

An element can be a text, a pattern of behaviour as part of habitus, a building, an organizational routine and so forth. It is the task of empirical analysis which elements actually obtain semiotic status in cultural creativity; an important point of access is the identification and analysis of rituals that govern the use of the signs qua elements. In other words, there is no predetermined set of phenomena or items that have 'cultural' properties.

This approach has important implications for cultural analysis. For almost two centuries, cultural analysis has suffered from the tension between atomistic and holistic approaches.[50] The latter emphasize the integrity and coherence of semiotic systems of culture and therefore treat 'cultures' as holistic, such as 'Chinese culture'. The former looks at cultural items and approaches culture as the activity of bricolage that operates on this open set of items. The holistic view emphasizes cultural resilience and stability through time; the atomistic view emphasises cultural change and syncretism. I claim that my approach helps resolve this conceptual tension. On the one hand, atomism is right in emphasizing the openness and fluidity of culture; on the other hand, as culture fixates individual identities, it becomes part and parcel of institutional equilibria in which there are manifold checks and balances that contain and channel cultural change, thus expressing the 'wholeness' of culture. In particular, culture is undergirded by rituals, which in turn have institutional causal powers, eventually also including the power of enforcement.

The important empirical consequence of this view is that we cannot impose any conceptual constraint upon what we conceive of as 'Chinese culture'. Chinese culture today is certainly not 'tradition' in any way, even if we observe the revival of tradition, such as of popular religion or of kinship rituals. Chinese culture today involves many signs that did not exist in Imperial China, such as modern consumer items, organizational routines of CCP, or foreign invested companies. All of these items are elements that can obtain a cultural status. For example, the heavy presence of foreign companies in China induces a trend towards professionalization among educated young urbanites, which directly affects their identities, and thus gives rise to new forms of ritualization of behaviour that is part and parcel of contemporary Chinese culture, but may or may not tie in with traditional notions of ritual.

Next, elements play an essential role in the mechanisms which underlie the emergence of 'patterns' that reflect institutions on the population level. Patterns are what we can observe, for example, as certain statistical regularities in economic phenomena, or certain systematic outcomes in behavioural data, such as increasing private economic activity. However, the generating forces of patterns are partly rooted in the cognitive processes of individuals; that is, patterns are based on perceptions, and hence are partly constructed by the actors who perceive the interplay of elements. In other words, patterns are expressions of sense-making. Patterns are dynamic, but they result in 'processes'. Processes go back to convergent individual actions and thus reflect mechanisms of aggregation. For example, elements may be particular consumer items, processes are the confluence of many individual demands into a market demand that drives the emergence of new structures of products, and technologies and consumption practices on the population level. Thus, market processes represent mechanisms of aggregation. I call the resulting structures 'states'. In my example, a state is the institutionalized set of consumption practices, production technologies, marketing activities and so forth which define a particular branch of industry or product group.

A state is the real-world reflection of the institution; that is, for example, the pattern of economic growth which emerges in a particular region of China and which is being embodied in certain outcomes, such as a distribution of income and profits among the population, a distribution of infrastructural assets across counties and so forth. Tellingly, this is reflected in the Chinese notion of models, 'moshi' (模式) on different levels of aggregation, with the 'China model' being treated with scepticism, but models on lower levels of aggregation proliferating, such as the Wenzhou model of private enterprise, the Jiangsu model of TVE development and subsequent privatization, or lower-level models even of single villages. Evidently, a state comes close to a medium-level theoretical term in the sense that it combines different mechanisms into a constitutive description of the institution. The explanatory circle is closed when we consider the fact that states can turn into elements in interpretive processes. For example, the institutions of urban China become embodied in certain states of urbanization, such as buildings and the design of cities. These states can become signs in themselves, and even their construction may have already been driven also by interpretive processes. Thus, the design of cities becomes an element that further drives the institutional process.[51]

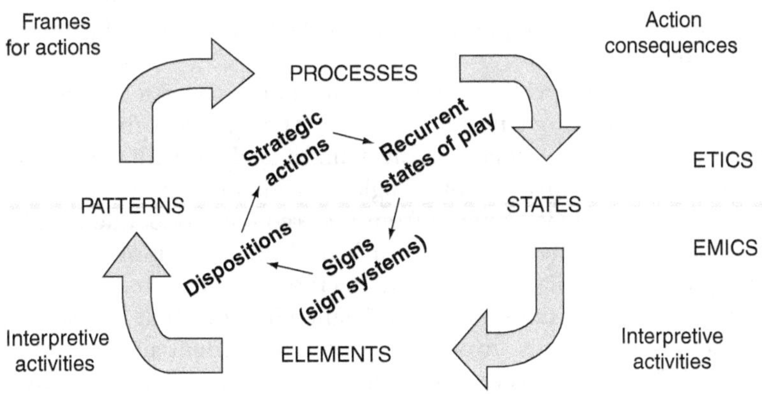

Figure 1.4 Cultural dynamics: the 'elements–patterns–processes–states' cycle.

I summarize and overview this discussion in Figure 1.4. Here, I relate my fourfold conceptual scheme 'elements–patterns–processes–states' to the original Aoki model. Basically, we can again distinguish between the performative and the distributed cognition part of the picture, which I also relate to the distinction between emic and etic. The performative part links the interpretive activities with action consequences in framing the decisions of actors. This is the part that connects signs with dispositions and hence the actions that result in recurrent states of play. Thus, performativity results in real-world consequences that we can analyse using etic methods, such as analysing divergent patterns of economic growth across Chinese regions. The distributed cognition part relates the recurrent states to the signs and the dispositions to act, and can only be analysed empirically in moving to the emic perspective. Figure 1.4 depicts the most general framework for understanding culture as a social mechanism. This framework can only be made empirically operational in detailing specific mechanisms, such as specific interpretive processes, certain dynamics of aggregation, or certain feedback loops that relate individual actions to individual outcomes.[52]

This approach can be most generally characterized as a network approach to culture. We consider culture as a dynamic network of elements which displays patterns and processes that coalesce into network states.[53] We consider two dimensions of networks. One is the network of elements that are activated as signs through the interactions between individuals, which in turn constitute a network in the second dimension. This perspective also allows one to further substantiate the relationship between culture and institutions, as we can say that institutions are aspects of networks of interactions. This in a twofold sense. First, institutions impose constraints upon the number and quality of interactions in networks of individuals; second, emergent patterns of behaviour in networks may result in institutionalization, in the sense of the Aoki model. With reference to culture, the constraints emerge as expressions of different identities of members of a population, such as being members of groups with different status.

The network perspective allows the introduction of a few additional theoretical notions for cultural analysis.[54] The first is path dependency, which is also a central category in mechanism analysis. Path dependency is a property of mechanisms, both single and interacting. In network analysis, path dependencies emerge from the frequency dependency of individual decision-making; in other words, individual decisions depend on the frequency of similar or matching decisions on the part of other individuals. Evidently, actions which maintain identities that are shared by other people necessarily involve frequency dependent phenomena. For example, if I adopt a certain way of dressing to indicate my identity, that depends on whether others who share this identity also adopt this style of dressing. If only a minority change their behaviour, this may not affect my decision. Thus, path dependency also involves critical mass phenomena which are process specific: once a critical mass is obtained, collective behaviour may shift abruptly.[55]

I have already critically assessed the widespread belief in cultural analysis that culture is about the persistence of the past in present social interactions. This, of course, begs the question how this persistence is actually happening, since we may otherwise assume that rational individuals will simply adapt to the circumstances. I argue that this persistence can be analytically grasped as path dependencies. Path dependencies are network phenomena sui generis which we can analyse on two levels, following the Aoki model. These two levels are the level of interactions and the cognitive level, which are connected via a specific kind of interaction, namely communication involving signs. In other words, we have path dependencies in the interactions between individuals that produce certain outcomes and which may, for example, be analysed by using tools of game theory. At the same time, the use of signs creates other kinds of path dependencies in communication, since individuals have to rely on certain shared interpretations of signs if they wish to communicate successfully.

Thus, we can distinguish between three kinds of path dependencies.[56]

- *Type A.* These result from individual choices of actions which directly relate to the frequency of this action in a population, such as in the aforementioned case of fashion.
- *Type B.* These are network externalities which result in any kind of communication system where interfaces play an important role, such that the success of communication depends on the shared use of certain media, signs, etc.
- *Type C.* These are interactions between the two levels, such that certain kinds of A and B path dependencies may be strengthened by path dependencies on the semiotic level; for example, we need to distinguish between decisions to adopt a certain style of dress and the conversations over fashion issues.

Type C path dependencies are of particular importance in stabilizing rituals, since rituals rely on shared uses of signs. Hence, ritualization also feeds back on type A and B path dependencies. However, on the semiotic level we can also observe path dependencies of types A and B, not regarding actions but regarding sign uses. We can then even speak of n'th order type C path dependencies once we consider the reflexive use of signs. I argue that this is where we can also speak of cultural phenomena once reflexivity also involves identities of actors.

This analysis is of great significance for institutional analysis, as I show in Figure 1.5. This is because many institutions are created by deliberate political action, especially in modern times. This is what I call institutional design, a process that is certainly essential in China since the CCP assumed

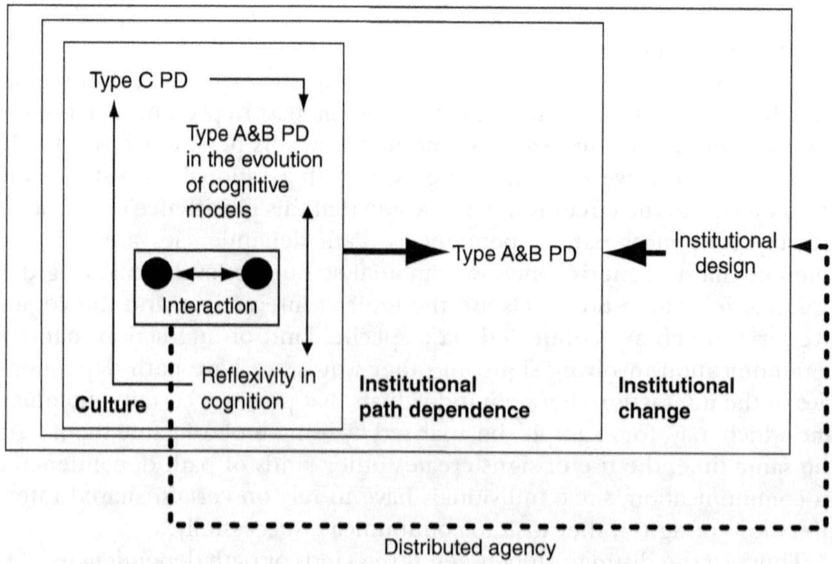

Figure 1.5 Path dependencies and institutional design.

power. The entire modernization effort of the CCP may be understood as a programme of institutional design. Path dependencies imply that design actions interact with forces that do not necessarily concur with the direction of the design. When paths are embedded in cognitive path dependencies, this effect can be particularly strong and is often referred to in the literature as tension between formal and informal institutions. In fact, this distinction is only relative to the design measure which claims the legitimacy of formalization, thus driving existing institutionalizations into the realm of informality. Yet, because of the strong interaction between institutional and cognitive path dependencies, the resulting paths can have institutional features that are as strong as in the case of formal enforcement.

Therefore, institutional design as such is insufficient to understand institutional change. Institutional design always aims at changing existing institutions. Existing institutions, however, manifest path dependencies because their main function is to maintain networks of interactions, and because the latter feedback on the institutions. Further, as we have seen, institutions may be partly internalized, in the sense of having defining functions for individual identities. The resulting networks of interactions generate resilient patterns that cannot be changed by institutional design unless sufficient critical mass would be created. However, as the aforementioned example of rural collectivization has shown, in the Aoki model the institutional path dependencies are embedded in cognitive path dependencies which are mediated via communication processes. On this level we also have path dependencies which, as shown in our example, may result in the resilience of kinship rituals in the interpretation of externally imposed institutions, which ultimately do not fully change the network interactions that are actually being covered by these institutions. Thus, type A and B institutional path dependencies, embedded in culture, result in the resilience of lineage structures in the shape of rural collectives.

There is an additional feedback loop which I label 'distributed agency'. In other words, the actors who implement institutional design may themselves be participants of the cultural processes. For example, cadres in People's Communes headquarters were relatives of the farmers whose behaviour they were expected to change. Thus, we cannot say that they are external actors, and we cannot even say that they have full control of the process, including their own actions. One way to grasp these interdependencies is to refer to the shared identities of actors, and also to the ways in which institutional change affects those identities. For example, in rural collectivization the CCP propaganda aimed at changing the kinship-based identities to class-based identities, thus aiming at separating the enforcers of institutional change from their previous identities. Hence, distributed agency closely relates with the analysis of status in the context of rituals. Institutional change often involves changes of status, and persistent status distinctions affect institutional change. Mechanism analysis thus goes beyond conventional analysis of class or interest groups in explaining institutional change, and focuses on status and status differences of actors in local contexts which result in collective action; this does not necessarily imply active involvement, but also acceptance and support.[57]

So, in summary, I argue that the shadow of history in cultural phenomena may be analysed in terms of path dependencies which are primarily cognitive and semiotic, but which interact with institutional path dependencies. Now, we can combine this with a more general phenomenon, which is the ubiquity of singular events, in order to introduce another core theoretical notion, 'historicity' (Figure 1.6). Singular events can be of two different kinds. One is simply the fact that many events happen without any regularity, especially in the sense of staying in no direct causal connection with the processes which they impact upon, and which may manifest a regular nature. For example, the eruption of a volcano is not causally connected with the economy, but may exert a strong singular impact upon it. The other kind of singularity reflects the complexity of the processes proper: if any actor in the system aims at predicting these events, she will fail to achieve this because of this complexity. As a consequence, actions based on these predictions are random forces with regard to the systemic causal mechanisms that impact upon them. A straightforward example is the failure to predict financial crises in complex market economies. This kind of complexity is a defining feature of all systems (both physical and social), which have many levels, change

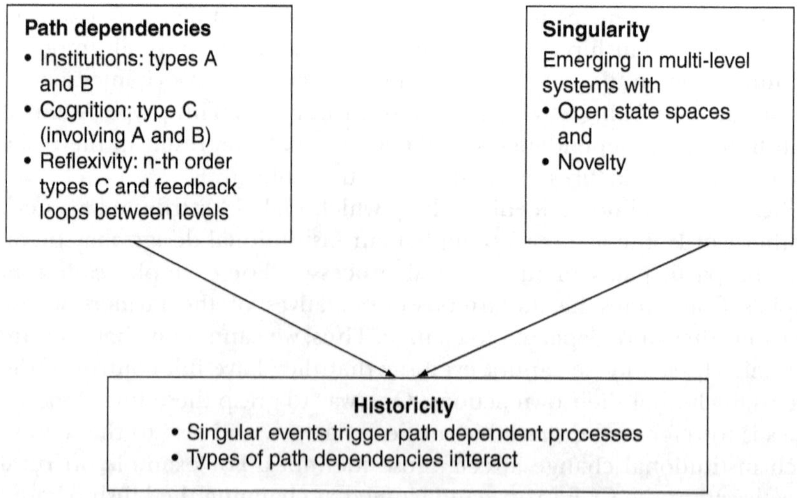

Figure 1.6 Historicity.

in an open space of possible states, and which include processes that create novelty (for example, an ecosystem is multi-level, is not bound to certain mechanistically available sets of states, and manifests novelty because of mutations on the organismic level).

Singular events combine with path dependencies in triggering certain trajectories of change which are self-reinforcing afterwards, but may not have been attainable without the occurrence of that event. Thus, singularity and path dependency together constitute what I call the 'historicity' of economic and institutional evolution. Historicity is often confused with the impact of 'culture' in the sense of the past shaping the present. Yet, this is not a cultural phenomenon at all, in the sense of my definition of 'culture'. Historicity is a property of current trajectories of evolution, and there are no causes in the past that directly determine these trajectories. However, culture comes into play if sense-making activities impose constraints upon possible trajectories via stabilizing the identities of actors.[58]

One basic conceptual distinction which is valuable in understanding historicity is between synchronic and diachronic analysis. If we consider particular institutions, they never stand on their own but are enmeshed in a web of institutions, both formal and informal. As shown in the discussion of path dependency, this creates functional requirements and constraints in combining institutions and creating and maintaining interfaces, if certain expectations regarding the performance of actions, conducted by the institutions, are to be met. In our example of rural collectivization, this refers to the interface between the formal institutions of the collectives and the institutions of extended kinship, which have been relegated to informal institutions by political force. However, in order to maintain commitments to cooperation, the actual implementation of the formal institutions had to dovetail with the informal institutions. If we consider a particular point in time, this is a synchronic phenomenon in the first place. In order to explain the existence of the informal institutions, we need to resort to diachronic analysis. However, since many elements of the old institutions were destroyed (such as formal lineage property), we cannot simply say that the past institutions have causal force on current institutions: this causal force only operates in the synchronic dimension. Diachronic factors come to the fore if we consider temporal interfaces. One problem here is the varying duration of certain mechanisms in terms of the realizing processes. For example, even though revolutionary institutional design has abolished lineage property as a formal institution, thus also affecting certain aspects of inheritance, this does not imply that certain assumptions about household structure have changed, such as the idea that households are represented by male household heads. This assumption may only change at the time scale of generations, whereas the abolition of lineage property can be done literally overnight. Male household leadership can be reflected in arrangements about land-use rights in collective landownership, thus even reinforcing traditional concepts.[59]

In conclusion, we can state that ritual and institutions play closely together, as ritual can be a substantial force in creating path dependencies of institutional change. Vice versa, institutions often undergird ritual because the creation and propagation of ritual is institutionalized. One important aspect of ritual is the reproduction of identities and status. This leads us to consider an additional expansion of our analytical toolbox.

Expanding the analytical toolbox: social capital and status orders

The second important concept in cultural network analysis is social capital. This may appear to be a narrow and very specific notion, but I argue that it is in fact very general if we consider the capabilities and functioning that individuals assume in network interactions, and which project beyond network relations, such as enabling certain economic activities.[60] The concept of social capital is powerful here because it keeps the basic economic assumption that individuals pursue their individual goals under constraints. Social capital is the accumulated stock of capabilities that they can use to exploit network relationships in order to achieve those goals, aside of other capabilities such as skills which are independent from network relations. These capabilities manifest another version of the tension between internalist and externalist views, since, on the one hand, capabilities may be individual in nature, such as my skills and education or other personal characteristics. However, the idea of social capital also recognizes the essential fact that my capabilities also depend on my position in networks, my relationships with others, and also on the interest others have in my capabilities. There is a well-developed analytical and quantitative subdiscipline in sociology dealing with networks that is only slowly being accepted in economics, although in sociology it has proven to be very fruitful in understanding larger patterns of behaviour and outcomes, especially in the economy.[61]

The different dimensions of networks highlighted in the pertinent research are summarized in Figure 1.7. This diagram describes the constitutive setting in which a large number of social mechanisms is arranged that link certain social states of individuals with outcomes of actions; thus we meet another instance of mechanistic explanation. It shows that, on the one hand, network structures are causal generators of the distribution of capabilities in a population of actors, which includes the accessibility of other resources via those networks, such as political power via personal connections. However, we also need to consider determinants of capabilities that are not directly linked with networks, and, in particular, we need to relate capabilities with sets of functioning. Functioning may be understood as roles or social positions that actors are expected to play, and can be generic or specific to these roles. As we see, social capital is also important for establishing the conceptual bridge to my previous analysis of ritual. On the one hand, status is an important determinant of social capital, but at the same time, power that results from social capital can feed back on status, thus establishing another kind of self-reinforcing feedback mechanism.

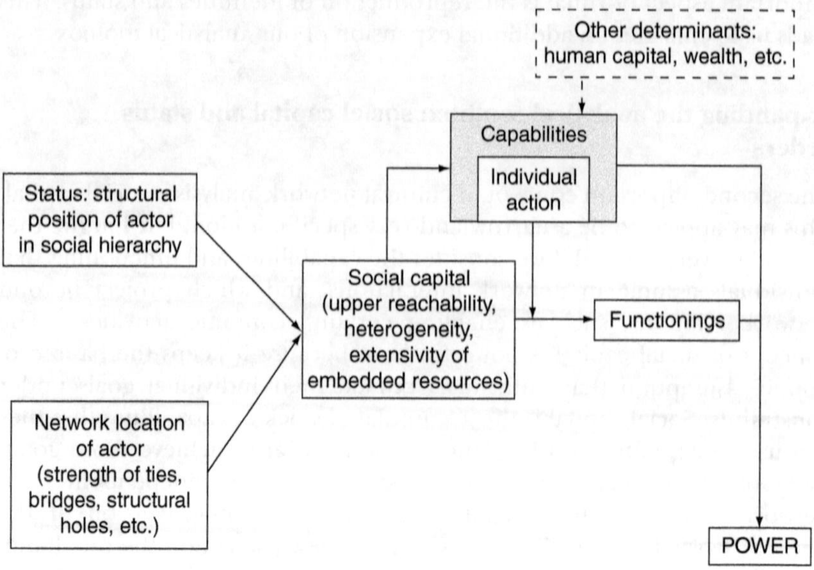

Figure 1.7 The structure of social capital.

Source: modified after Lin (2001).

Therefore, the distribution and evolution of social capital in a particular society can manifest path dependencies as analysed in the previous section. In other words, social capital has the property of historicity.

The social capital perspective is thoroughly individualistic in the sense that network analysis always treats individuals as primordial constituents of networks. This also applies in institutional analysis via the function of enforcement mechanisms in stabilizing institutions. We can say that ultimately the distribution of social capital in society determines the distribution of power which undergirds the institutions. This idea is operational if we include access to organizations and command of symbolic resources as aspects of network relationships. On the other hand, there are individual capabilities that do not directly connect with network structures, such as human capital and wealth. Thus, extending the concept does not result in arbitrary references.

For example, consider the changes in China's local society in the twentieth century. The starting point was a system where local elites such as lineage leaders had accumulated large amounts of social capital, which reflected their special position as intermediaries between the Imperial state and local society, undergirded by a whole range of symbolic actions which reflected their network position that was also directly engineered by the Imperial governance of rituals. With the collapse of the Imperial order, these elites were rapidly marginalized by newly emerging elites that mainly exploited wealth and command of violence in order to control local society; this also undermined state power. When the CCP gained control over China, a crucial political measure was the radical restructuring of rural elites, mainly based on class criteria, which also redefined the role of social capital. Relationships with the CCP became an important though not exclusive element in determining social capital. After decollectivization in the 1980s, the elements and determinants of social capital changed again, reinstating the role of wealth, but also partly reviving kinship as a network dimension; these developments, however, did not eclipse the importance of political connections to the CCP. This brief summary shows how social capital interacts with institutional changes in society, since at the grassroots level the enforcement of formal institutions depends ultimately on the social structures which propagate and enforce those institutions. Thus, for example, in Republican times social changes drove local society to the brink of collapse, and restoring order was a major reason why the CCP was able to gain supremacy in the civil war.

Similar as in the case of ritual, the social capital approach also results in illuminating reflections in the indigenous conceptualization of social relationships as networks. The network paradigm has always played an important though contested role in Chinese studies (for more on this, see Chapter 5). I argue that one reason is the insufficient grounding in generic theorizing. For example, approaching political power in China in terms of the social capital concept converges with Chinese studies approaches which try to understand political power and political change based on networks, factions and other groups within the organizational context of the Communist Party. It is important to supplement recent economic theories about the nature of the Chinese system relating to elite management and governance.[62]

Social capital is essential for cultural analysis since we can say that all network interactions are based on the identities of actors, and also feedback on these identities. Therefore, social capital analysis directly concurs with our working definition of culture. This is well recognized in the literature on China, even on the general level of 'Chineseness'. For example, diaspora Chinese capitalism is often portrayed as being embedded in dynamic business networks which are heavily imbued by ethnicity in terms of activating in-group/out-group boundaries (or, more precisely, on subethnicity, as Overseas Chinese networks build largely on shared regions of origin). Similarly, cultural diversity within China can be closely related to social capital analysis, such as when comparing the capabilities of farmers, migrants and urban populations, and their related functioning.[63]

The notions of social capital, status and ritual are closely connected. I introduce the notion of 'status order' to refer to a stable distribution of social capital across the members of a population through time, grasping the historicity of social capital in terms of its macro-expressions. Status orders may be identified by common methods of social network analysis, among other methods, and are expressed in many forms of institutionalized behavioural patterns. For example, consumption styles can express status orders, and hence are regulated by institutions in many societies, or settlement patterns can reflect status differences between different groups in society. In other words, social capital finds expression in rituals, which thereby transmit common knowledge about status orders in society. Thus, for example, distinct consumption styles of the native urban population and migrant workers reflect the status order that is also enshrined in the institutions of the household registration system.

Thus, in summary, I posit that there are two aspects of institutions that directly express the dynamics of networks, and which also become manifest as cultural phenomena. Both phenomena are important aspects of social mechanisms and therefore allow for a more focused and systematic approach in identifying the constitutive structure of cultural analysis. The first is path dependency, which occurs on both the level of interactions and the level of accompanying communication processes involving semiotic resources; the second is social capital and its implications for the distribution of power in society, which ties in with the enforcement of institutions, and relates to social structure in terms of the constitution and distribution of different groups in society. Evidently, social capital can therefore also manifest path dependencies, which can lend more detail to explanations of institutional resilience that may be perceived as a cultural phenomenon. The relationship between social capital, status and institutions is therefore an important analytical pattern that underlies the identification of forms of governmentality. If we make the two-level dynamics of path dependency explicit, meaning to account for the separate role of cognitive processes, we can complete this analytical picture.

For example, the aforementioned resilience of lineage structures in rural collectivization may be explained in terms of the restricted capacity of external intervening actors to transform the distribution of social capital in rural communities, often requiring resorting to violent means which itself create new social tensions and contradictions. Following the abolishment of the collective institutions, 'traditional' social networks re-emerged in many areas of China, partly reflected in the revival of cultural expressions of lineage authority in the rural areas. In my approach, we do not need to explain these phenomena in terms of certain 'ingrained' traditional values and beliefs, but as resulting from path dependencies and the distribution of social capital, which incentivizes certain actors to revive traditional symbolic means of expressing local identities. This is tantamount to reviving certain rituals, understood both in the generic theoretical sense and in the traditional Chinese sense. However, this does not imply that these rituals also express the same underlying social structure as in traditional China. Thus, social capital analysis in combination with path dependency allows for a proper weighing up of diachronic and synchronic aspects in constitutive explanations of certain social phenomena. We concentrate on the social reproduction and transformation of culture, and do not approach culture as a causal factor of its own.

The concept of 'economic style'

Putting the ideas of this chapter into the context of economics, I introduce a notion that is peculiar to a largely forgotten strand in economic research of German-speaking academia: the concept of 'economic style'. This concept tries to combine general economic laws with the observation of regularities that are specific to place and time, and thus anticipates the idea of medium-range theorizing in mechanism analysis. In economics, we often meet the difficulty that economists try to discover universal regularities which connect certain institutions with outcomes that can be related to a universal etic benchmark, such as efficiency or growth. However, in spite of the fact that certain universal propositions of economics appear almost intuitively true, the devil lies in the detail. China is of course a case that posits a particularly difficult challenge for economics, as her institutions appear to be highly deficient so far as standard assumptions about the institutions–performance link are concerned. The only way out of this conundrum is to approach these institutions as temporary and transitory ones, though recognizing that, with the increasing length of the so-called Chinese 'reforms', this argument becomes more and more tenuous. Thus, I propose that we can resolve this dilemma by introducing the concept of 'economic style'. In a nutshell, this means analysing the cultural dimension of the economic system, relying on the notion of culture as deployed thus far.[64]

The standard economic approach notoriously assumes that there is a generic benchmark for designing economic institutions, such that 'in the long run' institutional evolution across the globe may converge. This idea has been questioned by the literature devoted to the 'varieties of capitalism', which, however, is largely produced in the context of political science, whereas economists tend towards polar oppositions, such as opposing generic concepts of 'planned economy' versus 'market economy', or 'civil law' versus 'common law' regimes, or 'limited' versus 'open access orders', while assigning an elevated status to one of the poles. It is important to note the methodological differences between these approaches. The economic approach typically tries to characterize polar regimes by certain properties which can be measured and then aims at identifying the institutions–performance link via econometric analysis. Compared with this approach, the 'varieties of capitalism' school is much more geared towards a mechanism analysis; for example, in the context of studying governance mechanisms and their effect on labour markets and firm performance.[65]

The notion of economic style posits that any kind of institutions–performance link is culturally mediated, in the sense of being performed, with a range of variation that is circumscribed by the cultural medium. In this case, similar levels of performance may be achieved with diverse institutions, if the medium of culture varies. This can show up, for example, in the impact of diverse values upon the individual and collective responses to certain institutions and their generic incentives. If this is the case, there is a need for supplementing the economic theories with theoretical concepts of medium range. These concepts would identify certain mechanisms by which we explain the observations, but which have limited applicability in time and space, or, generally, are 'local' in nature.

I define a particular 'economic style' as an intermediate-level theoretical concept which results from the cultural analysis of economic institutions, as outlined in this chapter, and that applies to a particular region and period. Thus, for example, we can identify a peculiar 'Japanese economic style' that was prevalent after the Second World War and which is currently undergoing important changes, though still with an uncertain outcome. We need to distinguish between concepts that analyse single mechanisms, such as behavioural responses to certain property rights institutions, and concepts that aim at grasping the unity and coherence of a set of such mechanisms. This unity is derived from the construction of 'culture' as a process of sense-making in a universe of contested meanings and in a specific spatial and temporal context. In other words, we can analyse an 'economic system' such as the case of China in terms of generic institutional descriptions; for example, the distribution of ownership types in the economy. If we look at these descriptions from the angle of culture, and analyse distinct behavioural responses, we complement the analysis of the economic system by identifying the 'economic style'. Only by adding the cultural dimension to economic analysis can we fully describe the social mechanisms that work in the generation of economic performance. Thus, as in the example to which I have referred several times, describing property rights in Chinese rural areas would be incomplete if we only focus on the formal institutions (collective ownership) and apply universal economic theories about incentives and private vs. public goods in order to explain the economic consequences of this regime. We need to expand the analysis and analyse how these formal institutions are being interpreted in the context of local structures of kinship and community. Only then will we achieve a full-scale explanation of the economic mechanisms and causality.

However, this example also demonstrates that the complete analysis of mechanisms remains fundamentally local also in its explanatory claims. Thus, the case study is the archetypical method in this approach, which interestingly matches with the recent developments in China studies where case studies abound, facing the bewildering complexity and variety of China. If we ask for a general description of the economic style of China, the only way is to identify family resemblances across a series of case studies. This can be partly based on quantitative analysis; for example, we can construct a sample of localities and test econometrically for certain causal chains that involve both formal institutions and cultural factors, thus ending up with insights that can be generalized. However, these quantitative results only have empirical meaning if they can be substantiated by local mechanism analysis.[66]

Thus, an economic style is a more general notion of an open set of constitutive explanations with local grounding in the first place. If we relate this notion to the Aoki model, we can say that this model gives a universal framework for analysing mechanisms and putting them into context, whereas the style notion is the principle that guides the discovery of family resemblances that we can extract from a number of cases, both in the diachronic and the synchronic dimension.

If we want to identify family resemblances, we need a pivotal point that creates the perspective under which we perceive those resemblances. This pivotal point defines the 'style' of the economic system, and it is the expression of the observer's creative act in positing culture as a cross-cultural phenomenon. In this book, I will develop the central hypothesis that the unifying concept in identifying the Chinese economic style is the notion of 'ritual'. As we have seen, this view is actually two-pronged, and it is only because of this fact that we can use the notion of 'ritual' to identify the economic style. On the one hand, I refer to the generic meaning of ritual; on the other hand, I present ritual as a specific way to identify 'Chineseness' in the Chinese economic style, starting out from identifying family resemblances with the past, centring on historical meanings of 'ritual'. As I have already argued, this reference to ritual not only implies that the Chinese economic style is shaped by ritual, but also that current self-perceptions of Western economic systems suffer from a blind spot in failing to recognize ritual as a major determinant of economic processes apart from the formal institutions of the law. As we can see, this approach conjoins mechanism analysis with the hermeneutic perspective that is so far the most obvious methodology of cultural analysis. Constructing an economic style is an activity that explicitly and reflexively involves recurrent movements in the 'mirror of culture'.

Thus, on the generic level, I posit that in the analysis of economic systems, ritual is a universal, albeit so far neglected concept, and that it comes to the fore when we analyse any kind of economic style. Ritual as creating common knowledge refers to a wide range of phenomena. For example, economic systems might manifest peculiar business cultures and cultures of leadership. This is salient if we compare the role of executives in France, Germany and the USA, where distinct historical traditions in education and career patterns had emerged. In these respects, the role of managers is defined by certain rituals in business life. Compare, for example, the role of MBA education in the USA with the entirely different educational approach in Germany until most recently. Or, rituals refer to the expression and propagation of certain ideas about economic policy and institutions which may seem almost meaningless ideological commitments, but nevertheless appear to stabilize certain basic institutional patterns. If we take the case of the USA and Germany again, there are clear and fundamental divergences regarding beliefs about the role of government in guaranteeing a certain level of welfare for all members of society, which are recurrently expressed in political statements or in the media.[67]

So I argue that ritual is the defining characteristic of an economic style as compared to the analysis of the economic system in terms of formal institutions that is commonly the focus of economics. If we consider the breadth of the concept that has unfolded in this chapter, we can also pinpoint this role of ritual in being the public manifestation of a specific form of governmentality. This not only refers to the institutions of government that impact upon the economy, but also to broader aspects such as the status order in a particular society, the distribution of social capital, or the diffusion and maintenance of certain beliefs and ideas about economic life. Ritual is the medium by which governmentality is performed.

If we turn to China, ritual appears to be a category that is also an essential element in Chinese cultural and social history.[68] My claim is that this Chinese ritual indeed corresponds to the generic notion of ritual. Thus, if we analyse the Chinese economic style as a ritual economy, we pursue two analytical movements at the same time. One is to apply the generic notion of ritual; the other is to unfold the Chinese notion of ritual in the context of the modern economy, and making the mechanisms which connect ritual with economic processes explicit. I analyse the ritual economy of China in terms of the generic meaning of 'ritual', but I also try to understand the Chineseness of ritual based on the indigenous meaning of the term. In fact, as I have already argued, this bridge is easy to build, since we can say that the Chinese notion of ritual is a kind of vernacular version of the generic notion of ritual. This also applies for many concepts that I have introduced in this chapter, such as networks and social capital. All of these notions have direct indigenous complements in Chinese narratives about social interactions and structures.

I have previously stated that the study of economic style means to identify family resemblances in both the diachronic and the synchronic dimension. We always pay attention to the historicity of institutions; thus, a starting point is to study the historical conditions. In the Chinese context, this means that I will begin by outlining the ritual economy of Imperial China. This is relatively straightforward, as ritual was doubtless the defining aspect in Chinese culture and society until 1911. Yet, the relationship between ritual and the economy is a topic that only emerged relatively recently in historical research. Thus, defining and describing the ritual economy of the past remains a task that may lead to fresh insights. When doing this, the same methodological principles apply as in the case of synchronic research of present conditions: we need to concentrate on mechanisms in local contexts. Fortunately, this has also been a trend in historical research during recent times and indeed produced many new results that we can exploit for constructing the ritual economy as a historical type.

Identifying family resemblances with present conditions can then help define the modern ritual economy, which is certainly different from the past one. However, if we can identify mechanisms that work in a similar way, this is empirical evidence for grounding the modern system in historicity. There are three ways whereby this may be established. One is simply to identify formal homologies; that means similarities of functioning for which we can posit the hypothesis that they may therefore may be traced back to historical origins. Second, this may involve similar symbolic media, thus referring to a central element of the Aoki model. This connects most directly to conventional cultural analysis, such as when researchers explore the meaning of Confucian notions in China today. The third approach is tracking paths of change in local contexts. The most prominent examples are village studies that begin with conditions in Imperial times and reconstruct a narrative of change up until modern times.

However, I re-emphasize that grounding the analysis of the modern ritual economy in identifying family resemblances with the historical ritual economy does not mean that history is a determinant of the present. This is where great care is warranted in using the term 'Chinese ritual'. This may refer to historical notions of ritual and their continuity, in a twofold and different sense. One is the direct continuation of ritual, such as in popular religion. The other is ritual behaviours that are different in content, but appear to be similar in process, such as expressing status hierarchies in material consumption which is otherwise a manifestation of modernity. Yet, ritual may also include innovations, with the foremost example being the CCP and its rituals, such as the nomenclature system. That being said, we can even ask for those innovations whether there are analogies with the past or even homologies. In this example, an analogy may refer to the meticulous distinctions of internal administrative status that appears to be similar in modern nomenclature and ancient bureaucracy; so we might speculate why and how this analogy emerged. A homology would trace this back to events that actually connect the two models, such as when certain opinions about cadre behaviour clearly show Confucian antecedents (as in Liu Shaoqi's famous writings about 'How to be a good Communist').

In the end, the Chinese ritual economy is both. One is ritual as a phenomenon that links the past with the present; the other is ritual that defines differences between the Chinese economy and other economic systems in the present. Both meanings need not coincide, however. There may be ritual elements with historical roots that do not define differences between China and other systems today, and there may be ritual determinants of differences today that are not grounded in history. Yet the common perspective remains as 'ritual'.

Notes

1 In referring to Foucault's notion of 'gouvernementalité', in its reception the French word has often been misinterpreted as a combination between 'government' and 'mentality', which is wrong (see Senellart 2004); on applying the term, see Foucault (2004a: 119ff.). The root of the term is the French 'gouvernemental', like in 'musicalité' deriving from 'musical'. Governmentality is the manifestation of the power structures on which the rule of the state is based, and is accessible via the study of micro-structures of power, such as certain behaviours in the context of the family being shaped by public values and ideologies which are also supported by the state. As such, phenomena of governmentality always go hand in hand with specific forms of deviance or even resistance. In his lectures at the Collège de France where this concept was employed in detail, the market plays a special role in the analysis of German Ordoliberalism, compared with the French model of capitalism (see Foucault 2004b). Liberalism as a political and economic doctrine appears here as a form of 'biopolitics', another term of Foucault's which has achieved a certain prominence in China studies (cf. e.g. Greenhalgh and Winckler 2005). Biopolitics refers to the technologies of governing in large countries, based on notions of controlling aggregate phenomena such as the state of public health or the productivity of the economy. Ordoliberalism, in Foucault's view, grounds the liberal doctrine on the observation that there are principled limits to the capacity of government to access and process the necessary information for obtaining direct control of these aggregate phenomena. Therefore, the market itself becomes a means to stabilize the structures of power in the modern state: This is what in China studies is labelled the 'neoliberal' nature of government in

China today. As we shall see, this particular perspective on liberalism is useful in interpreting the most recent developments in Chinese politics.

2 The term governmentality has been applied in China studies in different contexts; for an exemplary discussion see Sigley (2006) and the collection of papers in the respective volume of *Economy and Society*. Typically, these studies are based on case studies that allow one to identify the micro-structures of government interference with individual behaviour, interacting with evolving personal values in China's modernizing society and the growing realm of individual autonomy. Sigley emphasizes the role of the 'complex socio-historical terrain of modern China' in understanding these phenomena and points out that it is of the utmost importance to analyse non-Western forms of governmentality in order to avoid certain misperceptions of the persistence of authoritarian aspects of rule in Western societies which understand their own history largely as a continuous process of unfolding individual liberty and the protection of individual rights. As Sigley emphasizes, one fundamental difference between the Western and the 'socialist' Chinese forms of modern governmentality seems to be that the socialist state claims a much more detailed and encompassing knowledge about the individual and society than liberal states, as exemplified in the Chinese approach to population policy. However, one important shift between the Maoist era and the reform era has been the current widespread use of the term 'governance' ('zhili' 治理) that is put into the context of a biopolitical perspective on the competition among nation states in the world. This recognizes certain limits of state intervention, but at the same time reinforces the role of scientific approaches in designing social and economic systems and processes. Market liberalization, seen against this background, is not simply 'pragmatism', but a conscious adaptation of the market to a socialist system of governing society. The same may be said of recent cooptations of civil society for local governance.

3 Recent surveys of the pertinent literature are Guiso *et al.* (2006) or Beugelsdijk and Maseland (2010); for a critical review, see Herrmann-Pillath (2010). The transmission of values across generations is an area of research that is particularly prominent in the USA, given its background of immigration (see e.g. Fernandez and Fogli 2009). A very sophisticated study and methodological discussion is presented by Tabellini (2008a). Tabellini makes the values explicit that are supposed to be transmitted by means of reference to the results of the 'general trust question' in the World Values Survey, which I also discuss in Chapter 5. He interprets this question in terms of a more fundamental distinction between 'generalized' and 'limited' morality, and argues that generalized morality is supportive of good governance and well-performing markets. He shows that these results differ significantly across third- and fourth-generation descendants of migrant populations, and correlate strongly with the existence of early institutions of representative and constitutionally bound government in their countries of origin. Thus, he claims that these values emerged under these conditions and were then transmitted through generations. He also presents a hypothesis familiar to anthropological students of culture, namely that such cultural differences may be rooted in different structures of language (see also Licht *et al.* 2007). Languages which do not distinguish between different forms of the second-person pronouns (such as the English 'you' in comparison to the German 'Du' and 'Sie') reveal a systematically higher level of trust. Finally, Tabellini argues that the existence of generalized morality is also a determinant of good governance in the present. Evidently these arguments are inconclusive regarding the role of synchronic and diachronic determinants of culture. So long as the language is still spoken by a group of migrants, the language effects are synchronic and do not necessarily point towards a

diachronic transmission of cultural values. That would only be clear if the language is no longer spoken, thus referring to past effects of language on culture. This example shows that treating culture as an exogenous determinant of current behaviour is actually hiding the complex dynamics of culture. That being said, Tabellini (2008b) also elaborates on the idea already implicit in the aforementioned argument: namely that values are also endogenous to institutions (for related experimental work, see Herrmann *et al.* 2008). This case for endogeneity raises difficult questions regarding the different time scales of cultural and institutional change, with authors such as Roland (2004) claiming that cultural change is always slower than institutional change, thus reinforcing the case for treating culture exogenously.

4 For an economic critique of views on culture as a determinant of economic and political systems performance and social processes, see Jones (2006). Jones approaches this issue as an economic historian and therefore concurs with anthropologists such as Hannerz (1991) who highlights the role of economic interactions in triggering cultural syncretism and creolism. This does not necessarily imply that culture is simply an ephemeral phenomenon of the underlying economic forces, such as posited by both structural views of Harris' (1979) 'Cultural Materialism' or the rational choice approaches that confronted the so-called 'substantivist' cultural views on economic behaviour (an overview of these early debates is Schneider 1974). However, Jones claims that the close interaction between economic actions and cultural activity implies that culture cannot be a force that obtains long-term stable causal powers relative to social phenomena. Jones (2006: 24f.) refers to Chinese business as a pertinent example and argues that the 'Chineseness' of Overseas Chinese business can be mainly explained as the active use of Chinese cultural legacies in adapting to environments which had become increasingly uncertain and threatening already in Late Qing times, and continued to be so in the regions where Chinese emigrants aimed for. Interestingly, this view concurs with those positions in China studies which criticize notions such as 'Confucian capitalism' (see e.g. Dirlik 1996). In conclusion, Jones (2006: 255ff.) presents culture as a process with moving equilibria; in an equilibrium, different forces result in a balance in which certain behavioural patterns and values are recurrently reproduced by individual actions. Thus, equilibrium is dynamic and not static.

5 This approach to culture is rarely deployed in economics; however, the so-called 'old institutionalists' rooted in American pragmatism had developed such a view; for a contemporary perspective see Mayhew (1994). In modern economics, a corresponding notion of rationality is Amartya Sen (2002: 588ff.), who argues that the standard approach treats human agents as 'rational fools' who are not able to reflect upon their preferences and choose among alternatives. For Sen, choosing preferences invokes more fundamental motivations such as the search for meaning, freedom or dignity. Approaching culture as sense-making comes close to a Weberian perspective which is especially relevant in the context of China studies. In Weber's (1985: 2) original definition of social interaction, mutual reference to the meaning and significance of the actions of others is an essential aspect. This 'sense-making' is based on cultural repertoires. Hence, Weber saw rationality as a historical phenomenon emerging out of a process of 'rationalization'. This idea was extremely influential on cultural explanations of economic development in China, especially with regard to explaining the absence of capitalist industrialization; for a contemporary view, see Landes (2006) and for a critical reflection see Lai (2015). However, Weberian rationality is not seen as a 'natural' property of individuals as in standard economics, but as a property of institutions which transform individual motivations into rational patterns of action. The

notion of sense-making is also seen as being fundamental in some modern sociological theories, in particular Fligstein and McAdam (2012).

6 Beugelsdijk and Maseland (2010: 13). The authors explicitly point to the aforementioned differences between current economic and anthropological approaches to culture; while concentrating on economic approaches, their definition is mainly informed by anthropology. It is important to highlight the fact that this definition is much narrower than many other definitions of culture, which often refer to a very broad range of values, customs and artefacts that are shared by a certain population, beginning with Tylor's classical definition. However, these definitions have proven extremely elusive, thus leading towards an emerging consensus in anthropology even going so far as abandoning the term as a focal analytical concept (cf. the discussion in Brumann 1999). One fundamental problem results from the distinctive contextualization of culture in two different discourses. One is the nature vs. nurture discourse between biology and anthropology, which overlaps with the use of 'civilization' in sociology. Here, culture is a universal and possibly even defining feature of humanity, and therefore the most general reference to cultural inheritance also supports broad definitions of culture, as in Richerson and Boyd (2005). This is an entirely different question from the use of culture in comparative studies of human societies, which is also a focus of the economics research on culture. The definition by Beugelsdijk and Maseland differs from broad definitions in emphasizing the role of culture as demarcating human groups from other groups by means of actively employing cultural items in constructing these identities. This means, for example, that an artefact that does not have this particular function but is still unique to that population would not count as culture, so long as it does not play this particular role. 'Construction' is also an activity of individuals interacting with others, thus avoiding cultural essentialism. In addition, the definition does not explicitly refer to artefacts as objects. Artefacts play a significant role only in being employed in certain behaviours, even though, as we shall see, the artefacts themselves may be materializations of ideational structures which guide behaviour. Recently, Hartley and Potts (2014) introduced an evolutionary approach to culture at the cross-disciplinary borderline between economics and cultural studies that also builds on this view.

7 The perception of ethnicity in China today is the result of an official recognition of this status in the Constitution, which entails a number of special rights, such as in the context of population policy. Interestingly, this entails the identification of Han ethnicity as a default setting, sometimes denounced as a form of negative discrimination or lack of proper recognition by certain Han-chauvinist groups (see Leibold 2010). However, this policy towards ethnicity cannot be based on simple historical, sociological or linguistic criteria. This also applies for the past, and in fact relates to a cultural phenomenon of its own, namely the interaction between the Imperial definition of proper rituals and local variations, which could be found in both Han Chinese and non-Han Chinese populations. As I shall detail later, this 'orthopractic' approach to ritual rendered irrelevant internalist views of culture as a defining feature of ethnic identity, which had become prominent in the efforts at building modern nation states in Europe, leading to theoretical approaches such as Herder's that treated culture as an inherent property of a group. So, for example, the Tu (or Monguor) minority in western parts of China did not recognize itself as non-Han, even though their language and rituals (especially funerals) did not match Han standards. However, the Imperial administration approached them simply as a variation of 'local customs'. This, of course, would also affect the standards for evaluating Han identity, which would therefore allow for a much larger variance in values and behaviour as suggested by Confucian norms

(on the Tu, see Brown 2007: 96ff.). In comparison, as Cohen (1994) points out, the Bai minority applied for recognition as a minority in the 1950s, even though they had adopted Confucian standards to a degree that one famous study of traditional Chinese culture, Francis Hsu's 'Under the Ancestors' Shadow' was based on their case. Again, remaining deviant features could be rationalized in terms of 'local customs'. This peculiar relationship between standards and variations is also reflected in the linguistic treatment of 'Chinese' as a language. For example, the Bai treated their language as a 'Chinese dialect', even though it is a separate language in the Sino-Tibetan family. As in the case of the Tu, this partly reflects the fact that the indigenous language had been creolized in adopting a large number of Chinese words. On the other hand, although the southern Chinese languages are sufficiently different from standard Chinese to be perfectly unintelligible for speakers of the other language, they are treated as 'dialects' in modern China. From the viewpoint of linguistics (see e.g. Norman 1988: 1ff.), 'Chinese' in this sense is a family of languages, which is factually recognized by public statements of the Chinese government that hundreds of millions of Chinese cannot properly speak standard Chinese, Putonghua (see www.bbc.co.uk/news/world-asia-china-23975037, accessed 25 September 2013). Looking at an area with well-established linguistic separation, Guangdong, however, we also find a strong affinity with orthodox Confucian norms, such as in lineage traditions.

8 The distinction between emic and etic is standard methodology in anthropology, but does not play any role in economic research on culture. The terms stem from the linguistic distinction between 'phonetics' and 'phonemics'. Phonetics is the analysis of language by methods of the natural sciences, such as acoustics, and thus is neutral to the positions of observers. In other words, etic is defined as referring to data which are commensurable across different positions of observers. For example, observers can agree on the acoustic properties of a language sound, even if they do not know the language. Phonemics approaches sounds of language only with respect to their function of distinguishing meanings of words. So, sounds that differ physically might be indistinguishable phonemically. This distinction can only be made if the meaning of the words of which the sounds are elements is known to the observer. So, this is the internal position. For an overview of the early debates about this methodological dichotomy, see Feleppa (1986) and Headland *et al.* (1990). Its importance follows from Quine's (1969) famous thesis of the indeterminacy of translation: even if external observers realize behavioural differences of verbal reactions to certain observations (such as, in Quine's famous example, calling a rabbit crossing 'gavagai'), they cannot unequivocally fix the meaning of the term (is it the rabbit, a part of the rabbit, and if so, what part, such as a leg, as compared to more complex notions such as 'rabbit passing by', etc.). Resolving the indeterminacy of translation requires the adoption of the emic viewpoint, hence the position of the internal observer. This is possible in conversing across languages; that is, in practising translations (cf. Ingold 1993). In the end, the researcher could only achieve an approximation to the 'real' meaning in involving herself as deeply as possible in the lifeworld in which the language is actually used. One should emphasize, however, that this problem does not entail the pessimistic notion that emic research would never lead to insights that are commensurable across different positions of observers, and hence would also approximate to an etic description. In fact, as we know from artistic creativity in poetry or the role of the judicial process in clarifying meanings of legal terms, the indeterminacy thesis also applies for understanding words within the same language.

9 This argument has been made forcefully by Baecker (2000: 11ff.), who follows Derrida in the remark that all culture was colonial in the beginning. In other

words, culture is always perceived and factually constructed as a cultural difference. Evidently, this also implies that one's own culture is a moving object, depending on the specific comparison that is actually being made. Yet, and to the contrary, in most approaches to cross-cultural management, for example, 'national cultures' are treated as existing independently from those comparisons, even though most advanced approaches such as Hofstede's recognize the importance of comparisons. But they start out from the idea that there is an etic standard (a set of survey questions) that may be used to achieve such an etic identification of culture. Only based on these results, cultures may be compared as fixed objects. In the perspective proposed here, every culture looks different when compared to another culture. Thus, the 'Western culture' is itself a result of comparisons, and in this sense is rooted in the history of colonial encounters. In this respect it is of the utmost importance to recognize the fact emphasized by Foucault (1997) that Western notions of universality of values such as certain conceptions of rights are themselves results of historical encounters and conflicts opposing different ethnic groups, such as the Anglo-Saxons and the Normans in the Middle Ages.

10 As I will discuss in Chapter 2, one difficulty in dealing with 'Chinese culture' lies in the fact that the Chinese Empire employed 'culturalism' as a distinct way to integrate the Empire politically, in spite of the ethnic and religious diversity. Culturalism is orthopractic enforcement of proper ritual, while allowing for much leeway in all other respects (see n.7 above). This was especially true for the last Imperial dynasty, the Qing, who were Manchu and actively implemented policies towards maintaining their ethnic identity and separateness, in spite of even further enhancing culturalist techniques of ruling. When in the twentieth century modernizing elites launched a wholesale attack against not only Confucianism as a state ideology, but also against popular culture, they created an idea of the 'nation' that was devoid of any cultural content, apart from the artificially created traditions of socialist modernization. Thus, Fitzgerald (1995) argues that the modern Chinese state does not establish a connection with a particular sort of 'people' in the sense of the 'nation', and hence appears as a 'nationless state'. However, we could also think of the modernist conception of the nation in terms of a new kind of ritual, with the modern state still operating along the principles of empire. This is most evident in the treatment of ethnicity, as a Chinese notion of 'nation' would certainly create problems in identifying with the peculiar traditions of Han Chinese. Therefore, the modern Chinese state actually follows the revolutionary concept of citizenship as it was created in the aftermath of the revolution in France, actually subduing any reference to particular previous historical traditions in a generalized idea of citizenship based on shared ideological values.

11 The term 'orientalism' was coined by Said (1978) and refers to the observation that in the history of Western perceptions of China, the constructed images of Asia were often implicitly reflecting self-perceptions of the West. In the context of China this has a long history, such as in the early descriptions of China by the Jesuits who used China as a reference for critical reflections about Western conditions (see Mungello 1999: 59ff.). In the Enlightenment, China served as a benchmark for assessing the quality of government under the *ancien régime.* This image underwent landslide changes when the industrializing imperialist nations developed their own images of superiority. This image was then reflected in Chinese self-perceptions, triggering the 'long century' of modernization that was launched by the late nineteenth-century intellectual debates, a clear instance of reverse orientalism. A classic case of 'reverse orientalism' is the theory of the 'Japanese' (nihon jin ron) that was triggered by seminal studies such as Benedict's deeply influential 'Chrysanthemum and the Sword'

which in fact only created the awareness of cultural distinctiveness in the Japanese academic discourse (see Befu and Kreiner 1992). In the context of the study of Overseas Chinese business, this problem has been highlighted and scrutinized by scholars such as Dirlik (1996) or Yao (2002). As Yao explains, the notion of 'Confucian capitalism' that emerged from works such as Redding (1990) fell on fertile ground in the frenzied activities of the 1990s in creating an Asia-Pacific economic space. Many academic conferences and political meetings included references to the networks of Chinese business driving the division of labour in the region, also contributing to an increasing self-awareness and assertiveness of Overseas Chinese after decades of ethnic discrimination or even violent suppression.

12 I developed this approach in Herrmann-Pillath (2000a). As the orientalism controversy illustrates, the underlying perspective is not new for anthropologists, but it has never been employed in economics so far as I know. However, there was a deep methodological awareness of these issues in early twentieth-century German-speaking economics, as I will show later in my discussion of the approach to 'economic styles'. The set of interactions depicted in Figure 1.2 is not complete, only to avoid cluttering. For example, internal participating observers can also reflect about their own culture via intermediation of external reflecting observers, such as when a Chinese manager attends a US executive MBA class where cross-cultural management is taught.

13 The 'general trust question' refers to the two possibilities 'most people can be trusted' and 'always need to be careful'. I report and discuss the data in detail in Chapter 5. The general trust data are often used in the context of research on social capital that aim to explain differences in economic performance across countries. If trust is high, transaction costs on markets are low, which undergirds the expansion of economic activity and the division of labour, hence also enabling higher levels of productivity. In social capital research, China often emerges as an outlier (see e.g. Bergren *et al.* 2008). This relates to the exceptional results in the general trust question which directly contradicts emic data on China. In Chinese self-descriptions, standard lore is to argue that trust is high among relatives and very close friends, but low in relations with strangers (see e.g. Gabrenya and Hwang 1996). Actually, this is confirmed by other questions in the WVS, in particular the question on whether one trusts people whom one meets for the first time. Yet, the problem remains that 'most people can be trusted' does not refer to relatives or friends, and in most other results this is also evident from the responses. So, for example, trust towards foreigners is much lower in China than in the USA, implying that the Chinese conclude that shared ethnicity increases trustworthiness. However, this reasoning would suggest that 'similarity' applies at a societal level, and not only to subgroups such as kin. Evidently, we can explain the results only by adding much more substance to the underlying presumptions on factors generating trust. Beugelsdijk (2006b) suggests that this would start out from distinguishing between trust emerging in social networks and trust in institutions, which matches more sophisticated analyses of trust such as Nooteboom's (2002). However, as we shall see in Chapter 5, this requires a more detailed scrutiny of network structures and dynamics in different cultural settings.

14 The most recent version of the Hofstede approach is Hofstede *et al.* (2010) which includes the extensions made by Minkov. The huge impact of this research is leveraged by the consultancy and training programmes (see www.geert-hofstede.com). The most comprehensive methodological critique has been presented by Behrens (2007), who also summarizes other contributions to the field. Even within the management sciences, there is also substantial criticism of Hofstede's method, such as pointing out that the dimensions actually

cover socioeconomic structures, but not culture (see e.g. Baskerville 2003). Regarding China, there are many issues, such as the differences across different 'Chinese' populations, or the interaction between supposed 'Chinese values' and environmental factors, such as when considering diaspora settings (for an exemplary study on Taiwanese, see Wu 2006).

15 It is important to note that there are a few dimensions which play an important role in almost all value studies, in particular individualism vs. collectivism and power distance. However, as Behrens (2007) argues, the dominance of these dimensions always leads to a reiteration of traditional accounts of modernization which confront a small number of 'Western' countries with the rest of the world. In comparison, most other categories appear to be less stable across different approaches. East Asia plays an interesting role in global values studies, because many studies refer explicitly to 'Confucianism'. For example, in another influential study, the GLOBE study (House *et al.* 2004), the 'Confucian countries' is the only region which is demarcated with reference to a philosophy or a religion, whereas all other regions are demarcated by geographical terms. The World Values Survey has supported a categorization of countries with reference to degrees of modernization, which maps onto the distribution of world religions. Again, East Asia is combined into a 'Confucian' region, hence evidently disregarding, for example, the role of Shintoism in Japanese religion. Thus, reference to 'Confucianism' in values studies is a clear instance of transferring Western perceptions into what is presented as an etic approach. Even if one were to stick to denoting the region as 'Confucian', the substantial differences across the region in terms of Confucian legacies are neglected; for example, Confucianism as a doctrine of the Chinese civilian state and Confucian values in the context of the military organization of Japanese samurai differ substantially (see the discussion in Rozman 1991). In the original research on the extensions of the Hofstede study taking better care of East Asian cultural contexts, the survey items were explicitly geared towards Confucian topics, such as 'shame', 'perseverance' or 'face', and termed 'Confucian work dynamism'. Thus, high scores for Chinese in this context appear to be more than plausible. Compared to the impact of these studies, it is remarkable that only 20 years later additional work was done, based on the World Values Survey (see the overview in Minkov and Hofstede 2012). Factor analysis led to results that correlate with the earlier 'Confucian' dimensions and therefore seem to support introducing additional dimensions. This protracted process implies an interaction between emic and etic perspectives, as the initial initiative on Chinese values was related to broader concerns about the indigenization of values studies by means of including survey items that are more sensitive to existing values as reflected in the indigenous worldviews. This concern was particularly articulate in Taiwan (see e.g. Yang 1989).

16 On this fundamental methodological limitation to values studies, see Beugelsdijk and Maseland (2010: sect. 5.3.2). Therefore, another much-cited study on values in the context of economics and business, the GLOBE study on leadership (House *et al.* 2004), explicitly distinguishes between two sets of questions: 'as is' and 'should be'. So, for example, in a category that is also employed by Hofstede, namely 'power distance', both China and Germany show a large distance between 'as is' and 'should be', while Germany has an even higher score in the 'as is' dimension than China. This needs a 'thick' explanation: For example, both countries may appreciate lower power distance, but perhaps in Germany this affects the assessment of the 'as is' differently than in China. There has been an intense methodological debate between Hofstede and the GLOBE researchers (see e.g. Javidan *et al.* 2006).

17 The experimental study of culture in economics was triggered by the seminal work of Henrich *et al.* (2005) which could show that in one of the simplest experimental set-ups, the ultimatum game, test persons from different 'small-scale societies' differ substantially in matching the 'rational solution'. In these approaches, the rational solutions appear to be the etic benchmark relative to which deviations may be determined as 'cultural'. As there is also substantial statistical variation in samples of test persons, in more sophisticated approaches detailed demographic surveys and value survey are added (for an exemplary study see Karlan 2005). However, whether and in which way this research actually encapsulates cultural variables is still difficult to assess. One problem is how test persons perceive the experiment, which is itself a cultural phenomenon. For example, as many experiments imply game-like behaviour under risk, a certain experiment may not be seen as testing for cooperation, but is actually viewed as gambling (on this, see again Karlan 2005). Or, as in Henrich *et al.*'s study, people might equate the experimental situation with situations in their real life. This creates the problem that the experiment is not actually seen as a one-shot test but as an instance in a larger set of recurrent and similar situations. As is well known from basic game theory (the so-called 'folk theorem'; see Binmore 1994: 115ff.), in these situations any kind of cooperative deviance from the rational benchmark may be interpreted as rational behaviour, thus invalidating the conclusion that the behaviour is 'cultural'. So, the borderline between 'cultural' and 'rational' behaviour is actually indeterminate because of a cultural process, namely assigning autonomous meaning to the experimental setting which is imposed by the researcher. This effect may only be avoided in experimental settings which cannot be interpreted as social interaction. Thus, one has to conceive of experiments as 'performances' that are subject to intentional efforts of control by the experimenter (see the detailed analysis by Guala (2007) and Muniesa and Callon (2007). The experimental approach to cognitive science comparative studies on Asia has been most systematically developed by Nisbett (2003), based on experimental work as in Ji *et al.* (2000, 2004). The 'rod and frame' test is a standard psychological experiment in which test persons are asked to judge the position of a rod relative to the ground floor and a moving frame on the screen. Chinese subjects typically reveal a much stronger impact of the frame on their assessment of position. As I discuss later, this has been interpreted as an indicator of 'field dependence' in social behaviour. In contrast, Caucasians seem to be better able to assess the position of the rod independent from the moving frame. There are other kinds of tests based on cognitive categorizations. Thus, East Asians tend to categorize objects in terms of relationships (such as combining 'monkey' with 'banana' because 'monkey eats banana') and not in terms of abstract categories (such as 'money' and 'dog' because both are animals). For a summary overview of all of these cognitive sciences results, see Ji *et al.* (2010).

18 On the Quine hypothesis, see n.8 above. In fact, this renders approaches such as Hofstede's more legitimate than it seems when considering their ethnocentric background. The Quine thesis implies that there is no other solution than to create the conceptual integration by an interpretive act which remains fundamentally subjective and is not accessible via empirical methods. So, if Hofstede introduces certain normative positions on 'Western' values, this is methodologically sound; it becomes problematic only if is combined with claims on etic validity. In other words, culture is ultimately a normative, and not an analytical or descriptive category, and individual reconstructions need only to be done in a transparent way, enabling debates over the underlying norms.

19 I have introduced this term into China studies in Herrmann-Pillath (1996). The term has been used by Wittgenstein (1958) in the context of classifying

parlour games and argues against any essentialist definition of a 'game'. In other words, games share a large number of properties, but never one single and unequivocal set of essential defining properties. Still, we can identify those shared properties, which might relate, for example, to a shared genealogy, as in natural families. But the resulting list of properties can be neither fixed extensionally (in terms of a complete list of properties) or intensionally (as a rule unequivocally defining essential properties). On culture, this applies both for indigenous views and comparative views. Thus, the Chinese would define their culture in terms of family resemblances across many different subcultures, with no list of properties claiming to be the prototype (which is done when referring to Confucianism as a core set of values), and in comparisons there would be no set of properties which are unique to Chinese culture or others. For example, as we will see in Chapter 5, 'individualism' does not unequivocally distinguish the 'West' from the 'East', but there are many different phenomena of individualism, some of which are shared, others not.

20 This discussion touches upon foundational issues in economics, which normally assumes that preferences are fixed and givens (the 'values' of psychological and sociological research correspond to 'preferences' in economics). This is necessary on methodological grounds, as the rational choice model is only empirically determinate when preferences are fixed. This is why normally cultural explanations would not be feasible in economics, so long as they are internalist. Internalization would refer to adaptive preferences in the sense of von Weizsäcker (2011). The analytical challenge of adaptive preferences is that they may lead towards a preference for the status quo, and so may involve inconsistency of valuations in the status quo as compared to changes in the status quo which entail improvements that are also valued ex post once preferences have been adapted (for a seminal discussion see Elster 1982). Sen (2002: 615ff.) argues that the assumption of stable preferences actually violates basic ideas of rationality as an expression of human reason. A rational person would be seen as being able to judge different sets of preferences and even choose from among preferences. Thus, adaptive preferences would be seen as a defining element of rationality.

21 It should be noted that the main protagonist of the economic rational choice approach, Gary Becker, actually turned to a much more sophisticated analysis in his more recent work on 'tastes' (Becker 1996). The notion of internalization is covered here by the term 'human capital'. In other words, Becker still sticks to the assumption that a certain set of preferences is fundamental and immutable across all human beings, but that one needs to add 'instrumental preferences' which are basically preferences over means to attaining states that satisfy those fundamental preferences. Instrumental preferences are learned via a process of socialization, resulting in the accumulation of human capital as a set of knowledge and skills in how to attain individual goals. So, for example, certain preferences for music might reflect a fundamental preference for music, but at the same time appreciation of particular kinds of music depends on experience and education. Evidently, this approach renders the general notion of rationality very problematic, because preferences become adaptive relative to human capital. It is impossible for an individual to decide rationally over future states where preferences have been formed by different tracks of building human capital. That would require second-order preferences over preferences and the conjugated contexts.

22 The ecological approach to culture has been developed by Yamagishi based on a long series of experiments largely comparing East Asian test persons with Americans (for an extensive overview see Yamagishi 2012). Yamagishi contrasts his view with internalist views on culture which posit that culture is a set of

inner beliefs and values. Instead, he argues that culture emerges from unintended consequences of individual actions which result in the construction of 'niches'; that is, sets of external constraints and patterns of incentivization to which individuals adapt their behaviour. This adaptation can be reflexive in the sense that individuals, once they recognize the context in which they take their decisions, can also choose behaviour that actively supports the maintenance of the niche (which would correspond to Sen's higher order rationality; see n. 20 above). In other words, unintended consequences lead to the establishment of games in which individuals adopt rational strategies, and they can opt for continuing these games. For example, in this research Yamagishi could clearly demonstrate that Japanese subjects are by no means less individualistic than American subjects, but that they respond sensitively to cues in the environment which foster cooperative and group-oriented behaviour. In one of the simplest experiments, subjects choose from among five pens, with one being different from the others. In the default scenario, many more Japanese than Americans choose the majority pen, thus apparently signalling group orientation; however, if both are told that they are the first to choose, the majority in both groups go for the majority pen, and if they are told that they are the last to choose, the majority go for the minority pen. Thus, in the second and the third scenarios there are no cultural differences; apparently, in the default scenario the Japanese tend to opt for the 'socially wise' behaviour, which means they compare this scenario with the second one. In experiments where these cues are missing, the Japanese turn even more individualistic in their behaviour than the Americans. Further, once they are aware of the fact that other players also have these perceptions, they actively contribute to maintaining these shared assumptions. Thus, the 'collectivist' orientation of Japanese is not a product of inner beliefs that can be carried on into arbitrarily determined environments, but reflects the peculiar structure of these environments. If Japanese interpret the default scenarios differently from Americans, this may reflect the result of learning, or internalization in the previously elaborated sense. This is a rational way of giving meaning to the experimental situation, and hence may transfer actual experiences in the Japanese environment to the experimental context, an effect known from experimental studies in general (see n. 17 above).

23 The distinction between field dependence and field independence has been very influential in Asian studies in terms of the closely related distinction between 'high context' and 'low context' cultures proposed by Hall (1976). Field dependence of cognition would imply, as in differential responses of Americans and Japanese on the default condition, that environmental cues are given stronger weight in what is otherwise rational behaviour. This can make interpretations of experiments very difficult: For example, Chen *et al.* (2007) show that idiocentrism and allocentrism (according to value survey results) mediate the response to a group norm on cooperation, so that allocentrists (Chinese) react on the group norm, whereas idiocentrists (US Americans) even exploit the group norm in cheating. This result, however, could also be interpreted in terms of field dependence, thus further strengthening the externalist reasoning. Yamagishi also discusses the thesis proposed by Nisbett (2003) that East Asian field dependence reflects the special conditions of cooperative agriculture in rice-growing societies: The causation in terms of agricultural ecology has been proposed also by anthropologists and biologists (see the brief overview by Boyd and Richerson 1985: 178ff.). In fact, it has a long pedigree in China studies, with authors such as Wilhelm (1930: 26ff.) and Eberhard (1971: 8ff.) emphasizing the impact of ecological conditions such as population density on Chinese culture. The problem with these explanations is, of course, in explaining this kind of persistence of ecological factors even when they no

longer apply, such as those resulting from urbanization. However, recent research on China (Talhelm *et al.* 2014) has offered the interesting insight that the large ecological divide in Chinese agriculture between the wheat-growing areas of the north and the rice-growing areas of the south is still reflected in significant differences between south and north Chinese even in cognitive tests such as the aforementioned linguistic classification tasks. Northerners are more likely than southerners to group concepts according to abstract categories than to relationships. Again, this converges with a very long cultural history of stereotypes about south and north in Chinese thinking (cf. Ting (1974) for an overview).

24 Yamagishi does not use the term 'performativity' but 'self-fulfilling prophecy'. By this he means that individuals produce certain incentives for others, based on certain beliefs they hold, fostering behaviours which ultimately confirm those beliefs; because these beliefs are based on observations, they also tend to be shared among members of a population. However, as the discussion in MacKenzie (2007) shows, there is an important difference between the Mertonian 'self-fulfilling prophecy' and performativity, since the latter can fail (the so-called 'counter-performativity'). In the context of economics, the notion of performativity has been developed in the narrower sense as performativity of economic theories, especially with reference to finance (see MacKenzie 2006, 2007). Broader notions such as Callon's (2008) include ideas about economic processes and structures which shape these notions in such a way that the ideas receive confirmation. I have developed an even broader foundational use of the term in Herrmann-Pillath and Boldyrev (2014) which converges with similar notions in sociology and anthropology, such as Butler's (2010). Against the background of the previous discussion, performativity as an extension of the philosophy of language relates to Searle's (1995, 2010) theory of institutions as 'observer-relative facts'. Searle speaks of 'declarations' which create a social ontology which, however, would not be accessible to etic analysis, because the facts only become constituted relative to a particular group of observers which share collective intentionality (for a similar approach, see Tuomela 1995, 2007; for a discussion of the differences, see Tuomela 2011). Thus, identifying the social ontology would require an emic approach on the empirical level. Although Searle does not analyse culture specifically, this conceptual model of institutions applies here as well. We can now appreciate the value of our definition of culture, as many institutions in general may share the property of being performative phenomena, but would not necessarily relate to establishing the identity of individuals in a group. Thus, we can say that culture is performing identity.

25 This point has been made seminally by Munz (1993: 25f., 169ff.). Munz deals with phenomena such as religion in creating and maintaining the identities of groups. He argues that beliefs that do not have empirical or functional content are the only ones which can play this role, because there would be no rational reason to imitate them. If these beliefs are costly, this effect is leveraged (such as long periods of learning proper rituals). Costly signals are also reliable indicators of identity, especially if there is no obvious benefit. This is a barrier to deceit by faking identities, known in biology as the 'handicap principle' (Zahavi and Zahavi 1997). This explains why many 'cultural' phenomena are non-functional or even dysfunctional. A seminal case study on these differential modes of diffusion is the research on canoes and their design among Pacific island populations presented by Rogers and Ehrlich (2008). The authors show that certain technological improvements of design spread much more rapidly than non-functional adornments of canoes across different populations; evidently, the non-functional items serve to identify groups at a distance. This

theory helps distinguish neatly between the two approaches to culture that I discussed previously: the general anthropological approach and the comparative approach (I have systematically elaborated on this theory in Herrmann-Pillath 2013a). For the general approach, we posit a universal human capacity for culture, which is rooted in the evolutionary advantages of creating and maintaining in-group/out-group boundaries. This capacity for culture gives rise to specific cultural phenomena that operate as group markers; in order to fulfil these functions, the criteria of low functional value and costly learning apply. The most universal phenomenon in this respect is human language, where even the smallest variants in phonetics and word repertoires can identify group boundaries, and certainly have disadvantages in functional terms.

26 In economics, mimetic processes have been placed at the centre of an alternative approach to preferences and choice developed by Orléans (2011) in the context of the 'economics of conventions'. This is not simply based on the idea that information is costly, so that copying others might save information costs. In anthropology, a related approach to culture has been developed earlier by Boyd and Richerson (1985) who detail different forms of copying, such as learning from model individuals which have a certain status in society. I have emphasized the role of ignorance about one's inner state in my own work (Herrmann-Pillath 2011, 2013a), building on experimental research such as that by Ariely and Norton (2007). In this research, individuals are taught to learn from their own choices which in turn may have been triggered by even arbitrary initiating events, resulting in 'self-herding'. My general model builds on Coleman's (1990) early application of a principal–agent model on choice, distinguishing between 'Object Self' (the evaluator of choices) and 'Acting Self' (the locus of agency). In this model, there is asymmetric information between the Acting Self and the Object Self. As a result, we can analyse consumption as an expression of one's identity as a person, thus even coming back to hypotheses such as the stability of preferences. However, this is not a given a priori as in standard economic methodology, but is explained by the more fundamental theory of identity. For a general approach to identity in economics matching this perspective, see Davis (2003, 2010).

27 The role of externalities in keeping up individual identities has been scrutinized in great analytical detail by Akerlof and Kranton (2000; 2005), thus providing additional support for Yamagishi's ecological approach. The simple point is that once individuals share an identity, Alter's actions that do not cause any direct impact upon Ego may nevertheless cause an externality if the actions violate certain expectations about identity. Thus, Ego's identity is affected by otherwise causally irrelevant actions. For example, in a strongly masculine group a man who confesses to be gay does not do any direct harm to other men, but indirectly questions their own identity as males. As a result, Ego may retaliate against Alter. This may be anticipated by Alter, so that he adapts his behaviour ex ante. Depending on perceived costs and benefits of these different actions, an equilibrium emerges which is a cultural pattern of shared identities. This approach may be based on a generic human property of 'groupishness' which is well established in social psychology, biology and experimental economics, seminally proposed by Taijfel's theory about in-group/out-group discrimination. This provides the basis for the phenomenon of 'moral aggression', which is difficult to explain in a simple rational choice approach, because by-standing third parties incur the costs of retaliating against deviators even if they do not suffer direct damage or do not reap any direct advantage. Moral aggression is a major channel for maintaining cultural cohesion in a group and thereby ensuring cooperation (cf. Bowles and Gintis 2001; Bowles *et al.* 2003).

28 The central role of identities in enabling welfare-improving solutions in sequential and nested games has been emphasized by Ross (2007). Ross relates this to the anthropological universal of language. Language enables cheating in strategic interactions, thus undermining any form of cooperation. However, language can also be the medium of establishing and communicating identities, especially via narratives that are being shared in a group. If these narratives connect with a sequence of costly actions in establishing identities (which actually includes learning a particular language), they create identities that are stable across different games. This allows the transfer of reputation between games. This point is made a central argument in the analysis of culture presented by Bednar and Page (2007). The authors show via agent-based modelling that the realistic assumption that agents have limited cognitive and computational capacities suffices to show that in sequential games, agents will adopt strategies which have the following five properties: (1) intra-individual consistency, so that strategies carry over to other games, (2) inter-agent consistency, meaning that agents of the same communities will adopt similar strategies in coping with similar problems, (3) contextual effects, so that agents of different communities react differently to the same problems, (4) behavioural stickiness, meaning that agents do not change strategies in the short term, and (5) suboptimal behaviour, meaning that because of the adoption of a constrained set of strategies they do not necessarily opt for the best strategy in a given game. These five properties are defining features of culture.

29 This analysis is helpful in avoiding a fallacy of cultural analysis that can lead to perceiving the world in terms of cultural areas which may even stay in tension, such as in Huntington's 'clash of civilizations' view. Sen (2007) is a critique of those views which suggest that these cultural aggregates also have a monopolizing influence on individual identities. This does not simply refer to statistical variation, such that one would possibly think of 'culture' as a sort of average in a normal distribution of traits of individuals. The point is that on the individual level, people have a large variety of identities in different contexts. This may include the activation of a 'prototypical' notion of group culture in a particular context, but this only dominates all other identities under conditions of strong stress, such as military conflict.

30 Tian and Dong (2011) present an analysis of Chinese consumers' perceptions of foreign brands based partly on interviews in which they ask about brand-related dreams. They show that the consumption of foreign brands is often embedded in broader visions of China's role in world society, and can therefore trigger complex emotional responses. For example, foreign brands can both relate to China's history of foreign dominance and humiliation or to dreams of freedom and individual enjoyment. Hence, consuming foreign brands is an action that involves deeper normative commitment, contributing to the emergence of what have been called the 'consumer citizens' of China (see e.g. Hooper 2005). This phenomenon can be put into historical perspective. As early as in the 1920s, and especially in Shanghai, responsible consumption of foreign brands was seen as a duty of the Chinese citizen, and creating national brands was perceived as a national goal that needed to be supported by individual consumers (for a detailed account see Gerth 2003). Therefore, brand management in China is a cultural activity *par excellence*, as analysed in great depth by Wang (2008).

31 In the context of the migration issue, the household registration system is often seen as the institutional determinant of discrimination against migrant workers. However, as Zhan (2011) shows, independent from these institutional factors there is a deep cultural gap between locals and migrants, which translates into exclusion from networks and hence reduced accessibility of social capital for

the migrants. The cultural gap is reflected, for example, in different ways of dressing which send cues about origin (Ngai 2003); this renders consumption (as discussed in n.30) into a cultural marker of identity. There are also immutable characteristics of persons such as the colour of their skin, which in places such as Shanghai even lead to discrimination among children in public schools (Lan 2014). In a work context, migrant workers are often put into entirely different organizational contexts, even in different buildings, such that within the same company a dualism in terms of corporate culture applies (Zhang *et al.* 2010).

32 Tensions between Western corporate culture and indigenous cultural perceptions of 'Chineseness' of social relations are widespread in cross-cultural management. For example, Walmart transfers its peculiar corporate culture to China which partly matches Chinese notions of patriarchal leadership; however, it also creates tensions owing to its puritan leanings (on this case see Davies 2007). Thus, Walmart imposes a rule that Walmart employees are not allowed to host clients for restaurant visits, which places them in an awkward position, given the ubiquitous expectation of hospitality. However, lavish expenses for meals and related entertainment are indeed also an import aspect of corruption in China. Similarly, commissions, kickbacks and gifts for customers can become a point of dispute between Chinese and foreign managers, with the latter often operating under US law with regard to bribery in foreign countries, even if they are not US companies by origin (Xin and Wang 2011).

33 This concept was developed in the neurosciences in order to explain regularities in the brain (see Craver 2007) and is only slowly being received in economics (for an application on the concept of routines, see Vromen 2011). The mechanism concept has also been used by Sperber (2011) in order to outline a naturalistic approach to culture, which is an alternative to the 'cultural studies' tradition mostly received in Chinese studies. In a similar way of thinking, Hartley and Potts (2014) therefore argue in favour of 'cultural science' as an alternative to 'cultural studies' (compare my own argument in Herrmann-Pillath 2011). This approach combines the epidemiology of cultural artefacts with the cognitive and neuroscience of behaviour relating to these artefacts. The fundamental difference between the mechanism view and the standard economic approach lies in the conceptualization of causation. In the standard view, the institution causes behaviour as an effect on the individual level, thus factually treating the institution as an external entity. In the mechanism view, behaviour is constituted as a complex multi-level mechanism that is observable on the individual level, but is ontologically constituted as a system.

34 For a comprehensive survey of research on mechanisms in sociology, see Hedström and Ylikoski (2010) and, in the context of the philosophy of science, see Craver and Tabery (2015). There is a wide range of researchers that might come under this category, even though they may not necessarily count themselves as representatives of the narrower strand that has been labelled 'analytical sociology'. There are also cross-disciplinary affinities. For example, a leading protagonist of a mechanism-based approach in historical science is Charles Tilly (see the overview by Schützeichel 2015). Further, in the context of the philosophy of science, so far the paradigmatic model of mechanism-based explanations is the neurosciences, as analysed by Craver's (2007) seminal work. In the case of the neurosciences there are already detailed expositions of how the pattern of constitutive explanations differs from regularity-based explanations which are so far dominant in economics (see Harbecke 2014). This shows that the mechanism approach is very general and is not confined to the social sciences. For the social sciences, this also implies that mechanism-based explanations are 'realist'; in other words, the constitutional conditions are seen

as being elements with ontological status (seminally, Bhaskar 1989). Therefore, in the social sciences, mechanism research also relates to approaches to social ontology that treat institutions as 'facts' (see next section).

35 This emphasis on local structures relates mechanism-based research to other previous approaches in sociology, which may otherwise be seen as alternatives, such as Giddens' (1984) theory of 'structuration' or Foucault's focus on power. The local orientation directly follows from the realist approach to causation while rejecting the straightforward possibility of identifying macro-level regularities by means of statistical extrapolations over a number of local cases. Only local studies allow for identifying constitutive structures in detail. This also applies in the sciences, such as the neurosciences, where brain architectures are local in nature. Generalization occur via the identification of similarities, often in terms of simple constituent mechanisms, as discussed in Craver (2007). This observation is of particular importance for Chinese studies, where local research has become the gold standard in empirical work, often raising the intricate question of how local studies generalize for China. In the mechanism paradigm, mechanisms are mainly embodied in local settings, and there must be a clear empirical reason why a 'China-level' factor obtains force in driving such mechanisms (for example, in economics the exchange rate may be a 'China-level' cause).

36 Interestingly, one of the early protagonists of the mechanism approach has been Daniel Little, who used Chinese case studies as a ground to deploy his more general methodological concerns (Little 1992). For example, he regarded Skinner's market system approach to Chinese rural society as a case in point, because Skinner linked certain general theories about location with specific mechanisms in Chinese society that result in patterns of settlement and social interactions in marketplaces.

37 In mechanism research there is a fundamental difference between reductionist and emergentist research. A leading researcher in the first is Elster (e.g. Elster 1989), who combines mechanisms with the position of methodological individualism, thus also establishing close affinity between sociology and economics. However, even in the neurosciences, reductionism is a position with very weak support (Craver 2007). Multi-level analysis in the social sciences means that entities other than 'individuals' may have causal status, a position seminally deployed by Bhaskar (1989). This is a necessary concomitant to process analysis, different from equilibrium analysis. In understanding mechanisms as processes, even if we can present an explanation of a supra-individual entity such as an institution in individualistic terms, this does not mean that in the specific local context the pertinent causal power of the institution is obsolete. The individualistic reduction would have to resort to another mechanism-based analysis that traces the emergence of the institution though history, without implying that this explanation applies to the present.

38 Mechanism research can therefore include a number of emic methodologies, such as narratives and identity research (see Schützeichel 2015: 116ff., again on Tilly). This is because in all mechanisms involving human subjects, their perceptions of themselves and the situational context obtain causal force in driving actions. So, mechanisms also include the production of symbols, narratives and other symbolic media which mediate those perceptions. Therefore, mechanism research can also integrate recent developments in political science which revived the interest in ideas as driving forces of political evolutions (see e.g. Blyth 2002; Mehta 2011).

39 My term 'institutionally guided behavioural patterns' is elaborated in Herrmann-Pillath (2013a). This term encapsulates the fact that in the first place, all institutions are only observable as regularities in behaviour that are

shared in human groups. In many economic conceptualizations of institutions, these appear to be external entities enforcing these regularities; this seems to violate methodological individualism, as in the case of culture. In my view, institutions, like a legal norm (such as a law forbidding theft), exist in terms of their shaping behaviour, and not only in the moment when they are enforced. So, we normally do not steal. The notion that an institution exists results from the observation that in case of deviance, certain mechanisms come into play by which the institution is enforced. However, on closer examination this is a complex set of additional institutions, such as the institutions regulating the behaviour of the police, the judges and so forth. Evidently, in these cases we refer again to behavioural regularities; institutions come into play as external entities when enforcement occurs after deviant behaviour. As we see, any single institution is a behavioural regularity that is embedded in a network of behavioural regularities that are in turn governed by institutions understood in this way, and so forth. This notion of IGBP goes back to Veblen (1914) who famously referred to institutions as 'habits of thought'; a related view was developed more recently by North (2005), emphasizing the cognitive grounding of behaviour governed by institutions.

40 The recent work by North *et al.* (2009) represents a final shift of focus in North's work on the theory of institutions. Whereas North (1981) started out from conventional property rights and transaction costs economics in his early work, only recognizing government as a special kind of agent equipped with enforcement power, North (1990) then moved on to considering the relationship between formal and informal institutions, hence culture, in his view, further substantiating this in his cognitive science-based approach in North (2005). Only in the most recent work does he fully analyse the role of government in institutional evolution. As a consequence, institutions are mainly seen as societal arrangements that reduce the cost of violent conflicts, and less as efficiency-enhancing devices in a market context. This central role of violence had long been neglected by economists, as they always started out from the market model of voluntary exchange, thus mainly analysing power in the context of imperfect markets. However, ideal typically, markets are the institutional alternative to forced exchange based on the threat of violence; there are always groups in society for which the application of violence is the cheaper way to access resources (see Hirshleifer 2001). Thus, markets presuppose institutional arrangements that reduce this threat. Since these arrangements also need to set incentives for groups controlling the means of violence to constrain their use, most societies are so-called 'limited access orders' in which elites control means of violence but also extract resources from society for their particularistic advantage. According to the authors, the transition to mature capitalism and market society requires the transition to 'open access orders' which further expand the scope of efficiency enhancing competition by limiting and abolishing market-distorting prerogatives of incumbent elites.

41 China has introduced most of the established formal institutions of capital markets and corporate governance in recent legislation (see Wang 2010). However, there are limitations that result from the power structure defined by the Communist Party, which causes a lack of independence of the different groups that are supposed to implement the mechanisms of corporate governance. But beyond that, we can also identify cultural factors. For example, traditional notions of face and social relationships affect the boardroom dynamics in corporate governance, even if foreign directors are members (a phenomenon also well known from Japan) (see Smith 2012). This requires certain sensitivities in dealing with different groups of shareholders or regulators. The importance of traditional assumptions about social relationships is also evident

in certain practices by which regulators enforce compliance. They may not rely solely on the formal institutions, but manipulate public perceptions in social networks (Liebman and Milhaupt 2007). Another issue is the role of professional cultures in groups whose work is essential for implementing corporate governance institutions, such as accountants and lawyers (Clarke 2010).

42 The most recent version of Aoki's model is Aoki (2011) which builds on earlier work (Aoki 2001, 2007). My approach has linked this model to the philosophy of institutions and theories of distributed cognition (see Herrmann-Pillath 2012a, 2013a). The most significant difference between those two versions is that in my view I minimize the role of deliberate choices in choosing certain behaviours, which mirrors Searle (1995) in treating behaviour that follows an institution as a disposition which is triggered by the signs and their interpretation by the actors.

43 The notion of performativity is implicit to Aoki's (2010) cognitive approach to the corporation and the institutions of corporate governance. Aoki argues that corporate governance institutions and the cognitive division of labour in a company need to match. The question is which cognitive assets are under control of which group, employees, managers, investors and so forth, and how far these assets contribute to the performance of the company. For example, if the cognitive assets are widely distributed among managers and employees, a corporate governance structure will be most efficient if it also includes employees as a group that is represented in some corporate governance body such as the supervisory board. Performativity comes into play because the corporate governance structure also sets incentives for the formation of cognitive assets. If employees think that their interests are not sufficiently represented in the corporate governance structure, they will not invest in the formation of specific cognitive assets. As a consequence, a corporate governance regime that does not allow their participation will emerge as the most efficient. Thus, the institutions and the cognitive assets mutually condition each other. This is a performative structure (for more on this see Herrmann-Pillath 2016).

44 In North's (2005) cognitive approach to institutions, 'shared mental models' play an essential role. This idea was seminally developed by Denzau and North (1994) and exerted strong influence on research on institutions. However, this approach adopts a misplaced internalism, because in fact institutions can function well without people sharing the same ideas and perceptions about their workings and purposes. For example, labour market institutions are certainly seen in a different light by workers and employers, yet they can work in terms of coordinating their actions. The Aoki model clearly distinguishes between the signs or public representations that are shared in a population by definition and the individual dispositions which might be caused by different interpretations, hence diverse 'mental models'. So, the Aoki model is strictly externalist. This way of thinking connects with the recent surge of interest in the role of ideas in politics, following seminal work by Blyth (2002) and others. At this point, we need to open up the black box of the model and explicitly analyse mechanisms that generate and propagate ideas, such as in Schmidt's (2008, 2011) 'discursive institutionalism'. In China studies, this relates to the institutional conditions of producing and disseminating certain ideologies, such as the Imperial examination system. As we see, analysing a particular institution always connects up with the analysis of other institutions, such as institutions in the semiotic domain.

45 The game-theoretic approach to ritual has been seminally elaborated by Chwe (2001). In game theoretic terms, common knowledge is essential to solving coordination problems (for a survey see Vanderschraaf and Sillari 2014). In economics, there is a long tradition of emphasizing the analytical model of the

'prisoners' dilemma' as the antipode of the 'invisible hand' model of markets; however, this model is in fact of limited analytical value, as Ostrom (1990) has emphasized in her work. Therefore, Skyrms (2004) argues that the prototypical model of social cooperation, including both markets and public goods, is Rousseau's stag hunt or the assurance game. At the heart of this structure lies a coordination problem. Thus, as Chwe argues, rituals are also of widespread and fundamental significance in all modern societies, and hence cannot be narrowed down to tradition or to peculiar social domains such as religion. For example, modern capital markets rely on rituals in many respects, such as the social organization of stock markets, the normative commitments of accountants and individuals implementing corporate governance institutions, and so forth (see Zaloom 2004). The analysis of performativity of markets such as in Çalışkan (2007) is actually the analysis of the rituals that create and establish those markets and generate common knowledge about their functioning. At the centre of this process stands the creation and confirmation of the identities of traders participating in the market as a group. Chwe's approach bears close resemblance with Barnes' (1995: 76ff.) interactionist approach which claims that collective action problems are resolved by means of symbolic communication and the implied capacities for sanctioning, such as approval, or despise as mere communicative acts. As I detailed previously, the power of those 'cheap' sanctions resides in their impact upon identities. Barnes does not use the term 'ritual', but his examples clearly show the importance of rituals in maintaining the symbolic repertoire that is necessary to enable the sanctions.

46 Hayek (1945) is the seminal source for understanding markets as systems of distributed knowledge which cannot be centralized in any single individual. This view was generalized on institutions in his later work, in particular Hayek (1973). In this work, Hayek distinguishes between 'cosmos' and 'taxis': taxis is the domain of man-made institutions, cosmos the domain of evolved institutions. Correspondingly, in law he distinguishes between 'nomos' as evolved law and 'thesis' as legislated law. In the Anglo-Saxon context, the former is common law, the latter public law. As we will see later, these Hayekian distinctions closely correspond to Chinese conceptions, such as in the distinction between administrative law and customary law. In Chapter 2 I will also refer to Fei Xiaotong's views, according to which we might equate 'ritual' as 'cosmos' and 'law' as 'taxis'; however, the notion of customary law seems to stay in tension with this, as well as the formalization of ritual in Imperial rule. Yet, one essential idea in the Chinese notion of ritual is exactly that it is seen as being a set of evolved social practices which define social order. This matches also with the game-theoretic notion of ritual. So, ritual girates towards the 'cosmos' pole and law towards the 'thesis' pole (the latter especially in continental law).

47 It is important to note that this neglect of ritual has influenced economics deeply, especially with regard to its philosophical foundations in liberalism and individualism. This mainly pops up in the context of reflecting upon the relationship between ethics and economics. Only in the past three decades have economists slowly rediscovered the essential role of morality for the functioning of markets, which are mainly seen as being governed by formal legal institutions; today, morality is recognized as another pillar of achieving successful and efficient coordination, if only because formal institutions are costly to establish and enforce (for one seminal and exemplary work see Platteau 1994). This bias has been created in the lopsided reception of founding father's work Adam Smith, well receiving the institutional analysis of the 'Wealth of Nations' but ignoring the 'Theory of Moral Sentiments' (cf. the assessment by Evensky 2005). As I have argued in Herrmann-Pillath (2015), many aspects of Smith's thinking converge with Confucian thought about the origins of ritual in a

'natural' morality of human beings. The intellectual bias has also prevented economics from receiving Hegel's philosophy as an alternative doctrine of liberal economics, as Fukuyama (1992) has pinpointed lucidly. Hegel's notion of liberalism and market society as civil society corresponds neatly with the Chinese dualism of ritual and law, with ritual corresponding to his notion of 'ethical life' (Sittlichkeit). Although Hegel created the concept of the 'Rechtsstaat' (constitutional state), he nevertheless believed that 'ethical life' provides its foundations. Interestingly, as I discuss in great detail in Herrmann-Pillath and Boldyrev (2014), Hegel's approach to 'Sittlichkeit' also dealt with the methodological problem that this is a generic concept, but can only become operational in the concrete context of particular societies. This idea was opposed to the Kantian effort at grounding ethics in universal notions of rational reasoning (the 'categorical imperative'). Thus, we meet the same methodological duality as in the term 'ritual'.

48 In economics, status had been highlighted as a central category already by Adam Smith (1759) in his 'Theory of Moral Sentiments': According to Smith, striving for status is the main motivation of human economic effort. However, status has since then been relegated to the domain of sociology, with important exceptions such as Veblen's (1899). Recently, Podolny (2005) has shown the ubiquitous relevance of status in ordering market relations such as in capital markets and investment banking. In his descriptions, the role of rituals is salient (for example, rituals in assigning certain positions of banks on public announcements of subscriptions to bond issues). The economic function of status results from the fact that status signals quality via costly signalling. However, status also creates the capacity to access social resources at lower cost because other agents wish to associate with high-status individuals, companies or groups. These competitive advantages makes status sustainable. In economics, status has been mainly highlighted in the context of consumption, following the track laid by Smith and Veblen (see e.g. Frank 1985; Hopkins and Kornienko 2004). The relationship between status and ritual is also salient in Barnes' (1995: 130ff.) sociological discussion of status groups. Barnes argues that symbolic communication is essential to maintaining status distinctions, given the fact that the essential mechanism is the exclusion of deviant members. However, exclusion is individually costly, so symbolic communication alleviates this issue. This point relates to the observation that a human universal is moral aggression; in other words, the willingness to act as a sanctioning third party without gaining direct advantage (see n. 27 above).

49 For a comprehensive overview, see Hartley (2003). Cultural studies emerged in Britain as a specialized subfield in sociology, political science and anthropology analysing the role of culture in modern societies, especially with regard to expressing and maintaining social structure and its undergirding power relations. One important subfield is media studies. Hartley and Potts (2014) continue with this tradition but develop a 'naturalistic' evolutionary alternative. Yet, the idea remains essential that culture serves as a marker of individual identities as being related to group and status boundaries. This tradition is immanent in my approach, especially with regard to the inclusion of media studies. If I highlight the role of signs in stabilizing institutions, the media are a particular institutional and technological setting in which the production of signs takes place.

50 This tension has been created by two founding fathers of modern anthropology, Tylor and Boas (for an extensive discussion see Ingold 1986: 29ff.). Tylor approached cultures as wholes, whereas Boas focused on the role of single artefacts. These different views imply that in the former case we can only understand elements properly if we place them into the entire context of

culture, which entails the Quine indeterminacy thesis and the impossibility of perfect translation (see n. 8 and n. 18 above). In the latter case, we can think of universal functions of culture which are realized in different ways in different societies, based on functionally equivalent artefacts. This implies that these elements can also be reshuffled more easily and de-contextualized across different cultures, which helps us understand phenomena such as cultural hybridization and culture change via culture contact.

51 In his analysis of cultural standardization in contemporary China, Kipnis (2012) refers to the observation that public buildings, especially government seats, reflect a shared symbolism of power. These symbols are also appropriated by state-owned companies, in particular if they operate on the periphery, see e.g. Cliff (2013) on the headquarters of energy companies in China's western provinces. In these contexts, architectural design may be directly seen as the embodiment of ritual. Indeed, this applies for modernist conceptions in general: Chinese cities manifest a very different urban design than most other metropolitan areas in the world, with considerable larger block sizes and reduced density of connections (see World Bank 2014a: 146ff.).

52 My approaches matches general methodological prescriptions of mechanistic explanations such as Schmid's (2011). Schmid distinguishes four steps in analysing social mechanisms: (1) the explanation of the individual action, (2) the analysis of the interaction patterns, (3) the aggregation process, and (4) the feedbacks between the aggregate level and individual action. These four steps relate to different theoretical resources, which also matches my exposition of the Aoki framework detailed elsewhere (Herrmann-Pillath 2013a). For example, the explanation of individual action may rely on psychology or microeconomics, the analysis of interactions on game theory. The aggregation process involves transitions between different levels, which is often obfuscated by economists in positing the so-called 'representative individual' in macroanalyses. Here and in the final stage, the feedback mechanisms, sociology may come into play, possibly tied up with mathematical methods such as complex adaptive systems.

53 This is inspired by the approach originating from White (2008) and is analytically enhanced by Mohr and Rawlings (2012); for an overview see DiMaggio (2011). The network approach to culture is a disaggregate analysis of semiotic structures, partly by means of applying social network analysis to the distribution of signs and their use in society. I have dubbed this approach 'bimodal' in Herrmann-Pillath (2013a), since it implies that we distinguish between social networks and semiotic networks. Social networks create semiotic networks via communication and interaction, and semiotic networks feedback on the social networks via the diffusion of signs and their effects on behaviour, such as expressing and maintaining group boundaries.

54 In the following, I may appear to be overly parsimonious in introducing more specific theoretical concepts as far as the empirical challenge of analysing economic systems in concerned, especially when compared to alternatives such as the 'varieties of capitalism' literature. However, if one looks at this literature in more detail (following the survey by Jackson and Deeg 2006), it springs to the eye that most concepts are descriptive generalizations that do not have theoretical status in the strict sense. The 'building blocks' that Jackson and Deeg identify (such as 'skill formation', 'corporate governance' or 'financial systems') are not even intermediate theoretical terms but just categories of empirical phenomena in particular fields of the economic system. The major theoretical innovations that Jackson and Deeg highlight are 'comparative institutional advantage' and 'institutional path dependency'. The former notion closely relates to my network approach in emphasizing the complementarity of

institutions, in the sense of a 'logic'. To grasp this logic, I argue that it is essential to do cultural analysis as expounded here.

55 This central role of critical mass phenomena in social change has been systematically elucidated by Kuran (1995) (for related approaches see e.g. Witt 2003a). Kuran distinguishes between private preferences, public preferences and publicly displayed preferences, and introduces the assumption that is also made by identity theorists, namely that one aspect of individual preferences is to conform to a group. So, in his model he retains the internalism of standard economic theory, but if we consider the notion of revealed preferences, only the publicly displayed preferences are observable. Thus, the distinction between publicly displayed and private preferences results from the fact that conformity is a distinct and universal determinant of individual utility. The frequency-dependent dynamics results from the fact that the distance between public preferences and private preferences creates individual costs, and that the public preferences reflect a statistical distribution of publicly displayed preferences. So, the single individual will assess individual costs and benefits, and may possibly switch the publicly displayed preferences which feedback on the public preferences; this effect changes the individual calculus, again resulting in critical mass phenomena. For a related argument see Schlicht (1998), who especially emphasizes the phenomenon of hysteresis. For example, maintaining normative commitments to tax compliance is a frequency-dependent phenomenon; once these commitments collapse, it is much more difficult to restore them. These approaches are particularly important in understanding the interaction between culture and institutions: institutions might enforce certain behaviours, such as tax compliance, but may only succeed if very high efforts are undertaken, when the frequency-dependent dynamics of actual behaviour works against them. In issues such as tax compliance and corruption, culture can play a role because the attitudes towards the government are influenced by perceptions and valuations of citizenship.

56 My classification follows Ackermann (2001). The notion of path dependency has been elaborated seminally by authors such as Arthur (1989), who focused on technological change. We can transfer these concepts to the analysis of institutions and culture, because in technology network effects are mostly emphasized, such as in communication networks or interface design in complementary technologies. This also applies for institutions, because institutions are also means to coordinate actions. For example, in regular transactions between businesspeople and government officials, certain expectations may be held regarding the prevalence of corruption. Businesspeople may fail to achieve their goals if they do not meet the expectations regarding bribes. This creates a frequency-dependent dynamics resulting in a stable configuration of the interface between businesspeople and officials. The notion of path dependency also has a prominent position in mechanism analysis, since positive feedback circuits are considered to be highly relevant in understanding the stability of mechanisms (see Schützeichel 2015: 91ff.). It is important to note that path dependency and institutionalization are different notions, but may be closely related. This happens when certain paths are stabilized via cognitive mechanisms that underpin enforcement of related behaviour. Thus, for example, racial segregation may emerge spontaneously in spite of relatively weak preferences for segregation, but may become enforced via the perception of the results and emerging supportive values that trigger enforcement actions (the classical analysis of these interdependencies is Schelling 1978).

57 In the analytical philosophy of institutions, this relates to the approaches by Searle (1995, 2010) and Tuomela (2007) who point towards the role of collective intentionality in explaining the institutionalization of behaviour. The

status notion allows us to combine this idea with differentials in enforcement power, such as third-party retaliation and so forth. This is also recognized in Searle's notion of a 'power creation operator': As a result of institutionalization, actors assume the status to exert power which is recognized by others, thus being able to enforce the institution. My notion of distributed agency corresponds to collective intentionality in eschewing the idea that even the most powerful designers of institutions (such as Mao Zedong during the 'Great Leap Forward') can actually monopolize the agency that drives institutionalization. No institutionalization is without collective intentionality, and hence even in this case the agency of institutional design is distributed across many actors, including those who appear to be the least powerful, such as the peasants.

58 In recent economic research on institutions, influential contributions have pinpointed the fact that current states of national economies can often be traced back to certain structural features of the past, such as the legacy of colonial history (Acemoglu *et al.* 2001, 2002). However, this merely establishes correlations between different sets of observations on past and present, and hence may be seen as a statistical way to identify family resemblances, and cannot reveal the specific mechanisms that generate them. So, these methods point to the historicity of institutions but cannot explain it. Blyth (2011) has highlighted the role of ideas in stabilizing certain regularities in complex social systems. However, this also means that the causal function of the ideas occurs in the present, even if they are transmitted from the past.

59 The distinction between synchronic and diachronic analysis is again taken from linguistics. In economics, this distinction has been given a prominent place in Aoki's comparative institutional analysis (see Aoki 2001: 207ff., 245ff.). An important unifying notion is 'complementarity'. Complementarity means that single institutions need to functionally complement other institutions synchronically, and that at the same time temporal sequences of institutions need to complement through time. So, complementarity imposes constraints upon institutional design that aims at single institutions. Most importantly for my later argument, in his analysis of complementarities, Aoki draws the conclusion that it can be impossible to rank sets of institutions on a unified performance scale.

60 There is a clear difference between sociology and economics in extending the notion of capital, which is also important for China studies. In sociology, influential authors such as Bourdieu use a number of different concepts of capital, such as 'symbolic capital', which are often also referred to in China studies but have never been received in economics. The only concept that transpired to economics is social capital, presumably because major contributors to the social capital literature in sociology had also adopted approaches close to economics, in particular Coleman (1990). Social capital then became very influential in the context of development economics, and, related to this, in empirical research on growth, with seminal contributions such as the edited volume by Dasgupta and Serageldin (2000) or the review article by Sobel (2002). My use of the term closely follows those contributions in sociology and economics which relate social capital to social networks, such as Lin (2001) or Dasgupta (2005), and less with aggregate analyses on civil society and values (as in Putnam 2000). The motivation for this does not lie in a methodological predilection for the economics perspective, but in the good match to the Aoki model and its focus on interactions. Further, I employ the categories introduced by Sen (1984). Functionings are individual performances relative to a given social structure. For example, an elementary functioning might be the role of fatherhood. In rural China today; this functioning is jeopardized for a growing number of low-status males, as a result of the one-child policy and the

lack of brides (see Greenhalgh 2012). Thus, we can say that they are lacking the necessary capabilities to fulfil these functionings. The capabilities include material aspects, such as individual income and wealth, but also network dimensions, such as relationships in extended kin groups or to middlemen in girl trafficking. Obviously, the set of functionings can be partly based on individual aspirations, thus involving the individual freedom of choice, or is partly reflecting role expectations in society. In Sen's framework, capabilities and freedoms are foundational categories and have been related by Nussbaum to a list of universal capabilities and functionings. Sen himself is more cautious and relates these to specific beliefs, ideas and norms in a given society. For overviews of the methodological debates on these Senian notions see Clark (2005) or Robeyns (2011).

61 Network analysis is only slowly gaining ground in economics (for a recent survey see Jackson 2014). This is the case even though the approach is geared towards formal modelling and quantitative analysis, and has produced important insights for specific fields in economics, such as labour economics, following early contributions by Granovetter (1985, 2005). Yet, the relationship between economics and sociology remains very biased to the disadvantage of sociology. The transfer of concepts is cleary unbalanced, with economics rarely importing concepts from sociology or citing sociologists (for bibliometric evidence on this see Fourcade *et al.* 2015).

62 For a classical approach see Pye (1981). As the analysis of career patterns of Central Comittee members by Shih *et al.* (2012) shows, these factors still count in modern Chinese politics. This compares to economic models that analyse the tournament structure of Chinese government, summarized by Xu (2011). In these models it is assumed that economic performance of jurisdictions determines the advancement of party officials that lead them. However, as Shih *et al.* show, factional ties with top leaders still matter, apart from other factors such as provincial revenue collection. This role of personal networks and social capital is also salient in more circumscribed contexts, such as the implementation of reform initiatives at the local level (see Tsai and Dean 2014).

63 Beugelsdjik and Maseland (2010) devote an entire chapter in their book on culture in economics to discussing the question of trust. Trust is a social phenomenon of great significance for economic transactions, as it saves transaction costs and stabilizes expectations. However, explaining country-level differences in trust is a tricky problem, as we will also see in Chapter 5. Research on trust is often closely related to social capital, as social capital can provide the foundation for trust. If I can safely rely on a rich set of network connections that help me achieve my goals, I entertain a high level of trust in my social environment. However, the relationship with identity is complex, as there are different conceptualizations of social capital which distinguish between homophilous and heterophilous relations (Lin 2001). On first sight, only the latter build on shared identities by definition. This underlies Coleman's (1990) approach to social capital as a public good that is shared in a community. A classical analysis of these layered circles of networks, social capital and business relations in the Chinese context is Landa (1994). The correspondences with indigenous notions are multifarious, such as business relations which are based on shared dialects, or the active constructions of social relations as 'capital' that may be exploited in future business transactions. I will discuss these matters in detail in Chapter 5.

64 The concept of economic style was proposed by Spiethoff (1932) in response to the ongoing debates among German economists about the relationship between Weberian 'ideal types' and 'real types' in approaching different economic systems, following up on the controversies about historism and its

theories of stages of economic development. Spiethoff proposed to distinguish between universal economic theories and theories that have an intermediate scope in space and time. This may be compared to recent proposals by Rodrik (2007) (also motivated by the Chinese case) distinguishing between general economics and specific conditions of application. The difference is that the 'economic styles' are also theoretical notions and not simply specific conditions of application. Further, the notion of style also implies that there is a strong subjective component in constructing these styles. This corresponds to the use of the term 'style' in the arts (for a contemporary view see Bechtel 1930). There, a 'style' is something that cannot be defined objectively, but by reference to perceptions of participating observers (the audience that appreciates a stylistic innovation) and to historical ex-post reconstructions by the art historian. Evidently, the methodology behind this comes very close to my use of 'family resemblances'. Interestingly, the notion of economic style was also used by Müller-Armack (1940) to develop the notion of the 'social market economy' that proved to be the guidepost for post-Second World War economic policy in Germany. In this case, 'style' also refers to the creative design of economic order, drawing explicitly upon cultural resources such as religion.

65 Dichotomic taxonomies of economic systems were dominating in periods of systems competition, in terms of the juxtaposition between 'planned economy' and 'market economy'. Alternatives were largely posited in terms of a 'third way', which, however, appeared to be elusive in real-world politics. Basically, this dichotomy also shapes Chinese and Western discourses about the Chinese transition 'from plan to market'. However, the Chinese case also demonstrates that the notion of 'planned economy' is by no means monolithic, since the Maoist system differed fundamentally from the Soviet model. The 'varieties of capitalism' view (for a seminal contribution see Berger and Dore 1996) gained ground following the collapse of the Cold War regime, highlighting the substantial differences between market economies of the Anglo-Saxon financial capitalism type, the so-called 'Rhenish' models, and the allegedly culturally peculiar ones such as the Japanese model. However, most economists still stick to dualist models, now translating into an opposition between the Anglo-Saxon model and the rest, as in the very influential 'legal origin' theory which sorts the economic systems in the world according to their roots in a common law or a civil law system, thereby neglecting the considerable institutional variety and variance in performance within the two categories. On this literature see La Porta *et al.* (1997, 1998) and the generalization by Djankov *et al.* (2003); for a devastating critique see Siems and Deakin (2010). Another recent dichotomic theory is North *et al.* (2009), which claims that there is a fundamental transition to 'open access orders' which, again, largely include the Anglo-Saxon economies and parts of Europe. This dichotomic historical analysis is also flawed empirically, as it excludes the possibility that an authoritarian political system can be combined with a liberal market economy. One important counterexample analysed by Wegner (2014) is Prussia in the early nineteenth century. The presumed tension between autocracy and market economy was only resolved following the debacle of Nazi rule and the Second World War. However, the tendency to divide the world of economic systems into polar opposites even affects the 'varieties of capitalism' literature, especially with reference to one extremely influential approach, that of Hall and Soskice, who introduced the distinction between 'liberal market economies' and 'coordinated market economies' (for an excellent overview of the different approaches in this literature see Jackson and Deeg 2006). This forced many contributions into sometimes stifling attempts at putting empirical cases into one of those two boxes (which is especially difficult for China: see Zhang and

Peck 2014), in spite of the fact that the descriptive and analytical toolbox is conceptually much richer than economic dualisms.

66 An excellent example is Tsai's (2007) research on the effects of formal democratic institutions on the performance in public goods production in Chinese villages. 'Western' theory predicts that democratic governance will also raise the quality of decision-making about the provision of public goods. However, Tsai cannot identify this causality, which may be explained by many observations about how elections are managed, how the Communist Party influences the results, etc. These observations would confirm the 'Western' theory because they would demonstrate that the democratic institutions are partly failing. However, Tsai can also show that public good provision functions well in those villages that have strong lineage organizations and temple-building associations. She argues that these traditional social structures enhance the accountability of local cadres independent from the formal democratic institutions.

67 On the long-term differences between the USA and Germany in terms of fundamental notions of business, economic policy and corporate practices see Abelshauser (2003) and Armbrüster (2005). One example is the different conceptualizations of managerial functions. In Germany, managerial functions have been traditionally associated with the formation of professional identities that are specific to particular industries. This is the notion of 'profession' 'Beruf' as 'calling' 'Berufung'. Correspondingly, until today, top executives have a background in the industries in which they are active, such as chemists in the chemical industry or engineers in automotives. By comparison, in the USA the idea emerged early that 'management' is a generic profession that may be applied without any specific industry background. This was reflected in the establishment of business schools and MBA programmes which gradually became very prestigious. In Germany, MBA programmes are still rare, and the standard 'Betriebswirtschaftslehre' as 'business administration' is not always seen as the king's way to top executive positions. Similar differences apply in other areas, such as the acceptance of income differentials or the public display of wealth. These differences mainly show up in political rituals, such as during electoral compaigns, which do not necessarily reflect actual policies. For example, even the Social Democratic government under Chancellor Schroeder recently implemented a liberalization of the labour market in Germany which is seen as undergirding the resurgence of the German economy over the past decade. Yet, these policies remain disputed today, and even the conservative party ponders re-regulations. This policy manoeuvring clearly shows the strong impact of general ideas about 'social' elements in economic policy that are deeply rooted in the notion of 'social market economy'.

68 In Chinese studies, the closest analogy to my work is Gates (1996). Gates builds on a different theoretical framework inspired by Marxism and introduces the notion of 'petty capitalism'. This results in a very different conceptualization than mine because Gates posits a dualist structure in which ritual dominates the 'tributary mode'. Both modes interact, but stay in tension and even competition with each other. My conceptualization of economic style is monistic: in terms of Gates' dualism, this would mean that I see her 'petty capitalism' as being governed by the same ritual principles as the tributary mode. In fact, many phenomena to which we refer are just the same ones, as Gates, for example, also recognizes the role of ritual in establishing the family as the basic unit of agency in 'petty capitalism'. Thus, her dualism is shaped by the theoretical presumption that there is a fundamental difference between 'capitalism' and 'ritual'. This dualism tends to downgrade important phenomena such as the fact that Chinese kinship enabled the growth of modern capitalist enterprises in Chinese overseas business conglomerates (which she simply includes

in the 'petty' dimension). In fact, these inconsistencies are most obvious in her treatment of regional differences in China, where the Jiangnan region features as a place where the petty capitalist mode is strong and the tributary mode weak. However, the Jiangnan region was also certainly a centre of cultural activity in Late Qing China that also produced the symbolic resources which sustained what is a ritual economy in my sense (for a concise summary of these characteristics see Naquin and Rawski 1987). For example, the vibrant merchant culture in the Jiangnan region was also strong in producing scholar-officials as members of the system: what Gates identifies as 'tributary mode'. So, in my view, the Jiangnan region was actually in a most advanced stage of the 'ritual economy'.

2 The Chinese ritual economy as historical type

Chinese thought and institutions: the meaning of ritual

In this chapter I will develop an analytical picture of the economic and social structure of the traditional Chinese economy that provides the ground for identifying family resemblances with current conditions. My picture is a theoretical construct and extracts certain general features from the historical literature that define the 'ritual economy' as a historical type; this allows for the establishment of family resemblances with the present. Thus, I will report what economists call 'stylized facts', which is often regarded as a basic methodological step in reconstructing social mechanisms, and I will add a strong dose of methodological and theoretical considerations. This chapter is not a piece of historical research or a summary thereof. I will touch upon many issues that are controversial; I will not discuss these in more detail but simply opt for one of the competing interpretations in the specialist literature. Thus, my picture is certainly biased, but it may be as justified as competing interpretations. In fact, I believe that these competing interpretations mainly portray the reflections and repercussions in the 'mirror of culture', thus actually also mirroring opinions about the implicit comparisons with European history, given the fact that the Chinese case is seen largely seen in the light of the European comparison by both Western and Chinese scholars. Recent Chinese economic and social history has often been written in the shadow of the question of why China failed to achieve indigenous modernization, and with an eye to the possible consequences for answering the question why and how China can catch up 'with the West'.[1]

I pay special attention to concepts that have emerged in this literature for grasping certain peculiar characteristics of China and which appear to be unique to China studies, since these concepts may be seen as pointing towards intermediate-level theoretical notions that would allow one to construct the economic style. These concepts encapsulate certain patterns of social interactions, such as Skinner's 'honeycomb' of local market systems or Watson's concept of 'orthopraxy' as the specific way how the Imperial bureaucracy supervised and regulated ritual in the context of local societies. These patterns correspond to certain mechanisms, as empirical specifications in the framework of the Aoki model, and hence manifest the institutional make-up of the traditional ritual economy. In past debates about social science approaches to history, those specific concepts often met with suspicion because they would make cross-region and inter-temporal comparisons difficult, and would certainly preclude the construction of general law-like propositions about historical developments. However, as I have argued in the previous chapter, it is those concepts which allow identifying certain types in terms of stylized facts that refer to causal mechanisms which may be ascertained via the study of local events and contexts; there we can directly access data and information about causes and effects without interpreting them as manifestations of macro-level structural features.[2] However, facing this bewildering richness of information about local studies that have been produced both by historical and contemporary China studies, we also need a unifying idea that helps us recognize family resemblances across these large sets of cases.

As we have already seen, the concept of ritual is indeed the most fundamental one in this endeavour. Recently in China studies this concept has been explicitly linked to the economy in coining the term 'ritual economy'.[3] This theoretical move reflects a strong revisionist trend in China studies that has been unfolding over past decades and which highlights the economic functions of many traditional institutions in the sense of establishing functional equivalences with legal institutions of market economies or capitalism; indeed, establishing functional equivalences is a hallmark of mechanism analysis.[4] For example, lineage organizations may be seen as functional equivalents of corporations. This literature is important in the context of the broader revisionist research that aims to explain the causes of why traditional China did not undergo an industrial revolution, in spite of the fact that economic, social and technological developments were far advanced compared to Europe in the Middle Ages. Again, in the ongoing debates over historical revisionism I adopt a specific position which remains contentious. Thus, as I outlined in Chapter 1, I actively construct a certain image of the past which is driven by my interest in identifying the relationship between culture and economy. I think that this debate does not simply reflect our still incomplete understanding of historical realities, but actually the diversity of trends and social forces that were emerging in Late Imperial China, and which partly failed to unfold because of the shocks that resulted from the challenge of Western modernity and Imperialism, ultimately leading towards the collapse of the Empire and a state of institutional destabilization, even chaos, that actually prevailed until 1978, when the CCP launched its reform process. I argue that it is extremely difficult to approach historical realities, because this endeavour needs largely to rely on all sorts of written sources that were always imbued with values and views of the literate elite. Looking through this cultural, or, as will become clear later, 'culturalist' veil was one of the major achievements of the revisionist literature.

Methodologically, this revisionist literature presents a radical departure from earlier structural and cultural explanations of China's development, and effectively completes the move towards mechanistic explanations, most seminally epitomized in the influential work of Skinner on markets as organizing principles of local society. In other words, whereas influential authors such as Max Weber referred to macro-patterns such as ideologies purportedly shaping the worldview of entire societies, the revisionist literature has been increasingly based on a large number of case studies that highlight the actual workings of the Chinese economy at the micro-level. On this level, mechanisms become observable, that is, the concrete way in which social interactions worked together and produced certain results. It is on this level that we can discover functional equivalences with patterns in European history and hence are enabled to debunk sweeping claims about structural or cultural forces as shaping China's fate in the past.[5]

These debates are of fundamental importance in understanding China's development up until the present day, as the single most important theme in Chinese political evolution in the twentieth century was the issue of 'modernization'. The idea of modernization reflected the belief, held by virtually all the groups and intellectual leaders competing for power and influence, that China's failure to industrialize has to be explained with reference to China's traditional culture, in the broadest sense. For example, in analysing the issue of rural development, many scholars and political leaders believed that the ritual commitments of rural elites caused a lack of investment in productive uses.[6] Therefore, the economic modernization of the countryside would also require a comprehensive cultural transformation of the entire social structure. Vice versa, the cultural transformation required a fundamental transformation of the economic foundations of social power. Thus, the CCP launched collectivization as a comprehensive approach towards modernization. Interestingly, in Taiwan land reform also aimed at breaking the hold of large lineage groups on local society, beyond developmental considerations, but maintained the relationship between family and ownership along traditional lines.

We need to pinpoint the fact that up until 1978 China remained in a state of institutional limbo, instability and outright chaos. This is especially true if we consider the alleged polar opposite to ritual: the law. The law was seen by most modernizing elites as a tool of modernization, and so Republican China saw great efforts in creating a modern legal system, mostly following German and Japanese precedent. However, given the political conditions of the time, these achievements failed to take root in society at large. For example, the series of laws installing the modern corporation never succeeded in changing practices of business, which almost entirely remained organized in the form of individual businesses or partnerships with full liability (see Chapter 6). After 1949, Maoist leaders effectively stalled legal development because the law was seen as being an element of bourgeois society: 'revolutionary law' was a far cry from law as understood in the context of economic theories of institutions. We therefore have to recognize the fact that the shadow of the Imperial past is long, especially if we consider the vast rural areas of China where the collapse of the Empire destroyed the foundations of local ritual order governed by elites imbued with Confucian values. As we know from hindsight, the attempts at a radical cultural transformation of rural society were only partly successful, and tensions between the rural little traditions and the socialist 'great tradition' are still visible. Thus, I argue that there is a *longue durée* of social transformation that spans the Imperial past and the present of reformed China. This does not refer to larger structures of social organization, but to particular elements, patterns, processes and states in the sense of the mechanism approach outlined in Chapter 1. This does not mean that elements may have exactly the same function in past and present; to the contrary, the ongoing Chinese modernization effort constantly re-contextualizes these elements and hence changes their cultural meaning and social functioning. But at the same time, we need to take notice of the revival of images, ideas and views from China's past, be this references to Chinese philosophy in official statements of political leaders, the success of historical television drama or be the creation of grassroots-level Confucian revival movements.[7] These observations suggest that there is also an ongoing process of reconstructing traditional culture as a newly emerging system of references for unfolding a Chinese version of modernity.

We can observe this process in many areas. One example of core interest in our context is the law. Contemporary legal studies in China mainly adopt a modernist perspective and almost completely ignore traditional Chinese law, thus continuing with the approaches that were dominant in the twentieth century. However, this effort often stays in tension with certain practices and values which are rooted in Chinese tradition, and thus trigger adaptations of legal practice to social realities.[8] But these observations raise the important and difficult question of how far the imposition of a so-called modern conception of law is factually contributing to improvements in economy and society. In standard economic explanations of the transition to capitalism and industrialization, the idea looms large that the emergence of the modern institutions of law were essential for achieving this transition. This refers to both general and specific aspects of law. In general terms, law is seen as having enabled the expansion of anonymous markets beyond the allegedly constraining factors of kinship and primordial communities, and safeguarding property rights against the obstructive intervention of power holders.[9] More specifically, certain legal innovations may have been essential for enabling new forms of economic organization, in particular the corporation.[10] It is illuminating to recognize that this sort of explanation concurs with similar judgements about current conditions in China: Observers believe that the further strengthening of the law and the establishment of more reliable structures of corporate governance are indispensable in completing the transition to the market economy. Therefore, analysing this argument for the case of old China also has implications for understanding present China.

Tellingly, we meet the same methodological issues when looking at the past and the present. This is a most revealing indicator that our approach to culture and economy in China may be influenced by implicitly assuming a specific perspective that is in turn cultural. In other words, in both cases we are involved in the mirror of culture, and the resulting constructions of culture may possibly show family resemblances. So, in assessing traditional Chinese law and, in particular, property rights in the economy, we may tend towards using modern economic theories in analysing historical circumstances, and thus identifying certain 'deficiencies' impeding the transition to states of higher efficiency and economic rationality. Similarly, in assessing the current status of property rights in China, we may draw similar conclusions. However, these conclusions are heavily influenced by a number of pivotal normative presumptions in the economic theory of property rights. For example, the economic theory of property rights focuses only on efficiency and incentivization, whereas we might also look at property rights from the angle of how societies resolve recurrent distributional conflicts, and how they internalize the ubiquitous externalities that result from any kind of economic action.[11]

In traditional China, law was seen as an alternative way to organize society as compared to ritual. Opposing these two fundamental concepts was a central issue in the intellectual debates of pre-Imperial China, in particular between the so-called 'Legalists' and the Confucians. Legalism was a major intellectual source for establishing Imperial authoritarianism in the third century BCE, which has remained a pattern at least until the end of the Empire but may actually also implicitly inspire contemporary ideas of 'rule by law'. It is important to recognize that the creation of the Legalist tradition was an act of establishing a modern state in the sense that law was seen as directly addressing the population and governing society, and not only as a system of rules ordering intra-elite relations, as in European feudalism. The so-called 'Confucianization' of law, especially under the Neoconfucian intellectual hegemony, did not change this approach, but emphasized the transformative role of law, in the sense that law should undergird the maintenance of ritual in society. This also implied that ritual obtained a legal dimension, so that ritual was also enforced by legal means, especially in the context of adjudication. Correspondingly, one cannot simply interpret the absence of civil law as a formal institution as leaving room for ritual as an informal institution.

Ritual was a major reference in a process of adjudication that itself followed strict and binding legal rules on court procedures.[12]

Yet, even Legalism shared with Confucianism the fundamental interest in the question of how a 'natural' order of society can be established, in the sense of societal self-organization matching certain general moral prescriptions, thus putting human society and cosmos in harmony. Legalist radicalism aimed at ultimately making actual enforcement of the law obsolete, as everybody would just follow the incentives created by the law. Thus, a more basic idea that emerged in the 'axis time' was the notion of 'wu wei' (无为); that is, government by non-action, most clearly articulated by Daoism, the intellectual current which also broadly shaped popular culture and religion until the advent of modernity. This idea of 'non-action' is probably the most direct equivalent to Western notions of freedom, though not being based on the idea of individual autonomy, but on the concept of harmony between the individual and the social and natural cosmos, in the sense of adapting spontaneously to the cosmic forces and thereby achieving equilibrium within and without.[13]

In contrast to the Legalists, a central tenet of Confucianism was to view ritual as the foundation of society, whereas law was seen as a special institutional device to organize government, and, on a more principled level, as being deficient in the sense that the need to enforce law reflects the failure of society to follow ritual. In other, almost Hayekian words, legal constructivism and interventionism of government reflects an overstretching of human capacities in designing society. In contrast, ritual was seen as a reservoir of culturally transmitted knowledge about the 'good society', defined in moral terms. This opinion is manifest in the peculiar characteristics of traditional Chinese law, which was largely developed in the realm of administrative and penal law, but did not recognize civil law. Matters of civil law were seen as the domain of ritual. However, even with reference to formal law, ritual was foundational in evaluative terms. The main task of government was to maintain and embody ritual, and many legal norms directly expressed ritual norms. In this sense, we can say that government in Imperial China saw itself positively as a system of 'governance' in modern terms.[14]

One possible way to understand the distinction between law and ritual in economic terms is to see law as formal institution and ritual as informal institution. In the narrower sense, ritual could also be interpreted as customary law. However, the problem with these distinctions is that ritual was also a formal institution in the sense of being enshrined in written sources and even being applied by formal institutions of enforcement, such as courts. If we reflect upon this definitional issue, we become aware of being entangled in the 'mirror of culture'. One central example of this, and one that is also highly relevant for understanding China's recent social transformation, is an essential aspect of Chinese ritual: the kinship group as 'lineage'. I continue with my discussion of this in the following section; in the current context, suffice it to mention that the Western view of the Chinese extended family was deeply influenced by the Confucian normative framework of kinship that was at the same time being matched with conceptions of lineages originating from Western anthropological research. The result was a picture of a tightly knit agnatic unit with severe patriarchal authority. This picture was slowly undermined by anthropological research that built on detailed local studies, yet continued to exert influence as a basic paradigm, because it was at the same time part and parcel of the Chinese project of modernization in the context of family and gender. But if we today diagnose 'social change', we largely adopt a reconstruction of the past which is based on this theoretical image. Yet, if we take the notion of ritual seriously, we have to ask about the real-world relevance of purely formalistic definitions of ritual as compared to actual social practices, even endorsed by formal processes. As we will see in this chapter, this means that we need to reset the purported starting point of social and economic changes triggered by the efforts at modernization. In the case of lineage, we need to acknowledge the broad scope of organizational and functional variants, the flexibility of kinship relations beyond the agnatic group, or the complexity of gender relations.[15]

Thus, if we want to understand the essence of ritual as compared to law, we need to move to a more abstract level. On this level, what has been thus far approached in terms of ideational foundations of the traditional order turns out to be an expression of fundamentally different cognitive stances. This point also comes to the fore when considering the Weberian account of Chinese culture and government as compared to Western development, which he famously characterized as a process of 'rationalization'. In this account, formal rationality stays at the centre, understood as a certain approach to general rules which are interpreted in terms of deductive logic, and in terms of a certain apparatus of enforcement, the 'rational bureaucracy' based on procedural formalism. However, we need to question this Weberian approach as possibly representing an immanent viewpoint that is itself an expression of Western culture, thus distorting our views on China.[16] This problem is straightforward if we consider an influential indigenous conceptualization of Chinese traditional culture and society, Fei Xiaotong's theory of *chaxu geju.* In doing this, I present a case study of triangulation in relating indigenous viewpoints to modern psychology, and referring this to historical conditions in identifying a pivotal point in the Aoki model, namely the specific causality that connects the processing of signs and symbols with actions via the mediating cognitive structures. As a result, we identify a fundamental type of mechanism that is central to understanding ritual as a feature of economic style.

Ideational and cognitive foundations of the ritual economy: Fei Xiaotong's theory of Chinese society

In this section, I adopt an unusual approach to reconstructing historical conditions as an empirical anchor for identifying family resemblances between past and present. I refer to contemporary psychology and cognitive science to explore the structural and normative foundations of these conditions so far as patterns of social interaction and institutions are concerned. This is an active movement in the mirror of culture, which is mediated via the indigenous reconstruction of traditional Chinese society by the eminent Chinese sociologist Fei Xiaotong. Although Fei mainly analyses Chinese society in the first part of the twentieth century, he claims to refer to stable patterns that have persisted over centuries, if not millennia. In turn, this perspective on the very long run is echoed in modern psychology and cognitive science in terms of the hypothesis that certain fundamental structures of social cooperation in the context of agro-ecosystems have shaped psychological features of individuals in groups since very early times.[17]

Fei Xiaotong proposed a Chinese neologism to describe the traditional order of Chinese society, 'chaxu geju' (差绪格局), which has been translated as 'differential mode of association'.[18] This conceptual innovation is extremely suggestive as an ideational movement in the mirror of culture, since it is an indigenous construction that is explicitly put into the context of a comparison between Western and Chinese culture. In this comparison, Fei did not emphasize notions that receive priority attention in Western self-descriptions, such as 'individualism', but analysed distinct modes of creating social relationships in groups. According to Fei, Western society manifests the feature of 'tuanti zhuyi' (团体主义) 'groupism'. By this he refers to the idea that individuals are ascribed to abstract categories of groups, whereas in Chinese society individuals are elements in concrete groups defined by ongoing interactions he denotes as 'circles', 'quanzi' (圈子). Groups as categories are closed in the sense of clear membership criteria and, being abstract, in treating all individuals as equal in relationship to these criteria; on the other hand, membership to abstract groups does not necessarily imply that all members of the group are actually connected via social interactions. Groups as 'circles' are open and inclusive, since membership criteria are contextualized respective to local conditions, and they are bound together by actualized, albeit often indirect social relations. It is important to note that this distinction is not simply one between 'universalism' and 'particularism', as categorial groups are also of non-universal scope and size.

Thus, as depicted in Figure 2.1, Fei actually identifies two different types of forming social networks: The 'Western' network neatly distinguishes between individuals and relationships, and further assigns individuals to clearly demarcated categories of groups, whereas the 'Chinese'

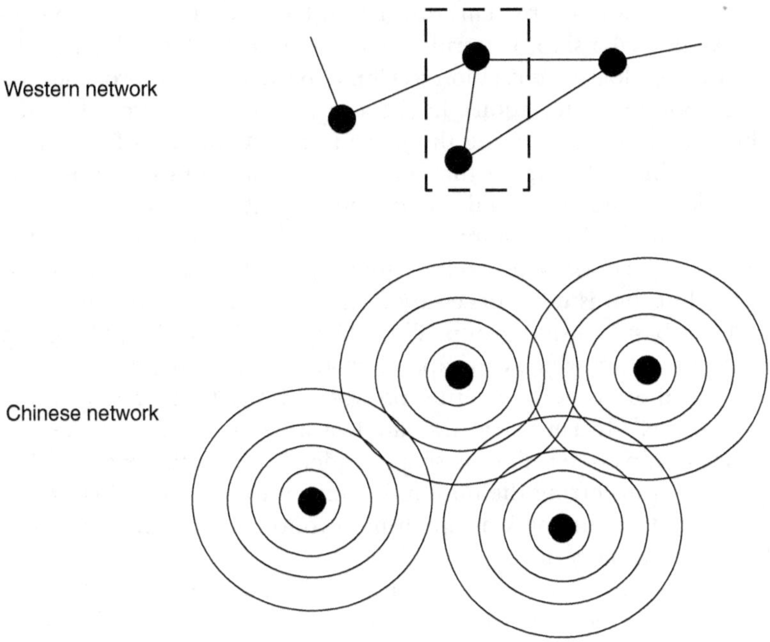

Figure 2.1 Fei Xiaotong's comparison between Western and Chinese social relations.

network sees individuals and relationships as mutually constitutive, and perceives groups as overlapping and open circles. In other words, in the Western case, group assignment is based on shared abstract properties of individuals, who do not necessarily interact with all the other members of the group. For example, being a believer of a religion is based on membership of a church, defined via certain general features such as a written orthodoxy. In contrast, the Chinese network is based on concrete and actual relationships between individuals, including indirectly mediated ones. Taking the example of religion, therefore, ascription to certain abstract groups determined by certain shared beliefs does not define a religious group, but actual relationships between the individual and other religious entities, such as ancestors who are worshipped on a regular basis, and hence even turn into ghosts if this interaction is not maintained, or deities in temples who depend on the ongoing flow of believers offering incense for nurturing their existence.

Fei argues that against the background of this fundamental difference in approaching groups, great care is necessary in using even the simplest and most basic terms for denoting groups in cross-cultural comparisons. Thus, we meet an important instance of the 'mirror of culture'. One of his examples is salient in the current context of understanding the traditional Chinese social and economic order, namely the 'family'. Fei argues that the 'family' in the Western sense is seen as a category, whereas in China it is a network of relationships. This distinction becomes evident when considering extended kinship. Fei criticizes the use of the term 'lineage' by Western anthropologists in relation to China, because this approaches lineages as corporate organizations, hence as a category. This would be the term 'shizu' (氏族). Considering the more fundamental term for 'family' ('jia' 家) in Chinese, he argues that one needs to distinguish between the 'jiating' (家庭) as the actual unit of cohabitating family members, generally the nuclear family or joint family, and the 'jiazu' (家族) as the extended family. The *jiazu* as extended family can be organized as a corporate unit, but that is not a necessary form and therefore not a defining feature of the basic kinship group. Thus, 'family' means a flexible group of actual relationships which can expand or shrink according to functional needs, so that there is no fixed criterion who belongs to the family in the categorical sense.[19] In Fei's view, the family is a system of 'circles', so that actual relationships determine its scope. Indeed, this is the basis for the many forms of transferring the notion of family into other social contexts, also in terms of transferring kinship terms beyond the biological or genealogical criteria of relatedness.

As we will see, these questions are of fundamental importance for conceptually grasping the actual trajectory of social and economic changes from Imperial times up until the present. For example, the standard notion that beyond the 'family' there was a social desert where strangers met with deep mutual suspicion directly translates the Western concept of the family into alleged Chinese notions of social structure, drawing a neat boundary where actually there was very large scope for all forms of intermediate cooperation and closer interaction. More generally, however, we also note that Fei actually describes two fundamentally different types of mechanisms in Western and Chinese society. These mechanisms are of universal relevance in understanding more complex social interactions and the resulting structures.

The distinction between different network principles may be related to fundamental assumptions about how society is structured cognitively, and which have been shaping the development of Western philosophy and social science in the past, at least in the sense of opposing a 'mainstream' and a 'non-mainstream' line of thinking. The 'mainstream' line of thinking is analytical and atomistic, in the sense of supposing that in reflecting upon the relationship between the individual and society it is possible to distinguish neatly between the two levels, and ultimately assuming that the society level can be reduced to the individual level. This belief has been developed both as a positive and a normative theory. Positively, this means that explanations of social phenomena have to proceed in reference to individuals as the exclusive element of social ontology; normatively, it means that society should at least hypothetically be constituted by reference to individual benefit and consent. These ideas underlie Western notions of market economy and democracy, and opposing views, though often articulated, are largely relegated to narratives that locate 'organic' notions of agency and community in conservative strands of thought that would ultimately hold back general social progress. The dualistic view on individual and society also allowed for radical emphases on the society pole, with the most explicit expression in Marxism, thus providing the basis for the emergence of twentieth-century totalitarian models of state. Yet even these ideologies remain rooted in the analytical separation between individual and society.[20]

In the term *chaxu geju* proposed by Fei Xiaotong, the expansion and interaction of circles is the 'pattern' *geju*, whereas the *chaxu* refers to the status order that governs the interactions between individuals in circles. This is the manifestation of ritual: In contrast to Western categorial groupism, in Chinese social interactions individuals are never seen as being equal in principle, but as unequal in the sense of occupying different positions of status. However, this status order is itself local, because even if there is an external benchmark assigning status, the action consequences of status are always determined by the relative status that the individual represents in a specific situation. Ritual provides orientation of how to adapt behaviour properly to these locally embodied status orders. Clearly, ritual in this sense is universalistic in the same way as law is universalistic. The difference lies in the idea that ritual regulates concrete interactions, and is not based on abstract notions of group membership. Thus, according to Fei, the legal universalism of Western society is rooted in the abstract ascription to groups. Indeed, this created the perennial tension in relationship to cosmopolitanism, as the most inclusive group, humanity, was only seen as ascriptive reference in theory but not in practice (epitomized in phenomena such a slavery and racial discrimination). This is a clear hint at recognizing the difference between intellectual history and factual history, especially with regard to path dependencies. It is clearly true that China did not develop comparable theoretical and philosophical approaches to individualism and subjective rights in the context of abstract groups, but at the same time we also note general moral ideas about humanity.[21] Combining these intellectual trends with actual historical developments certainly leads analysis astray: one could even argue that Chinese ideologies did reflect actual practices more closely than Western theorizing, and therefore were empirically more powerful than the latter.

The reflection of ritual in everyday life was traditionally labelled with an expression that is still being used in China, in particular in the rural areas, namely 'li shang wanglai' (礼上往来). This means that in social interactions ('wanglai') one always has to observe the standards of proper behaviour ('li shang'), in particular in the sense of reciprocal obligations. In discussing the distinction between ritual and law in a comparative context, Fei therefore argues that the Western polarity between 'rule of law' and 'rule by man' is misleading, because it suggests that absence or weakness of law directly has the latter as a consequence. Instead, ritual is a tertium datur, also imposing tight constraints upon 'rule by man', that is, arbitrary power.[22] However, these standards, though universal, only apply in a local context. Thus we can speak of the universalization of localism or particularism. This means, however, that the fundamental difference between ritual and law is not the fact of whether they are abstract principles, but the different ways of contextualization. At this point we are back with Fei's distinction between West and East. The law refers to abstract categories of groups as contexts, whereas ritual is a higher order principle for concrete interactions in groups that are established by relationships.[23]

Referring back to the previous discussion of a major aspect of traditional ritual, kinship organization, the *li shang wanglai* model actually puts kinship in a secondary position in highlighting the generative role of social interaction. Ritual would manifest all kinds of customary ideas and norms about proper social interaction, especially with regard to norms of reciprocity which result in stable patterns of relationships that are recurrently maintained and expanded via interactions. So, as we have already seen, there is no fixed notion of 'family' beyond what actually constitutes the nuclear and joint family, and the expansion of the family (indeed, in his own work Fei does not use the term 'extended family' but 'expanded family') is itself governed by customary rules of different shapes and by the underlying norms of reciprocity. Reciprocity implies that this expansion is mainly driven by functional needs, which would even include the ritual dimensions of the family in the context of religion, namely ancestor worship. In this broadest sense, ritual does indeed have an economic meaning.[24]

I posit that this phenomenon may be traced back to a different cognitive logic in perceiving and constructing social relationships. In modern cognitive sciences, this distinct logic has been coined 'field dependence' as opposed to 'field independence'. There is ample experimental evidence that modern Chinese subjects reveal a high degree of field dependence even in the most simple of cognitive operations. Field dependence means that cognitive operations pay close attention to contextual cues and emphasize contextualized relationships, both between perceptual items and between concepts.[25] Field dependence may be a feature of cognition that reflects ecological determinants of economic activity. Thus, specifically, it has been argued that traditional rice agriculture rewards cooperation and requires complex regulation of joint production activities and the willingness to participate and maintain collective goods; as a result, individuals develop a special sensitivity to contextualize their perception of social situations. This argument cannot neatly distinguish what are the prime movers of the emergence of field-dependent cognitive patterns, whether cognition drives social interaction patterns or vice versa. However, it is standard lore of generalizations in comparative cultural studies and has also recently been vindicated in experimental studies. It is important in our context because, independent from what we regard to be the prime movers, the presumed causal interdependence is a constant over very long historical periods, and thus can provide a linchpin for positing propositions about family resemblances between China's past and present.

It is important to reflect upon such arguments methodologically. In the context of the Aoki model, they refer to the interaction between signs and individual-level cognitive characteristics, which in turn determines behavioural dispositions. The individual-level characteristics are seen as being embedded in certain social environments that are in turn shaped by material conditions in the economy. This argument is synchronic in the first place, but would apply for the entire time span through which these conditions held. In closer detail, one might look at historical processes in which rice agriculture actually emerged as a major element in the traditional economy, together with accompanying population movements and the concentration of population in certain places. Interestingly, behavioural and cognitive differences between north and south China belong to the oldest stereotypes in Chinese folklore. However, if we relate these observations to modern experiments in cognitive sciences, we cannot rely on synchronic explanations, but need to refer to diachronic explanations, and path dependency in particular, because modern test persons would generally not live and work in the context of rice agriculture. In the Aoki model, it is possible to develop such hypotheses, because in the completely closed causal structure there can also be an impact of signs upon cognitive stances, with the signs being transmitted through time. Behind this transmission there are complex interconnected institutional settings, such as in education. However, this does not necessarily refer to the direct transmission of certain cognitive stances, although this certainly also happened. Consider, for example, the long intellectual traditions in China that deny the possibility of a precise and absolute distinction between subject and object, and therefore envisage the possibility of an intuitive kind of knowledge about objects which can be gained through meditation.

A potential determinant of field dependence with a much broader impact is Chinese writing. The possible causal interaction between artefacts and cognition has been elucidated in recent research on distributed cognition; thus we can refer back to a sound theoretical foundation.[26] Given the extremely long history of Chinese writing, and the relatively high levels of semi-literacy since Song times, we can therefore surmise that the Chinese script influenced cognitive styles. The essential point here is the modularity of the Chinese script. In other words, standardized simple elements combine into coherent wholes following a certain ritualized sequence of insertion, thus opening up an unlimited combinatorial space for creating new characters. This differs fundamentally from the analytical and linear-sequential approach of the Western alphabets. Modularization implies context dependency of the meaning and function of single constituent elements. Further, modularization also implies an organization of the semantic space which appears to correspond to the notion of open circles in Fei's analysis of groups. In other words, by combining elements into characters while opening up different dimensions in phonetic and semantic functions of elements, the meaning of characters is itself open and depends in turn on the context in a sentence, by which certain aspects might be activated or not.

It is straightforward to discover aspects of modularization in all expressions of Chinese aesthetics; aesthetics may be seen as a material reflection of fundamental cognitive principles. For example, Chinese landscape painting over centuries applied modularization in combining certain elements (trees, mountains, poems, etc.) into an aesthetic arrangement that as a whole carries the meaning of the artwork. One can even argue that Chinese food culture is shaped by these principles: a dish is an element of an arrangement for an entire group enjoying the meal, and it combines into that whole as well as being arranged via individual selection. However, the most important aspect of modularization, in my view, is traditional popular religion, since we can say that religious thinking and behaviour reflect more fundamental cognitive stances. I will come back to popular religion many times in this book, so suffice it to state the fundamental principle of 'polytropy'; i.e. 'religion' is not defined according to categories that encompass a clearly determined set of beliefs and categories, but as an open and fuzzy set of practices that relate to different kinds of religious needs and therefore also to different sources of knowledge. Therefore, individual religious practice is not subsumed to a certain 'confession', but is modularizing the different practices and combining them into idiosyncratic, even individualized sets. In polytropic religious behaviour, the individual switches between different modalities of religion and therefore activates many different 'categories' of religion, such as different sources from Daoism or Buddhism, which are themselves organized in terms of particular sets of beliefs. I will argue that this modularization of religion in the sense of polytropy also exerts a strong impact upon cognitive and behavioural patterns in the non-religious domain.[27]

As I have noted, we can relate the notion of field dependence to Fei Xiaotong's indigenous comparison between Western and Chinese society. Then, 'circles' represent the dynamics of social interaction under the conditions of field dependence, whereas categorial groups manifest field independence. One final observation is about the notion of the individual that stands at the centre of the networks, and, hence, the notion of the 'self'. This is important in the context of my approach, since it relates to the way in which identities are formed and expressed. In the Chinese network, the boundaries of the self are not neatly circumscribed, as the relationships are also constitutive of the self. Yet, if we look at the ideational foundations of moral conceptions of sociality in Confucian thought, this does not mean that the individual is simply merged with the social body in which it is embedded. On the contrary, the individual is seen as a moral agent, who, in the most developed stage of maturation, assumes a fully autonomous role in expressing moral judgements and pursuing corresponding actions. Beyond these philosophical dimensions, this is also evident in the practical approach to networking in Chinese society, which we will study in more detail in Chapter 5. Here, the individual is the carrier of agency in developing an expanding web of relationships. In other words, if we consider the question how far the Chinese conception of ritual also involves a universal inclusion of individuals into one overarching status order, we have to conclude that ritual is the framework of the unfolding of multipolar network relations, ultimately rooted in individual agency.[28]

In conclusion, we can oppose ritual with law, and we may say that both are simply two manifestations of the concept of general rules under the two different cognitive regimes. This differs from Fei's own interpretation: Fei argues that the ritual order is the order of a local society under conditions of immobility, in which all behavioural rules can be learned by observation and are enforced through continuous social interaction. These were the conditions in Chinese rural society, and so Fei believes that ritual is actually reflecting the predominantly rural nature of pre-modernization China. Once China transits to urban society, she would need to move to the regime of law which matches the functional requirements of a highly mobile and anonymous society. Thus, Fei ultimately upholds the standard modernization paradigm. Yet, considering the social structure of Imperial China, it is difficult to take these ideas for granted, especially in terms of the comparison with Europe. On the one hand, one cannot simply classify the conditions in relatively small European cities as 'anonymous', considering, for example, the social interactions in tightly knit merchant communities or artisan guilds in the places where modern notions of law originated. On the other hand, there were plenty of cities in Late Imperial China which were of similar size to European metropolitan cities, even the most central ones such as London or Paris. These cities were targets of inter-regional migration in all strata, from ordinary workers to rich merchants. Yet, they were also the places were the culture of ritual was further developed and enhanced. In other words, even a most simple comparison cannot support the idea that urbanization and law necessarily go hand in hand, rendering ritual obsolete. The simple reason is that urban organization itself can follow different developmental tracks.[29]

In stating this, we may also surmise that the ritual economy may be an alternative regime of organizing economic activities compared to the market economy governed by law. This statement may apply for historical periods, and may then raise the question of how far the Whiggish reconstruction of early capitalism actually matches social realities, including legal practice. But when we ask this question, we may also ponder how far the ritual economy will persist in the present context of Chinese modernity. In order to respond to this question, we need to explore in more detail the mechanisms that worked in the historical ritual economy, grounded in the general cognitive mechanisms and ideational patterns identified in this section.

Ritual, law and kinship in institutionalizing the economy

The previous section presented an abstract and ideal-typical pattern of the ideational foundations of Chinese society, apparently approaching a timeless ideal type. As such, this picture does not claim to be an empirical description but is actually a theoretical hypothesis, providing deeper foundations for other concepts that have been generated in the context of China studies, such as 'orthopraxy'. I have pursued this abstract and ahistorical reasoning here because I think this approach may unearth deeper reasons for the insights that have been gathered by the revisionist historical literature, which has accumulated an impressive amount of what may count as empirical evidence in this context. In a nutshell, this literature asserts that we cannot argue that a deficiency of institutions was the major cause of the failure to industrialize in Late Imperial China. This assessment has to be seen against the background of a long tradition of claims that deficient institutions, embedded in traditional Chinese culture, have been the main cause of perceived 'failure'.

In this literature, Max Weber is a towering figure who has presented a view on China that is deeply influenced by his view on Western 'rationalization', against which Chinese institutions appear to be 'irrational', in particular in Late Imperial China. This evaluation continues to reflect the Western disenchantment with China, after the Enlightenment writers had extolled the rational and advanced nature of government in China, deeply influenced by the reports of the Jesuits who found comrades in spirit in their interactions with Confucian bureaucrats.[30] However, once China turned out to be another 'sick man' in world history, perhaps the disappointment was especially pronounced, resulting in a stark pessimism about traditional Chinese culture. This cultural pessimism continues to shape even the most recent attempts at explaining the failure of China to evolve into 'modernity'.[31]

The problem with this kind of universal history is that it is based on certain assumptions about the entire Chinese social structure and cultural system when viewed as a whole. Many authors generalize over certain aspects and assign the role of a prime mover to them. On the contrary, much of the revisionist literature is driven by detailed case studies of local histories or single organizations and institutions. In other words, in this literature we see mechanisms at work, which need to be put into the context of a larger system of course. But this is where the methodological issues lurk, and where ultimately we can only rely on theoretical models which may fall into the trap of being entangled in our own cultural framework. We can often look at the same mechanisms in a very different light, depending on which theory illuminates our thinking. Clearly, we need to achieve generalization, because otherwise we may see only the trees and not the forest. Yet, in analysing the mechanisms, we need to avoid premature conclusions. One important difficulty is that in theorizing we easily construct parallelisms with the revolutionary changes that China underwent in the twentieth century, thus seeing disruptions and radical change on the macro level, but overlooking continuities and stability on the level of mechanisms.

For tracking these continuities, it is often most useful to look at artefacts that are used in everyday life activities. Methodologically, this was recognized by recent historical research on China in pursuing meticulous and difficult work in studying the archives of local governments, such as documents of court proceedings. One phenomenon that was only discovered in the past 30 years is the ubiquitous use of contracts in almost all social domains, which belies common perceptions of informality, networking and trust-based interactions in Chinese contexts. So, the study of contracts is an important means by which we can better understand Chinese society in the past. At the same time, once this pivotal role of contracting is recognized, we also note that contracts played an essential role in Chinese economic reforms after 1978. For example, the allocation of land-use rights in agricultural reforms was implemented via household-based contracting, or the relationship between state-owned companies, general managers and government departments was regulated via contracts in the so-called 'enterprise responsibility system'.[32] Thus, there is a class of artefacts which displays a remarkable resilience in recent Chinese history, and which had not even been recognized in earlier literature as an element in Chinese traditional society. There are kinds of contracts which stay directly in a tradition with the past, such as the contracts used in the countryside to arrange family divisions.[33] Other kinds of contracts – such as those between government agencies and economic units – are institutional innovations. Further, we need to consider considerable changes in meaning and function. Yet, the observations on contracts deserve much attention for understanding the economic style, past and present, and formulating hypotheses about family resemblances. The notion of family resemblances can cover both the continuities and the differences in the role of contracts as artefacts in organizing social relations in China.

If we start out from the previous discussion of law versus ritual, one core question is how economic transactions were actually regulated, and how property rights were defined, given the fact that there was no separate body of civil law. In a nutshell, the standard history of Western capitalism is about private property rights in different forms, including corporate organizations and financial markets. In conventional views, it is argued that the lack of clearly defined and secure property rights is one of the most important obstacles to economic growth. In this regard, our picture of Chinese conditions in the past has recently undergone major revisions. Since Song times, China had evolved a highly complex social practice of contractual relations, as pinpointed previously. Contracts were based on customary law embedded in ritual, and in cases of litigation were also enforced by the courts. Customary law and formal jurisdiction were connected by many channels, such as opting for the registration of contracts with the local magistrate, or lodging records of local practices with the magistrate's office.[34]

Hence, we cannot simply distinguish between 'formal' and 'informal institutions' here. The contract is certainly a formal document, but it does not refer to legal prescriptions, which is a major reason why contracts were as detailed as possible. Indeed, one could also argue that it was the absence of legal default rules that generated the need for explicit contracting. On the other hand, there is a chicken-and-egg problem: the early spread of contracting since Song times also lessened the need for government intervention in legal design, because contractual practices were embedded in ritual, given the fact that the majority of contracts involved relationships governed by societal institutions, in particular the family and other primordial communities. Thus, contracts were not legal documents in the first place, but arrangements of social relationships that were cast into written form. Therefore, we have to submit a major revision of Fei's original model which claims that ritual is informal and even tacit knowledge. In fact, social relations as shaped by ritual were expressed in the medium of contracts, and hence in written and public form.

An important vehicle through which this was achieved was the institution of the witness.[35] Witnesses also signed the contract and were recruited from the social context in which the parties lived. In other words, the major medium of enforcement of the contract was the social network of the contracting parties. The content of the contract was known to the witnesses, and, in case of conflicts among the parties, this knowledge could be mobilized by the efforts of mediation via persons of reputation, such as lineage elders and village leaders. But at the same time, the contract could achieve legal quality in the event that social mediation did not work. Given the sheer number of cases filed with the magistrates, this was by no means a rare event. Then, contracts were interpreted in the light of the evidence supplied by the witnesses, among others, and in the light of legal norms. Although it is true that there was no explicit civil law, many conflicts might ultimately also relate to criminal law because, for example, breach of contract can be interpreted as fraud or theft. So, ultimately, matters of ritual as functional equivalent of civil law were partly under the shadow of the penal code, hence a well-elaborated formal institution. Thus, we have to conclude that ritual and law were by no means opposites in traditional China. Yet, the law interacted strongly with ritual as the norms of proper behaviour in social contexts.[36]

We can approach these practices in terms of the notion of field dependency elucidated in the previous section, thus linking the observations with a general feature of social mechanisms.[37] In other words, I approach contracts as an artefact that mediates institutions and actions along the lines of the Aoki model, grounded in fundamental cognitive mechanisms. This may be shown in the many ways in which contracts were used and interpreted. Over the centuries, contracts evolved into certain customary patterns which were also documented via archiving at local magistrates (which allows research today). In business relations, this knowledge was largely maintained and transmitted via persons of authority, such as the so-called 'head merchants' in certain trades which were also licensed and authorized by the government. Although there were certain provisions in the Qing law code regarding obligations, for example, among family members in the context of criminal offences, and which also highlighted proper ritual obligations, these left much leeway for local variation. Therefore, if we look at the practice in litigation, contracts were initially approached as stand-alone written arrangements. A judge had to consider the actual context of the contract in assessing the mutual obligations and responsibilities of the different parties involved while following precise legal institutions of court procedure. As a first stage of adjudication, this has often been received in the literature as 'mediation'; however, this term may falsely suggest an informal arrangement relative to a formal framework, as in the Western traditions of mediation. In Chinese tradition, it is the contract itself that obtains the role of a legal reference, almost achieving a status of sanctity. This is because the underlying patterns are seen as storages of past experiences, and in terms of their support by respected authorities as matching the requirements of the local social context. Thus, we may argue that contracts were themselves a repository of customary law. This is why the Chinese practice diverged both from common law (namely without a substantial case law) and civil law (without a detailed set of legal prescriptions).[38]

Field dependence is also expressed in the contextualization of contracts relative to the social setting in which the underlying transactions take place. Here, the important point is that legal enforcement even of judicial decisions was very weak in China, given the lack of administrative means at the local level (I come back to this later). In other words, the binding force of a judgment had to result largely from the acceptance of that judgment by the different parties and the sanctioning by their peers. By implication, judges had to anticipate this and therefore consider not only legal aspects but also the social context in terms of the enforceability and the sustainability of a decision. Many decisions therefore came in the form of 'adjudicated mediation'; again, this peculiar arrangement is not covered by the term 'mediation' because a decision is formally announced, and the contract is interpreted strictly. Yet, enforcement itself may lead towards further complexities of arranging the conflicting interests in a new stable pattern of social interaction, such as in the context of disputes over land and irrigation systems.[39]

Contracts largely regulated relationships of ownership and property, such as in the partitioning of land in family division. There was a well-developed land market with complex ownership arrangements. Given the strong binding role of contracts here, we cannot speak of weak property rights only because there is no tight backing by formal civil law. In litigation, contractual arrangements were meticulously discussed and interpreted, which reflects the fact that in the ordinary course of actions, contracts were sufficient to fix property relations. This is also evident from the universal practice to even arrange family matters in contractual terms. Essential events in the family life cycle such as marriage and family division were always put into contractual terms. Therefore, the Chinese case calls the Weberian idea into doubt that legally binding arrangements presuppose the existence of a separate body of formal law. On the contrary, we recognize an important lacuna in Weber's framework, namely that 'rationality' of law is only defined in formal terms, but not in material and substantive terms. The Chinese model of universal contracting means that in the process of adjudication material rationality counts most, and that formal rationality refers to procedural rationality in the sense of the methods that are applied to discover the truth.[40]

If one directly concludes therefore that property rights were only customary rights, this would partly distort reality. In addition, in the case of the most essential asset, namely land, property rights were directly backed by the government via the payment of taxes. According to legal practice, presenting formal documents on tax payment was considered to be the strongest proof of ownership. Thus, in spite of the fact that the Kangxi Emperor had frozen the land registers in the early eighteenth century, this did not imply that property rights were not formally established and recorded. Again, we meet a case of field dependence because it was left to the individuals whether they wanted to incur the costs of receiving full formal backing of their rights. But if they did, in most circumstances the property rights were reliable and, above all, enforceable. In other words, we may argue that taxes were treated as a fee for obtaining the government service of enforcing the pertinent property rights. In fact, property rights and obligations to pay taxes were intimately connected. This belief was rooted in the physiocratic economic theories of the Confucians which conceived agriculture as the only productive source in the economy, and of course in the fundamental notion that ultimately all land belongs to the Emperor, in the sense of encompassing the sacred territory of Chinese civilization.[41]

It is interesting to note that in case of landownership with complex multi-layered tenancy arrangements, the top-level owner of a larger estate also paid the taxes, thus making his property rights enforceable by the government. Lower-level tenancy rights were regulated by contracts and customary law, which often respected the role of labour in establishing rights of possession for tenants. Thus, conflicts between landlords and tenants could be regulated by mediation, but if the landlords claimed their rights in court, these largely prevailed. This intermingling of social context, ritual obligation and formal institutions was enabled by complex conceptualizations of property rights, such as distinguishing between rights on the surface (the 'skin') and ultimate ownership rights (on the 'bones') as well as distinguishing between 'dead' and 'alive' rights. So, even when only considering these two dimensions, actual ownership rights could assume complex forms. In particular, sales of land rights might keep rights of the original owners 'alive', which means that they have rights to redeem or repurchase the land. This was particularly important in balancing the needs of individuals in certain economic circumstances and their role as stewards of what is sacred property of the family.[42]

In addition, many property rights on land were regulated in the context of kinship groups, which included the emergence of more complex organizations via the lineage estates and trusts. In these cases, property rights were shareholder rights that were embedded in ritual obligations, thus in fact even obtaining religious legitimacy. Since lineage rules were also strongly supported and partly shaped by the legal code, this confirms the view that property rights were ultimately backed by the state. The government only resorted to expropriative measures in special contexts, such as irrigation systems and water engineering. Land property rights explicitly assigned to kinship groups, however, had close to sacred status, and were thus protected by the state. As we saw above, this was partly an exchange of legal protection for taxation. Therefore, we need to recognize that kinship institutions were part and parcel of the formal institutional framework of property rights, which is further evidence that the juxtaposition of ritual and law is erroneous. Yet, lineages were certainly ritual units in the first place. But the formal protection of lineage property rights supported the growth of formal organization in business, often in the shape of lineage trusts, 'tang' (堂).[43]

This being said, we cannot conclude that property rights had the same nature as property rights in Europe, if only because their ideological status was certainly different, as China was lacking the corresponding traditions in political philosophy. But this does not imply that there were no first principles in customary law. In the local practices, the different economic functions of property rights were clearly recognized and regulated by ritual obligations. These were most evident in the context of the extended family: probably the most fundamental difference between Chinese and Western concepts of property was that in China the family was seen as representing the owner but not the individual. This does not imply collective possession and control, as the family is also represented by its leading authority, the head of the family. Yet, we can only speak of a sort of individual stewardship here. This also implies that other family members cannot independently enter economic transactions without the consent of the family head.[44] There were also general principles, such as effectively giving almost inalienable rights of possession to the tenants who work on the land, and separating these from the financial rights to the land rent, which could be divided and allocated in complex ownership arrangements. Thus, in practice, certain moral rules on the role of labour in maintaining the economic usability of land and safeguarding the livelihood of people were putting limits on absolute ownership rights.

To summarize, if we want to extract the political philosophy of property in traditional China, we might highlight three aspects. First, the subject of property is the family, which includes complex nested ownership formalized in shares; second, property is expressed in labour exerted on it, thus establishing actual possession; and third, formal expression of ownership is linked to the payment of taxes.

Especially in the most advanced regions of China, such as the Jiangnan region, this difference between relative and absolute property rights was most obvious. The contractual instruments enabled complex nested structures of sub-tenancy and alternating positions of landlord vs. tenant, in which individual rights were relative in nature. Relative property rights constrained individual decisions over the use of property in terms of ritualistic obligations towards kin and the local community, such as limiting the fungibility of land in land markets. However, when in Qing times the economy underwent a deep commercialization process, these limitations eroded slowly. The institutional model of land property rights was also applied in arranging shareholding structures related to other assets, such as salt yards. Here, the ritual limitations were virtually absent, often also involving non-kin as shareholders. However, the shareholding model was ubiquitous, thus manifesting many different ways of how to arrange social relations in economic transactions.[45]

Thus, kinship organizations as a ritual frame of property rights allowed for the emergence of corporate structures also beyond the management of landownership. Basically, lineage trusts provided a model for open shareholder engagement in investing in business operations also beyond agriculture, without implicating the same ritual cross-generational obligations. Thus they also allowed for non-hierarchical forms of cooperation, in the sense of shareholding structures with equality among the members. In this context, it is very important to properly evaluate the role of formal lineage organization. We can distinguish between the horizontal and the vertical meaning of kinship, and how kin relationships are actually identified. In this context, the distinction between 'lineage' as *jiazu* and 'clan' as *zongzu* is often used in a confusing manner. There are various possibilities as to how the different notions can combine. One matches Fei Xiaotong's model of 'circles' and hence his notion of *jiazu*. This is mainly horizontal in the sense that interacting relatives are in focus, and in terms of ritual the relationship with a common ancestor is based on real genetic closeness. Yet, this does not imply a strong formal lineage organization. This would emerge when reference to a common ancestor is dominating real circles of interaction, which leads to the paradoxical result that strong formalization can also imply low degrees of genetic closeness, as in many large-scale southern Chinese clans. For this reason, it is the formal pattern of clan organization that could also evolve into corporate structures in business. As a result, there were two organizational modes in traditional kinship, the generational mode and the associational mode, which were activated or dominant under certain contextual conditions (such as different levels of agricultural productivity and hence surplus) and in different functional environments (such as lineage trusts managing land vs. other ritual associations funding festivals).[46]

So, if we take the two aspects of contracts and kinship organization together, we can understand why ritual could serve as a framework for economic organization. This is because the religious nature of kinship allowed for the abstraction and hence the transfer of associational structures into other domains. So, one track is the direct extension of the family into those other domains, which is enabled by the flexible boundaries of the kinship network, hence the *jiazu.* The other track is the extension of the shareholding model of the *zongzu* and the lineage trusts. Both tracks allowed for the inclusion of non-kin into economic organization, the first via quasi-kinship, the second via abstracting from kinship in the shareholder institution. There are many intermediate forms which build on and at the same time transcend kinship.[47]

If one asks where the crucial difference between these Chinese forms of corporate organization and Western forms might be located, then this is probably the role of limited liability. But this does not straightforwardly apply for the transition to industrialization. The Chinese corporate structures did not evolve the feature of limited liability, although in principle they could be 'perpetual' entities, given the cross-generational sustainability of the extended family. This implies, however, that individual family members could possibly create legal obligations for other family members in non-related business. Yet, if we look at the diffusion of legal forms, we need to take notice of the fact that even when the appropriate legal forms were developed and promoted, they were not received in practice (see Chapter 6). At the same time, the evolution of contractual forms also manifested solutions to the problems with liability in more complex ownership arrangements.[48]

So far I have equated ritual with kinship organization. This perspective would mislead the inquiry if I stopped there. As we have seen, kinship organization manifests fuzzy borderlines with corporate structures in which kin principles were weaker, even though the formal framework was maintained. Beyond this phenomenon, we have to take note that the associational forms of lineage also represented organizational principles that could be exploited in non-kin settings. One example of this are functional lineage organizations that build exclusively on the shareholding logic, such as when lineages set up separate bodies for organizing certain religious activities. This transition is most easy to recognize when considering the case of single lineage villages, where by definition any kind of functional organization also involved the lineage members. For example, a village specializing in certain economic activities might establish a local market which requires investment in market infrastructure. This investment would be channelled through a separate organization in which lineage members are shareholders.[49]

The fundamental pattern of these organizations may be designated as the 'hui' (会), which therefore classifies as another principle of Chinese ritual organization apart from kinship. A *hui* features certain general characteristics, in particular the shareholding principle involving equal status of members, if only modified by the extent of the contribution, rotating leadership, decision by consensus and hierarchical organization of committees in larger organizations with extended spatial scope. Thus, these organizations differ from formal lineage organizations in excluding genealogical hierarchy from determining the allocation of power. All of these organizations have a strong ritual component, with transitional forms extending from kinship. One simple example are surname associations which could have large territorial scope because they fulfil the function of networking among members, while referring to the surname as a quasi-kinship term. Ritual functions are obvious in the case of temple associations which often mobilize substantial amounts of money and require continuous management of ritual activities.[50]

Associational structures were particularly salient in the context of organizing long-distance trade and investment, and they activated cultural resources beyond kinship, such as shared native place. Associations of itinerant merchants increasingly not only provided a range of services for their members (such as lodging or managing transfers of funds), but also played an important role in the production of local public goods at their places of residence (such as fire protection or welfare provision). Further, they operated as representing local society towards government. As I will discuss in the final section of this chapter, this role created a specific pattern of governmentality, considering the simple fact that in Late Imperial China the number of cities by far outgrew the number of administrative centres. An economically vibrant place was built on a thick associational infrastructure of institutions, often recruited from the complex relationships between different groups of migrants, travellers and locals, and combining different principles of association that activated ritual resources. For example, a native place association of travelling merchants could also internally reflect the power structures of lineage organization in the native place, thus transferring ritual organization to geographically separate places. Chinese religious ritual enabled the voluntary cooperation of all these different groups in temple associations which express the territorial identity of the place of sojourning, such as the City God. Thus, Chinese cities allowed for the ritual expression of diverse identities in the same symbolic system, thereby contributing to the unity of ritual all over China, in spite of the particularistic nature of the fundamental kinship principles.[51]

If we summarize the discussion in this section from a theoretical perspective, we can say that Chinese ritual obtained a multitude of functions in organizing the economy, thus establishing a close relationship between function and meaning. Ritual proved to be adaptive in response to solving problems of economic coordination, in particular with regard to property rights and in enabling more complex structures of economic cooperation. This was undergirded by the institution of the contract, which to a large extent was not a ritual institution per se, but which activated ritual context via establishing a formalized relationship between the parties, the witnesses and the middlemen. Thus, we cannot say that the difference between ritual and law lies in the degree of formalization; that is, the distinction between 'informal' and 'formal' institutions. Instead, we observe a deeper impact of the two polar cognitive modes, with the Chinese case revealing a high degree of field dependence. This is reflected in a different conceptualization of law in terms of substantive rationality, thus revealing a white spot in the Weberian tradition of interpreting Chinese institutions. Thus, I claim that the institution of the contract, embedded in larger patterns of kinship organizations and associational structures, stays at the centre of a wider range of mechanisms which we can arrange in a constitutive picture of the Chinese ritual economy as economic style.

The family in the Smithian economy of Late Imperial China

Having considered extensively certain selected mechanisms of social organization in traditional China, I will now move back to the macro-level as a point of entry, partly anticipating the discussion in the following sections, in a brief and succinct characterization of China's traditional ritual economy. This is necessary to keep the overall picture of the ritual economy in mind, while discussing details of mechanisms.

If we reflect upon the previous considerations about ritual and law, we reach the conclusion that these and other complementary practices allowed both for the emergence of complex and even nationally integrated markets and the aggregation and organization of capital under control of single corporate units. In the Aoki model, these are states of the ritual economy which may be ascertained as 'social facts' (such as the national convergence of rice prices on regional markets). I will discuss markets in the following section, so suffice it to notice here that the institutional structures I have described so far did not amount to a 'rule of law' in the Western sense, yet appeared to enable a complex division of labour and a high level of economic performance. This macro-level observation can only be properly evaluated in the context of considering a fundamental type of social mechanism in the traditional Chinese economy, the hierarchy of local and regional market systems, which provided the channels through which, on the one hand, flows of funds from urban centres supported local production in family units embedded in a local and regional division of labour; on the other hand, the products of family production were distributed to final consumers, especially in the urban areas. In other words, traditional China combined the feature of commercial capitalism, including even incipient features of financial capitalism, with maintaining the family as the basic unit of production. The two basic types of institutions that enabled this were the contract and the association, with the latter including the basic structures of kinship organization beyond the family. The major distinction between this system and the Western one emerging after industrialization appears to be the absence of corporate structures with limited liability and the absence of certain fully fledged institutions of financial markets and the monetary economy, such as more advanced techniques to track financial assets and to compare financial returns across different kinds of assets, and more sophisticated financial instruments. In particular, China never developed the instrument of government debt which stood at the core of the growth of the financial sector in Western Europe, and mainly relied on external inflows of species via the international trade balance to provide the necessary monetary means for sustaining a growing economy in the Late Empire.[52]

This pattern has been labelled a 'Smithian economy' in the sense of enabling a complex, society-wide division of labour, epitomized in the large variety of professions and specialized markets for a wide range of products. In other words, there is no reason to assume that institutional deficiencies were the major cause for the absence of industrial capitalism in Late Imperial China. In positive terms, we can say that China evolved a 'ritual economy'; that is, a pattern of organization of economic activities based on ritual, and more specifically customary law, and not mainly on formal law and institutions directly promulgated and enforced by the Imperial government. In this ritual economy, the symbolic resources of traditional kinship and community organization were activated for the organization of economic activities that went beyond the confines of kinship.

This position receives strong support by comparative studies of industrialization. In this regard, we have to recognize that any theory of industrialization cannot simply compare large units such as 'China' and 'Western Europe', because we have to distinguish neatly between the conditions of the emergence of industrial capitalism and its diffusion once it had been established. Industrial capitalism (as distinguished from 'financial' or 'commercial') in the sense of a peculiar combination of capitalist institutions and technological innovation emerged in England. The single most important distinctive feature of England as compared to other European countries and China was the sharply diverging costs of energy, namely coal, in the early centres of industrialization, and the specific match of the new general purpose technology, the steam engine, with the specific needs of mining and transport under the local conditions. Once that model had emerged in England it could be imitated in other places, with the result that improvements in technology gradually changed the cost structure that was a constraint on industrialization in other places, ultimately enabling the diffusion of industrial capitalism in Europe. Against the background of this analysis, we may conclude that the absence of industrial capitalism in China was reflecting a rational and efficient adaptation to the prevailing conditions of production, hence relative factor prices.[53]

In other words, we could even argue that the high level of market development provided for an effective processing of information about relative factor prices and hence the efficient adaptation of production. Then, what further counts for explaining alternative institutional trajectories is the level of induced transaction costs. In China, the ritual economy contributed to a low level of transactions costs of markets, such that alternative arrangements of economic activity, especially the subordination of production activities to hierarchical organizational structures, were not competitive vis-à-vis the market. Thus, for the traditional economic style, the interaction between family and market was the essential pattern, embedded in ritual.

In previous discussions I have elaborated on some aspects of Chinese kinship organization. If we now turn to the 'family' proper, which represents the most basic and abstract notion, my use directly refers to the Chinese term 'jia' (家). In one sense, this is the most overarching and hence abstract term; in the other sense, it refers to the fact that the extended family represented an ideal norm and reference in social life, but the vast majority of Chinese families were conjugal or joint families of small size, with family division always leading to the separation of the families of brothers. Thus, the extended family as a ritual norm is a means to extend the scope of economic cooperation along kinship lines; but if we consider the basic structures of production, the family as based on the conjugal unit is the essential building block. In other words, in terms of theorizing about the ritual economy, we can distinguish between the family as a unit of production on the one hand, and on the other hand extended kinship or associational structures as units of market organization, activating the specific institution of the contract. This dualism of production and market, reflected in the dualism of family and wider associational mechanisms, is fundamental to understanding the ritual economy of China.

Considering the ritual nature of the family, it is essential to emphasize its religious role. In Chinese popular religion, the family is the most basic unit of worship. This includes worshipping the ancestors, but also any other religious activities both within and outside the residential unit.

In the context of formal ritual, the male household head was the only representative of the family, but with regard to domestic religious activities and many other public activities such as burning incense in temples, women played a major role. The elementary family was also a unit in the territorial hierarchy of the officially legitimized pantheon of Chinese gods, with the 'Kitchen God' actually monitoring the behaviour of its members and reporting back to the Jade Emperor. The family was seen as a link in the chain of generational succession, and preserving the family and continuing the family line was a religious duty that was deeply enmeshed in everyday life, independent from the formal rituals of extended kinship.[54]

Many observers have therefore stated a fundamental difference between Western 'individualism' and 'family individualism' or 'familism' in China. In other words, and as we have seen in the context of property rights, the fundamental unit of decision-making and the carrier of rights is not the individual but the family. This interpretation may be questioned from the viewpoint of gender studies, since the family is represented by the household head. The gender perspective is ambivalent, however. On the one hand, women were clearly subordinate to the authority of the patriarch, with immediate economic consequences. In Late Imperial China, the widespread practice of foot binding actually confined many women to work in the household, which however opened up the possibility to engage in homework, such as silk weaving, a major industry in the twentieth century. Thus, the asymmetric power relationship was a determinant of the emergence of peculiar patterns of sideline production in Chinese villages, bolstered by the expansion of the market system. This partly explains one element of the economic models of the Chinese family that I scrutinize below, namely the low marginal costs and hence wages in these sectors that made them competitive against Western competitors until the advent of full-scale industrial systems. This gives a special and very concrete meaning to the idea of the ritual economy, as the ritual gender division of power and labour is a structural factor in the economy. This would imply, however, that 'family individualism' is actually male hegemonic individualism.

On the other hand, we know that even the strongly ritualized power asymmetry between the genders was contextualized. This refers to the widespread use of 'atypical' patterns of marriage, including uxorilocal forms or the delay or even refusal of marriage in the case of economically productive groups of women, as in south Chinese sericulture. In our context, however, what matters most is the structural tensions in the standard model of the Chinese family which has always been a major driver of early family division and a destabilizing force in cooperation in the larger agnatic group, especially between brothers. Psychologically, this structural tension was grounded in the relationship between wife and mother-in-law, and could find full expression when the wife had produced the male progenitor, thus fulfilling the central religious function of reproducing the family line. Therefore, Chinese joint families mostly divided long before the passing of the parents, thus resulting in the practice of contract-based family division. Therefore, we may argue that the conjugal relation indeed stands at the centre of Chinese familism and cannot be simply reduced to patriarchy, thus simply substituting 'familism' with 'patriarchal individualism'. Chinese ritual generated 'family individualism' as an expression of the ritual dynamics in generational change. This perspective can explain the pervasive use of contracts in managing relationships between extended kin and the economic functionalism of expanding the *jia* into larger *jiazu* structures. In other words, economic functionality determines the actual interpretation of the 'family', and there is no preconceived boundary of the group, even the most elemental domestic one. The family as a 'circle' is a unit that integrates economic and social relationships. One manifestation of this is the distinction between the ritual head of the family, the 'jiazhang' (家长), and the 'family manager', the 'dangjia' (当家). Thus, the economic functionality of the larger kinship groups is a manifestation of the fundamental familism of the conjugal unit.[55]

In economic theories about the traditional Chinese economy, the family in the current sense plays an essential role. The argument on energy has to be seen in the light of relative prices of labour and energy, with labour largely provided in the context of families as production units. In this respect, the notion of the ritual economy adds an important twist to the analysis of the Smithian economy of China. There have been different theoretical approaches to the family as a production unit, so I just generalize to highlight one essential point. Chinese ritual provides a very strong normative foundation for maintaining the family as a social unit and of subordinating possibly divergent individual interests to the collective good of the family as a hierarchical structure. In theoretical terms, the 'family' is approached as an elementary unit that consists of parents and children, possibly including grandparents. This is justified against the previously highlighted background that in Chinese practice, although the extended family was considered to be an ideal pattern, family division was a universal phenomenon, establishing the elementary family as the basic unit of society and economy.

Now, the theoretical point is that the family is a unit that manifests economies of scale of consumption and therefore mitigates individual risks in participating in market activities. This implies that individuals can offer labour at a wage that does not need to cover marginal costs under the assumption of individual supply of labour.[56] Hence, families can outcompete individual suppliers in the market system as well as any more complex economic organization that relies on individuals for supply of labour. This reasoning may explain why a most remarkable trend in the evolution of the Chinese ritual economy was the evanescence of large-scale organizations, such as the manor, and at the same time the absence of factories.

Even when economic activity was concentrated in single locations, the basic unit of production remained the family.[57]

Given the normative concepts of the family in Chinese ritual, this also created a strong demand for labour and hence created an incentive for raising the rate of reproduction. In this sense, the Chinese Smithian economy was also a Malthusian one. This observation is of great significance also for analysing contemporary China, as we also have to recognize the role of demography and population issues in understanding the present. The Chinese ritual economy created a demographic pattern, with early marriages, early childbirth and potentially high rates of reproduction that directly engendered the strong expansion of the population in the long, peaceful periods of Qing rule. The corresponding growth of the labour supply further exacerbated the trade-off between prices of energy and wages, and is the single most important factor for explaining the stagnation of per-capita GDP relative to Europe since the Middle Ages. These diverging demographic patterns have also been exacerbated by unique historical conditions in Europe, in particular the plague and the continuous military conflicts that enhanced the local scarcity of labour by the high numbers of casualties and destruction. In comparison, the Chinese constellation has been coined a 'high-level equilibrium trap', with the notion of 'trap' simply reflecting the ex-post judgment that China lost out in comparison with the West.[58]

This mechanics of demography and economic growth was embedded in an ideological system that expressed a very strong moral obligation of sons towards their family to procreate the largest possible number of sons who would continue the family line. The marriage practices in Europe significantly diverged from China in this respect, for example, in supporting delayed marriage and reproduction, and also maintaining a relatively high level of bachelorhood and spinsterhood, especially in rural society. The religious dimension of this development should not be overlooked in comparison with China, since, after all, celibacy was a central value in Christianity but was often regarded to be problematic in China, in the context of Buddhism as a 'foreign' religion, and in conjunction with Daoist beliefs about sexuality and procreation. In addition, Europe also featured the slow expansion of primogeniture, starting out from England. Equal division of land among brothers was the major mechanism in China that directly connected population growth, family and agricultural production.[59] The essential importance of the family line was highlighted in traditional popular religion, which included a central role of ancestor worship. Even though ancestor worship is one of the oldest elements in Chinese religion, the central place in local practices was not simply the result of societal forces but was strongly supported by the Imperial State, especially after the rise of Neoconfucianism and the final establishment of Imperial Confucianism. Even though the extended family could also emerge as a local power structure that obstructed the enforcement of Imperial rule, ultimately the balance always worked in the direction of official support of family ideology and especially lineage cults. The integration of ancestor worship into state ideology resulted in a specific form of 'universalizing particularism'; in other words, in putting filial piety at the centre of ritual, the government created a universalistic foundation for the resilience of the traditional family.[60]

Thus, we can say that ideological and economic forces played together in sustaining the Smithian economy without achieving a technological breakthrough. Considering the interaction between religion, family structure and demography we could even restate the Weberian hypothesis that religion is an essential element in understanding Chinese economic growth in history. This differs from the original view, however, since to a considerable degree the Chinese conditions appear to be similar to the original thesis on Protestantism in emphasizing the deep penetration between everyday life, in particular economic behaviour and popular religion, and also highlighting the 'rational' nature of this pattern. So, I wish to conclude this section with a few general remarks about religion and economic development; I cannot go into detail, but wish to mention that these brief impressions dovetail with the general analysis of cognition in the second section of this chapter. We have already noticed that the specific mechanism of economic growth, given the prevailing relative factor prices, may not have produced demand for technological change. We might add that religion may also have supported a particular stance towards the use of technology in society and, especially, the systematic development of science as related to technological practice. This role of religion transcends the notion of ritual as related to social order, but also connects to certain cosmological foundations of ritual.

In Confucian thinking ritual not only related to human matters, but also contributed to maintaining the natural order. This connectivity between the social and the natural was also reflected in geomantic beliefs, according to which, for example, the spatial structure of a village and the location of its temples and other religious sites such as graves actually made up a symbolic representation of the underlying cosmic forces, thus turning territory as such into a religious space. Vice versa, disorder in human social relations, especially as reflected in uprooting material structures such as settlements, could also contribute to creating cosmic imbalances. In this sense, nature itself assumed a moral, hence ritual meaning.[61]

The question why China did not industrialize is closely connected to the so-called 'Needham puzzle' in recognizing the failure of modern science to develop in China based on what was a highly developed body of knowledge of natural processes in earlier times. One general factor was certainly that the traditional worldview did not develop the general idea of 'progress' as a basic condition of society, but highlighted the ideal conditions in historical times, against which Confucian thinkers saw the present as a morally deficient state. More specifically, traditional Chinese philosophy and religion did not develop the idea of a dualism between matter and mind, and thinking of the material world as having a 'design' that was created by an external agency, the Creator God, and which can be decoded by scientific research. In contrast, the Chinese view saw man and world as a unity in the flow of cosmic forces, and thus approached nature also as a moral phenomenon. This also implies that moral knowledge and religious practice directly allows access to the essence of the world. The aim of human practice is not to improve the human condition, but to contribute to these cosmic balances. In this ideological theatre, the separation between subject and object in scientific research cannot hold, and in more pragmatic terms, science cannot be perceived as giving guidance to technology. Thus, the pinnacles of Chinese artisanship at the Imperial Court were devoted to creating magnificent toys to represent this idea of balance.[62]

Against this background, we realize that one of the most far-reaching cultural changes in the transition to the twentieth century was the adoption and widespread diffusion of a modernist worldview that centred on the idea of progress, often even in the utopian sense introduced by Marxism. As we shall see in the final section of this chapter, this was combined with the idea that government has to transform society which would otherwise be locked up in its involutionary dynamics. Accordingly, transforming the family was a core element in this modernist approach, culminating in the imposition of the one-child policy after 1978.

Pulling together the strands of reasoning so far, the central claim is that the absence of industrialization in China may be explained by certain mechanisms that produce economic actions which did not trigger technological innovations in local contexts. For this, the family as a ritual phenomenon is essential, together with systemic determinants such as relative factor scarcities. These mechanisms have to be neatly distinguished from the market mechanisms by which those systemic determinants were actually transformed into relative factor prices. Therefore, I now turn to the role of markets in Imperial China.

Markets as forms and expressions of ritual

In this section we will explore the role of markets in the traditional ritual economy. The fact is essential that the previous analytical view on the relationship between the family and economic structure presupposes the existence of a fully fledged market system, because only the possibility of expanding the division of labour creates the conditions for sustaining the corresponding expansion of the population, given the traditional structures of the family. Technically speaking, the involutionary pattern of traditional China reflects the expansion of markets with the absence of economies of scale in applying technology and creating corresponding large-scale organizations. This raises the question in what sense the market proper is also constitutive for the entire institutional set-up. In economic analysis, the view often prevails to approach markets as technologies of allocation and to treat institutions as exogenous mechanisms of regulating market activities. This idea extends to the observation that exchange is a universal human activity such that markets are just larger scale systems of exchange, and market institutions simply transform these systems. The alternative view is that markets themselves are institutional arrangements which create new forms of social interaction that transcend exchange, and also build on peculiar ideational and cognitive resources, such as certain moral commitments. Thus, markets cannot be separated from social context.

There are different expressions of these ideas in the literature, and I cannot survey them here. Suffice it to notice that the first view is largely maintained by economists who pursue a generic model of economic behaviour, in particular the rational choice paradigm: Then, the transition from the traditional economy to the market economy is possible without major frictions, mostly determined by certain capacities such as human and social capital. For the second view there are many different approaches, such as the Marxist analysis that has always exerted a strong influence on Chinese studies, though in a more diluted conceptual framework that sees 'capitalism' as a distinct social formation as compared to traditional society, or in terms of Polanyi's 'Great Transformation' which emphasizes the different patterns of social embeddedness of economic activity. In contrast to these macro-level approaches, the concept of economic style follows recent developments in anthropology and sociology that see markets and even 'the economy' as complex constructs that co-exist with other forms of social interaction such that in so-called traditional societies markets are also recognized as social structures in social ontology. In other words, markets are being constructed by means of different elements, such as theories about markets, market institutions and certain material artefacts that enable market exchange. As a consequence, one cannot simply contrast traditional forms of exchange and markets, because they can interrelate in many forms. So, research has to focus on particular mechanisms and artefacts that mediate different forms of social interaction and valuation.[63]

In this section, I outline the unique role of markets in the Chinese ritual economy. In other words, I do not separate markets as a distinct social domain related to the modern economy, or argue about whether the traditional system was 'capitalist' or not. Indeed, the market-based perspective renders concepts such as 'capitalism' almost meaningless, unless they are substantiated in terms of specific mechanisms that do or do not exist (such as particular forms of financial markets). What counts is the existence of markets as social artefacts over very long time horizons, with the early beginnings in the so-called axis time, which in China went along with the secular decline of feudal forms of social organization.[64] Markets in the sense of marketplaces grew significantly during the Song 'medieval economic revolution' and triggered the emergence of a fundamental dualism in Chinese settlement patterns, with a hierarchy of economic areas on the one hand and the system of administrative centres on the other, which of course were identical in the latter case, but not co-extensive.[65] This implies that in contrast to the conditions during Tang times, most marketplaces were no longer subject to the physical constraints of administrative centres (such as being approved and controlled by the government within the city walls), but were the ground on which a large and complex system of cities and townships developed which were only indirectly subject to administrative supervision and control. Therefore, markets also played an integral part in the governmentality of traditional China, as I explore in the following section. This observation is essential to avoid a conceptual fallacy that is inherent in the Western tradition of economics and political thought, namely juxtaposing government and market. The notion that overcomes this dualism is ritual. In the Chinese ritual economy, markets are elements of ritual, and ritual is also constitutive of markets.

When studying social relations, anthropologists often use the term 'commoditization' in describing the fact that in traditional China markets penetrated society deeply. This can be directly recognized in the content of contracts which were meticulously detailed in listing the mutual obligations of the parties. Hence, commoditization is reflected in quantification, even if no market transaction is involved. So, for example, marriage customs tended towards brideprice arrangements, and there was a diffuse borderline to market-mediated exchange of girls and women, for example, when families sold daughters to brothels. There were precise ideas about the costs of educating children and about the corresponding value of the support children should give parents during their old age.[66]

However, the term 'commoditization' is linked to certain theoretical commitments that would possibly bias comparisons between China and other cases. In my approach to economic style, it is more fruitful to relate these phenomena to a more specific feature of Chinese social interaction. This is the role of money in exchange. Whereas the term 'commodity' is generic, in the Chinese context money is an artefact with a clear functional and symbolic role in ritual behaviour. Therefore, I argue that the relationship between markets and ritual is partly mediated via the ritual functions of money. This is most evident in the religious role of money and wealth. Tellingly, in the orthopractical transformations of the Gods of Wealth, a secular transition took place that gradually elicited all demonic and morally suspect features of money and only highlighted the role of wealth in securing the livelihood of the family line.[67] Wealth is an essential factor in maintaining the family line via the division of assets among brothers, and assumes transcendental status in also being shared with the ancestors during the ancestral cults. Up until today, money has played a central role in many expressions of Chinese popular beliefs, embodied in the widespread though in Mainland China often hidden use of myriad varieties of 'ghost money'. According to these beliefs, money is an indispensable medium in establishing reciprocity between the living and the ancestors and other members of the afterworld. Of course, the money that is burned as a donation is fake money, but this fact highlights the role of labour in producing paper money that is used in establishing reciprocity with the afterworld. The paper money ultimately represents the effort that individuals invest in producing and folding the large quantity of essentially worthless 'banknotes from hell'. Paradoxically, in modern times 'hell money' itself became commoditized in being printed and sold on the marketplace.[68]

This observation represents the central value of effort in Chinese ritual, hence a cultural value of 'ritual labour', representing the core economic role of labour in the pattern of growth and economic activity of traditional China (as opposed, for example, to the role of land or capital), thus matching the fundamental economic structures of familism. The ritual status of labour is an essential means of overcoming incentive and monitoring problems in labour-intensive family production. In the narrower domain of the paper money custom, the original practices involve the onerous folding of large amounts of paper into the bills, so that what is in fact delivered to the afterworld is the labour that has been invested in the production of what is essentially worthless pieces of paper. On a more fundamental level, this effort expresses the seriousness of ritual actions. Thus, the custom fits into a general semantic field of traditional Chinese notions that focus on the 'sincerity' of ritual behaviour, as opposed to the underlying beliefs.[69]

If we further delve into the cultural complexity of money in China, this relationship between fundamental notions of reciprocity and the religious role of money shows how markets are ultimately embedded in general systems of exchange that are undergirded by moral norms of reciprocity. I will analyse this further in Chapter 5, when we discuss the relationship between markets and networks. At this point, suffice it to say that up until now, essential events in ritual are always accompanied by sending gifts, namely the 'red envelopes' that contain a certain amount of money. These gifts are documented in detailed accounts in every household, thus establishing a collective system of measuring the quality and intensity of social relations. Given the long periods that might pass between important events in different households (such as marriage or children), these flows of gifts establish long-term reciprocity.[70]

In this case, we can also clarify the distinction between the role of money in ritual and commoditization. One conspicuous feature of social reciprocity is the exchange of labour, such as when building a house. Traditionally, this would be mostly realized within kinship groups. The alternative is to hire wage labour. Yet, in this case, reciprocity in labour exchange is not measured in monetary categories. The decline of those systems of labour exchange in Chinese villages is one of the most important aspects of the commoditization of labour in these contexts, which is of course accompanied by assessing the value of labour in monetary terms.[71] So, we see that commoditization and monetization of aspects of ritual are different phenomena. In the ritual economy money plays an ambivalent role, being the medium of markets on the one hand, and an expression of values in the religious domain on the other. I posit that the religious valuation of money was an important determinant of the orientation of economic activities in the market context.

Turning to the relationship between markets and ritual, we need to consider one of the most influential paradigms in China studies: Skinner's analysis of regional systems in China. In the current context, the many receptions of this idea tend to concentrate on the regional economics and geographical part of the argument, whereas Skinner's original contribution also emphasized a more fundamental point, namely the fact that the market deeply penetrated all domains of social life.[72] Therefore, I argue that the market was part and parcel of the ritual order of traditional Chinese society. This is straightforward to recognize in treating markets as mechanisms that are embodied and scaffolded in material structures. In Skinner's models, these are mainly the geographic structures of the regional marketing systems, but we also have to consider the artefacts of the corresponding settlement systems, which include not only marketplaces in the narrow sense, but also, for example, temples as sites of festivals and fairs. In studying markets as mechanisms, we need further to consider their embeddedness in social and cultural structures, such as lineages. Finally, the mechanisms of markets also impact upon these contextual elements, such as in the penetration of other social domains by the artefact of money. It is these patterns that make up the position of markets in the ritual economy.[73]

In order to elucidate this argument, we need briefly to outline the principles of social organization of the basic units of traditional society, the villages. The ritual aspect looms especially large when we consider the religious foundations of the pertinent social practices, and how they became embodied in material structures. On the local level, four fundamental patterns of social interaction shaped everyday life: 'xueyuan' (血缘) as kinship, 'diyuan' (地缘) as local community, markets and government. The fourth element of government as 'governance' is the topic of the following section. In understanding Chinese ritual, *xueyuan* and *diyuan* are conventionally emphasized, whereas the market is not seen as being constitutive. Skinner's contribution was to shed light on the role of the market in the Chinese social formation.

Up until today, one of the most damaging misperceptions of traditional Chinese society has been the claim that family and kinship is the dominant principle, thus creating the image of a polarity with the Imperial state being the other pole, with virtually no intermediary structures. This perception is certainly bolstered by certain aspects of the traditional ideology that conceived of government along the lines of family, and which actively promoted the family as the ideal type of all social relations. However, even on the most basic level, the village, the two principles of kinship and locality worked together in creating social structure, also epitomized in traditional religion and its material manifestations. Indeed, if we look at traditional religion, we may conclude that the salient role of ancestor worship was partly reflecting the impact of Neoconfucian civilizational efforts in spreading the values undergirding the Confucian view of the family. However, popular religion *in toto* emphasized the role of the community in managing the relationship between community and nature and the broader social context, with no central significance given to the family in the narrow sense. Even more so, we can even say that many manifestations of popular religion actually highlight the needs and concerns of the individual as a member of the larger local community. This is evident, for example, in the essential expressions of religious ritual during the recurrent festivals of the lunar calendar, which often require the mobilization of community efforts, and celebrate the community as opposed to the external world. Community efforts are central to one of the most visible manifestations of popular religion, the local temples. So, the co-existence of *xueyuan* and *diyuan* is directly reflected in the two types of religious buildings, namely ancestral halls and temples, which tellingly have undergone a strong revival in China today, with significant regional variations.[74]

If we look only at the kinship side, the village appears to be a loose spatial collection of elementary families that organize themselves into larger units, the lineages, depending on the richness of local resources which can be mobilized to maintain those larger units materially, such as ancestral halls, lineage trusts supplying certain public goods such as schools, or enabling redistribution on the occasion of festivals. This is reflected in the organization of religious activities, with the elementary family as the unit of daily rituals, also represented in particular deities and family altars, and the lineage as the unit of the rituals related with the descent groups, such as ancestral halls. However, in considering this ritual organization, it is important that kinship transcends the village in two senses, so that we cannot simply think of a hierarchy with the family as the units and the village as the encompassing entity. One is that the family and the collective organization of the village fall apart and can stay in tension, a constellation that has been coined 'family individualism'.[75] The other is that the reach of economic activities can go far beyond the village, as lineages can be multi-local or expand their activities via the migration of members or entire families. In other words, the *xueyuan* principle is an essential feature of the village social structure, but in economic activities such as migration it reaches far beyond the village. This also shows that kinship and market mutually interact.

This interaction can be based on the analysis of Chinese kinship presented in the previous section. Kinship organization responds flexibly to the needs of economic organization. As we have seen, the core notion, that of the *jia*, refers to a unit of economic activity, and as such may be expanded to activate closer or more distant kin relationships. In other words, markets and kinship organization can be co-extensive, in the sense of the latter offering an institutional support for market transactions, and the former activating the functional capacities of kinship. This observation goes beyond the aspect that lineages can become models of corporate organization. Kinship structures can also become essential elements of market organization via many direct and indirect means. For example, lineages set up associations that organize markets in a certain physical space.[76]

Turning back to the village, the village also reflects the *diyuan* principle, which is embodied in ritual activities that are directly centred on representations of the locality independent from kinship. These representations are also essential for embedding the local community in the commonwealth of the Empire, as I will discuss in the following section. The ritual of the locality establishes clear demarcations of 'in-group' and 'out-group', reflected in the numerous beliefs about hostile spiritual forces in the surroundings of the locality, which are typically scrutinized, for example, in 'fengshui' (风水) practices. Thus, the village, in spite of being possibly internally divided along kinship lines, emerges as a social unit towards the external world and as a force of cooperation within its confines. In this sense, the village is separate from the market system, and indeed the pertinent local religious practices may be seen as undergirding the collective capacities to generate cooperation, such as in maintaining local irrigation systems, representing local interests in sustaining the embedding regional systems or organizing self-defence militias. In other words, whereas the market relates individual activities to private interests, mostly interpreted in terms of the family, the village is the institutional framework where public interests may be pursued.[77]

In comparison to common characterizations of traditional villages as being closed 'moral communities', however, in traditional China family individualism and markets played tightly together. This fact was Skinner's essential insight. In spatial terms, Skinner analysed the regional structures of markets in the rural areas, coming up with his famous 'honeycomb' structure (Figure 2.2). The honeycomb structure is a generic economic model of spatial economics that appears to apply approximately to the rural economy of China. The remarkable feature of this model is that it envisages villages as being centred on local market towns, which are in competition with each other if trading activities are sufficiently frequent and dense. Markets provide the conditions for increasing division of labour with families as basic units of production, and in turn growing production for the markets triggers further deepening of the regional market

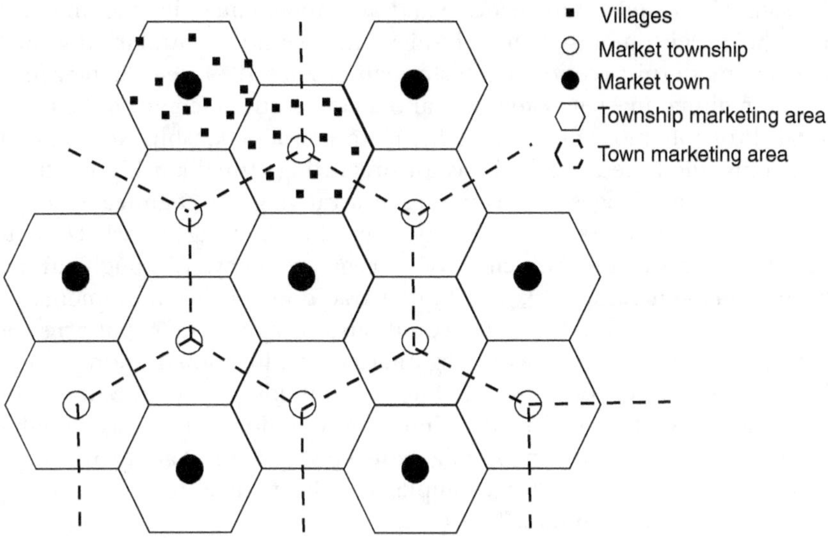

Figure 2.2 Skinner's model of regional marketing systems.

system. This implies that the market system emerged as a functional substitute for hierarchical units of production, such as manors or factories. Thus, the market system contributed essentially to the pattern of the 'high-level equilibrium trap'. We can say that economies of scale worked on the level of market organization, such that transaction costs were further diminished via the numerous trading activities processing information, thus obviating the need to introduce hierarchical organization in production. So, the market system was the essential infrastructural element of commercial capitalism in China, especially in the most developed areas, such as the Jiangnan region.[78]

The market system also provided the structural foundations for a most salient structural feature of traditional Chinese society: the lack of boundaries between urban and rural areas. On the one hand, the landownership system enabled landowning elites sojourning to Chinese towns and cities, and on the other hand, landownership also kept these elites culturally connected with the rural areas. This cultural integration was bolstered by the lack of the specific European feature of legal and corporate autonomy of cities in the political power structure, in spite of the fact that in Late Qing China, many urban areas evolved into settlement units which were clearly dominated by non-agricultural economic activities and were largely self-administered, beyond the seats of county magistrates. So, structurally, small towns were a distinctive feature of the Chinese societal fabric, also supporting a shared cultural context essential for the Chinese model of governance that I discuss in the next section. This fact is of particular significance against the backdrop of the rigid institutional separation between cities and countryside that was implemented by the modern household registration system and which has become a central institutional aspect of modernist economic transformation since 1949 (see Chapter 3).[79]

The regional market system was also a constitutive element in Chinese ritual. Probably most fundamentally, if we consider kinship, the market system provided the material basis for organizing affinal kinship relations across different villages, for example, in arranging for channels of communication and flows of information in the 'marriage market'. This reflects the normative principle of lineage exogamy. Although affinal kinship was generally weak in Chinese tradition, in fact movements of brides in the regional system could also trigger wider patterns of cooperation and support, as in regional crises with mobilization of self-defence forces, and serve as a medium for unfolding general patterns of association. We also need to take into consideration that the Neoconfucian emphasis and enforcement of agnatic kinship was not always reflected in local practices, which, for example, saw the regular return of young brides to their natal families.[80]

Indeed, it is important to note that the market system was undergirded by a plethora of associational structures that transcended kinship, but which were largely built on organizational principles that are also manifest in certain economic transpositions of traditional lineages, as we have already seen. One of the core institutions were local temples as the ritual complement to markets, which were built and maintained under the auspices of local associations, often explicitly as temple associations. Local temples were the rallying point of regular trade fairs and periodic markets, and thus were directly connected to economic activities. Beyond that, market towns adopted a multitude of functions in the social fabric of traditional China, such as is represented in the roles of matchmakers, moneylenders or religious experts. In other words, major activities of individual households were actually disembedded from the village and embedded in the local market system, centring on the market towns. This fact laid the structural foundation for the aforementioned cultural integration between rural and urban areas. If we look at urban agglomerations on higher levels of the market system, we notice a further differentiation of these associational principles, especially with regard to migration and travel. In Late Qing China, the regional hierarchy was not simply reflecting the organization of the state, as most emerging urban centres were not seats of higher level administrations at the same time. Therefore, the ritual economy provided the seedbed for local self-organization in terms of an incipient civil society. Associations such as the chambers of itinerant merchants assumed many roles in fulfilling para-governmental functions in the provision of local public goods.[81]

In analysing these traditional structures, we are confronted with the serious difficulty that we cannot reliably present counterfactual trajectories of development. In the late eighteenth and early nineteenth century, the Chinese economy was entering a stage of serious Malthusian strains, which were exacerbated by the slow deterioration in the quality of government, with growing corruption even at on highest levels. So, we can say that in meeting the challenge of Western Imperialism the Empire stood on feet of clay, resulting in an under-provision of public goods by formal government.[82] However, given the rise of civil society, it is difficult to evaluate this state, because with regard to the market system, economics tends to see lower levels of government intervention as a positive phenomenon. So, we face a fundamental difficulty in assessing the economic role of government in Late Imperial China. On the one hand, the revisionist literature has turned away from emphasizing bureaucratic fetters of growth to pinpointing deficiencies of public good production, hence substituting the picture of a strong interventionist state with one of a weak state that did not support the economy sufficiently. This picture of a weak state, however, may also be seen as a complement to the vigorous Chinese market economy, and hence in a more positive light. Interestingly, this may be seen as being both an interpretive ambiguity from the viewpoint of modern observers and from the perspective of historical observers.

This ambiguity points towards the role of ideas and attitudes in performing the ritual economy and mediating its real effects on growth and behaviour. One of the core observations is that markets were not seen as an independent source or carrier of values. There was no foundational idea of the freedom of markets which gradually evolved in Europe, in the sense of identifying 'the economy' as a separate social domain with its own functionality and laws. In the ritual economy, the market is lacking autonomy vis-à-vis society and politics. Indeed, it has often been noted that in China a 'liberal' ideology never emerged, with no direct conceptual equivalent to the Western notion of 'economic freedom', especially with reference to the individual. This corresponds to the contrast between relative and absolute notions of rights. Whereas Europe developed the notion of absolute and inalienable rights of individuals, and correspondingly absolute individual rights of property, the Chinese notion emphasized the relational nature of any individual right, and hence the balance between rights and obligations. In this context, 'freedom' in the Western sense appears as a partly deficient state, namely an unordered expression of individual whims which need to be shaped by moral education.[83]

However, that being said, we also need to take note of the fact that in the original tension between the Legalists and the Confucians, the latter adopted a critical stance towards monopolies of the government. In a sense, actual practice throughout the Empire reflected a compromise solution, with the government actively supporting the institution of brokerage with licensing, including the assignment of monopoly rights to selected groups of merchants, such as in the salt trade. With regard to the ideological dimension, we can safely state that Imperial governments in principle backed private ownership as a backbone of people's livelihoods and markets as a major social institution, and therefore in economic policy was mainly concerned about market order, fair pricing and product quality, thus standard roles of government in modern liberal doctrines.[84]

Up until today, many commentators have referred to the low level of social valuation merchants received in the Confucian canon. However, this tends to neglect the supportive attitude towards markets that was already evident in the famous Han dynasty disputes over salt and iron, where the Confucians voted against government monopolies that were favoured by the Legalists.[85] In Qing dynasty China, the non-interventionist approach to markets was reflected in limiting taxes on trading activities, and the decision to freeze the land registers for taxing agriculture. In other words, the traditional Chinese state, at least since its high point of institutional evolution under the Tang dynasty, intentionally allowed market society to unfold its dynamics, including various forms of self-organization. These forms of self-organization were the object of ritual supervision and standardization, as we see in the following section. This view was also reflected in the emergence of Confucian schools of thought that explicitly supported commerce and appreciated business, building on earlier traditions, such as Mencius' thought on the duty of government to take care of people's livelihoods. These ideas clearly distinguish between the lives of ordinary people, who may pursue their individual interests without any moral shame, and the lofty moral commitments of the Confucian gentleman who is obliged to concentrate on the public interest.[86]

The pejorative moral stance towards merchants did not reflect social reality in local contexts, but must be mainly seen as a normative commitment of political elites to emphasize moral values relative to expedience and individual interests. Already in the discourses over salt and iron, the Confucian rejection of government monopolies was based, among other arguments, on the fear that this would introduce a profit motivation into government action, which would corrode the moral foundations of government. In traditional Chinese conceptualizations of the body politic, the juxtaposition of 'li' (利) and 'yi' (义), and of 'si' (私) and 'gong' (公) played a decisive role. In ideal terms, the government and its representatives should represent the highest values of public interests, which entails a pejorative view on private commercial interests. But this did not mean that those private interests did not deserve proper recognition as a powerful motivation in the lives and efforts of ordinary people.

In terms of market organization, these ideological viewpoints were reflected in the institution of brokerage. Brokers were an essential element of the traditional market system across almost all product categories and trades. The system reflected the hierarchy of markets, with wholesale traders at the top and petty traders at the bottom who connected producers with the market system. The concerns of the government about market order led very early on to the establishment of a system of government-licensed brokers. The goals pursued by this system varied throughout the centuries. On the one hand, government aimed at controlling markets, often adding the task of taxation to the activities of brokers, which towards the end of the Empire and in the early twentieth century morphed into a tax farming system in many areas (see the following section for more details). On the other hand, the goal was to establish market order in curbing the scope of profit-seeking activities via the limitation of the number of brokers and the fee system. This clearly reflected the philosophical concerns about markets in recognizing the vital role of markets for people's livelihoods, but at the same time establishing a role for government in enforcing market order.

The brokerage system evolved into a symbiotic system of governmental and local market order in which ritual and markets were deeply integrated. Local merchants assuming the functions of brokers were often members of powerful lineages which closely adhered to Neoconfucian doctrines, while maintaining a strong interest in commercial activities. As I mentioned previously, local markets were often investments by lineages and other merchant associations who had a stake in the respective economic activities. The Imperial government was well aware of the many problems with direct intervention in the market system, as this might also trigger abuses of power by local-level government representatives. So, the local lineages struck a balance between government intervention and market liberalization in assuming the function of enforcers of market order. In Qing dynasty China, this combined with the general policy of lowering the tax burden for the population in explicit systems of ritual markets in which local merchant elites negotiated a tax-free policy for the local market, while agreeing on delivering a quota to the government and on enforcing market order.[87]

So, in conclusion, we can say that markets were indeed an essential element in the ritual economy: Markets were a means to secure the livelihood of the people and were therefore protected by the Imperial government; markets were created through local initiative, contextualized by the norms of kinship and associations. In this ritual economy, there was no opposition between government and market, so that a distinct idea of 'economic freedom' did not emerge. Markets were seen as an essential element of the ritual order, as they were a natural way to arrange economic activities, especially in enabling the economic sustainability of the fundamental unit of society: the family. We can also identify a distinct institution that connects ritual with market processes, thus highlighting a specific cultural shape of market mechanism, namely brokerage. The institution of brokerage is also closely connected to another institution that is central to organizing market interactions: the contract. As we have seen, middlemen were often directly included as witnesses or guarantors in contracts. So, ritually grounded brokerage is another part of the picture of the strangely missing civil law in the historical ritual economy of China.

Governmentality and market system: the Empire and its local states

When assessing the role of ritual in the ritual economy we need to distinguish neatly between the ritual practices in social organization and ritual as a means of enforcing Imperial rule in the vast territory of China. This distinction comes close to the dichotomy of 'little' and 'great tradition', although in China the core issue lies in understanding the interaction between the two poles. In this respect, Chinese writing again offers a conceptual model. The Chinese script does not correspond to a particular language, but to a family of languages which also underwent long-term linguistic changes, involving, for example, creolization in the context of migration in territories with non-Chinese native populations, especially in south China. This has to be seen against the fact that the Chinese Empire was factually multi-ethnic, thus indeed matching the standard conceptualization of empires as opposed to modern nation states. In contrast to Europe, where alphabetic scripts allowed for the gradual emergence of regional identities of vernaculars, ultimately creating cultural conditions for grounding nation states in constructed national identities, these remained autonomous in China because the standardization of the script could proceed independently. However, this also removed any obstacles both to the free diffusion of this script and to its enforcement by the Imperial state. Since the use of pictorial characters allows for any kind of gradual literacy, reaching from knowledge of single characters in their ritual uses, posters and signs, advertisements, etc. to the fully fledged capability to read and write texts, the standardized script could also smoothly integrate 'little and 'great tradition'. Correspondingly, written materials served as a medium of diffusing elite concepts of social and political order, such as honorary steles extolling virtuous officials, censored booklets with scripts for local operas, or village compacts that define the responsibilities and duties of local communities.[88]

In understanding the relationship between 'great' and 'little tradition', the role of Confucianism in the traditional body politic certainly stays at the centre of attention. On the one hand, Confucianism clearly emphasizes ritual as a principle of subsidiarity in enforcing social order, but at the same time authoritarian rule also exerted very tight control of ritual on occasions. This phenomenon has been approached in Chinese studies by means of a concept peculiar to this field: 'orthopraxy'. The claim is made that in Western society, especially in the context of the secular conflicts about religion, orthodoxy mattered most, whereas in China the question of true beliefs was secondary to following the proper rules of ritual conduct, and expressing sincerity in fulfilling those ritual obligations.[89] Indeed, this notion of sincerity corresponds to the concept of 'ritual labour' that I introduced previously. As a result of proper ritual action, moral transformation follows closely.

The Confucian state sometimes observed very strict principles in enforcing proper ritual, however, by focusing only on parts of it, which were considered especially sensitive, and also largely neglecting questions of proper beliefs that undergird the ritual practice. To use the metaphor of language and script, proper writing is more important than proper speaking. In other words, whereas Western 'orthodoxy' emphasizes the movement from inside to the outside, in Chinese orthopraxy the assumption is made that following the ritual also has transformative powers relative to the inner state. Chinese notions of religious ritual are deeply externalistic in philosophical terms, and differ fundamentally from European internalism and expressivism. This conviction has deeper roots in fundamental anthropological concepts of the sociality of human individuals, who enter society without a preconceived set of capabilities and rights, and only develop into mature individuals through socialization and education.[90]

Therefore, we need to note that characterizing traditional Chinese culture as 'Confucian' is highly misleading. This is a vast topic, but we need at the very least to accentuate the role of religion. The interaction between 'great' and 'little tradition' was one of civilizational effort, epitomized in the notion of 'jiaohua' (教化) that is still being used today in Confucian contexts. In spite of the fact that Imperial Confucianism also adopted religious rituals and was also deeply religious in terms of the cosmological views on Imperial rule, with regard to popular religion it adopted a sceptical and rationalistic attitude. I have already emphasized the modular and household-centred nature of popular religion, where the syncretism of Daoist, Buddhist or Shamanistic beliefs and practices were freely combined in local and even individual contexts, and where the religious experts were mainly acting as providers of religious services. This constellation was a seedbed of recurrent cultural creativity in creating new forms of belief, often coalescing into religious movements and the formation of sects. The Imperial administration imposed strict controls on these activities, yet at the same time accommodated many religious innovations by co-opting them into the Imperial pantheon, thus expressing moral judgements about the quality of these beliefs.[91]

It is important to note the integration of popular religion into a pantheon that was conceived as an afterworld replica of the Imperial administration, with the Yellow Emperor on top, and with celestial administrators even reaching the individual family in the shape of the Kitchen God. Yet, this did not suppress the fundamental ambiguity of local practices, even when focusing on rituals that were also embedded in notions of hierarchical ordering of the body politic. On a deeper level, this also reflects the cultural archetypes of 'wen' (文) versus 'wu' (武). The Empire builds on civilization as a fundamentally civilian and civilizing endeavour, whereas martial virtues always carry the dangerous potential of violence and disorder. Popular religious practices, such as including sword fights, martial arts and other forms of performing violent acts, therefore always also signal the potential of individual and community deviance, or at least also the need for the local community to defend itself against threats from the outside world. As a matter of fact, the Imperial military forces were also a part of this potentially dangerous world.

I highlight these aspects, because we can relate them to the parallel process of civilizing and containing violence in the Western world. The interaction between 'great' and 'little tradition' in China actually centres on this pacifying endeavour, and one of the deepest ruptures in the cultural and social fabric of China in the late nineteenth and twentieth century, continuing even up until the Cultural Revolution, was the collapse of its cultural framework. Militarization and endemic violence at the local level overturned the traditional social order, and the Communist revolution was also accompanied by waves of erupting, partly uncontrolled violence, such as during the first waves of land reform and during the Cultural Revolution.[92]

These observations may be summarized in conceptualizing a distinctly Chinese approach in conceiving the role of government in society, which has been dubbed 'culturalism'. Culturalism refers to governance mechanisms that emphasize the ritual and cultural integration of the Empire as opposed to bureaucratic and legal integration. This was undergirded by certain aspects of the official state cult in which the proper conduct of Imperial rituals on different levels of government, from the Imperial Court to the County Magistrate, was seen as essential in maintaining social order in society at large. In comparison, enforcement of law was seen as a secondary activity; that is, it was regarded as the expression of failure in properly maintaining ritual in society. In other words, culturalism approaches governance as a continuous process of civilizational transformation of the population that is led by ruling elites.[93]

A most remarkable fact about Late Imperial China is the amazing discrepancy between the scope and reach of state power as mediated by culturalism and the extreme thinness of local administrative structures. At the lowest level, the county, only one formal representative of the Imperial government, the Magistrate, ruled over a large territory relying on what was basically a privately arranged supportive staff. This pattern went along with systematic corruption, thus actually enshrining moral failure in the very foundations of governance at the local level. On the one hand, this was simply a manifestation of the fact that the expansion of the Empire, together with the strong growth of the population, overstretched administrative capacities; on the other hand, however, this was also the outcome of conscious decisions to refrain from a deeper bureaucratic penetration of society. Therefore, we need to recognize the county as a pivotal element of the ritual economy. Indeed, the county is one of the most stable elements of administration that even connects the Imperial past with the modern era.[94] In Imperial times, the county is essential in the ritual order of the Empire, as the Imperial Rites were replicated by the

Magistrate who therefore served as a direct image of the Emperor, thus playing a distinct role compared with other personnel in the field administration. At the same time, at the county level the formal representative of the Empire interacted with the local elites to establish the Confucian concept of moral order, based on shared values.[95]

This system could only work efficiently because the Magistrate could establish cooperation with local elites whose members partly also received Confucian education in aspiring to public office. The number of students who finally failed to achieve public office was much larger than the number of officials, but they had often received decades of education in classical literature, ritual and the arts. Thus, culturalism in practice meant the co-optation and integration of local elites into the broader stream of elite 'great tradition'. Obliging local elites to maintain the ritual and social order was essential for the institutional stability of the Empire. This is evident, for example, in the public support of lineage authority in Confucian governance, in spite of the fact that lineage feuds were often also a source of local violence and disorder. Yet, a social contract emerged in which local lineages could bolster their local power and authority, in exchange for assuming para-governmental functions in enforcing social order. Thus, governance in Imperial China was actually two-modal, top-down and bottom-up, with the local elites assuming the pivotal role in coordinating and mediating these two modes.[96]

The impact of this form of governance upon the economy may be best illustrated in the way taxation was organized. Late Imperial China saw the transition from a traditional tax system based on in-kind payments and corvée labour to a monetary tax system, thus manifesting the growing significance of markets. However, local elites and the government negotiated the way in which government intervened with markets in enforcing taxation. In the ritual economy, this was cast in moral terms as an obligation of local communities towards the state. Leaders in the local market system agreed to deliver a certain amount of taxes, and the government refrained from interfering directly with markets. In fact, the importance of markets was recognized to such a degree that the Imperial administrators even opted in favour of monetary payments in order to activate market supply in case of famines and other emergencies. Thus, we can say that taxation was mainly organized as a ritual obligation towards the Empire.[97]

As we have already seen in the discussion of the brokerage system, we meet another ambiguity here. On the one hand, the way the tax system was organized points towards the structures of a 'patrimonial state' as analysed by Max Weber. In other words, the Imperial government extended privileges to certain groups in return for assuming collective responsibility in paying taxes. This kind of tax system was labelled 'liturgical' ('leiturgisch') by Weber and is opposed to the rational tax bureaucracies of modernizing capitalist countries.[98] The ambiguity stems from the fact that the tax burden of Imperial China was extremely low in international comparison. This remains true even if we include the role of arbitrary levies and even corruption in county administration. There are two factors that can explain this phenomenon. One is that the costs of taxation were high under Chinese conditions. This argument can only be properly assessed if we consider the central challenge to the Imperial government which certainly differs from the European case, namely holding the Empire together. This resulted in a specific constellation, namely that the core areas of military investment were peripheral in economic terms, and hence could not offer a strong tax base. Yet, the administrative and military apparatus had to be strong exactly in these areas. Therefore, in considering the optimal use of scarce administrative resources, the government had to establish a unique combination of relatively weak but effective administrative structures in the most prosperous regions, based on close cooperation with local elites. The other factor is ideology, as we have seen. In other words, in the cooperation between the Empire and local elites both parties were aware of the Confucian norm of low taxation and the duty of the Emperor to safeguard the livelihood of the people. In the confluence of both forces, the low tax regime of Late Imperial China emerged.[99]

So, by implication, we cannot straightforwardly interpret the 'liturgical' system in the conventional Weberian way, because of the obvious normative constraints on expanding taxation. This is why I argue that the Chinese system may be characterized as 'ritual economy'. In the domain of taxation, this means that there was an implicit constraint upon government intervention in the economy; this was not based on the notion of subjective rights evolving in Europe but on ritual obligations that were binding for both sides. Regarding the side of the local elites and the population, this was reflected in the emerging combination of free markets and local self-governance. It is crucial to recognize that this occurred mainly in the most developed regions of China, and hence has to be regarded as a transformative process that encompassed both the economy and the body politic.

This system was undergoing systematic change when in the mid-nineteenth century the infamous 'likin' taxes were introduced, which directly taxed inter-regional commerce and often mutated into a gamut of arbitrary levies, tolls, etc. The legacy of this incomplete transition was visible throughout the twentieth century up until today. The Republican government failed in setting up a reliable and accountable system of local taxes, resulting in a disordered imposition of charges and levies, which experienced a reincarnation in the arbitrary rural taxes in the 1990s. In the *longue durée*, this reveals the slow progress in substituting the ritual economy with an economic system comprising bureaucratic and legally grounded fiscal systems. I will discuss these developments in detail in Chapter 4.[100]

Thus, an essential feature of the traditional Chinese body politic was the co-existence of a local state grounded on ritual and a central state, the

Imperial bureaucracy. The Imperial bureaucracy largely followed Legalist principles, hence emphasizing bureaucratic mechanisms and formal legal rules in its internal operations. Yet, one fundamental dilemma of Imperial rule since the strengthening of its authoritarian and even despotic features in Ming times was that the representatives of this bureaucracy also embodied the Confucian beliefs in moral commitments, thus potentially clashing with the individual interests of the Emperor and his family. This typically resulted in the creation of a parallel power structure at the Emperor's court, such as the role of Eunuchs in Ming times, a pattern strengthened by the ethnic division between Manchu rulers and mainly Han bureaucrats in Qing times. The implicit dualism of Confucian bureaucracy and 'inner' organization of power as embodied in the Imperial family obtained a defining role for Qing politics.[101]

Thus, ritual and bureaucracy stood in potential tension on the central level. In the local context, the source of tension was the potential rupture between local practice and orthopractic regulation. In this sense, we can use a term that has so far applied only to modern China: the 'local state'. The local state is not integrated bureaucratically into the central state, and so remains partly autonomous, yet it is subject to ritualistic governance, mediated via the interaction between bureaucracy and local elites that is grounded in culturalistic governance, institutionalized in the system of Imperial examinations. Relative to the local state, the Magistrate acted as a representative of the moral and religious power of the Emperor. His main duty was to impose ritualistic governance upon the local self-organization of a society centred on village communities and the regional market system and its commercial hubs on different levels, with the market towns at the bottom. Compared with this ideal-typical picture, the actual messy administrative interferences of the Magistrate and his para-governmental, often irregular staff were close to a state of failure in achieving social order. This produced immense tension in the bureaucracy whose identity was built on Confucian moral convictions.[102]

The local state is an essential part of the Chinese ritual economy. We can approach this term as a medium-range theoretical term encapsulating a constitutive pattern that integrates a large number of mechanisms, such as the structured social interactions between local elites and the Magistrate, the interaction between taxation schemes and markets, and so forth. Ritual in this context is a form of governmentality; I portray its basic structure in Figure 2.3. In the literature, the concept that comes closest to this is Duara's notion of the 'cultural nexus of power'. In Foucault's conception, governmentality essentially includes the regulation and standardization of forms of knowledge and the whole range of local and individual mechanisms that undergird the enforcement of governmental power in a large, complex and growing society. Duara's 'cultural nexus' highlights certain aspects of these mechanisms, in particular the distinction between 'entrepreneurial' and 'protective state brokerage'. I treat these terms as labels for a set of peculiar mechanisms that manifest a process perspective on the local state. The notion of brokerage directly relates to the interaction between the county level and the village level, and emphasizes the need to intermediate and negotiate state power there. On contrast to direct bureaucratic governance, which prevails between the Imperial state and the county level, intermediation builds on particular groups of people: the 'brokers'. Hence, we meet an interesting parallelism between the notion of brokerage in market organization and in the state, which should be kept analytically distinct, but may often be fulfilled by the same group of people. This is one of the most important indicators of markets being part and parcel of ritual governance, namely the overlapping roles of brokers in the market system and brokers between local society and the Imperial state.[103]

In Figure 2.3 I distinguish between administrative, ritualistic and culturalistic governance, and between the Imperial state and the local state. The local state is not only embedded into but even constituted by the market system, and is materially embodied in the distribution of market towns and counties, with the counties representing the interface between local state and Imperial state. This reflects the Skinnerian idea that the fundamental unit of traditional society was not the village, but the market system; however, in understanding governmentality we need to explicitly include the dimension of the state, because the Magistrate is the agent of culturalistic governance, which ultimately centres on the system of taxation as the

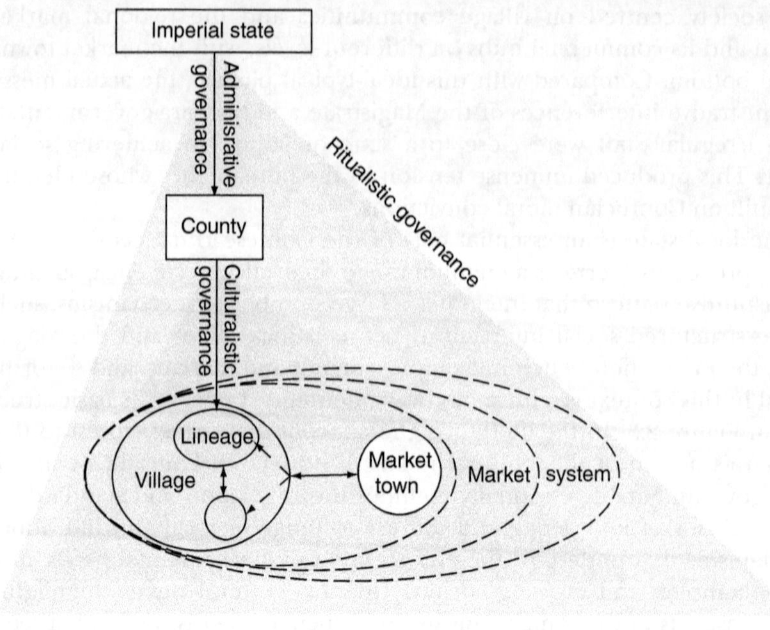

Figure 2.3 China's local state in Imperial times.

main manifestation. Market towns are not only economic centres, but also cultural centres in the sense of being the theatres of local ritual, such as in activities of temple building, festivals or the representation of lineage authority beyond the village. The village and the lineage represent the grassroots level of the local state, and reflect the principles of *diyuan* and *xueyuan*, respectively. Culturalistic governance at the grassroots level focuses especially on the rituals of kinship and lineage, whereas ritualistic governance reaches further and encompasses the market system, as far as it is mirrored in the corresponding patterns of ritual, in particular popular religion. At this interface, culturalism and ritual also encompassed specific forms of government interference with the local state, in particular in taxation, epitomized in unique forms of 'liturgical' taxation, as we have seen.

The distinction between culturalism and ritualism may appear to be somewhat arbitrary. However, I propose to refer the former to the cultural integration of local and Imperial elites, whereas the latter refers to the much broader orthopractic control of the population, thus also implying a much broader scope of the effects of integration. This results in what has often been emphasized as the paradoxical relation between large local variety and high degrees of national integration, at the same time.[104] In terms of governmentality, culturalism is therefore a special form of regulating knowledge in society, whereas ritual control focuses directly on behavioural patterns. This distinction is evident from the pivotal role of the Imperial exams in recruiting members of the culturalist elites, which clearly focused on knowledge.[105] These distinctions are important in understanding the actual mechanisms that shape the realization of brokerage between the Imperial state and the population of the local states. If we follow Duara's distinction between two modes of brokerage, ritualistic governance is the breeding ground for the emergence of protective state brokerage. In this case, local elites strive to represent the interests of the local population vis-à-vis the Imperial state, and to mediate solutions which position both sides in a sustainable pattern of interaction, such as when arranging 'tax-free markets'. So, as this example clearly demonstrates, protective state brokerage is an essential element in safeguarding the autonomy of the market system vis-à-vis the state: this is how ritual embedded the market. In contrast, entrepreneurial state brokerage mainly emerges from dysfunctional developments in the culturalist governance structure, directly violating certain premises regarding the relationship between *li* and *yi*. In this case, the state brokers aim at gaining as much personal advantage and profit as possible from the relationship with the Imperial state, and therefore also undermine its ritualistic representation towards the population. The most dysfunctional expression of this is the evolution of profit-oriented tax farming, which in the early twentieth century reflected the collapse of the Imperial order, thereby destroying the culturalist constraints upon exploiting local power. Beginning with the introduction of the *likin* tax, these dysfunctional phenomena also contributed to increasing frictions in the workings of the market system.

We can therefore state that this peculiar governmentality of the local state was the central and defining element of the Chinese ritual economy, thus resulting in the unique economic style of Imperial China. In modern terms, we may also say that the ritual economy is political economy in a straightforward meaning; that is, the market and the state build a unified institutional pattern, with the political domain obtaining a primordial role, mediated in the unique form of ritual. However, as we have seen, this deviates fundamentally from the Western pattern of political economy which up until today assumes a distinction and even contradiction between the market and the state. In Imperial China, markets were part and parcel of the body politic, and the political domain undergirded the workings of markets in driving the evolution of the social division of labour.

If we try to analytically summarize the resulting pattern of development, two notions in the recent literature loom large. One is 'economic involution', the other is 'state involution'.[106] What has been referred to as 'Great Divergence' may be conceived of as a pattern where state involution became a force reinforcing economic involution, and vice versa. However, these terms may claim to be too broad in scope, so I propose using the terms 'market involution' and 'government involution' instead. The term 'involution' characterizes a particular kind of mechanism, and in narrowing down its meaning I suggest that we concentrate more on the details of the mechanisms, and avoid the fallacy of larger scale structural explanations. In my view, it is necessary to distinguish neatly between the 'economy' and the 'market', and between 'state' and 'government'. In the former case, this distinction allows for identifying transformative potential in structures that are not market mechanisms per se, such as the lineage corporations, but are also part and parcel of the economy. In the latter, we recognize that 'government' refers to the formal institutions of the state; if we approach the state in terms of 'governance', then, again, we are able to see the transformative potential of informal institutions. In other words, my terms focus more explicitly on particular mechanisms that drive the phenomena referred to by the broader terms.

The term 'market involution' means that the ritual economy undergirded economic growth up until the nineteenth century, but without sustainable growth of per capita income, major innovations in technology and material culture, and without disruptive emergences of new forms of social organization. The increasing sophistication of traditional agriculture and the expansion of the market system enabled strong population growth, a pattern that was embedded in ritualistic notions of family and kinship. These ritualistic notions were part and parcel of a larger system of ritual that also governed state–society interactions. Ritual was therefore a functional equivalent to law, and in this respect undergirded the role of contracts and property in enabling the expansion of markets. Thus, the apparent paradox in China's traditional regime is growth of markets without triggering substantial qualitative change in the material conditions of the economy. As we have seen, the explanation for this phenomenon may lie in material factors such as the dearth of cheap energy, and may not relate to the institutional structures per se. Thus, we cannot support the broader claim of economic involution, because the system was highly efficient, both in terms of allocation and adaptation, and also highly productive, as manifest in the substantial expansion of the carrying capacity in demographic terms. At the same time, we also avoid regarding the entire set of institutions affecting the workings of the economy as involutionary. The involutionary mechanisms are working at the interface between market and non-market domains, in particular the family. This implies that under different ecological conditions evolutionary processes may emerge, in the sense of emergent novelty.[107]

This distinction is necessary in explaining the fact of the immense entrepreneurial dynamics that was unleashed by Chinese families outside of Mainland China, with no principled obstacles to entering modern industries, finance or the global economy in general. A particularly important case in point is Taiwan, where economic and social modernization has been accompanied by the resilience of many aspects of traditional Chinese culture. This clearly shows that it is the precise nature of market signals and mechanisms that determines the transformative potential of the ritual economy. Thus, we identify involution as a particular kind of mechanism that is mainly mediated via markets, and is local in nature, though summing up to aggregate results.

The apparent contradiction between Chinese success outside Mainland China and failure within Mainland China was often attributed to the differences between political institutions. However, with regard to the conditions in Taiwan during the transformative stages in export-oriented industrialization, these differences in terms of formal institutions were not that substantial, as might appear when observers confront 'Communist' rule with Guomindang rule. The Guomindang operated as a Leninist party with deep penetration of the economy, controlling a large state-owned sector, and imposing economic dualism on the society separated into the groups of Mainlanders and Taiwan-born population. In other words, the structures of the state did not differ in that substantial way which was suggested by the Cold War polarity, even including aspects such as corruption.[108] Now, the term 'state involution' with reference to Mainland China originally meant that ritualistic notions of government limited the growth of government in terms of bureaucratic integration that would enable the state to control an increasing share of economic product via taxation. The ultimate reason for the persistence of the low tax regime in China co-existing with the spiralling out of local irregular public expropriation was the fact that once the government adopted a more interventionist approach, the costs of supervision and enforcement increased, for two reasons. First, local resistance against the intrusion of government became stronger, hence increasing governance costs. Second, enhancing government intervention also increased the internal agency costs of government, as incentives for abusing administrative power at the local level grew stronger. So, as a result, the growing costs of governance tended to eradicate the additional benefits from higher taxes for the central government. These problems became much more serious following the erosion of the political foundations of the ritual economy in the twentieth century. However, this shows that it is important to distinguish between 'state' and 'government'. The outlined involutionary phenomena refer to government, but not necessarily to the state. The dilemma of the twentieth century was that the ritual foundations of the state had been destroyed via radical reforms without putting a functionally equivalent structure in place. Therefore, we cannot diagnose an involutionary dynamics per se, but only the collapse of an essential part of the traditional order, adding the effects of external aggression and internal civil war. So, it is analytically necessary to limit the involutionary analysis to formal government institutions in the narrow sense.

In other words, we need to distinguish neatly between government and governmentality, which partly overlaps with the distinction between formal institutions and ritualistic institutions of governance. Government involution in the late nineteenth and early twentieth century was mainly driven by internal deficiencies of government administration, thus resulting in rapidly declining net fiscal benefits from expanding the administrative capacities. The instability of the state was partly caused by this, but also by the erosion of the cultural nexus of power, hence a particular form of governmentality, supported by formal institutions of ritual in Imperial times. In considering this erosion, however, it is important to neatly distinguish between different mechanisms of governmentality. For example, up until 1949 we cannot diagnose a fundamental disruption of lineage structures in Chinese society, but a dissolution of the link between formal government and local elites via culturalist governance. In other words, the erosion of governmentality largely resulted from the disruption of culturalist mechanisms, but did not fully affect ritualistic governance, insofar that this was partly autonomously implemented via many social practices, such as in popular religion. This observation is essential in understanding the continuity of culture in the evolution of the ritual economy. From that perspective, we can further specify the analysis in temporal terms: market involution is a process that characterizes economic development in Qing times, whereas government involution is a process that was speeding up in the twentieth century, probably triggered much earlier by the catastrophic event of the Taiping rebellion.

Looking at this interaction by way of counter-factual history, certainly the most intriguing insight is that in the second half of the nineteenth century a federalist movement emerged out of the structures of the ritual economy which was aborted with the collapse of the Empire and the dominance of political movements that aimed to strengthen the role of the centre and the unity of China in Republican times, culminating in the establishment of a formally highly centralized institutional regime of Communism in 1949. The federalist movement clearly shows that the ritual economy also had transformative potential in terms of innovations in governance. This is because the ritual organizations rapidly evolved into modern institutions of local governance in many Chinese urban areas, in the shape of Chambers of Commerce and other institutions of urban administration. These developments were major counterpoints of the provincial self-strengthening movement dominated by the traditional political elites of the Empire.[109]

Theoretical reprise

In this chapter, I have explored the idea that the economic style of Late Imperial China may be specified as a 'ritual economy'. If we reflect upon this analysis from the perspective of the theoretical notions that I advanced in Chapter 1, the appropriate starting point is the observation that writing an economic and social history of China is an endeavour deeply entangled in the mirror of culture.

This applies both for contemporary research and for the historical conditions. When China launched her modernization process, certain concepts and ideas were imported from Western countries that served as an analytical beacon to understand her own historical situation. For example, the concept of the 'nation' was received and applied in order to envisage necessary steps towards political transformation, or the notion of 'capitalism' was introduced in order to assess the status of the development of the Chinese economy. All these concepts originated in self-descriptions of Western societies, which were then taken as the lense through which Chinese realities were perceived and evaluated. They assumed a pivotal role in the immense transformative efforts that were expended in the twentieth century in order to progress the Chinese modernization process. However, today we have to acknowledge that these descriptions may have presented a deeply distorted picture of these historical realities. Taking the two examples cited above, we may need to consider that the tight integration between Imperial rule and local practices via culturalism and ritualism in fact may have resulted in what were incipient structures of a modern nation state in Late Imperial China, building on the precocious modernity of the Legalist empire established in 221 BCE; or, the market system of the traditional Chinese economy may have resulted in unique forms of commercial capitalism in the absence of certain forms of technological transformation due mainly to factor endowments and the resulting price relations, hence an efficient adaptation to the constraints under which the Chinese economy operated.

The mirror of culture shines everywhere in the study of Imperial China, resulting in the creation of distinct theoretical constructs of medium range which appear to be central achievements of recent historical research, such as the notions of 'orthopraxy', 'culturalism' or 'marketing system' (as a Skinnerian terminus technicus). I take these notions as conceptual building blocks in constructing the economic style of Imperial China as a 'ritual economy'. In doing so, we touch upon what is probably the most fundamental aspect of the mirror of culture, namely the distinction between 'ritual' and 'law'. This leads us to reconsider most basic paradigms of Western development, such as the Weberian notion of 'rationalization'. In the mirror of culture, we have to ask whether these notions not only distort the perception of historical conditions in China, but also of the West. Thus, ultimately, the methodological challenge lies in the normative nature of most theories in the social sciences; in other words, in concepts which are designed as being objective analytical instruments, we nevertheless always carry a normative excess meaning. 'Rationalization' is a notion which also refers to emerging Western notions that societies should be 'rational'. In other words, past structural and institutional changes are always deeply enmeshed with normative notions, and the scientific theories often fail to disentangle these two elements. The same applies for China. Describing Imperial China as 'Confucian' is not only reflecting objectively given social and political structures, but also the normative commitment of past elites to transform Chinese society into a Confucian order. Thus, in both cases we face considerable difficulties in distilling reality from historical information. In order to achieve this, medium-level theoretical terms are of central importance, with 'ritual' being the most essential, and aforementioned terms such as 'orthopraxy' being further specifications. In other words, we can arrange many important concepts of Chinese studies into a coherent medium-range theory of the ritual economy.

Medium-level theoretical terms serve to identify and generalize over mechanisms. This can be straightforward. A most evident case of mechanism analysis is Skinner's model of local and regional marketing systems. These include a large scope of specific and concrete social interactions that obtain causal forces, such as arbitrage activities of local traders or production decisions of local farmers. Yet, the Skinner model also suggests that these mechanisms cannot simply determine social structure in the sense of a materialistic economic determinism. Cultural creativity is always at play; we saw that 'the market' is both a material structure and a cultural construct in the Skinner model, properly understood. A foremost example is the role of brokers. On the one hand, we can easily explain the function of brokers by applying economic models of mechanisms that include transaction costs. However, who specifically obtains the role of a broker cannot be explained by referring to that function alone. Thus, the economic explanation would commit the methodological fallacy of taking functions as causes. The cause of the emergence of the brokerage function can only be identified if we expand the explanation by referring to social capital. Brokers are people with a particular endowment of social capital. But this also implies that the market structure, even the topography of markets, becomes endogenous to the process of cultural creativity: The distribution of social capital in space and time determines the specific direction and flow of brokerage activities. For example, whether a particular market town may obtain a central role in regional trade of bamboo cannot be explained only by reference to economic data such as transport costs; what is essential is whether local lineages invest their social capital into creating the respective institutions that undergird market activity.

So, one theoretical condensation of my analysis is that ritual is a determinant of the production and reproduction of social capital. This applies in many different forms, and so requires another step in mechanism analysis. Elaborating further on the example of brokerage, brokerage roles can emerge endogenously as a result of recurrent market transactions in which some traders accumulate a reputation as being trustworthy and reliable. There are many game theoretic models that would only refer to economic mechanisms in order to explain this transition. Once we include the perspective on ritual, however, we may also argue that brokerage is grounded in complementary moral commitments, such as norms of trust, and the corresponding societal expectations that also induce sanctions in case of deviance. Thus, the endogenous mechanism of intermediation is embedded in moral norms that are part and parcel of ritual. In addition, brokerage may be grounded in ritual assignments of elite status to certain groups. This is the case when powerful lineages invest in commerce, thus fostering the emergence of local merchant elites. These elites often assume brokerage roles as means to close and control the market; thus they do not necessarily follow moral norms of brokerage. However, at the same time their own legitimacy rests partly on their alignment with the government, which in turn often pursues interests in enforcing market order in terms of containing profiteering and unfair behaviour. Thus, the local Magistrate may play a substantial role in guiding the behaviour of local lineages, which at the same time increases their trustworthiness vis-à-vis the population. As a result, the lineage-based organizations contribute to enhancing the efficiency of markets via large-scale brokerage functions connecting local and regional systems.

So, the theoretical notion of social capital helps disentangle the cultural nexus of power analytically. Reconsidering Figure 2.3 in this context, we note that Imperial rule imposed a unique network structure upon the Chinese local state via the examination system, since the system created a large group of graduates with no official position, who nevertheless obtained a pivotal role in mediating between bureaucracy and local society, since they had obtained the human capital that undergirded culturalistic governance. This network structure overlapped with local structures, in particular with the lineages. For the lineages, activating the symbolic resources of the Imperial state was an important means to build social capital in local society and in the local and regional market system. Hence, culturally embedded social capital became an important element of the market process, creating the conditions for successful repeated interactions without explicit reference to law. The market process fed back on the formation of social capital and power positions via the accumulation of wealth which resulted in the formation of a social stratum of merchant families that fulfilled both commercial and culturalistic roles, even in recruiting talent for the Imperial administration.

In these processes, the formation of identities was the core element. Ritual, especially in the sense of Fei Xiaotong's ideas, is a medium in which identities are fixated and related to the societal status order. Therefore, we can summarize the analysis of social capital thus far in the sense that in the ritual economy there is a society-wide process of the production, formation and maintenance of social capital that is part and parcel of the system of governance. This is why the examination system has to be regarded as probably the most essential part of the formal institutions of government in Imperial China, a fact that transpires when we consider that the Emperor himself presided over the final Palace exams. This is a major difference to Western developmental pathways that focus on the role of law. The discovery of social capital in Western economics in the 1980s was mainly seen as making informal institutions more explicit in dealing with markets. In the Chinese ritual economy, ritual is in fact a formal institution centring on the production and reproduction of social capital. In recognizing this, it is a straightforward process to organize the empirical observations into a theoretical pattern; for example, as we have seen, because social capital is a major determinant of market interactions and structures, it directly relates with the Skinnerian notion of market system.

These examples show how mechanism analysis allows us to disentangle the notion of economic style into constituent structures and elements. If we apply the general Aoki model here, we also see why and how elements of ritual can obtain different functions, especially at the interface between markets and society. This helps us avoid misunderstandings that result from differentiating between certain kinds of organization on the macro level, such as kinship groups versus corporations. If we move down to the mechanism level, we realize that certain symbolic means – signs in the Aoki model – can change their function in responding to certain adaptive pressures on the population level. Thus, for example, there are certain public representations of shareholding practices in lineages: These signs can obtain functions in organizing economic processes that result in the pooling of resources, establishing differentiated management roles, or organizing the distribution of profits; thus, in sum, this results in functional equivalences with the Western corporation. Thus, mechanism analysis helps lift the conceptual veil of macro-level institutional concepts such as the 'corporation'. As we have seen, this also helps sharpen the analytical focus, since one can identify more specific mechanistic differences between China and the West (one example in the context of the corporation is the absence of the institution of limited liability in China).

Further extending the Aoki model when applied to the analysis in this chapter, I accentuate the mediating role of cognitive structures which link public representations with behaviour. We have seen that field dependency is a central phenomenon here: This is crucial in identifying family resemblances between past and present, since there is much evidence that this cognitive structure has been a stable phenomenon until recent times, as is reflected in pertinent psychological studies. Field dependency directly connects with medium-level theoretical terms in China studies. Orthopraxy may be seen as a reflection of field dependency when generalizing over different sets of local data that are the direct empirical manifestations of mechanisms. In other words, the notion of orthopraxy encapsulates the fact that field dependency causes a relatively large variation between signs and behavioural expressions, without jeopardizing the institution in terms of the entire feedback circuit of the Aoki model. So, we see how a term specific to China studies connects up with mechanism analysis. On the other hand, the Aoki model also allows us to approach shifting equilibria at the population level of interactions. For example, the oscillations between protective and entrepreneurial state brokerage may be analysed in these terms, once we consider the destruction of social capital embedded in formal institutions triggered by the collapse of the Empire. This example also highlights the need to consider diachronic and synchronic interdependencies between different institutions. Thus, the breakdown of administrative governance after 1911 created a drift towards entrepreneurial state brokerage, which resulted in even larger local variations of social and political conditions.

The Aoki model also allows for correcting one principled misperception in comparing Western and Chinese developments: This relates to the role of public representations, and here in particular religion. For Western societies, the dualism of political and religious symbolic domains and structures of power had obtained a defining role since early medieval times. In the mirror of culture, this has trapped the analysis of Chinese religion into many misunderstandings, such as overly emphasizing its rational and civil nature as a legacy of the Jesuit encounter with Confucian bureaucrats at the Imperial court. Against such interpretations, the Aoki model directs attention to the role of popular religion in mediating institutions in local contexts, which implies that religion and the lifeworld are seen as being deeply integrated. As we have seen, popular religion was an integral part of regulating behaviour in many facets, reaching from the role of money in markets over ancestor worship regulating lineage structures to reflections of the Imperial bureaucracy in religious rituals. It is also important to note the regulatory efforts of the Imperial state directed at supervising and shaping the symbolic domain of popular religion. So, we need to analyse religion in the context of a larger set of cognitive mechanisms that undergird the institutions of the ritual economy. In particular, we have to approach popular religion as a complex medium of governmentality in Imperial China, which partly played an autonomous role, and therefore may also be an important medium of path dependencies linking past and present. This aspect is easily overlooked when one concentrates on Confucianism as the official ideology of the Imperial state.

If we want to apply the Aoki model in more detail, we have to refer to the elements–patterns–processes–states framework. An important example is the contract. Taken as such, contracts are economic artefacts found in all societies with a complex division of labour. In the Chinese case, we recognize a unique dynamic in the evolution of contracts. Since Song times contracts emerged and diffused as elements throughout the Chinese economy and society, enabling a multitude of different types (hence, patterns) of processes in the market system, such as the increasing use of contracts in arranging family and kin relationships or in enabling economic transactions in the market system. This resulted in a fundamental feature of the traditional Chinese economic style, hence a 'state', namely the pivotal role of the institution of contract independent from formal law as a regulating institutional framework. In order to understand this pattern, it is necessary to look at the unique social mechanisms at work. One important feature of contracts was the explicit inclusion of the social networks of the parties via the roles of witnesses and middlemen. So, we can relate the institution of contract to the concept of social capital. Contracts partly embodied information about the social capital of the parties involved and hence created corresponding incentives to fulfil contracts. Thus, contracts were strongly contextualized, with implications for conflict resolution and enforcement. These patterns coalesced into states, which may be analysed as basic structures of adjudication in Imperial China. Here, interactions with other institutions are again important. A central fact is the absence of formal civil law in China, which gives the institution of the contract a pivotal role in the legal process, and opens the way for a strong emphasis on material aspects of justice in adjudication. This emergence of 'substantive rationality' in the judicial process manifests strong contextualization and field dependency. If we therefore characterize a certain pattern of adjudication as a state, we also have to consider this state as an emergent element in the political structure of the Empire. So, we end up with the diagnosis that the institution of contract was part and parcel of the ritual economy.

It is straightforward to recognize that this analysis has far-reaching implications for the comparison with Western developments. The role of contracts in traditional Chinese society has only been discovered and properly assessed in the past three decades of historical research. Contracts are formal documents and obtained a legal status in adjudication. So, we cannot simply characterize ritual as being opposed to law along the lines of 'informal' vs. 'formal institutions'. If we wanted to consider macro-level typologies again, what we meet is an alternative developmental track that differs from both the common law and the civil law regimes in the Western world. This corresponds to the blind spot in the Weberian paradigm that focuses on formal rationality and neglects material or substantive rationality of the legal process. Therefore, our mechanism-focused analysis clearly shows the deficiencies of macro-level theoretical conceptualizations. Yet, at the same time, these can be helpful in pinpointing certain general characteristics of economic style once we have established family resemblances over a larger number of local data and cases. So, for example, highlighting the role of material rationality and justice is a result of considering a larger number of adjudicative processes, which may then be interpreted in the light of more fundamental notions such as field dependency.

All these observations also point to the path dependent nature of institutional changes. In Western and modernist Chinese views on the Imperial state, the impression of stagnation prevails. However, local studies clearly show that this impression is mistaken, if we consider, for example, the rise of the merchant class in local and indirectly also national elite formation in Late Imperial China. The transformative potential of this process becomes visible in the vast number of urban areas that were not administrative seats, so were purest cases of culturalistic and ritualistic governance as a framework for societal self-organization. In other words, the picture of stagnant China fails to recognize the diversity and the dynamics of the local state or local states in the narrow sense. In the final decades of the Empire, this potential found expression in the first steps of bottom-up transitions to local self-government and incipient participatory institutions.

So, what we really refer to when falsely perceiving stagnation and resilience of traditions are patterns of path dependent changes and historicity of institutions. Historicity as reflected in Imperial ideologies creates an image of stasis, yet historicity as a social fact it is a dynamic phenomenon. In this regard, cognitive path dependencies were clearly driving forces, since the ideas and values of culturalistic and ritualistic governance were deeply imbued in individual thought and public discourse, especially in popular religion and related social practices. This fact is certainly reflected in the radical way in which modernist ideologies rapidly became dominant in the twentieth century, explicitly aiming at breaking these cognitive path dependencies. One of the clearest expressions of this was the radical movement against popular religion that gained momentum throughout the twentieth century, reaching a climax during the Cultural Revolution, and only slowly abating in most recent times. As we saw, popular religion is a core symbolic medium by which the different elements of the ritual economy were integrated, such as the family and kinship, the market system and culturalistic governance. Thus, one task of the subsequent chapters is to explore the interaction between institutional design and path dependency in the modernist transformation of the ritual economy. Considering path dependencies in the Imperial era, however, we need to draw attention to the fact that Confucian rule itself was a transformative project that was pursued over centuries. So, one aspect of cognitive path dependency is to look at continuities between this transformative project and the modernist project of the twentieth century.

Path dependencies in the Imperial era certainly include aspects such as the brokerage systems, in which ritual assumed an economic function, so that economic development, in particular the growth of markets, actually contributed to the resilience of ritual. Brokerage builds on social capital, and the formation of social capital is a frequency-dependent network process, because determinants such as reputation and status loom large. So, path dependencies are a manifestation of the mutual reinforcement of markets, social capital and the societal status order. Formal and informal institutions worked together in creating the path dependencies that were actually stabilizing forces in China's local society, and hence the local states, beyond the disruptions of the central state in the nineteenth and twentieth century. Certainly one of the core institutions in this context is the family. The Chinese family was a social and religious institution at the same time, thus differing substantially from the Western model, where religious roles were embedded in the community of believers. The resilience of the family was a constitutive element in the mechanisms of market involution, and the resulting demographic patterns fed back on sustaining the institution of the family via economic incentives. The vehemence with which modernist policies aimed at transforming the Chinese family in the twentieth century reflects the strength of the underlying path dependencies.

Yet, even in this context, path dependencies did not preclude change. One factor is that we should avoid the fallacy to take Confucian models of the family as reality, thus overlooking the flexibility of the institution of the family across various local contexts. This also applies for the larger structures of extended kinship. Local variety allowed for many degrees of freedom in adapting the family to economic circumstances, thus even enabling the evolution of functional equivalences to certain institutions in European modernization, which were however expressed in the idiom of ritual. Considering the sophistication of the traditional market system, this is an important insight because it removes one of the crucial elements of standard institutional explanations of 'failure' in the transition to capitalism. The ritual economy featured markets and corporate structures, and was based on the ubiquity of contracts as a transactional means. In fact, we should say that the institutional path dependencies supported the growth of the market system precisely because they created stability of interactional contexts. In other words, if lineages obtain corporate functions, this is path dependent change in an exemplary way, and we should not take the stability of the symbolic media as an indicator of stasis.

So, summing up, we can arrange a large number of elements that are often associated with 'culture' when referring to Imperial China into a more detailed and complex picture of mechanisms that unfold a dynamics captured by the general framework developed in Chapter 1. This framework leads us to construct an economic style that I call the 'Chinese ritual economy'. To repeat a fundamental point made earlier, this term has a double meaning. One is that I specify Chinese culture in terms of Chinese ritual, the other is that I analyse the specific way in which ritual in the generic and universal sense is manifest in the economic system. Both aspects tie up, because we can say that the difference between the Chinese and the 'Western' economic style may be exactly the way in which the generic functions of ritual are mobilized and deployed by the specific form of Chinese ritual. This double-faced nature of my analysis shows the way to understanding and analysing the transformations of the Chinese ritual economy up until the present.

Notes

1 A salient recent example is the excellent survey by Brandt *et al.* (2014). which explicitly tries to understand the consequences of China's Imperial system in terms of modern China's current economic development, and draws up a list of institutional continuities vs. discontinuities. In this list, certain important features are seen as persisting, especially the authoritarian system and the 'patronage economy' with rampant corruption and irregular taxation, which is diagnosed as one of the most important reasons for China's failure in the past. New elements include the developmental vision and ideology of government (aka 'modernization'), globalization and much greater state capacity in modern China. However, in conclusion, the authors grant that as far as the modern economy is concerned, many observers 'underestimated the strength of China's unconventional system'. One wonders why this does not apply to the Imperial system as well, with the only counter-argument being the proven fact of failure. Success breeds explanations of success, failure suggests explanations of failure. Against this background, it is not convincing that the authors think that the standard explanations based on insecure property rights and corruption are still the strongest ones. Doubts may be justified, even when adopting an immanent position of critique. For example, the authors refer to some works which show that extra tax burdens in old China may have amounted to more than 50 per cent of the official quota. However, at the same time they show that the average tax burden in China was about 3 per cent of the English and the Dutch burdens in the second half of the eighteenth century, and about 7 per cent of the French burden. So, even if the true burden of extra tax payments and corruption was several times higher than the official tax statistics suggest, this would still add up to a much lower burden than in Europe. Actually, the only other substantial evidence offered on the alleged exploitation of the private economy by officials is the study of gentry income by Chang (1962), which of course includes all other sources of

income. Further, the authors also argue that insecure property rights impeded the development of financial instruments. This is just a counter-factual hypothesis, because after all the Imperial government was neither forced nor compelled to develop public debt, which was a prime mover in the emergence of financial markets in Europe, in spite of high risks of default in the context of the competing system of states. So, in sum, this survey of the historical evidence is clearly biased towards the standard Western views on institutional conditions of the rise of the West.

2 For example, Watson's (2004; also Watson and Rawski 1988) notion of 'orthopraxy' was developed partly on the basis of detailed studies of funeral rites in China, investigating the ways in which these were standardized by the Imperial government (for a similar use of the term, see Schmidt-Glintzer 1983). Watson concludes that these practices imply that it did not matter very much what the actual content of the beliefs was that the participants of rites entertain. New ideas and beliefs were highlighted when they induced the emergence of new elements of rites, such as new deities and gods, but if they could be combined with the existing rites this did not matter. Thus, Watson concludes that 'orthodoxy' in the sense of European confessional tensions and conflicts was not an essential value in China. In the sense of Foucault, orthopraxy is hence a specific mechanism of governmentality, especially with regard to the expression and management of local systems of knowledge. However, this remains a hypothesis that may be tested against evidence gained from other local studies, such as Pomeranz (2007), who claims to show that local discourses indeed also made questions of true belief explicit. Interestingly, in his critique, Pomeranz argues that a certain pattern of behaviour is an 'equilibrium' that is undergirded by the interests of different parties involved. So, a notion such as 'orthopraxy' may also become over-generalized, once it is recognized that in local practices the agents of standardization may pursue interests that differ from the Imperial government. In the current context, these critiques may be interpreted as positive evidence about the status of 'orthopraxy' as a hypothesis about mechanisms that can be falsified.

3 Without directly employing the term 'ritual economy', the most important contribution to this view on Chinese economic history is Faure (2006: 3, 93ff.). Faure refers to ritual as a notion that is more narrow and clearly defined as common uses which refer to interpersonal relationships in general, such as in emphasizing 'face' as a core principle in organizing Chinese society. In Faure's view, ritual relates to the principles of kinship organization and hence, specifically, to the forms of incorporation of economic activities and the institutions of property, especially in the context of inheritance. Against this backdrop, he agrees with much of the recent revisionist scholarship on the traditional Chinese economy that highlights the commercial dynamism and the complexity of market organization. In his view, ritual only proved an obstacle to capitalist development in impeding the emergence of modern institutions of financial markets. The term 'ritual economy' proper was employed by Yang (2007) in referring to the fact that in places such as Wenzhou, the rise of unbridled capitalism and the private economy is accompanied by a strong resurgence of popular religion. Popular religion is deeply enmeshed with economic activities, as it requires pecuniary engagements in many forms, such as contributing to temple building. Stafford (2006) uses the term more broadly in referring to Yang's (1994) earlier work on *guanxi*, hence the role of reciprocity and mutual favours in social relationships, and also with reference to Gates' (1996) proposal to analyse the traditional economy as dualist, namely a market economy segment ('petty capitalism') and a segment based on tributary relationships, namely a 'gift economy'. I pull these

different uses of the term 'ritual' together into one coherent concept. For a critical discussion of Gates' alternative dualist model, see Chapter 1, n. 68.

4 This view emerged out of the aforementioned work by Faure (2006) and has been formulated most explicitly by Zelin (2009). Zelin points to two problems in historical research on the past Chinese economy. One is that a lot of information used in earlier times was mediated via the views of early twentieth-century observers, who had already adopted a modernist stance and did not rely on evidence from earlier sources as historians do today; further, experience with Overseas Chinese business was simply extrapolated into the past of Mainland China. The other is that comparisons between Chinese and Western business mostly overlook the fact that Western business operating in China was organized in a very similar way to Chinese business (for example, Jardine & Matheson was a family company involving brothers and cousins), and that therefore the Chinese could actually adopt the 'Western' institutions easily, including allegedly 'modern' ones such as insurance. This observation shows that the actual workings of the traditional institutions were not properly recognized in the historical literature until most recently. So, Zelin shows that if one explores the relatively rare detailed records on actual Chinese business practices in Late Qing China, the alleged differences with Western business at the same time simply evaporate. For example, there were shareholding structures, notions of legal persons and employment of professional managers.

5 This methodological shift is explicitly recognized in Little's (1992) philosophical work on studies of the traditional economy of China. In the general literature on mechanistic explanations in sociology, Little is recognized as one of the early protagonists of the movement of analytical sociology, though mainly for his accompanying methodological work, and less for the China studies part (see e.g. Hedström and Yilikoski 2010; Demeulenaire 2011). Yet, his methodological work is largely shaped by the detailed analysis of research on China. Little argues explicitly against earlier macro-level explanations of Chinese development and especially criticizes any attempt at modelling those explanations according to the covering law notion in the sciences. Instead, he proposes that explanations need to identify causality in terms of specific mechanisms that generate outcomes. This may be related to the analysis of social types, but not in the sense of larger scale macro-aggregates, such as certain notions of 'rational bureaucracy' featuring prominently in Weber's account of European history as 'rationalization'. In other words, researchers should not aim at generalizations about purported macro patterns such as certain kinds of political systems, but look at local-level micro patterns which may be reduplicated in many places, thus resulting in the identification of medium-range causal mechanisms. These could be reinstated cautiously as 'social types', but these types would be much more narrow in scope, such as certain ways of organizing ownership on land or, as in the previous examples, certain ways to supervise and enforce religious behaviours and knowledge. One can identify family resemblances across societies based on such types, but these would never result in society-level comparative propositions.

6 These debates played a major role in early assessments of the Communist revolution. For example, Riskin (1975) distinguished between a 'technological' and a 'distributionist' school in explaining agricultural stagnation in China. These distinctions go back to earlier debates in the 1920s and 1930s, summarized by Myers (1970: 13ff.), who identifies 'distributionist' and 'eclectic theories'. All distributionist schools certainly opted for a radical transformation of ownership in the countryside; however, that might include either land reform or collectivization. Many protagonists of the debate directly linked the issue of distribution to traditional patterns of social structure and

behaviour, as reflected in ritual, in emphasizing the lack of entrepreneurial and technological motivation on the part of the rural elites, who, according to this view, invested surplus mainly in ritual expenses and private consumption which may also be seen as ritualized status consumption. Therefore, the CCP did not expect much from mere land reform without simultaneously radically revolutionizing social structure, i.e. modernizing rural society. These competing explanations of agricultural underdevelopment remain influential to this day, so that the discussion has never been finally resolved (compare the overview in Richardson 1999: 6ff.).

7 The ubiquity of symbols of old China is evident to everyone who switches on Chinese TV and stumbles into one of the historical drama series. However, even highest level leaders refer to traditional Chinese philosophy, such as Hu Jintao when explaining the concept of 'harmony' in recent Chinese politics, directly quoting the Confucian expression 'he wei gui' (和为贵) (www.china.com.cn/chinese/news/899546.htm (accessed 15 May 2014)). It should be noted that this kind of reference is not just ideological phrasing but goes hand in hand with many grassroots-level activities. I will go into more detail later, but with reference to Confucianism suffice it to mention the spread of Confucian movements and academies such as the *Yidan xuetang* (see Billioud 2011), the organization of Confucian summer schools and reading clubs for schoolchildren (Zhao 2013) or the use of Confucianism in efforts to build corporate culture, with highly visible examples such as the FOTILE corporation (Fang 2013).

8 Huang (2015) gives the important example of the continuing synthesis between formal law and traditional morality in the context of family law. According to traditional conceptions, the patrilineal family line dominates the marriage relationship. Although in modern Chinese law gender equality is enshrined, there are important aspects in inheritance regulations which still maintain the traditional assumptions. For instance, regarding home ownership there is no right for the spouse to directly claim the shared home with her partner in case of passing ('joint tenancy with right of survivorship'). Huang argues that this is not simply a resilience of particular traditional values, but manifests a systematic alternative to the Weberian notion of formal-rational law, coined 'substantive-rational' law by Huang. Interestingly, this difference is also reflected in popular opinions (see Davis 2010): Whereas the new Marriage Law introduces strong notions of individual property and contractual arrangements in regulating conflicts over the allocation of assets in case of divorce, popular opinion highlights moral aspects, such as future needs of parties. Since most conflicts are regulated without invoking courts, these moral notions may have a stronger impact on the actual workings of property rights mechanisms than the formal law.

9 This idea is upheld by most economists, and has been most clearly defined by North (1990). North is important in our context because he recognizes the two principles of social organization, namely formal and informal institutions, and accepts the ordering role of the latter. But he claims that these can only maintain a 'bazaar economy', that is, a commercial economy, but not industrial capitalism. This opinion is shared by many authors, even if they show, as in Greif (1994), that in a similar context (here, medievial long-distance trade) formal and informal institutions can be functionally equivalent. However, Greif also states that only the formal institutions allow for the continuous expansion of scope and reach of markets (on his anthropological misperceptions of the Arabic traders' extended kinship networks, see White (2011), who, similar to the recent revisionist literature on China, emphasizes the functional equivalences). So, Greif also concludes in the case of China (Greif and

Tabellini 2010) that particularistic ethics enshrined in kinship norms was a major obstacle to development in Imperial China.

10 In the long list of competing explanations of the 'European miracle', in a number of papers Kuran (e.g. 2012) has highlighted the role of corporatization, historically going back to the establishment of formal organizations by the Catholic church. This model was then transferred into a business organization and created the notion of a 'legal person', thus partly cutting the link between personal wealth and corporate assets, thereby allowing for the emergence of legal constructs such as limited liability. However, apparently this theory also suffers from weaknesses in terms of identifying causal mechanisms properly. In fact, corporatization may have evolved early in terms of legal creations, but it played a small factual role in the emergence of capitalism, only serving as a stabilizing factor in its later expansion. The vast majority of firms in British industrialization were family companies or partnerships with full liability; in fact, as a result of earlier financial crises the government was reluctant to allow for the application of the legal construct of 'corporation' for private business, reflected in legal measures such as the so-called 'Bubble Act' (cf. Mokyr 2009: 357f.). The legal framework for joint stock companies was only created in 1844, and limited liability was only introduced in 1855. In other words, these legal phenomena cannot be an essential part of explaining the Industrial Revolution. Furthermore, businesspeople applied many legal tricks to circumvent these restrictions, so that this is even evidence undermining the institutional explanation of industrialization. The resulting businesses operated without legal protection and had to rely on a moral code of honour in order to be effective. So, business organizations did not differ substantially from the Chinese case (see Zelin 2009; cf. Gardella 2004). This explains the ease with which British and Chinese merchants could cooperate across linguistic and cultural borders, with Chinese merchants actually dominating the British trade with China, even in terms of financial arrangements (see Hao 1986: 216ff., 245ff.).

11 Ocko (2004) evaluates the common claims that one central impediment of capitalist development in China was the opaqueness and limited enforcement of property rights. In doing this, he recognizes that such evaluations reflect the central normative role of property in Western political philosophy and ideology. This is not fully reflected in Western realities, as in particular the theorists of relational contracting have emphasized. Seminal contributions such as Ellickson (1991) have shown that also in Western countries, customary rules or contextualized arrangements for resolving social conflicts often dominate formal law. So, we meet a 'mirror of culture' constellation where Western theories even cause misperceptions of Western realities, and corresponding accounts of Chinese development actually serve to support the normative view of the Western system. Further, many Chinese practices appear to be rational and efficient arrangements in distinguishing neatly between different aspects of property rights, especially with regard to land transactions, on which the revisionist view was seminally launched by Chen and Myers (1970), and were submitted to court procedures depending on the perceived costs and benefits of these transactions by the different affected parties. In addition, many customary rules ('informal institutions' according to North) were actually cast into written form and even partly submitted to courts as reference material. Thus, Chinese practice simply reflected a different standard for prioritizing aspects of social and political order, such as the maintenance of stable social relationships through time, especially in local society. In other words, in China the enforcement of formal institutions explicitly paid attention to local conflict resolution mechanisms that Ellickson diagnoses as being

the blind spot in Western economic theories of law. Kennedy (2013b) adopts the same position with regard to modern China in criticizing the mainstream economic literature on property rights that emphasizes efficiency. He argues that this reflects the neglect of the role of property rights in resolving social conflicts and defining an initial distribution of assets and benefits in society. 'Clarity' of property rights can also contribute to heightened levels of social and legal conflicts in society, such that participants may rationally avoid this in order to enable contextualized solutions, which effectively increase efficiency.

12 Under the founding dynasty, the Qin, the precedent was set that law is an instrument of the state to impose public order upon society based on punishment. So, this tradition survived in the penal code and also in administrative law, but in all other domains the Confucians aimed at legal minimalism, in the sense of keeping the number and extent of laws as small as possible, and also refraining from establishing a systematic role for the judiciary. As Vandermeersch (1985) explains in great detail, however, this does not mean that formal regulations played no role. On the contrary, the Empire was governed based on an evolving collection of edicts and other rules promulgated by the Emperor, and which were expressions of ritual. These collections mainly define administrative praxis, hence state–society relations, and reflected the belief that the state represents the cosmic order of society. However, they were not used to promulgate laws in the narrow sense, especially as default regulations of relationships between citizens. That being said, it is also necessary to recognize that the term for law, *fa*, is in fact referring to a generic notion of rule, so that Yao (2012a) introduces the term 'li fa' (礼法) when referring to ritual. For example, many conflicts in the civil domain would be regulated in the lineage context, based on formal lineage rules. But these rules were also strongly shaped by the Imperial state in setting standards. Therefore, earlier authors such as Bünger (1983) were already highly cognitive of the special nature of law in China and its high level of development, though on a different track than the European one. Partly, one can certainly account for this legal minimalism as an efficient and adaptive response to governing a large and growing society, especially under the Qing. Huang (2008) therefore coined the term 'centralized minimalism' to characterize this system. Specifically, this refers to the activation of semi-formal local elites in governing society who actively mediate between local customs and context on the one hand and the formal bureaucracy and the law on the other. This approach amounts to a kind of 'Confucianized Legalism'.

13 As Vandermeersch (1985) also emphasizes, the central difference between law as in instrument of rule and ritual is the notion that ritual is followed 'naturally', 'ziran' (自然). This means, on the one hand, that notions such as 'liberty' or 'rights' do not play a role, yet the ritual is not enforced in society, as it reflects a natural order of cosmos and society. In this sense, the Chinese concept also includes a place for liberty. Bünger (1983: 160) makes the important point that this different concept may reflect the fact that especially in comparison to England, the state was never as intrusive towards local society in China, so that similar notions of positioning and battling for rights may not have been necessary intellectual responses. Indeed, as Foucault (1997) has elaborated in great detail, the early English emergence of notions of rights may actually reflect the ethnic tensions between Anglo-Saxons and Normans in the early Middle Ages, and hence the specific history of confronting competing claims on legitimacy and dominance. Similar tensions may not have worked out in Chinese history. The notion of a natural order and the specific idea of 'wu wei' may even have influenced the emergence of Western

liberalism, in particular via the physiocrats, as has been argued by Chinese (Sheng 2010) and Western (Gerlach 2005) scholars. There was a direct intellectual impact of Confucianism and the reports about Chinese government practices by the Jesuits upon pivotal thinkers such as Quesnay (Priddat 2001: 87ff.), and notions of natural order also transpired via Chinese aesthetics, such as the images, as Gerlach points out, on pieces of Chinese porcelain that were especially appreciated in the regions where modern capitalism originated, such as the Netherlands, depicting nature as a harmoniously balanced aesthetic experience, thus reflecting the notion of *ziran*.

14 One of the most evident expressions of the ritualistic notion of law was the adaption of penal grades to the relative ritual status of individuals, such that, for example, a crime committed by a son against his father would be punished by much harsher means than the same crime committed by the father against his son. The notion of 'governance', 'zhili' (治理) is championed in Yao's (2012a, 2012b) approach to 'constitutionalism' in feudal and Imperial China. This matches the aforementioned other conceptual approaches, such as the 'centralized minimalism' notion put forward by Huang (2008). Whereas 'government' would be seen as directly designing and intervening in society reaching down to the local and grassroots level, 'governance' focuses on indirect rule mediated by social norms and customary law, thus shaping the incentives and constraints under which societal self-organization operates.

15 The perception of Chinese lineages in the Western literature was strongly biased by Maurice Freedman's work on lineages in Hong Kong. Historically, as Faure (2007) has shown, Guangdong was a region in China where Neoconfucian ideas about kinship exerted a strong impact, reflecting the aim of the Imperial government to create stable social conditions in a frontier region. In propagating those norms, officials met with positive responses from local elites who could bolster their power position in relying on such official sources of legitimacy. So, Faure even suggests that these norms come close to incipient concepts of 'national citizenship'. Freedman combined these notions with established concepts of lineages in existing anthropological research in his time, which was strongly influenced by the British school working on African lineages (Watson and Watson 2004: 274). As Stafford (2000) shows, in doing this, he created a picture that is highly biased in terms of actual social structures. As I discuss in the following section, one important aspect is regional variation, which, against the backdrop of Freedman's model, has been largely interpreted as the absence of lineages in North China. However, as Cohen (1990) made clear, this may also indicate that the underlying model of kinship structures was misleading. The same applies for gender relations, where we also face the difficulty of how regional variations relate to the basic model: are they 'local deviations', or are they falsifications of the model? For example, Stafford points towards Wolf's (1972) concept of the 'uterine family' and argues that the model itself operates as a filter of the ethnographic data, simply neglecting the wealth of information, even cast into paradigmatic terms such as Wolf's, that contradicts the standard model. For example, beyond the uterine family, in real-world Chinese kinship interactions, affinal ties are almost as important as agnatic ties, and wives have often maintained close interactions with their native places (seminally on this: Judd 1989). In Xiao's (2001: 60f., 415) comparative study of nine villages in Jiangxi and Anhui there are many forms of interaction between both agnatic and affinal kin, such as mutual help. Interestingly, this is also true for historical times: Ebrey (1986: 45ff.) notes that one major motivation for developing the practice of genealogies was not tracing agnatic descent, but keeping an overview about the affinal relationships created via marriage.

16 The debates about the validity of Weber's views on China have a long pedigree; see the overview by Schluchter (1983). The fundamental problem with Weber's views is that on the one hand, he recognized the fundamentally different nature of the Chinese society and body politic in comparison with the Western developments; yet he ultimately obtained normative standards for evaluating Chinese realities only from the latter. As a result, he fell back on a quasi-Hegelian linear concept of history in which China assumed a particularly negative role, in the sense of incorporating 'irrationality' despite the presence of advanced political and administrative structures. So, for example, for him the complex interplay between formal and customary law boiled down to quadi justice; or, the inner-worldly orientation of Confucianism was interpreted as a complete lack of transformative tension and effort. Weber's views were certainly partly influenced by the fact that his description of China was a mix of references to early stages of development and some fragmentary observation on more recent periods. So, he was unaware of the dynamism after the Song dynasty, and could not appreciate developments such as urbanization in the context of the market system (Elvin 1983). He also lacked insight into the actual practices and perceptions of bureaucratic elites (Metzger 1973). Yet, it is this tension that is internal to the Weberian picture which allows one to reconstruct a positive Weberian evaluation of China. Recently, Lai (2015) follows up with Philip Huang's ideas about the blind spot in Weber's thought that does not recognize a possible role for substantive rationality. This corresponds to deeper strands in European intellectual history highlighted by Hayek's distinction between constructivist law and evolving rules. The Weberian picture of rationalization only emphasizes the former; this implies that we can turn Weber's blind spot into a positive insight about a fully fledged alternative to Western developments.

17 This hypothesis has been proposed in a very systematic way by Nisbett (2003) and is referred to by many influential researchers, such as Yamagishi (2012). I have already outlined the basic reasoning in Chapter 1, n.23: the idea is that living in agricultural communities which centre on rice agriculture fosters high cognitive sensitivity for context. It is important to note that this argument does not presuppose that individuals are active in rice agriculture, but that there are path dependencies which shape certain attitudes and cognitive stances in the respective communities. Needless to say, in the Chinese case the argument raises interesting questions because rice agriculture was only becoming dominant after shifting the economic centre of gravity to the south, thus creating the ecological dichotomy between north and south China, which would imply that in north China a lesser degree of field dependence has prevailed also in the past, as has been confirmed empirically for modern conditions by Talhelm *et al.* (2014). After all, Fei Xiaotong himself grew up in Jiangsu province, so would have received the impact of 'rice culture'. I discussed the theoretical foundation of these arguments in Chapter 1. At this point, I only add that ultimately evolutionary explanations hold, along the lines of Hallpike's (1986: 288ff.) analysis of 'core principles' of societies which emerge during early periods and which exert a deep channelling impact upon further institutional and cultural developments.

18 Fei Xiaotong belonged to the early generation of Chinese scholars who received academic education in the West, studying for a Ph.D. in anthropology at London School of Economics under the supervision of eminent scholars such as Radcliffe-Brown and Malinowksi. He later returned to China, implementing classical village studies (Fei 1939; Fei and Chi 1945). In 1947, he published his short book *Xiangtu zhongguo* which was eventually translated into English and published in 1988. In this work, he raised a number of

substantial comparative points; however, the reception was mostly driven by his approach to China. His term is widely cited by Chinese researchers, yet it has not had a great impact on Western literature, especially beyond the narrow field of Chinese anthropology (cf. the discussion by Harrell 2011). Harrell points out that the leading scholar in shaping Western views on Chinese kinship as a core of Chinese society, Maurice Freedman, never read Chinese, so he was not aware of the highly original contribution by Fei that directly discussed the problems of using the established notions of 'lineage' with regard to China.

19 Corresponding to Fei's reasoning, there is considerable confusion about the proper translation of 'lineage' into Chinese, so that, vice versa, the identification of 'lineages' in the Chinese context can also be difficult, depending on the usages of Chinese terms. This question is of considerable significance in assessing historical developments, also in terms of their consequences for the present. One aspect of this problem is the common view that lineages have been weak in north China and strong in south China, especially in areas such as Fujian and Guangdong. However, this observation largely refers to organizations denoted as 'clans', 'zongzu' (宗族). Fei does not use this term at all, whereas today the term is the standard one used by Chinese anthropologists writing about lineages (see e.g. Zhou 2003). Historically, Clans were largely urban phenomena (see Baker 1977). In fact, the *zongzu* refers to what Fei calls *shizu*, and corresponds to the notion of lineage in Maurice Freedman's work that has shaped Western China studies for decades (see n. 15 above). Historically, Ebrey (1986) speaks of 'descent groups' which corresponds to the most general notion of 'agnate', 'zu' (族). Over the centuries, descent groups developed group identities via certain shared rituals, especially regarding worshipping ancestors at graveyards on the occasion of the *Qingming* holiday. In comparison, in early times the *jia* was seen as a co-residential kinship group, which was elevated to an ideal referring back to the *zong* of pre-Imperial times. However, this ideal was rarely realized even by the elites who propagated it. The notion of lineage in the sense of the Western anthropological literature on China only emerged after Song times, connected to the practice of establishing endowments and lineage estates. So, as indicated by Ebrey and Watson (1986), the conceptual muddle may be clarified for the historical etymology in the following way. The *jia* is an economically active kin group in managing collective assets, the *zu* is the group of agnates (however, including the perspective on the matrilateral connection), and the *zong* is the formal principle of agnatic descent. In practice, this implied that a *zong* would be a higher level aggregation of lineages or even a grouping that is not based on genuine kinship but on surname only (which relates to the term *shi* which Fei uses, and which historically was only referring to a group sharing the same surname). Coming back to the distinction between north and south China, this clearly reflects a great variety of kinship structures and patterns of group formation in both historical and recent times (Watson and Watson 2004). Taken together, these more recent conceptual developments confirm Fei's fundamental theoretical viewpoint.

20 Of course, this is a very superficial account of Western intellectual history. One of the most explicit treatments supporting this interpretation is Elias (1969a: xlviff.). Elias uses the term '*homo clausus*', referring to the secular trend towards analytical atomism in understanding human social life. This is also what Taylor (1989: 195ff., 305ff.) emphasizes. The mainstream trend in Western thinking is focused on the individual, its expressions of inner states, its subjective rights and so forth. The sidestream movement, with recurrent expressions, such as in recent communitarian thinking in the US context, is

what Taylor calls the 'republican' or 'civic-humanist' approach which sees individuals as being embedded in civic communities, and which therefore have certain moral priorities in terms of civic duties. In Elias' account, this is linked to larger patterns of civilizational development, in the sense of increasing constraints of physical interactions between individuals, such as in social mores about hygiene and eating, or interpersonal violence (for a modern confirming view on this, see Pinker 2011: 59). In social thought, the *homo clausus* assumption means that individuals are constituted independent from social context, thus, for example, claiming individual rights as a precondition of entering sociality. This is certainly the leading idea in economics, but here we may also observe how certain cultural developments even lead towards a biased reconstruction of intellectual history. So, economists normally claim Adam Smith as being the father of the individualist approach, but actually the 'Theory of Moral Sentiments' posits a primordial sociality of the human person. I cannot go into detail here (see Herrmann-Pillath 2015), but suffice it to say that atomism permeates all theorizing in social theory until the present day, such as in the shape of dualisms as 'agency vs. structure'. Attempts at dissolving the individualist focus largely assume apparently radical shapes, such as in recent Actor–Network Theory (Latour 2005). The notion of 'agencement' explicitly dissolves the clear boundary between network structure and individual, and posits that agency is located in localized network processes. In comparison, standard social network theory assumes that nodes and connections are analytically separable. Interestingly, Chau (2013) applies ANT to the case of popular religion in Taiwan, thus revealing possibly affinities in conceptual deep structures between ANT and Chinese perceptions of agency in networks.

21 There have been long and intensive debates about the nature of Chinese ethics, which often also refer back to Weber's opinion that there was a lack of 'rationality' and 'tension' in Chinese ethical thinking. However, one can certainly say that Confucianism entails a set of universalistic ethical notions that directly compare with similar notions in Western ethics, such as the much-cited Golden Rule. The Golden rule builds on a universal notion of humanity, epitomized in the concept of 'ren' (仁). *Ren* is not simply a particularistic norm, although its concretization operates via the fulfilment of obligations in contextualized social environments. In his careful assessment, Roetz (1992) argues that Chinese ethics had already entered a 'post-conventionalist' stage with the early Confucian thinkers who focused on the Self as an autonomous moral agent, with notions such as 'perfecting the Self' or 'scrutinizing the Self'. Bloom (2004) supports this view in highlighting the many instances where early Confucian thinkers referred to their inner thoughts and emotions when expressing tension with the moral decay of the outer world and the need to take expressive action against this, later typically symbolized in remonstrations of ministers in the face of the Emperor. Ultimately, ethical norms relate to a universalistic moral notion of cosmological status, the 'dao' (道) (this point is central to modern restatements of Confucianism as ethical doctrine; see e.g. the Taiwanese philosopher Li Ruiquan (2014)). Metzger (1977) therefore has convincingly argued that Confucian ethics were based on an 'inner-worldly tension', which in a sense was resolved with even stronger moral rigidity precisely because Chinese ethics requires the recognition of the currently prevailing moral order as a basic condition for sociality, thus closing the door to transcendental escapism and redemption.

22 On this point, see Fei (1947: 30ff.). Following Fei Xiaotong, in modern Chinese studies the term *li shang wanglai* has been made the linchpin of Chang's (2010) analysis of social relations in the rural areas. Chang puts it in

contrast to other research on social networks, mostly emphasizing *guanxi*. She argues that the notion of ritual in this context is far broader, both in terms of scope (for example, even including the afterworld) and detail. The term *li shang wanglai* originates from the prototypical text about rites, the Li Ji (礼记，曲礼), with the famous expression: 往而不来非礼也。来而不往亦非礼也. In this context, it referred to the web of mutual obligation among the elites in China's pre-Imperial feudal society. Therefore, in terms of ideological history we need to recognize similar interactions between early social structure and ideology in European feudalism, such as with reference to the role of contracts. Therefore, it would be very misleading to see ritual as informal institutions. In fact, as Yao (2012a: 71) argues and mentioned previously, the rites are a formal institution as well, and therefore uses the term 'lifa' (礼法); for example (Yao 2012b: 623ff.), there were formal organizations enforcing the rites, there were ritual experts and so forth. The difference between Fei's and Yao's view lies in Fei referring to the rural context exclusively, although he also emphasizes the role of customary law. Yao also refers to customary law, but that does not preclude formalization. So, what Fei describes is the truncated version of ritual that remained once the revolution of 1911 and the efforts at modernization had abolished the governmental and educational superstructure. Following Vandermeersch (1985), it is therefore important to establish the proper references for the traditional Chinese terms. *Fa* is a term denoting formal institutions, but not 'law' in the sense of particular legal norms (which are 'lü' (律)). So, Yao puts the term *fa* on the same level as the Western notion of constitution. He refers the ideas directly to the Hayekian distinction between *nomos* and *thesis*, with *nomos* referring to historically evolved rules, and *thesis* to designed institutions, hence *li* as *nomos* and *fa* as *thesis* (cf. Chapter 1, n. 46).

23 In the Western philosophical tradition, the question of universality of law looms large, following up the Kantian legacy in ethics. In this view, particularism is always secondary and less preferable to universalism. Although this opinion is certainly the dominant view, especially in the more popularized versions such as the common thinking about human rights, it was finally refuted by Hegel in his Kant critique. Interestingly, Hegel's view is deeply economic, as he shows that mere universalistic rules will always suffer from a deficit in setting working incentives for action following the rules. Incentivization always implies contextualization. So, in spite of the fact that Hegel is a strict and rigorous philosopher of the 'rule of law' and of 'civil society', he also shows that law needs to be rooted in notions of 'ethical life' which are peculiar to time and space. Ethical life are the evolved norms of certain people in history, and thus appear to be particularistic on first sight. Yet, only ethical life and law together can establish social order. As I argued Chapter 1, we can therefore equate ethical life with ritual (see Chapter 1, n. 47). Hegel's ideas are experiencing a strong revival today in practical ethics (e.g. Pippin 2008) or in dealing with the problem of global norms facing cultural diversity (e.g. Buchwalter 2012).

24 Stafford (2000) therefore proposes a different model which is also reciprocated by Chang (2010). According to this model, the central notion is the term 'yang' (养), which means to 'nourish', 'grow' or even 'create'. We can directly relate this term to the notion of social capital and hence simply argue that Chinese ritual is the set of rules in how to create social capital. These activities are governed by reciprocity. For example, even within the family the general idea is that parents care for their children, and that therefore children are obliged to take care of their parents in old age. According to Stafford, this is not fully congruent with the notion of filial piety, as it can also

apply for non-kin. Thus, it can be *yang* activities that create quasi-kinship, and kinship may lose force if there is no *yang*. Interestingly, Gui (2014: 30ff.) argues that there is a close correlation between the degree of 'modernization' and the activation of reciprocal exchange across villages with different social structures. Villages with strong kinship organization do not do as many and as regular *wanglai* activities compared to villages with higher mobility and fragmented kinship structure. So, according to this perspective, modernization actually fosters the allegiance to traditional forms of social relations beyond kinship.

25 On this and the following, see Chapter 1, n. 17, n. 22 and n. 23. In cross-cultural research, the notion of field dependence resembles Hall's (1976) classical distinction between 'low context' and 'high context' societies. However, the term in cognitive science is more closely related to anthropology and biology, and is based on experimental evidence of different sorts. As already reported in Chapter 1, n. 17, this includes classical experiments such as the 'rod and frame' test, where test persons assess the slope of a vertical line relative to the floor in a moving frame. Field-dependent cognition means that people are strongly biased by the frame in these assessments, whereas field-independent cognition is evident in people assessing the slope correctly independent of the frame. In the corresponding linguistic tests, field-dependent individuals emphasize relationships against categorial assignments. In his comprehensive overview of these experiments, Nisbett (2003) gives an interpretation that provides the basis for my use in the context of this chapter. Yamagishi (2012; see Chapter 1, n.22) seems to concur, even though in his ecological approach to culture he argues that certain value orientations of people are contextualized via incentives. Yet, he also thinks that the way these incentives are perceived may be determined by more foundational cognitive stances.

26 Distributed cognition or extended mind theorists question the standard equation between mind and brain, beginning with seminal contributions such as Clark and Chalmers (1998). The general idea is that cognitive operations often involve external entities in order to save operation costs or to open up qualitatively new operations. This can simply mean that cognition operates indirectly in analysing certain properties of the world, such as when predicting the ballistic curve of a flying object. In our context, it refers more narrowly to the creation of artefacts that interact with the brain in enabling new cognitive performances. For example, inventing numbers and relating these to certain objects such as coins enables quantitative valuations of otherwise incommensurable objects (on numbers, see Clark 2011: 50ff.). Writing is an artefact which enables new reflexive operations of thought, thus creating opportunities for increasing complexity, among other effects (Menary 2007). Further, distributed cognition also involves social interaction, as has been recognized in Hutchins' (1995) classical study of navigation. This implies that there is also feedback between social organization and cognition, which may also be relevant for the Chinese case. I am not aware of any applications of this argument to different writing technologies, however.

27 My argument closely follows Ledderose (2000). Ledderose shows how Chinese arts, handicrafts and architecture basically reflect the technology of writing: The general idea is that a limited number of 'modules' allows for the unlimited generation of individual variants of composites. For example, in architecture the basic wooden building blocks of temples were often standardized, but could be arranged in flexible ways to create a unique building. In porcelain manufacture, design features such as flowers could be multiplied in many ways, thus enabling veritable mass production in spite of failing to achieve economies of scale in a factory type of production. The notion of religious

polytropy has been explored by Chau (2011, 2012) in a number of papers. The term has been coined by the anthropologist Carrithers with reference to India. In the Chinese context, polytropy means that there are different 'modalities in doing religion', as Chau puts it, such as textual modalities, or activities related to events in the life cycle. So, for particular purposes, individuals might approach Buddhist ritual experts (especially for 'white' events, namely funerals), and for others, Daoists (such as health-related concerns and exorcisms).

28 I will discuss the issue of 'individualism' extensively in Chapter 5. The background to the philosophical debates about the Chinese self were the theories about 'dependency' that had been proposed in the 1960s and 1970s in order to explain the phenomenon of Maoism, in particular Solomon (1971). These were matched with theories about a lack of moral autonomy, as aired by scholars such as Wilson (1981), who referred to theories about moral development, in particular Kohlberg's, which would classify Chinese moral behaviour as staying in the 'conventional' stage (see Roetz 1992). However, as I have already pointed out, these opinions were refuted by scholars such as Metzger (1977) who posited 'interdependence' as a paradigm for understanding moral autonomy of the individual in China. Hall and Ames (1998) present their analysis of the 'focus field self' in emphasizing the externalist and expressivist thinking of traditional Chinese philosophy: in other words, 'inner' and 'outer' are not separated, and ritual is a medium through which the self can create itself via action. In this deeply interactionist setting, values such as 'sincerity' and 'truthfulness' clearly indicate the deep moral tension which drives the aspirations of the individual to become a 'genuine person' or 'gentleman'. However, these tensions were not placed in a transcendental context, but remained embedded in this-worldly action.

29 The classical study of ritual in urban organization is Rowe (1989). One can trace back the evolution of pre-modern urban systems partly also to social conflict about prerogatives of scholar-officials in the Imperial state, with complex outcomes (see e.g. von Glahn 1991a). Conflicts over taxation and labour service pitted local populations, local elites and the Imperial state against each other, which partly also contributed to the general tax reforms under the Ming dynasty. Although these movements did not result in establishing a formal legal role for cities, it certainly contributed to the emergence of merchants as a core group in urban governance, as described by Rowe. A most interesting more recent example is colonial Hong Kong. Clearly, the British government introduced the Western law into local society, thereby fostering the emergence of a hybrid regime (for a detailed account, see Chan 1991). Hong Kong society emerged out of a continuous inflow of migrants from all over China, but this resulted in sheer complexity and opaqueness of local conditions, such that the colonial rulers had to rely on the co-optation of local elites in imposing order. These merchant elites did not rely on Western law in establishing cooperation and civilizing local society, but on ritual, even to the extent that merchants actively pursued insignia and status by the Imperial Court, and posed as scholar-officials in local society. Typical patterns also known from other Chinese cities emerged, such as centring local governance on the organization of welfare activities, which were rallying points of what we would call 'civil society' today.

30 For a detailed account of the role of the Jesuits in shaping the European picture of China, see Mungello (1999). Lagerwey (2010: 2ff.) analyses the intellectual foundations of this exchange. At the Imperial Court the Jesuits met with the Neoconfucian elite who maintained a critical distance from popular religion and Daoism, aiming at a civilizational transformation of the

lifeworld of the Chinese people top-down. In adopting this attitude, they converged with the Jesuits' understanding of their own role in the Catholic Church. Therefore, the Jesuits easily received an interpretation of the Imperial Rites as a civic ritual, thus downplaying its religious dimensions. This resulted in the classification of the ancestral cult as a transformational project without essential transcendental meanings, but mainly as a form of practical ethics. This matched the Confucian aim of 'educating' the people. Clearly, this picture conformed to a rationalist interpretation of the Chinese body politic, which was then extolled by leading thinkers of the European enlightenment, such as in Germany Wolff or in France Voltaire (Mungello 1999: 87ff.). Neoconfucianism was seen as coming close to the Deist thinking favoured by the rationalists. Indeed, intellectual distance from popular rites was already a hallmark of Confucius himself who did not express the belief that in the ancestral rites ancestors would really be present as transcendental beings. This attitude was consistently expressed in Neoconfucian efforts to control and even transform popular religion. Interestingly, in this European literature the physiocrats, with Quesnay as an intellectual leader, received the Confucian idea that the state should concentrate on agriculture as the basis of the economy and should adopt a non-interventionist approach. So, China appeared as a model of the modern Western state, with a rational civil service and a liberal economy.

31 A very pronounced, even polemic statement in this line of thinking is Landes (2006). Landes highlights the intellectual inertia of the Chinese elites in developing the indigenous potential of scientific and technological knowledge as well as in receiving Western technology. This account matches the version of European economic history presented by Mokyr (2009) which also emphasizes the intellectual and social underpinnings of European industrialization, such as the widespread belief in progress and the idea that science can contribute to the improvement of the living conditions of mankind. In this respect, Landes certainly catches an important aspect of Chinese history, as demand for sophisticated technology was largely driven by the appreciation of luxury products for the Imperial elites. The best example is watchmaking. In Europe, pocket watches became a product that served as an investment and savings vehicle and as a status also for the broad masses, simultaneously spreading values in appreciating technological sophistication and rationalizing time management (see De Vries 2008: 1ff.), whereas watches in China were a favourite object of Imperial collections. This is just one aspect of the fact that China did not develop many of the institutions that supported the diffusion of technological knowledge in England, in particular, such as educational bodies, professional associations or scientific clubs of laypeople, as described by Mokyr. Indeed, one of the impressions that Europeans noted after the Jesuit period in cross-cultural contact was the absence of progressivist attitudes in China and the widespread belief in civilizational supremacy which fostered the conviction that China already represented a zenith of human development.

32 Faure (2006: 73ff.) points out that the historical correspondence of the modern term for contract, 'hetong' (合同) is the term 'bao' (包), which is also used in 'chengbao' (承包) in modern China to describe the arrangements in the responsibility system. Many practices in the countryside that were instituted as reforms actually reproduced patterns of contractual relations before 1949, such as when lineage trusts auctioned off use rights of fish-ponds (see Potter and Potter 1990: 173f.). I will discuss these similarities later in detail. The *chengbao* model was also followed in the different ways of quasi-privatizing township and village enterprises as transformations of the rural

industries of the People's Communes. In the state-owned sector, contracts were introduced as the first step of reforms, such as in defining enlarged autonomy of directors in factory-based responsibility systems. As long as SOEs delivered both taxes and profits to government agencies, contracts were the main medium in which those obligations were defined, thus partly obfuscating the boundaries between tax and profit.

33 For exemplary studies of the continuities in using contracts, see Cohen's work on contracts of family division in rural China which allows us to track these continuities directly. Cohen (2004) offers a detailed study of contracts in a Taiwan area during the nineteenth century that were used by Hakka settlers speaking Han-Chinese. These contracts covered all important aspects of family life, with marriage according to standard Confucian norms displaying a more ritual and religious dimension, and most other types of economic arrangements expressed in more mundane and practical terms. Contracts about family division were generally signed before the death of parents and hence are arrangements between parents and sons about both the division of the family assets and the provisioning of support for parents in old age. Ritual obligations loom large in terms of perceiving the family assets as being owned by the family and not by the individual family members. However, obviously these obligations did not suffice to make them sufficiently binding, so that the contractual medium was almost always used. In comparison, Cohen (1992) offers detailed information about family division in Hebei in the 1980s (for another example of a family division contract, see Xiao 2001: 72f.). As in the Taiwan case, Hebei villagers regarded the family as the unit of ownership and often resorted to contracts in arranging the division of family assets. These contracts are signed by the brothers and arrange for the relationship between communal and private property and for the support of the parents. The contracts are very similar to the contracts drawn up in nineteenth-century Taiwan, especially with regard to the degree of detail and also the role of witnesses.

34 Many observers have noted the strange fact that in spite of the universal use of contracts in Chinese society, the Qing legal code was silent on this institution (Zelin 2004a). The rapid diffusion of the institution of contracts in Song times has been studied extensively by Hansen (1995), which reflected the general trend of marketization and innovation. Contracts differed in their nature depending on the role of official recognition. For the most important kinds of contracts, those on land transactions, a distinction was made between ordinary contracts and those with a magistrate's 'red' seal; the latter also implied registration for tax purposes (Osborne 2004). It is important to recognize that over the centuries standard forms of contract evolved that were specific to different kinds of transactions, such as loans or land transactions, and which were uniform across the country (for a study of different contract types in nineteenth-century Taiwan, see Brockman 1980/1996). In other words, these standards served as a functional substitute for explicit legal regulations.

35 Apart from witnesses, another important group of people who signed a contract even though they were not parties themselves are the middlemen (see many examples in Chen and Myers 1976a, 1976b). I will discuss the role of middlemen in the following section, so suffice it to note here that in both cases the social network that undergirds and contextualizes the underlying transaction is explicitly formalized. Thus, these groups could be summoned by judges in case of legal conflicts; this also gave them a role in efforts of mediating between the parties. A special kind of middlemen were the guarantors in loan transactions. According to Duara (1988: 181ff.), middlemen could come from a different background, including professional agents, but were

often people with a local reputation, so that aspects of social networks such as face were directly activated in the contractual construction.

36 Huang (1993) therefore introduced the notion of the 'third realm'. He distinguishes between formal and informal justice and argues that the state and society were mainly interacting within the third realm in which both were combined. Certainly some areas of social life were mainly regulated by ritual and might rarely come into contact with formal adjudication, such as family division in the lineage context. But even then one should not forget that lineage rules were deeply shaped by the state over centuries. When parties submitted a case to the Magistrate, the third domain was apparent in the strong role of processes of mediation that were triggered by that very act. Thus, even without formal adjudication the parties acted 'under the shadow of the law', which, in this case, is embodied in the Magistrate. Here, as Buoye (2004) has forcefully argued, Weber's notion of 'qadi justice' is seriously misleading, as the magistrates referred to the Qing code where possible, and normally collected information meticulously in order to establish the truth (see also Allee 2004: 173). In this context, written documents such as contracts assumed a central role. Other media of the third domain were the activities of the so-called 'xiangbao' (乡保), members of local elites who were nominated by the communities and approved by the Magistrate as their representatives in dealing with matters of government. One should note, as Brockman (1980/1996) emphasizes, that the 'third realm', contra Fei Xiaotong, does not refer to a circle of people who are familiar with each other. Contracts in traditional China also mediated dense interactions between people only connected by the 'weak ties' of commerce.

37 In his classical study of Chinese customary law as recorded in the late 1920s, Kroker (1959) adopts a very similar view in arguing that the Chinese notion of property can only be properly understood if one distinguishes between the Chinese way of thinking, which he calls 'coordinative', and the Western one, which he labels 'subordinative', distinctions which dovetail with the notions of field dependency vs. independency (and the related Western penchant for closed categorizations as highlighted by Fei Xiaotong). This 'coordinative' thinking is expressed in cosmological and religious notions of valuing property (such as *fengshui* assessments of location, or the presence of graves), or in the explicit consideration of social context in land transactions; for example, neighbours would be present when concluding a sale of land, so that possible claims resulting from boundary issues might be avoided, and also claims resulting from the special location of the land which might affect use of contiguous land. Generally, land purchase by strangers was tightly constrained and always involved the possibility of redemption. However, this did not imply that transactions were not following market valuations, because often middlemen were involved who established and mediated fair prices that were oriented towards market prices. So, middlemen played an important 'coordinative' role as well.

38 This special position of Chinese legal practice has been highlighted in Huang's (2006a, 2006b) work on mediation and adjudication. Huang emphasizes that court-assisted mediation is just a first step in adjudication; vice versa, adjudication, as Brockman (1980/1996) also emphasized, could go without punishment if the parties accepted the judge's decision. Huang points out that the fundamental difference between Western civil law and Chinese law is that the latter does not move from abstract principles towards application, but distils those principles from practical examples and application. This procedure allows for both strict application of principles (which was often possible because contracts were kept as simple and as clear as possible) and for

adapting to the circumstances of the case. This adaptation invokes moral judgement. So, Huang argues that one should not take the Confucian ideology of mediation at face value. Yet, at the same time judges could rarely directly refer to legal norms when deciding about disputes in the domain of civil law. One example of the interaction between formal law and contextualization is the distinction between irrevocable and conditional sale of land, which reflects lineage norms on protecting ultimate rights of ownership on sacred property of the family line; this often led to conflicts, as parties might claim supplemental payments if they did not redeem the land (Buoye 2004). In this important case, judges could refer to formal law, and even the Imperial government issued further regulations.

39 For an intriguing analysis of these complexities, see Schoppa (1989), who traces the history of a local irrigation system and lake over several centuries. In these contexts, legal issues over land rights might emerge because there are always strong incentives to reclaim land from lakes that at the same time have considerable value as collective resources in the irrigation system. Magistrates often played a pivotal role in balancing private and public interests, but they could not simply rely on legal rules and enforcement in establishing sustainable solutions. Therefore, in dealing with single legal issues, they had to take the long-term consequences into consideration.

40 Bünger (1983: 149ff., 161ff.) emphasizes the role of administrative law in safeguarding the procedural quality of the process of adjudication and highlights the priority of material justice. In other words, whereas the judge had considerable leeway in adapting his judgment to the local context, he had to follow formal procedures. This is also emphasized in Lai's (2015) critique of the Weberian approach which does not consider the possibility of 'substantive rationality'.

41 The role of tax payment in formally establishing ownership has been elaborated by Osborne (2004). One very simple context is land reclamation or new settlements where ownership rights might be directly created by governmental fiat, and would be formally recognized in accepting the tax duty. These acts could assume a substantial role after times of civil unrest or when migration explored new territories. Recognizing tax duties was also even a means of illegally claiming land in case of competing informal rights. Thus, one has to take note of the deep enmeshment of property and tax regimes in traditional China. Zhou (2014: 11ff.) offers an interesting case study of an early modern Guangzhou village where the tax-paying units were the lineages, organized in lineage trusts, 'tang' (堂). In this case, property rights were arranged internally via the customary kinship norms, mostly governed by the rules of family division, inheritance and marriage. The lineages arranged the tax payment via agreements with the local magistrate, and paid the duties out of the income generated by the communal land owned by the trust, as well as the rents paid by the tenants who were members of the lineage. Thus, the state clearly recognized the formal status of lineage rights, without at the same time directly formally recognizing the rights at the level of the individual families. From that perspective, limitations of trading land rights were also in the interest of the government in safeguarding the tax base.

42 On these distinctions, see Kroker (1959). This implies that selling land would first occur in the closer circle of relatives and neighbours, thus keeping the original right 'alive'. Tan (2010: 171, 234) reports that this distinction is still in use in rural areas today, often for referring to the distinction between actual possession and the underlying collective land rights. On the rights of tenants vis-à-vis the owners, see the classical study by Chen and Myers (1976a). There was even the notion of perpetual tenancy rights resulting from

long-term investment in the land, meaning, for example, that once a tenant paid the rent, owners could not simply sell the land, with new owners cancelling the tenancy contract. Further, customary levels of rent were lower, taking efforts of tenants into consideration. On the other hand, tenants could also sell the 'surface' rights to others, while keeping the rent paid to the owner who also remained responsible for paying the land tax.

43 The evolutionary transition, as Faure (2007: 218ff.) explains, started out from the ritual rules of inheritance which might include the possibility of setting up shared ownership for particular assets related to ritual, such as buying land for setting up an ancestral temple. This created the need for contractual arrangements, thus linking lineage ritual with the institution of the contract. Such contracts provided the basis for incipient notions of corporatization. Ritual, on the other hand, became an important element in executing and reaffirming the validity of the contract. Out of this a model of corporatization emerged that could be directly employed in many different commercial activities that lineages pursued. It is important to note that such practices did not simply emerge without any intervention from the Imperial government. Already in Ming times, the Imperial authorities spent considerable effort in standardizing and propagating models for lineage rituals. Scholar-officials produced substantial literature and practical guidebooks on the specific design and organization of lineages (Faure 2007: 110ff.). In other words, in spite of the fact that there was no formal legal framework for corporatization, there was a role for government-led standardization that could also be invoked in clarifying legal disputes.

44 This may best be illustrated in the terminology that has been used until most recently in arranging family divisions (see Gui 2014: 152ff.). Even if a simple joint family splits, the transition of property is not between the patriarch and the sons as individuals, but the sons are merely representing new 'branches', 'fang' (房), through which the original family line (*zong*) is perpetuated. The term *fang* is of almost arbitrary scope, so can simply be the nuclear family of the next generation, or a large subunit of a clan with hundreds of members. This shows, however, that the family is also a corporate unit, which was recognized as such in Chinese legal practice. Thus, *fang* could set up trusts, *tang*, without necessarily fully congruent sets of members. In many larger scale shareholding structures, *tang* were often the shareholders, if only emerging from earlier family divisions. This meant, however, that nested ownership also often implied complex corporate structures in which *tang* were involved (Zelin 2004c).

45 In her meticulous study of nineteenth- and early twentieth-century salt yards in Sichuan, Zelin (2004c) shows how the traditional shareholding model adapted to the growing complexity and the changing financial needs of salt production. In these structures, often lineage trusts, *tang*, were shareholders in the yards, which implies that the lineage members could also be involved in many different businesses. Accordingly, as I discuss in Chapter 6 in more detail, the business units also manifested a process of professionalization, such as hiring professional managers. In fact, in the salt industry this process had already gone far beyond the practices in the USA at the same time, with shareholders mainly having a voice in the annual shareholder meetings. In comparison, many uses of the shareholding model were simpler. For example, peasant families might agree on raising a pig together, because no single family could afford the investment (Zhou 2014: 22). Interestingly, in this case the joint investment was not simply an economic one but served to fulfil ritual obligations in hosting relatives on certain occasions.

46 On this distinction between horizontal and vertical kinship, see the discussion in Gui (2014: 74ff.) who refers this also to other distinctions, in particular

descent as vertical relationship and identity as horizontal one. The relationship between the two dimensions can only be properly understood if the religious and hence ritual nature of the *zong* is recognized. In comparison, Cohen (1990) argues that there is a generic notion of lineage (which is the *jiazu*) as a patrilineal descent group, but that there are two different basic modes of lineage organization, even adding supplementary modes. One is the 'associational mode' in which all descent lines are of equal status, which provides the basis for branching into segments, in which members have access to collective goods of the lineage or the segments based in equal status. This mode is dominant in southeastern China and provided the subject for the classical Freedman model of the Chinese lineage. Combined with political support and sources of legitimacy, this model also includes the establishment of clans which are based on artificial kinship. Hence, the term *zongzu* originally only referred to these organizations and was apparently then extended to all kinds of lineages in the associational mode (cf. Baker (1979), who distinguishes neatly between clan and lineage but unfortunately does not give the Chinese equivalents). The other is the fixed genealogical mode, in which status within the descent group is strictly determined by genealogical seniority. This form has been prevalent in north China. One distinguishing feature is that in the associational mode, lineages also own corporate holdings, which was also the basis for economic organization as business entities (Faure 1996a, 1996b). Yet, the northern variant was also a medium of lineage solidarity and cooperation. Beyond these two modes, lineage organization can also be enhanced by associations in the broader sense, such as in Cohen's case study the *Qingming* associations, in which the genealogical status differences do not count. This analysis shows the conceptual foundations of the corporatization of kinship in China, which motivated Gates (1996) to coin the term 'patricorporation'.

47 In comparing Japanese and Chinese notions of the family, it has often been emphasized (e.g. Pelzel 1970) that the Japanese 'ie' (家) is a corporate organization that easily includes non-kin, for example, via adoption. However, if we distinguish the two tracks in the Chinese case, we need to take note that the Chinese 'zijiaren' also included non-kin, if only via the extension of kin terms to non-kin (see Baker 1979: 162ff.). This happened frequently in the context of traditional apprenticeship, when families sent their sons to artisanal masters in order to learn a craft. Lineages could also directly use adoption or uxorilocal marriage in order to enhance their manpower (Gates 1996: 111). On the other hand, lineage trusts were often managed by professional non-kin, who might nevertheless develop a close relationship with lineage members. Therefore, the borderline between kin and non-kin was permeable to a large degree. One important example that goes beyond economic organization but activates economic resources is the cooperation between lineages in multi-lineage villages that could also be connected via affinal ties (for a seminal case study, see Strauch 1983). Different lineages could build common trusts which would therefore reflect the village as a community, though using the kinship idiom (such as addressing members of other lineages as 'brothers').

48 Faure (2006: 47f.) points out that in England limited liability as a legal form was only created in the mid-nineteenth century and diffused slowly in practice. In fact, as Mokyr (2009: 357f.) also mentions, even in Britain the demand for new legal forms was weak in the early decades of industrialization. The idea that limited liability might be an essential distinctive criterion in comparing Chinese and European developments has been proposed early by Bünger (1983: 160f.) and is also emphasized by Zelin (2004c). Zelin also provides examples of how Chinese institutions coped with the resulting legal issues in developing case-specific contractual arrangements.

49 The organization of markets relates to the topic of the market system that I will discuss in a later section. Here, we need to approach 'markets' as material structures which require certain investments, in particular the land on which the market is located; further, the Imperial government also paid close attention to market order, which was also one of the rare aspects of civil law that appears in the Qing Code (such as on deceit and fakes). In other words, setting up a market also implies that the responsible group must assume some supervisory function and a role in the resolution of conflicts in the marketplace. Therefore, markets were often set up by powerful lineages, or, as Zhou (2014: 24f.) discusses, through cooperation among a number of neighbouring villages. Markets were an important aspect of competition between lineages, since they would undergird reputation and often also monopolistic positions, especially with regard to markets that focus on certain products. For an illuminating case study, see Mann (1988: 74ff.), which shows how lineage activity could even overcome infrastructural weaknesses of market locations in focusing on long-term developments of certain industries. Lineages would design and adapt their strategies over many generations, thus contributing to the development of local markets. As Faure (2007: 227ff.) reports, this role of lineages in shaping the market system has been overlooked because the lineage genealogies generally only report on the underlying land transactions but do not mention the business behind them. A direct source of income provided by markets is the rents that tenants pay to the market owners, which is formally analogue to land rent.

50 The seminal study of these phenomena is Sangren (1984) who strongly emphasizes the differences between kinship organization and associations as bedrocks of traditional Chinese society, while arguing that this dualism also reveals the flexible nature of kinship in China. So, what has often been regarded as 'local' variants of certain standard principles of kinship turns out to be an expression of more general and abstract principles of social organization. In other words, the presence of associations reveals the flexible nature of lineage organization proper, so that we also need to reconsider standard notions of the agnatic group. This is further evidence for the thesis that what has been regarded as traditional Chinese kinship is in fact the institutions that were moulded by Neo-confucian interventions over centuries, thus in fact representing legal structures, and not only informal customs. The Chinese organizational principles allowed for a large variety of combinations, such as when lineages set up religious associations. Such associations often had many tasks beyond the narrow religious functions in providing public services, such as schools or hospitals, but also local self-defence. Tan (2010: 66ff.) presents a long list of associations, 'gong hui' (公会) in a traditional village that often invest in land in order to fund shared activities, such as lavish banquets on certain holidays, or jointly raise a pig for the same purpose. They could be created by different underlying social networks, such as lineages, friends or village elites.

51 In studying the city of Hankow, Rowe (1989) is a *locus classicus* for understanding this increasing role of self-organized corporations in urban management. It is essential to note again the merger of ritual and functional roles of certain symbolic activities, such as organizing temples. In his general assessment, Rowe highlights the intriguing fact that large Chinese cities manifested many signs of modernity as did European early modern cities, such as the emergence of an urban proletariat, but a much lower frequency of violent conflicts, in spite of clearly demarcated different interests and social groups. This was the case in spite of the fact that in Hankow the government was not directly represented, since it was not a county seat. So, what comes to the fore is the power of ritual in creating an urban community.

52 For a concise summary of the institutional features of the traditional economy that come close to the pre-industrial European economy, dubbed 'Smithian', see Arrighi (2007). Building on his analysis of the traditional institutions of kinship and contract, Faure (2006) argues that the absence of financial instruments and capital accounting was the crucial factor impeding the emergence of modern capitalism in China. This argument is partly reflected in Brandt *et al.* (2014). Regarding the accounting methods, much depends on how to interpret classical studies such as Gardella (1992). Gardella shows that a native version of double-entry bookkeeping was used for centuries even up until the mid-twentieth century, which, however, manifested certain weaknesses in profit and loss accounting and adapting to more complex business ventures. However, he also points out that Western practice did not differ greatly in the nineteenth century, and that one certainly cannot argue that innovations in bookkeeping were a triggering force of capitalism. In other words, in both China and the West's accounting practices the functional needs of business were more prominent than theoretical considerations. Zelin's (2004c) study of the salt business shows how this happened in the context of dealing with liability issues and debt. Thus, probably what remains of the argument is the underdevelopment of financial markets in the narrow sense. However, this downplays the central significance of government debt in the evolution of banking and financial markets in Europe and also ignores the fact that monetary institutions in Europe were also weak, especially in the early transition to capitalism. For example, in England there was a serious dearth of currency in maintaining everyday market transactions over a long period, thus creating the need for informal credit relations to maintain the flow of business (Mokyr 2009: 373ff., 446ff.). Hence, also in this respect, the comparison with China supports the argument of institutional convergence. Thus, with regard to more complex financial instruments, in fact one could argue that fiscal conservatism was the major impediment in the transition to capitalism, if at all. But this is certainly a problem for liberal accounts of economic development in which government debt and inflation are largely seen as disruptive forces of market order. This essential role of government restraint was also evident from the fact that the Imperial administration refrained from using the Song invention of paper money after the Yuan inflation. Therefore, the inflow of Mexican silver dollars was a major driving force of the secular inflationary trend in Qing dynasty China which proved to be supportive of economic growth. Accordingly, the sudden outflow of silver following the Opium Wars was an external shock that could not be softened by the financial institutions and monetary management, thus causing a major depression (for a concise summary of these developments, see Eastman 1988: 123ff.).

53 Economic and ecological theories about the 'Great Divergence' were first deployed by Elvin (1973) as an alternative to institutional and cultural theories. The more specific argument on coal stays at the centre of Pomeranz' (2000) account, alongside the role of colonialism. It is important to emphasize that this explanation narrows down the theory to local mechanisms that relate local availability of resources to locally adaptive technologies and relative prices, so focusing on the initial stages of industrialization in England. Thus, it not only explains the difference between China and 'the West', but also the differential developments in Europe, where countries such as France initially struggled to keep up with the English development. This analysis is deployed in great detail in Allen (2009). Allen shows that the relative prices of energy and labour varied considerably across Europe, with an extremely low value in Newcastle. In China, energy was very expensive relative to labour. Interestingly, this perspective also differs from the conventional emphasis of the

relationship between land and labour. The coal theory is much more detailed and explicit about the mechanisms that produce a certain developmental pattern, and also particular technological developments. For example, Allen shows that the construction of kilns was very different in England and in China, adapting to the different availability and costs of energy. Mokyr (2009: 268ff.) is one of the foremost critics of the coal theory, arguing that coal prices are endogenous to economic and technological change, and pointing out that wages also reflected higher levels of skills, such that technology did not mainly aim at saving labour. Although this may apply to the intra-European comparison, it does not invalidate the comparison with China. These ecological theories may be extended to include other factors, in particular the diffusion of high-energy and capital-intensive agriculture in North European countries (see Broadberry 2014). On the one hand, this includes the much greater importance of livestock in European agriculture, hence extensive land use for herding that was restricted in China, and, on the other hand, the increasing importance of capital goods complementary to draft animals which created the demand for 'proto-industrial' production (Hesse 1982, 1991).

54 In classical treatments of the Chinese family, there is a clear tendency to separate the sociological and the religious perspective, as in Baker (1979), where the ancestral cult is only treated in a separate chapter. Similarly, Eastman (1988) clearly identifies the role of the family as a religious unit, but does not specify this in analysing the family in sociological terms, whereas the chapter on religion deals only with ancestor worship as one aspect of religion in general, without considering the essential role of the family. This distorts the religious status of the family in two senses. First, the religious nature of the most fundamental notions such as descent is not recognized as a determinant of the social phenomena, and second, ancestor worship is seen as the only religious aspect of the family. The latter is problematic because, on the one hand, this may overestimate the role of ancestor worship in Chinese religion (as Lagerwey (2010) emphasizes), and, on the other hand, this does not recognize the fundamental role of the family in religious activity beyond ancestor worship. The latter perspective has been recently highlighted by Chau (2014) in discussing the differences between Christianity and Chinese popular religion. In Christianity Christ hosts the believers, and the community is primordial, whereas in China the household hosts the Gods, both in the context of domestic worship as in the case of external activities. Chau even claims that modern phenomena such as the Christian 'house churches' are partly influenced by this form of religious sovereignty of the family. The religious nature of the family is also emphasized in Gui's analysis of contemporary rural society (2013, 2014). Gui posits that in rural society, the religious or 'sacred' sphere is inextricably enmeshed with daily life ('spending the days', 'guo rizi' (过日子)), and that descent *zong* is the core religious notion that directly relates the individual to the religious sphere (cf. Xiao 2001: 143, 419). Therefore, in his view, 'familism' is not only an ethical notion relating to ritual in a sociological sense, but the religious nature of the family is expressed in everyday ritual. Correspondingly, the family is also the place of religious creativity. So, Gui even argues that 'socialism' obtains a religious dimension, as, for example, when families approach political leaders such as Mao Zedong as deities. The religious nature of the family is most clearly expressed in the central role of funerals and grave sites. Funeral reform was a major policy in transforming 'superstition' in Communist China, only ending up in the current mix of modernist approaches such as cremation and the new expansion of cemeteries where urns would be placed. In 2008, the traditional

Qingming festival, the clearing of the graves, was declared as a national holiday (see Goossaert and Palmer 2011: 236ff.). In 2012, when Zhoukou county in Henan launched a campaign to return grave sites to agricultural use, this triggered a national debate and widespread public criticism, ultimately forcing the Ministry of Agriculture to intervene and stop the campaign (Zhao 2013: 182f.).

55 The two possible interpretations are both well supported by empirical observations, and the resulting ambivalences are well reflected in Gates' (1996) analysis of the family and gender relations which presents a balanced picture. Patriarchal individualism is most evident in the many ways in which women were treated as economic assets in traditional China, with repercussions until the present, such as in girl trafficking. Household heads were free to sell their daughters to other families, into prostitution or as servants; this could even apply to their wives, especially if they did not fulfil the ritual duties of producing male progenitors. In these transactions, there were clear notions about the economic value of females in the different contexts, and this was reflected in the contracted prices. There was even an explicit notion of how much the parental investment in daughters was worth in pecuniary terms. On the other hand, the specific role of women in the family has even led anthropologists to coin the term 'uterine family' in order to highlight the autonomous role of wives in shaping the family. A classical treatment of the structural dynamics of the Chinese family is Baker (1979: 18ff.). The entire topic is difficult to deal with, as it certainly manifests very strong phenomena of orthopraxy, since certain topics were considered as core elements of Confucian ritual, such as the chastity of widows, and therefore were objects of intensive propaganda on the part of the Imperial elites. So, the great variety of so-called 'local practices' may in fact also hide a systematic divergence from these ritual norms in the underlying value system. As I will discuss later, this also affects the assessment of recent developments. For example, in Chinese rural areas, 'wedding gifts' have exploded recently (e.g. Gui 2014: 246; *The Economist*, 30 November 2013), which could be interpreted directly as a manifestation of the imbalanced sex ratio. But this phenomenon also occurs in urban areas, where it is expected that the groom's family raises funds for an apartment, a car and other items of modern middle-class life. The difficult question here is whether this can be interpreted as a persistence of ritual patterns of brideprice, which were, according to Gates, also predominant in what she identifies as centres of the 'petty capitalist mode', that is, the Jiangnan region.

56 Economic theories about the Chinese family so far divide into neoclassical ones and Chayanovian ones (Richardson 1999: 78). Chayanov's model was used, among others, in the influential work of Philip Huang. These models (for an analytical survey, see Ellis 1988: 106ff.) assume that peasants follow a consumption norm and optimize over the trade-off between the disutility of farm work and additional income. Given the consumption norm, this means that the peasant household will expand labour supply until the household consumption norm is met; this depends on the composition of the household, namely the relationship between working and non-working members. When the availability of labour increases, work output will grow, as land is flexibly available. An essential precondition for applying the model is that there is no labour market, because the household will expand labour output beyond the efficient point of equalizing marginal costs of labour and the wage rate which would be set on the labour market. So whether the model applies to China is a question of how to evaluate different institutional practices. One is that traditional social relations also included reciprocity of labour exchange and thus avoidance of the labour market. Indeed, the retreat of labour exchange is a

major element of social change in modern Chinese villages (see e.g. Zhou 2014: 125). On the other hand, Chayanov considered the unlimited supply of land in Russia, which certainly does not apply to China. Adaptation of land supply to availability of labour largely happened via the shifting distribution of tenancy relationships in a village, such that families with low labour supply might rent out land to families with higher labour supply. In my reasoning, I follow the neoclassical model presented in Chao (1986), which seems to be less restrictive with regard to the interpretation of institutional practices. Chao presents a neoclassical model that is only modified by the simplest assumptions about family norms, namely the norm governing family reproduction and internal sharing that follows on from that. So, peasant households can offer labour below the subsistence wage in both agriculture and sideline production. In other words, as long as the handicraft sector operates with traditional technologies, it cannot compete against sideline production with wage labour. So, the economy converges on the Malthusian scenario on a high level of total production, without generating incentives for technological change.

57 The observation that larger scale production units evanesced in the course of Chinese history is a central argument in Elvin's (1973) seminal launch of the revisionist view of the 'Great Divergence'. This refers first to the manor, with far-reaching implications for technological change, as in Song times owners of manors were still actively involved in introducing new technologies. Later, owners became detached from the production process, often living in urban areas, and the tenants ran the rented land as small-scale family firms. This pattern was also typical for manufacturing. For example, even large-scale units such as the Imperial porcelain manufacturers were organized with artisan families as basic production units.

58 The notion of a 'high-level equilibrium trap' was seminally introduced by Elvin (1973) and refers to a model of Chinese development which highlights the intensive exploitation of traditional technology in order to maintain a continuous growth of population that is governed by traditional family norms. A related notion is the term 'involution' coined by Huang (1990). In the European comparison, the Malthusian factor has been recently emphasized again by Voigtländer and Voth (2013). They argue that the 'Great Divergence' was actually triggered by the 'First Divergence' which resulted from the suppression of population growth both through recurrent wars and by certain emerging social norms of late marriage. In fact, however, as the comparative data in Feuerwerker (1990) show, China manifested even sharper cycles, including periods of population shrinkage, resulting from the havoc of internal civil wars, foreign invasions and dynastic change. In particular, as Broadberry (2014) also discusses, the role of the Black Death is ambigious, which clearly shifted demand and supply of labour in many European countries, thus triggering wages increases; yet, this effect was mediated by contextual factors (for example, in Europe, Spain did not show these effects). This may also explain why the Chinese response to such demographic shocks was also different. Therefore, it seems necessary to include the ritual dimension into the analysis; that is, the different cultural norms of marriage and reproduction. These have been condensed seminally in the influential notion of the 'European marriage pattern' by Hajnal and relate to secular changes in the composition and the behavioural norms of households in Europe, seen as launchpads of the 'Industrious Revolution' by De Vries (2008: 14ff.). Broadberry (2014) also emphasizes the role of marriage patterns as one important explanatory factor of the 'Great Divergence'. In general, the question of the 'Great Divergence' has been discussed controversially in the past 30 years. The so-called 'California School' (Wong 1997; Pomeranz 2000) has offered

many historical observations that China was on a par with Europe up until the eighteenth century. This picture was not supported by the first systematic attempt at putting global comparative data on growth together in Maddison's (2007) influential work. Maddison compared China and Western Europe and showed that already with the 'First Divergence' Europe shifted to a different track. This picture has been further emphasized by more recent detailed analysis of available data (see Bolt and van Zanden 2013; Broadberry *et al.* 2015). This work could show that the relative peak of Chinese economic performance was during the Song dynasty (thus confirming Elvin's account), followed by a long process of relative decline. However, one problem that is well recognized in this literature is the different sizes of the geographic units compared, as regions such as Holland were just larger metropolitan regions in Imperial China. Further, the advancement of Europe was marked by complex waves of relative acceleration and decline for single countries, such as Holland as compared to Southern Europe (Fouquet and Broadberry 2015). Thus, a fair and relevant comparison would be to look at the Jiangnan region. The new research posits the Jiangnan region at approximately 50 per cent of the Netherlands in the early nineteenth century, and probably on a par with the richest regions in Europe in the seventeenth and early eighteenth century. This kind of comparison has to make many assumptions that affect the comparisons. For example, Broadberry *et al.* (2015) construct a benchmark comparison between China and Britain in 1840 where China has just about one-quarter of per capita GDP. However, this hinges on the estimation of the exchange rate. With the explosion of the opium trade, China experienced massive silver outflows, which may have affected the exchange rate relative to the earlier periods with large surpluses in the trade balance. The authors correct the exchange rate by means of internal price data, thus also including purchasing power parity considerations. However, given the fragmented nature of the Chinese monetary system, and the dualism of silver and copper for accounting and transaction purposes, respectively, these calculations are fraught with great uncertainty. So, the dispute over the California school is not yet settled, in my view, if we take appropriate regional comparisons and the climax of Qing development as a reference point (i.e. the mid-eighteenth century).

59 The central significance of primogeniture for the rise of capitalism in England has been elaborated on by Goody (1983). The comparison with China is of special significance here, because Goody argues that in the early Middle Ages the Church actively promoted more narrow lines of inheritance and ultimately primogeniture in order to break the local power of extended kin groups which were also a hotbed for popular pagan beliefs. Primogeniture was a major factor in structural change of the economy, especially in conjunction with gender. This is because minor sons were driven into other occupations, thus indirectly raising the social reputation of the latter. In China, important parts of sideline production remained feminized. Thus, we note that in both China and Europe family structure was complementary to certain structures of public power: in Europe the Church, in China the Empire. As mentioned in the previous note, the Church therefore also played an important role in the transition to the European marriage pattern that defined the demographic conditions for growth.

60 As Faure (2007) has shown in great detail, the spread of lineage ideology was to a large extent reflecting governmental action. In the early Empire, the ancestral cult was a monopoly of the rulers or the Imperial family. In this sense, as Lagerwey (2010) emphasizes, it would be misleading to characterize the ancestral cult as 'the religion of China'. Formal ritual and popular beliefs about the presence of ancestors must be neatly distinguished. Therefore, the

active support of ancestral cults in the population was an essential part of transformational efforts of the Neoconfucian (see Ebrey 1985). We might even speak of a 'democratization' of the Neoconfucian value system that was initially driven by the claims of elite families to extend the Imperial prerogatives to them. Faure (2007) therefore argues that in Ming times, the notion of lineage assumed the status of a feature of 'citizenship' defined by the Imperial state along the lines of modern nation states. This is because lineage ritual became a marker of being a recognized member of the Chinese Empire.

61 This religious nature of space and place has been particularly emphasized by Lagerwey (2010) in his claim that China is a 'religious state', at least up until recent times. One must emphasize that geomancy is a belief system that bridges the 'Great' and 'Little traditions' of China. As such, *fengshui* may not be regarded as a religious practice, as it is conducted by experts that have no religious function in the sense of claiming sacred status. Yet, the underlying cosmological ideas have deep connections to most general patterns in Chinese religiosity. For a short but informative sketch see Weller (2011).

62 A concise description of the intellectual changes beginning in Ming times is Elvin (1973: 225ff.). One instructive comparison is between the Neoconfucian philosopher Zhu Xi and the Ming philosopher Wang Yangming, who in fact also supported the rise of market-friendly ideas (see n.86 below). Whereas Zhu Xi believed that principles can be investigated in external phenomena, Wang believed that they can only be discovered by introspection. This is possible because human mind and matter are ultimately co-substantial and epiphenomena of the more fundamental cosmic forces that constantly work towards establishing balance. One result of this belief, as Elvin points out, is that observations which appear to contradict expectations can always be explained as indicators of dynamic adaptation and therefore be 'explained away'. This thinking was fundamentally different from the Cartesian shift to dualism, which stated a separation between mind and matter, thus opening up the way for the extension of the mechanistic paradigm of physics even to the human body. This created the different tracks taken by Chinese and Western medicine and biology. These intellectual developments concurred with the divergence of social structures undergirding the interaction between science and technology. As was seminally proposed by Zilsel (1976), in Europe scholars and artisans cooperated closely, thus creating the basic practical conditions for scientific work, such as sophisticated devices for measurement. In China, even when the Jesuits introduced modern scientific ideas at the Imperial court, these remained confined to elite circles. Mokyr's (2009) study of the Industrial Revolution in England clearly shows that it was not science as such that contributed to technological change but the widespread diffusion of progressivist ideas among the general population. Many groups were active in searching for propagation technological solutions to practical issues. However, whether these ideas were absent in China is an open question. No lesser a scholar than Joseph Needham himself (Needham 1977: 236ff.) has presented evidence of the fact that at least in the Middle Ages Chinese scholars contributing to knowledge domains such as pharmacology perceived themselves as being actors in a cumulative and collective effort of expanding human knowledge.

63 This approach has been aptly overviewed by Çalışkan and Callon (2009, 2010). In anthropology, the relevant classical debate was between 'formalists' and 'substantivists', with the former mainly building on neoclassical economics and the latter assuming that the economy is constituted by institutions of different non-economic domains such as the polity. In Asian studies, a related debate took place between the rational choice theorists and the protagonists of the 'moral economy' (see e.g. Feeny (1983) for a contemporary

view). Çalışkan and Callon argue that these theoretical oppositions have been overcome from both directions, because on the one hand the economists today recognize the essential role of institutions and norms in enabling successful economic transactions (e.g. Platteau 1994) and, on the other hand, the sociologists have included a micro-level analysis of agency in embedded markets (e.g. Granovetter 2002). These views are compatible with the mechanism approach championed in this book.

64 This discussion is particularly salient in Chinese studies, in which the issue of the 'Great Divergence' suggests the existence of a fundamental break between two socioeconomic regimes, with one often dubbed as 'capitalism' or, in the context of the current social system, as 'socialism'. In Chinese historiography, therefore research into the 'sprouts of capitalism' was an important issue. If one focuses on markets as particular kinds of artefacts, however, authors such as Chao (1986: 2ff.) have emphasized that there is overwhelming evidence that markets have existed in China since early times, and equally early assumed a central role in social organization. As I also emphasize below, one simple indicator is the well-documented existence of market prices for almost any kind of artefact. It is also important to note that in spite of the fact that China did not develop an independent body of economic theory, there is an early compendium of knowledge about the movement of prices, the *Guan Zi*, which itself is a mirror of the ubiquity of markets even in Pre-Imperial times. The *Guan Zi* is a Daoist classic with strong Legalist leanings, which contains chapters about economic phenomena, in particular related to the impact of government actions in market equilibria as reflected in price movements.

65 The classical study of this phenomenon is Skinner (1977c). Skinner showed how the Imperial government adapted administrative structures in the growing Empire to certain functional needs, so that, especially in the economically advanced regions, spans of control were wide. This reflected the aim of creating an effective tax administration, in which a relatively strong and reliable higher level administrative centre would cover a larger region. In contrast, in border regions with military functions, spans of control were shorter and administrative control of lower level units tighter. In other words, in the economically advanced regions the administration operated via a relatively small number of large prefectures that could be more easily supervised by the Imperial Court. This approach presupposed a complex system of informal governance where local elites in the advanced regions cooperated with the administration in critical areas, such as taxation. I will scrutinize this in the next section. As a result, many urban areas in China resembled structurally the city of Hankow as studied by Rowe (1989) (see n.51 above).

66 Examples of contracts on the sale of daughters and even wives may be found in Chen and Myers (1976b: 342ff.) where the precise monetary value is always given. These observations are central to Gates' (1996: 121ff.) analysis of dowry and brideprice in China. In her conceptual scheme (see Chapter 1, n. 68) the fluent borderline between brideprice and sales is a defining aspect of the so-called 'petty capitalist mode', whereas the dominance of dowry characterizes the 'tributary mode'. Bates shows that the former mode was most prevalent in those regions of China such as the Jiangnan area where the economy was most developed. If girls were directly sold at a younger age to other families or for other uses, the prices reflected the costs of rearing and the conditions for generating cash income from the girls' work. In many marriage transactions, brideprice was not paid in the form of bridewealth (that is, valuable objects) but in cash, which implies that the generated income is fungible and may be used for any kind of investment. Certainly one channel could be indirect dowry, so that the money would be invested in household equipment for

the daughter's use. This is the track explaining how social change affected traditional arrangements, manifesting changing gender valuations. However, these possibilities were all present in the traditional ritual scheme.

67 Von Glahn (1991b) traces the history of the modern Chinese 'God of Wealth'. This god goes back to a Song dynasty god named Wutong, who had truly devilish features, similar to Christian stories about the relationship between money and the devil. In particular, Wutong traded sexual favours of women with money, thereby creating havoc for traditional families and the fates of young girls. This picture was dominant until Ming times, and triggered a series of official responses which aimed at suppressing the cult which had many features of black magic. In Qing times, with secular economic growth and the stabilization of the market economy, the god evolved into the 'God of Wealth' who represents all the virtues of small businesses, such as thrift and diligence. Wealth as a religious attribute is widespread in China and is also often mixed up with other religious entities, even with the most widespread and influential ones, such as the Goddess Guandi.

68 For contemporary descriptions of the ritual uses of paper money in Chinese villages see Xiao (2001: 464) or Gui (2014: 122ff.). In these cases, there are different kinds of paper money ('yellow', i.e. golden, and 'white', i.e. silver) which are donated to different circles of recipients, ancestors, gods or ghosts, and in clearly demarcated different environments, such as graves at *Qingming* festival, temples or inside vs. outside the home. Paper money that is burned to cater to the needs of ancestors is explicitly seen as a medium to provide for their 'material' needs. Thus, on the one hand, paper money reflects the 'commoditization' of the afterworld, also with respect to relationships of debt, but on the other hand it also signals different ritual domains, especially delimiting the circles of related and unrelated people. Gates (1996: 170ff.) emphasizes the relationship between money and debt, epitomized in the idea that the afterworld also has a bank. In ideas about reincarnation, ancestors have incurred a virtual debt that needs to be partly repaid by their living relatives in order to ensure proper rebirth. Hence, the ritual uses of paper money even include the implicit notion of accumulation. Blake (2011) offers a comprehensive historical and anthropological analysis of the custom, which dates back at least a millennium and is ultimately grounded in ritual prescriptions of the Book of Rites. Against this background, the custom has multifaceted meanings. For example, on the one hand it matches Confucian requirements of the frugality of ritual, but on the other hand it is also a mockery of ritual. That may depend on the kind of money used, such as 'white money' as an explicit attempt at cheating the ghosts about the true value of the donations. Blake's analysis emphasizes the correspondence between the flow of real-world money in the continuous efforts to create wealth through exchange and the flow of paper money in the relationship to the afterworld, where this money is also used in transactions. However, he criticizes Gates for assigning the custom to the 'petty capitalist mode' exclusively. His point is that precisely in the custom of paper money the fact is ritually manifest that markets in old China were 'monetized', but not 'commoditized'. In other words, Blake finds that Gates' 'tributary mode' actually permeates ordinary market transactions. Thus, he proposes (Blake 2011: 102) the notion of a 'cash–nexus-based social economy' which would actually be a very advanced form of feudalism. Needless to say, in my view this is another failed attempt at using generic macro-level concepts to designate social formations in China. Blake's analysis of paper money can most parsimoniously support the notion of a 'ritual economy'.

69 On the importance of effort in producing paper money, see Blake (2011: 48ff., 126ff.) (cf. Xiao 2001: 464). The semantic field to which I refer relates

to the classical Confucian notion of 'gongfu' (功夫) (see Metzger 1977: 123ff.). *Gongfu* is the serious individual moral effort to overcome constraints and dilemmas of action without fundamentally challenging these conditions by means of unconstrained individual creativity. This term is generally known to a Western audience as an expression describing traditional martial arts. If we consider their origin in festivals of popular religion, martial arts are elements of ritual activities mostly realized by individuals living at the margins of Chinese society, and thus failing to participate in the proper cycles of labour and familial reproduction. In displaying prowess and the willingness to suffer pain (for instance, while walking through massive explosions of firecrackers), these individuals express moral effort to become part of the local community (on this interpretation, see Boretz 2011: ch. 2). Effort is also an essential value in the mindset of Chinese entrepreneurs, often referred to as a special 'spirit', 'jingshen'(精神) which is expressed in daily toil, which, after all, may often just be sitting behind a counter and waiting for customers (see Yao 2002: 28). I argue that these different notions as a semantic field hark back to the fundamental notion of 'cheng' (诚) in the Confucian concepts of ritual, as interpreted by Sutton (2007: 14). *Cheng* is not simply an internal state of mind but a bodily phenomenon, understood as tension, effort and perseverance. Compare Pye (1988: 50ff.), who also emphasizes the relationship between ritual and sincerity. On the one hand, ritual fosters feigned compliance, which results in endemic suspicions about true motives and thoughts; effort in sincerity is the means by which authenticity is signalled through ritual action.

70 Classical studies of these phenomena in contemporary rural society are Yan (1996a) or Kipnis (1996). I will discuss these phenomena in more detail in Chapter 5. At this point, however, it is important to emphasize an observation made by Wilson (2002) with reference to modern Chinese villages that appears to apply to the past as well. In Yan's discussion of gift exchange, there is the conventional distinction between 'expressive' and 'instrumental' gift giving, with the latter increasingly dominated by the 'cash nexus'. This view appears to reiterate narratives of social change following Polanyi's 'Great transformation'. However, Wilson realizes that in his fieldwork, even the closest relationships were also imbued with the cash nexus, with families meticulously recording the flow of gifts, mainly motivated by fears of 'losing face' when violating norms of reciprocity. So, one cannot say that the money medium defines the difference between 'expressive' and 'instrumental' relations. I argue that in fact these conditions in modern Chinese villages manifest family resemblances with historical conditions, rooted in the ritual meaning of money. In sum, the Chinese case vindicates Zelizer's (1997) influential sociological account of money that invalidates the simple dichotomic view about the 'modernizing' role of money, such as Simmel's. In fact, ritual aspects of money loom large in all societies, as in the early twentieth century US case scrutinized by Zelizer.

71 On this decline of labour exchange, see Zhou (2013: 125). Again, Wilson's (2002) aforementioned fieldwork gives important hints at reinterpreting some observations regarding social change. For example, even though labour exchange in the context of house construction has declined substantially in reform China, this does not mean that social exchange on this occasion has lost significance. People may employ wage labour to build their homes, but they receive cash gifts and low-interest loans from their relatives as a functional equivalent of labour input. Again, money assumes a ritual function.

72 For a comprehensive assessment of the Skinner model, see Cartier (2002). The Skinner model actually consists of different hypotheses, in particular the

hypotheses about the structural relations between villages and market towns, and the hypotheses about higher level aggregate structures; that is, the marketing system and the macro-region approach. Cartier summarizes the critical aspects, which often start out from identifying deviations between the hypotheses and the factual geographic and economic patterns. For example, the notion of macro-regions, combined with the marketing system hypothesis, downplays the role of inter-regional commerce directly embedding lower level markets into trans-regional trading patterns. Cartier also presents an important theoretical argument against Skinner's theory, which is based on more recent reasoning in geography. He seems to suggest a materialistic conditioning of geographic factors by economic determinants such as transport costs, and thus does not pay attention to the reverse causation by human cultural creativity. My use of the Skinner model is not affected by these criticisms, because I mainly concentrate on the village–market link, and neglect the macro-regions part, and because my argument on the ritual economy implies that there is feedback from culture on geographical patterns. The local market as a cultural phenomenom also shapes the workings of economic determinants, so that we would indeed expect that geography not only reflects 'material' economic determinants. Thus, the economic determinants become endogenous to the entire institutional set-up. Correspondingly, we could no longer use isolated data on supposed economic determinants (such as data on topography and transport costs) in refutations of the Skinner model.

73 The original contribution is Skinner (1964/1965). This work was continued in the highly influential work on urban systems in China (Skinner 1977a, 1977b, 1977c), thus shaping China studies with regard to many different levels of analysis, both at the micro-level (that is, the relationship between villages and markets), and at the large-scale level of establishing macro-regions in Chinese history (Skinner 1985a). The Skinner model has been analysed methodologically by Little (1992: 68ff.) as an example of medium-level modelling of mechanisms that can adapt to many specific modifications, such as including inter-regional trade. Regional systems play an essential role in the diversity of cultural patterns in China, such as variations of lineage structures. This is an argument in Gates' (1996: 65ff., 122ff.) critique of the Skinner model that she reduces to the economic logic of the marketing system. Instead, she argues that the two modes, the petty capitalist and the tributary mode, were actually reflected in the distribution of the cities, with administrative centres operating in the latter and thereby also affecting the economic processes. For example, over the centuries the infrastructural transformations created by the Imperial administration according to the tributary logic also changed the economic determinants of the marketing system. At the same time, realms of a purely economic logic would be the smaller cities and townships where the petty capitalist mode dominated. The mix of the modes would define macro-regions according to Gates, such as the North China Plain where the tributary mode dominated, or the Jiangnan region, where the petty capitalist mode would have been strong. Although Gates certainly makes a valid point, Skinner's original reasoning about the coevolution between administrative structure and the economy does not in my view contradict her points. The notion of the ritual economy resolves this apparent conflict, considering, for example, that the strong and rich merchant families of the Jiangnan region with many scholar-officials in their pedigree certainly do not appear to be 'petty capitalists', but a pillar of culturalist rule in China.

74 The fundamental dualism in the religious landscape of Chinese villages has been succinctly depicted by Lagerwey (2011: 6ff., 153ff.). Lagerwey argues that this dualism goes back to sources as early as the Rites of Zhou, and he

constructs an ideal-typical model that builds on central dualisms in Chinese ritual, namely Yin and Yang, Wu and Wen, or Red and White. These dualisms correspond in the first of the pairs with a territorial dimension, which is embodied in the altar of the Earth God, and the second, which is embodied in the ancestral temple. The religious dualism reflects the Janus-faced nature of social relations in the village. In a multi-lineage village, there are two levels of competition within the lineages: between the lineages; and between the families. At the same time, the village needs to cooperate against outside enemies, which may include both forces of disorder such as roving bandits, but also the Imperial forces that might endanger the village for reasons of taxation or religious control (see Watson and Watson 2004: 423ff.). Hence, in the religious sphere the world is perceived as a complex system of flows of negative and positive forces, which present human beings with an unpredictable fate. Therefore, divination plays a central role in popular religion, with the concomitant activity of gambling.

75 A most pronounced argument along these lines was presented by Stover (1974). However, as Strauch's (1983) seminal case study of a multi-lineage village in Hong Kong also shows, lineages could also activate quasi-kinship ties in order to undergird the *diyuan* community. In this case, for example, the annual festivals clearly distinguished between community rituals and lineage rituals, interweaving both family-related activities and village-based activities, with alternating circles of participants. Interestingly, the village-level activities even overcome gender distinctions, as both males and females are involved, distinct from the lineage activities.

76 As an interesting case, see Zhou (2003: 308ff.). In Le'an county, Fuzhou prefecture of Jiangxi province, the Dong lineage controlled and managed the entire trade of bamboo and wood in the region. For that purpose, the lineage created a separate association, the 'mu gang hui' (木纲会) which had branches in the different marketplaces. In these activities, ritual and economic practices were inextricably enmeshed, even to the degree that certain customs in popular religion were shaped. The merger of ritual and commerce was supported by the spread of new Confucian schools that put a positive value on merchant activities, which went hand in hand with a leading role of the merchants in lineage organization. Lineages bolstered this symbiosis by investing in education and placing talented members in the carrier track of officials. The *mu gang hui* certainly monopolized regional trade, although in the larger regional system there were also competing organizations. For example, lineage rules constrained trade with non-lineage members and effectively closed the transport business to outsiders, thus controlling a sensitive service in trading with logs. On the other hand, the lineage put a high emphasis on business ethics, thus directly translating ritual into social capital that could be mobilized for sustaining their competitive advantages and commercial networks. Another case in point is described by Siu about the Fan Palm Guild in Huicheng (Siu 1989: 62ff.). Lineage estates invested in land and generated rent income that was then reinvested in commercial enterprises that involved certain agricultural products, often in creating vertically integrated structures via long-term contracts with growers. Markets were controlled via product-related guilds that operated until the advent of Communist rule, with a complex structure of specialized sub-associations for different stages of specializations of the palm business. The guild acted as a public body supporting a variety of public services and was therefore a major link between the government and local society.

77 As Lagerwey (2010) analyses in depth, this is reflected in the ritual infrastructure of villages, as central religious places such as temples are collective goods

of the villages, thus representing village identity vis-à-vis other villages, although cooperative ventures between different villages in establishing shared religious places were also widespread. Temple building is a major cooperative effort which in terms of ritual mirrors other important forms of village-level and inter-village cooperation, in particular in irrigation systems. In his critical view on the Skinner model, Wu (2014: 11ff., 40f.) presents arguments as to why the irrigation system is the most important determinant of marriage patterns in his data about the twentieth-century history of a Fujian village, thus arguing that the market system is not the dominant context of organizing the marriage market, as Skinner believed. As Schoppa (1989) demonstrates, maintaining irrigation systems and water reservoirs was explicitly reflected as a public task in Imperial times, thus involving high moral stakes, often pitting family interests against public interests; therefore, county magistrates often exerted great effort into educating the population in this respect.

78 A classical study of the interaction between markets and manufacturing in urban systems is Shiba's (1977) study of Ningbo. Shiba emphasizes that commerce and production are often difficult to separate analytically. Often production was organized in a complex regional putting-out system (for example, umbrellas, furniture or straw hats), which might include not only finished products but also intermediate products, similar to the production networks in international trade today. At the top of the marketing and production hierarchy were the wholesalers, who often also operated retail stores in many places and interacted with the final producers via middlemen, peddlers and other agents in the marketing system. For example, the bamboo ribs for umbrellas were produced by farmers and prepared by their wives, and were then traded via the market town; wholesalers would buy the paper and the oil needed to make it watertight with other sources, and finally give the task of producing the umbrella to family artisans. It is important to emphasize that this activity also had a substantial financial dimension, as the wholesalers often bought large quantities of inputs (such as straw for straw mats) in advance and supplied them to the family producers via the network of agents.

79 According to Lu (2010), in the late nineteenth century there were about 11,000 'small towns' in China, which generally corresponded to standard markets or intermediate markets in the Skinner model. Such 'small towns' could easily have tens of thousands of residents and sometimes were much larger than the administrative seats, the counties. These urban areas were deeply integrated with the countryside, both via the interactions between villages and markets and via the residential patterns of the landowning elites who kept a lifestyle that expressed their identification with the rural society. At the same time, there was a perception of social distinctiveness of people living in larger urban centres which reflects the continuum of rural and urban in the case of the towns. If we consider that more than 50 per cent of the entire urban population lived in these places, we can certainly confirm Skinner's (1977b) early assessment that in China the cultural distinctiveness of urban life was only weakly expressed. Sociologically, the small towns were the hinge that connected the Imperial government with the rural population via the role of local elites, mostly powerful lineages, often active in commerce, who assumed 'liturgical' roles, as I analyse in the following section. This was exacerbated by the role of returnees in shaping local cultural and political life. Often members of the Imperial elites returned to their native areas after retirement and contributed to the establishment and maintenance of academies, schools and other cultural institutions. Thus, the market system remained deeply connected with ritual concepts of ancestor worship, mediated via memories of native places and local history. This could directly relate

to market activities. One favourite expression of elite sponsorship driven by affection for one's native place was the donation of funds for building bridges. The role of the rural/urban dichotomy is especially important against the background of Max Weber's (1991) views, who seminally pointed out that the emergence of the city as an autonomous legal body may have been a crucial factor in the rise of capitalism in Europe. Weber argued that in comparison, villages in China may be seen as self-governed bodies, though being subject to fetters of tradition. This view overlooks the intermediate role of the towns, which were actually of the same size and often larger than the corporate cities in Europe.

80 A classical study of the mobility of young wives after marriage is Judd (1989), who refers to 'traditions' cited by twentieth-century farmers. Wu (2014: 299ff.) offers a contemporary record of practices in Fujian where this regular interchange between the families of husband and wife is highly ritualized in the context of the recurrent holidays of the lunar calendar. This could often include long stays with their natal families, thus creating many opportunities for establishing social networks via affinal kinship. In Skinner's ideal-typical model, the marketing area is also endogamous, as the market town is a place where people exchange information about opportunities for accessing brides, for example, involving the services of matchmakers, sometimes even professionals. This thesis has been often criticized, since marriage alliances may be formed via many other channels (see Wu's (2014) aforementioned observation on irrigation systems as contexts for marriage patterns: n. 77 above). Duara (1988: 21ff.) argues that the marketing area may be endogamous, but the relationships may not be necessarily mediated via the market town. After all, once affinal relations are established, they can be activated in arranging marriages, thus no longer involving the market town. Still, the conclusion remains valid that the standard market corresponds to networks of affinal kinship, which is often underestimated in the conventional picture of agnatic kinship in China.

81 See n. 29 and n. 51 above, referring to Rowe's work.

82 Jones (1988) is a foremost example for the change of perspective. Whereas in his earlier work on the 'European miracle' he had put much emphasis on the conventional property rights and institutional explanations, he later turned to a 'weak government' hypothesis in conjunction with the role of economic and military competition among European states. This competition created incentives to enhance the infrastructural powers of the states, and therefore also triggered the strengthening of fiscal administration.

83 The semantic field of freedom, 'ziyou' (自由) is discussed by Bauer (1974: 200ff.). Fairbank (1992: 257ff.) points out that therefore no 'liberal' political line of thought and corresponding social forces emerged. This problematic status of 'freedom' persists up until this day (see e.g. Kelly 2013); especially since in the twentieth century the term was comingled with 'liberation', 'jiefang' (解放), which refers to the status of China as a nation, with the individual being a part of this whole entity. In n. 13 above I discussed the term *ziran* as another conceptual complement of traditional notions of freedom. Here, freedom means to follow natural cosmological forces. This is different from Western individualistic notions of freedom, as it actually even implies that final dissolution of the individual into these forces. On this ambivalence, see Bauer (1990: 202ff.). The term *ziran* refers to the notion of 'self', 'zi' (自), thus apparently suggesting a movement from interior to exterior, as 'being self through oneself'. Yet, in Daoist thinking in particular, this means that the self follows nature, since the interior states are expressions of the larger exterior cosmos. This is most visible in the images of Daoist saints who often

represent highly individualistic habitus and body characteristics, also almost anarchistic lifestyles, but at the same time almost merge with nature into one being.

84 In my previous discussion of contracts and property, I have already shown how the Imperial government protected private property. When certain central aspects of property remained conflict-ridden in private arbitration, such as in the case of the distinction between conditional and irrevocable sales, the government even took regulatory action. I add the observation that the Qing Code, though being mostly silent on civil law matters, did include specific regulations on market order, namely regulating the role of brokers, the use of weights and standards, the sale of defective products, and fraud (cf. Zelin 2004a, 2004b).

85 For a comprehensive description and analysis of this source, see Schefold (2002) with contributions by von Mende and Vogel. Von Mende emphasizes the deep impact that these sources had, together with other sources such as the chapters on economics and famous merchants in the classic of *Shiji.* The *Yantie lun* was a direct reflection of the expansionary policies of Emperor Wu, which required the strengthening of extractive capacities of the state. Thus, the *Yantie lun* was a detailed and extensive discussion of the role of the state in the economy, centred on the arguments of the Legalist government advisor Sang Hongyang (153–80 BCE). In the dialogues, Sang directly identifies his critics as 'Confucians'. Later, important modernist reformers such as the Song dynasty chancellor Wang Anshi referred back to Sang's arguments, who, for example. argued in favour of a professional education of civil servants and fiscal strengthening of the state. In contrast, the Confucians believed that government should take care of people's livelihood first, which presupposes fiscal constraint. Sang argued that fiscal strength enables government infrastructure investment and thereby also contributes to raising the living standards of the general population. So, we see a striking modernity in these arguments. It is important to recognize that the policies of Emperor Wu Di did nor result in a full-scale government-controlled iron and salt sector, but co-opted rich merchants by giving them positions in the bureaucracy. This mixing between private and public interests incited the outrage of the Confucians. Therefore, we can cleary diagnose the moral status of markets in Confucian thinking: open and free markets are a means to secure the people's livelihood and constrain expropriation by private interests.

86 In the course of the Ming and Qing dynasties many scholars began to develop notions that allowed for the combination of commercial life and the fulfilment of gentlemanly ideals. Thus, for example, one of the towering figures in Neoconfucianism, Wang Yangming, explicitly stated that commercial activity does not stand in the way of becoming a sage, and the founder of the Taizhou School, Wang Gen, praised commerce and accepted many merchants as students. These teachings were eagerly received by the newly emerging merchant elites (Zhou 2003: 311). The Jiangnan region was a breeding ground for many related scholars and schools, which can be traced back to the intellectual ferment of Eastern Zhejiang in Song times, thus reflecting the socioeconomic changes of the medieval economic revolution (see overview in Wang and Zhu 1996: 10ff.). The spread of Neoconfucianism was combined with a pragmatist turn that praised the application of knowledge in action, systematized as 'shigongxue' (事功学). This pragmatist turn also led to the endorsement of commerce, contrary to the traditional view that agriculture is the only source of value.

87 The classical study of these developments is Mann (1988). The major institutional phenomenon is the expansion of 'benevolent markets', 'yiji' (义集),

which were tax-free in the sense that the brokerage functions were no longer fulfilled by state-licensed brokers but by local merchant families, that is, powerful lineages. In return, they paid the brokerage fees and other local taxes and took care of market supervision. These activities even included essential markets such as local grain markets. The term *yi* was used in many different contexts, always referring to some public good (such as 'charitable granaries', 'yicang') that is provided jointly by Imperial authorities and local elites.

88 On using the Chinese script as a formal analogue to understanding orthopractic enforcement of ritual in China, see Sutton (2007: 11). Especially when considering indigenous views on the Chinese language, the use of the term 'dialect' often suggests a higher degree of linguistic homogeneity than is warranted. As Norman (1988: 1ff., 187ff.) discusses (who also opts for using the term 'dialect', however), Chinese is actually a language family that may be compared to the family of Romance languages, also in the sense of reflecting the history of empire. Thus, in fact, the peculiar tradition of writing Chinese even affects the linguistic classification, as probably the lack of written vernaculars is the ultimate reason why the different variants of Chinese only count as dialects.

89 For a survey of the debates about orthopraxy, see Sutton (2007), and see n. 2 above.

90 I cannot go into detail here. It is illuminating to go back on classical analyses of Chinese philosophical thought, such as those collected in Moore's (1967) volume, with contributions by influential Chinese scholars of the times, such as Y.P. Mei or Wing-Tsit Chan. There are differences in weighing the balances, but most thinkers would agree that in traditional Chinese thinking, the individual is clearly recognized as an autonomous source of action and valuation, but at the same time there is no sharp borderline between subject and object, thus indeed reflecting the cognitive stance of field dependence. Applied to the relationship between individual and society, this is tantamount to stating 'interdependence' as a fundamental principle, as is also elaborated in Metzger (1977).

91 For an overview of the regulation of religion in historical times, see Goossaert and Palmer (2011: 27ff.). Basically, many Confucians approached religion from the moral point of view, thus accepting a wide variety of beliefs as long as they conformed to fundamental moral notions upheld by them. At the same time, however, religion played an essential role in defining China as a civilizational entity, reflected in the complex and comprehensive Imperial rituals which included rituals on the local level that were conducted by the magistrates. Local practice diverged widely and went far beyond these limits, but at the same time the symbolic realm of popular religion also partly reflected the Imperial order (Feuchtwang 1992). One important aspect is that the difference between the cultural centre and the local variety was also cast in the difference between the civilizational forces *wen* and the potentially violent and disruptive forces of *wu*; the latter were mostly domesticated in Daoist rites, but, as Feuchtwang discusses, therefore the apparent conformist symbolic structure of popular religion also contained the possibility of deviance and resistance (cf. Boretz 2011: 21ff.). On the other hand, as Watson and Watson (2004) discuss, even auspicious symbols such as the dragon representing Imperial power could turn into an unpredictable threat of destruction.

92 In Pinker's (2011) authoritative treatment of the secular decline of levels of violence in the world, China remains a blank spot as far as the institutional details are concerned, as Pinker himself notices (ibid.: 88). He cites an observation made decades ago by the sociologist Norbert Elias who argued that one

aspect of civilizing violence in Western countries was the spread of knife taboos or special rules on how to handle knives when eating. In this perspective, the use of chopsticks is a most advanced form of knife taboo, since the use of knives is exclusively in the kitchen where the meals are prepared. However, looking at Pinker's lists of atrocities (e.g. ibid.: 195), of death-tolls in singular events of war, civil war, etc., five of the 'top ten' occurred in China, such as the Taiping rebellion, the An Lushan revolt or the Great Leap Forward. This matches the aforementioned observation (n. 52 above) that China's population growth showed much sharper cycles than the European pattern. However, this does not invalidate the observation that China's civilization from early times valued civilian power higher than military power (see Hallpike (1986) for a theoretical generalization on this). This is confirmed also by analysing local religious practices, in which violence plays an important role but is embedded in ritual, signalling the eventual integration of potential disorder in the community (on Boretz's 2011 pertinent analysis, see n.91 and n. 69 above). Thus, we may conclude that the containment of violence is a primordial motive in conceiving of social order as created by the state; that is, a most essential element in the threat of 'chaos'. On the different dimensions and types of violence in China, see Harrell (1990).

93 The term 'culturalism' was introduced into China studies by Levenson (1968) (for a survey of its reception and meaning see Townsend 1992). The original use was to reflect the debates of Chinese intellectuals in the late nineteenth century about the status of a Chinese 'nation' such as in the contributions of Liang Qichao. So, culturalism is a theoretical counter-pole of 'nationalism'.

94 On the institutional resilience of county-level government see Lam (2010) and Zhou (2014: 17ff.). There are many counties that maintained their basic shape over centuries, which is also reflected in a special branch of historiography, the county gazetteers, 'xianzhi' (县志). However, as Skinner (1977a) emphasized early on, this is not representative of the general trend. Throughout Imperial history, the total number of counties vacillated between 1000 and 1500, notwithstanding the different sizes of the Imperial units and the tremendous growth of the population. So, there was also a lot of restructuring going on, and certainly the scope of the administration in terms of population under the jurisdiction of a magistrate expanded continuously. As I have already mentioned elsewhere, in Qing times often neighbouring market towns could easily outgrow county seats. As Zhou Qingzhi (2014) also emphasizes, what makes the county level unique is the fact that both higher level and lower level administrative units showed much higher levels of instability. In particular, there were recurrent changes in grassroots-level organizations which mainly reflected the tension between the bureaucratic ideal of directly integrating the population in centrally designed structures such as the *baojia* or *lija* systems, also driven largely by ideas about functional optimization of taxation, on the one hand, and on the other hand the practical limitations of such schemes under the conditions of pre-modern technology. So, there were periods in Chinese history when there was no administrative structure at all below the county level. This is especially interesting with regard to the level of the 'xiang' (乡), since this played a crucial role in recurrent attempts to establish administrative structures below the county level. In the late Qing dynasty, the first attempt was made to establish the *xiang* as a self-governed level of the state.

95 In this context, the failure of the Song dynasty reforms launched by Wang Anshi was the turning point, because in the broadest sense Wang designed an expansion of a legalist Imperial state to the grassroots level, based on enhanced powers of taxation and administrative capacities for interventions

(for a concise evaluation of these reforms, see Huang 1988: 116ff.). Wang revived the modernist potential of legalist Imperial institutions as designed during the establishment of the Empire. Fiscal and monetary policies stood at the centre; for example, Wang designed a full registration of taxable land according to different grades of productivity and wanted to use the proceeds in order to extend government bureaucracy to the grassroots level. He also proposed that the emergency storage system of the government be used to manage credit for the farmers. However, after failing to finally implement these reforms in face of mounting Neoconfucian resistance, the Empire continued to rest upon a combination of informal and formal organization until its demise. For a concise summary of these stable characteristics of local government, see Fairbank (1978: 20ff.). In his authoritative analysis of the county magistrate, Watt combines the two insights that are essential in our context. The first (Watt 1972: 17) is the fact that the county was seen as a ritual miniature of the Empire; the second (Watt 1977: 364) is that the administration appears to 'sell government services at the highest marketable rate'. These two apparently contradictory observations may reflect the essence of the ritual economy in the context of government, in the sense of the marketization of public services.

96 This two-modal model has been emphasized by Fei Xiaotong in his works (see Zhou Qingzhi 2014: 36f.). Faure (2007) goes so far as to say that in Ming times this 'social contract' qualified China as probably even the first modern nation state in the world. Interestingly, he distinguishes this from the conditions under the Qing dynasty which clearly established ethnicity as an organizing principle of 'nationhood'. Under the Han-Chinese rule during Ming times, the notion of lineage was promulgated orthopractically as a notion of 'citizenship' in the sense that Neoconfucian norms defined certain general rules for local government. Apart from standardizing lineage rituals, this included a number of other institutional innovations, in spite of the fact that many could not be implemented completely, such as the 'baojia' (保甲) structures of communal self-government and collective responsibility, or the 'xiangyue' (乡约) village compact system designed by the philosopher Wang Yangming, which was further elaborated under the Qing dynasty (see Watt 1972: 145ff.). Faure's viewpoint supports the interpretation of ritual as a formal institution different from Western conception of law and legality. I think that this interpretation may even be supported yet modified in also considering the general philosophy of taxation, as Zhou Qingzhi does (2014: 26ff.). With the formula 'bianhu qimin' (编户齐民), the Imperial state claimed in principle to be the ultimate owner of all land and hence taxable resources, and therefore at least in theory established a direct relationship with taxpayers via the registration of land and population. In doing this, the state treated all its subjects as being equal, so that one could also speak of an incipient notion of citizenship.

97 On the deliberate activation of markets as mediating institutions for emergency measures, see Will (1990: 212ff., 294ff.). Often the Emperors directly acted against the more interventionist policies adopted by governors in disaster-stricken areas. As long as there were no excessive profits, the activity of merchants was seen as 'first best' in maintaining the 'natural circulation' of goods, even including means of subsistence. Under the Qing dynasty, even the system of emergency granaries was gradually hollowing out, as the administrators believed that it was more efficient to hand out cash to the people in distress such that regular demand was maintained to keep markets operating. Merchants were often directly assigned to the role of managing official relief measures.

98 Liturgical taxation is the typical form of taxation in advanced patrimonial systems of rule (see Weber 1985: 116ff., 584ff.). The resulting interpretive problems may stem from the inadvertent extension of Western legal concepts to the Chinese context, as Hamilton (2014) explains. Weber's notion of 'patrimonial rule' is an extension of the more general patriarchal rule in the simple household economy, the *oikos*, under the conditions of much the larger size of extended empires. In other words, Weber extends the institutional conceptions of patriarchy in Roman Law (*patria potestas*) to the notion of patrimony. Hamilton argues that the role of the Emperor in China cannot be properly understood with reference to this legal construction. The Emperor is bound by ritual and the corresponding cosmic forces, and is therefore constrained in his exercise of power, despite the despotic potential.

99 I have already discussed Skinner's (1977c) analysis of the design of field administration, see n.65 above. One example of how negotiating the low tax state occurred locally is reported by Mann (1988: 58ff.). On the one hand, the government had tried to control markets via state-licensed brokers, who also partly assumed tax-farming roles. But at the same time, the government was very aware of the resulting risks in abusing those special rights. So, the Qing administration, in spite of maintaining the system, also supported local elites in working against these abuses. The administration even supported the creation of 'tax-free markets', as mentioned previously. Interestingly, this pattern was partly driven by the endogenous dynamics of the marketing system, as in regions with dense markets there was locational competition. Local leaders were keen to suppress exploitative structures in order to attract traders. I have already referred to the problems of how to comparatively assess the tax burden in Imperial China (n.1 above). According to the data in Brandt *et al.* (2014), the tax burden per capita dropped between Song (taken as index = 100) to only 15 per cent in 1776, which is equivalent to only 0.12 shi of rice per annum, and also corresponds to an absolute decline of taxes by roughly half, in spite of the much bigger population. In the international comparison, the per capita tax revenue in grams of silver was about 4.2 in the early eighteenth century, compared to 12.9 grams in the Ottoman Empire, 21.0 in Russia and 158.4 grams in England. So, as I argued in n.1 above, even if we double this burden by including a rough estimate of informal taxation, this would also apply for the other cases, and would still make China exceptional in a global comparison.

100 In her analysis of the transition, Mann (1988: 158ff.) emphasizes the phenomenon that the government did not consistently pursue a strategy of bureaucratization of the local tax administration, in spite of the fact that new organizations had emerged on the local level with modernist claims, the chambers of commerce. Instead, tax responsibility systems were implemented which continued with the practice to assign local elites to the task of guaranteeing the revenue of the state. In other words, as long as the Qing government existed, the conventional notions of ritual constraints remained strong on both sides. These morphed into outright tax-farming systems in Republican times. At the same time (1988: 175ff.) the new business taxes would have needed to access the complex local systems of brokers who operated largely along traditional lines, and which were dominated by wholesale traders operating according to customary law and kinship norms, as we have seen previously. So, the attempts at bureaucratic expansion met with the resistance of local groups, and where these groups slowly receded as a manifestation of general trends in social change and instability, professional tax farming emerged out of the traditional liturgical structures. These developments have to be seen in the context of general administrative reforms that aimed at

strengthening formal administration below the county level (see Duara 1988: 58ff.). However, these did not transform the central feature of the traditional tax system, namely its reliance on informal fees and levies; these were called 'tankuan' (摊款) (cf. Siu 1989: 88ff.) and continued to be negotiated collectively between the villages and the county. In the *longue durée* it is fascinating to realize that these structures survived up until the twenty-first century, even connected with a similar term, 'tanpai' (摊派) (see Bowen II and Rose 1998; Kennedy 2007).

101 For a brief outline, see Fairbank (1976: 26). There was a distinction between 'outer court' and 'inner court', and the latter was institutionalized in the office of the 'Grand Councillor'. It is important to note that this dualism was even reflected in fiscal terms, as the Imperial family also had a special office to manage and supervise its personal property, which therefore is factually distinct from the theoretical notion that all taxable resources belong to the Emperor.

102 This has to be seen against the background of an extensive and thorough system of disciplining and punishing officials for misbehaviour, which may include many aspects that are not directly controlled by them, such as social unrest. Experiencing disciplinary punishments deeply affected the officials' sense of honour; see Metzger (1973: 249ff.). For an illuminating case study for the challenges that officials met in governing society, see Kuhn's (1990) account and analysis of a sorcery scare in 1768, where the Emperor himself invested strong efforts into getting his bureaucracy in line in order for what was seen as an upsurge of political crimes and social unrest.

103 Duara's (1988) work is one of the most influential in the contemporary literature on local government in modernizing China, also often referred to by Chinese researchers (e.g. Zhou Qingzhi 2014). His distinction between forms of brokerage relates to the dualism of *diyuan* and *xueyuan* in the sense that the *diyuan* principle emphasizes the local community, and hence favours protective state brokerage, whereas the *xueyuan* principle entails the fundamental tension between community and familism. Beyond this dualism, Duara emphasizes the role of popular religion as a means of how different actors define their identities, in particular how local elites create and exploit symbolic resources to stabilize their power position. Further, popular religion was also a mediator of social interactions extending the village, such as in the context of the market system and market towns and, more specifically, in organizing activities such as pilgrimages. The latter are an important example of how popular religion also posits egalitarian structures against the prevailing hierarchical structures. Hierarchical structures are also directly reflected in popular religion, such as in the different territorial cults.

104 This is emphasized by Cohen (1994). Cohen highlights the high degree of cultural integration in Imperial China that resulted from the standardization of the symbolic domain. There are many examples to hand, such as the universal role of the lunar calendar and the festivals, or the widespread presence of Daoist rituals in many shapes, though relying on shared repositories of texts. Yet, we also need to recognize the variety of behavioural patterns, such as the large variety of marriage models where it is in fact difficult to distinguish neatly between the reality of the mainstream model and the reality of local variants, which actually would possibly also define a local mainstream.

105 In the context of this chapter, I cannot go into all the details of ritual in Imperial China. The Imperial examination system was certainly a pillar of the reproduction of ritual via the selection and stabilization of a certain social structure in which education was the central indicator of status. This is another instance that shows how misleading the characterization of ritual as

'informal institution' actually is. With the transition in Song times, the examination system triggered a fundamental transformation of the structure of elites, henceforth minimizing the role of inherited privilege, though at the same time also stabilizing status as embodied in the symbiosis of elites in the local state and the stratum of Imperial administrators, which increasingly included wealth as a determinant. For a detailed analysis, see Elman (1991). Thus, we can say that the examination system was a formal institution regulating the production and allocation of social capital in the ritual economy.

106 'State involution' is another core analytical term in Duara's (1988) work. The term 'economic involution' originates from Huang (1990). Both authors draw upon earlier uses of the term 'involution' in the anthropological literature, such as Geertz. The shared meaning is that there is a dynamic process which does not result in the emergence of new structures, but only in the perfection and stabilization of existing structures. Thus, both terms have a normative component in referring to an alternative that is implicitly valued in positive terms, thus implying failure. In the case of state involution this reference is the integrated bureaucratic structure of the modern state, and in the case of economic involution this is capitalism. Yet, the negative reference is stronger in the former case, as the conditions of 1930s China partly resemble failed states, especially on the local level. In comparison, the second case comes closer to the previously mentioned notion of a 'high-level equilibrium trap'.

107 This refers to the much-debated question how far industrialization took off in Republican times. In his classical treatment, Rawski (1989) adopted a positive perspective, which is controversial however, given the immense difficulties in interpreting statistical data of these times (see Richardson 1999: 25ff.). Yet, it is important to note that he assigns a special causal role to energy prices that fits with related views on European catch-up in Allen (2009). The introduction of railways into China as exogenous technological change caused a fall in coal prices that evidently gave a boost to local industrial development (Rawski 1989: 223ff.).

108 On this, see Wedeman (2012). Wedeman even argues that the Guomindang exerted a more penetrating and encompassing control of economic resources than the CCP, in the sense of merging state and party, and directly managing party-owned companies. This relates to the specific political conditions under military rule (i.e. the sub-ethnic differentiation of political power).

109 Unfortunately, space is lacking to add more details. A classical study of these developments is Min (1989) who emphasizes the continuity of presumably 'modern' Western ideas of Parliament and democracy with traditional ideas, especially in the context of opposing the 'feng jian' (封建) system with the centralized system of Imperial rule that had emerged since Tang times. Many leading Confucian thinkers had advocated a strengthening of local self-government, of course, with reference to local elites, but always also referring to the responsibility of local elites for the general welfare of the local population. These ideas served as a context into which modernist notions such as parliaments were embedded. In terms of social structure, pertinent initiatives were indeed often supported by those local elites, such as holders of low degrees in urban areas, which met with the top-down initiatives of provincial governors and hence higher ranked officials. These local initiatives were aborted by both the Republican and Communist governments, continuing with the Late Imperial tradition of the centralization of power, now a major element in strengthening the Chinese state against foreign intruders.

3 Institutions, ideas and ritual in the modern Chinese political economy

Modernism and the persistence of the Chinese growth model

With the collapse of the Empire in 1911, China embarked on a radical modernization programme that has continued up until the present, though with extreme alternations in constellations of political power and the concomitant agendas of modernization. The transitional period between 1911 and 1949 saw the dissolution of the traditional ritual economy and the disruption of the relationship between the central and the local state. As we have seen, this resulted from the erosion of the ritual foundation of the local state, and the following emergence of power structures that rested upon exploiting resources of violence and wealth for private advantage, thus also destroying the institutional foundations of the local and regional market systems. Before the CCP-guided land reforms speeded up and turned violent, one of the hallmarks of CCP policy in the liberated areas was to restore local order and to revive the market system, thus creating legitimacy with the local population. In understanding the unfolding of the Chinese economic style under Communist rule it is essential to look at the many ways in which markets have recurrently been used deliberately as a means to integrate society and improve living conditions, while at the same time recognizing the tensions between the core values of the new political order and the behavioural norms nurtured by market competition.[1] So, more recently, the transition from Maoist policies to the reform era was a shift in the moral framework of markets. It is highly significant that Maoism did not approach the question of markets and capitalism from a Marxist viewpoint, namely to see capitalism or capitalist practices as reflections of the material development of economic substructures, but as an ideological and ultimately moral issue. In this sense, socialism was always seen as the dominance of *gong* over *si*, of *yi* over *li*. In Maoist times, the alleged detrimental effect of markets on moral attitudes was a driving force of recurrent campaigns against 'petty capitalist' activities on the local level, especially in the rural areas, where the administrative controls of the planned economy were less tight than in the urban areas.[2]

After 1949, the CCP implemented a wholesale transformation of the institutional order of society, including the suppression of markets. However, as I analyse in my general model of institutional change, this attempt at institutional design interacted with the existing institutions and cultural patterns. The result was a transformation, but also a revitalization of the ritual economy after 1978. As we will see, a key process in these developments was the radical imposition of collectivization and the household registration system in the rural areas, thus blocking rural–urban migration as well as suppressing the market system up until 1978. To an unprecedented degree, these measures created an institutional separation between rural and urban society on the level of the local state, thus contributing to the 'cellularization' of the Chinese society and the economy. These institutions, I will argue, provided the elements by which the cultural process resulted in a transformation, but also a revival of the ritual economy after 1978. Correspondingly, we need to recognize the continuities that not only connect the Imperial past with the present, but also the Maoist era with the reform era. The apparent radical ruptures in the macro-perspective often block the view of continuities at the local level.

In terms of our general model of historicity, we need to consider at least three layers in analysing contemporary institutions; these correspond to different phases of the transformation in the past, and in which complex path dependencies hold place:

- the interaction between Maoist institutional design and the remnants of the ritual economy in mid-twentieth-century China;
- the interaction between reformist institutional design and the legacies of the Maoist period;
- the current interactions between institutional transformations across different domains.

On these three layers, respectively, it is necessary to consider the interaction with cognitive path dependencies.

In the Aoki approach, this corresponds to a combination of diachronic and synchronic contextualization and correspondences. For example, the post-1978 liberalization of markets started out from unique structural features of planning in the Mao era (regional decentralization), or the reforms of the state-ownership system were strongly influenced by the emergence of township and village enterprises in the 1980s, which in turn were rooted in the People's Communes. In analysing such processes, we can make the historicity of institutions explicit; this enables us to develop hypotheses about the evolving economic style.

In understanding this institutional evolution, it is of the utmost importance to explore the ideational dimension of economic policy after 1949. In terms of theory, we need to consider explicitly the cognitive path dependencies that connect the Imperial era with China's present. This ideational dimension is reflected in the worldview of 'modernism': I present this term as a medium-range theoretical term encapsulating one defining element of the Chinese economic style. Modernism emerged as a universal ideational stance of Chinese elites after the May Fourth Movement. I refer to the idea that the task of a new political and intellectual elite is to transform China into a 'modern country'. The term 'modern' refers partly to the material infrastructure; that is, economic and military modernization, in particular, and to certain civilizational standards, which were seen as becoming a wholesale substitute of traditional Chinese culture. In this sense, modernism has continued to be a foundational idea in Chinese politics also after 1978, with the first four, later five and even six 'modernizations' being perceived and communicated as a project of civilizational transformation. This emphasis on civilizational transformation reflected the belief that the previous period of Maoism did not fulfil the promise of modernization. Thus, in contemporary China the notion of 'civilization', 'wenming' (文明), stands at the centre of the modernist agenda. This most general notion is applied in different contexts, such as initially in the dualism of 'material' and 'spiritual civilization', and more recently in contexts such as 'political civilization' or 'environmental civilization'. In connecting the modernist agenda with the educational claims for leadership in the civilizational process, the CCP has created an ideological umbrella that also integrates the idea of socialism with the market.[3]

In my understanding, the term 'modernism' not only refers to certain ideas and ideologies, but also to the material infrastructures that express these and which also feedback to the consciousness of actors as being symbols and signs of modernity. Because of these feedback mechanisms, modernism is an important aspect of Chinese institutions. However, in considering path dependencies that operate on the different layers identified previously, we have to recognize that these institutions remain diachronically embedded. One crucial insight is that the idea of modernism directly ties up with the traditional notion that there is a stratum in the population that defines the agenda of cultural transformation and is therefore legitimized to 'educate' the population in order to raise their civilizational standards. However, whereas the Confucian transformational effort started out from a set of ideas that was to a large degree coherent with the values and institutions of popular culture, the modernist effort of the CCP in the first three decades after 1949 directly aimed at transforming popular culture in a radical and comprehensive way, not only including the so-called 'feudal' customs such as popular religion and kinship organization, but also the practices undergirding the market system, which were denounced as being potential seeds of a resurgence of capitalism. So, modernist thinking stood in deep tension with the ritual economy.

These radical modernist efforts were gradually toned down after 1978, but changed only partly in emphasis and direction. In this regard, the radical population policy adopted at the beginning of the reform period has to be acknowledged as a major aspect in the continuity of the modernist transformational agenda across the apparent ideological divide between Mao and Deng. The enforcement of the one-child policy is a most articulate expression of state power in modern China, because it directly reached through to individual decision-making and also clashed with fundamental norms of the traditional Chinese family. Therefore, population policy is at the same time a policy tool as an expression of modernism. In Foucault's terms, population policy is part and parcel of a 'biopolitics' of development. Together with the resilient growth model, it is therefore a fundamental cultural feature of Chinese reforms.[4] Imposing a constraint upon the number of children in order to push economic progress was achieved by the same political and administrative means that were also a defining feature of Maoist policies, such as campaigns or setting binding targets for local administrators. On the other hand, population policy is highly significant for assessing the path dependencies of ritual practices and ideas, because the reduction of the number of progeny certainly changed the material conditions for the continuity of ritual, especially in the context of extended kinship, and it undermined essential values of the traditional family in terms of the priority of continuing the family line and the emphasis on patriarchal order and male primacy. Therefore, population policy is a measure of modernist cultural transformation that does not differ in method from earlier measures directed against markets and capitalism, deeply affecting popular perceptions of social order and morality. In a sense it is even more radical, as it more deeply penetrated into a core domain of private lives. Therefore, population policy may be seen as a key element of the modern ritual economy. It directly transforms ritual foundations of society, yet was designed as a purely economic policy measure aiming at balancing population growth and productivity of the economy.[5]

The example of population policy, however, is also important in making us aware of the complex structure of the interactions among the various levels of path dependency. Consider the traditional family as a unit of production. When reforms were launched, the traditional family was still in its prime, reflecting the pronatalist policies of the Maoist leadership. In other words, in terms of historicity of changes we have to pay attention to the generational time frame. The one-child policy caused changes in the size of the family only after 1978, and therefore initially directly affected only the marriage patterns and reproductive decisions of families. The effects on children's socialization only find expression in rhythms of decades, whereas the effects on extended kinship and economic organization emerge after only one generation, such as when family companies are handed over to the second generation where all peers are mostly single children, and, for example, issues of family division no longer loom large. So, the different layers are also manifest in particular temporal structures of the changes, resulting in complex interdependencies and unintended consequences.[6]

On the other hand, we need to consider the complex configurations of the ritual economy in the past, where simple generalizations did not hold, as we have seen. So, in assessing the effects of modernist transformations on the family, we also need to be aware of the flexibility of the traditional structure. For example, 'minor marriages' with elements such as uxorilocal residence were part and parcel of the traditional pattern, so that we cannot simply classify a greater prevalence under conditions of scarcity of brides, reflecting the distorted sex ratio, as a manifestation of cultural changes, or a transformation of ritual. Yet, this does not mean that there are no effects on the social and even psychological conditions of an increasing number of males who may need to accept these deviations from what is seen as the standard form of marriage.[7]

Thus, the example of population policy is an excellent case for demonstrating the deep interactions among the modernist agenda and social structures and agency, thus qualifying it as an essential part of governmentality. On the one hand, there are the formal institutions of population policy, but these interact with pre-existing norms and behavioural patterns, eventually resulting in new states that were not necessarily intended by the designers of the policy. As I will discuss in the following section, one important example is the effects on gender valuations, since, on the one hand, the population policy even reinforced the perception that the reproductive role is a defining feature of the female gender, assigning the entire responsibility for implementing it to the female side; on the other hand, the resulting distortions of the sex ratio greatly shifted the valuation of genders towards the female side, thus supporting value change in society.

I have started my discussion of modernism with the example of population policy because in this case the continuities and the ruptures between the Maoist and the reform era are straightforward to see. The modernist claims of the state on leading society towards improvements remain the same; only the goal has shifted.[8] However, on an even deeper level it has to be recognized that both pronatalist and birth control policies were seen as subordinate to the goal of economic development. In this sense, we need to put it into the larger context of the growth model that is the material counterpart to the economic style. In both the Maoist and the Dengist paradigm, economic growth represented a core goal of modernist transformation. I submit the claim that this model is the most important institutional continuity across the break of reform policies in 1978, and persists even today. Then, we can also understand that the current debates about changing the growth model actually have to be seen in a long-term context, and even have a cultural meaning as well. This adds deeper perspectives on what is currently a macroeconomic discourse, highlighting the need to rely more on consumption as a driver of growth, in place of investments as a primary driver and exports as a secondary driver (where, after all, foreign consumption plays the decisive role). Therefore, again, my subsequent analysis provides the background for understanding most recent policy debates and measures as a part of the modernist agenda, and hence as expressions of economic style.[9]

Regarding growth as a central concern of modernism, however, we have to recognize the pivotal position of the state as being seen as promoter and agent of economic transformation. This raises the question of how the state can appropriate the resources necessary to fulfil this role of the avant-garde of growth. Seen in the light of the previous chapter, this relates to the issue of economic or market involution. Indeed, collectivization was seen as a major means to break up involutionary patterns of the traditional ritual economy, and, in turn, marketization after 1978 was seen as countering those involutionary forces that had unintentiously been created by collectivization. So, if we look at the side of resource appropriation by the state, the question of the growth model is essentially connected with the issue of taxation, and hence ultimately the relationship between the central and the local state. This is where in the traditional system market and government involution played together. This is also a defining pattern for understanding the economic style up until the present day. If the state is seen as an avant-garde of economic modernization, how can the necessary resources for exerting this function be generated, and how can possibly negative effects on growth be avoided that result from extractive interventions?[10]

As we have seen, under Republican rule taxation morphed into a system of entrepreneurial state brokerage. Correspondingly, we have to interpret collectivization as an institutional means of eradicating entrepreneurial state brokerage and directly accessing the farming population in order to extract resources for the state, thus even bypassing the local state.[11] This was made possible by the comprehensive militarization and mobilization of the rural society, albeit at high costs in terms of eventually jeopardizing productive motivation and efficiency. This perspective leads us also to reconsider reforms under the aspect of how the reforms affected this capacity of the central state to harness fiscal resources. The major issue here was that the Maoist institutions failed in terms of setting up a modern taxation system, thus merely relying on direct control of production and distribution. The question after 1978 was how these extractive institutions would need to be designed if at the same time productivity of the economy needs to be enhanced, and how the required institutions for this interact with the institutions of taxation. So, my claim is that the key to understanding market transition after 1978 is the institutional transformation of the tax system. As we have seen, the organization of taxation reaches far beyond the scope of the formal institutions of the fiscal system and involves governmentality in the broadest sense, especially the role of the local state in relation to both the population and central government.

In considering taxation, we note one fundamental difference between modernist and traditional ideas about taxation. The Confucian ideology as well as the practices of the Qing central state in principle supported the idea of frugal fiscal policy and keeping taxation at a level that does not jeopardize the people's livelihood. The escalation of local taxes in the late eighteenth and early nineteenth century under the auspices of Heshen was therefore clearly seen as a violation of fundamental principles of Imperial statecraft. This relates to a leitmotiv in Chinese discussions of taxation that persists today, namely the role of the local state in driving a wedge between formal institutions of taxation and practices of taxation at the grassroots level, and hence the narrative of local government failure, corruption and arbitrary abuse of power. I will analyse this part of the picture in Chapter 4 in greater detail. At the moment, we have to keep it in mind as a background for the ongoing analysis.

In contrast, modernism is a position that pursues the goal to maximize the fiscal capacity of the central state in order to enable it to push forward the economic modernization of society. In modernism, people's livelihoods are only a secondary goal or simply a constraint on the modernization programme. What counts first is the material transformation of the economic foundations of state power. This idea emerged from the violent conflict with Western Imperialism in the nineteenth century and has actually been a constant across the apparent ideological divide of 1978. Until very recent times, the goals of 'wealth and power' have been seen as closely related, and the welfare of society at large is only seen as a concomitant result, although after 1978 rising living standards were also interpreted in the context of civilizational progress. Yet, consumption is not the ultimate aim of the economic process, in the modernist view. Therefore, heightening the role of consumption in the macroeconomy according to the 'new growth model' is not simply a measure of economic adjustment, but would possibly transform fundamental premises of modernist economic policy.

The basic idea of the Chinese growth model between the 1950s and 1980s was that economic modernization and growth can only be achieved if the rate of accumulation is as high as possible, or, in non-Marxist terms, the investment rate.[12] This corresponds with a high savings rate and low consumption. So, the major difference between the Maoist era and the reform era does not lie in the growth model as such, but in the fact that the mechanisms achieving this aim differ, with command economy levers dominating in the first period, and market mediated mechanisms in the second period. However, there are also institutional features that connect the two manifestations of the growth model, of which the most important are the household registration system and the system of state-owned companies, including, in particular, a government-controlled financial sector.

In the first period, the suppression of the traditional market system and the use of command economy guidance resulted in a system of forced procurement of agricultural products at low prices. This forced procurement is therefore the pivotal institution of the Maoist system of taxation and the means to directly access the fiscal capacity of the rural society, bypassing all intermediate levels that could possibly interfere in the process. The procurement prices on the one hand suppressed rural consumption and savings, but also enabled the enforcement of low wages in the urban industrial economy, thus eventually making high rates of industrial investment possible. This also implied that rural investment had to rely mainly on labour, such as building irrigation systems by means of quasi corvée labour, which therefore also counts as a means of taxation, ominously representing the revival of traditional institutions of labour service in the Empire. The strong disincentives in agriculture were partly and temporarily overcome by ideological mobilization, which worked effectively in the context of strengthening the household registration system, because people could not avoid local social pressures and surveillance. This system effectively blocked inter-regional movements of rural labour even at the local level (for example, moving from villages to nearby market towns). Therefore, the institutional separation between urban and rural society was part and parcel of the system of fiscal extraction. As we shall see below, by this the modernist effort also created an essential ingredient of the ritual economy of the present, namely the status distinction between rural and urban society in general, but also among urban areas of different hierarchical positions in the national urban system.

As a result, China entered the reform era with a severe structural distortion. China had already achieved a relatively high level of industrialization as measured by the share of industry in GDP, but it still showed a much lower share of industrial labour as compared to agriculture.[13] At the same time, the suppression of markets did not provide space for the development of the tertiary sector. So, the forced industrialization model created a dualist economic and social structure that cut through the social fabric that was supporting the traditional market system, in particular in terms of the cultural integration between the rural and urban areas. This structural dualism is essential in understanding the dynamics of economic reforms, in particular the rise of township and village enterprises and the concomitant rural urbanization processes, which created path dependencies that have influenced development up until the present day, and the role of migrant labour in creating the competitiveness of industrial export clusters in the coastal areas. However, these structural factors also have a deeper significance in terms of cultural and institutional patterns. First, therefore, the long-term effects of cellularization of rural society have also shaped cultural changes in more recent times, with close to 80 per cent of the Chinese population in 1978 living in confined and semi-autarkic local communities; this implies that social changes in the context of urbanization are shaped by the cultural dynamics of generational transitions in the rural areas. Second, since the rural population lives under the jurisdiction of the local state, hence the county level, any kind of institutional differentiation between the local and the central state is therefore also a constitutive element of the economic style.

The basic structure of the Chinese growth model up until 1978 is depicted in the upper part of Figure 3.1. This is a description of the formal institutions, and thus should not be mistaken for the description of the entire institutional make-up. In other words, we look at the institutional design part of the picture, and so far leave out institutional path dependencies. Considering the aforementioned structural consequences of these institutions, on the theoretical level we need to consider complete and comprehensive loops of elements–patterns–processes–states. Thus,

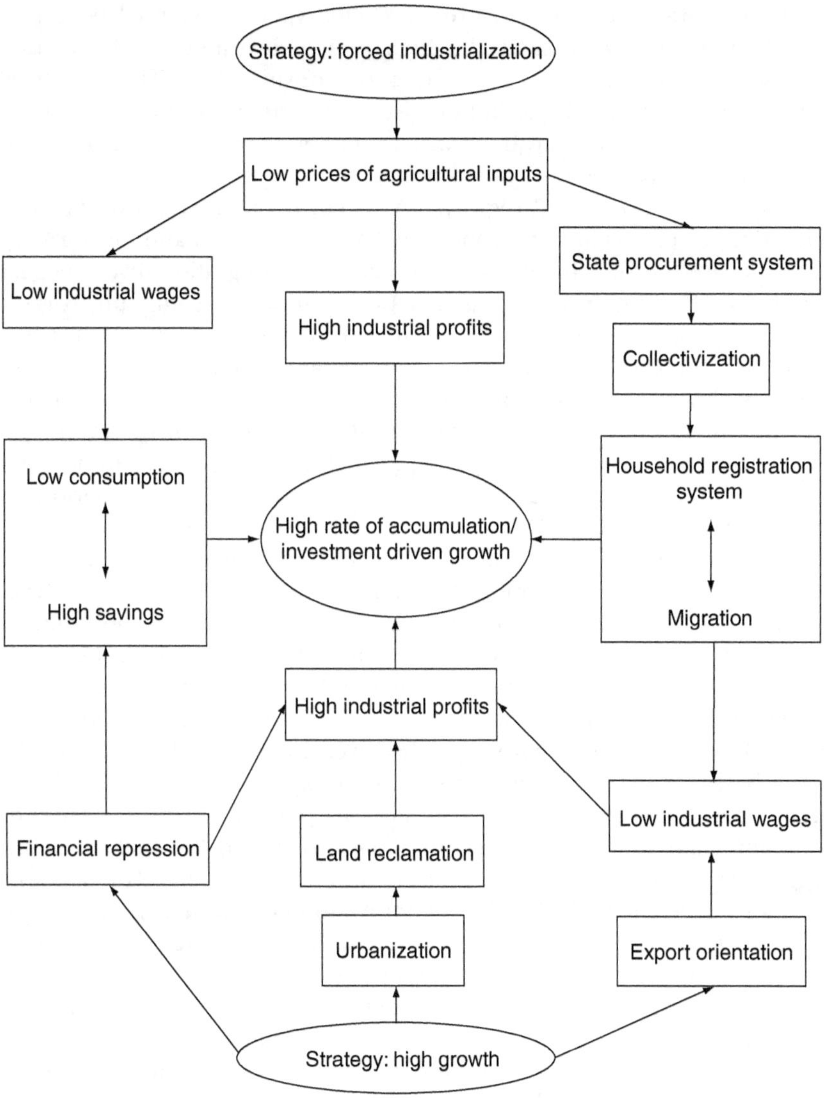

Figure 3.1 The Chinese growth model, 1949 to the present.

cellularization is a state that resulted from the interaction between formal institutions and traditional institutions, mainly driven into informality because of the withdrawal of legitimacy in the Communist state. I will analyse this in the third section of this chapter.

An important observation here is that, first, even though formal institutions were drastically changed in the course of reforms, the basic mechanisms remained the same. This shows that a core aspect of these institutions is the pattern of resource extraction under modernist auspices. The lower part of Figure 3.1 shows main elements of the growth model of the reform era. The two parts are connected via one essential feature of growth performance, namely the high rate of investment. This feature necessarily combines with a low rate of consumption. The structural dualism created by the household registration system represents the essential institutional continuity; there are a number of important background conditions, such as the population policy.

Whereas the household registration system in the first period blocked migration, its effects in the second area have persisted in another form up until the present day. In releasing the fetters on migration, over decades China could maintain a wage gap between urban and migrant workers even in the cities, since migrants are disenfranchised of a range of urban privileges, such as access to social services and insurance. This means, however, that the low-wage pattern of the old model could persist, including the distributional effects on industrial profits, even in the more specific sense of a rural–urban wage gap, which shows up as a gap between urban inhabitants and migrants. This is also reflected in the abnormally low share of wages in GDP: since the 1990s, the wage share has been retreating to below 45 per cent, only recovering a little most recently, thus being far lower than the standard 70 per cent in developed capitalist economies. It is important to note that this low share includes the imputed remuneration in agriculture and self-employed sectors; that is, the entire informal economy. The wage rate for employed persons, hence of the formal sector, hovers at around 34 per cent. From this it follows that the decline of the wage share is partly driven by the developments in the family-based economy.[14] Another structural expression of this fact is the high savings rate in China. Approximately 50 per cent of this is savings by companies and the government, in stark contrast to 'normal' capitalist economies where companies are net debtors and households net savers. In other words, the high share of corporate and government savings in the economy is the core indicator of the persistence of the traditional growth model in spite of comprehensive market reforms.[15]

The high savings rate of China also reflects financial repression favouring industrial enterprises via the state banks. Financial repression is particularly pronounced in the rural areas and is manifest in the low interest rate for savings and a lack of alternative investments. Together with the erosion of collective institutions of social services in the countryside, this creates very strong incentives for 'Keynesian' savings. In other words, in rural areas, but also mostly in urban areas, individuals save for structural and habitual reasons independent from the interest rate, such as for education, emergencies or housing. The low interest rate enables the state banks to offer cheap credit to companies, thus further reducing the costs of investment. In summary, we can classify the savings in China as 'forced savings' in the sense that they are reflecting the lack of alternative savings vehicles, such as capital exports. Since savings are generally even higher than the investment rate, capital exports are realized by companies and government, the latter in the form of accumulating vast amounts of currency reserves. In macroeconomic terms, financial repression is also the means by which investment assumes the prior causal role in determining the high savings. Thus, consumption is passively adapting to investment which is in turn not mainly driven by market factors but by decisions taken on different levels of the administrative system (which I study in Chapter 4).[16]

Finally, the structural distortion of the Chinese economy on the eve of reforms was also manifest in the low level of urbanization, which, in comparative terms, persists until today, in spite of the rapid urban growth in recent times. Accordingly, the rise of migration after the onset of reforms pushes urbanization. Especially after the 1990s, a major mechanism of urbanization was land conversion. Land conversion is another form of redistributing funds from the rural areas to the urban industrial economy, today also including urban services, since it mostly occurs at artificially low prices for agricultural land. This is reflected in the urban sprawl; that is, in spite of the rapid ongoing urbanization, cities tend to grow extensively, indicating less efficient use of urban land because of depressed prices which create rents for developers and other commercial users. Since urban land is state-owned, the government can directly allocate rents between itself and other users. If the government does not fully charge land users such as SOEs, ultimately resources are redistributed directly from the original rural owners to urban industries and services.[17]

All these observations boil down to one fundamental institutional fact, namely the dualism between rural and urban society and the economy. In the Maoist era, this went hand in hand with the cellularization pattern; this pattern was broken in the reform era via marketization. Yet, the rural/urban dualism continued to be enshrined in the institutional structures. With the rise of migration, and reforms in the state-owned sector, dualism is expressed in the co-existence of the informal and the formal economy, directly reflected in the labour market, in which the migrants build a bridge between rural and urban. The formal economy is manifest in labour market arrangements which allow participation in social security institutions and other special arrangements such as in housing, and where formal labour contracts are also enforced by the legal system. This system emerged from the Maoist urban system mainly in the context of the state-owned sector and in the foreign-invested sector, gradually transforming urban privileges of the command economy mode into privileged access to social security institutions which are compatible with markets. The most recent expansion of these formal institutions towards full inclusiveness in the urban areas meets with resistance in the informal sector and thus remains contested until today, with many employers using legal means to avoid the transition to the formal economy for a substantial number of employees. As a result, when in former times the urban population represented just 20 to 30 per cent of the entire Chinese population, today, after many rural dwellers have moved to the cities, a similar proportion defines the dualism of the formal versus the informal economy.[18]

The informal economy is a major element in the persistence of the forced industrialization model up until recent times. This is most directly visible in the fact that the wage differential is essential for maintaining China's comparative advantage in the export sector, especially in South China, and also for maintaining high levels of investment in construction and infrastructure. Although, in recent years, urban minimum wages have risen considerably, and also mandatory and inclusive social insurance has been imposed, there are many ways in which the corporate sector can adapt and maintain low wages, often with accommodating attitudes of local governments who want to keep industries in place (for example, overtime practices can hollow out minimum wages). Further, the informal economy has been essential for the expansion of urban services, thus allowing for a rise in real urban living standards without a proportional increase of the wage level, thus also enabling a continuing depression of wages in the formal economy.[19]

So, in summary, we can say that the growth model of the reform era is a replica of the Maoist model, if not in terms of form then in substance. As I have explained, this perspective is immediately transparent if we consider the institutional structures in terms of extractive functions. In this sense, in both periods it would be highly misleading to differentiate analytically between formal fiscal institutions and institutions of the economy in general. In the second period of the modernist growth model, the extractive functions were indirectly mediated via the market system, such as via the interest rate, or via the discriminatory pricing of rural land assets during the urbanization process. The core expression of this functional convergence is the high rate of accumulation. In terms of the Aoki model this is an etic datum, which defines a 'state' of the economy, with a mutual determination of economic structures and institutions. In this state, the modernist metamorphoses of the growth model have created a specific form of governmentality in which the market assumes a central position. This observation suggests approaching 'informality' as a systematic feature of the modernist ritual economy which emerges from the interaction between the modernist formal institutions and decentralized economic decisions by individuals. This interaction is in turn mediated by ritual phenomena that shape those individual decisions, and which reflect the modernist ideational frame.

The 'quality' of modernity: the market as a form of governmentality in the status order of the ritual economy

The differentiation of the ritual economy into a formal and an informal domain is tantamount to establishing a status order of modernism. This finds expression in the notion of the 'quality' *suzhi* of population that has been a pivotal idea in Chinese population policy in recent decades. The central aspect is the distinction between different strata of society, partly reflected in residential differentiation, according to different civilizational levels and hence degrees of 'modernity'. This distinction relates to claims on cultural leadership in the modernization effort. In this sense, modernism partly replicates the patterns of culturalism in Imperial times. As we have seen, a particular distribution of status and social capital was the pillar of the traditional order. We can identify similar mechanisms in the context of the modernist growth model, thus recognizing the workings of cognitive path dependencies. This relates, first, to the notion that a culturalist avant-garde leads the process of civilizational transformation, and second, to the strong interaction between formal institutions, on the one hand, and the production and distribution of social capital in society on the other. Social capital in modern China is partly influenced by formal institutions, but there is the more fundamental impact of modernism as a cognitive-institutional complex.

The modernist order assigns high social status to the urban population.[20] Generally speaking, the urbanite has higher *suzhi* than the rural dweller. This term refers to civilizational advancement in terms of education, manners, lifestyle or material culture. This status distinction has been enshrined in the formal institutions of the household registration system, giving a number of privileges to the urban population *in toto*, but also differentiating between different levels in the urban hierarchy; that is, giving higher status to metropolitan areas as compared to smaller cities. As a result of blocking migration and urbanization in the Maoist era, and the social patterns of migration in the reform era, a cultural dualism has emerged that not only distinguishes between rural and urban society in formal terms, but also in habitus and even corporeal characteristics such as colour of skin. For example, second-generation children of migrants are easy to spot in elementary schools, and often segmented social interactions emerge, such as assortative matching in play.[21] This matching is grounded in physical characteristics of the different groups, even simply the different complexion of skin ('white' vs. 'dark'). Indeed, the notion of *suzhi*, though mainly referring to the civilizational and cultural characteristics of a person, is also interpreted in physical terms: habitus finds expression in movements, discipline may be mirrored in bodily shape, especially of females, and so forth.[22]

This cultural distinction induces the segmentation of urban society under conditions of migration, even if the constraints of the formal institutions are released. In fact, the status order is reflected in a differential distribution of social capital across various segments of the population, which is visible, for example, in the segmentation of the labour market or settlement patterns. This segmentation is increasingly independent from formal institutions. In fact, in medium-level cities migrant workers often do not even want to change their formal registration from rural to urban, because the formal rights and claims are no longer essential for their social differentiation. The differential distribution of social capital is undergirded by many supplementary institutions, especially in the educational system.[23]

As a consequence, we may say that the institutional underpinnings of the modernist growth model have gradually coalesced into a ritual order of society, reflected in the pattern of the distribution of social capital. This ritual order is status based and highlights different civilizational levels, thus directly tying in with related ideas in Imperial China, though in modernist metamorphosis. The most important difference is the creation of a sharp cultural dichotomy between urban and rural society. This can be easily recognized in cultural icons. Whereas in traditional China bucolic and even wild landscapes were essential cultural images, these have been substituted by images of urban modernity such as skyscrapers or airports. If we look at the determinants of this resilience of a civilizational status order, the crucial insight is that it is no longer exclusively determined by the formal institutions of the *hukou* system, but reflects a differential distribution of human and social capital that is mediated by the market, such as when migrant workers concentrate in particular urban jobs and professions. It is market signals that evaluate 'civilizational' differences and therefore also contribute to their resilience. So, they have become an aspect of the ritual economy in the genuine sense.

After successfully enforcing a reduction of the growth rate of the population in the 1980s, population policy turned to measures that aimed at increasing the 'quality' of the population. However, looking at the conditions prevailing in the rural areas, this did not imply that the government invested more resources, for example, into the education sector. On the contrary, one of the core features of social and political change in the countryside was the retreat of government from the provision of social services, and the growing importance of markets. This is largely interpreted as a default solution, in the sense that markets were the only feasible alternative to a diminishing fiscal basis for the supply of public services, together with the erosion of other means of public organization, as in the case of the community-based health workers. But we also need to recognize that markets gradually turned into a central element of governmentality, in the sense that they became a central element in the rural social fabric. This means, for example, that migration was interpreted as a lever of opening up rural society to modernity, and hence contributing to the efforts to increase the quality of the population.[24]

The full complexity of this process can only be properly understood once we consider the local state in Chapter 4. At this point, suffice it to mention that the retreat of government from the public sector in the rural areas went hand in hand with the resurgence of the local state under modernist auspices. In other words, the task of modernization and economic growth was partly decentralized and relegated to local authorities, which had to adapt to the growing role of markets in their economic environment. So, the active recognition of the market on the part of the local state was also translated into the active involvement of the rural individual with the market, often in close interaction between government and individual, as in actively promoting migration as a means to release the pressure of rural underemployment.

So, taken together with the modernist status order that is pivotal to the growth model, quality as *suzhi* may be regarded as a core notion in the cultural transformation of the ritual economy. Reflecting upon this, we realize that it is not a rupture with the past, but actually reinstates the role of markets in the traditional ritual economy. The difference lies in their conceptualization. In the traditional ritual economy, markets were not activated as a medium of the civilizing effort of the government; they were just accepted as being part and parcel of the living world of ordinary people. Markets were not seen as being an element of elite culture, though often being the means by which the economic basis for this status was created, as in the case of strong merchant lineages including scholar-official pedigree. Today, markets are part and parcel of the modernist project. In other words, market reforms have to be seen as a *jiaohua* effort, and not simply as a means to enhance efficiency and productivity in the economy. Markets are central sites of modernism in action. This creates a distinct, possibly even paradoxical approach to markets, at least from the view of certain Western observers who are deeply influenced by the liberal tradition. Whereas in most liberal doctrines markets are 'natural' outcomes of the free pursuit of enterprise, in the modernist view markets are institutional devices created and implemented by the government in order to transform society. As we will see later, this not only applies for the rural–urban distinction we have discussed so far, but, for example, also for the modernization of state-owned companies that 'go global' and therefore undergo the modernization of management and organization via the mediation of the global markets.[25]

So, the civilizational function of markets applies for both the rural and urban areas. In the rural areas and with regard to migrant workers, markets are the medium through which individuals may raise their *suzhi* by adopting more independent and risk-oriented behaviours and adapting their behaviour to the urban lifestyles and the workplace standards in modern enterprises. Thus, government agencies are often involved in the process of selecting migrants and channelling them to modernizing urban places. As we will see in Chapter 6, this translates into specific approaches to labour management in companies, which interestingly focus on 'Legalist' disciplinary mechanisms in order to achieve the necessary behavioural changes. This often reinstates the status order in the context of companies, as migrant workers and regular employees even experience very different contexts of corporate culture and leadership styles. A typical pattern is that migrant workers dominate the production process, whereas urbanites dominate the white-collar jobs in the company. It is important to realize that in these human resource management approaches, interfaces between the formal and the informal economy are created in spite of the fact that the companies operate in the formal economy, thus creating an integrative mechanism in the ritual economy.[26]

The corresponding cultural dualism is largely visible in the 'professionalization' of the urban workforce, especially in the white-collar segment. Here, internationalization and modern education are hallmarks of the emerging urban middle class, and local governments strive to play a leading role via the educational system and the management of the labour market for 'talents'. These efforts reflect a similar transition in labour market mechanisms as in the rural areas and the informal economy. Today, jobs for graduates of higher education are mostly allocated via the market, so that market-based criteria offer the standard for professionalism to which the largely government-based educational system has to adapt. In cooperation with universities, local governments are often actively involved in setting up job fairs, markets for talent and providing counselling or other services to graduates. Again, government and market are inextricably enmeshed, and the standards of modernism are deduced from market practices. For graduates, the adoption of these standards is not only seen as a means to launch individual careers, but they are also aspects of citizenship in a modernist state. Consequently, professionalism in China today has become a manifestation of governmentality.

This has to be seen in the larger context of the gradual convergence between the imposed limitation of family size and the market-guided preferences of couples. The one-child policy in the urban areas caused a significant interaction between modern and traditional family values that directly influences the larger patterns of consumption practices which is also shaped by the influence of the market on family decisions. This is because professionalization goes hand in hand with intensification of labour market competition which rewards higher levels of education that increase the costs of raising children. Thus, in spite of the continuing enforcement of population policy, market frames largely also create strong incentives to reduce the number of children. This is another manifestation of population policy morphing into a form of governmentality.

Increasingly, the couples' preferences match with the regulations, thus apparently turning reproductive decisions into voluntary ones. The main reason is the exploding costs of raising children in an increasingly competitive urban environment. This begins even with the early stages of childhood socialization: 'quality mothers' are seen as investing in single 'quality children' who as early as possible accumulate the human capital that is necessary to be a modern subject in the market economy. This also creates links between the modern consumer society and education, as children are being nurtured and equipped with the best possible consumer goods that might help increase their quality of life. It is also important to notice that the resulting overindulgence towards single children is partly shaped by the traditional ideas about filial piety: investing in the quality of life of children hopefully creates reciprocity between the generations, such that filial children will later assume responsibility for their parents.[27]

However, as I stated in the previous section, labour market outcomes are strongly influenced by the distribution of social capital, undergirded by other institutions. As transpired in previous paragraphs, the educational system is of central significance here. This is because the labour market is ordered by status distinctions, and symbolic representations of educational status reflect these distinctions. The rural–urban dualism is increasingly connected with a pattern of differential access to institutions of higher education, which can be only partly made up by market-mediated measures such as investing in children's education. The status bifurcation is visible, for example, in the impact of the household registration system upon differential success in the university entrance examinations and even the transition to secondary high school. Migrant workers have to send back their children to the place of registration of the parents, since children have to take the entry exams there. So, they typically enter lower quality schools and suffer from other detrimental conditions such as the separation of families. As a result, contrary to the more egalitarian early post-Mao institutions that equalized access to higher education, the current system has created a long-run tendency of an increasingly uneven distribution of human capital between the urban and rural areas. Now, since education is also a hallmark of civilizational advancement, this actually bolsters the effects of the unequal distribution of social capital. However, it should be noted that these status distinctions also apply for urban areas, as the *hukou* status is actually broken down to the district level. The best schools are often concentrated in particular areas of cities and thus may not be open to children with a *hukou* of another district. These barriers can be overcome by special relationships, 'donations' to the schools and other informal means. Yet, the educational system as a whole therefore directly undergirds the stratification of society into fine-grained status groups.[28]

These different observations are important because they show that the simple abolition of the formal institutions of the urban–rural dichotomy would not necessarily change the status order that is now embodied in the distribution of human and social capital. On the contrary, market forces may even exacerbate these effects in cementing the institutional differentiation between the formal and the informal economy and between different social strata. This is because educational status is a signalling device, corresponding exactly to the notion of *suzhi*, and hence creates differential conditions across groups with different status, which feed back into salary structures and career patterns. In other words, in the marketplace the status order becomes performative. This performativity is evident if we consider the feedback to educational careers of children whose parents have already built their own careers in the context of the status order. Parents with low-paid jobs and working in more disadvantaged sectors or regions in the economy would lack the resources to support their children's educational careers in turn. This is a crucial insight. In the ritual economy, what was originally enforced institutional change morphs into a performative institutional structure, in which ideational determinants (such as modernist appreciation of urban lifestyles), material factors (such as corporeal distinctions across different groups in society or residential patterns) and intentional actions of different actors come together in reproducing the status order that stands at the core of the ritual economy. In the element–pattern–process–state explanatory framework, this means that the *hukou* system as an element is transformed into a state that turns into a cultural element of its own.

We may count this as a central mechanism in the modern ritual economy, which is already having long-term consequences. The formal institutions of the household registration system as elements have resulted in patterns and processes that have created states of unequal status that are performative, given the current institutional conditions in the educational system. This is also where the fiscal system comes into play, hence the organization of modernist extractive mechanisms. In regions where fiscal resources are weak, educational investment will be relatively low, impacting upon the career prospects of local children at all levels. In other words, educational status obtains an essential significance in defining the status order. In this context it deserves mentioning that the CCP increasingly treats educational status as an important criterion for admission to the party. I come back to this point in Chapter 4.

This central role of education bears strong family resemblances with the traditional ritual economy. Traditional and modernist education are functionally equivalent in defining the societal status order in ritual terms. I posit that in the context of professionalism, but also the corporate socialization of migrant workers, we can also meaningfully speak of 'ritual work' in terms of establishing an orthopraxy of the market. In other words, professional standards such as submitting a curriculum vitae, learning about rules of conduct or dressing in the appropriate way are behavioural patterns that manifest the 'sincerity' by which modernity is accepted and put into practice. Ritual work does not necessarily mean that individuals actually adopt the corresponding 'inner stance' which comes to the fore when non-standard situations emerge, or when actual work also requires one to be creative in terms of rearranging established standards. This is reflected in often-cited complaints by international employers in China about a certain lack of soft skills, individual responsibility and creativity on the part of the younger cohorts of university graduates. Interestingly, another complaint directly matches certain traditional attitudes towards education, namely that university graduates lack practical knowledge and experience in how to apply the acquired knowledge, which has often been accumulated as a mere formal set of knowledge items, thus actually turning knowledge proper into a ritual pattern, displayed generally in the context of examinations.[29]

It is important to note that in these determinants of the status order there are strong interactions with the urban marriage market. I claim that the marriage market is an essential element in reproducing certain structures of the ritual economy which bear close family resemblances with the past, thus replicating the pivotal position of the family in it, though in a modernist form. This fact reflects the highly unique role of the population policy in determining structural and dynamic features of the economy. As a result of population policy, there is a surplus of males searching for brides, which has shifted the balance towards increasing flows of assets from the grooms' families to the brides in constituting the new household. Families with sons need to increase their investment in the relative status of sons, which has to be complemented by investment in appropriate consumer goods which effectively operate like a brideprice: the urban marriage market partly replicates traditional norms of arranging marriages according to status. This is a major factor driving investments into residential real estate, cars and education, since attractive jobs are also a status symbol in the marriage market. This typically requires a professional background, such as working in advanced urban sectors, finance or international companies. So, professionalism and status converge in the marriage market as well. As a consequence, the marriage market increasingly shows patterns of assortative matching along status lines, with education, quality of jobs and household registration sustaining the status order. This assortative matching defines a substantial difference in traditional marriage patterns because the status of women is considerably enhanced. But at the same time, social status distinctions in terms of civilizational qualities are becoming more firmly entrenched and are reflected in changing patterns of modernist status consumption.

Since education also relates to a status order of job placements, a close family resemblance to conditions in Imperial China is the increasing gap between graduates who enter the expected careers and those who lose out, mostly with a low-quality bachelor's degree, such as bachelor degrees from local universities. This reveals the variation of the status order within urban society and across different urban places. The Chinese system of tertiary education produces a growing number of graduates who remain urbanites, but cannot enter attractive careers. These males struggle in the marriage market, and typically fail to win attractive brides. So, in the Chinese public debate it has been often noticed that the population policy resulted into a partial revival of traditional gender roles, with males aspiring to wealth and professional success, which is highly appreciated by many females, and focus on physical attractiveness on the male side. Social changes triggered by education may also be recognized, as an increasing number of females opt for professional careers and therefore delay marriage beyond traditional concepts. In fact, the population policy has also caused a change in gender valuations, with parents of daughters actively supporting their careers. This in turn leverages the growing scarcity of brides on the marriage market. Thus, we can say that in spite of the fact that gender valuations have changed tremendously in balancing the appreciation of daughters and sons, at the same time the traditional pressure for relatively early family formation persists, especially also on sons. In fact, whereas in earlier phases of population policy the preference for sons caused negative impacts upon women, in more recent times the pressure on men also increased in facing the threat of being unable to establish a family.[30]

So, we observe cohort differences in attitudes, which nevertheless result in a resilience of important elements of the traditional family, in particular regarding its centrality in life cycle decisions. This is reflected even in macroeconomic patterns, thus coming together with the Chinese growth model. The mechanism that drives these phenomena is status competition. As is well known from economic theory, status competition in general is a zero-sum game or Red Queen race; in other words, there is no point of saturation of preferences, since only the relative distance to competitors for status counts, and the status positions are in limited supply, depending on the structural diversity of reference groups. The marriage market shows some interesting features here, because it is not necessarily structured along more detailed lines of group distinctions, such as different professions. In other words, there are group distinctions such as between different social domains, in particular rural and urban, and distinctions in the general status hierarchy of society, such as is defined by wealth and education. Within these larger reference groups, the status positions are necessarily in limited supply, because the top positions are always fixed. In particular, the supply of status positions is not determined by absolute levels of prosperity. In the Chinese case, the interaction between economic growth and population policy means that status competition in the marriage market has been becoming increasingly tense, reflecting the increasing sex-ratio imbalances.

Status competition on the marriage market is largely driven by long-term investments, because these are essential for signalling relative status between prospective partners, and because family formation is a long-term investment. In other words, beyond signalling attractiveness via consumer goods such as fashion and fancy devices, durable consumer goods and education that translates into attractive jobs count most. This creates very strong incentives for saving, thus complementing the investment-driven savings in the state-led sector. This applies for both parents and children. Parents will save more to invest in marriage prospects of their sons, and sons will do the same, if at all possible. Since the marriage market is a status order, this also results in a Red Queen pattern or an arms race. One important consequence of this is that the individual savings rate is driven beyond individually optimal points of consumption. So, this is functionally equivalent to forced savings, thus reinforcing an essential feature of the Chinese growth model. For example, in the rural areas the brideprice has been exploding in the past two decades, in relatively backward areas easily approaching the sum of many annual incomes, not including the costs of the wedding ceremony.[31]

Thus, we reach a very important conclusion: population policy, marriage market and economic decisions come together in performing the high-investment Chinese growth pattern. Population policy certainly directly contributed to achieving high rates of growth in the past three decades. However, this increasing prosperity was accompanied by heightened competition on the marriage market. This came together with the government-led investment drive, thus establishing a close interaction between macroeconomic policies and social change. I see this as a direct reflection of ritual aspects of the economic style. Although there is substantial value change in society, especially with regard to gender and internal allocation of power in the family, traditional norms about the centrality of family formation in the life cycle persist even in the urban areas, and certainly in the rural areas. The economic mechanism that establishes the connection between macroeconomic developments and the marriage market is the upward pressure on implicit prices of marriage opportunities for males, which in the rural areas translates directly into brideprice (as in traditional China, this is often explained as being compensation for the costs of raising a daughter). This results in a strong pressure to increase individual savings. This veritable 'savings glut', which is independent from interest rates, drives down the costs of investment, thus supporting the high investment rate in the Chinese economy. So, we may regard the investment rate as a manifestation of the ritual economy, and in particular of the pattern of governmentality and market that I identified in the concluding paragraphs of the previous section. The high investment rate is imposed by the modernist growth model and its institutions, and is also supported by decentralized decisions of the individual market actors. Modernist ritual and traditional ritual come together in producing and reproducing this state of the modern ritual economy.

On the one hand, this mechanism partly suppresses individual consumption. This stays in paradoxical tension with the rise of a consumer society in modern China. Even if the marriage market contributes to a high savings rate, at the same time it is a key determinant in driving consumption patterns, such as the demand for apartments including household equipment, furniture, or for cars; all kinds of personal consumption can also be indicators of relative status. Therefore, the desire for status goods is a central motivation in Chinese consumer behaviour. However, this also means that in China's contemporary consumer society the market plays a pivotal role in generating the standards which regulate the expressive means for status. More generally, ultimately the market becomes the standard by which the achievements of societal modernization and individual advancement are evaluated. Often this is seen as an expression of plain and simple materialism and hedonism. On the contrary, I venture the hypothesis that consumption in China is also a manifestation of ritual, thus reaching beyond these simplistic interpretations. Indigenous criticism of these phenomena may be seen as the expression of traditional moral concerns about 'private' versus 'public' and are thus also implicit expressions of ritual.[32]

In envisaging the market as a civilizational project, consumer behaviour assumes a pivotal position in the modernist ritual economy. This was supported by the idea that modernization of industry would also mean that Chinese products might become competitive against Western consumer products, which were mainly imported. Already in early Republican China, the adoption of a modern lifestyle was seen as an essential element in the national effort of modernization. Consumption was interpreted as an expression of new forms of self-control (such as in hygiene), but also (as in boycott movements) as a political statement. These ideas became closely intertwined with the 'New Life Movement' launched by Chiang Kai-shek. Shanghai in particular assumed the position of a cultural avant-garde. Although these efforts did not basically change the patterns of international trade and investment in Republican times, there was a deep cultural impact upon Chinese society, linking individual consumption with ideas about national revival and modernization. In particular, these movements and activities deeply intruded upon even the most sensitive and private matters, such as very early on in touching on the sensitive issue of the male queue when adopting Western suits as the new standard for male dressing, or when female household management practices were addressed, thus putting the female gender even at a pivotal position in the campaign for national awareness in consumption styles. Here the link between consumption and governmentality becomes most evident.

The building of a consumer society was also accompanied by the emergence of civil society initiatives devoted to the modernization of the Chinese economy and society. This politicized individual consumption in many nationwide campaigns, such as creating networks of stores that only sell 'national products', or in a series of large exhibitions displaying Chinese industrial success stories. This pattern is observable today:

consumer associations represent a part of government-sponsored civil society in China, with a national umbrella organization and numerous associations on the provincial and local level. Government organizations on every level launch initiatives that foster Chinese brands, such as annual awards.[33]

In the reform era, consumer behaviour and governmental policies have been closely interacting, thus continuing with the historical precedent. Since the late 1990s, the government has undertaken many measures that have actively supported the rise of the consumer society. This reflects the discovery of the 'middle class' in Chinese politics, which is devoid of political references, but is clearly defined in economic terms. The rise of this stratum was partly socially engineered by the comprehensive privatization of the urban stock of publicly owned housing, which amounted to a massive redistribution of wealth among the urban population via subsidized prices. A broad range of policy measures enhanced consumption opportunities, such as introducing credit cards and consumer credit. In the government sector, this included targeted increases of salaries, for example.[34]

To a considerable extent, this pattern prevails today, epitomized in the role of the 'consumer citizen'. Modernism is expressed both in relation to the rural areas and the international context. Modernization of behaviour is an expression of urban 'quality', such as in adopting modern cosmetics luxury products which highlight distinctions such as the colour of skin.[35] The capability of affording global luxury products is also a manifestation of status, which, however, may sometimes stay in tension with national aspirations to competitiveness. Thus, modernism is also visible in national policies towards creating Chinese brands, both domestic and global. Buying and handling famous brands is also an individual endeavour that is often the result of deliberate decisions. In scrutinizing these decisions, one may observe a high level of contextualization along the lines of the political meaning of consumer behaviour in early Republican times. So, we realize another instance of field dependency: individual consumption decisions are often put in the context of the narrative of China's modernization, suggesting individual responsibility for the implications that individual consumption may have for national development. This does not necessarily translate into crude denigration of Western brands for patriotic reasons. On the contrary, Western brands are seen as positive models to emulate and also as symbols of China's future of modernization; yet this also engenders high expectations and an implicit moralization of consumption.[36]

In this context, two remarkable tendencies loom large. One is that therefore modernist aspirations need to be met also by claims on quality. Global luxury brands manifest high quality, whereas national brands and products often fail to meet expectations. So, consumerism can obtain a political dimension, as in the case of scandals regarding fake products that even cause serious damage to health and life. Government regulation takes the role of civilizing Chinese producers, and hence consumerism may actually combine together with the political system aiming at constructing markets as civilizational ventures. Then, government may actually support civil society engagements in consumer protection, or may adopt a paternalistic role in supervising industries for the sake of the consumer. In this context, global brands set references for quality standards, but also have to meet high moral standards. Chinese consumers appreciate the global brands, but are easily upset if their high expectations are not met. In these cases, patriotic outrage can shift the balance easily to the detriment of global brands. Hence, we take note that in the Chinese consumer society patterns of governmentality loom large.[37]

In this context, the opposition between national and foreign brands often focuses on the possibility of counterfeiting, fakes and outright deception. However, this is also a general problem beyond deception about brand identities. In the recent years, one particularly sensitive issue was the series of food scandals, with sometimes very serious health consequences and a large number of victims. Food is a central concern in Chinese culture, and therefore worries about food quality can have a deep impact upon daily lives. These scandals clearly involve the regulatory responsibility of government supervisory agencies, so that the role of government in regulating the market becomes ambivalent. Then, choosing foreign brands is also an expression of distrust in public order. This is the other side of governmentality in Chinese consumer society. In both senses one may say that government and market are perceived as inextricably related, and failures of supervision are largely seen as moral failure of government, thus actually reproducing traditional notions about the moral superiority of government in the sense of representing the public interest. It is important to note that the problems in the food industry result partly from the fact that the majority of firms are small-scale family firms, thus directly reflecting economic structures of the traditional ritual economy.[38]

The case of food scandals is different from many other cases of counterfeiting because nobody would knowingly consume poisonous food, whereas the use of counterfeit luxury goods is often done intentionally, although there is certainly also a high incidence of straightforward deception (an example in the food industry is fake red wine[39]). Consuming counterfeit luxury or expensive goods is a reaction of consumers to the prevailing rat race in status consumption, in two senses. One is that counterfeit goods would be used to deceive others about one's true status, thus distorting status signalling. The other is that this is also a form of mockery about status goods consumption. Hence, in the latter case consuming counterfeit goods is also a form of cultural creativity, as in the case of so-called 'shanzhai' (山寨) production. *Shanzhai* production makes certain product features available to low-income consumers (for example, smartphones for migrant workers), but at the same time it is a political statement in often imitating foreign brands while openly revealing the imitation to the buyer (for example, by slight variations of the product name or logo). The interesting observation is that although Western producers of luxury products always complain about these violations of their rights, in fact one cannot say that they lose business, since this low-income demand would be inaccessible for them anyway. So, a major effect of these imitations is actually familiarizing low-income consumers with international brands. Eventually, many users of imitations strive to achieve the civilizational high point in owning and displaying a genuine original.

Shanzhai production may therefore be interpreted as another constitutive element of the ritual economy. *Shanzhai* simultaneously confirms the ritual order of brand consumption and makes a mockery out of it, thus reinstating the dual nature of many rites in traditional Chinese popular culture. And indeed, *Shanzhai* production is also perceived as a cultural activity in the narrow sense, today even including artwork and influencing artists' projects and agendas. So, even the mockery and parody of *shanzhai* in fact confirms the ritual nature of the brand standards that provide the reference. Beyond that, the relationship between *shanzhai* and the ritual economy is also evident if we consider the production side: *shanzhai* producers are generally informal family businesses. This peculiar economic structure also enables a constant flow of highly unique and even individualized forms and imaginaries of consumption.[40]

To sum up this section, I argue that the modern consumer society is an essential part of the ritual economy of modernism. For one, this refers to the fact that consumption in China is strongly driven by competing over positional goods. This status competition is embedded in a particular form of governmentality, namely the close interaction between formal institutions and cognitive beliefs in creating and maintaining a modernist status order, on the larger aggregate level differentiating between rural and urban society, also migrants of different origin, and on the more disggregate level differentiating among wealth, education and professional status. The modernist worldview collapses all these distinctions into one single dimension, namely 'quality' as *suzhi*. Quality is also a central concern in modernist population policy, which therefore also qualifies as an essential aspect of modernist ritual. Path dependencies with the traditional ritual economy are especially visible in the marriage market, where modern functional equivalents of brideprice in status-based matching of partners result in the distinct state of the extremely high individual savings rate in China.

The resurgence of the ritual economy in rural society

The original uses of the term 'ritual economy' were explicitly referring to the traditional economy and the resurgence of certain of its features in the rural areas in particular.[41] Specifically, this highlights phenomena such as the mutual embeddedness of traditional forms of religion and the economy, such as in temple building, or the revival of status goods consumption in the gift economy and in the context of the family life cycle. In this section, I look at some of these observations in more detail in order to discover path dependencies. This requires an interpretation of the Maoist era in a fresh way, namely as a medium through which certain aspects of ritual were actually passed over to the period of modernist reforms. In realizing this, one can also lend some new interpretations to the early literature on the political culture of Maoism which often tried to connect this radical approach to societal transformation with aspects of traditional China.

Certainly, our discussion of modernism as a defining feature of economic style has to start out from taking stock of the modernist programme as pursued up until 1978. The reformist leadership diagnosed a failure of these policies not only in terms of economic progress, but also in terms of civilizational transformation. This delay in modernization, even defined from the perspective of Chinese political elites, can be pinpointed in two observations that also relate to seminal contributions to modern Chinese studies. The first observation is the diagnosis of 'cellularization' of the rural economy and society as a result of Maoist institutions, and the corresponding institutional separation between rural and urban society; the second observation refers to the establishment of authoritarian relations of dependence in the urban areas. In this chapter, I concentrate on the former question and leave the discussion of the second question to Chapter 6.

The cellularization of the rural society was the direct result of collectivization as a major project of institutional transformation in the 1950s. Collectivization had induced the cellularization of rural society, and market liberalization was a means to break up this pattern again: this is a central manifestation of the market as a form of governmentality. We have already seen that in the setting of rural migration, the market partly assumes the role of a modernizing, hence civilizing medium. In the current context, we have to expand this notion in seeing the market as a means of re-embedding rural society into a national body politic that defines itself as a modernist state.[42] Rural collectivization exerted a deep impact on rural society, as it had cut the villages off from the regional market system. However, this system was transformed into the administrative structure of brigades and People's Communes, which were largely identical to earlier market towns. This structural isomorphism is important in understanding the dynamics of rural reforms in the 1980s, which re-instituted the old functions of the market system, together with reviving the traditional administrative distinctions of market townships and towns ('xiang' (乡) and 'zhen' (镇)). In this process, economic modernization, path dependencies and administrative reforms closely interacted in shaping the emergence of a modern system of markets. Thus, for example, the rapidly increasing growth of demand for market services pushed the transformation of the traditional periodic marketing system into a modern structure of wholesale and retail logistics. Yet, these transformations started out from the traditional regional hierarchy, thus structuring lower level urbanization in lending it a particular direction.[43]

A unique pattern of urbanization emerged, especially in areas which were more advanced economically in the past, such as in the Jiangnan region. A case in point is Fujian province, where we observe urbanization that is not driven by migration from rural to urban areas, but which starts out from the grassroots level, such as turning traditional market towns into urban areas, while gradually growing together via urban sprawl. So, in the neighbourhood of cities one may observe a quasi-suburbanization of what are still rural areas in administrative terms.[44] In the context of our investigations into the ritual economy, this means that in sociological and cultural terms, places that are urban in infrastructural and technological dimensions can still retain a social and institutional context that creates path dependencies in societal modernization. However, these developments certainly vary tremendously across China, and we need to take note of recent developments that follow the launch of the initiative 'Building a New Socialist Countryside', 'shehuizhuyi xin nongcun jianshe' (社会主义新农村建设). This programme is another example of direct 'modernizing' interventions by the central state, being mediated by the local states in implementing it. The modernist goals are evident from applying urban principles of zoning and settlement restructuring to rural areas. In these activities, villages are often radically restructured in order to enable the more efficient use of the land, which means that villagers move to newly built residential areas which have very different structures of settlement and individual housing. This implies that material carriers of ritual are also destroyed, such as the structures of temples and lineage halls or the spatial distribution of lineages in the territory. This creates highly diverse conditions for path dependencies even within the same regions of China, which would appear to be similar in other respects. In particular, the standard approach in creating model villages of social transformation which are then supposed to be copied by others leads towards considerable variety, because model villages are much better endowed with financial means to realize the projects, so that less well-endowed villages would search for alternative tracks.[45]

In order to properly understand these developments, it is important to put the radical transformations of the property rights structure since 1949 into perspective. As we have seen previously, collectivization was a pivotal institutional feature in the forced industrialization model of Maoism and, to a certain extent, was a necessary consequence of designing a system by which resources would be extracted from the rural areas for raising the rate of accumulation in order to speed up industrialization. However, in the Chinese context, collectivization was also a project of cultural and social transformation. It was also the political means by which the local power of lineages should be broken, since their economic basis in land-ownership was destroyed. In this regard, redistribution of land in the previous land reform was not sufficient, since in principle also a small-holder peasant agriculture would support the resurgence of lineage practices. Actually, this was predicted by Marxism-inspired ideas about petty capitalism that was so characteristic of the Chinese countryside. Therefore, in the view of Maoism, economic transformation and cultural modernization were two sides of the same coin, such as mobilizing female labour in the People's Communes and thereby supporting the transformation of the traditional family.

However, an intricate aspect of collectivization was that locally the assignment of farmers and land to teams and brigades often replicated the traditional kinship structures, partly because they were embodied in settlement patterns. So, one could also interpret collectivization in the sense of actually strengthening extended kinship vis-à-vis the individual families in terms of the 'collective' being a group of males connected via the descent line, and sharing certain property rights, both individually and collectively, and living together in a certain territory. In fact, the notion of collective ownership partly replicated traditional ideas about land property rights, especially when, in the early 1960s, the household land lease rights were extended for the first time in some areas of China such that the collective assumed the economic function of a landlord and the family the position of a quasi-tenant.[46] In this sense, collectivization even strengthened the hold of agnatic authority upon village life, further bolstered by the weakening of affinal ties that traditionally were often mediated via the market system. So, one perspective on collectivization could be to interpret it as a revolutionary transformation of traditional kinship structures only to the extent that it turned more egalitarian, without at the same time changing its basic structures. These egalitarian structures are visible in the equal distribution of explicit or implicit ownership rights to land in different phases of collectivization and de-collectivization, and in the concomitant egalitarian structures of the arrangements of marriage and family. As a result, the rural reforms after 1978 reinstituted the smallholding family farm as the basic unit of the rural economy and society, exactly reproducing its pivotal role in the traditional system.[47]

One simple though highly significant indicator of this revival of tradition is the pattern of interaction between population policy and the sex ratio at birth that results from the individual decisions made by families. In rural society, the one-child policy was a major assault on traditional concepts of the family, especially with regard to the continuation of the family line via male descendants. This principle had not been changed by the Maoist transformation, after some failed attempts at doing even that. So, in this sense, the population policy was a much more radical attack against the traditional rural family than even collectivization. The result of this were highly dysfunctional phenomena such as the widespread use of female infanticide or targeted abortions in order to fulfil the wish for a male descendant. Now, what is important in the current context is the fact that in spite of the relaxation and the administrative improvements in enforcing the policy, the imbalance of the sex ratio has been heightening in the 1990s and the 2000s. In particular, this applies for the birth order. Whereas the sex ratio for the first child has remained stable, though biased towards boys, the sex ratio for second and higher order births is strongly biased towards boys, and this trend is becoming even more pronounced. In addition, one has to consider the regional differences across China. Here we can use the sex-ratio data as an indirect indicator for the intensity by which traditional concepts of the family have been reviving differentially across regions. So, it is highly significant that the most distorted sex ratios occur today in regions which had a strong lineage tradition in the past. So, the southern provinces of China and in particular Guangdong province manifest areas with the highest sex ratios in national comparison. This observation about a correlation between different historical conditions with the current sex ratio is strong evidence of the general trend of the revival of traditional concepts.[48]

The interaction between socialist institutions and traditional family structures may be shown in many instances, such as when treating male household heads as representing the family, for example, in assigning ownership of private plots, or in the maintenance of a pronatalist population policy under Mao, which reinstated the Confucian norms of continuing the descent line. In other words, collectivization resulted in the cellularization of traditional kinship, but not in its wholesale transformation. This was reflected, for example, in increasing frequencies of village and lineage endogamy, or in the strengthening of local dialects. These effects may be straightforwardly explained by considering the consequences of curtailing the scope of the regional marketing system while at the same time restricting the mobility of peasants. As stated in the Skinner model elucidated in Chapter 2, this also implied that many social networks and interactions were severely compressed in spatial scope, and also important events such as regional temple fairs were no longer held.[49]

Yet, this process did not necessarily directly translate into the restoration of traditional lineage authority, but in the first place focused social and economic processes on the village level, often via the inward orientation of social conflicts and political struggle, which however focused on traditional divisions and fault lines in social structure. In this sense, cellularization was mainly a process in the *diyuan* dimension, leaving the *xueyuan* dimension truncated and transformed. Communist social transformation also meant that the traditional status order was turned upside-down. The institutional mechanism was the party hierarchy and the institution of the rural cadre. This is most significant if we make the comparison with the traditional order, especially in its state of erosion in the twentieth century. As I will discuss in Chapter 4, one of the most significant continuities between the old order and the modern Chinese state is the fact that the county level continues to demarcate the central and the local state, even in constitutional terms. Below the county level, rural communities are self-governed in principle, and are also the owners of the land. In other words, the formal administration of the central state has only advanced gradually down to the grassroots level of Chinese rural society, with the Party secretary as the spearhead, and the local, village-funded cadre as the intermediator. Both roles could be played by members of kinship groups, yet were to be fulfilled by individuals with a clean class background. This meant that old landowning elites and their families were excluded from obtaining positions of power in local society. So, whereas prior to 1949 mostly lineage elders played the central role in governing villages, this role was now overtaken by a new stratum of intermediators: the cadres. But this revolution of social and political status does not mean that the structures of kinship were also transformed, since cadres with a poor peasant background could also be members of lineages, especially, of course, in villages that only had few lineages or even a single lineage. These assignments could actually also reflect old lineage rivalries, with low-status lineages gaining an advantage over high-status lineages. Therefore, collective ownership of land factually established the continuity even of the economic foundations of traditional kinship. In some sense, kinship turned more inward-looking and hence probably gained even more salience, since the widespread pattern of absentee landlords residing in the towns was broken.[50]

It is important to note that market liberalization after 1978 did not necessarily reverse this trend of cellularization of kinship, in spite of the original intention. This creates important path dependencies in cultural change, and is caused by the effects of the one-child policy on the marriage market. With the increasing value of brides, relatively poor villages are especially strongly affected. Brides from richer areas would not like to move to poorer areas following the norms of patrilocal marriage. As a consequence, families from poor areas are forced either to rely on endogamous marriage in order to continue the family line, or to resort to other means such as trafficking brides even from other countries.

This analysis shows how institutional design interacts with local conditions. On the other hand, this implies that we cannot easily achieve generalizations over China. So, as we saw in Chapter 2, the role of lineages varied across the regions of old China, with South China, in particular Guangdong, being especially prominent. It is illuminating to note that in these regions, the ritual economy proved to be resilient and provides the ground for the evolution of peculiar patterns of development even in the context of the rapid urbanization process today. Considering a typical pattern, this happens when the administrative and the economic structure are separated organizationally, such that the local economy becomes increasingly governed by private actors, which are effectively often extended kinship groups in local society. This means, on the one hand, that the market is a medium of transforming and reversing the cellularization of rural society, but, on the other hand, it cannot be simply seen as a modernizing force that is neutral towards traditional kinship. In fact, the market is also the medium through which these traditional structures are partly revived. This is a central empirical phenomenon in the continuity of the ritual economy across the revolutionary changes in past decades.

I will study these phenomena in more detail in Chapter 5, so suffice it to note here that this is easily to be explained against the background of economic theory. During the first decades of reforms, in the rural areas there was a particularly high level of institutional uncertainty, so relying on kinship relations or other social connections was an essential means for reducing transaction costs. Thus, the expansion of market opportunities actually also created strong incentives for reviving traditional patterns of social interaction. This would suggest that the revival is a transitional phenomenon and would whither away with institutional consolidation. However, this analysis overlooks the fact that partly deeper cultural resources are being recreated and reconstructed which play a constitutive role in the socialization of social and economic agents. Market growth induces the formation of social capital that is itself of a more enduring nature than is suggested by its current functionalities. However, there are also economic forces that are being generated by the market process, given the current institutional conditions. A pivotal issue is the consolidation of certain positions in the distribution of wealth, hence the interaction among the formation of capital in the different dimensions, economic, social and others. The core issue in this area is the role of landownership. As we have seen, collectivization created a structure of landownership which partly transformed but also partly reinstated traditional structures of extended kinship, with regional variations. So, collectivization created a collective asset, and privatization is still constrained via the legal framework of landownership in China. This supports the reformation and transformation of lineage structures, while also undergirding their resurgence and resilience.[51]

The background of this development is the diffuse arrangement of formal property rights of land in the rural areas. These are assigned to the grassroots-level communities, but under post-reform conditions the constitution leaves open which level below the county level may be regarded as such. Thus, there are competing claims of control between townships and villages, or even subgroups within the villages, with the former mainly represented by government cadres having an urban registration, and the latter, if lineages are strong, by village cadres and lineage leaders. This institutional ambiguity partly reflects ideological concerns and differences in the leadership of the Communist Party, but during past decades also conflicting interests of the farmers. In fact, in many areas, full-scale privatization is not the most preferred policy alternative, because this is seen as giving up the implicit social welfare function of collective landownership, especially with regard to the family life cycle (provision for old age, employment guarantees for children). These attitudes may change rapidly in the course of the decline of agriculture as a major source of income, yet, at the same time in places where agricultural land plays a central role in the urbanization process, this also creates opposite incentives.[52]

Now, if historically brigades continued to reflect lineage structures, this allowed for the emergence of landholding lineages in many areas. They can separate their control from the administrative structure in establishing special economic organizations for land management and village development that are formally owned by the village, but are effectively controlled by lineages. Hence, we meet another instance of market institutions actually enhancing path dependencies in institutional development. The general model bears a strong resemblance with traditional lineage trusts. This is the so-called 'cooperative shareholding system', 'gufen hezuo zhidu' (股份合作制度), in which every member receives shares of the collective assets (which may be land or other economic assets such as companies). A share gives members the right to participate in the income generated and possibly also to take part in a shareholder council, but it cannot be sold to parties who are not members of the original collective. Clearly, this concept of a 'share' is very similar to the shares in traditional associations and trusts, as I briefly introduced in Chapter 2. A most important case in point is the corporatization of collective property rights in land. In terms of modernization, this step is ambivalent. During the transition, the cooperative shareholding system was a formal umbrella which allowed for wide variety in actually implementing this general idea. However, more recently these corporate structures have needed to adopt legal forms that entail a set of regulations staying in tension with the interpretations that hold under the ambiguity between formal institutions and traditional concepts. For example, if a cooperative shareholding corporation is a holding company of a set of enterprises, it would have to adopt legal forms of the Company Law, which would require one to apply the relevant regulations. This may conflict with local practices and triggers dynamic processes of adaptation.[53]

Hence, the legacy of Maoist institutions is a major determinant of the revival of lineage identity in the urbanization process, thus actually combining a societal process of modernization with strengthening a major element of the ritual economy. This is bolstered by the role of kinship ties in foreign direct investment that, particularly in the first two decades of the reform period, was dominated by Overseas Chinese activities. For example, lineage traditions and popular religion had remained strong in Hong Kong, and when Hong Kong entrepreneurs who emigrated from Guangdong earlier returned to their native places, they often donated money for the reconstruction of traditional religious sites. This is also true for Overseas Chinese in Southeast Asia, especially in areas which were focal regions of origin of emigration in the past, even back to the nineteenth century. These social interactions therefore simultaneously opened up the view on modern business and contributed to the revival of tradition.[54] These developments do not imply that the new reconstruction of ancestral halls, often under the title of 'old age homes', directly reflect a revival of traditional values and social structures. However, it does reveal a complex social power balance between local society and the state as represented by the urban administration.

It is difficult to assess the significance of such phenomena on the national scale. If we look at recorded cases which are certainly individual in terms of local histories and conditions, in the Pearl River Delta we frequently observe a pattern where, in an urbanized context, the villages and their lineages continue to hold strong positions as landowners. Riding on the waves of foreign direct investment into the region, lineages emerged as a rentier group. Since no individual can claim the income streams from land rent directly, the rent is allocated to new developmental projects and public services, and partly distributed on a per-capita basis to the members. This does not necessarily mean that the lineage leaders also dominate the local administration, but the control of important economic resources remains with them. As a result, local society evolved a formal status order, as lineage wealth allows for very significant distinctions between locals and migrants, with the latter vastly outnumbering the former. For example, special hospitals might be reserved for locals only, or being only accessible at much higher cost for non-locals. So, in these and comparable cases the ritual economy combines together with economic trends such as globalization and migration in actually sustaining a ritual order, contributing to a revival of extended kinship structures and to the creation of a local status order. The foundations for this development were created by the socialist institutions of collectivization, and the specific local shape of these institutions emerged often as a result of political conflicts over the distribution of resources between local lineages and the local state.[55]

Generally speaking, kinship groups can often be involved in conflicts over power and resources. However, if we consider the traditional order, we need to take the different principles of village organization into consideration. Then, the resurgence of the ritual economy cannot only be equated with the revival of lineage structures. On the contrary, this may be a phenomenon restricted to certain regions and places, thus expressing strong path dependencies in institutional change. Another aspect of the rural ritual economy is therefore the resurgence of popular religion, visible, in particular, in temple-building activities. Indeed, these activities are especially strong in areas such as Fujian, where traditional notions of kinship also loom large. This revival of traditional popular religion is difficult to assess, since temples as a form of material manifestation have also always been the object of political struggles over religion. Often they undergo cycles of reconstruction and destruction, such that the true extent of religious activity is not directly reflected in existing temples and other religious sites. Further, given the nature of popular religion, it is highly dispersed and merged with everyday life activities, the seasonal cycle of holidays and festivals, and the recurrence of life cycle events. This results in a peculiar linguistic stance towards popular religion, which is largely treated as 'local custom' even by the practitioners themselves. In this sense, temples are the material artefact that demarcate the borderline between the notion of 'customs' and 'religion'. They are also an expression of the creativity of local religion, such as when local temples may even be devoted to political leaders such as Mao Zedong.[56]

Regarding the status of popular religion, it is important to note that the situation is extremely complex and in transition. Whereas in the past the CCP mostly fought against popular religion as 'superstition', this assessment has been changing recently, although often camouflaged as 'protection of cultural legacy', and with attempts at expanding official control over temples and other religious activities such as large local processions at important festivals, partly driven by the increasing economic benefits resulting from rapidly growing tourism in China. The motivation results from the recognition that popular religion is an essential element in defining traditional Chinese culture and hence national identity. There are already local-level associations of popular religion that add to the associations for the five official religions thus far recognized. Most importantly, popular religion is increasingly seen as a medium in which 'Chineseness' is defined on a global scale. The previously mentioned role of Overseas Chinese in setting up lineage temples is today only one part of even official activities that connect religious organizations outside Mainland China with temples on the Mainland. This is particularly significant in relations with Taiwan. Large organizations such as the Mazu Temple Association establish official relations with the historically older temples on the Mainland, and relationships obtain a religious meaning in 'dividing the incenses'. Hence, popular religion obtains an important role in expressing the shared national identity of Taiwan and the Mainland. Taking all these different aspects together, we can safely assume that the general revival of popular religion in China will be gradually accompanied by increasing institutionalization. By implication, we have to pay proper attention to its role in the ritual economy.[57]

However, we need to avoid the conclusion that only institutionalization would reflect the relative strength of popular religion in the ritual economy, because this would only reproduce the earlier difficulties in properly recognizing the nature of popular religion in China. Its foremost characteristic has always been the integration between religion and social life, such that 'religion' simply does not manifest itself as a separate institutional domain. This also allows for the current approaches of re-instituting legitimacy, in terms of 'local customs' or 'cultural legacy', thus avoiding the derogative term 'superstition'. For instance, in the rural areas, the merger of religion and everyday life is reflected in the religious meaning of the locations in the village, often determined by past *fengshui* activities, and in the religious aspects of the flow of gifts on different occasions in the yearly cycle of family events and festivals. In both cases, ideas about moral reciprocity loom large, and particular items are imbued with a religious meaning. Thus, one aspect of the ritual economy in the rural areas is the network of reciprocity that connects people among themselves and with the entities of the spiritual world. The economic effects are visible, for example, in the networks of mutual support that can be mobilized, with important events such as the formation of a new family or the construction of a new house. Thus, the central notion in both the social and the religious domain is reciprocal exchange, embedded in ideas about long-term relationships of mutual debt and trust, efficacy of interactions, and the role of complex forces that determine individual fate. So, for example, in religious activities divination and requests for support are essential concerns in individual rituals. In this context, it is evident that the increasing role of markets in social life actually works together with the need for religious orientations, as the market is a complex environment that cannot be overseen by individuals and is governed by forces that cannot be fully controlled by those individuals; there is a major factor of luck and chance in succeeding in the marketplace.[58]

In the institution of the temple as a sanctuary, this diffused nature of popular religion finds a concentrated expression. Temples are places of worship where reciprocal relations between individuals and deities are mediated. It has been pointed out that in the Chinese context, the 'religious markets' paradigm applies with a vengeance, since the individual does not relate to temples in community or confessional terms. Temples wax and wane according to their 'efficacy', 'ling' (灵) in providing 'services' to believers. This relationship is even directly based on exchange, with believers offering 'currency' to the deities, which range from incense paid for by donations to the temple over gifts presented at festivals to the burning of ritual money; they expect support in exchange, such as healing, success in examinations or profits from business. Thus, the relationship between believers and temples is highly individualized in terms of individual relations of reciprocity and experiences about positive relationships. This includes network effects, culminating in strong reputations of single temples, thus resulting in increasing numbers of visitors, which may end up forming institutionalized patterns such as large festivals or regular pilgrimages. So, in the ritual economy religion is also patterned as a 'quasi-market', where different providers of services compete for the attention and ultimately also for the payments of believers, the latter understood both literally and metaphorically. Thus, the types of providers range from individual spirit media to itinerant Daoist priests to large temples with a long historical record. For all of them, the experience of *ling* determines their role in the religious marketplace.[59]

Traditional temple building was often a manifestation of cooperation in the local community, undergirded by the official recognition of temples by the Imperial administration, and the explicit parallelism between certain temples (such as the Earth God) and the territorial organization of the Empire. This relationship was broken in modern China, yet there remains a strong relationship between community and local temples. If we compare the Mainland development with Taiwan, rapid economic development was also accompanied by a strong revival of temple building in Taiwan. Local religious organizations were also rallying points for early democratic movements, such as environmental groups.[60] We can explain this phenomenon when considering the creation and accumulation of social capital that goes hand in hand with mobilizing collective resources for temple building, both on the part of the groups involved and the leaders. Therefore, local leaders often get involved with temple building not by merely showing religious zeal. Temples are an expression of leadership and of the status of the local community relative to other communities. This status symbol also ties in with other activities that piggyback on temples as rallying points, such as local festivals. These can also become factors in local development in attracting visitors, and indirectly supporting the formation of networks that can be activated in business relations. Thus, even today temples can become another interface between local population and local government in China's local state.[61]

Correspondingly, we observe a strong resurgence of temple building in rural China. This not only fosters a resurgence of traditional religion, but also other forms of religion. For example, in Wenzhou, a famous place of private business, local business leaders often invest in the construction of Christian churches and assume roles of leaders of the parish. In doing so, the organizational approaches of business and church management converge, as churches are actually major investment projects. In this case, the simultaneous formation of social capital is most obvious. This even applies for the strong national and global activities of Wenzhou merchants, who often establish churches in the places where they meet, thus replicating a well-known pattern of China's past. In this particular case we may also note the relationship between religion and the civilizational project of modernism, as Christianity has been perceived as a 'modern' religion already in Republican times, and leadership in Christian communities is again seen as a matter of *suzhi*; *suzhi* finds expression in entrepreneurial and managerial capabilities that are embodied in the building projects.[62]

Beyond this particular case we can say that temple building is often not only an expression of local prosperity, but actually contributes to local development via the creation, utilization and leveraging of social capital. This ties up with the effects on the accountability of local leaders and cadres. For local cadres, handling religious matters can be sensitive. As a matter of fact, the CCP often acts aggressively against expressions of traditional popular religion which is seen as mere 'superstition'. However, this puts local communities and leaders in an awkward relationship if there is a strong demand for the services of religion. Thus, temple building may be put into another context, such as tourism, in order to neutralize the topic. In this case, possible conflicts over controlling the religious resource may persist, but local elites may also become actively involved, such as assuming leadership positions in temple-building associations.[63]

There is a potential side effect of such phenomena which becomes discernible if we compare those traditional forms of expressing cooperative relationships within the village with the newly established institutions of village democracy. Village elections have become a widespread feature in China, though with very different performances. The CCP supports the introduction of local-level democracy for different reasons, although this is constrained by maintaining the claim on controlling governmental power. One motivation is to establish checks and balances against the misbehaviour of local cadres and collusive local elites. Generally speaking, villagers express strong interest in democratic participation and highly value voting rights. Yet, in spite of formally establishing village democracy, the elections often remain under the control of the CCP; however, in the local context this may only reflect the result of local power struggles, even involving groups that simply pursue their own interests. Therefore, village elections do not necessarily help to create democratic accountability in office. Far too often the result is that local power brokers pursue their own aims to the detriment of the local community, with business interests and party representatives colluding. This is visible in the combination of private wealth and public poverty in many local communities.[64]

In comparison, we often observe that communities with a vibrant popular religion also manifest a better supply of public goods. One possible explanation is that the institutions of religion create additional mechanisms of accountability. For example, consider a temple association following traditional principles. This is based on voluntary contributions of its members, who also have equal rights in participating, traditionally including rotation of leadership positions. If a local cadre gets involved, this adds to (mostly) his local reputation; at the same time, additional accountability is established also beyond the scope of this project. The same applies for many lineage-related activities. Thus, beyond the formal mechanism of village democracy, local leaders become embedded in a multi-dimensional web of local social relationships which constrain their behaviour. As a result, public opinion is expressed via many channels and influences local decision-making, probably gearing it towards a more inclusive and careful investment in local projects. So, the interdependence between formal institutions of governance and the institutions of traditional religion may be regarded as an important manifestation of the ritual economy in the public sector.[65]

I conclude my analysis of the resurgence of the ritual economy in the rural areas at this point, but will pick up this thread again in Chapters 5 and 6. So far, I have left out the role of traditional concepts of social relations, in particular kinship, in the organization of markets and companies. I will discuss these aspects in the respective chapters. At this point, let me just mention two examples in order to highlight one general aspect that is often alluded to in the literature. The two examples are informal finance in the domain of markets and family business in the domain of organizations. In both contexts, we can often find a particular reasoning informed by institutional economic theory claiming that the resurgence of tradition is a response to the deficiencies of the formal institutional framework, and partly of the outright policy discrimination especially of the rural areas. In this view, ritual is a complement of formal institutions, and will therefore become obsolete when these institutions are further transformed and improved. In other words, the dualist structure of the Chinese economy would imply that the ritual economy is restricted to informal domains. In its simplest form, the ritual economy would appear to be mainly rooted in the rural economy, and urbanization would lead to an increasing formalization of institutions.

An important manifestation of the ritual economy in the organization of business is the provision of credit. Here, we can indeed see how the ritual economy emerges as an adaptation to the institutional context and its deficiencies. This institutional context has been directly determined by the growth model that I scrutinized in the first section, featuring financial repression as an important policy pattern. Throughout the reform period, the Chinese banking sector was dominated by the state-owned banks, which do not readily extend credit to private business, especially in the countryside. The rural credit cooperatives were never allowed to adopt a more active role in the credit business, and alternative organizational approaches, such as the rural credit foundations that were blossoming in the late 1990s, were suppressed when some of them went bust. Conditions have changed only recently. In this institutional context, traditional means of providing credit were a natural alternative. This includes the revival of traditional organizations, such as the pawnbrokers and the rotating credit associations. Yet, probably the most important means of obtaining credit is the mobilization of funds in the extended family, both agnatic and affinal. So, informal finance clearly emerges as a response to financial repression, and contributes to the resilience of traditional ritual in the undergirdning social relations. Whether we can generalize this observation I will discuss in Chapter 5.

However, this argument does not seem to hold for the other example, namely family business, which is of course also closely related to the case of informal finance, as financing family business often recurs on extended kinship networks. Family business in the rural areas builds on the traditional economic role of the *jia*. This is by no means a pattern that is peculiar to China, as the involvement of family members in the company is the defining feature of family business all over the world. Yet, the particular form of the family business is certainly influenced by the specific structure of the Chinese family, given the deep impact of population policy. There is no clear presumption that the family will whither away as a framework for business in the course of societal modernization, as even the most advanced economies such as Germany manifest a pivotal role of family business in the economic structure. This resilience of the family rests upon generic competitive advantages, such as the long-term orientation of decision-making and the special incentive structures governing managerial behaviour. Therefore, we might expect that the Chinese family as a central constitutive element in the ritual economy will also continue to be important in the future, even if the formal institutional framework improves. This question will be scrutinized in Chapter 6.

So, the argument that the ritual economy may be circumscribed to the rural economy and society is not necessarily true. It falls into the conceptual trap of interpreting 'ritual' in the traditional sense only, thus overlooking the generic meaning of ritual as discussed in Chapter 1. Thus, in the next section I look at aspects of ritual that emerge in the context of formal institutions.

Localism and the status order of ownership

Having considered the revival of the ritual economy in the rural areas, the final observations of the previous section raise the question whether the ritual economy is indeed a comprehensive phenomenon, in the sense of also encompassing the formal institutions that govern the economy. For example, in the case of popular religion, formal institutions clearly limit its role, or in case of the family, formal institutions clearly enshrine gender equality, such that the resilience of traditional forms appears to be a deviance that may be only a transitional phenomenon. On the other hand, we have seen that forms of modernity such as the rise of the consumer society may also be interpreted as manifestations of the ritual economy. In this section, I pursue a line of reasoning that has already been laid down in the previous section; this relates to the role of ownership in the ritual economy. In this context, we need to distinguish neatly between path dependencies and disruptive institutional innovations, but we have to recognize, first, that the latter may also be accompanied by ritual innovations, and second, that path dependencies may operate on different levels, especially including the cognitive level, such that in spite of radical innovations of formal institutions certain path dependencies may emerge even in cases of ritual innovations.

As a point of entry, I refer back to the analysis of ownership in the rural areas, as actualized in the context of urbanization. Path dependencies emerged from the interaction between formal institutional innovations (i.e. collectivization), and the interaction with cognitive patterns (i.e. interpretations as mediated by material artefacts, such as settlement patterns); this resulted in the reconstitution of collective ownership as lineage ownership in some regions of China, which in turn translated into certain patterns of urban political economy, in which lineages emerged as a new group of landlords. It is illuminating to observe how these developments are in turn reflected in material structures of settlement, in this case the widespread phenomenon of 'urban villages', 'cheng zhong cun' (城中村). This has raised many conflicts about the civilizational status of urban lifestyles and sometimes serious conflicts about modernist urban planning and reconstruction.

The materiality of the 'quality' of modernism and its institutional foundations is embodied in Chinese urbanism that is simultaneously shaped by consumerism and by state-led urban design. Chinese cities reflect the role of the state in designing structural features, such as the unusually large blocks and the salience of architectures that represent the government or government-affiliated organizations. These architectures are visible signs of a homogeneous national idea of modernization and the role of government in leading the process of societal transformation; so, in one sense we can say that the material structure of Chinese cities mirrors the role of formal institutional design in economy and society. This is a phenomenon that relates to the general diffusion of architectural designs in China, with government organizations expressing their status with certain design features, such as open spaces in front of a building, gates and so forth. Design features diffuse from the top to the bottom level, such that lower level authorities try to enhance their status in local contexts imitating upper level designs. Interestingly, and reflecting another instance of the market as impinging upon forms of governmentality, in this process imitation is also supported by the fact that architectural standardization is often also a way to economize on costs, both on the side of the decision-makers and the developers.[66]

Yet, this process of modernist standardization also meets certain constraints, which partly reflect the dualism of formal and informal economy, and points towards the tension between modernist claims and path dependencies of social evolution. In South China in particular, unregulated urban settlements compete for the control of urban space with government-led endeavours of modernization, such as redeveloped downtown areas as temples of consumerism. The ideal-typical expression is the construction of the shopping mall on land from which low-income migrant dwellers are evicted. Depending on local balances of power, urban spaces evolve in different ways; as we will see in Chapter 4, this also reflects structural diversity of the local state. The most salient phenomenon is the 'urban villages', which have emerged as a special organizational pattern in the urban sprawl that is driven by migration. In other words, if former agricultural areas are transformed into urban spaces, the existing rural grassroots-level power structure is reflected in maintaining the village as a unit in the urban space, visible in construction that is partly autonomous from formal urban planning. This autonomy is directly manifest in distinct architectural features, such as cramped housing with little distance between buildings, wires and pipes openly visible, and deficient sewage management.[67]

This constellation is complex because it interacts with the *hukou* system. In places where urban villages are an important part of urban infrastructure, demand is largely driven by migrant workers, both for urban dwellings and for accompanying infrastructure, such as healthcare provision. Often, the land provided for residential units comes from two different sources. One is state-owned land, for example, controlled by state-owned units as joint-venture partners, which is largely invested in dormitories which can be of huge size, hosting ten of thousands of workers. However, these are mainly used by young and transient workers, whereas iterant or second-generation migrants aspire to an urban lifestyle and hence prefer rented flats, even if of lower quality. Since earnings are lower than the average urban wage, most cannot afford regular apartments anyway, and they are sometimes lacking formal access rights because of their registration. Therefore, migrants largely move to urban villages at a lower cost, but also low-status residential areas. In other words, the internal residential pattern of urban areas not only reflects the different status of ownership rights, but also the different status of *hukou* of the majority of inhabitants.

It is essential to recognize that this leads to very different urban dynamics when compared with urban squatting in most metropolitan areas in the world. This is because the urban villages stay in a continuous negotiation process with the urban authorities on reconstruction and redevelopment projects, and because they are represented by management units that pursue the interest of the original landowning collectives. As I briefly described in the previous section, these shareholding companies assume parapolitical functions, thus establishing social order in the urban villages in close symbiosis with state agencies. They also often take active part in redevelopment, because they can negotiate high profits for their members, thus actually colluding with urban authorities, with the migrants having no voice.

Thus, the urban villages are an expression of the status hierarchy of urban locations that is enshrined in the household registration system, and which directly reflects the economic valuation of urban areas. Because of their registration and low income, migrant workers can generally only access these residential areas, apart from dormitories on factory premises. Changing their registration in order to become full urban citizens, however, is often tightly constrained, especially if the urban location is highly valuable in terms of economic, social and political opportunities. In recent reforms of the *hukou* system, this translates into regulated access to urban registration that directly reflects the 'quality' of candidates, thus even linking urban status with notions of individual quality and status.

This basically resembles international systems of regulating immigration according to economic criteria, such as giving privileged access to individuals with high levels of education. Restrictions to in-migration allow relatively easier movements on the same administrative level and within a province, but limit permanent movement to higher level cities. Status is measurable in the different point systems that have been recently introduced by many metropolitan cities, and which are most demanding and restrictive in the highest level cities. Thus, attempts at actually liberalizing the migration regime factually enhance status differences within the Chinese population, with inhabitants of higher level areas also claiming higher status in comparison to migrants without permanent settlement rights.[68]

As I have analysed in the previous section, these material phenomena partly reflect the institutional structure of ownership, with urban sprawl increasingly devouring territorial assets of rural collectives. Yet, the expansion of urban planning into sub-urbanizing rural areas also requires the transformation of ownership, from collective to state owned. This transformation is therefore also a modernist civilizational transformation: the unregulated growth of urban dwellings with decentralized, spontaneous patterns of organization are crowded out, literally in the form of demolition, by 'rational' urban planning and construction. So, the transformation of a migrant enclave into a shopping mall also expresses symbolically the transformation of ownership. The dualism of state and collective ownership is also a status order of ownership rights.

Now, I claim that this phenomenon is only one example of the comprehensive status order of ownership in China. The status order of ownership is a very distinct phenomenon of the formal institutions of socialism in China and thus cannot be related to any aspect of Chinese tradition. On the other hand, however, this formal institution interacts with the dynamics of the resurgence of the market system. This interaction, which is always accompanied by recurrent interventions of the state on different levels, reproduces the status order of ownership. Therefore, I argue that the status order of ownership is an essential element of the ritual economy in China, which represents a ritual innovation to a large degree. At the rural grassroots level, this status order interacts with traditional elements of kinship and community in creating path dependencies of institutional evolution. In the urban and urbanizing contexts, the status order is mainly a phenomenon of modernity, although deviating in principle from most institutions that so far have been identified as 'modern' in the Western context.

What is of interest here is the fact that ownership and political or administrative status overlap to a considerable degree. This is already evident in the institutional distinction between urban and rural areas and the respective assignment of landownership rights. In the urbanization process, reassigning agricultural land to urban uses implies the change of status and effectively a 'nationalization' of collective land rights, since all urban land is state owned. As such, urban land is of higher value, since it may be used for purposes other than agriculture, and is controlled by higher level authorities. However, the category of state ownership is much more complex than this simple legal transformation suggests.

State ownership is only formally assigned to the national level, in the sense that in abstract constitutional terms, the central government would represent 'the people' as the ultimate reference for identifying 'the state'. One of the most intricate features of the Chinese economy is the persistence of a 'regional property rights system'. This means that public ownership is administratively fragmented, with different property rights assigned to different levels of territorial administration. So, for example, a state-owned company may belong to the central, the provincial or the municipal level. In principle, these ownership rights could be reshuffled at will by the national authorities, because all these rights are state owned. But factually, the system was and still is stabilized by the emergence and recognition of factual rights of possession, in particular rights of *usufructus*. The latter are embodied in the structure of the tax system, with regional owners remaining the beneficiaries of the revenue that is generated by the companies which fall under their jurisdiction; hence, the tax system is in fact an essential element in allocating and recognizing ownership rights.[69]

This system of regional property rights is a ritual one, as it is not simply a legal arrangement, but is partly maintained by conventions. In fact, there is no formal entitlement of certain government units to particular ownership rights; these have emerged out of past decisions and interactions among different levels of government and are only indirectly formally constituted, such as via the assignment of taxes. These conventions are rooted in unique path dependencies that resulted from the institutional dynamics of planning in the Maoist era. In principle, the assignment of companies to particular levels of government may be decided by the central government as ultimate authority. However, quasi-property rights can be claimed by governments on any level, based on historical precedence and past investments. The resilience of this system is most visible in the recent reforms of assigning the supervision of state-owned companies to special government agencies, the SASACs. I will deal with these in more detail in Chapter 6, so suffice it to state that this re-allocation of certain aspects of ownership rights to a new 'system' specializing in this task did not simultaneously abolish the regional structure of ownership, because SASACs were constituted at every level of government. This replicates the dualism of 'line' versus 'block' authorities, namely vertical versus horizontal administrative relationships that I will analyse in Chapter 4; thus, the horizontal (i.e. regional) realization of ownership rights is also reproduced.

Historically, this system originated from the diverse decentralization measures that were initiated during the Great Leap Forward, and represented a major departure from the Soviet model of central planning. These measures were partly aimed at minimizing transaction costs in the planning system, but were also driven by non-economic, especially military considerations. So, the regional property rights system is also intimately linked with the unique structural characteristics of the Chinese economy at the outset of reforms, namely the similarity of industrial structures across provinces. This reflects the entirely different framework of planning compared to the Soviet Union. In standard centrally planned economies, planners would prefer highly concentrated industrial structures in order to minimize the costs of coordination between those units. Decentralization would mainly occur via internal organizational decentralization in those units, but less so in regional terms. In China, however, the idea prevailed that regions should be capable of maintaining full-scale comprehensive industrial systems in order to fend off a possible foreign invasion and lessen vulnerability of sensitive industries concentrated in particular areas. This policy was further accentuated with the so-called 'Third Front' policy by which large-scale industrial capacities were built in the interior provinces.[70]

So, this structural fragmentation was an exogenous given for planners who therefore opted for decentralization in order to economize on transaction costs. Industrial fragmentation turned regional governments into stakeholders and even quasi-owners of these state-owned units. During marketization, one important motivation to identify with the local industries was the employment that was safeguarded by them. Aside from that, as I mentioned before and will scrutinize in Chapter 4 in more detail, the local governments directly participated in the taxes and profits of the enterprises under their jurisdiction. Throughout the evolution of this system, local governments could also turn into investors in the local units, which reinstated or gave them rights of control. In other words, we observe a further instance where marketization started out from certain unique structural and institutional features of the Maoist era and actually created incentives to maintain certain of its aspects. With marketization, local governments in the first place perceived an increased value of the assets under their control. Only after the difficulties in surviving market competition became more evident during the 1990s did local governments opt for ways to divest from these assets, which were sometimes 'stranded' in the genuine sense, because they were created under the severely distorted price system of earlier times. However, at the same time they kept an interest in maintaining the local economic structure.

As I will argue in more detail in Chapter 6, this system may therefore be characterized as a stakeholder model of corporate governance of state-owned companies, with claims of different stakeholders approaching the status of ownership rights. On the theoretical level, it is important to distinguish these rights from what is conventionally seen as formal property rights with reference to Western developed market economies, as these rights are not the object of legal institutions, even in the context of

Chinese law. So, I propose to call these rights 'entitlements'. In this sense, the 'regional property rights' system is a system of entitlements assigned to different levels and units of government; this system is an essential part of the ritual economy, and hence is constituted by ritual. The notion of entitlement is broader than the notion of property right and relates to the status of a stakeholder. However, local government is not an ordinary stakeholder in the Western sense, as it combines many roles, reaching from regulatory roles to ownership roles, such as regarding land. In particular, local government also stands in political relation with the other government units that might control a company located in their jurisdiction, but which is not owned by the local government. So, if we say that local government holds stakes in local employment provided by a company, this may be seen as an entitlement that can be an object of bargaining.[71]

Historically, the system of entitlements was mainly a structure of competing claims of different government units on certain assets or outputs of a state-owned unit, designated in the picturesque way as 'many mothers-in-law'. This construction may be theorized as a 'multiple principal' model where different principals pursue different goals which are not necessarily congruent. This unique translation of a system of entitlements in a mechanism of corporate control was the reason why the Chinese central planning system had the unique feature of 'soft planning' allowing for slack. Only by leaving room for autonomous adaptation to different goals were the state-owned units able to mediate between the different claims of their governmental stakeholders. As a result, the existence of slack enabled many SOEs to respond swiftly and flexibly to the introduction of the 'double-track' system in the mid-1980s, which allowed SOEs to sell above-quota production via markets and market prices. From the viewpoint of corporate governance, the system therefore early constituted a domain of corporate autonomy even within the planned sector, manifest in the continuous bargaining process between SOEs and their different stakeholders.

With the ongoing modernization of the legal and administrative framework of SOEs, this system became more complicated, especially with the step towards 'corporatization' initiated in the mid-1990s. Corporatization means that SOEs adopt the legal status of corporations, such as publicly listed entities, and therefore obtain the status of a legal person also in the context of property law. In other words, the SOE is an owner of its own legal status, but these ownership rights are only derivatives of the ultimate ownership rights of the government. Theoretically, these rights would be managed by the SASACs, but in fact the original entitlements remain valid, partly manifest in shareholder arrangements, partly visible as stakeholder claims. In the current context this is important, since it introduces another complication in the ritual nature of ownership. An SOE at a particular location has a formal status of its own as a corporate entity, and the factual strength and the factual capacities that result from this formal status are determined by the relative status of the different stakeholders that are engaged with the unit and that claim certain entitlements of any kind of output, performance or action taken by the SOE. In other words, we cannot simply interpret the current ownership system in terms of the conventional regional property rights system, even though many of its aspects remain valid. However, one important conclusion is that the ritual nature of the regional property rights system is even further enhanced in the new shape, as the complicated relationship between the corporate unit and the stakeholders is mainly regulated via status mechanisms.

In this context, it is therefore important that the regional property rights system does not imply that all companies within a certain territory belong to the respective jurisdiction. In fact, the regional property rights system is even independent from the spatial organization, which has been further accentuated during market reforms which enhanced the autonomy of companies in their investment activities. In other words, considering a particular municipality, the state-owned units that are located in this territory may be assigned to different levels of the administrative hierarchy, both vertically and horizontally. Thus, a company may not belong to the provincial level where the municipality is located, but to another province. As a result, in the same territory units with highly diverse status of ownership may co-exist. These complex conditions were created, most importantly, via the efforts at restructuring the SOE sector in the past three decades, which were initially guided by ideas about creating 'trusts', later 'enterprise groups', and finally applying modern approaches to M&A as a means to restructure SOEs and enhance their competitiveness. Right from the beginning, the explicit aim of restructuring was to break through the 'cellularization' pattern that was also implicit in the regional property rights system (for more details, see Chapter 4). So, for example, in automotive industries inefficient small-scale regional factories might be merged with a large enterprise group and would assume the role of a supplier. Under these arrangements many variants would be possible, such as maintaining a partly autonomous status in a group, or changing into a branch factory and so forth. As a result, the status of a company at a particular location might become independent from the regional administrative structure. Yet, in these processes of restructuring, regional governments would often strive to protect certain entitlements via special arrangements. For example, they might explicitly turn into shareholders of the new entity, they might keep their taxation authority and hence claims on profits, or they might claim guarantees of local employment.[72]

In this complex system, the status of ownership reflects the different status of stakeholders as administrative units on different levels. This status is reflected in many arrangements, such as in rights to receive higher level subsidies, rights to approve infrastructure investments of a certain size, and the status of mayors and other top-level administrators in the nomenclature and so forth. These status differences in administrative structure directly translate into status differences of the organizations that are assigned to the respective levels. So, a state-owned company on the central level has higher status than an SOE on the local level. In the next chapter I will also detail the role of the nomenclature in reflecting this status hierarchy, since the status of organizations is always defined in terms of the status of the leading positions in the nomenclature. At this point, we should note that leadership positions in any kind of public organization are part of the CCP nomenclature and hence correspond to certain positions in the party hierarchy. So, the status of a certain organizational unit is not only determined by its status in the administrative hierarchy, but also by the status of the leadership position in the nomenclature. Evidently, this status also determines the relative status of individuals that represent different organizations.

If we want to generalize over these observations, we have to consider the relative status of the individuals that represent certain social entities such as companies or government units. So, the analysis of ownership in the ritual economy has to proceed to the individuals that actually take the decisions and actions that are enabled by certain entitlements that are linked to certain units. It is the relative status of individuals that counts in the ritual economy. Therefore, as I will detail in Chapter 5, in an important sense, ownership is embedded in the networks of individuals which are governed by relative status, or, more specifically, by relative endowments of social capital. Therefore, we can even draw a direct parallel with Fei Xiaotong's notion of *chaxu geju*: ownership as manifest in the distribution of entitlements is eventually governed by status differences between individuals. This also reflects a weakness of formal institutions that govern ownership, and is therefore another reason to use the term 'entitlements' instead. Entitlements relate to organizational units, but they can only be actualized by the individuals that represent the units, based on the relative endowment with social capital. Considering this fact, it also becomes evident that the actualization of ritual is only happening in local contexts where individuals with different status positions meet. Therefore, we notice another instance of the notion of field dependency. Although we can speak of a 'national' status order, this only becomes actual in local contexts.

In most general terms, we can therefore depict the status order of socialist ownership as a system of entitlements as shown in Figure 3.2. The status order is three-dimensional, with the dimensions of the 'system', 'xitong' (系统), the 'territory', 'difang' (地方) and the 'rank', 'dengji' (等级) in the nomenclature. The rank order in the nomenclature translates into different designations, such as the 'CEO' of a company or a 'bureau chief' in the government administration. So, one cannot immediately recognize the relative rank just from knowing these positions, although the rank order partly correlates with the relative status of territories. So, for example, a municipal mayor is necessarily below the status of

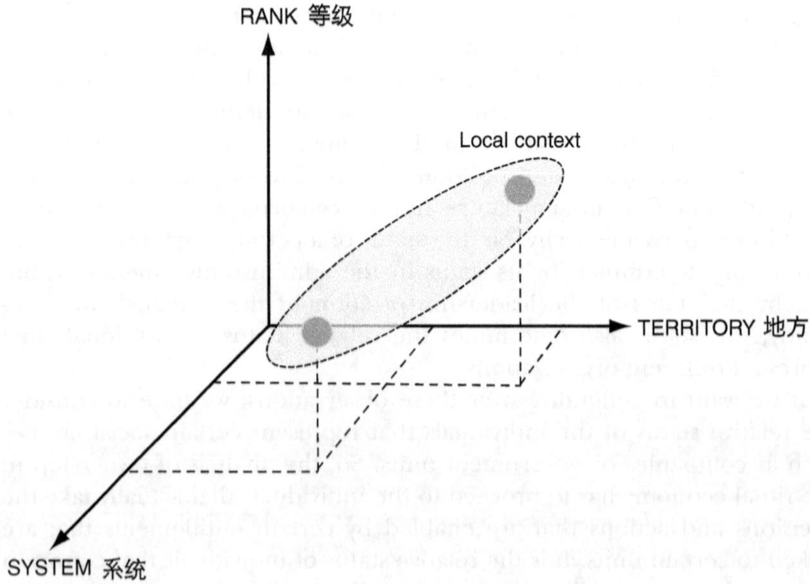

Figure 3.2 Dimensions of the status order of socialist ownership.

a provincial governor also in terms of rank. However, a relatively low position in the provincial administration may have a status that is above a high position on the municipal level, as projected in the general rank order of the nomenclature. This situation is further complicated by adding the third dimension, the system. The importance of systems is mainly determined on the national level and reflects the internal status order in the central government, with different ministries having different impact and reputation, resulting from historical developments, current policies, measures of restructuring and so forth. So, a certain representative of a system with high status may have a relatively low status in rank, but works on the central level, which gives him a relatively high status in local contexts. A relatively high rank may come together with a low status in the dimension of system, thus defining status differences on the same territorial level. In fact, however, it is the nomenclature that at least partly reduces the resulting complexities by means of referring to a commensurable and coherent rank order in the CCP as an encompassing national institution; for example, the CEOs of the largest SOEs on the central level, also belonging to strategically significant systems such as energy, would have the same rank as a vice minister in the central government hierarchy.

This complex dimensionality of the actual status order and its contextualized nature is one of the most important reasons for the path dependency of the process of implementing central government policies at the local level, even if, formally, only the domain of state ownership is involved. The actual distribution of entitlements of organizational units interacts with the status order of the individuals who represent them, and the outcome of policies is determined by the interactions and bargaining processes in the local context. This is what I identify as the ritual economy in the domain of formal institutions. Clearly, the status distinction between rural and urban domains is just one expression of this more general phenomenon, yet certainly a most essential one.

I argue that this interaction between status order and formal institutions is a constitutive element of another defining feature of the Chinese economic style, which I explore in much more detail in Chapter 4, namely 'localism'. Localism as a medium-range theoretical notion is an extension of the notion of the regional property rights system in recognizing the more complex conditions of the contemporary market economy. Localism results from the fact that the effects of the status order on social and economic interactions are always contextualized locally, since relative status emerges only via the mutual recognition of status among the particular actors involved. In other words, I claim that ritual is necessarily related to localism. This is clearly different from the idea of law as a formal institution. General and abstract law as constituting ownership relationships is explicitly designed to be de-contextualized, whereas entitlements defined by ritual are contextualized. As I will show in the next chapter, this contextualization also has an economic function, namely defining and enabling the essential feature of experimentalism of Chinese reforms. Localism enables the adaptation of policies to local conditions, mainly via the discursive framing of decisions among the different stakeholders in the local economy.

As I have already elucidated, localism entails a status order of ownership as defined in formal institutions. This has been evident in the de facto privatization process of the past two decades, which was launched in the second half of the 1990s under the slogan 'Grasping the big, and letting the small go', 'zhuada fangxiao' (抓大放小). Generally, status correlates with scale, although, as a result of Maoist decentralization policies, sometimes even very large SOEs were assigned to the local level. In other words, the new policy implied a centralization process in state ownership, since many lower level administrations were forced to close their SOEs, effectively to privatize them, or to merge with other SOEs. In the 2000s, the central government also launched the initiative to create global champions, which often meant that central-level SOEs received additional support and became part and parcel of the modernization via globalization effort. This is particularly true for industries which remained strategically under control of the government, such as petrochemicals or banking. This policy was actively supported by mergers and acquisitions, with central SOEs often acquiring provincial-level SOEs. As a result of this policy, we can state a general trend towards concentration of state ownership in high-status domains of the ritual economy, as reflected in size, leadership position and the relative status of stakeholders. One expression of high status of particular state-owned units may be that the CEOs become members of the National People's Congress. In addition, as I discuss extensively in Chapter 6, the distinction between state ownership and private ownership is a distinction of status, increasingly also in terms of modernization. Industrial restructuring aims to establish the role of the government as avant-garde of modernization, hence putting SOEs in front of the globalization effort. Yet, the status of private business can also be enhanced by political co-optation, again in People's Congress memberships on the different territorial levels.[73]

Against the background of my previous discussion of landownership in the rural areas, it is illuminating to look at the urban management of state-owned land in the context of localism and the status order of socialist ownership. Formally, urban land is state owned, namely with the State Council as the ultimate principal, and all other subordinate units as agents. In fact, in a particular city there are different land rights with different status, since in the same place organizations co-exist that are assigned to different levels of government with different status, both in terms of territory and system. So, for example, in a prefectural-level city, certain parts of the urban land may be controlled by the municipal government, but other parts belong to state-owned companies of different status, including central-level ones. This implies that some decisions over local land use may be even taken on the level of central decision-makers. This has the important implication that one cannot assess the factual effect of fiscal and administrative decentralization measures simply by looking at the change of formal institutions. Since in the late 1990s and 2000s land has become a major source of revenue for local governments, their actual degree of autonomy depends on the bargaining processes between the different organizational units and their representatives in the local context. Thus, we see localism at work.

We cannot understand the actual functions of state ownership of urban land without considering the ritual nature of the entitlements that different parties have in a local context. This corresponds to the previous observations on the urban villages. In other words, again we can state that the development of the material infrastructure of urban areas reflects the interactions in the ritual economy. This results in complex conditions for urban planning and hence path dependencies of local urbanization and modernization processes. Often, the different decision-makers have different status in the nomenclature, with, for example, the top executives of central SOEs having higher status than the mayors and Party secretaries of municipalities. So, if the latter want to pursue a local planning process, in spite of the fact that all land is state owned, they have to bargain across status differences, and with the different groups not necessarily converging on consensus. This also applies for other kinds of economic decisions, such as the restructuring of local and central SOEs, which may include

M&A of local by central SOEs. The relative status of corporate units can be directly expressed in the handling of their land assets. Again, we meet an instance where architecture is a signal that reproduces the status order, for example, when a large central SOE with operations in a peripheral area would set up a local headquarters with a large public square, thus appropriating the symbolism of government.[74]

To conclude, I argue that Chinese localism reflects the status order of the ritual economy of the modernizing socialist state, and that this has even been strengthened during the reform period. It is important to note that this form of localism is not necessarily converging with regional cultures in the traditional sense. This reflects a fact that, in turn, stands in continuity with the administrative structure of Imperial China. Also during that time, the administrative structure often deliberately cut across economic, natural or cultural borders among regions on different levels, in order to insulate government policy from potentially centrifugal forces of regionalism. This remains true for today, and we cannot easily show that the formal status order is converging with cultural borders, such as borders of local and regional dialects. One of the litmus tests is the phenomenon of local protectionism, which is clearly undergirded by provincial-level administrative borders, but not by traditional regional socioeconomic and cultural distinctions.[75] So, in this sense, localism is a phenomenon that originates in formal institutions, and even reflects institutional design. But at the same time, as we have seen, it cannot be approached as a category of law, but is an expression of ritual.

Theoretical reprise

In this chapter I have analysed how the ritual economy becomes manifest in the modernization of the Chinese economy and society. It lays the foundation for further analysing the contemporary Chinese economy in the course of the next three chapters. This analysis overcomes dualisms that often overlook the importance of interactions between what is identified as two segments or domains in the economy. Most importantly, the notion of ritual makes the distinction between 'informal' and 'formal institutions' analytically obsolete, which might suggest that there are two different economic systems in China, namely the 'formal economy' and the 'informal economy', which would also further suggest that the Chinese economy operates like many other economies in the developing world, featuring large 'informal sectors'. This would be a misplaced comparison, in the same way as the comparison between Chinese 'urban villages' and 'urban slums' would be erroneous. A Chinese urban village is not 'informal' in the genuine sense, since it is largely governed by corporate organizations that follow local regulations in their operations and assume parapolitical functions, and reflects the constitutional distinction between collectively owned and state-owned land. So, what appears to be a distinction between 'formal' and 'informal' is actually the manifestation of a status order in the ritual economy, which also formally distinguishes between different qualities of ownership rights or the status of citizens in the household registration system.

It is certainly true that many phenomena of ritual today appear to be 'informal' because there are formal institutions that explicitly contain or even negate them. For example, if government regulations denounce popular religion as 'superstition' and thereby trigger many activities of local officials aiming at suppressing its expressions, popular religion is driven into informality. But at the same time we cannot classify a temple that is led by a temple boss and a temple association and which operates with a charter as an 'informal institution', as it is based on formal regulations and is recognized by the local government. The situation is even more complicated when we consider collective ownership rights in the rural areas and note that these formal rights are partly interpreted by the actors in the light of traditional lineage structures. In this case, it would be misleading to approach this interpretation as 'informal', because actually there is no additional pattern of social interaction beyond the scope of the formal institution. From the analytical perspective of ritual, it is the formal institution that is synthesized with traditional notions into what may be approached as the 'actualized institution'. In the Aoki model, this tension is easy to resolve. The 'formal institution' is only the public representation, a sign that is itself being interpreted in the process of institutional reproduction. So, the 'institution' is this entire causal feedback loop, and cannot be reduced to the sign as such.

The notion of 'economic style' overcomes such misplaced analytical dualisms. Thus, in this chapter, we have collected the first building blocks in identifying the economic style of contemporary China. If we reflect upon such issues in theoretical terms, in the first place we consider the role of ideas in institutional change. Formal institutions express certain ideas that drive institutional design. The towering idea in recent Chinese history is certainly modernization, which is the intellectual response to the Western challenge. However, if we want to understand its role in economic style, we do not write intellectual history but try to understand how this idea affects institutional change, and how institutional change in turn influences ideas. The central theoretical paradigm here is path dependencies in institutional change, triggered by institutional design. The fundamental analytical mistake of the aforementioned dualisms is to take institutional design as reality, or at least as the benchmark for sorting reality into different domains.

Modernist thought has guided institutional design in many respects during recent decades. One important theoretical lesson of this chapter is that this does not necessarily also change cognitive path dependencies. An illuminating example is the Chinese family and the interaction with population policy since 1978. The one-child policy is a thoroughly modernist institution which aims at raising the growth potential via limiting the size of families. However, as we have seen, this administrative intervention interacts with traditional beliefs about family and gender, causing unintended effects of the policy which will continue to unfold during the decades to come. One mechanism from which these effects result is the shift of the sex ratio at birth, hence a material phenomenon. The sex ratio influences the marriage market, and, via the marriage market, even macroeconomic patterns such as the savings rate. These effects are mediated via cognitive path dependencies. So, for example, the imposed limitation of the number of children combines with conceptions of the value of gender, causing the bias in the sex ratio. However, the resulting imbalance feeds back to these standard notions, such as when rural parents begin to recognize that daughters are essential for their well-being in old age. This valuation is also reflected in the relative value of females in the marriage market. In the long run, these endogenous changes of beliefs interact with long-standing policies that aim at the modernization of the institutions of the family and marriage and at creating the conditions for gender equality. Thus, we can say that the institution of the one-child policy is actually embedded in a complex network of cognitive phenomena and related institutions, and therefore is an essential element of the economic style, and certainly is not just a macroeconomic policy intervention with mere quantitative dimensions. If we want to understand these complex interactions, the notion of ritual is essential, in both senses. For one, we have to consider traditional Chinese ritual, such as certain conceptions of marriage; at the same time, in the interaction, modernist conceptions become manifest in behavioural norms and values that are ritualistic in the generic sense, such as the sex ratio. This analysis of the one-child policy is therefore also important from a theoretical perspective. Because of the manifold institutional connectivities, the one-child policy has to be regarded as a constitutive element of the contemporary Chinese economic style, as it has also been transpiring earlier in its Foucaultian interpretations as 'biopolitics'.

Indeed, if we focus only on ideas, it is straightforward to see how the status order of modernist ritual also establishes a distinction between different kinds of knowledge, with modernist ideas assuming high status and other domains of knowledge turning into 'savoir assujeti' in the sense of Foucault, such as traditional notions of gender. These 'low-status' ideas cannot be simply seen as being disconnected from social reality, or as having no positive functionality. For example, the decline of public services in the rural areas evidently fosters the belief that the family can be an ultimate institution of support, thus actually disproving modernist ideas, and resulting in severe tensions over the implementation of related policies. One essential aspect of the ritual economy is this interaction between different kinds of knowledge with different status, with the status defined relative to the benchmark of modernism.

One important leitmotiv of this chapter is that modernism is mediated via material structures. After all, the sex ratio is a material structure. In theoretical terms, this means that we approach material structures as signs that are constitutive for the causal mechanisms of institutional reproduction. In doing so, we have to be very careful in empirically fixing the causality and therefore properly identifying the semiotic mechanisms. Signs always have a double side: one is the expressive, the other the interpretation. If signs are produced intentionally, the expression and the interpretation do not necessarily converge. Interpretations lead to certain actions that may in turn influence the reproduction of the expressive function of signs. So, there is large leeway of the causal processes that might relate to a sign that by itself may be relatively easy to identify in etic terms.

In this chapter, the foremost example for this is settlement patterns and architectural design. Modern urban architecture is an expression of modernism which is part and parcel of institutional design that is led by the notion of 'civilization' as a quality. The difference between urban and rural settlement patterns is therefore also a distinction of status, and thus expresses a ritual dimension of contemporary Chinese society which is also enshrined in institutions such as the *hukou* system. Modern urban planning is the material expression of modernist economic planning, whereas the urban villages are the manifestation of migration and rural social structures in the midst of modernist urban projects. These material distinctions reinforce status notions of modernism, with the chaotic infrastructure of urban villages also expressing the low civilizational status of migrants. Thus, we can say that the existence of urban villages feeds back on the norms and values that maintain these perceptions and expressions of status, and thus are an essential aspect of ritual. Correspondingly, the rural reconstruction projects that relocate villagers in a 'New Socialist Countryside' are a manifestation of modernist ideas, presupposing advanced knowledge of economic planners and administrators about which lifestyles and social settings are most desirable for the rural population. However, in this case it is not straightforward whether this intentional action, namely viewing reconstructed settlements as expressions of civilizational advancement, is being interpreted correspondingly by the relocated villagers.

In this chapter, there is a crucial example of such a gap between expression and interpretation, also related to settlement patterns. This is the unintended effects of collectivization, which, as we have seen, have had long-run causal effects, for example, on the emergence of urban villages. Collectivization did not affect the settlement patterns, which means that the material structure of a collectivized village continued to embody the historical patterns of extended kinship and group formation. The settlement pattern produced what were economic effects in the first place, such as influencing ease of coordination or costs of movements and transportation. Yet, these effects also reproduced traditional interpretations of the settlement structures. As we saw in Chapter 2, Chinese villages were actually also religious domains, with settlements expressing perceived cosmic forces of auspicious locations, with temples and lineage halls expressing the regular course of ritual actions throughout the year. Collectivization changed the names of the corresponding artefacts as well as their uses, turning lineage temples into warehouses, but did not eradicate these interpretive dimensions. Therefore, a deep gap between expression and interpretation emerged, which contributed to the rapid resurgence of traditional ritual in the rural areas after de-collectivization was launched.

So, in understanding these developments, it is essential to combine the perspectives of the theoretical models of path dependency and the analysis of signs in the Aoki approach. The Aoki model focuses our attention on the role of material structures in the reproduction of ritual. Therefore, for example, rural reconstruction and relocation would be seen as possibly contributing to a further transformation of ritual. For the time being, these may be primarily seen as the risk of anomic decay of social life; yet the long-run consequences are not obvious. In the case of collectivization, the Aoki model implies that it would be wrong to reduce the description of the institutions of collectivization only in terms of the formal institutions implemented by government design. The settlement patterns and the cognitive path dependencies worked together in the emergence of a different institutional setting, such as described by the notion of 'cellularization'. In this notion, traditional kinship looms large, hence a ritual dimension *par excellence.* So, against dualistic approaches I would argue that 'cellularization' was a defining element of socialist institutions in the transition from the Maoist era to the reform era, and therefore a building block of the ritual economy.

Therefore, one of the important insights of this chapter is that there is not that radical rupture between the Maoist and the reformist period as is normally suggested. Two factors contribute to the continuities. One is the unintended consequences of Maoist policies, such as cellularization. The other is the modernist cognitive framework. As I have shown, we can say that the modernist framework unifies the growth models of the two periods in a very fundamental sense, namely centring on maximizing the investment rate as a driver of growth. Marketization is just another means to achieve this goal without jeopardizing incentives. Yet, there are also institutions of marketization which are directly influenced by the Maoist institutional legacy, with the foremost example of the *hukou* system.

The *hukou* system was an institutional innovation that directly broke apart what was a sociocultural continuum in the Chinese past. I have argued that, being a radical change of formal institutions in the first place, it has turned into an important element of modernist ritual in the reform period. The central variable here is social capital interacting with markets. Formally, the system defines certain rights and obligations. However, once people respond to these constraints and incentives, they create social capital while aiming at exploiting opportunities that are increasingly opened up by marketization. This results in path dependencies in the formation of social capital; thus, specific forms of agency emerge that crystallize into a status order that becomes partly independent from the original formal institutions. As a result, formal institutions partly lose their constraining nature, because they become endogenous and even internalized in the newly forming ritual order of society.

This observation points towards the role of modernism in shaping specific forms of governmentality in the ritual economy. The mechanisms by which these forms are generated can be theorized in the 'elements–patterns–processes–states' framework that builds on the Aoki model. As I emphasized in Chapter 2, in understanding ritual it is important to realize that elements can be any kind of social phenomenon, and thus are by no means related to certain phenomena that are conventionally associated with 'traditional culture'. The *hukou* system was certainly a radical institutional innovation, but it has engendered a number of social patterns and resulting processes that have coalesced into states. States are visible, for example, in the urban villages, and thereby become elements in further processes of institutional change. Thus, a radically new formal institution turns into a cultural phenomenon of its own, and assumes an independent causal role in subsequent patterns and processes.

This framework is most useful for understanding many aspects of 'modernity' in contemporary Chinese society in terms of ritual. My analysis of the consumer society and urban professionalism is a case in point, which is part and parcel of expressing and living the status order of the ritual economy. In the economic context, the most important contribution certainly lies in identifying the ritual essence of ownership in China today. It would be very misleading to approach ownership in terms of formal institutions and the law. Therefore, I introduce the term 'entitlements' which I refer to as 'states' in my theoretical paradigm. Formal institutions are elements that are interpreted in the course of social action, and only as a result constitute what is a property right in terms of entitlement, with the latter qualifying as 'states'. Economic analysis has to focus on these, and, with reference to China, we note the ritual nature of entitlements. Many observers have pointed out that property rights in China evolve informally, in spite of the increasing number of pertinent laws. But that would throw the baby out with the bath water and unnecessarily downgrade the role of formal institutions. This view would also wrongly suggest a necessarily evolutionary trend towards further strengthening certain formal forms of ownership. For example, in current reforms of SOEs, the idea of 'hybrid ownership' has been adopted officially: I would suggest that this even extends the scope of ritualistic determination of entitlements. The litmus test in the chapter was landownership. Land plays an essential role in the current stage of economic development because of its specific functions in maintaining the growth model centred on high rates of investment. Barring revolutionary changes in the Chinese political system, we may safely assume that public ownership of land will remain a stable constitutional feature of the Chinese political system. So, the status order of ownership will reproduce itself in a gradual evolutionary fashion, most visible in the particular ways in which urbanization is being actualized and literally materialized across China.

The status order of ownership is a state that emerges out of the evolutionary institutional dynamics. I have argued that one essential characteristic of this state is 'localism'. Again, localism is not another dualism. This is often suggested by observers who relate 'central' government to the source of formal institutions and then put forward the diagnosis that 'localities' adopt deviant strategies, which would amount to 'informality'. In contrast, localism refers to the fact that it is constitutive for the Chinese economic style, as the ritual order of ownership can only be constituted in local terms, being ultimately based in actual status distinctions among agents who represent different social and organizational entities. In the most general sense, this reflects cognitive and institutional patterns that are 'field dependent'. One instructive example is collective landownership, where the formal institutions do not lend a clear meaning to the notion of 'collective'. This kind of ambiguity is a characteristic feature of many laws and formal institutions. However, it is by no means evident that this ambiguity constitutes a difference or even 'deficiency' as compared to legal regulations and terms in the Western economies. After all, these are often highly abstract, and the entire system of legal adjudication serves the purpose of clarifying their meaning in specific cases. Localism in the ritual economy implies that this meaning is continuously negotiated among the different parties involved in the local context, but also in interaction with other systemic levels, such as central government. In this process, legal adjudication can also be involved, but then the question is how far this process also lends attention to the local meanings, which often appears to be the case. As a result, the proposed notion of entitlements refers to the local nature of property rights.

A stark case in point is the fact that farmers in China appear to have very different entitlements regarding collective land across different locations, resulting in different structures of power and local political economy. The difficulty in assessing this fact is that there is no way to relate this state with a hypothetical reference case of individually assigned property rights. Every fixation of entitlements is to a certain degree therefore without precedent. In the status order of ownership, farmers may face a low status in bargaining over land rights with the local states which assume the role of the modernizing agent, aiming at raising the civilizational level of rural areas. At the same time, local farmers may see themselves as high-status individuals relative to migrant workers who flock into industrializing and urbanizing rural localities. All the different groups claim different entitlements, and the final allocation is local in nature. As we have seen, in many respects this is also true for the state-owned sector.

To sum up, in drawing upon theoretical notions such as path dependency, social capital or signs as constitutive parts of institutional mechanisms, we can approach the modern Chinese economy as a 'ritual economy', and we understand this term as a unified and coherent identification of economic style. Then, the question comes up naturally: In what sense can we identify family resemblances with the ritual economy of Imperial China? To a large extent, it is too early to give a qualified response to this question. In one sense, many observations in the chapter point towards dissimilarities. The two most important discontinuities are certainly modernism and the institutional divide between the rural and the urban areas which is constitutive for the growth model. Regarding the former, however, it would be misleading to approach modernism based only on its own terms, defining itself in opposition to 'old China'. The status order of contemporary China includes the existence of a privileged stratum of officials who claim superior knowledge about society and who aim to transform society according to their own ideas. Modernism as *jiaohua* effort therefore has a paradoxical nature, rejecting traditional ideas but also adopting them in the very process of rejection. On the other hand, in spite of ideologically praising its rural origins, the CCP has implemented a growth model that creates and builds on a modernist status order that explicitly assigns low status to the rural population, enshrined in the *hukou* system.

One difficult question is the role of the market, because there is a tension between the revival of the material structure of markets and the market as an idea. This is a topic that I need to further explore in Chapter 4. As we have seen, in many respects the revival of tradition is also linked to the revival of the traditional market system as a material infrastructure of the Chinese body politic. Maoist cellularization obviated this role of the market; reforms reinstated it. On the other hand, and very different from traditional notions, the market is today given a modernist interpretation. For example, globalization is seen as a driver of civilizational advancement, and market-driven migration as a means to upgrade the quality of the population. This is a rupture with the past, when markets were seen as necessary conditions for material welfare, but were not seen as a defining element of culture. I have described this as markets assuming an essential role in modern Chinese governmentality. This defines a major difference in the ideational foundations of economic style in China and the liberal Western tradition. In the latter, markets and state are often seen as different domains, and markets often define the realm of freedom that needs to be protected against incursions of the state. In China, for a long time, markets were regarded as a morally ambiguous domain; in fact, Maoism may be seen as radically accentuating traditional concerns about the missing morality of markets. In twenty-first-century China, markets have become a defining element of economic style, and are part and parcel of governmentality.

Notes

1 For a detailed discussion of the CCP policies towards markets in the rural areas, see Thaxton (1983: 109ff.). Thaxton emphasizes the gradual adaptation of the policies to the traditional values and behavioural standards of the peasants, focusing on the restoration of smallholder family farming and opening up markets. The CCP actively engaged in brokerage roles, such as providing information or easing transport channels. It abolished most of the irregular taxes, especially on trade, and allowed for free pricing of goods. The market obtained a strategic role in undermining Japanese attempts at controlling the flow of economic resources. These activities were often explicitly related to the institutions of the traditional ritual economy. For example, the CCP supported temple fairs, clearly also a medium of political mobilization, but also in fostering the traditional market activities. Thaxton therefore concludes that prior to the onset of collectivization, the CCP policies were an ideological merger between socialist ideas and traditional norms of the peasant economy. This observation is important in understanding the rapid resurgence of independent economic activity in the cautious attempts at restoring family farms in the aftermath of the Great Leap Forward and with the eventual onset of reforms since 1978. With the latter, the CCP directly returned to its roots in the 1940s.

2 The classical study of the moral dimension of Maoist policies is Madsen (1984). This goes back to the radical transformation of Marxist ideology that took place early under Mao's leadership, initially launched by leading intellectuals such as Li Dazhao, and was soon criticized by Soviet observers as voluntarism and unscientific, an evaluation that was tellingly repeated with reference to the Chinese reforms of 1978 (see Herrmann-Pillath 1986). The main idea was that the notion of class was extended to entire nations, so that China, in spite of still being in a pre-industrial state, could be seen as suffering from capitalist exploitation on a global scale. Thus, the cases of the socialist revolution and the liberation of China from external aggressors could be merged. As a consequence, ideological righteousness became the central concern for maintaining the stamina of revolutionary effort. In the rural areas, as Madsen amply demonstrated, this turned the question of market-oriented behaviours and individual economic interest into a moral one, which was heightened by the recurrent ideological campaigns sweeping the countryside. In this view, the market was seen as a seductive force, reviving moral attitudes of profit seeking and egoism. It is fascinating to see how Metzger (1977: 231ff.) puts Maoism in the context of Neoconfucian concerns about moral rectitude and the resulting tensions of inner-wordly actions. Metzger correctly anticipated that once the tension is lost, reflecting the political realities, a return to the traditional view may be the necessary outcome, adopting what he calls 'moderate realism' and recognition of the world as partial moral failure. That would include the revival of 'capitalist' practices.

3 In referring to 'modernism', it is important to note that this term is not indigenous, in spite of the fact that 'modernism' had been widely used in Japan in different variants, such as *gendai shugi*, in order to denote modern lifestyles or modern urban architectures; however, the corresponding term 'xiandaizhuyi' (现代主义) did not diffuse to China and apparently is only used in the context of 'postmodernism', 'hou xiandaizhuyi' (后现代主义) (Evelyn Schubert, personal communication). Modernism became an important notion in cultural studies on Chinese literature, cinema and the arts of the 1980s, but mainly in the context of comparative studies in these narrower fields of aesthetics (see e.g. Hayot 2012). On the history of the 'civilizational' agenda see Dynon

(2008), and as an example of the actual relevance in indigenous theorizing about Chinese developments see Guo (2015); the term may be regarded as an essential piece in 'Dengist' ideology, as Deng Xiaoping himself introduced the initial distinction between 'material' and 'spiritual' civilization. Western observers tend to discard these conceptual frameworks as mere propaganda, yet they played an important role in defining ideational anchors for political leadership across all levels. For example, with the advent of the Hu and Wen leadership, the term 'social civilization' gained some prominence, thus highlighting the concern for social disparities. There have been countless initiatives, events and communications over the decades in which narratives are constructed that detail the meaning of such terms. One core idea is 'balance', thus being reminiscent of traditional Chinese thinking, tied up with the notion of progress, which is not. It is important to note the distinction between *wenming* and 'culture', 'wenhua' (文化) in this context; if used together with the notion of China, *wenhua* refers to Chinese essences, whereas *wenming* is clearly modernist in often suggesting references to 'best practices' which continue to be 'Western'. Often material and spiritual components of civilization actually come together, such as in the propagation of certain sanitary standards when launching urban renewal projects. But this also reveals the comprehensive evaluation of individual and social practices in a moral dimension.

4 The term 'biopolitics' was introduced by Foucault (2004b) as referring to the diffusion of new practices of governments that focus on macro-level characteristics of the population of a territory, based largely on statistical data covering those characteristics. These practices pursue certain goals that relate to the stabilization and enhancement of state power, in particular with reference to economic aspects. In this sense, all modern states pursue biopolitics, for instance, when governments adopt macropolicies in targeting economic growth or healthcare policies. In the Chinese context, as is shown in Greenhalgh and Winckler (2005), who directly refer to this term in the title of their book-length analysis of Chinese population policies, the term also raises a number of narrower 'biologistic' associations, since population policy may also include even eugenic considerations or refer explicitly to issues such as territory, population growth and availability of resources in long-range developmental plans.

5 For a detailed and extensive analysis of Chinese population policy in the larger context, see Greenhalgh and Winckler (2005). The campaign style was most prevalent in the first decade, also leading to excesses that attracted the attention of Western media, in particular violence against women, forced abortions and so forth, also driving cadres and the rural population into a difficult and conflict-ridden situation. More recently, the institutions and methods have been considerably overhauled, such as in putting implementation into the general context of counselling and individual family planning. Yet, the coercive nature of the policy has not changed in principle, and is now mainly expressed in high fines and other economic sanctions on violators. Greenhalgh and Winckler (2005: 252ff.) also discuss the deep psychological effects, even traumas, that were caused by population policy. With responsibility for contraception largely laid on the shoulders of women, many women had to undergo repeated abortions and developed anxieties related to sexual intercourse. In past decades, China has seen an extraordinarily high suicide rate of women (in most countries, male suicides are more frequent than female ones), generally connected to population policy and its ramifications, such as in the context of rural migration, when fathers leave the village and mothers stay at home with daughters-only families, thus feeling shame and loss of face, in spite of being mothers. Tellingly, the numbers have substantially improved recently (*The Economist*, 28 June 2014), apparently because of the increasing number of young

females who leave villages and migrate to urban areas, thus freeing themselves from the fetters of village traditions.

6 In popular perceptions, the one-child policy has led to the rise of 'little emperors', referring to children who are being spoiled by too much care from parents and grandparents. There is empirical evidence that the cohorts of children born in the years before and after the introduction of the one-child policy indeed show differences in values and attitudes. In particular, they appear to be more risk-averse, and less trustworthy and trustful (see Cameron *et al.* 2013). The question of the generational transition in family business attracts much public attention today (see e.g. Zhou Xibing 2014). One problem is the different value orientation of the two generations. This not only relates to the fact that many entrepreneurs have only one child, but also to the different experiences. For example, many entrepreneurs have sent their children abroad to earn a degree, but this changes also the motivation to continue with the father's traditional business. Entrepreneurs often have to accept daughters as successors, although they would like to stick to the traditional male line of inheritance. However, the traditional separation between the family head and the family manager also allows for more flexible arrangements, such as marrying in sons-in-law who would cooperate with the daughter in continuing the family business.

7 Greenhalgh (2012) offers an extensive analysis of the 'bare bones' issue in rural society, which has a cultural history, as also in the past bachelors who could not afford formal marriage often joined marginal groups in society, such as secret brotherhoods. Today, the issue is neglected in the context of population policy which centres on the female role in terms of rights campaigns. Bachelors are often depicted as a threat to society, especially since they generally belong to the poor and illiterate stratum of society. The growing scarcity of brides especially in the less developed regions has triggered many changes in marriage customs; for example, lineages are often forced to give up the principle of lineage exogamy because families cannot afford the escalating brideprices and cannot attract brides from areas with higher levels of development.

8 Population policy was a central issue in the political controversies on the eve of the Great Leap Forward and hence the radicalization of the Maoist programme. Matching the subsequent discussion of the growth model, it was seen against the background of different conceptualizations of economic growth. A major academic role was played by the economist Ma Yinchu, who had earned a Ph.D. in the USA before returning to China (Herrmann-Pillath 2009b). Ma recommended the adoption of a Keynesian policy that would use rural development in order to increase demand for industrial products, thus engendering a virtuous cycle of consumption and industrialization. Limiting population growth in the rural areas was seen as major means to raise rural living standards (see Ma 1981). Mao himself criticized Ma who was therefore facing political persecution, only to be rehabilitated after 1978, also in terms of adopting his policy ideas in combining rural market reforms with tight interventions in population policy.

9 The debates about the new Chinese growth model have wide circulation and are also part of the official agenda of economic policy (see e.g. Huang Yasheng 2013). It is an essential element of thinking about the long-term agenda, as it transpires in the World Bank (2012) 'China 2030' report that was completed in close collaboration with the Development Research Center of the State Council. The idea of a new growth model conjoins many different aspects, the core being to change the drivers of growth while paying attention to the wider 'civilizational' context of growth, such as balancing growth with environmental aspects (so-called 'green GDP').

10 In Huang's (1990) approach to economic involution population, family and involutionary growth are closely connected phenomena in both the traditional and the collectivist Maoist economy. The simple reason is that the collectives operated as families writ large, especially regarding the role of surplus labour in driving the implicit price of labour below a ficticious market wage rate, and maintaining internal redistributive mechanisms. As a result, collectives continued to offer labour even with marginal productivities converging against zero, thus also creating incentives to prevent technological innovation. He strongly emphasizes that this mechanism is therefore independent from 'socialist' or 'capitalist' institutions, because it operates within both market and non-market contexts. This involutionary dynamics could only be broken via the external push towards industrialization that was launched by the township and village industries in the 1980s, building on collective industries of the communes. Therefore, government intervention remained essential for the growth model, in spite of marketization and liberalization. As we will see, this also puts the resource extraction devices at the centre of attention.

11 It is important to recognize that these ideas have a very long pedigree in Chinese political thought and were also perennially pursued by Imperial governments. In this respect, the Legalist and the Confucian ideologies even converged, though with different emphases. The classical model is the 'well field system' of groups of peasant smallholders who are collectively responsible for paying their duties to the state. This model (normally referred to as the 'juntian' (均田) system) was often actively pursued in times of dynastic renewal, such as under the Sui (see Twitchett 1979: 24f.), because the government could distribute large areas of land that were laid waste because of depopulation caused by military conflicts. Kuhn (2002: 102ff.) makes a convincing point that collectivization may be interpreted as a radical attempt at creating a resource extraction system that bypasses all intermediate levels via direct government purchasing of agricultural products at fixed prices. He also emphasizes that in this system the rural cadres, especially the leading cadres of the *xiang* level (mostly headquarters of communes), actually assumed the role of tax agents. This is important in order to understand the impact of marketization on this system, as these cadres could now obtain a similar structural position in the local state as tax farmers of earlier times. I come back to this point in Chapter 4. The idea of putting taxation at the centre of understanding the economic system is shared by an increasing number of Chinese authors. For example, in his analysis of *xian*-level government Zhou Qingzhi (2014: 16) also cites Kuhn approvingly.

12 The emergence of this growth model may be explained by Marxist economics, where capitalist accumulation always stays in direct competition with the wage fund and hence consumption. The capitalists have to keep wages as low as possible in order to raise the profit rate. This simple growth model was also applied to the socialist institutions, the only difference being that accumulation is now controlled by the state. As I have already mentioned in n.8 above, there were alternative growth models available in the 1950s, such as in the policy proposals by Ma Yinchu, which emphasized the role of consumption in creating the demand for industrial products (Ma 1981). These ideas were often related to the rural question, which explains why the CCP adopted many of these ideas after 1978. In the early years of reforms, rural marketization was accompanied also by changes in industrial policy, emphasizing so-called 'light industries', largely consumer goods industries.

13 This point has been emphasized by many authors as a major difference in the conditions in the former Soviet Union at the beginning of market transition; a recent argument is made by Bosworth and Collins (2008). In 1978, China was

already advanced in industrialization, with 48 per cent of GDP generated in industry. However, at the same time 71 per cent of the working population was employed in agriculture that produced only 28 per cent of GDP. The existence of a vast surplus labour pool has been a shaping factor of structural changes in the Chinese economy until most recently. In the mid-2000s, the share of agriculture in GDP had shrunk to 9 per cent of GDP, while 47 per cent of the working population are still statistically working in agriculture. The most recent data (Zhongguo tongji nianjian 2013: 121) reveal that 33.6 per cent of employed persons still work in primary industry. This question relates to an important analytical issue in the transition to the so-called 'new growth model', which is the identification of the so-called 'Lewis turning point'. This point indicates the disappearance of rural surplus labour and hence the conditions for raising wage levels because of tightening labour supply. The wage pressures in South China in recent years have motivated many Chinese observers that this point has been already achieved, thus driving the transition of the growth model (see e.g. Zhang *et al.* 2011). The IMF study by Das and N'Diaye (2013) claims that this point is still a decade away; this would better match the aforementioned structural data on the composition of the labour force.

14 Qi (2014) presents the complete statistical analysis. So, in his Marxist analysis he argues explicitly that the reproduction of the formal workforce essentially depends on the supplementary incomes generated in the informal sector. Therefore, on the macroeconomic level one defining feature of the traditional ritual economy persists, which Huang has labelled 'economic involution'. On the family level, this is reflected in the internal division of labour, with some family members opting for migrant work and others retaining agricultural and sideline employment. In these patterns, the informal sector, including migrant labour, faces consistent downward pressure on wages (on the specific mechanisms in the firm context see Chan and Siu 2009). According to the World Bank report (2014: 267), the downward trend of the 2000s was reversed only in the past few years; the authors claim that this already reflects the Lewis turning point. According to cited research, it may also be shown that there is no longer a systematic wage discrimination because of the status of a migrant. Yet, wage differences persist because migrants are largely employed in sectors and ownership types with generally lower wages. This observation does not invalidate Qi's argument because those sectors are also closely related to formal sectors. For example, in many labour-intensive industries there are outsourcing structures with a main producer with formal legal status as a corporation and a large number of family firms which employ migrants in a more irregular and informal way. The World Bank report (2014: 109) also shows that the declining share of consumption in GDP in the 2000s results from both an increase of savings and a decline in household income share. Migrants play an essential role here, as they have a much higher propensity to save than do urban households. This reflects their lack of access to many essential urban services.

15 For a detailed analysis see Yang (2012). In the late 2000s, companies and households saved approximately 20 per cent of GDP each. Further, the share of government has been rising consistently since the late 1990s. The savings of companies is the difference between value added and the sum of wages, production taxes, net asset payments and net transfer payments. Since companies do not consume, these savings are manifest in the increased profitability of companies. Many companies retain profits in order to invest. Private companies save because they are lacking easy access to official sources of credit, and state-owned companies often do not need to pay dividends. Meanwhile, the government could expand its revenues considerably because the scope of government services does not grow as fast; for example, welfare payments have been lower

than received social insurance fees. On the other hand, private savings remain high for several reasons; one is directly related to population policy, as ageing parents cannot expect that they will receive sufficient support from their single children.

16 This argument is deployed by Eckaus (2014) going back to a classical definition of forced savings by Bentham, who, interestingly, also counts this as an indirect means of taxation. Basically, there are two types of forced savings. The first is directly imposed upon private agents via government regulations, such as compulsory contributions to a housing fund that effectively conducts the savings operations for the households (the Singapore model). The second operates via indirect macroeconomic mechanisms that link increases of investment with induced increases of savings, which can happen via Keynesian mechanisms that adapt the savings via the concomitant income effects of the investments. According to Eckaus, both forms of forced savings exist in China. The first relates to n. 15 above, because, for example, retained profits would normally have to be distributed to private owners, so that the state-owned sector may be directly interpreted as a vehicle for forced savings. The second is reflected in the expanding credit volumes which drive the growth of the money supply. Eckaus points out that this was accompanied by a decline in the velocity of money, so increasing periods of holding cash in bank accounts.

17 OECD (2013: 64ff.) compares Chinese urbanization levels with global averages. China lies consistently below typical values for countries with similar per capita GDP, partly reflecting the backlog of structural adaptation resulting from the freezing of the urban population up until the 1980s. Yet, even the predictions keep China at a relatively low value. The World Bank (2014: 99ff.) shows that the current urbanization process was accompanied by falling population densities, which reflects the ongoing relevance of the *hukou* system in restricting urban in-migration. This may be interpreted as a distortion because of the low prices paid to farmers during land conversion, thus reducing cost pressures of land scarcity. Interestingly, the authors show that the regions where this effect is particularly salient also manifest high investment rates, thus revealing the role of land conversion in the growth model. The mechanisms of land conversion are described and analysed in the same report (World Bank 2014: 38ff., 188ff.).

18 This argument is explored in detail by Huang (2009, 2013). Huang points out that the share of 'not registered' labour relations has increased tremendously in recent decades, mostly fed by migrant workers and laid-off workers from the formal economy. 'Registration' means that there are formal labour contracts which entitle workers to claims on social security or provide special protection against layoffs. In spite of the recent tightening of the Labour Law, there are many ways to circumvent its regulations, such as via labour service companies that regularly rotate workers to keep employment short term. Further, the Labour Law only applies for firms incorporated according to the Company Law, which excludes the majority of small-scale family businesses in labour-intensive industries or services. Therefore, Huang argues that in the initial reform period 'informal' labour was mainly confined to the rural areas, whereas today it is an essential part of the urban economy.

19 Following the financial crisis of 2008, many export-oriented companies in South China were facing cost pressures. Therefore, they struggled to maintain the existing wage relations (see Lüthje 2013). This is even true for companies that are suppliers to leading multinational companies, as Chan and Siu (2009) report in great detail. There are many ways in which wages are kept down. One is to increase the share of small-scale informal businesses in the supply chain which pay systematically lower wages, thus undermining the existing regulations on labour standards in the multinational sector. The other is to

apply non-transparent overtime systems, which often even enable employers to impose lower hourly wages. As for the workers, there is often pressure to earn a maximum amount of money, since they want to maintain certain benchmarks, for example, for remittances to their families, for savings, etc. Thus, they often accept overtime arrangements, even though these undermine the minimum wage regulations. Growing dissatisfaction incites wildcat strikes and other forms of worker resistance. Given these these circumstances, local governments are under strong pressure to suppress conflicts, often resorting to coercive actions, thus actually colluding with employers.

20 For a multifaceted treatment of rural–urban dualism, see the edited volume by Whyte (2010) entitled *One Country, Two Societies*. Interestingly, one contribution in this volume by Wu (2010) directly relates this to the notion of *chaxu geju* proposed by Fei Xiaotong. The common element is the notion of 'differential citizenship'. This means that the *hukou* system established a comprehensive and fine-grained distinction of citizenship status, partly also hidden behind more detailed administrative regulations. For example, all urban inhabitants enjoy a status advantage relative to rural people, but there is also the impact of the urban hierarchy upon the relative status of urban citizens; for example, constraining their rights and opportunities to move up from lower level urban places to higher level ones. On the other hand, the status of rural citizens is also not homogeneous, because there are sharp distinctions between the status of farmer and local cadre, for example (cf. Chapter 4). In urban society, the distinction between natives with full registration and non-natives covers much more variety than just the migrant workers. Wu identifies a special group of 'denizens', meaning people with higher educational status who nevertheless have only limited and temporal rights of residence, which can be revoked at any time.

21 On the distinctions in habitus and dress see Ngai (2003). For example, many young female migrant workers in South China have few opportunities to leave the premises of the large factories where their dormitories are also located. In their spare time they often visit the urban temples of consumption, the shopping malls, but normally do not buy items there because they are too expensive. Their dress style is notably different from those of the urbanites, so that the groups of young women are easy to spot. A case study on discrimination at Shanghai schools is Lan (2014). Generally speaking, there is differential access to schools anyway, with migrant children mainly accessing lower quality schools (see World Bank 2014: 289ff.). As Wu (2010) emphasizes, the label 'peasant workers' children' is even an official category in public policy, and it reflects the fact that these children inherit the *hukou* status from their parents, even if they have been born and live in the cities. In other words, even if these policies often have the character of affirmative action measures, they still reinforce the status distinction, especially in cultural terms. Lan therefore introduces the term 'segmented incorporation' and distinguishes between 'institutional' and 'cultural incorporation' which can proceed at different speeds and even directions. For example, local authorities may set up special schools for migrant workers' children which tellingly pay much attention to lifting their 'quality' by means of many non-curricular activities, often in the context of boarding schools which take almost total control of the children's lives; as an example, see Lin (2011; cf. the seminal study by Murphy (2004)). Yet, even if the children are enrolled at the same schools, children realize assortative matching, because the migrant children are easy to spot, given physical differences between native Shanghainese and migrants from interior areas of China, as well as dialectal differences. So, migrant children realize their separateness from the native children, which results in spatial patterns of behaviour, with

migrant children playing together in certain areas of the schoolyard. However, Lan also reports on 'apartheid' practices of even separating migrant and native children by putting them in different classrooms, which is justified by the different 'quality' that they bring with them into the educational process. Discrimination between urban dwellers and in-migrants has a long tradition, such as the case of Subei people in Shanghai studied by Honig (1990). Certain areas in urban Shanghai have been occupied by Subei people in the past, but today this distinction has gradually disappeared, and new migrants and other marginal groups have taken their place (see Zhu Jiangang 2010: 52ff.).

22 For a bibliometric analysis of the rise and current use of *suzhi* see Kipnis (2006). The term has semantic relations with traditional ideas about the perfection of the self and hence certainly represents an ideational continuity with Chinese cultural history. This is also obvious from the fact that since the 1990s the term has played a major role in education, with specific elements in the curriculum related to *suzhi* education, 'suzhi jiaoyu' (素质教育) (Yan Hairong 2003). Kipnis points out that there is also a substantial 'anti *suzhi*' literature, for example, by the influential author Wang Shuo who makes a mockery of the radical attempts by a young man to transform himself into a perfect fighter, so alluding to widespread motives of martial arts and other cultural narratives. Therefore, it is important to include the physical dimension in interpreting the relationship between *suzhi* and modernization, as Anagnost (2004) has also elaborated upon. Artists have picked up on this dimension, as in the much-cited reconstruction of the stele in front of the Forbidden City by using human fat as a material that was collected at beauty farms (see Holmes 2014). In this case the connection to cultural narratives of civilizing China is very straightforward.

23 For a pertinent case study, see Zhan (2011). Giving up rural registration also means losing particular rights in the rural communities, especially claims on land, both for agricultural use, but also for private plots, including residential uses. Since an important part of migration in China is regional, this means that within one province, relations to native areas may still be important, even for long-term urban sojourners. At the same time, many of the original privileges of the urban population have been diminishing because market-based supply has superseded public supply. For example, housing allocation is increasingly market based, so that rural migrants are not systematically excluded. Yet, as Zhan shows, this does not mean that discrimination is receding. This has partly resulted from voluntary decisions by migrants. For example, a migrant may opt for saving to invest in a new home in the countryside and therefore lives in substandard urban residential areas; if many choose this option, the migrants gradually concentrate in separate residential communities. Job opportunities may be determined by human capital in the first place, but are also accessible via social networks. Even if rural migrants invest in education and training, they often fail to access better jobs because their social networks are separate from the networks of urban natives.

24 On this, see Yan Hairong (2003). As early as in the 1980s local authorities developed the view that entering the national labour market is also a means to increase the civilizational levels of the rural population. Rural migrants would need to adapt to the standards of modern industry and would therefore undergo a 'modernizing' educational experience. This even included aspects of attitudes, such as willingness to face the uncertainties of migration. Correspondingly, contrary to the often-cited image of the 'blind waves' of migrant workers, there were often well-organized movements, with local authorities involved in establishing the connections to receiving places and supporting the hiring process, for example, by screening the candidates. Often this is also

done by specialist labour recruitment companies that closely cooperate with local authorities. Akin to protestant attitudes in European industrialization, poverty is often also explained by low *suzhi*, which partly points to subjective factors (such as 'feudal thought') and thus assigns the responsibility to overcome poverty to the subjects themselves. When successful migrants return home, they are seen as living examples of *suzhi* improvement. It is also interesting to notice that the official and semi-official agencies of labour recruitment stay in competition with traditional networks that channel chain migration, such as native place networks. These traditional networks are often seen as problematic by employers because they would enable collective action among workers. Therefore, companies such as Foxconn often adopt explicit strategies in order to suppress these channels.

25 To a certain extent, the modernist concept of markets appears akin to the ordoliberal position in German economics which has also attracted Foucault's attention (see Foucault 2004b), a connection that is sometimes recognized in the China literature (e.g. Anagnost 2004). The Ordoliberals did not believe that the market is a 'spontaneous' pattern of social organization, but may always succumb to the forces of special interests and collusions of powerful groups, thus stifling competition, which is the major feature of markets working for the general welfare of society. Therefore, they believed that the market has to be orchestrated by the government, especially via the 'visible hand' of competition policy. So, the market requires strong government, though remaining aloof from the market process; that is, by adopting a non-interventionist stance. The current position of the CCP towards economic policy closely resembles the ordoliberal view, such as in the resolution of the Central Committee of 15 November 2013 where the government is explicitly assigned to the roles of a watchdog of competition, and the market economy is seen as the defining feature. However, as Foucault already notes in his discussion of Ordoliberalism, the 'liberal' part of the position is also grounded in certain views in the Freiburg school of economics that closely relate to so-called 'Austrian' views, a relationship that is reflected in the ambivalent role of Hayek in both strands of thought. This refers to the idea that government does not have sufficient information for designing interventionist policies, for principled reasons, and therefore should stay clear of the economy. On the contrary, the modernist view of markets assumes that the government is avant-garde even of the market process. This is reflected, for instance, in the idea that state-owned companies should play a significant role as leaders in globalizing the Chinese economy.

26 On the separate treatment of migrant workers in company organization, see Zhang *et al.* (2010) who talk about '*hukou*-based HRM systems'. This is called the 'one factory, two systems' approach in China. Regarding the formal/informal distinction, the important point is that most employees with a rural *hukou* would only receive short-term contracts which do not entitle them to full rights according to the Labour Law, as Huang (2013) also takes as a criterion. Many migrants also work as 'rented workers'. I discuss the 'Legalist' approach to management in Chapter 6. The assumption behind this approach is that migrant workers lack self-discipline and therefore need close and constant supervision. This is combined with tight rules of linking performance and payment. The behavioural controls reach into the private sphere, as many migrants live in dormitories where many rules affect their daily lives, such as in the context of staff canteens. These employment conditions are perpetuated by many practices, such as giving migrant workers less or no access to training programmes, which also influences their opportunities for promotion. Zhang *et al.* (2010) point out that although the original distinction of *hukou* is a formal institution, many consequences are mediated by cognitive beliefs.

27 For a book-length study of these phenomena, see Hoffman (2010). Hoffman explicitly refers to Foucault in her anthropological analysis of urban job markets. She also emphasizes the role of 'culture' in assessing the 'quality' of job candidates. Clearly, these cultural features manifest a strong impact of social background, such as the role of parents in investing in the capabilities of their children via the plenitude of services offered in developing skills such as playing the piano or further raising their level of English. Middle-income families have a headstart in this, which further reinforces social discrimination along the traditional status order. On quality education in general, see Greenhalgh and Winckler (2005: 237ff.). In urban areas, parents directly aim at international careers for their children, beginning in early years, as epitomized in legendary figures such as the 'tiger mothers' and the 'Harvard girls'. Personal aspirations can be interlaced with national visions of 'standing up', as in the widespread craze for English language education, where the capability to act in international contexts is also a way in which citizens can contribute to express China's rising status in the world (for an interesting case see the lively report in Osnos 2014). Greenhalgh and Winckler also elaborate on the role of intergenerational reciprocity: showering their children with 'gifts' is intended to create obligations to reciprocate in the future. This demonstrates the deep structures of traditional ideas interacting with modernist beliefs.

28 For detailed data on the discrimination among rural and urban people and migrants in the educational system, see World Bank (2013: 325ff., 2014: 289ff.), Hannum *et al.* (2010) or Li *et al.* (2015). In order to assess this it is important to understand that within the same territory there are different qualities of schools which are ranked according to the administrative status of the supervising and funding body (cf. the section on localism). In other words, the administrative status order overlaps and reinforces the social status order. There are provincial-level, city-level or district-level schools as well as basic regular schools. Migrant children mostly attend the lowest level schools. However, there are also many barriers to even entering the public school system, where the government has announced a policy that nominally cancels tuition fees for migrants. One obstacle is that, as opposed to residents, migrants have to present a certain number of documents, for instance, related to vaccination, which is often difficult (for example, they may need to return to their native place to retrieve these documents). In fact, access to public schools requires relationships and other forms of 'support'. According to the World Bank data, this discrimination leads to the result that children with rural *hukou* enjoy a substantially lower chance to advance from junior high school to secondary high school. This means that, in the past decades the gap between the endowments of human capital has increased dramatically between urban and rural areas, in spite of the improvements in basic rural education. This difference also translates into differential access to higher levels of education, as Li *et al.* (2015) show. On the differential access to education within the category of urban residents, see Li and Li (2010). There is a grade system of public schools which partly corresponds to location in the city for historical reasons; at the same time, the quality of *hukou* is different depending on location. For example, in many cities a suburban *hukou* would not allow children to attend the best public schools in the central districts unless the parents pay an additional fee. In the case of Guangzhou in the mid-2000s, this fee could amount to RMB40,000 per annum.

29 Most recently, the Chinese government launched a wholesale transformation of the system of tertiary education that directly aims at changing its ritual foundations (see Schmidt-Dörr 2015). The goal is to transform a large number of lower level universities into universities of applied technology, hence tertiary institutions of vocational education which can also issue Bachelor degrees. This

responds to the paradox that university graduates increasingly face unemployment in spite of a strong demand for qualified professionals. However, so far vocational colleges suffer from widespread prejudice. Thus, the new reforms would need to radically change the popular perceptions of higher education as a status marker.

30 For lively accounts of this situation, see Goethe-Institute Online Magazine at www.goethe.de/ins/cn/lp/kul/mag/dis/diao/deindex.htm (accessed 29 April 2014) and *The Economist*, 19 April 2014, p. 49) on the 'diaosi' (屌丝), the 'lost pubic hairs', referring to male graduates with low-income jobs who cannot succeed in the urban marriage market, and Osnos (2014) on the many service businesses that have emerged in urban society as a result. These matchmaking agencies provide extensive lists of criteria that future grooms have to fulfil, in which material status matters a great deal. This reflects the fact that the social pressure to marry at an appropriate age is still very high even in the most advanced urban areas. This causes psychological tension for female professionals who delay their age of marriage beyond socially acceptable norms, thus turning into 'superfluous' women ('shengnu' (剩女)); see http://baike.baidu.com/subview/404328/16873573.htm (accessed 12 October 2015), which of course even further increases the imbalances on the marriage market. As Greenhalgh (2012) noted with reference to the rural areas, in both the rural and the urban domain we observe a downward concentration of the gaps in the availability of marriage opportunities. Low-status males are defined as men with low educational attainments, relative to their reference group. In the rural areas, this means that illiterate and semi-literate men remain bachelors.

31 On the exploding costs of marriage in the rural areas, see *The Economist*, 30 November 2013, or Gui (2014: 246). Gui reports that the value of gifts in the context of rural marriages grows continuously, independent of the fact that marriages are increasingly based on 'romantic' relations. In his case studies, the standard was 60 to 80,000 Yuan. The argument on the savings rate has been detailed by Wei and Zhang (2011). The theoretical point is that in a marriage market where wealth determines men's marriage chances, there is a strong incentive for males and their families to save. This leads into a standard micro-macro dilemma, because if all men individually increase their savings, they cannot improve their marriage chances because the benchmark levels move up for everyone. For women, the situation is ambivalent, because they may just free-ride on men's savings, but also may consider that bringing wealth into marriage would increase their bargaining power within the relationship. The authors confirm this hypothesis by statistical evidence showing that the savings ratio varies with the regional sex-ratio imbalance across provinces, a phenomenon which could not be explained by alternative theories about savings, such as life cycle theory. Further evidence are systematic differences between families with sons and families with daughters. Interestingly, there is even an effect on housing prices in the cities, which vary with the sex-ratio imbalance. Clearly, this argument takes certain traditional features of marriage in China as a given, which allows one to interpret these observations in terms of ritual.

32 The moral aspects of status consumption also transpire in the context of the marriage market, however, in another sense. This is the widespread resurgence of the custom of secondary 'wives' or concubines. This differs from occasional marital infidelity or prostitution in the sense that men invest in a secondary sexual partner on a more stable basis; that is, providing the woman with an apartment and all the necessary lifestyle equipment on a longer term basis (on this, see Gerth (2010: 51ff.); see also the observations in Osnos 2014). These modern concubines are a male status symbol, the value of which is signalled by the expensive status goods that they consume conspicuously. Clearly, the rising

scarcity of brides in the regular marriage market is even further heightened by these practices, which are probably reinforced in turn because of the increasing value of the status symbol. There are no aggregate data about the relevance of this phenomenon, which, interestingly, has also been driven by foreign direct investment, with many Hong Kong and Taiwan entrepreneurs setting up even second families on the Mainland. Phenomena like these are largely interpreted as a serious decline of moral order: Wang (2002) sketches the picture of the 'post-Communist personality' which combines hedonism without individualism, the latter being officially interpreted as 'bourgeois' by the ruling party. At the same time, official ideology has been devalued as a source of moral order. As I argue here, these views partly overlook the culturalist embeddedness of consumption.

33 For an extensive treatment of this role of modernizing consumption in the effort to restore national integrity and status in the global society, see Gerth (2003). Immediately after the establishment of the Republic, the Chinese Association for the Protection of National Products, 'Zhonghua guohuo weichi hui' (中华国货维持会), was founded and remained very active throughout Republican times. A sensitive issue was the strong position of Japanese companies in the consumer goods markets, thus linking up with boycott movements. The propaganda was often deeply moralistic in tone, such as denigrating women who wear Western imported fashion as prostituting themselves. Gerth argues that these activities created a deep cultural structure of linking nationalism and consumption that was also driving Chinese Communists' policies, especially in the initial years, before the strict Maoist austerity campaigns against conspicuous consumption were launched. The contemporary Consumer Associations are no longer involved in fostering patriotic consumption and focus on consumer rights, yet there is also the general idea of civilizing consumption practices; for a brief discussion, see Gerth (2010: 148ff.).

34 On the social engineering of an urban middle class see Tomba (2004). This even included the construction of newly built housing complexes which were then bought and resold by public agents, such as state-owned companies, at lower prices. In more recent times the government invested in housing programmes with the explicit aim of stabilizing consumption via weakening one important savings motive. On the general measures of incentivizing consumption, see Gerth (2010: 5) which included, for example, the extension of holidays to so-called 'Golden weeks' and the general shortening of the weekly work schedule, especially freeing up Saturdays. Following the financial crisis of 2008, the government even subsidized purchases of durable consumer goods in the rural areas as a macroeconomic stabilization measure.

35 As Gerth (2010: 4f.) points out, cosmetics and fashion products represent a very large share in the Chinese consumer goods market, especially at the high end. In the mid-2000s, this industry came in as the fifth largest in the Chinese economy after real estate, automotives, tourism and information technology. Interestingly, in cosmetics, new brands have been emerging that especially focus on the skin complexion of Chinese women, such as Yue Sai Cosmetics, which was sold to L'Oreal in 2004. This brand was founded by a Chinese-American celebrity, Yue-Sai Kan (Jin Yuxi (靳羽西)), who also launched Chinese variants of Barbie dolls and other cultural products that aim at globalizing Chineseness in consumption styles (see Herrmann-Pillath 2009a). I have already pointed to the observation (Lan 2014) that even second-generation migrant children recognize that the colour of their skin is an indicator of their origin.

36 These complexities of the citizen consumer are explored in detail by Tian and Dong (2011), who even use accounts of dreams as a source for empirical

research. It has been well established in empirical marketing research that Chinese consumers generally do not display straightforward preferences for national vs. foreign brands. However, the narrative of Chinese modernization plays an essential role and is bound into four different perspectives, as Tian and Dong argue. On the one hand, this includes the two polar positions: one is that Western brands signal Chinese inferiority and humiliation, the other is that they represent adventure, freedom and modernity. But there are also more sophisticated views, such as perceiving Western brands as standards which Chinese brands can successfully aspire to and often have already succeeded in matching, and the other as ways to establish cooperative relations between Western and Chinese companies. Depending on context, one of these perspectives can dominate, such as in the sensitive case of Japanese products which sometimes face sudden market slumps following particular political events, but generally maintain a high reputation. The materials presented by the authors show that often the individual consumer actually reflects upon these different perspectives and achieves her or his individual contextualization. It is this individual process which qualifies the consumption decision as 'consumer citizen' behaviour. For a related analysis, see Hooper (2005), who perceives the consumer citizen similar to Tian and Dong, namely as a personality who contextualizes individual consumption in narratives of China's modernization. On the one hand, this means that there is also a strong potential for civil society initiatives; on the other hand, since many aspects of quality require government supervision, this heightens the awareness of the role of government in safeguarding the fulfilment of consumers' expectations and desires. This view transcends the mere hedonistic interpretation of consumption and therefore stays in tension with the views on rampant hedonism highlighted by Wang (2002). The hedonism view often reflects moral concerns of intellectual elites and is certainly also undergirded by the dynamics of popular culture often deeply intertwined with advertising campaigns which link dynamic urban subculture formation with distinctive fads in consumer behaviour (see Wang (2008) for an extensive analysis). Yet, as Wang shows, for example, in China the notion of brands is often less focused on product brands than on corporate brands: the latter are also images of national revival and strength.

37 For example, managing the brand of BMW in China can be a tricky task, as BMW drivers often appear to be people who put the value of their car above everything else, such as the case of the woman who refused to smash the window of her BMW in order to rescue her son from inside the car; see www.straitstimes.com/asia/east-asia/woman-in-china-refuses-to-rescue-trapped-son-because-it-would-damage-her-bmw (accessed 24 February 2016). This is particularly difficult in the internet community, where emotions are released freely. BMW drivers are often mentioned in the context of outrageous cases of even intentionally killing others, such as in the recently exposed cases of killing victims of accidents in order to save costs of compensation; see www.businessinsider.com/chinese-drivers-kill-pedestrians-intentionally-2015–9?IR=T (accessed 24 February 2016).

38 This is also emphasized by Yan Yunxiang (2012), who analyses much-cited cases such as the milk powder scandal which was particularly sensitive, since one of the most precious treasures in Chinese lives was affected, namely children, and a direct consequence was that consumers switched to Western suppliers and brands because of quality concerns. This case is also an example of how the Chinese internet mediates between different groups, in this case the consumers, the companies and the government. Yan distinguishes this from Western concepts of the 'risk society' in which general risks of scientific progress and complexity are highlighted, whereas the Chinese consumer emphasizes the

moral responsibility of government. The Sanlu incident was also sensitive because the case was reported to the government by the foreign joint venture partner; see the background information reported by McGregor (2012: 184ff.).

39 China sometimes consumes more French red wine of a certain kind than is produced by the respective French brands. This is a very interesting case showing the mechanism of status consumption, because one problem for exporters is that many Chinese consumers lack the sophistication to appreciate differences in taste and smell that define the quality differences of red wine. So, price is the main criterion in using red wine as a status good. This even opens up the possibility that consumers do not really care about deception as long as the supply of fake wines is limited, because the price signal works independent from the genuine quality difference. On this case see e.g. www.jancisrobinson.com/articles/a20131106.html; www.businessweek.com/articles/2012–09–27/chinas-fine-wine-counteroffensive (accessed 22 July 2014).

40 On the one hand, *Shanzhai* production is a peculiar form of industrial organization; I analyse this aspect in some detail in Chapter 6 (see Booz&Co 2009; Shih *et al.* 2010). In the current context, the character as a popular counter-culture needs emphasis, partly even challenging established patterns of status consumption; for examples, see www.chinasmack.com/2008/pictures/funny-clever-chinese-shanzhai-brands.html (accessed 24 July 2014). There is also a connection to the distinct Chinese cultural tradition of imitations as a form of mastering the cultural legacy, which is often invoked when discussing Chinese violations of intellectual property rights (see e.g. Gregory 2003). As such, *shanzhai* is a form of cultural production; thus, for example, there are also *shanzhai* television shows (mocking even events such as the annual New Year television shows). These activities even partly combine with the 'consumer citizen' stance in being interpreted as challenging the power of Western brands, thus even claiming that piracy is a kind of national duty of the Chinese in fighting against Western dominance of global business (one comment on the above cited webpage is 'There is no such thing as most "shanzhai", only more "shanzhai". The Chinese people is great, Chinese people's creativity is limitless, Long live the Chinese people, Resolutely attack legitimate products, support pirate products'). Increasingly, this Chinese counter-culture is also embraced by Western artists, creating a new form of artistic expression; see e.g. www.highsnobiety.com/2014/01/08/the-artof-shanzhai/ (accessed 24 July 2014). A hotbed of such cultural mergers is the city of Shenzhen, and actually the term *shanzhai* is sometimes explained as resulting from the Cantonese pronunciation of 'Shenzhen'.

41 See Chapter 2, n. 3.

42 The notion of 'cellularization' was originally developed in analysing the Maoist economic system (see Donnithorne 1972). I will discuss this aspect in the next section. It connects with the use of the term by Shue (1988), which is my central reference in the current discussion, in the context of the increasing devolution of the control of economic and fiscal resources at the county and commune level in the 1970s, as a result of the diverse approaches to local self-reliance. Shue explicitly relates her model of cellularization, which she dubs 'honeycomb' (thus paying homage to Skinner), to the social and political structures in Qing dynasty China which I have described as the 'local state' in my portrayal of the governance system. In her view, cellularization was enabled through certain economic conditions, and emerged out of the continuous conflicts between localities and the central state over ideological issues and mobilization agendas, in which local cadres slowly evolved into a stratum of local elites who managed to mediate state power relative to local interests. This resulted in stalemate in the late 1970s, when the standard policy tools of the

Maoist central state lost efficacy. Against this background, marketization was actually an instrument of enhancing state power. In fact, this agenda was also visible in many initiatives of the 1980s and 1990s which aimed to establish economic links between rural areas and cities via certain organizational means, such as establishing supply chains with specialized production bases, which proceeded simultaneously with diverse efforts at administrative reorganization, increasing the role of townships and counties in administrating the grassroots-level units. I look at these developments in Chapter 4.

43 This transition has been analysed by Skinner (1988). It is important to note that the Maoist transformation was a dynamic process that never fully abolished the regional marketing system. In radical phases such as the Great Leap Forward, market activities might have almost come to an end, but phases of economic recovery also implied a resurgence of markets. In part, the resilience of markets also reflects the fact that the CCP applied indirect means to diminish their role, such as destroying the interactions among the different levels of the hierarchy by means of synchronizing their schedules or prohibiting the use of tractors for transporting goods to the markets. So, one may say that the market system remained a stable cognitive-institutional reference throughout the Maoist era, periodically activated in years with more relaxed ideological conditions. Thus, on the eve of the Cultural Revolution there were still about 37,000 rural markets and about 33,000 before the advent of reforms. Within only five years, this number grew to 43,000. In a more recent analysis, Rozelle *et al.* (2003) refute Skinner's prediction that periodic markets would rapidly vanish in modernizing reform China. In fact, the number further expanded to 83,000 in 1995. In addition, a remarkable fact is that the numbers grew even stronger in the most urbanized areas, thus directly contradicting the modernization hypothesis. The authors present some explanations for this, such as the limited access to land and credit for traders, so that they were unable to invest in larger and more stable marketing structures, and aspects of taxation. Yet, they also ponder whether modern logistics might also support conventional markets because of the improved ease of transport and communication. Probably what plays a role is a factor that has been emphasized also by Skinner in his analysis of the traditional model. This is the competition among marketplaces, which also includes efforts to establish new markets that therefore need to fit into the spatial and temporal niches of the existing system. Niche creation maintains these structures. This interacts with administrative reforms. Many townships try to bolster their administrative roles and economic functions by setting up special markets which connect with the wholesale trading system (see e.g. Carrillo 2011: 56ff.).

44 Zhu *et al.* (2013) call this process '*in situ* urbanization'. They present observations on Fujian province, arguing that this process is driven by the high population densities in the rural areas which already in the 1980s had supported the administrative mergers of villages into conglomerate structures (the so-called 'piancun' (片村)). In these 'rural agglomerations' residents are not counted as 'urban population'. The authors argue that this leads to a statistical misrepresentation of urbanization and propose to use the data on non-agricultural employment as an indirect indicator for the degree of urbanization in sociological terms. Within only eight years, this share has grown from 53.2 per cent in 2000 to 68.9 per cent in 2008. So, for example, Xianyou county in Putian prefecture, a place with strong lineage traditions, statistically had a share of urban population of 26.8 per cent in 2007, but if one considers non-agricultural employment, this number would need to be corrected upward to 63 per cent. OECD (2013: 68) attempts a definition of 'urban' that is also independent of administrative classifications, as there is also the opposite case, namely that a

city may administratively cover areas which remain rural. The criterion is that a 'metropolitan area' is defined as administrative units with more than 300,000 inhabitants, and a population density of more than 500 people per square kilometre on the lowest administrative level, i.e. the county. For China as a whole, this implies that in 2010 about 45 per cent of the population were living in metropolitan areas.

45 I will discuss this programme in more detail in Chapter 4. As Thøgerson (2011) argues, it stays in the long twentieth-century tradition of initiatives in transforming rural communities not only in economic aspects, but also culturally. Ahlers and Schubert (2009, 2013) generally assess the programme as being successful in the sense that policy objectives were factually made operational and many new measures were created and implemented. For a discussion of the planning approach to resettlement, see Bray (2013). For example, strict zoning regulations imply that farmers can no longer keep animals close to their dwellings as is usual. These activities have been accelerating recently, since many villages suffer from 'hollowing out' as a result of out-migration. This has led to the policy creating so-called 'concentrated villages' by means of resettlement (see Ong 2014). The problem with the policy is that it is often driven by the motivation to overcome the limitations to the expansion of non-agricultural land by means of converting agricultural land. The land for housing can be converted, however, so that the resettlement opens up new fiscal resources. Thus, as I will discuss in Chapter 4, the entire process of structural change and cultural transformation is often directly driven by fiscal measures, which in turn reflect particular aspects of the fiscal system. Generally speaking, the interaction between modernist transformation and traditional concepts is difficult to decipher, since, for example, lineage halls may be renamed as 'recreational centres' or similar entities, even though the villagers may retain the original interpretation (see Looney 2015). In Xiao's (2001) comparative study of nine villages in Jiangxi and Anhui, many places saw a resurgence of traditional lineage-related infrastructure, such as ancestral temples, often driven by competition among lineages.

46 This interpretation was proposed by Potter and Potter (1990: 261ff., 334). A similar point was made in the classic study of Parish and Whyte (1978: 304f.), who argued that collectivization actually enhanced lineage control of resources, also via the consolidation of land holdings which previously might be more scattered and interspersed. The close relationship between settlement patterns and lineage relations, even in cases where lineages are weak, is also noted in Xiao's comparative study of nine villages in Jiangxi and Anhui (e.g. Xiao 2001: 79, 486). Potter and Potter suggested that the current system of landownership basically replicates the legal forms of traditional private ownership in the context of lineages (see Chapter 2). In other words, a modern collective would be seen as being functionally equivalent to a lineage trust which is owned collectively by the lineage members. Landownership refers to what has been traditionally called the subsurface rights (the 'bones'), and the individual farmers own the surface rights (the 'skin'). The more recent reforms that aim at strengthening the latter, such as enabling its use in mortgages, would only further converge with the old system. So, the only difference would be a social structural one, namely that there are no large private landlords, but only collectives. However, as I will discuss below, these collectives can be very different social entities, with lineages only being prevalent in the minority of areas, and in many regions of China being represented by the government and the CCP, in terms of acting as local elites. Yet, we can grasp this differentiation in terms of the *xueyuan* vs. *diyuan* polarity. A touchstone for the Potter and Potter interpretation is the practice of inheritance. In many rural places of China, in

spite of the regulations in the marriage law, women are factually excluded from rights to collective property of their native area if they marry out. That may even include outright resistance to matrilocal residence in marriage. These conflicts between traditional customs and modern legal frameworks also occur when (see below in more detail) ownership rights in collective property are formalized as shares in shareholding cooperatives. In the contemporary Cantonese villages investigated by Zhou (2013: 130f.), shares are seen as the property of the descent line (even called 'tai gong gu' (太公股); the *tai gong* is the founder of a lineage), and there are struggles over claims of out-married women to these shares in cases where there is no male descendant. The Chinese term refers back to the 'tai gong tian' (太公田), which were the lineage controlled properties. In the case study, this land amounted to 50 per cent of village land. Income generated from the land was redistributed among the lineage members in different forms, such as food during festivals (the expression was 'when dividing the pork, everyone gets his share' (太公分猪肉，人人有份) (Zhou 2013: 12f., 28f.). This was explicitly considered to be a kind of insurance. Zhou (2013: 67) also reports that many peasants did not like the idea of distributing all the lineage land to members on an individual basis. The persistence of such ideas is easily understood if one considers the fact that is also highlighted by Potter and Potter. Often the reorganization of villages according to production teams and brigades simply reflected the settlement structure, and this in turn mirrored the distribution according to lineages. So, neighbours often worked together in teams, and brigades corresponded to lineages, so that a brigade would consist of farmers with the same surname; for another example, see Zhou *et al.* (2003: 120).

47 This interpretation was first developed by feminist scholars in particular. For a seminal approach, see Stacey (1983). Stacey argued that Chinese communism actually resulted in the democratization of traditional patriarchy. So, for example, the modernization of marriage did free the individual family from the control of lineage leaders and abolished polygamy, but at the same time the basic feature of patriarchy was retained in the context of the nuclear and stem family. In terms of economic and public policy, the land reforms clearly supported the resurgence of the traditional rural family economy. As I argue in this chapter and Stacey seminally proposed, even collectivization simply amounted to the reinstatement of lineage structures, though subverting its hierarchical dimension. The only policy that fundamentally challenged the traditional system was the Great Leap Forward. Its failure actually prepared the ground for the reforms of 1978, although two decades of internal political struggle in the CCP leadership delayed this return to the original synthesis of socialism and tradition. This synthesis was visible throughout the Chinese Communist movement; for example, class status was seen as being inherited via the male line, or the moral puritanism of Maoism translated into upholding traditional norms about marriage while just changing the roles of matchmakers, for example. Interestingly, Stacey (1983: 192) even states that the CCP aimed to establish a new 'ritual', 'li'. In the rural areas, this meant that most marriages still involved a strong role of the family (i.e. the parents), and followed traditional patterns, such as employing brideprice and dowry. For example, the CCP never questioned traditional principles such as patrilocality, in spite of promulgating the new legal framework for marriage. Stacey's interpretation is supported by more recent analyses of constancy and change in the Chinese marriage system, such as Huang (2011b).

48 The data are presented and analysed by Eberstadt (2011). Whereas the sex ratio for the first child hovers around 105 for the first birth, it went consistently upward for the second birth after the introduction of the policy, approaching

150 in 2000. For third and fourth births, it went beyond 160. The trend accelerated after 1990, presumably because of the more widespread availability of technologies to identify the sex of a child before birth, thus resulting in targeted abortions. Eberstadt only presents regional data for the overall sex ratio. There is a variation of the sex ratio which includes areas in which it approaches 150 and higher values. The sex ratio converges against natural values in the northeastern provinces, whereas there are concentrations of very high values, for example, in certain areas of Jiangxi and Hubei and in Guangdong province. These are also regions where historically lineage organizations were strong. In the coastal southern provinces, there is a pattern with lower levels in the poorer inland areas and higher ones on the coast; this is an interesting fact, because evidently higher levels of economic development on the coast even reinforce traditional behaviour.

49 This localization of marriage had been noted in early studies such as Parish and Whyte (1978: 54). Stacey (1983: 223) emphasized that in fact the socialist institutions strengthened residential patterns such as the three-generation family and enhanced local orientation. Huang (2011b) shows that in the mid-1990s, at least 25 per cent of all rural families were three-generation families where a married son lived together with his parents in one residential unit. An interesting case reflecting this compression of social space is Wu's (2014: 8ff.) study of a Fujian village. In comparison to pre-1949 marriage patterns, the average distance between the parental homes of the groom and the bride had shrunk from 6.2 to 2.5 kilometres. At the same time, the basic mechanisms of marriage had not been basically transformed, with matchmakers involved in 88 per cent of the cases, and with more than 50 per cent of even post-1982 marriages being mediated via brideprice arrangements (only 2.6 per cent of marriages were based on 'love') (for a similar resilience of traditional marriage customs, even in more developed villages, see Xiao 2001: 135, 470). The reason for this resilience of tradition is that the village remained largely agricultural, although its main economic specialization was jewellery. This business was realized by itinerant artisans of the village in many other areas of China. So, there was an interest in marrying in capable women who might contribute to maintaining the agricultural basis of the village. Wu shows that in pre-liberation times the regional economy was much more tightly integrated via activities of itinerant peddlers and artisans in the market system, which was a major channel of providing information about brides. At the same time, he criticizes the Skinner model and argues that in more recent times it was not the marketing system that was a shaping force of the 'marriage circle' but the irrigation system, which establishes connections between nearby places. This applies in both senses of attraction and repulsion, because villages with which there were often conflicts about irrigation issues were not part of the marriage circle.

50 The classical longitudinal case study of these phenomena is by Chan *et al.* (2009) of 'Chen village', which was originally a study of a rural community under Mao and was extended to the reform era in a new edition. The drama of collectivization unfolded against the background of traditional social structure and traditional concepts of morality (see also Madsen (1984) and Chapter 4, n. 32).Two village leaders represented two different principles, Qingfa and Longyong, with the former being more closely connected to more powerful segments of the Chen lineage, also with a problematic 'class background' going back to his grandparents who owned certain land holdings and therefore could afford better education for their children. Throughout the collectivization period, and later with a vengeance after reforms had been launched, Qingfa pursued his own interests and also supported closer kin, for example, in arranging the production team structure and in allotting land to the teams.

According to traditional notions of morality, this behaviour was partly seen as legitimate, but came under pressure with the enforcement of Maoist ideology, especially after sent-down youths arrived in the village and pushed the 'Cultural Revolution'. In contrast, Longyong was less well connected and with better class status, thus assuming leading positions in the brigade. This differential endowment of social capital led Longyong to adopt the 'collectivist' strategy in representing the interest of the brigade; however, he also pitted the village interest against the larger interests of the Commune, which also caused trouble with the political authorities. So, Maoist policies were always interpreted and made instrumental in internal social interactions, conflicts and social-structural patterns.

51 The classical argument on the role of kinship in reducing market transaction costs is Landa (1994), also with reference to the Chinese case. I discuss this in more detail in Chapter 5. Methodologically, it is important to emphasize that the Landa argument only runs from kinship to market organization, whereas a full explanation also needs to consider the reverse impacts. This implies that the whole structure becomes performative.

52 As is shown by Kung and Liu (1997), in the mid-1990s the majority of farmers with high incomes in non-agricultural activities were in favour of maintaining collective ownership. One motivation is that collective ownership allows for the adaptation of the allocation of land-use rights according to demographic criteria, thus equalizing access to land as a functional equivalent to insurance and as an asset. At the time, the majority of farmers opposed the extension of land-use rights to 30 years, in spite of simultaneously requesting the possibility of inheriting the land for their children. Ho (2001) introduces the notion of 'deliberate institutional ambiguity' with reference to national political schemes, which refers to the lack of clear central-level guidelines about the interpretation of the meaning of 'collective', which is of course essential. This ambiguity is a defining line of many conflicts about the conversion of land in the 2000s. Typically, the question is whether the collective is a 'natural village' or even a hamlet, the 'cun' (村) or the administrative village, 'xiang' (乡). Administrative villages are under the control of the township governments, and depending on the context of urbanization the assignment of land-use rights at this level implies that eventually the local government can appropriate the collective land rights in the name of the 'collective'. On the contrary, if the rights belong to the village, this expresses the assignment of the rights to the grassroots level. The majority of villagers follow this second interpretation and therefore often aggressively try to protect their claims when the state interferes with their perceived rights. Ho argues that this reflects the fact that the central leadership is divided about the approach to this question. Therefore, the specific arrangements on landownership are highly diverse across localities, as Brandt *et al.* (2002) show. There are certain commonalities (for example, after 1988 in most localities it was permitted to lease out land-use rights by the original holders, but only a minority actually used this right), but no clear trend towards one model. Brandt *et al.* therefore conclude that the decisions about the particular system were mainly taken at the local level, hence the village cadres, under guidance by the next higher authority. Prosterman (2013) shows that the prolongation of land-use rights to 30 years was still incompletely implemented in the mid-2000s, in spite of the fact that this had been announced as a political goal already in 1993. In many cases, farmers did not possess the relevant documents. Hence, the central government continuously increased efforts in clarifying the system of landownership, especially in the context of the new Property Law of 1997. Often, these policies are announced in the so-called 'Documents No. 1' which the CCP releases at the beginning of each year, and which are

traditionally devoted to agriculture. Following the decisions of the eighteenth Party congress in the autumn of 2013, 'Document No. 1' of 2014 announced the final completion of landownership under the general principle of *chengbao*, which means that collective ownership is maintained, but the scope of land-use rights is further extended to include rights transfers and the use of land-use rights as a collateral, and setting up full registries of land-use rights. Prosterman argues that such a system would amount to a system of private property rights.

53 These transformations of the landownership system are often triggered by the urbanization process. The most explicit form may be found in Guangdong province, a region with strong lineage traditions (for a comparison with other regions, see Tang 2015). As Chung and Unger (2013) show, in the context of urban sprawl many villages have actually become fully integrated into the urban infrastructure of the neighbouring city. Thus, urban planners start the transformation of a village into an urban district. However, this creates the legal problem that rural land is collectively owned, whereas urban land is state owned. In many areas of China, this is exactly how the farmers are being expropriated by urban commercial interests by offering low compensation for the converted land. In Guangdong province, the local lineages were powerful enough to design their own response to the urbanization strategies of local governments. They separate the economic and political organization of the village in creating a corporation as a 'shareholding limited liability company', 'gufen youxian gongsi' (股份有限公司). This was based on general regulations released in 1991 by the provincial government about the cooperative shareholding system. In some cases, because of the limited resources of the local governments, these corporations in turn develop political functions. For example, if they own substantial real estate and housing for migrant workers, the companies may assume parapolitical functions, such as organizing a local security force. This is one extreme example of the widespread practice of shifting the control of land property rights to cooperative institutions that are partly independent from the administrative hierarchy, thus potentially strengthening the property rights of the grassroots-level collectives (on these 'land cooperative shareholding companies', 'tudi gufen hezuoshe' (土地股份合作社) or 'tudi liuchuan hezuoshe' (土地流转合作社) see Trappel 2011). For a fascinating case study, see Zhou (2013). Zhou shows in great detail how the availability of new institutional forms via provincial-level regulations triggered local responses in reshaping the ownership system in terms of corporatization, which were partly mediated by intermediate-level administrative regulations (this meant, for example, that the aforementioned provincial-level regulations of 1991 were further specified by district-level regulations in 1994 which gave more precise definitions). In this case as in others (see e.g. Saich and Hu 2012), the lead role in the process was assumed by village party cadres who perceived the opportunity to activate land resources in order to attract investment into industrial facilities. Thus, the corporatization of the land also supported the process of rural industrialization (see Pei 2002). In this process, an intensive local discourse about corporatization took place. For example (Zhou 2013: 92), there were tricky issues as to who might count as a member of the local collective (e.g. depending on the time of moving in), and many farmers argued that ultimately the shares were rooted in landownership, which in turn went back to lineage property (Zhou 2013: 110). So, the villagers directly requested to apply the traditional rule 'to share the pork' (太公分猪肉) in arranging the allocation of shares. This led to conflicts, for example, about the rights of in-married women, which led to interventions by local government that requested the observation of legal stipulations on gender equality; however, these were

strongly resisted by many villagers (Zhou 2013: 131). Once the cooperative is fully transformed into a corporation, formally the Property Law and the Company Law fully applies, which defines clear individual property rights on the share. This creates serious difficulties in considering demographic change, as the original allocation of shares gradually disenfranchises the young generation from rights of ownership (Zhou 2013: 117). There were many conflicts about ritual issues in the context of corporate control, such as the question whether profits of the company should be invested in building lineage temples, which was considered problematic because the village had residents with different surnames who were also shareholders.

54 Such cases were often reported in the literature (see e.g. Woon 1989; Kuah 1999; Chen 2004: 163ff.). It is important to note that these activities are increasingly supported by the Chinese government, especially in the context of Mainland–Taiwan relations (see Chen (2013) for detailed information). The context is the activation of popular religion for creating a sense of shared cultural identity.

55 The outcomes of these developments can even vary widely within one territory, such as the Pearl River Delta. For example, Ip (2014) shows how land transformation gradually turned local villagers into an urban lower class, because during the high peak of transformation many villagers did expect a lot from marketization and the resulting business opportunities, so that they did not push for higher compensation. When recognizing these effects, the villagers actively pursued the revival of lineage traditions in order to demarcate themselves from the migrants and in order to build a power base vis-à-vis the local government. This was physically manifest in the construction of a 'cultural centre' that was named after the old lineage hall and was even bigger than the seat of the district administration. These tensions only abated after the leaders of the villagers were co-opted into the local political system, for instance, by being elected into the local People's Congress. In other cases, such as reported by Saich and Hu (2012), the villagers kept control of the land property rights and hence could build a comprehensive public infrastructure that only catered to the needs of the native local population. This could result in the absorption of the grassroots-level government organization into the economic organization of the village, as reported by Chung and Unger (2013), or as an extreme case by Hu (2007: 216ff.). In the latter case of Hubei province near Wuhan, an entire village was merged with a company that had been developing out of the original rural industries, even adopting the name of the company. Village cadres are partly paid by the company, as a form of local quasi-tax. In the Pearl River Delta, the merging of local land-holding cooperative shareholding companies with the district administration is visible, for example, in the fact that local public security guards are employees of the company. Wong (2015) diagnoses a general trend in growing village autonomy vis-à-vis the local state resulting from these institutional changes, based on exerting collective land rights.

56 In Fujian province, the number of reconstructed temples approached the same magnitude as reported for the early twentieth century; that is, there is one temple for 400 inhabitants (see Goossaert and Palmer 2011: 241f.). The religious status of temples is different depending on size and local significance. Often small temples are constructed by local communities that are devoted to local deities, which generally have a connection with established deities in the pantheon of popular religion, thus merging with Daoist or Buddhist deities. Larger temples have to be supervised by the local administration and are required to have a resident representative of the officially registered religions, namely Buddhist or Daoist, so that they would count correspondingly. On the

spread of temples devoted to Communist Party leaders, especially Mao Zedong, see Chen (2013: 236f.). Chau (2006: 51) believes that this is a trend that, however, can often be explained by giving legitimacy to the temples which often host these special shrines. Yet, the practice has been sufficiently widespread to be mentioned in the cited bluebook on religion. One should note that this is a normal development in Chinese popular religion, as most deities emerged from historical figures which were said to have achieved some important and miraculous feats. So, given the stature of Chairman Mao, even including his negative sides, this would certainly match the historical precedents.

57 For a detailed account of these developments, see Chen (2013). The role of Taiwan is also salient in the expansion of new religious organizations to Mainland China, for example, in the context of disaster relief. A foremost example is *Yiguandao* (I Kuan-tao) (一贯道) which was prohibited also in Taiwan and is one of the largest and most globalized Chinese redemptionst religious organizations in the world. *Yiguandao* is a syncretist belief that strongly emphasizes traditional Chinese values while adopting a global outlook on the peaceful coexistence of religions. Today, *Yiguandao* is again also active in the revival of local temples in Mainland China. This development is remarkable, as the CCP had launched a radical campaign against the sect in the 1950s which completely eradicated it in the Mainland (for an exemplary account see DuBois 2005: 138ff.).

58 For a detailed description of these interdependencies see Chang's (2011) study of the current conditions in Kaixiangong, the village that was also the site of Fei Xiaotong's early fieldwork. As an example, Chang (2011: 204) describes the religious meaning of many activities that are part of family reunions during the New Year period, when certain gifts such as apples are also religious symbols, or villagers visit local temples. The unifying core activity is gift giving, both in the shape of gifts that flow among people and offerings given to deities. For example (Chang 2011: 142f.), when families divide, establishing the new home for the new family is not only accompanied by gifts of mutual support and help among people, but also by offerings to the Kitchen God. This is also an example of the diffuse nature of popular religion, since many everyday activities are realized 'in passing' at home. This fact is also important in understanding the mechanisms that resulted in the revival of religion. If temples are destroyed and rituals such as processions are prohibited, religious activities are simply retreating into the context of private lives at home. Yet, these activities are also of crucial relevance in the entire set-up of traditional religion. This deep fusion of religion and everyday life is also emphasized by Gui Hua (2011), who refers to the expression 'guo rizi' (过日子) in order to explain the idea that the ordinary course of life itself is imbued with religious meaning. For an overview of traditional village religion, see Tam (2011), who also explains the moral dimension of *fengshui* practices in the rural areas. There is a range of generic concepts in popular culture that reflect this penetration of religious ideas into everyday life, often related to fate. For example, the notion of 'yuanfen' (缘分) is an idea that refers to the intuitive understanding that particular people match each other, reflecting some predestination resulting from the forces of fate, often supporting the immediate establishment of relations of trust (see Xiao 2010: 243). The argument that markets actually enhance the need for religious orientations is made by Yang (2011).

59 This perspective on Chinese popular religion has been elaborated in great detail, both empirically and theoretically, by Chau (2006, 2011). The 'religious market' approach has been developed by economists and was later adopted by sociologists of religion; for an application on Taiwan, see Lu *et al.* (2008). I

have referred to this already in the context of the discussion of 'polytropy' in Chapter 2 (see n. 27). On the notion of *ling*, see Dean (2003), who analyses the case of an individual spirit medium in rural areas. In Chapter 5 I come back to these topics, especially to the notion of the 'religious market'. *Ling* may be seen as an indicator of performance, in the sense of the individual utility of a religious service. This creates a 'demand and supply' framework, in which religious polytropy reigns.

60 On this role of popular religion in the democratization of Taiwan, see Weller (2004). During the era of Martial Law, many independent religious organizations were prohibited, and local popular religion was tightly controlled. After the lifting of Martial Law there was a strong resurgence of religion in general, especially also including redemptive societies and new Buddhist lay organizations such as *Ciji gongde hui*. It should be noted that this development was also highly gender-biased, with women playing a leading and active role, which today may also be observed in the Mainland. For example, many spirit media today are women, whereas in earlier times they were mostly males. Pennarz (1992) shows how the strength of local communities in Taiwan correlates with the vigour of temple organizations, which reflects the role of popular religion in the competition among different localities. Decline of a location goes hand in hand with the decline of the local temple, with causality working in both directions. For example, heads of temple associations were often also heads of villages, thus establishing links to political organizations. Weller (2004) shows how the environmental movement in the transition to democracy was often intertwined with local temples, with religious activities such as divination also playing an important role in inciting collective action. So, temple associations often served as informal channels for political action, including the mediation of interests between different parties, such as the local population, local government and business that comes from outside.

61 For an important case study, see Chau's (2006) description and analysis of the 'Black Dragon King Temple' in a Shaanbei village which may be seen as representative of many activities in temple reconstruction in China. In this particular case, a local temple was revived by establishing a network of neighbouring villages. The local temple boss himself was a successful businessman who eventually devoted all his time to this position, without assuming any official capacity, not even as a party member. This reflects a common feature of temple organization, which always needs to be built on a business model, as the construction of a large temple is a very expensive investment, and organizing related activities requires considerable management resources. One important source of income is the organization of temple festivals and pilgrimages. Hence, the capacity of launching such a project is a sign of the underlying social capital of the organizing groups, and it creates opportunities for expanding this social capital. What is also evident in this case is the deep embeddedness of religion in socioeconomic life, with no fixed patterns of religious expression. This means that there is a plenitude of local deities and worthies which might become the object of such expansionary investments, remaining small relicts otherwise. So, temple building is an expression of territorial competition between communities. DuBois (2005) also emphasizes the fact that temples and other communal religious activities build on collective efforts, but do not necessarily presuppose shared religious beliefs and practices. Social capital is manifest in the publicly displayed contributions of all members of the community.

62 On this Wenzhou example, see Cao (2008, 2009). Cao reports in detail about the financial arrangements and governance structure of these churches, where we may observe a fusion of business practices and traditions. On the one hand,

church leaders transfer organizational models from their business, for example, in arranging funding for the churches. On the other hand, many aspects of organization also reflect structures of traditional temple associations, thus also revealing their commonalities with traditional business organization. The churches in Wenzhou may be of very large size and closely copy Western-style architecture. Recently, there has been a wave of demolitions as the images of Christianity became very visible in city life, thus inciting the anger of CCP officials.

63 For a case study on the minority areas, see Kang (2009). This case is interesting because it shows in detail how a temple with a complex history becomes the object of different groups and individuals who struggle over the interpretation and control of legitimizing sources, with very different motivations. Whereas temple revival is often the initiative of individuals, sometimes even marginal individuals, concomitant with the revival, competing claims are made by religious groups and local interest groups. This results in a phenomenon that has already been highlighted by Siu (1995), namely that the same cultural artefacts can be interpreted in a very different manner by different groups, which is made even more complicated, since expressed attitudes and factual attitudes may differ. For example, officials may uphold a politically correct attitude, but visit temples privately and after sunset in order to minimize visibility. Generally, as in the case study, the policy on tourism and protection of cultural legacy allows for active interference and participation of local governments in temple management, which often means that commercial interests prevail, thus also leading towards cooperation with business leaders who adopt an active role in temple associations. This can result in tensions with the interests of religious groups who pursue the revival of the religious functions of a temple. In the case study, this is complicated by the fact that in many temples different deities are placed together, often in different shrines, which relate to different religious groups, such as Daoists, or, in this case, Tibetan Buddhists.

64 On the motivation for introducing grassroots-level elections, see O'Brien and Li (2000). Kennedy and Shi (2011) analyse a national survey of 2005 which clearly highlights farmers' preferences for democratic elections, although interestingly the respondents expressed strongest trust in the institution of the Party secretary who cannot be elected by the population. The large scope of local conditions and performances of elections is discussed by O'Brien and Han (2009). For example, they point towards dysfunctional phenomena such as vote buying, by which local business can support their political partners. An illuminating case study is Yao (2013). Construction and infrastructure is an area where corruption and collusion between politics and business interests are salient, which is central in the efforts of modernizing the rural areas.

65 This is the result of an extensive study by Tsai (2007). Tsai analyses a sample of 316 villages in Shanxi, Hebei, Fujian and Jiangxi which were selected in terms of sharing certain structural characteristics, thus establishing similar environmental conditions for development. Yet, there is a very significant variation in the provision of infrastructure and public services even in the case of villages which are close neighbours and appear to be similar in most socioeconomic characteristics. Tsai shows that the existence of local-level elections and their respective type does not have any significant effect on public performance; this also applies for the degree of bureaucratic penetration; that is, the role of upper level administration. She clearly demonstrates that the existence of temples and lineages, as reflected in the corresponding artefacts and associations, has a much stronger impact on performance. Her theoretical explanation is that voting alone does not necessarily improve performance as long as ex-post monitoring and accountability is weak. Therefore, she even argues that

improving accountability by means of traditional channels of accountability can weaken demand for democratic institutions, especially if their implementation is deficient. These results are also confirmed by other studies, such as Lu (2012). Lu shows that democratic elections work well in villages which have a relatively low rate of out-migration and which have strong and competitive kinship groups, thus confirming that embeddedness of democratic institutions in social capital is essential. In this sense, this echoes the strong interaction between traditional popular religion and civil society in Taiwan, as Weller (2004) has also pointed out (n.60 above).

66 Kipnis (2012) calls this phenomenon 'mimetic urban spaces'. This happens via the diffusion of certain standards in the urban planning process and is expressed in the similarities of certain arrangements of public squares, parks or university campuses. Kipnis clearly emphasizes the role of modernist ideas in these processes, and also mentions the example of the 'New Socialist Countryside' policy which leads towards the standardization of the suburbanization of rural areas, explicitly interpreted as a civilizational process. Further, Kipnis points out that this architectural standardization also entails the partial standardization of social actions that take place in their context. His example is the squares and plazas which may often express political authority, being in front of buildings with a certain significance, but that are also appropriated by the local population for spare-time activities, which however have begun to spread across China, such as skating. On the peculiarity of urban space in China, see World Bank (2014: 142ff.). The main phenomenon is the 'superblocks' which go back to the traditional *danwei* structures, where typically public units such as an SOE may have a campus-like structure, with factories and residential areas enclosed in one walled compound. For example, blocks in large Chinese cities may have a side length of between 400 and 800 metres, whereas one of the largest metropolitan areas in the world, Tokyo, only features 50 metres. A historically grown city such as Turin has a much denser use of urban space, also with a much higher complexity of land use. For example, in one square kilometre, Turin has 152 intersections of pathways, whereas new areas in Beijing have only 14. Ominously, the traditional *hutong* in Beijing have 119 intersections.

67 For an illuminating case study, see Chung and Unger (2013). The loss of control of top-down urban planning happened in spite of the fact that, as I discussed in the previous section, shareholding companies tended to collaborate with urban authorities in urban redevelopment. This is because land transformation only affected agricultural land but not the residential land owned by the villagers. So, most villagers enjoy the dividends generated by the shares, but also started to pull down their homes and to erect multi-storey buildings instead, so that they could rent out flats to migrant workers. In fact, this is also a transient phenomenon, as often the living conditions deteriorated considerably in these cramped and unregulated urban spaces. However, this leads towards serious conflicts of interests among the migrants, who form the majority of residents, and the villagers, who earn sufficient income to enjoy the advantages of moving to newly built residential compounds.

68 On the role of migration in the development of urban villages, see the fascinating case study by Cheng (2014) of Shenzhen. Shenzhen is certainly one of the most urbanized and modern areas in China, but at the same time it had 320 urban villages in 2005, with 5.02 million inhabitants, of which 4.69 million were migrants. As a sort of 'artificial' urban space, aside from the urban villages, the units that represent state ownership play an important role, which I also discuss below. These belong to different 'systems', *xitong*, which have invested in Shenzhen, and which are owners of state-owned companies, such as the

China Merchant Group as the original developer. Dormitory construction was a major activity for these units, often in collaboration with foreign investors. This even reproduces the traditional socialist *danwei* structures to a certain degree. These units continue to hold these facilities because, with economic growth, their value has increased continuously. The organization of urban villages follows the model of shareholding companies as outlined in the previous section. On the systems that currently govern migration and the change of *hukou* status in Chinese metropolitan areas, see OECD (2013: 94ff.) and World Bank (2014: 363ff.). There is a clear correlation between the level of economic prosperity and the degree of constraints on the conversion of *hukou*, both rural to urban and lower level urban to higher level urban. Existing approaches to *hukou* reform generally do not liberalize the conversion but standardize it. So, a typical approach is to introduce a point system which recognizes certain individual features as qualifying for the urban *hukou*. Then, for instance, a benchmark may be defined which can be easily surpassed by university graduates or technicians, but is difficult to achieve for workers or farmers unless they can also invest substantially in business projects.

69 The concept of 'regional property rights' was seminally developed by Granick (1990) and is a central theoretical notion in Herrmann-Pillath (1991). Granick's approach is phenomenological, as there is no formal institution that fixates those rights. He argues that the Chinese system of planning, before the advent of reforms and in the mid-1980s, was substantially different from the Soviet Union, and that these differences can only be explained by introducing the regional property rights structure as a hypothesis. So, we meet a medium-level theoretical term. In Granick's view, the current distribution of rights is determined by past investments of different government bodies and the company itself on the one hand, and on the other hand, by historical decisions about assignments of responsibilities. Therefore, he introduces a multiple-principal model to analyse this system. The major empirical anomalies that can only be explained in this way are: the existence of multiple principals with different claims on the enterprise; the slack in planning and the large share of above-quota production; the existence of multiple prices, or merging the roles of decision-maker and supervisor in the nomenclature (i.e. Party secretaries are often also factory directors). Granick adds the observation that the Chinese planning system was therefore much more geared towards hard budget constraints because regional authorities do not necessarily have direct access to the centrally controlled banking and monetary system. I come back to this analysis in Chapter 6.

70 On the systematic role of military considerations in Maoist industrial policy, see Naughton (1988, 2007: 73ff.). These ideas went back to the 'people's war' strategy facing technological gaps relative to the main military enemies, the USA and the Soviet Union, which directly threatened the maritime and the continental borders, respectively. Therefore, investment was even reduced in coastal provinces, especially in Guangdong and Fujian (opposing Taiwan) and redirected into provinces such as Sichuan, Ningxia and Yunnan. Naughton also summarized the major resulting differences between the Maoist approach and the Soviet approach: militarization, decentralization, local autarchy, absence of direct material incentives and very low mobility of labour.

71 On the analysis of property rights as entitlements, see Schlicht (1998). Schlicht's argument on 'custom' comes very close to my analysis of ritual. He argues that 'law' is a refinement and clarification of custom that is itself based on a set of customary relations involving lawyers, courts and so forth, and which puts formal reasoning over entitlements and obligations at the centre. However, entitlements and obligations remain at the core of the institutional

set-up, in particular since the majority of property relations are never tested or enforced by legal action, and may often even stay in tension with law. Schlicht defines 'entitlements' as subjective rights which go along with the readiness to defend those rights, and probably also with mutual recognition. Thus, he believes that cognitive mechanisms are essential in defining rights, such as features of clarity of rules. Based on Schlicht's ideas, it is simple to put Granick's notion of 'regional property rights' on a firm theoretical foundation which matches Aoki's approach.

72 A seminal study of enterprise groups, 'qiye jituan' (企业集团), is Keister (2000). Keister emphasizes the fact that enterprise groups show highly centralized control by the core firm, thus actually relinquishing other principals of their entitlements. This was partly motivated by their recognition that local SOEs may have lost competitiveness and actually became a fiscal burden. Yet, there remained substantial interests in employment and indirect fiscal benefits or disadvantages. Lee (2007) shows that supplier relations and subsidiary arrangements are strongly influenced by administrative ties or personal relations that reflect previous official positions of management in enterprise group members, thus establishing strong intra-regional biases. For an illuminating case study, see Lin and Chen (2013). The authors show that a local government can exert substantial pressure even on central government SOEs in extracting a lot of compensating measures, even including influencing the ways in which corporatization is used for restructuring. One reason is that the large SOEs often maintained a high level of employment with many social services that they aimed to reduce via restructuring, thus leaving the burden of adjustment to the local government. So, the local government might negotiate special prices for provisioning products and services from the SOE or they might extract surtaxes for supporting local public services.

73 Brødsgaard (2012) offers a detailed study of the role of SOE leading cadres in the CCP Central Committee. On the one hand, at the time of the report there were 121 SOE business groups which fall under control of the organization department of the Central Committee, such as China Telecom, Sinopec or Air China. These positions rotate, so that CEOs may move to other positions in government after a certain period. At the same time, 17 CEOs were also members of the Central Committee. This constellation leaves much room both for CCP control and CCP capture by business interests. Similar constellations also apply to lower level political hierarchies. For example, even private businesspeople in Guangdong aspire to become members of local political bodies, which gives them status and provides legitimacy, and also provides access to political leaders. In a recent survey, the vast majority of business owners said that it is very important for them to attain positions in the People's Consultative Conference or the People's Congresses (see Unirule Institute 2015).

74 On the use of architecture as a status symbol in the ownership system, see Cliff (2013) on the case of Korla in the Tarim Basin, where the Tarim Oil Company has created an exclusive area in the city with administrative and residential functions. Interestingly, the high salaries of the central SOE also drive the consumer culture, thus connecting with my analysis of consumption in an earlier part of this chapter. My analysis of the relationship between land and the local status order is inspired by Hsing's (2006) seminal analysis. Hsing distinguishes between municipal governments and what she calls 'socialist land masters'. The latter are all kinds of entities belonging to certain *xitong* embedded in higher level administration, such as state-owned enterprises or central-level universities. They play an extremely important role in the process of urban development because many of them are located in the inner part of the cities,

for historical reasons. They control industrial estates and residential compounds, the latter as a legacy of the *danwei* system. Theoretically, the entire urban area is owned by the State Council, but factually the 'socialist land masters' claim the ownership rights vis-à-vis the municipal governments. These units often set up their own development corporations and even expand their assets by buying land from other SOEs in the city that close down or aim to restructure. So, in this case, the *xitong* status severely curtails the capacities of municipal governments to control urban land. This translates into difficulties in imposing strict procedures of urban planning upon the different parties involved. These are further accentuated by the fact that the municipal governments themselves, especially in large cities, are also complex composite organizations, in which land is factually controlled by subunits with different status and influence. Rithmire (2013) offers an illuminating comparative study of the cities of Harbin and Dalian, also arguing that landownership is mainly actualized in informal terms, which I interpret as ritual. Dalian implemented a highly centralized urban planning regime, probably because of the high rank of the then Dalian mayor Bo Xilai, who was able to win external financial support for creating a development zone to which central level SOEs could be attracted. In Harbin the municipal government had to negotiate with many affected groups, even including citizens who live in public residential compounds. This led to a dispersion of factual ownership rights among these different interest groups. The different realizations of ritual are highly visible in the distinct urban infrastructure of the two cities, with Dalian showing off modern, entirely newly designed urban districts, whereas development in Harbin is haphazard and patchy. Yet, this does not necessarily lead to general dissatisfaction among the population, as this pattern often reflects a successful realization of partial interests. Interestingly, this was also accompanied by a more salient role of the privatization of land-use rights to small and medium-sized businesses.

75 For more on this, see Chapter 4 on industrial policy.

4 Local state, ritual and territorial competition

State building and the transformation of the Chinese fiscal state

In the previous chapter I analysed localism as a manifestation of the ritual economy. In this chapter I explore the institutional structure of the Chinese state in more detail. The central argument is that we can only adequately understand the Chinese reforms and their outcome as a reflection of the state-building effort that was launched in the late nineteenth century. In this process, a concept peculiar to Chinese studies looms large: the 'local state'.

In the *longue durée*, we approach the local state as a contemporary institutional legacy of the traditional structures of empire. The term 'local state' has been introduced in the context of contemporary Chinese studies in order to grasp the peculiar dynamics between central government and 'local government'.[1] It has been rarely used with reference to Imperial China, as I did in Chapter 2. However, if we distinguish between the Chinese and the Western uses of the term 'local government' and compare this with the term 'local state', the historical continuity that lurks behind the many family resemblances across historical watersheds is evident, since the term 'local state' mainly refers to the level of the county, and thus relates to the urban vs. rural borderline that is constitutive for the institutional structure of the modern Chinese state. In comparison, the Chinese term 'local government', 'difang zhengfu' (地方政府), covers all levels of government that are not assigned to the central level, thus including even the provinces. Comparing this use with the Imperial situation, we recognize that in fact the relationship between higher level 'local governments' and the central level bears many resemblances, but there are also important differences.

As we have seen, in Imperial times the Imperial administration exerted tight control on the entire bureaucratic system down to the county level, but left the level below to culturalistic governance via intermediary local elites. This constitutional dualism also partly applies to contemporary China, which highlights the continuing role of the county level in separating two distinct types of sociopolitical systems. Yet, the fundamental difference between contemporary and Imperial China is the increasing bureaucratic penetration of local society by governmental institutions emanating from the county level. This is why we talk about a 'local state', which did not exist in Imperial times yet continues to bear the mark of Imperial times. On the one hand, the county level remains a special institutional structure in the entire governmental set-up, but at the same time it is the engine of the formalization of grassroots-level government. In this sense, the local state stays at the centre of the evolution of Chinese governmentality in the course of modernization.

Yet, a parallel process is that, in modern China, the provinces emerged as a distinct level of Chinese politics, so that the direct lines of bureaucratic control have been blurred by the dynamics of political bargaining and representation of regional interests. Indeed, for many macro-level phenomena of Chinese economic growth, the level of provinces is crucial to understanding their specific dynamics, such as being driven by structural and institutional differences across provinces. However, as I will argue, this role of the provinces unfolds as a manifestation of certain organizational structures in the central state, thus also remaining tightly constrained by these structures. Therefore, the Chinese meaning of 'local government' blurs a very significant distinction between the structural dynamics on the level of the provinces and the level of the county. The former is a central state phenomenon, the latter a local state phenomenon.[2]

Thus, the traditional structures of Empire cast a long shadow over the formal institutions of the modern Chinese state, and are only gradually dissolving in more recent times via the extension of the government bureaucracy to the township level and even to the villages. In order to investigate this phenomenon, we need to focus on the 'local state', hence the county level. At the same time, Chinese modernism implied that the urban areas were placed under much tighter administrative control, thus aligning the urban system with the structures of centralized government. Historically, this may be related to the failure of federalist movements in China, which had been strong in the late nineteenth and early twentieth century, and were promoting the idea of provincial self-government based on the social structures of the modernizing urban areas. For some time, these movements worked together with the factual weakening of the national power structure, and the fact that competing political forces had to rely on local resources and support in order to fight for their cause, ultimately resulting in the dysfunctional state of urban-based Warlordism. After 1949, regaining and cementing control of urban society was a central challenge to the Communist Party which had 'encircled the cities from the villages', according to Mao Zedong's famous dictum. As a result, a distinct role of urban areas in the political economy of China is only re-emerging gradually in recent times, so that, thus far, the administrative structure in terms of the division of the country into provinces exerts a strong impact upon the dynamics of the national political economy.[3]

In the course of the twentieth century, the alternative way of modernizing the Chinese state as a federal system based on the provinces and their urban centres was effectively blocked, and almost all urban elites opted in favour of a strong central state. Against this background, one of the most influential conceptual paradigms in understanding the dynamics of Chinese reforms, the idea of 'quasi-federalism', is seriously misguided as far as it suggests a high degree of informal autonomy on the level of the provinces. In fact, the modern Chinese state continued with the Imperial tradition of tight control of the provincial level, so that we should avoid merging the local state and the provinces into one concept of 'local government', as the Chinese term insinuates. This control is institutionally based on the deep penetration of urban society by the institutional structures of the central state, so that there is no independent social-structural basis for provincial-level autonomy. In the first decade of reforms, this pattern was mainly stabilized by the continuing centrality of state ownership in the urban economies, and therefore the *danwei* system integrating work environment and private lives. This social-structural weakness of urban social and cultural dynamics has only started to change in the aftermath of the renewed reform dynamics in the 1990s, creating what has been labelled an emerging middle class. However, this middle class remains tightly bound to the structures of the central party state. As we will see, therefore, what appears to be autonomous policy space on the provincial level is mainly generated by the internal political economy of the central state bureaucracy.[4]

Yet, the state-building effort on the national level faced serious constraints of administrative and institutional resources, so that this institutional complex of the central state covering urban China is still being contrasted with the structures of the local state rooted in rural society. So, I posit that what effectively happened after 1949 until the turn of the millennium was a modernist transmutation of Imperial structures of governance without changing their basic functions. In other words, one can interpret the collectivization movement during Maoist times as an attempt to freeze the political and social dynamics of the rural areas in order to enable the extension and stabilization of the central state in the urban areas, which was reflected in the cellularization pattern discussed in the previous chapter. Once the institutional constraints in the countryside were released, the local state reinstated itself with a vengeance. As a result, the major challenge to Chinese state building in the past three decades has been the further extension of the central state to the sub-county level. As we have seen in the previous chapter, modernist urbanization is therefore not simply a modernization in economic terms, but also a means to integrate rural society institutionally into the modern state. In other words, ongoing urbanization is a key process in the eventual obsolescence of the Imperial legacy in governing China.

However, in this context urbanization is a coin with two sides as far as the local state is concerned. As we have noted, the term largely refers to the county level, and hence is an analytical category applying to the rural areas, including the urban areas that are administrative centres. However, in the course of the rapid urbanization process, with rural areas transforming into urban agglomerations, we have to consider that newly emerging municipalities can also become manifestations of the local state. In other words, the urbanization of rural areas is actually driven by two forces: the extension of the central state into the rural society on the one hand, and the expansion of the local state on the other hand, with the latter actually emerging from a complex mixture of top-down and bottom-up social forces. We have already scrutinized one special case, which is the interaction between villages and municipal administration in the context of 'urban villages', but more generally we may surmise that the central areas in the traditional market system obtain a pivotal role in the ongoing state-building process. This is reflected in the immense variety of local urban political economies that has been emerging in recent times. For example, formerly rural counties have been transformed into large urban areas, together with administrative upgrading. These administrative changes increasingly blur the lines in the conventional hierarchy of territorial administration which clearly subordinates urban places to the provincial administration. As a result, urban local areas have been emerging which pursue distinct localist policies and interests that are no longer linked with a rural socioeconomic structure. In this sense, we may say that new degrees of freedom in the national political economy are emerging in which urban places assume a more independent role. This implies that local state and modernism increasingly form a functional alliance in driving economic and social change.[5]

This may also be true if we consider metropolitan municipalities which have an elevated administrative structure, even on a provincial level, such as Shanghai or Chongqing. The case of Chongqing has received much attention because of the political scandals related to the person of Bo Xilai. Yet, Chongqing demonstrates the potential of localization of Chinese politics, precisely because even this very sharp tension between local politics and central government control could build up, when an individual leader exploits the local state for building his power position in national-level politics. These special circumstances should not obscure the fact that Chongqing is a case that shows the degrees of freedom in policy-making on a metropolitan level, thus possibly qualifying as a local state. As I will discuss below, these degrees of freedom certainly relate to the phenomenon of experimentalism in Chinese policy-making, yet we can also see how the local state can assert spaces of autonomy which partly loosen the administrative control that went hand in hand with modernist centralism which was installed after 1949.[6]

So, we can say that the term 'local state' today covers two different phenomena in the context of Chinese state building. One is the growing politicization of the relationship between larger urban places and upper level administration which transforms the bargaining relationship between higher and lower levels into a political process implying a distinct diversity of the political economy of local states. In the *longue durée*, we may therefore speculate whether this development also ties in with the emerging role of urban areas in the incipient modernization of China in the nineteenth century. Regarding the second phenomenon, however, we do not need to rely on speculation, since this has already been visible for decades, namely the growing intrusion of higher level administrative structures into the rural grassroots level. This process is driven by the county level, for sure, thus completing the long-term process of overcoming the institutional dualism of the Imperial state. Yet, this raises the question whether this is mainly extending the local state or whether this automatically also implies a strengthening of a direct grip of the central state in the rural areas.

In order to understand these complex transformations, the most promising object of investigation is the tax system on different levels. As we have seen in Chapter 2, the tax system of the Chinese Empire was explicitly built on a systematic distinction between central-level taxes and the informal funding of the local state, i.e. the county administration. This dualism was a major aspect of the traditional ritual economy. So, the question is how far the modern transformations of the tax system have changed these aspects of ritual, in three senses. The first is whether elements of the traditional system have survived, the second is whether the Chinese state effectively proceeded with a Weberian rationalization of the tax system under central control, and the third is whether traditional forms of ritual have been substituted or complemented by modern forms of ritual. Subsequently, I will not go into the details of the tax reforms, as they have been the object of numerous studies, but highlight a number of analytically relevant stylized facts.[7]

As a point of departure, the Maoist tax system not only clearly replicated the structures of the Imperial tax system, but was even atavistic in the sense that the rural areas were taxed in terms of direct levies that were implicated in the price controls of the state procurement system, as we saw in the previous chapter. In other words, whereas the reforms installed by the Ming and Qing emperors completed a monetization of rural taxation, the implementation of the planned economy actually meant a revival of traditional forms of taxation based on levies in kind and even corvée labour that was implicit in the many campaigns of mobilizing peasants for rural infrastructure projects. Demonetization of the tax system went hand in hand with the suppression of the traditional marketing system, thus also stripping the peasants of most opportunities for gaining pecuniary income. When the rural reforms were launched in 1978, this atavistic tax system was continued in the shape of the household responsibility system. The contracts governing the lease of land-use rights inevitably included certain quantitative obligations to deliver a certain amount of agricultural produce to the collective entities, which channelled them further into the state procurement system, and would also oblige the peasants to contribute a certain amount of labour days to the collective. Thus, interestingly, even the feature of the traditional tax system was reproduced where rights on land were directly tied to tax duties. In the so-called 'agricultural responsibility system', the contracts regulating land lease and thus guaranteeing land-use rights were factually fixing the amount of taxes to be paid to the government.

With the growing marketization of the rural economy, rural taxation was still organized in close resemblance to the traditional system, distinguishing between the agricultural tax and mandatory procurement that went to the higher level government, and diverse local surtaxes, fees and other contributions mainly funding local infrastructure and local administration. In this pattern, the traditional dualism also survived which placed the intermediate rural elites into a pivotal position as 'brokers' between the central state and the local population. In other words, after dismantling the People's Communes the system started out from the condition that even most of the grassroots-level cadres were paid out of the budget of collectives, i.e. (administrative) villages. The funding of local public services applied until most recently, even while at the same time extending bureaucratic control to the township and even village level. In fact, what occurred was a transformation of the Maoist system of collective funding of grassroots-level government and public services into a mixed system with very large regional variations, in which almost all public services are provided via independent funding by specific fees. Here, we need to distinguish between fees in the sense of levies that are imposed upon the rural population and user fees that are charged as a quasi-market price for certain services by entities that have been institutionally separated from formal government as so-called 'service units', 'shiye danwei' (事业单位). This is significant because only the former would fall under the general category of 'tax'; yet the service units are not private companies but remain under the control of the local state.[8]

So, we can even state that the pattern of government involution that was characteristic for Republican times continued to prevail in many areas of China. On the one hand, townships and villages were being integrated into the structure of the state in terms of enhancing bureaucratic control of funds. For example, today most important cadre positions in the rural areas are also included in the budget of the superordinate township; at the same time, townships have to administrate their budget via accounts on the county level. Yet, at the turn of the millennium, the CCP recognized that the phenomenon of irregular levies and taxes was rampant in the countryside, constituting a major burden for the farmers. So, the new Hu and Wen leadership launched a major tax reform initiative, abolishing the agricultural tax and prohibiting the use of irregular levies. Against the background of the previous discussion of family resemblances with Imperial conditions, we can therefore safely say that only this tax reform eventually declared the goal to put an end to the Imperial system, since the agricultural tax represented the local tax due to the national hence ultimately central level, and the irregular taxes served to fund the local administration. Yet, if we take this together with the aforementioned trend of a growing commercialization of public services, we note strong evidence for a continuing dynamics of government involution, as the extension of the government bureaucracy is accompanied by a diminishment or even crisis if not breakdown of the public provision of government services, even in sensitive areas such as healthcare.[9]

So, in the first three decades of reforms, the Chinese fiscal administration directly replicated the dual nature of the Chinese state, since the rural areas remained outside the scope of formal tax administration, and urban industry was taxed in the context of the regional property rights system. Urban taxation was based on uniform laws and regulations, but revenue was assigned to the different levels that claimed ownership rights to the economic entities under their control. The fragmentation of the central state into a hierarchy of jurisdictions was a new phenomenon as far as their explicit economic function is concerned. This is why, in the previous chapter, we introduced the regional property rights system as a new feature of the ritual economy. On the county level, the two systems actually met, because as a legacy of the Maoist period, the county level also mustered a number of small-scale state-owned companies. As we have seen, the regional property rights system created the conditions for the emergence of the complex political economy of urban growth.

This system experienced a deep crisis in the mid-1990s, triggering a comprehensive tax reform in the urban domain. This effort was further deepened by the rural tax reforms of the early 2000s. In both cases, fiscal crisis was a motivating force. In my discussion, I interpret these crises as crises of governmentality, thus actually being manifestations of deeper level institutional and social-structural aspects of state building in China on both the central and local state levels.

In the first half of the 1990s, the share of central government in total revenues had fallen to an unprecedented level. This was mainly caused by the fact that the reforms had triggered economic growth in domains which either remained outside the formal tax system, namely rural industries and township and village enterprises, or where local authorities were major beneficiaries in the context of the regional property rights system. This was bolstered by the extension of the system of extra-budgetary funds which were also funded by other levies and fees, apart from regular taxes, on all levels of government. Obviously, the growth of local-level fiscal resources outside the national tax system was the strongest in the most prosperous regions. As a consequence, the share of government in GDP also declined. This diagnosis put the role of the central state as a modernizing agent seriously into question, and even seemed to endanger the unity of the state, as the central government's power to redistribute fiscal resources among the regions was weakened substantially. This development played together with the rapid globalization of the Chinese economy which deepened the geo-economic fissures between the macro-regions, such as the southern coastal provinces and the inner provinces.[10]

We approach this crisis as a crisis of the ritual economy, in the sense that the root was located in a pattern of norms, expectations and behavioural regularities that were only partly also reflected in formal institutions. For example, considering the extra-budgetary funds, these had emerged as a pervasive feature of the fiscal system going back to the late 1950s when local authorities obtained the right to levy surcharges on national taxes in order to fund local public services, such as in education. When marketization spread after 1978, local government entities on every level and in every system could exploit this formal precedent in order to create a large number of additional fiscal accounts that could be funded by a bewilderingly wide variety of local fees, surtaxes and other forms of revenue. It is important to consider this in more general and abstract terms as manifesting the degree of autonomy of the local state in China, thus reflecting a constitutive phenomenon in the ritual economy that would be misinterpreted if we just see it as a form of deviance in terms of formal institutions of the central state. This is visible in the recurrent conflicts between the local states and the central fiscal administration over the control of those funds, and the many ways in which new forms of autonomous fiscal powers emerged on the local level, with the latest manifestation in the 'local government investment vehicles' that I discuss below.[11]

This interpretation receives strong support in the particular shape of tax reforms in 1994 that aimed at centralizing control over local revenues. In order to countervail centrifugal tendencies, the central government implemented a tax reform which created a fiscal system that is unique across the world. This tax reform strongly centralized formal revenues, but kept the expenditure side very decentralized until today. Since the constitutional rule was continued prohibiting local debt, this implied that local governments became increasingly dependent on fiscal redistribution from higher level governments. On the one hand, this bolstered the bargaining power of the central government, but we can also interpret this measure as an implicit recognition of the autonomous fiscal powers of local governments, because leaving such a large share of expenditure with the local states implies that the central level not only recognizes local powers to fund its activities, but actually even incentivized them. In other words, as long as central-level redistribution does not only imply comprehensive central planning of local expenditures, revenue centralization does not fundamentally challenge the existence of local states, but only shifts the power balance in favour of the central state. Yet, this strategy cements and recognizes the role of the local states in the entire set-up of government while strengthening the centre at the same time. Therefore, I argue that the peculiar formal structure of the fiscal system actually manifests the strong continuity of Chinese governmentality, together with ongoing efforts to block the forces of government involution.[12]

The strategic significance of the 1994 tax reforms is also reflected in their dynamic effects. These largely surfaced on the level below the province, because central-level redistribution focused on the relationship between the provinces and the central government. In other words, the interpretation of the 1994 reforms needs to pay close attention to the distinction between the 'local state' and the 'local government' in the sense of our initial discussion in this chapter. The new redistributive powers were mainly directed at shifting the power balance between the central and the provincial government, thus in fact reconstituting the internal coherence of the central state as opposed to the local state. The resulting imbalance between revenues and expenditures mainly affects the local state, and thus entities below the provincial level, and in particular the county level. Facing the gap between revenues and expenditures, and the growing need for infrastructure investment supporting rapid economic growth, local states were forced to implement savings and activate new forms of revenue.[13]

This explains two major phenomena in the recent reform process. First, the de facto privatization of the late 1990s was mainly driven by the motivation of local states to get rid of loss-making SOEs under their control. In the longer run, this was a major impetus for modernizing the SOE sector and enhancing the role of higher level entities, that is, the provincial and central level. In this perspective, the 1994 tax reform was an indirect means to enforce a privatization programme without actually formally implementing it as a central policy, which was supported by the slogan of 'keeping the big and letting the small go'. Correspondingly, the tax reform triggered the emergence of a new dichotomy in the ritual economy. These are the correspondences between the institutional scope of the local state with the market economy and the private sector, and between the central state and the state-owned sector, though also operating increasingly in a market context. Yet, this system did not finally abolish the regional property rights structure behind the assignment of fiscal rights. Thus, measures such as the restructuring of SOEs still remain affected by the conflicts about fiscal resources or, generally, stakeholder rights. This means, for example, that the local state might give up ownership rights to SOEs during their restructuring and integration into higher level entities, but retain stakeholder rights in terms of claims on employment or contributions to public services, which may include even the re-introduction of forms of local taxation as compensation for the lost direct revenue rights related to regional property rights.[14]

Second, the 1994 reforms set strong incentives to exploit land-use rights as a source of revenue, thus speeding up the urbanization process as a side effect. Compared with the privatization push, this may be seen as an unintended consequence, because central government always tried to impose strict constraints on the conversion of agricultural land into urban land. But within the scope of urban land administration, local authorities could find many ways even to exploit the revenue potential of existing urban land, such as when moving administrative buildings out of downtown areas and opening up the estates for urban redevelopment. In this sense, funding the local state by activating land rights is simply a transformation of previous patterns of extra-budgetary funds and other forms of autonomous funding of the local state. The central difference lies in establishing a direct link between the fiscal system and the financial sector. This is because, in one of the institutional forms of activating land rights, these rights are basically used as collateral in funding local infrastructure and urban development by means of loans that are provided to especially established 'local government investment vehicles', thus also obviating the need for extra-budgetary accounts. This has resulted in a very strong expansion of local government debt, in spite of the constitutional prohibition of formal debt below the central level. In other words, we can interpret the current status of factual local government debt as an expression of the dichotomy of local vs. central state. Correspondingly, the next step in regulating this relationship is necessarily the regulation of local government debt, which means more specifically the extension of current experiments with municipal-level bonds.[15]

In understanding the dynamics of tax reforms in their relationship to the ritual economy, it is important to delve more deeply into the details of administrative structure. Based on the results of the 1994 reforms, in the 2000s the most important aspect of national reforms was the centralization of tax administration on the provincial level. Traditionally, there has always been an organizational distinction between the tax administration and the fiscal administration, because the latter also included the entire financial management of state-owned assets. This has resulted in complex structures that are only fully visible if one looks at the details of organizational arrangements which affect the internal organization of both and their relationship. In this context, the regional property rights system interacts with the so-called 'tiao kuai' (条块) principle in administration.

The *tiao kuai* distinction is a central aspect of the internal power distribution in the Chinese government bureaucracy. Therefore, I approach it as a central aspect of ritual in the Chinese political process. The reason for this is that there is no provision in terms of constitutional arrangements that clearly defines this allocation of power in Chinese government, although it effectively determines what has been called the 'quasi-federalism' of the Chinese state, especially with regard to the economic system. This *tiao kuai* is a matrix organization with the two dimensions of functional and regional lines of control and command, and has held sway throughout the history of the People's Republic. This means, for example, that if we consider a certain function of government such as financial administration or environmental policy, these functions are part of a functional hierarchy that starts out from the central level and reaches down to the lowest level, such that in principle the structure of central level government is replicated on lower level governments. However, this does not necessarily mean that the hierarchical relationship is also a line of command. This is because the function is part of the respective territorial government which may also exert control in different ways. So, a fundamental issue in administrative design is how the different aspects of administrative power are allocated in the two dimensions. Traditionally, these are also defined in a conceptual dualism, namely 'lingdao guanxi' (领导关系) relations, which is direct control, and 'yewu guanxi' (业务关系) relations, which is regulatory control. The two dimensions can vary in degree; for example, regulatory control may refer only to higher level issuance of certain guidelines for administrative practice or tighter control in terms of policy evaluation, etc.[16]

Traditionally, in many policy domains the regional line has dominated the functional line. In other words, funding and personnel management take place on the regional level, and professional and regulatory guidance run via the functional level connecting up to higher levels. This implies that independent from functional governance, regional control is consistently more powerful, since functional departments need to rely on local resources. This is bolstered by the nomenclature system which I scrutinize in the following section, and which means that in relations among different representatives, the status order applies that I described in the previous chapter.This means that in the same territorial rank the relative positions of systems and nomenclature determine the relative status of members of different administrative departments. So, for example, if on the central level the environmental administration is a relatively weak system, this is replicated on the lower territorial level. At the same time, in the nomenclature dimension the rank of a bureau chief is typically lower than the rank of a territorial leader. Thus, in terms of status, this means that the *kuai* dimension is normally stronger than the *tiao* dimension. However, this does not imply that the territorial unit as such has constitutionally guaranteed rights of autonomy in any policy domain. Therefore, great care is warranted in comparing this system with federal arrangements. The degree of autonomy of local-level governments is only an expression of the more fundamental power structures in what remains a centralized government in formal terms. I argue that this is another expression of the ritual economy, which is fundamentally different from a formal federalist system. The distribution of power across territorial levels of hierarchy is determined by the internal ritual allocation of power in what is formally a centralized and unified administration.

I wish to emphasize that this is different from a mere principal–agent issue, as has already been emphasized in analysing the regional property rights system, because it is the power distribution that defines a multiple–principal structure, which may be analysed in terms of the principal–agent model only in the second step. This means that we cannot simply explain the emergence of regional autonomy as an outcome of the information asymmetries and conflicts between the central government as principal and the local governments as agents. In fact, the central government is often well informed about the situation on the local level and could exploit its power in order to enforce control, as it has easily done with the tax reform of 1994. So, as I did in analysing the regional property rights system, we have to recognize the ritual nature of the actual distribution of power which then becomes manifest in forms of local autonomy which may partly be seen as corresponding to similar phenomena in federalist systems.[17]

Against the background of the *tiao kuai* structure, the administrative embeddedness of tax authority is obviously an essential determinant of the actual performance of the tax system. Traditionally, the tax administration was in a weaker position than the financial administration, as only the latter was in charge of state-owned assets, and direct flows of revenue were more important than regular taxes. Further, tax administration was subordinate to the respective territorial government. Accordingly, the implementation of national tax laws was weak, because the local tax offices were under the control of local governments. With the tax reform of 1994, this turned out to be the Achilles heel of the policy, since major taxes were centralized formally, yet implementation remained under local supervision and control. This would have weakened tax efforts on the local level, so that a necessary complementary policy was the centralization of tax administration, thus effectively shifting administrative powers from the *kuai* to the *tiao* dimension. Only by achieving this did the centralization of taxation become viable. However, this was done by separating the tax administration along the two dimensions, leaving the local taxes under the administration of a local tax office. In the course of implementing the reforms, this was also accompanied by redesigning the channels of flows of funds, especially with regard to the extra-budgetary funds.[18]

However, the result of this process was not simply centralization with reference to the central government, but the strengthening of the provincial level vis-à-vis both the superordinate and the subordinate level. So, in fact, the centralization did not unequivocally bolster the position of the central government, but of the central state *in toto* as opposed to the local state. Thus, provinces and central government continue to bargain internally over the allocation of funds collected centrally and to be redistributed across the provinces. At the same time the centralization of tax administration strengthened the provincial level vis-à-vis the local state. This centralization effort has been diffusing downwards to the county level. Since counties are the government entities which have been most strongly affected by tax reforms, with a majority factually running deficits, the county level strives to extend fiscal control to the township level, thus allowing access to grassroots-level revenue capacities. So, we observe an institutional dynamic of expanding the scope of central-level fiscal institutions, with the ultimate state integrating county-level institutions directly into provincial level institutions. This would achieve an institutional innovation of historical significance, since for the first time a bureaucratically integrated tax administration would be created that directly extends from the provincial level to the rural areas via the county level. In other words, if the ongoing tax reforms succeed, the local state would wither away as an institutional phenomenon. However, this process is still a going concern, with major steps in reforming budget management only announced in 2014, and planned to be completed in 2020. In this sense, we need to interpret the current emphasis on further fiscal reforms as reflecting the factual resilience of the ritual economy in spite of all previous fiscal reforms.[19]

Now, the extension of the tax bureaucracy to the township level works together with the reforms of the rural fiscal system launched in the early 2000s. As I mentioned previously, this system maintained major aspects of the traditional fiscal system and its transmutations in the early twentieth century in mainly building on irregular fees and other surcharges or contributions in order to fund local government. This system contributed to the improvement of rural public services in those places where township and village industries were strong, but failed in other areas without that development.[20] With the privatization of TVEs in the second half of the 1990s, the informal nature of local finance was further strengthened, while at the same time driving rapid urbanization of rural areas in the most developed regions of China. It is important to note that this 'informal' nature is partly a transfiguration of what was collectively owned property before. A TVE may have been under direct control of a village government until the mid-1990s, thus directly channelling profits into local-level budgets; after privatization, these contributions may have taken the shape of irregular levies and fees, though actually being based on a shared understanding of the resulting private economy being part and parcel of the local body politic, that is, the local state. As I discussed in the previous chapter, these complex interactions could even result in the corporate structures incorporating the public sector, even its governmental functions, as in some 'villages within the cities'.

Hence, we may say that fiscal administration and the development of the private economy were deeply interconnected in the course of reforms. On the one hand, the Chinese central state had accumulated political and administrative power to a degree that is unique in Chinese history. At the same time, it allowed for the partial autonomy of the local state in managing the local economy. One explanation for this is an implicit bargaining position where higher level authorities leave partial fiscal autonomy to the local state, because the local state has incentives to tap the fiscal potential of the local economy. This in turn implies that the local state will also cooperate with business in order to maintain incentives for investment and growth, thus effectively protecting private property rights. On the other hand, if local businesses flourish, this will also increase the revenue of local governments that is partly shared with higher level governments. The result of this bargaining game between governments on different levels and private actors corresponds to what I have called 'localism'. Localism is the cultural complement of the local state in the ritual economy and refers to the unique interaction between formal and informal institutions, especially in the rural areas. As a pattern, localism is not enshrined in any specific set of formal institutions which even formally constrain it, such as with the constitutional prohibition of local debt. The entire legal construction of the fiscal system runs against localism. Therefore, localism is a direct manifestation of the ritual economy, in two particular senses. First, localism is a manifestation of the status order of the Chinese state, and second, it is maintained in a set of conventions and informal institutions which are undergirded by certain beliefs about policy-making.[21]

This means that, considering the ongoing reforms of the fiscal system, it is indeed crucial to observe what grassroots-level centralization will imply for the local state, especially with regard to the county level. As I have said, there are in fact two interlocking centralization processes which do not necessarily converge. One is the centralization of the local state on the county level, and the other is the centralization of the central state including the provincial level. The climax of institutional change with regard to the latter would be to directly subordinate the county level to the provincial level, which is an unfinished though actively pursued agenda of reform. Considering the fact that the county level is also the level on which future urbanization will proceed most intensively, this would eventually refer to the actual degree of fiscal autonomy of the municipal level in the organization of the Chinese state. This is being negotiated between the provincial and county levels, as is already happening in the reform areas.[22]

The other centralization process is the inclusion of the village level into county-level fiscal administration. As we have already seen in discussing the role of temple building in reflecting certain patterns of accountability on the local level, localism is most directly expressed in the role of informal practices in funding infrastructure and other public goods, especially on the village level. One of the most significant expressions is informal government debt. This is running mainly via two channels: formal credit given to local projects and involved organizations, and supplier credit. In both cases, local governments do not directly run fiscal deficits, but factually borrow funds or act as guarantors. On the lowest level, namely the villages and small townships, this is most directly embedded in the ritual economy in the sense that personal relations between cadres and creditors enable the borrowings. For example, a village cadre may have to implement government programmes to modernize roads, but since there are no funds available he approaches local construction companies to see whether they may be willing to invest and would get reimbursed later. That promise may be based on the assumption that the new road will create new business opportunities, hence increase local revenues, or may offer new business opportunities which may be partly controlled by the local government, which would give preferential access to them to the original creditor. In this case there would be no direct repayment of the borrowed funds.[23]

These mutual obligations are embedded in norms of reciprocity (that I will analyse in Chapter 5), and hence generally in ritual. Clearly, the borderline to corruption is porous under these circumstances, as the ritual obligations are heavily personalized. Incentives for corruption are especially strong when agricultural land is transformed into urban territory during urbanization processes. In this case, status differences add to the complexity of ritual embeddedness, because cadres are involved who may have an urban *hukou* and are well connected in the towns and cities. They confront farmers with a lower social status. The pressure on mobilizing fiscal resources and increasing local GDP intermingles with opportunities for personal enrichment. Hence, the status order translates into the enforcement of unfair contracts on lower status farmers.[24]

To summarize this section, state building is an essential element in defining the economic style of contemporary China. This fact has been recognized by many important scholarly contributions under headings such as 'quasi-federalism' or 'regionally decentralized authoritarianism', but these notions appear to be overly static, and they leave important aspects out of the picture, which reflect the specific governmentality that connects past and present. First, we have to approach state building as a dynamic process in which the state gradually proceeds in penetrating the economy and society, overcoming the patterns of cellularization; however, this process also creates many unintended consequences which feedback on its direction. It is still open as to what the final status will look like, as we still observe strong forces of government involution, mainly manifest in the fiscal structures of the local state. Second, the opposition between 'central' and 'local government' defines the wrong borderline in the Chinese body politic, since we have to regard provinces as a part of the 'central state' vis-à-vis the local state on the level of rapidly transforming counties and municipalities. On the central level, we therefore need to include organizational routines and administrative practices into the analysis of the economic style. Third, we have to acknowledge the special role of the Chinese Communist Party, which is certainly covered in the often used term 'party state', but which is still underestimated in many characterizations of the Chinese economy as opposed to Chinese politics. Therefore, I turn to this topic next.

The Chinese Communist Party as a ritual organization

In this section, I look in more detail at the status order of the local state. This status order is determined by the structural feature of the parallelism of party organization and government organization, which is however partly disconnected on the grassroots level. This was a systematic feature of state building in the Maoist period. Whereas the Communist Party aimed to penetrate the rural grassroots level as deeply as possible, the government administration was not extended in the same way, and was even obstructed in a number of political campaigns. In other words, on the grassroots level rural cadres were mainly funded by the collectives and were not included in the government budget, with the exception of certain core administrators. Therefore, as we have seen in the previous section, state building in the reform era has been manifest in the gradual extension of the government bureaucracy at the lowest level and hence the inclusion even of rural cadres into the formal budget, with the township level as the core site of (local) state building.

One central feature of this system is that leading positions in the government bureaucracy are mainly held by members of the Communist Party. On the lowest level, the slow advance of government implied that the central position is the Party secretary who is not necessarily the village head. This distinction is important because the widespread introduction of elections on the village level means that village heads may be elected in a democratic procedure with different degrees of genuine political competition, whereas the Party Secretary is determined by the internal procedures of the CCP organization department. As a result, the Party secretary is typically of higher status than the village leaders. Throughout the history of the PRC, this status difference enabled direct interventions of higher level authorities into village life, in the Maoist era mainly via campaigns and other forms of mobilization. Yet, this does not imply that the Party secretary was also a member of the government bureaucracy.

The process of state building has proceeded along the structures of the traditional marketing system, which, as we have already seen, had also been reproduced via the structure of the People's Communes. In other words, state building works via the interaction between the county and the township level, with townships gradually extending their control downwards to the villages. In this structure, the role of the CCP is reflected in the distinction between 'leading' cadres and ordinary cadres, with the former typically being recruited from CCP members. The Party secretary on the county level is the pivotal figure in this structure.

The basic structure of the leadership in the local state is outlined in Figure 4.1.[25] One of the most significant facts about internal administrative structure in China is that the line of command between the county and the upper level unit, the prefecture, is relatively weak in the sense that the prefecture leaves large leeway for decision-making on the county level.

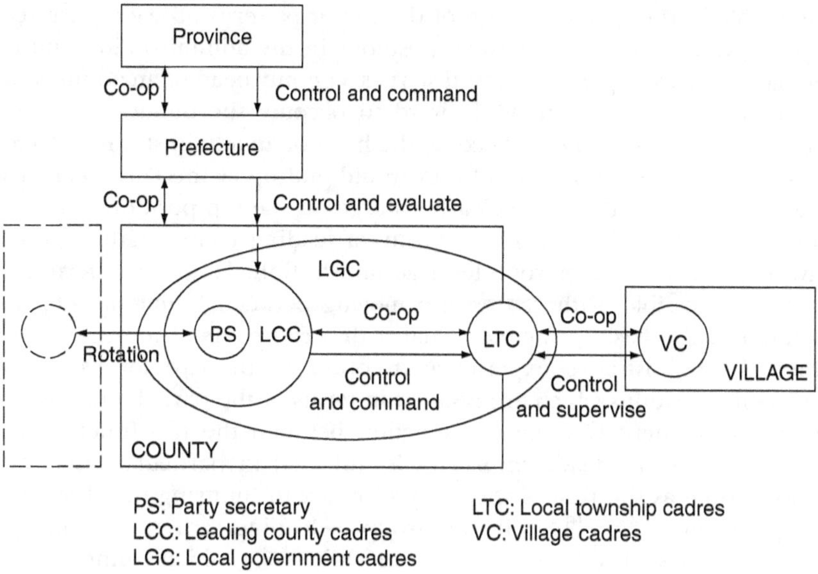

Figure 4.1 Institutional structure of local leadership.

This constellation is also preserved in the reform model directly subordinating the county to the province, and is possibly even strengthened. So, upper levels often only set certain general policy goals, but they do not determine the specific measures that need to be taken. The grip of the upper level becomes tight when it comes to the evaluation of the performance of leading cadres. In the nomenclature system, the upper level also controls the assignment of leading cadres to their positions. This specific feature of cadre administration establishes the relative autonomy of the local state which, as we will see in the following section, also relates to the notion of experimentalism and localism. In other words, the general idea in nurturing cadres is that leading cadres should have extensive experience in grassroots-level work so that they are able to adapt general policies to local conditions, both in terms of design and in ways of implementation.

So, we may say that a defining feature of government in China is the duality of leadership and administration. Whereas the administration is responsible for implementing policies, the party and its representatives assume the leadership position in defining strategies and directions. This applies to the different levels, but especially to the county level. Subsequently, I develop the idea that ritual is an essential aspect of leadership, thus turning the duality of ritual and formal administration into a defining feature of Chinese governmentality.

This dynamic relationship between leadership and administration is also visible in the specific design of the career patterns of leading cadres. Aspiring cadres alternate between positions in the administration and in the party. For example, they would start as a deputy head of an administrative village (*xiang*) and move forward to become the deputy Party secretary; only then would they become the head of an administrative village. This alternation continues until they would end up as the Party secretary of a county, which therefore clearly emerges as the top position, 'di yi ba shou' (第一把手). In fact, the majority of leading county cadres would have experience of grassroots-level administration. However, alternative tracks are possible, with cadres also moving between functional departments. Yet, the basic principle remains that cadres need to accumulate practical administrative experience in order to prepare for assuming leadership positions which are defined in terms of the party hierarchy. In other words, there is a status distinction between the two functions of administration and leadership. This is reflected in particular ritualistic notions, such as the role of the Party secretary in 'unifying the thought', 'tongyi sixiang' (统一思想) in the group of leading cadres; a 'thinking' can further crystallize into a 'model', 'moshi' (模式), which connects with similar approaches in other places and with policy preferences on higher levels of government.

Thus, Party secretaries assume the position of strategic leaders of the local state, with large leeway in determining local policies. The relative autonomy in county-level policy-making is combined with a low degree of mobility between the county level and the upper level of the administration. This is an essential fact about the administration in China, because in explaining the Chinese 'miracle' the hypothesis has been presented that tournaments incentivize the decision-makers in the administration to enhance the economic potential of their jurisdiction (see below). However, looking at the county level, it is true that evaluation takes place, but success rarely helps to move up from the county to upper levels of the administration. There are two reasons for this. One relates to political control at higher levels, which results in the fact that administrators of higher levels, but not yet in leading positions, are often sent down to the prefecture level in order to gain leadership experience. This also ensures provincial control of prefectures; that is, municipalities. For this kind of position there are also educational requirements that county-level cadres often do not fulfil, given their particular career pattern which requires extensive experience of grassroots-level work in rural areas. Only a majority of county-level leading cadres have a university degree, which is largely required in assuming higher level positions.[26]

As a result, the low upward mobility of county cadres is also reflecting a status difference vis-à-vis upper level administrators. Leading cadres of the local state have a distinct identity in relation to cadres of the central state, which is mainly represented as provincial administration mediated via prefecture-level administration. Since there are many reforms which establish a direct administrative subordination of counties to the provinces, also reflecting the rapid urbanization of counties in many places, the borderline between the central and the local state is manifest in two different groups of government cadres. Careers of leaders in the local state largely unfold in horizontal rotation, which is a general practice anyway in the context of 'avoidance' policies which aims at keeping corruption down. In this rotation, the status differences among the various government units and locations matter. There are government departments which have a high political valuation and others that would actually imply a degradation, even when the cadre rank would formally be the same. These status differences are reflected in the quality of equipment, the size of budget and other fringe benefits for leading cadres. In a similar vein, within higher level jurisdictions, different townships and counties have different status in the sense of being focal places or peripheral, which of course directly influences the fiscal buoyance and hence the resources that are invested in local government premises and fringe benefits. These two dimensions of status allow for many degrees of freedom in shaping individual careers within the local state and corresponding patterns of incentivization. Finally, there are also distinct regional identities of cadres. In Maoist times, county-level cadres often stemmed from other areas of China because there was a huge reshuffling of cadres in extending the political control of the CCP nationwide; in reform times, in spite of the 'avoidance' policy, an increasing share of leading cadres comes from the prefecture in which a county is located and even from within the county.[27]

So, the relative autonomy of the local state is inherent to the organization of the internal administration and implies a very strong position of the county Party secretary which manifests an amazing family resemblance with the position of the county Magistrate in Imperial China.[28] In contrast to the Imperial administration, however, the formal county administration reaches further down to the township level. In particular, the 'leading cadres' on both levels closely interact, and there is a tight command relationship between the county and the township. This allows for the ongoing process of centralization on the county level, as we have seen in the context of fiscal administration. Between the village and the township, there is a weak administrative connection in terms of direct subordination, because formally the villages are self-administered. However, villages do not have their own fiscal accounts and are therefore dependent on the township administration, unless they mobilize funding for certain measures independently. Evidently, this lack of budgetary autonomy is a serious constraint upon the role of grassroots-level elections, since village heads have no control over village budgets. This creates the conditions for the widespread occurrence of informal debt that we have discussed in the previous section.[29]

So, what we observe is a status order between county, township and village, with the respective cadres displaying corresponding habitus, including access to different resources such as cars, certain buildings, etc. This status order is a major factor shaping the political economy in the rural areas, especially in the context of urbanization, as we have seen in the case of land management. Leading cadres embody higher *suzhi* relative to the farmers, and therefore adopt an authoritarian attitude in pushing forward with projects of economic development and modernization, such as in urbanizing rural areas while at the same time appropriating collective land for modernist endeavours. One important aspect of this status difference is the *hukou* status which distinguishes government administrators from the rural population, since leading cadres obtain urban *hukou* or have already inherited this from their parents and do not live in the villages. So, the *hukou* status marks the elite position of the leading cadre group, which is often bolstered by informal relationships. One aspect relates to the 'political families'; that is, cadre families whose members have different positions in the administration, often centring on one leading individual. This does not necessarily reflect nepotism, but the fact is that once a certain status is reached, the children of leading cadres will obtain an especially good education and can therefore more easily enter important government departments. If we look at the early periods of reforms, this was leveraged by the practice of *danwei* guarantees for the employment of *danwei* members' children, gradually phasing out in the 1980s. The impact of family relations upon status is certainly also retreating because of the one-child policy; however, quasi-kin relations mattered until today. This means that a leading cadre may 'adopt' a child of a related person and act as that child's mentor and sponsor accordingly.[30]

Considering the general situation, one may observe that the cadre stratum reproduces itself via socialization, as most cadres have parents who are also cadres, and most parents already have urban *hukou*. Therefore, there is a clear status distinction between the village level and the township level, with farmers having a low probability of entering the cadre stratum. This is in stark contrast to the conditions of Maoist times; however, one has to take into consideration that the stronger position of farmers resulted also from the fact that a larger share of cadre positions was funded by the villages. With the abolition of the People's Communes, the township and county cadres have emerged as an urbanizing elite which is basically closed to farmers, thus reproducing the urban/rural status distinction of modernism also in the context of grassroots-level administration. With the increasing differentiation in the educational system, these status differences harden, since farmers' children face growing difficulties in entering better quality schools. So, the cadre stratum excels in accumulating social and human capital that stabilizes its power in the local state.

Beyond the context of the local state, the notion of status is deeply ingrained in the administrative hierarchy of China and has the special and important feature of being merged with the status order of the Communist Party. In spite of the fact that reforms have implemented a clear formal separation between Party and government administration, the fact remains that the CCP nomenclature integrates all important career patterns across most political, economic and social domains in China. The nomenclature is controlled by the Organization Department of the CCP. We do not need to look at the details here, which include a comprehensive system of personal files containing full records of all relevant individual activities of members. What is important in the current context is that the nomenclature regulates the assignments of individuals to positions of leadership on different levels and in different domains. In doing so, a general system of classifying positions is applied that I have already briefly outlined in Chapter 3. In the local state, the nomenclature covers the group of the leading cadres and the candidates for those positions. This has many practical consequences; for example, there is a special directory which is only accessible to this group that allows for speedy, direct and confidential interactions. I have already pointed out that the relationship between party nomenclature and administration is directly reflected in the career patterns of leading cadres which always involve an alternation between party and government offices. In these patterns, it is always clear that advancement happens via moving up in the general nomenclature hierarchy which is controlled by the party.

This system has two important consequences which make the Chinese political economy unique in a global comparison, and which I highlighted in Chapter 3. The first is that, by implication, two positions in two different domains are exactly comparable in terms of relative status. Thus, for example, the status of a mayor in a third-tier city may be compared with the status of the CEO of a large central government SOE which has a branch in that city. If the CEO visits the place, her or his status is higher than the status of the mayor. In other words, in China status is fungible and measurable, unlike the situation in most other countries. Everywhere comparisons of social reputation are possible, for instance, between a university president and a CEO; but if the two meet, there is no direct and exact way to compare their status. In China, the two would know exactly on which position in the nomenclature they are located. It is also important to note that this implies that the relative positions of the organizations which the leaders represent are also comparable. Actually, we can say that it is the nomenclature which also defines a status order on the organizational level across all social domains. With regard to government or military organization this is straightforward, since there is a direct correspondence between the nomenclature hierarchy and the hierarchy of jurisdictions, for example. But considering corporations or other civil organizations such as universities, this is not immediately evident. Then, the exact nomenclature position of the leader of a particular organization is also a marker that signals the general importance and status of the organization in the context of Chinese politics, as these valuations are ultimately conducted by the Communist Party. So, for example, the presidents of various universities located in Beijing will have very different nomenclature status, thus signalling the importance of their respective organizations in the educational domain as embedded in general policy contexts. This is also salient when strategic policy directions are changed, as this is often accompanied by reshuffling the rank order of the leading positions in different organizations. If a certain government function and the respective administrative structure is deemed to become more important strategically, the rank of the leading position is enhanced.

Further, we have already seen that career patterns are defined in the nomenclature, and not necessarily in terms of the domains. In other words, an individual can easily move across domains when moving upward. This creates a high permeability between the domains. For example, a deputy mayor may become the president of a local university. In addition, this also means that career aspirations are never entirely tied up with a particular domain or organization. In other words, a successful leader in China always has to expect that success implies that in moving up the career path she or he will leave the current organization and may even move to another domain. This is a major difference between private companies and state-owned companies, as we will see in Chapter 6. As a result, many Chinese leaders are trained as generalists, accumulating experience in different domains. So, assigning a deputy mayor to the position of a university president by no means signals any qualification in science, but may reflect the strategic goals of higher level leaders in developing and enhancing the role of the university in regional economic development. For this, the new president would certainly need good knowledge of regional economic structures and trends, and should be well connected to industry and politics. If the new role also implies an upgrading of the nomenclature location of the president, this sends a strong signal about the strategic intentions of higher level leaders.

To sum up, and continuing with the general argument advanced in Chapter 3, I argue that the CCP is a ritual organization in the sense that it is the Party which defines and implements a status order that encompasses the entire political, economic and social systems of China. It is straightforward to see that we cannot count this as an 'informal institution' unless we adopt the viewpoint of political systems in Western industrial nations, where this kind of Party impact may be seen as informal, such as when government office is allocated based on Party membership and certain norms of reciprocity between the different parties. In China, I argue, the CCP is the organization which implements a status order that is formally independent from the structure of government, and which is effectively driving the power distinctions in the entire system. Then, if the CCP, for many years now, advances the notion of separating government and party, this in fact even strengthens this ritual function of the party because it accentuates the distinctions between ordinary administrators and those who are Party members.

It should be noted that the ritual assignment of positions to certain organizations is therefore an important means to shape the complex bargaining processes among different organizations in larger policy domains, based on the implicated status of those organizations. This fact has been becoming more and more significant with the liberalization of the economic and social system. In most societal domains, the CCP no longer directly exerts control via mandatory directives. However, the Party still raises the modernist claim that it is the avant-garde of social, economic and cultural development. So, the status order of the nomenclature is a signalling system which translates strategic valuations of the party into a status order of organizations that implement those goals or are seen as having to follow and adapt to these goals. Then, the assigned status partly determines the outcome of negotiations between the organizations. In other words, the status order of the nomenclature contextualizes interactions among formally autonomous organizations in such a way that, on the one hand, many degrees of freedom regarding the outcomes are maintained, but at the same time the strategic orientations of the party are also realized. So, we meet a clear case of the confluence of the two notions of ritual: the ritual of the CCP status order operates as a ritual that turns its strategic orientations into common knowledge of actors in bargaining processes. Therefore, I argue that policy implementation in China is ritualized to a large degree: thus, we can speak of ritualistic economic policy. This is mainly achieved in conceiving economic policy as a task in leadership. This leadership function materializes in the complex institutional network of government, especially as being shaped by the different dimensions of *tiao* vs. *kuai* and *lingdao* vs. *yewu guanxi*.[31]

In this sense, the CCP is a political organization whose members are qualifying for leadership, and who take responsibility in implementing the strategic orientations of the Party. The mechanism that achieves this is controlling and enforcing the political status order on Chinese society. Therefore, I claim that a major political function of the CCP is defining and controlling ritual. If we adopt this perspective, the family resemblances with Imperial China spring to mind. The ritual function of the CCP was already most salient in the Maoist era, when ideological radicalism highlighted the moral status of Party members, partly linked with criteria for status that were aligned with family history and class status. For example, in the rural areas revolutionary status was assigned to poor peasants, who were also expected to show moral rigidity in fostering collectivist values and behaviours when assuming cadre positions. This highlights the role of ritual in an extreme way, as at the same time political leaders struggled against the perceived trend of the bureaucratization of government, thus actually playing havoc with formal government institutions.

In this sense, we may say that there were two dimensions to state building in China, with the CCP extending the ritual order as a lead process, and bureaucratic integration only following on gradually, being still incomplete today, especially in the local state. Remarkably, in Maoist times, this ritual order partly integrated traditional notions of ritual: for example, the idea that class status is inherited by children from their parents was actually reproducing traditional notions of inheritance via the paternal line. Conceiving of the social status order as a moral order also replicated Confucian notions of the primacy of the moral dimension in exerting the power of government. So, the Party member, in particular in a leadership position, was expected to be a moral model for the ordinary population. In this sense, the Maoist radical rejection of markets also reflected traditional concerns about the erosion of moral commitment in pursuing private profit.[32]

This emphasis on moral behaviour in ritual has been substantially weakened in the reform era. In its place, education has emerged as a major criterion in marking the elevated role of CCP members vis-à-vis the general population. However, this obviously does not invalidate the hypothesis of family resemblances with the Imperial past where education loomed large in the form of the examination system in the Civil Service. This already applies for admission to the party, and continues on higher levels of careers. In recent times, recruitment policy has focused on education, with the largest share of new members coming from universities. Political criteria continue to matter, of course, with a moral dimension still applying in terms of civic attitudes. In other words, the CCP is evolving into an elite organization, with educational level being an essential status signal, and the general expectation that Party members display political loyalty and civic responsibility. This applies on every level. The conditions in the local state are of special interest here, because the glass ceiling between the county level and the higher levels is also defined by educational level, as most leading cadres on the county level joined the official career path without a university degree, which would be necessary to move up to higher levels. However, at the same time, educational levels mark distinctions within the local state. Taking these different aspects together, we may say that ideological control in the CCP still has a distinct ritualistic character, which goes beyond the perceptions of many Western observers who only see widespread cynicism in following ideological norms. Indeed, we might relate this to the distinct form of expressivism in terms of the 'sincerity' of publicly displayed behaviour.[33]

After admission to the party, intra-party education continues in a nation-wide system of Party schools on all administrative levels. Party schools are of different quality, depending on location and administrative level, but, generally speaking, they offer professional education together with ideological indoctrination and behavioural standardization. On the highest levels, this system has shifted to an approach that is reminiscent of business schools, especially in the USA. This means that, programmes include a heavy input on business administration, management and public policy, even offering degree programmes, but at the same time networking is essential. Advancement within the status hierarchy is impossible without running through the appropriate programmes at Party schools. Every career step is accompanied by educational programmes matching this step in terms of content, but also confirming and reinforcing political and ideological loyality. The system is increasingly showing disparities in quality between the local and the central state, and also between provinces and regions on different levels of development. This reinforces its role in creating a national elite as opposed to the local elites, and accentuates status distinctions in habitus and social capital. For example, high-level party schools often actively promote a globalized outlook of students and offer access to the latest intellectual trends in business, which differs substantially from the conditions of local-level schools which emphasize traditional ideological training.[34]

One important function of Party schools is to bring leaders from different localities and regions together who otherwise would rarely meet. In the context of ideological sessions they may be forced to evaluate their own work openly, thus sharing private and status-sensitive information with strangers. So, this experience also creates personal bonds between the participants. As a result, the Party schools are hotbeds for creating network relations, as is analysed in Chapter 5. These networks obtain different functions. For example, they are channels through which policy models and local experience are diffused nationwide, they enable investment contacts and business projects, and, most importantly, they also create connectivity across the status hierarchy. The latter can be important in mobilizing support for policy experiments (see the following section). The educational process also serves in unifying the habitus of party elites and enhancing the awareness of elevated status in society, especially in the sense of representing a modernist avant-garde.

These networks are also essential for enabling 'soft' guidance even in national policy-making. Thus, they are another means as to how the ritual order influences policy design and implementation (see the following section). If political institutions such as People's Congresses often appear to be rubber stamp organizations, this hides the fact that in the often very long processes of decision-making and law-making, informal processes take place in leaders' networks (compare the discussion of the planning process in the following section). Through these networks, guiding opinions of national leaders may diffuse nationwide, and may also meet comments and reactions. One outward manifestation of this phenomenon is the speed by which sometimes simple utterances of national leaders can trigger very fast shifts in local-level decision-making. Messages, assessments and opinions flow quickly through networks, today mediated via smartphones.

So, we can say that the CCP implements a culturalist approach to integrating national policy-making and policy design mediated via the design and management of cadre careers. Culturalism is expressed in the role of ideology in national leadership. It is important to distinguish between form and content here, especially with reference to economic matters. In practice, the CCP has given up most fundamental tenets of Marxism and adopted what is more or less a neoliberal doctrine of economic policy, with some important exceptions, such as maintaining a significant share of state ownership in strategically important sectors. The organizational approach as a leaders' organization has even changed admission policy in co-opting entrepreneurs and businessmen, hence the archetypical capitalists. As a consequence, what remains of ideology is an emphasis on very general cultural notions. This has been mainly covered in the propagation of different models of 'civilization', which from time to time also include 'spiritual' control, as is evident in the most recent campaigns against government critics and civil society. However, generally speaking the emphasis is on modernism as a cultural notion, with a strong bent towards loyalty to the nation and the party.[35]

Hence, in particular, the most recent campaigns against corruption may be seen as a measure of culturalistic and ritualistic control. Corruption in China operates partly in a grey area which is circumscribed by another element of ritual and status order, namely conspicuous consumption and gift-giving. I take a closer look at this in Chapter 5, but anticipate one point here, namely that in spite of standard comments by Western observers, corruption has not yet achieved a systemic dimension, but remains a local and personal deviance, though being widespread. This image is certainly also necessary for Chinese policy-makers in order to create a bulwark towards further erosion of commitments against corruption, and is cast into the dualism between 'local' and 'central', as most forms of corruption are in fact or in public images local misbehaviours which are actually cleaned up by the central power; so, the centre represents the systemic capacity to contain individual moral failure.[36] But, in fact, in the grey area it can be difficult to clearly identify the specific flow of benefits, such as when businesspeople invest into good relations with local officials by means of invitations to lavish restaurants and fancy karaoke bars. This sort of status consumption is itself an aspect of the ritual economy, and hence clashes with rituals as defined by purist Communist ideology. So, we cannot simply say that the disruption of the luxury goods market in China following the launch of the anti-corruption campaigns directly reflects the extent of corruption in the economy. But the anti-corruption campaign imposes ritualistic control upon the individual behaviour of party members in society.

The ritual role of the CCP is also strengthened via the recent developments in the relationship between Party and civil society, which has even been labelled 'retreat of government' and 'advancement of the party'; although generalizations are difficult to make, with vanguard areas such as Guangdong province where the CCP has supported the growth of civil society organizations within certain limits, and a partial backlash with the tightening of authoritarian controls in the first years of the Xi Jinping leadership. The general idea is that in the course of the rapid urbanization processes, ongoing structural changes in the economy and the increasing number and growing qualitative scope of societal tensions and conflicts makes it increasingly difficult for the local state to handle local society. Indeed, the local state plays a pivotal role here, since all social conflicts are first of all local phenomena, and, correspondingly, the performance assessment of local cadres places a high priority on their capacity to handle these phenomena.

One approach being pursued is to enhance the entire administrative apparatus that deals with issues of social stability, both in the local state and in the national security apparatus. This happens in two different ways. The first is to enhance the number of staff and increase the resources devoted to the security apparatus. The second is to create structures which also have a preventive function: one way is to develop close networks between the administration and grassroots society via the activation of citizens in surveying and handling potential for tensions. The two measures are often integrated under the umbrella of one coordinating agency, such as 'zonghe ban' (综合办), which covers the classical security apparatus and other departments, for example, handling petitions, and includes 'part-time workers' in social organizations such as schools.[37] The other approach is to allow for the emergence of civil society initiatives that would largely focus on relieving social strain and scarcity of resources that may help ease social tensions. Naturally, civil society initiatives in these areas would often also adopt a moralistic language of support and harmony, as, for example, in the upsurge of initiatives devoted to educational issues, such as catering for the needs of migrant children, or in arranging emergency relief during disasters. Interestingly, these initiatives may also be related to religious motives, reaching from Christianity to Buddhism and also Confucianism, the latter interpreted as a civic and secular moral belief system. In the latter case, there is also the explicit reference to the notion that Chinese society needs civilizational efforts which includes moral improvement.[38]

With regard to the CCP, civil society is partly co-opted, but may also be the target of direct organizational design, with the party actively promoting the creation of non-governmental organizations. In these cases, Party members also assume a leading role in developing those organizations. In other cases, the CCP may exert pressure to involve party members in the organization and potentially also surveillance of NGO activities. Without claiming general validity of this point, this means that the CCP increasingly assumes the role of ritually defining and circumscribing civil society in China, thus providing the arena in which these activities might unfold, at the same time increasing autonomous spaces in the public sphere, but also limiting their scope and reach. Whether this will unfold into a systematic pattern is not clear for the time being. But in vanguard areas of reforms the slogan 'Big party, small government, big society' is explicitly used as a counterpart to the formula 'Small government, big society'. Thus, I claim that what emerges is a ritualistic form of civil society, with ritual embodied in the organization of the CCP. This pattern would actually stand in the tradition of 'orthopractic' control of society, since it would leave room for alternative beliefs, such as opening up space for religious organizations. Yet, what counts is proper behaviour, as displayed in public actions. This allows for the emergence of a new form of authoritarian government, which has been aptly labelled as 'consultative authoritarianism' or 'responsive authoritarianism'. By using these terms observers wish to express that the extension of networks between the Party and society not only means that the Party enhances indirect control of society, but also becomes more open to flows of information and public opinion.[39]

One area where these developments also impact upon the economy and hence may further unfold its ritual nature is the labour market. Although China is formally following the tripartite model of regulating the relationship between employers and employees, the activities of trade unions are tightly constrained, with no possibility to set up autonomous trade unions outside the framework of the CCP-controlled national union organization. So, in fact, China approaches a 'quadripartite system' in which workers form partly autonomous pressure groups which are not directly represented by unions. In case of tensions, the local government adopts a pivotal role, given the fact that containing social unrest is a policy priority. Then, the labour unions are mostly assigned to the role of mediators between aggrieved workers and employers. However, this model has come under strain with the increasing role of foreign direct investment and private business especially in areas where these are concentrated, such as Guangdong province. This found expression in the strong growth of incidents involving wildcat strikes and other forms of labour conflicts, mostly involving migrant workers. This problem was exacerbated following the financial crisis which created strong pressure on industrial restructuring and challenged the traditional model of low wages as a pivot of competitive advantage. So we meet a specific issue of economic policy which sits at the core of the traditional growth model and relates to the notion of strategically steering the model towards consumption-based growth, which requires an increase in the share of wages in the distribution of GDP, as we have already seen in Chapter 3. However, the difficulty is that there is no arena in which wage bargaining can take place which would result in the required increase in the wage share.[40]

The local state is in a quandary here, because the goals that drive the behaviour of its cadres focus on growth and social stability, which are both endangered by increasing tensions on the labour market. So far, this has resulted in the alignment of interests between the local state and employers, hence government and capital, vis-à-vis labour. This amounts to a paradoxical role of the CCP and its affiliated trade unions. Therefore, we observe first steps towards strengthening the tripartite system, which would imply that the official trade unions more directly represent workers in a formal wage bargaining process. Considering the existing cases, this would imply that the CCP assumes the role of a moderator and facilitator which would exert strategic leadership in decentralized wage bargaining procedures. This leadership would be based on the authority of the leaders of the local state. In other words, reforming the Chinese labour market would result in establishing a ritual order for the relationship between labour and capital. Again, this would imply a retreat of formal government organizations, akin to the aforementioned developments in civil society. There are different possible tracks of further evolution, reaching from the establishment of forms of collective bargaining towards the revival of mediation. Mediation is of special interest here, as it builds on a central idea in the design of the juridical system of modern China that partly continues with Imperial traditions, and which accentuates the role of the local state in conflict resolution. This means that mediation is an explicit formal element in conflict resolution before and even simultaneous with formal litigation, thus partly obviating direct reliance on formal law. In the context of the local state, this means that labour conflicts are being resolved with an explicit consideration for the strategic interests and goals of the local state, often reinstating the importance of developmental goals against the interests of workers.[41]

In concluding this section, I keep as an essential insight one of the pillars of ritual in the Chinese economic style: the Communist Party; this is embodied in the nomenclature and its impact upon the status order of organizational entities. Political ideology is a medium of culturalistic governance, in particular in the local state. The CCP is a centralizing force, but this does not imply bureaucratic centralization, thus manifesting strong family resemblances with Imperial times. Therefore, the role of the CCP as a ritual organization combines with another major feature of policy-making in China, namely the much-cited experimentalism.

Chinese experimentalism and economic policy-making

In Chapter 3 I outlined the basic structures of localism and regional property rights that define the interface between government and the economy in China. Many observers have noted that one of the most important features of the Chinese economic system has emerged from this peculiar structure, which is the intense locational competition among territorial units on different levels. This phenomenon raises the important question of how this competition is regulated. As a matter of fact, there is no formal constitutional framework that establishes this regulation in a stable way. One case in point is the fiscal system considered in the previous section. On the one hand, the 'tax-sharing system' establishes a clear division of taxes along the levels of government, but at the same time entitlements to certain amounts of taxes are still governed by the regional property rights structure that has historically evolved. This reflects the universal validity of the *tiao kuai* dualism: the *tiao* line may imply regulatory centralization, but this does not necessarily restrict territorial autonomy in important respects. This is one reason why non-funded mandates play such an important role in establishing central policy authority. The *tiao kuai* dynamics results in what I call a territorial status order. Hence, I surmise that territorial competition in China is mainly regulated in ritual form.

One of the distinctive features of the administrative hierarchy of China is the status distinction of jurisdictions that only partly reproduces the formal administrative hierarchy. This status distinction may be determined by economic criteria, in particular the distinction between central and peripheral territories. Economic criteria also underlie possible changes in the formal status of jurisdictions, such as when upgrading a county to a higher level urban entity. This matters in terms of economic policy, as jurisdictions with different status typically have different degrees of freedom in economic planning and project implementation; and it defines the scope of inter-jurisdictional competition for status: leaders may aspire to ultimately achieving a change of status of their jurisdiction, thus enjoying an extension of rights of local policy-making.

In other words, we can say that there is also a status order of local states in China. This status order of local states is projected into a system of giving certain rights of economic policy-making to certain jurisdictions. These rights may be generic with reference to the level of administration, which means that higher level jurisdictions also have more rights in terms of making decisions, for example, about infrastructure projects. They may also be specific to certain strategic programmes defined by the central state, both the central government and the provincial governments, such as when particular jurisdictions obtain special rights in implementing experimental economic policies. Finally, there is an informal dimension of rights which emerges out of historical trajectories and bargaining processes and which may be reflected in certain reputations of particular places, such as when Zhejiang province and Wenzhou in particular have gained the reputation as being the avant-garde of private business, which implies that they may adopt partially autonomous strategic orientations in economic policies favouring private business.

Basically, we can say that territorial competition occurs on two levels. One is the competition among local states, which includes both the county and the municipality level, with a high dynamics of feedback. This means that success in territorial competition determines the relative administrative and ritual status of local states, for example, when counties are upgraded to municipalities. The other is competition among provinces, which happens within the structures of the central state. This implies that formal regulation is stronger. A distinct mechanism is that many central- and national-level laws leave room for interpretation and explicitly require completion by more detailed legal and administrative regulations, which are largely designed and implemented on the provincial level. In comparison, local states do not operate mainly via this form of formal legal measures, but only through administrative measures which, however, may even transcend or stay in tension with central-level legal norms.

The status order of local states is embedded in a distinct style of leading economic policy on the central and provincial level which we can clearly identify as culturalistic. This characterization refers to the role of 'models' in advancing certain policies. A particularly interesting case is the guidance of local state policies via the announcement and propagation of models. For example, in the general framework of 'Building a New Socialist Countryside', certain counties may be identified as model counties in implementing the policy. On the one hand, this reflects the fact that the policy itself is only defined in very general terms, thus leaving much policy leeway for specifying measures in particular local contexts. On the other hand, selecting a particular model leads directly to very detailed and contextualized policies of individual cases, which often cannot be transferred to other contexts without substantial modifications. Model counties also receive special financial and other kinds of policy support which further constrains direct transfers of their experience, lacking these additional resources. Yet, this approach means that the general policy is finally substantiated via a number of exemplars which diffuse nationally and inspire imitation and adaptation in other places. This is a form of culturalistic policy implementation, since these transfers happen without actually limiting the scope of policy autonomy of local states. It is also a ritualistic form, since the distinction between model cases and ordinary cases establishes a status distinction. This status distinction is a major driver of competition between jurisdictions. Achieving model status can ultimately result also in formal changes of status if economic development is sustainable and also leads to significant structural changes.[42]

The role of models in communicating strategic orientations of economic policy relates to the pivotal role of experimentation during the reform period. However, this goes back even to the Yan'an period when the CCP developed a distinct policy style that emphasized the interaction between centrally designed policies and local conditions. So, experimentation also relates to the fundamental dualism of the central vs. local state. Going back to these times, a distinct policy process emerged in China which remained characteristic even across the ruptures of radical Maoism and reforms. In this policy process, there is principled recognition of autonomous action on the local level, provided that certain very general strategic orientations would be observed. I venture the hypothesis that this attitude has deep cultural roots that may be traced back to notions of local efficacy in popular religion, such as is reflected in *fengshui* practices. This means that successful action is only seen as becoming enabled by paying attention to the confluence of forces at a particular place and time, which therefore requires a deep understanding of these local conditions. Imposing certain general solutions designed irrespective of these conditions is doomed to failure. Therefore, implementing general strategies requires a delicate balance between top-down and bottom-up processes, which can only be based on accumulating experiences with a series of local experiments. This may even include deviant action, although, as in the management of popular religion, this always entails the risk of backlash by the authorities. Yet, if local experimentation proves to be successful, it may be gradually recognized and finally acknowledged as a 'model'. Achieving this status means that the local experiment becomes an element in communicating the scope and content of strategic orientations on the national level. This process is guided by an explicit normative framework cast into specific language that allows for reflecting about the degrees of deviance from standards, the threshold when this pattern may be more formally recognized, and when it may be accepted as a model.[43]

Putting this into an even more abstract context, I argue that experimentalism in Chinese economic policy reflects the fundamental cognitive stance of field dependence as analysed in Chapter 2. It is of the utmost importance to realize that this gives a distinct meaning to 'experimentalism' which may otherwise be seen as only pragmatic muddling through and a trial-and-error process. In fact, field dependence means that experimentalism also implies the contextualized application of general principles, and so may also be characterized as 'experience-based policy implementation'. Therefore, we can relate ritual, culturalism and field dependence in one explanatory approach that identifies mechanisms of policy design and implementation in China. In this approach, ritual is assigned to the evaluative aspect of economic policy and to establishing common knowledge about these valuations among the community of actors across different local states and the central state. For example, a 'model' might be established as legitimate policy reference for 'unifying the thinking' among policy-makers, often communicated via documents that do not represent administrative acts but are 'opinions', 'yijian' (意见) or 'explanations', 'shuoming' (说明). As I discussed in the previous section, a locality might assume model status and hence also receive an upgrade in the administrative hierarchy which goes together with a promotion of its leaders, probably also including the transfer to another unit with even higher status. In the networks of leading cadres, this is a signal that rapidly communicates the model nationwide, often also supported by regular study trips of cadres to this model location. Eventually, these processes result in the convergence of national policy which may be finally recognized by issuing laws and regulations that fix the institutional status quo achieved.

Experimentalism is a defining feature of Chinese policy-making, resulting in a peculiar policy cycle that we can often observe in China. Local experiments happen, almost always with the consent of higher level authorities, even central-level ones. If they are successful they may be studied and copied in other areas. If they remain successful, the experience is evaluated on the highest level, and possibly cast into national recommendations, regulations and laws. Typically, laws often remain very general and even opaque, awaiting more detailed administrative specifications which are often done initially on the provincial level. So, even a legal fixation explicitly allows for further experimentation. This distinct policy process should be seen also in the light of the structures of the CCP hierarchy. Although there are cases for that, it seems unlikely that higher level leaders are rarely involved as sponsors of local experiments. On the contrary, experiments that appear politically sensitive are largely supported or even suggested by high-level leaders and implemented via their personal networks in the CCP. This kind of communication is difficult to observe and prove after the fact. Yet, we may assume that local experiments are often supported by higher level leaders. We can detail this mechanism only with the help of the additional insights into personal networks achieved in Chapter 5, but we note at this point that high-status individuals in the CCP reach through the entire hierarchy in suggesting and supporting local experiments.[44]

It is interesting to note that experimentalism is also part and parcel of the formal policy process throughout the reform period, as in the case of the officially pronounced special economic zones that were a central policy pattern in the early years of reforms and continue to be so, with the latest example the Shanghai Free Trade Zone. The latter example reveals an interesting basic principle in Chinese policy-making which also appears to relate to cognitive features of field dependence. Local experiments can in fact suffer from functional inconsistency which even triggers deviant action. Therefore, most Western observers would say that only a systematic and comprehensive approach will work. The Chinese approach is heavily contextualized in the sense that experiments are seen as part of a contextual shift, and the resulting actions may show the way for further developments, even if they reveal inconsistencies in the beginning and hence appear to be dysfunctional. In comparison, the field independent approach would require a consistent and comprehensive design which takes into consideration in advance all possible dysfunctional side effects. In the Chinese approach, these side effects, though difficult to control, are seen as important elements in changing the contextual forces of further developments, thus actually working as triggers for further change.

This approach is often termed 'Crossing the river by groping the stones', so allegedly claiming that there is no blueprint. However, if we look at early documents of reforms such as the one promulgating the Socialist Market Economy for the first time in 1993, these are detailed and explicit in identifying the goal. Thus, it seems that Chinese experimentalism is mainly an expression of a strategic approach to policy-making, and thus actually reflects the permanent features of the ritual economy. In other words, experiments serve to identify measures that are useful in changing local contexts of decision-making, such that certain broadly defined policy goals are 'spontaneously' fulfilled by local decision-makers. We have already met one important example. When the fiscal reforms of 1994 were implemented, the context for dealing with local SOEs was changed fundamentally, creating strong incentives for privatizing them. In this case, the central government did not have to announce a national privatization policy, but in fact triggered it. The role of central policy was mainly one of culturalistic leadership, with slogans that emphasized efficiency, modernity and so forth, but avoided or even outlawed the term 'privatization'. Other important examples include the so-called 'double-track' system of the 1980s and 1990s, in which market prices and plan allocation co-existed, thus creating strong incentives for improving capacity utilization in order to benefit the profit opportunities from market pricing. This also induced much corruption, but this was also a side effect of creating incentives for lower level cadres to open up markets and start organizational changes in SOEs, which suffered from the competitive pressures created by the surge of TVE development.[45]

So, the characterization of economic policies during the reform period as 'transitional' misleadingly applies field-independent cognitive characterizations of policies in the Chinese case. The Chinese approach does not aim at setting up consistent systemic frameworks for action, but at strategic consistency in a constantly changing environment, not the least because of the impacts triggered by the policy. Strategy implementation takes inconsistencies into account as even a positive determinant of incentivizing further changes.

One of the most principled strategic decisions at the beginning of the reform period was to subordinate most policy domains to the general goal of achieving growth and development. This decision was in accordance with the modernist growth model that we studied in the previous chapter. As a result, we can interpret many measures of economic policy and the ways of implementation as a form of ritual, in the sense of establishing common knowledge regarding this policy priority. The most direct expression of this ritualization of economic growth may be discerned in the evaluation of leading cadres, where the economic growth achieved in their jurisdiction is a central criterion of evaluating their performance and determining their careers. The ritualization of the growth target is visible in many forms of public representations, such as the annual reports of different territorial units or the policy announcements. One specific example is the publication of rankings of localities in terms of growth performance, which amounts to a 'naming-and-shaming' mechanism, thus directly activating also network mechanisms of face and reputation that I analyse in Chapter 5. This is particularly relevant in the context of the local state, such as in the relationships among the groups of leading cadres at both township and county level. So, one of the essential mechanisms of incentivizing local cadres is a ritual one and does not draw upon direct administrative guidance, thus keeping an autonomous space for individual decision-making in spite of tight evaluation.[46]

Generally, there is a set of criteria in assessing cadre performance which distinguishes between 'veto' criteria and more fungible and substitutable criteria. For example, maintaining social and political stability is a veto criterion in the sense that political unrest will certainly jeopardize a career. In the reform era, achieving a certain level of economic growth also moved to a central position in determining career perspectives, though not exclusively. In closely aligning growth performance and nomenclature, the former achieves the function of a status marker and hence is a ritualistic notion. Interestingly, when the central government recently announced the 'new normal' with reduced expectations about economic growth, this was accompanied by intensive efforts in political communication in order to change this perception of ritualistic obligations. In other words, the goal of economic growth has been part and parcel of common knowledge in the domain of the economy, encompassing the behavioural patterns of cadres and other leading actors.

This is an essential element in the competition models that have been developed to explain the success of China in terms of growth and development. On all levels of the nomenclature, competitions between leaders take place, in which the most successful leader will advance up the career ladder. This has many implications for policy design. In particular, local leaders will tend to favour projects that directly affect economic development, and will neglect projects that have only long-term effects or do not show up in GDP. This implies that the status order in the cadre evaluation process also creates a status order of policy domains. A standard example for this is the relatively weak position of environmental policy bureaux in the local state, in spite of the fact that 'greening growth' has been a central government concern since the turn of the millennium. Since environmental goals have low priority in the cadre evaluation criteria, they are in an unfavourable trade-off with growth objectives, thus leading towards comparative neglect. Therefore, we may also speak of the ritualization of economic policy in terms of a status hierarchy among policy domains. By implication, this means that achieving a shift in policy focus towards the environment also requires one to redefine the ritual order of criteria in cadre assessment.[47]

The analysis thus far is lacking considerable detail, however, which is also important in assessing the general nature of economic policy-making in China. This even refers to the fundamental question of how market and plan relate in practice, which I will discuss in more detail in the following section. At this point, it is important to realize that the retreat of mandatory planning did not imply that detailed goal setting would also be abolished in the cadre assessment system.

Since the 1980s the internal administration of government has adopted a system of 'managing by objectives' which is institutionally implemented in the widespread use of internal contracts between principals and agents. This appears to tie in with a central aspect of the ritual economy in Imperial times, in which contracts played a central role. In other words, beyond the role of certain core indicators such as economic growth, administrators were subject to a detailed and very comprehensive system of goal setting. This applies for both the central and the local state. It is essential in understanding the way in which the county leadership is actually implemented. Lower level cadres are bound into a system of agreements and contracts about achieving particular goals in their area of responsibility. This is remarkable, since we can also observe that the retreat of economic planning and the corresponding growth of the market was especially fast and comprehensive on the level of the local state, with state-owned companies increasingly becoming a feature of the central state and the urban economy. Yet, this did not imply the reduction of goal setting in the government bureaucracy of the local state. The county government sets an extremely high number of goals for the township-level governments which include all kinds of economic activity and social indicators. However, this does not mean that the county government directly issues mandatory plans of implementation. In other words, it remains the task of the local administration to design measures that may help achieve the goals. On the one hand, this may be seen as an expression of the experimental approach, but we need to note that this approach also applies for regular policy implementation. So, there is a systematic tension between the tightness of the goal system and the open nature of the system of implementation, which places lower level administrators under very high performance pressure.[48]

This puts the reduction of mandatory planning into perspective, since management by objectives certainly encourages all kinds of governmental intervention in the local economy. Therefore, we have to judge the retreat of the plan in the context of the ritual economy, in the sense that the competition system and the status hierarchy of cadres continues to undergird a strong role of government even in the market context. This role is also based on the strong centralization of the policy process, culminating in the person of the Party secretary of the county. So, the aforementioned strategic role of this position is also reflected in the detailed system of management by objectives that guides the behaviour on all subordinate levels. Goal fulfilment is not only assessed internally, but is also reflected in publicly available information. As I have already mentioned, annual reports of counties will inevitably contain a rank order of townships in their jurisdiction which reflects the overall success of local measures in economic policy. This means that since it is common knowledge that local economic performance is a central criterion of cadre evaluation, there is an immediate impact upon the responsible local cadres. So, again, we observe an important role of rank and status distinctions that will also affect the career prospects of officials. If certain localities manage to come up with a top position over a number of years, this will substantially improve the promotion prospects of the top cadres. Since success breeds success, the important side effect in terms of regional development is that typically there emerges also a status distinction between 'elite' townships and average or peripheral ones, since the former also attract more support or attention by higher level authorities, including the role of former cadres promoted from there. This often results also in policy preferences, such as larger amounts of subsidies for local projects transferred from higher level administrations.

This public nature of performance evaluation activates the role of face in the networks of leading cadres, as I have indicated previously. Reported economic performance becomes an element in the personal reputation of the responsible leading cadres vis-à-vis their peers, and less in the sense of accountability towards the local population. However, as we have seen in the earlier discussion of local-level accountability, this can be also a strong determinant of cadre behaviour at the grassroots level. At higher levels, peer groups matter most. Low performance of local jurisdictions implies loss of face and shame for responsible leading cadres, the anticipation of which may be regarded even as the strongest incentive to achieve local growth, independent from the preferences of the local population. This fact leads to the phenomenon that growth-oriented policy measures are often a major trigger for expressions of local dissatisfaction by authorities, such as when land is requisitioned for urbanization projects, local environmental conditions are neglected in order to keep costs of local enterprises low, or when local cadres collude with local companies in labour disputes. In other words, what has often been designated as 'state capitalism' is a manifestation of underlying ritual practices and routines in the cadre management system.

As a result, the ritual nomenclature mechanism creates strong competition among jurisdictions on every level, relative to the peers. So, for example, townships within a county may compete against each other, as the result will finally show up in the county-level ranking of townships; counties within a prefecture compete against each other, and so forth. This also drives experimentalism and autonomous policy initiatives at the respective levels. One important effect of this system is that policies are shaped by the regular rhythms of tenure in public office, an effect that can be compared to the electoral cycles in democratic systems. In case of the latter, what matters is policies that cater to certain needs and expectations of the electorate; in case of China peer groups and superordinate authorities matter more than the interests of citizens. The resulting policy process is therefore shaped by a project management-type approach; this particularly applies to the Party secretary leading the local state. Typically, the Party secretary will identify a number of projects that can be managed within the period of his tenure and which aim at pushing economic development ahead. These projects should be different from those pursued by his predecessor, at least in the sense of focal policies, and they would be seen as improving economic performance relative to other counties and to the predecessor. So, we realize that the cadre competition also features the essential property of status competition, which is operating with the Red Queen mechanism or as an 'arms race'. Since status comparison with others is crucial, a ratchet effect emerges that explains the extremely rapid diffusion of policy models in China. Once a policy proves to be successful in one jurisdiction, many other jurisdictions will aim at copying this success for fear of losing out in the status comparison.

Interestingly, the Red Queen dynamics also implies that leading cadres would tend to make the mistake of taking models out of their context, thus just copying the policy measure and violating the principles of experimentalism. So, there are many dysfunctional effects of status competition that are manifest in local policy failures. Ritual politics therefore fosters the ritual copying of policies irrespective of local conditions. This phenomenon has driven processes such as the many failed attempts at rural industrialization in remote counties which are intended to copy the tremendous success of TVEs in regions such as Jiangsu province, or the outright policy mania in setting up industrial and technology parks all over the country. This requires intervention by central authorities and has actually driven the re-strengthening of alternative approaches to planning that I analyse in the following section.[49]

In this ritual dimension of territorial competition driven by status considerations, one particularly salient phenomenon is the role of statistics. Up until today, Chinese statistics suffers from distortions, biases and outright fakes. In the 2000s, the gap between the aggregate provincial-level GDP data and the national GDP has increased each year by more than 10 per cent. Only following an extensive process of revisions and corrections have the final official data been released in the *National Statistical Yearbook*. This process reveals the ritualistic nature of the data, especially as produced by the local states. Since GDP is also a signal of personal success and relative status, numbers often drift upward in local reports and statements. So, the dualism of statistics, local versus central, and for that matter also between *tiao* and *kuai*, defines peculiar features of the national statistical system which therefore cannot fully rely on a standard procedure collecting data at the grassroots level and simply aggregating these data.[50]

We may discern a cultural bias here reminiscent of the distinction between orthodoxy and orthopraxy in studies of Imperial China. Statistics are not necessarily seen as a tool to depict reality in a most truthful sense; the numbers should reflect proper behaviour in following strategic orientations which are cast into ritual obligations. For example, this may imply that higher level authorities manipulate data at the local level if they can achieve an aggregate balance in terms of goal fulfilment. This means that local successes and failures, deficits and surpluses may be balanced out intentionally, justified by contextualized reasoning about the causes. So, what matters is not the correct description of reality at the local level, but whether the higher level leaders achieve a satisfying outcome in the balance. Thereby, they can also protect grassroots-level leaders from facing severe criticism, which would also partly appear to be a problem in their own evaluation as superiors. Thus, the aggregate statistics already contain an evaluative component. This implies that national statistical authorities are involved in a complex and nationwide activity of correcting local-level data. For example, local reporting may be accompanied by national-level direct data collection based on statistically robust sampling, so that the accuracy of aggregate data based on local reports may be better assessed. This means that the overall quality of aggregate data may be good, in spite of the ritualistic production at the local level.[51]

From a scientific perspective, this may be seen simply as outright falsification of statistics, but I argue that this would partly misinterpret the motivations of the actors. Chinese statistics has improved considerably over recent decades, yet it remains imbued with normative considerations. One expression of this is that there is an ambiguity between the term 'model' and the idea of an 'average'. Clearly, the model is not the average, but normatively it suggests that the average should move towards the model. Accordingly, announcing the model as a benchmark will also move the statistics towards the model via myriad local actions that respond to the normative signals. So, we may say that statistics is part and parcel of the modernizing agenda in contemporary China, with the distinction of the local vs. the central state being manifest in the ritual production of statistics in the local state and the scientific use of statistics on the central level. Both levels, however, interact, as policies announced at the central level also influence the statistical rituals at the local level.

In sum, I claim that ritual and experimentalism are two sides of economic policy-making in China, as it is ritual practices that define strategic guidance on every level, partly mediated via the cadre system and the mechanisms of policy evaluation. Within these constraints, there is much leeway for autonomous action in the shape of experimental policies. This view differs from common interpretations of experimentalism being a transitory phenomenon in the gradual establishment of the market economy. Instead, I argue that this is a permanent feature of economic style, ultimately rooted in most general patterns such as cognitive field dependency; hence experimentalism also combines with other features such as localism. One aspect of this is the claim often made by observers that the transition to the market also implies the retreat of planning. In fact, planning has remained strong, largely under the label of 'industrial policy' or 'regional policy'. So, the distinct economic style also puts the application of standard categories in describing economic systems into perspective, such as the much-cited idea that China moves towards the model of a 'regulatory state'.

Industrial policy, regulatory state and political leadership

In spite of the transition from a planned economy to a market economy, the Chinese government continues to play a decisive role in determining and shaping the course of economic development. This applies on every level of the territorial hierarchy, with different scope and direction. This has the important implication that central-level industrial policies not only directly address actors in markets, but also and often predominantly lower level jurisdictions. Again, we can put this into the dualism of central vs. local state: the county-level government exerts manifold industrial policies in its jurisdiction, but it is constrained in its actions by higher level regulations and strategic goals. However, this principle also applies to the higher levels, in particular the relationship between the provinces and central government. In this case there is the important aspect that industrial policy partially targets the state-owned sector, which is organized in the regional property rights structure. Thus, in considering the relationship between market actors and the government, the latter has to be conceived of along the lines of a multiple principal framework, with a complex and sometimes conflict-ridden relationship between the principals.

The typical pattern of these tensions is that lower level governments more directly face the consequences of any kind of strategic decision made on the central level, especially with regard to the effects on economic growth and employment. With reference to employment, local governments face a direct trade-off between higher level goals of industrial policy and employment, because the latter may also affect another 'veto' goal in the cadre evaluation system, which is maintaining social stability. This trade-off has a broad scope: for example, in the financial system banks may be under pressure to refinance non-performing loans if a local crisis in employment looms. Correspondingly, we may say that whereas strategic decision-making in industrial policy has been centralized over recent years, the specific shape and direction is only determined by the complex interactions across the hierarchy of jurisdictions. This is particularly relevant in assessing the scope and significance of the recent evolutions towards the 'regulatory state'. This is institutionally represented in the establishment of a number of industry regulators, such as in banking, electricity or financial markets, which is supposed to define a clear difference between regulation and direct policy intervention. However, given the complex goal structure of Chinese economic policy, the legal independence of these regulators, though formally established, is by no means manifest in practice. Many regulators also remain under the direct supervision of the NDRC and therefore are not even legally conceived of as independent regulators.[52]

This fundamental pattern in Chinese industrial policy is another path dependent structure that has its roots in the specific model of planning that emerged in the Maoist period. The Maoist approach to planning may be characterized as a command economy without full national integration into a central plan. As such, the planning system may be regarded as the historical origin of the regional property rights system, as it allowed for the accumulation of lower level entitlements in the system of territorial administration. In contrast to the Soviet Union, where experiments with regional planning were abandoned in the late 1950s, China embarked on a regionalization approach during the Great Leap Forward and the Cultural Revolution, which drove cellularization on different levels. In other words, on every level there was a tendency to increase the self-sufficiency of the respective territorial economies. Partly, this certainly also reflected the political strain under which the system operated over two decades, beginning with the Great Leap. During the Cultural Revolution, radical leftists even denounced accounting and statistics in monetary categories as instigators of the resurgence of capitalism, so that the resources devoted to the administrative apparatus necessary for full-scale planning were far too small. Thus, the devolution of planning to lower level jurisdictions was also an adaptation to the administrative constraints under which the system was operating. As a result, the higher level administrations largely concentrated on planning the flows between lower level entities, and refrained from direct interventions in the lower level entities. The system was akin to planning external trade between regional units. This was supplemented by the national strategic planning of investment, such as in the context of 'third front' industrial policies which created large industrial capacity in inland provinces. These measures were largely motivated by military objectives. Regionalization and cellularization were intended to reduce the vulnerability of China in case of foreign invasion, which would start in certain areas. During the Cultural Revolution, most of the industrial capacity of China was governed by regional planning procedures.[53]

The legacy of this special institutional feature is well known. In the Soviet Union as in other centrally planned economies, such as the GDR, integrated national planning led to the regional concentration of industrial capacity, because central planners prefer large production units and monopolized industries to reduce the information costs of planning. In China, regional authorities were motivated to invest in many independent regional capacities in order to become autonomous from imports, so that in the 1980s China had an industrial structure with a high share of parallel and duplicate production facilities across all the provinces. This complex industrial structure made central planning even more difficult, but also reduced its necessity. At the same time, it created a specific challenge for central-level industrial policy which since the launch of the reforms was unequivocally directed at the modernization of industrial structures. Modernization would inevitably affect the interests of local-level jurisdictions, as it would lead towards closures and corporate restructuring with direct implications for local interests.[54]

Thus, the decentralized industrial structure created special conditions for economic growth during reforms. There was a high share of excess capacity on a low level of efficiency, because many production units were operating below the technologically optimal scale, especially once modern technological equipment was introduced. Market openings immediately created competitive pressure to enhance capacity utilization, thus putting regional authorities in competition with each other. This also caused protectionist tendencies, because regional authorities had to rely on their own industries in order to safeguard revenue sources and local employment. As a result, national planning was gradually transformed into a system governing investment activities and implementing industrial policies in the context of territorial competition. This was complementary to the reduction of mandatory planning on goods allocation via the introduction of the dual-track system. In other words, if we only look at the latter in order to assess the role of planning in China, this would be misleading. In fact, Chinese economic reforms may be interpreted in a twofold but not contradictory way: one is the expansion of the market, the other is the devolution of the planning system, which does not necessarily imply less government intervention in the economy. One of the most conspicuous phenomena in this regard is local protectionism, which would directly reflect local government intervention in the economy, and therefore could be seen as an indicator of the resilience of the planning system, together with indicators of regional specialization that would denote the structural effects of local planning. As a matter of fact, up until today there is evidence for the existence of these phenomena, thus indirectly proving the resilience of planning.[55]

In other words, the expansion of the market via the double-track system did not simply reduce government intervention in the economy, since the additional opportunities of economic development were in the interest of local governments which therefore perceived incentives for shaping the direction of local development. The most visible phenomenon in this regard was the plunge of the local states into developing the township and village enterprise sector in the 1980s, which actually built on the collective rural industries of the Maoist era. In fact, this market dynamic even enhanced the interventionist role of the local state owing to the competitive success of the TVE sector in competing with the SOE sector, especially on the lower territorial level. This was reflected in the scholarly literature of the 1990s which identified a new pattern of corporatist leadership on the local level, thus turning many county governments into autonomous entities of industrial policy-making.[56]

In this regard, it is important to note that the status order of ownership played a decisive role in shaping the dynamics of the TVE sector. In the 1980s, its expansion was directly supported by the availability of credit from the state-owned banking sector, in particular the Agricultural Bank. The massive restructuring and de facto privatization that started in the mid-1990s was accompanied by the drying up of these funds, thus establishing the status order in the financial sector with state banks supplying credit mainly to the state-owned industries and other public entities, and with industries in the rural areas having to rely largely on alternative means of funding. However, this shift did not necessarily affect the role of the local states in shaping and supporting what has now been emerging as the private sector economy in China.

The rise and fall of the TVE sector is one glaring example of how the central government is able to exert national control of basic patterns of economic development and institutional structures, especially via the allocation of credit in the still vastly dominant state-owned financial system. However, we need to scrutinize in more detail these planning capacities at the central level, realizing that the capacities to implement national plans differ considerably across different domains. One example where planning has been almost comprehensive recently is birth control. The central government was able to shift the entire pattern of demographic reproduction within a few years, reaching through to the level of individual decision-making even in the rural areas. The most important tool is the formulation of national goals which can be easily broken down to goals for cadre action on the local level. It is easy to determine the number of births locally, so that there is no additional need for complex structures of supervision and direct process management. However, this led to many expressions of deviance in terms of methods of goal implementation (such as forced abortions and violence against women) which were more difficult to control. Yet, overall goal implementation was successful. This is an almost ideal-typical example of the relationship between management by objectives and local policy autonomy discussed in the previous section. The targets of birth control could be easily disaggregated even on the grassroots level, but at the same time there was no central direction on how these targets should be achieved, and, above all, there was no specialized and integrated national-level bureaucracy that implemented the goals. This resulted in intensive interaction across the different levels of policy design, which we interpret as a learning process. In other words, local states might develop their own approaches to implement the policy, provinces might interfere in further developing these approaches in identifying and promulgating model cases, and the central level might recurrently launch regulatory interventions in issuing central-level guidelines for policy intervention. As a result, Chinese population policy gradually became more sophisticated and also balanced individual interests and rights with national policy objectives.[57]

This example clearly differs in terms of complexity from planning and governing corporate structures, industrial supply chains or technological change. In this case, indirect interventions into industrial structure are more efficient, such as guiding mergers among companies. However, compared to population policy, the internal contradictions in the administration may have a much stronger impact on plan implementation. For example, in case of a merger, local authorities may be concerned about negative effects on local employment and may therefore resist. This is why a pervasive feature of the policy process in China are the tensions and conflicts of interests between the local states and central government. However, given the approach outlined in the previous section, simply opting for a full-scale centralization of decision-making is not a feasible and appropriate strategy in the Chinese context. Yet, there is one shared feature of all approaches, which is the relationship between planning and cadre evaluation.[58]

As we have seen in the previous section, a major aspect of planning in China up until today is linking the plan with the system of cadre evaluation. The higher levels do not necessarily intervene directly in the economic process, but cadres have to fulfil certain targets, and so they will strive to discover methods to achieve this. So, planning and experimentation are intimately intertwined. This is important when considering, for example, the move from emphasizing GDP to environmental targets in more recent times. With GDP targets being binding targets and environmental targets being only supplementary indicators, it is straightforward to explain why 'environmental authoritarianism' in China failed to perform well. For local authorities, environmental regulation was even of negative value, both in terms of trade-offs with mandatory GDP targets, as in terms of local interests in employment and revenue. So, in spite of the fact that China developed a modern environmental law and regulations, and notwithstanding the existence of a national administrative body implementing these laws, it was not possible to pursue environmental goals reliably and consistently. This is only changing currently, with environmental targets achieving binding power and becoming more important for cadre evaluation. One special aspect is the direct targeting of particular industries, such as renewable energy, which allows for activating traditional tools of planned interventions, such as via credit allocations.[59]

At this point the ritual aspect of planning becomes evident. A national plan is a frame for partly autonomous decision-making, and plan implementation often takes the shape of a 'campaign'. Although the term 'campaign' is rarely used today, in fact campaign-like policies are very frequent, such as after the eruption of the financial crisis in 2008 or in the recent anti-corruption drive. The defining feature of campaigns is that the higher level authority expresses priority and urgency for certain goals without committing itself to a specific strategy of intervention. Lower level authorities may also perceive the probability of tough sanctions in case of failure. So, campaigns and experimentation are closely connected, since in a situation of heightened awareness, local authorities explore many methods as to how to fulfil the goals. Quasi-campaigns may be launched by shifting status positions in the government hierarchy. A characteristic measure is to set up additional committees headed by high-profile cadres and which operate aside of the formal government hierarchy, so that they have no direct competencies of issuing orders to lower levels. However, their main task is to change strategic orientations across all levels of administration.[60]

Against this background, a major policy instrument governing these dynamic forms of planning is the financial system and the system of approving investments. One of the early ideas about planning in the 1980s was to free up markets but to keep government control of investments.[61] This has been a feasible strategy up until the present, since capital markets remain a small source of funding, especially for state-owned companies. Chinese companies rely heavily on bank credit, so that control of this channel is an important means to implement government policies, both macroeconomic and industrial. This combines with planning industrial policy so as to identify certain areas of priority or restriction, such that, for example, the central government is able to create conditions for pursuing the goal of expanding renewable energies and related industries. In other words, the credit sector is an important lever by which the rank order of goals in the cadre assessment system and the priorities of higher level industrial policies may be aligned, since loans are an important resource through which the local-level authorities can implement their otherwise autonomous industrial policies. The other important resource is land, which is under more direct control of the local states, as we have seen. So, beyond general funding needs, the management of state-owned land is an important means by which lower level governments can directly influence economic development in structural terms.

Summing up the discussion thus far, we can posit the hypothesis that the reform era is falsely described as a transition from plan to market, since the scope and reach of planning has been expanding on all levels, especially in the context of industrial policy and development. On the one hand, this reflects the basic continuity of the growth model and the modernist leadership of the state in the ritual economy. On the other hand, this cannot be interpreted as a continuation of traditional socialist planning. In other words, the nature and approach of planning have changed fundamentally, but this does not imply a retreat. This does not even mean that mandatory targets have lost their significance, as we have seen, since they continue to play an essential role in the cadre evaluation system. The difference with a system of socialist central planning is that plans do not directly interfere with the markets for goods and services. So, we diagnose a simultaneous transformation of market and plan. In fact, this is also reflected in the quantitative expansion of plans on the different levels of government. The national plan has dissolved into a large number of decentralized plans, some of which, however, have even strengthened their mandatory character.

Formally, this has been reflected in the changing organization of planning, which is now guided by the National Development and Reform Commission established in 2003. Meanwhile, the basic structure of the Five-year

Plan framework has been maintained, but in 2006 the plans were renamed 'Guidelines of development', 'fazhan guihua' (发展规划), thus signalling that they do not have a mandatory character. However, this only applies in the sense that the plan no longer directly determines the structure of interactions among economic actors. In fact, many targets that are named in the plan are still mandatory in the sense that they lead to individual sanctions if they are not met. In positive terms, therefore, we can re-emphasize a point made earlier that national planning is basically a framework for territorial competition, thus regulating the planning activities of lower level administrations, partly via the cadre evaluation system. This clearly reflects the traditional structure of fragmented and cellularized planning in the context of a radically different system of allocation and structural transformation that is governed by market relationships. One indicator of this effect is that there is an increasing number of macro-regional plans. In the old cellularized system, the national plan would focus only on the relationship between the disaggregate units, whereas in a more integrated economy there is also a growing need for the coordination of local-level government interventions, often manifest in local protectionism. Therefore, macro-regional plans have multiplied.[62]

Generally speaking, we can therefore catch the complexities of planning in China today in a multidimensional framework that combines the *tiao kuai* dimensions with the nomenclature dimension, which I depict in a highly compressed, simplified and abstract form in Figure 4.2. There are different kinds of fundamental interactions in the system. One is the definition and enforcement of goals in the cadre system or the nomenclature. This is strictly hierarchic and covers activities in great detail, even down to the grassroots level. However, this does not imply that those goals are set on the central level, of course. We have a cascading system in which the next highest authorities translate their own goals into disaggregate goals for the next lowest level.

In Figure 4.2, the two strands of government and party are shown as separate, but in fact they overlap, as the nomenclature covers the positions in government, especially the positions of decision-makers. Therefore, the activity type of 'decision' is assigned to the nomenclature, whereas the activity type of 'intervention' is on the side of the government. This reflects the fundamental distinction between the leadership function and the administrative function on every level of government. As we have seen, the typical organizational pattern that reflects this is the establishment of 'leading groups' which gather high-ranking individuals across different administrative departments. This separates the decision function from the implementation function.

The *tiao* dimension is reflected in the regional economic systems nested hierarchy, with the province as the pivot. The continuous arrows with different thickness show that on the national level, typically less and more aggregate targets are transmitted downward in the administration, with

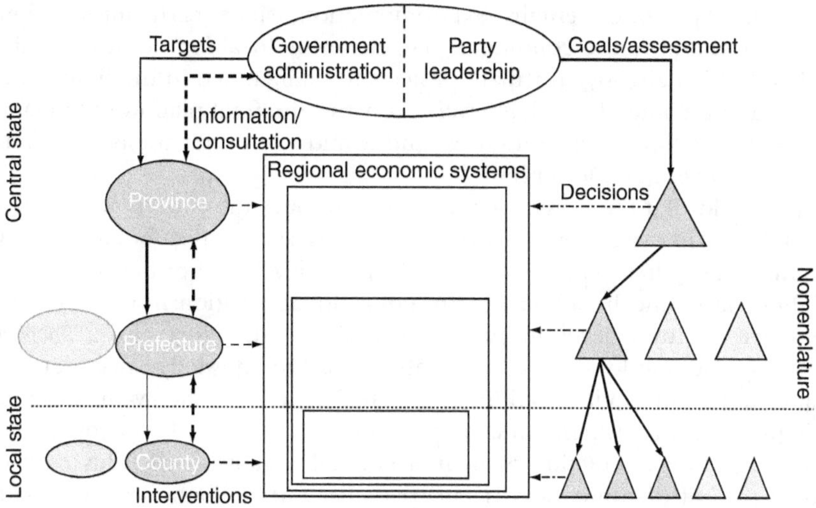

Figure 4.2 Basic structure of planning.

the province as the central node at which these are translated into more detailed targets (thicker arrows) which are then transmitted further downward. The diagram still depicts the traditional hierarchy; in other words, it does not directly subordinate counties to provinces. Therefore, the traditional planning system still reflects the division between the central and local states, since the county level receives less detailed targets (thin arrow). As we know, in case of direct subordination to the province, this feature may even be reinforced.

Looking at the actual implementation of this kind of planning, we can characterize it as a deliberative process of policy-making with sectoral and regional specialization; this is indicated in Figure 4.2 by the double broken line arrows which show that information flows and bargaining run in both directions. The absence of a mandatory national plan goes hand in hand with the expansion of what may be called 'decentralized planning'. However, decentralized planning takes place under the control of higher level authorities which always need to approve lower level plans. In practice, this means, as in the case of national plans, that the most important part of planning is the process, not the result. So, for example, the drafting of a Five-year Plan for a large municipality would be a process involving provincial authorities, and often, if the municipality is of national importance, central government authorities. So, the NDRC takes on the role of a consulting agency for lower level authorities, akin to a standardizing body issuing certificates for meeting standards. In this continuous flow of communication between the levels, local authorities receive a large amount of information about context and central government aims and criteria which allow them to develop a local plan that balances different interests. This often entails experimentation, since early information about aims and future conditions may incite the local level to test certain policies which already anticipate projects to be included in the final plan. So, as an outcome of the deliberative process, the final plan would ideally reflect a developmental consensus, and would not simply impose central-level objectives upon lower levels.

If we add that the nomenclature system imbues the process with status considerations, we can even consider planning as an aspect of culturalism in the sense that representatives of upper level authorities represent higher status, and hence stay in an 'educational' relationship with representatives of lower level authorities. Planning is therefore also a *jiaohua* process, instilling lower level authorities with the knowledge necessary to fulfil the task of modernization. The NDRC represents the avant-garde of this process, with a high concentration of expertise and knowledge, also involving close interaction with international organizations. This educational role of planning is part and parcel of the deliberative process of negotiating over the plan. Therefore, it would be entirely misguided to see the national-level plan as the outcome of a national-level decision process that is being implemented top-down. In fact, the plan is a stock-taking exercise that reflects the process during which many activities that are covered in the plan already unfold.[63]

It is important to recognize that national-level planning by itself is also a complex process because different organizations are involved. This is especially complicated in the case of modern SOEs, because formally they are controlled by the SASACs (see Chapter 6), which represent the government as an owner. In the standard model of planning, ministries enacted the ownership role. So, in the past, the structure of industry was reflected in a large number of branch ministries. In the course of market liberalization, this number was reduced considerably, with new generalist ministries embodying the role of government as a regulator, standard setter and planner of structure and development. However, since SASACs represent the ownership function relative to a large number of companies, they also include sectoral concerns in their decision-making which would also be part of a sectoral and regional plan. Thus, the ownership and the regulatory function stay in tension, in particular in the context of competition policy. Competition policy is an interesting case, because ultimately competition policy would have to represent consumers' interests in cheap prices, product diversity and quality. However, if government remains as owner of industries, it represents producers' interests, and this in a fragmented administrative structure. As a result, the relative impact of different agencies upon final planning is driven by power balances and conflicts among them, with, for example, SASACs sometimes prevailing over ministries, or ministries easily falling into the trap of regulatory capture if powerful SOEs are involved.[64]

So, a more general feature of planning in China is the prevalence of producer interests over consumer interests, which is bolstered by the ideological foundation of modernism. Planning represents the government as avant-garde of modernism, equipped with superior knowledge and expertise. The latter assumption may be partly true in the relationship between higher level and lower level authorities, a common issue in large countries with decentralized local administration. In this context, the role of private industry could be to strike a balance between consumer and producer interests. This was certainly true in the expansion of TVEs, which aimed mainly at consumer goods and hence put considerable pressure on SOEs up until the mid-1990s. By definition, private industry would remain outside the scope of government planning. However, beyond a certain size, private industry would meet specific constraints which could only be relieved by government support, in particular regarding industrial estates and credit by state banks. So, planning can indirectly channel the direction in which private investment flows.

There is one aspect of government–private sector interaction which has been evolving since the early years of reforms. This is the role of industrial associations in industrial policy, which has to be seen partly in the context of the previous discussion about civil society, but is also of a different kind, precisely because industry associations represent producers' interests and hence are in principle congruent with the aims of government on every level, in particular the local state. So, industry associations and specialized chambers of commerce play an important role in policy coordination and implementation. In the local state, industry associations are often directly established and also supervised by government agencies, with membership even being compulsory. In the organization of the associations, status distinctions matter a great deal. On the one hand, local leaders of industry may be co-opted into the party and may even obtain official status, for example, as members of the regional People's Consultative Conference. On the other hand, officials may assume roles as honorary members or members of advisory boards. So, we have a clear case of state corporatism, where government uses associations as an instrument to communicate industrial policy goals, enforce certain regulations such as on tax compliance, or delegates certain tasks in regulating labour conflicts. This state-corporatist approach has been promoted since the early years of reforms.[65]

These associations differ from those that are established independently from the government, although these often cannot assume full formal roles as legal persons, such as local industry organizations with a regional background (for example, the Wenzhou Chamber of Commerce in Shenzhen). This also reflects the multiple goals of associations, partly related to diverging interests of different actors. So, for example, government agencies are interested in assigning governance functions to associations, such as in regulating corruption or labour issues, whereas industry representatives may aim at lobbyism or wish to foster intra-industry networking. This diversity of goals may result in competing organizations with different status and impact. For example, the aforementioned regional associations may focus on networking, thus even explicitly shunning the government-controlled official associations. The local state has much leeway in shaping the developmental patterns of these structures, using tools such as the requirements for registration and subordination to a particular government agency and registration at the tax bureau.[66]

We can also describe this structure as 'corporatist' in general terms, and hence propose to add this term as another descriptive item in the characterization of the ritual economy. The analytical issue is how far this is geared towards 'state corporatism' or whether 'social corporatism' also plays a role, similar to the ambiguities of civil society in general, as we have seen. With regard to planning, corporatist structures imply an extension of the scope of deliberative processes to the emerging private industry, with a leading role of government representatives that emanates from their elevated status. In these processes, a developmental consensus may emerge which can then be implemented also with supporting measures of the government, such as providing credit or acting as an intermediator in establishing business relations. Therefore, we certainly meet a variant of state corporatism here, since even in the case of autonomous associations their factual status is shaped by the responsible government authorities. However, the question remains whether corporatism is a feature of the local or the central state. As a matter of fact, the central state actively contains the emergence of national-level associations apart from those entities that are directly controlled by the CCP. The typical structure is that of a 'federation', such as the All-China Federation of Industries (中華全國工商業聯合會), which was established in 1953 as a successor organization to the Chambers of Commerce in pre-1949 China and is under the supervision of the United Front Department of the CCP. Leaders of this federation also obtain the highest positions in structures of the state, such as the People's Consultative Conference, while the organization is factually an association of more than 3000 chambers on the level of local government and local state. It mainly targets private business.

However, private business also creates many independent associations, often in the context of regional interest groups or specialized branches and even product categories, which may not be registered officially. The local state may be permissive towards the growth of these independent associations, but they are constrained in setting up national structures. For example, there are many regional and even native place associations on the level of the local state, but they are not allowed to create formal allied structures on the national level, even though factually many semi-formal activities may take place. This is even often supported by local states, namely because local states also pursue the goal to represent their own regional interests in other areas. In this context, there is an illuminating family resemblance between these and modern Chambers of Commerce, 'shanghui' (商会), as compared to 'xiehui' (协会). Given the increasing fluidity and inter-regional activity of regional business, local states even up to the provincial level support the representation of local business interests at other locations. This raises the intricate issue of where the regulatory competence for these associations may be assigned to. This phenomenon is especially relevant in areas where many migrants and outside investors from other regions come together, such as in the Pearl River Delta, but also large metropolitan areas such as Chongqing. These developments emerge out of manifold activities related to migration and travel in reforming China which often go back to the 1980s, in the shape of 'friendship associations' of travellers from a particular area, with different geographical scope, reaching from particular localities or regions to the provinces. So, we meet a similar dynamic as in the evolution of modern Chambers of Commerce out of native place associations in nineteenth-century urbanizing China.[67]

In this sense, we may further qualify Chinese corporatism as 'local state corporatism'. This term differs from earlier uses in referring to a much larger variety of local patterns, and including autonomous civil society developments, thus putting much more emphasis on the side of society and business and its autonomous forces. One should add that these corporatist structures are also increasingly relevant in the state-owned sector. However, interaction between government and business is also driven partly by the internal processes of the cadre management system, as there is a substantial mutual flow of cadres between government and SOEs. In particular, a certain share of leading cadres is typically recruited from top managers in the SOE sector, which implies that they are able to activate their business networks in exerting their status-based influence on industry when pursuing strategic goals for local economic development. Beyond these informal factors, however, industry associations on higher territorial levels also include the SOEs, so that there is a formal corporatist setting for industrial policy. I come back to these aspects in the next chapter.[68]

These complex institutional patterns imply that 'industrial policy' in China is not simply defined and imposed by the government on any level, in spite of the fact that there are many direct and indirect mechanisms and levers by which the government can pursue its goals even relative to the private sector. Instead, I propose that even central government planners adopt an approach that might be called 'competitive industrial policy'. This principle applies within the context of territorial competition in general and to private–public competition. Both dimensions partly overlap. For example, if a private sector agent launches a new industrial project that stays in competition with state-owned industry, this can be supported by the regional authority where the investment is placed, thus challenging market incumbents located in other regions. Central-level authorities regulate this competition indirectly, at least via their influence on the regional authority. We know several very significant cases where central-level authorities allowed for the emergence of private companies successfully challenging incumbent SOEs. This reflects the fact that the reforms of the planning system indeed weakened the ties of interest between central ministries and companies, the so-called 'zhengqi fenkai' (政企分开) approach. In other words, the territorial competition between government units in China intermingles in complex ways with market competition among units with different ownership status, or, within the SOE sector, with different regional affiliations.[69]

Against this background, the central-level Five-year Plan is still an important lever by which the central government imposes certain disciplines upon central-level ministries and other economic interest groups. In this context, leadership is crucial, which is often expressed in setting up high-level work groups which are chaired by senior party leaders, and which might include 'business representatives' who are actually CCP members of high rank, possibly even with a previous career in government (for example, top managers in the power industry have been provincial governors before). In these groups and committees, sectoral interests are negotiated and aligned with overarching objectives. So, if we take a bird's-eye view of the entire planning process, we realize that it is immensely political in nature, and less determined by bureaucratic factors.

In conclusion, we may say that planning remains an integral part of the Chinese economic style, but is deeply shaped by the governmentality of modernizing China. This refers to fundamental aspects such as the dualism between the local and the central state, the educational relationship and culturalist governance exerted by the centre on local states and, increasingly, civil society structures such as business associations, or the impact of the CCP-determined status order upon strategic priorities and the resulting bargaining process among different entities.

Theoretical reprise

The theoretical reprise of the previous chapter emphasized the role of markets in defining the economic style of contemporary China. This did not refer to a disguised 'neoliberal' paradigm, as is often suspected in China studies, but to the fact that markets became part and parcel of Chinese governmentality, including the important aspect of a resurgence of the market system as an integral element of traditional culture in Imperial times. In this chapter I focus on the side of government organization in understanding this governmentality. In the literature, the peculiarity of the Chinese model during the past 30 years has been recognized by many authors, leading towards the characterization by means of newly coined medium-level theoretical terms. The most recent and also the most sophisticated one is the concept of 'regionally decentralized authoritarianism'. This notion pulls together two strands of China research: the first is the research on territorial or inter-jurisdictional competition in economics; the second is the political science research on 'fragmented authoritarianism'.[70]

This chapter has shown that all of these characterizations suffer from oversimplification and analytical bias, and fail to recognize certain essential elements of the Chinese state, past and present. For example, the notion of decentralization is inherently unidimensional and overlooks the complexity of the relationship between central and subnational governments, which also includes a strong central power in a systematic way. In this chapter, I have tried to take this complexity into account. From a theoretical perspective, one central concern is to understand and analytically detail the specific mechanisms of path dependency which result in a number of family resemblances between modern, Imperial and, in this respect, also Republican China.

These path dependencies have emerged in the process of state building that has taken place since the fall of the Empire; yet, from a certain perspective, we might even say that this process only started in 1978, since many political events of the Mao era were actually obstructive to state building. This is why I have assigned a pivotal role to fiscal institutions in the analyses included in this chapter. Fiscal institutions also stood at the centre of analysing government involution in the late nineteenth and early twentieth century. This concept also has the status of a medium-level theoretical term, as it designates a particular kind of institutional mechanism, namely a pattern in which the extension of government institutions is accompanied by increasing costs of enforcing and implementing policies, so that the net benefit to society is actually declining, and hence the stability of the entire body politic is under threat. In contemporary China there are a number of indicators that government involution is still persisting, in particular the increasing costs of containing and suppressing social conflicts across many domains, reflected, on the one hand, in the inflation of the public security apparatus at large, and on the other hand the commercialization of public finance in spite of vigorous attempts to reform the fiscal system and the growing fiscal resources under control of the central government. Government involution is manifest in the role of parapolitical 'service units' across all areas, the privatization of healthcare or education, or the eminent role of informal government debt channelled via 'local government investment vehicles' and based on the management of public land by the local states. However, as all these trends occur on the local level, the question is how state building on the central and the local levels relate to one other. Clearly, the resolution of the fiscal crisis of the early 1990s focused on restoring the developmental capacities of the central state, but left many local states in a fiscal quandary, thus triggering the phenomenon of government involution. Yet, this also contributed to the emergence of a wide variety of local states across China, which have been identified in the scholarly literature as 'developmental', 'predatory', 'entrepreneurial' and so forth. In this sense, Chinese governmentality seems to defy coherent and simple characterizations.

So, if we dig deeper analytically, the resilient forces of government involution are embedded in the persistence of the dualism between local and central state in modern China. However, this does not simply mean that certain institutional structures of the Imperial state persist. This is because there is a deep impact of one fundamental institutional innovation of the 1920s, namely the Leninist organizational patterns of the one-party state (which, by the way, applies to both leading political organizations in Chinese modern history, the CCP and the Guomindang, and hence is independent from the specific content of their political ideology). In theoretical terms, we might refer to the concept of 'routines' here. This term is used in organization studies to describe organizational patterns that shape the behaviour of agents often with a strong component of tacit knowledge, having accumulated over the entire time span of the existence of an organization, and which therefore save internal information and organization costs.[71] New members of organizations are socialized in this context and thus carry on with implementing the routines, which also make up the identity of the organization and its members. In the Aoki model and in particular in the elements–patterns–processes–state circuit, we can refer to routines as elements that become part and parcel of the economic style at large. That is to say, on the one hand, the CCP is an element that came into existence by fiat and therefore is by definition a 'modernist' organization. Yet, it has also turned into an institution, in the sense that organizational routines of the CCP mould institutions in the economy which are not themselves part of the CCP organization. In the model of path dependency, we can pay respect to this effect in considering the CCP as an agent of institutional design. Design actions are also influenced by routines, and design interacts with the other forces of path dependence. In the elements–patterns–processes–states circuit this means that the routines result in certain patterns of behaviour, and that these trigger processes in the economy which result in institutions as states that also include the reproduction of the routines.

We have met several instances of this unusual effect of routines. The first is that the cadre evaluation system is strongly geared towards economic growth which matches the modernist culturalism analysed in Chapter 3. Thus, the routines of the evaluation system bolster the culture of growth. We have seen that this is not simply reflecting growth-related performance criteria, as the evidence on these more specific effects is not fully convincing. But there are also many interdependencies between different performance criteria, such as the veto criterion of social stability, which may often be endangered by events emanating from trends that relate to the economy, such as lay-offs. These interdependencies result in the salience of the growth criterion for channelling and coordinating the behaviour of cadres. So, the routines drive the institutionalization of growth, which is embedded in a wide range of modernist ideas and symbols, thus linking concrete cognitive frames with specific behavioural incentives. Second, the cadre evaluation system is an integral part of the planning system in China, which puts the simple idea into perspective that reforms have proceeded as a transition from plan to market. In fact, here we observe a very strong effect of routines on institutions, thus questioning the aforementioned 'neoliberal' interpretation of marketization in China. The central point is that the cadre evaluation system continues with identifying certain outcomes of the economic process as a goal, but does not specify certain mechanisms of intervention. This fundamentally changes the nature of planning, indeed allowing much leeway to markets in the sense of autonomous interactions among economic agents, but at the same time instigating a relatively strong role of government intervention and participation in the market process. This may be labelled in different ways, such as 'industrial policy' or 'regulation', but implies anyway that market outcomes are determined both by markets and government. I argue that this establishes a unique kind of 'market governmentality' defining the economic style. As has been pointed out repeatedly in the theoretical literature on East Asian development, on first sight this bears close resemblance to the 'developmental state' paradigm that was introduced as part of the unusual conditions in the catching-up process of Japan or Taiwan, but this characterization would certainly fail to recognize the central/local duality in the case of Mainland China. The developmental state paradigm emphasizes the direct interaction between a central state bureaucracy and the market. Instead, Chinese market governmentality is shaped by ritual, and hence is a defining feature of the ritual economy.

As we have seen, this market governmentality is reflected in the continuing importance of the institution of the 'plan' in the Chinese economy. A plan is a document that specifies outcomes, and as such is a public representation in the context of the Aoki model. This perspective helps us understand how plans actually operate, if we see this together with our previous analysis of field-dependent cognition. Then, a plan sets up a cognitive field that channels the actions of agents even without directly determining their actions (actually, the term 'guidance' captures this neatly). If this works together with the cadre evaluation system, it is straightforward to see how interactions among market agents and government agents may result in an outcome that meets the requirements of the plan and therefore reproduces the implied state of the economy. We can designate this interaction with a term that is also important for the self-perception of the Party, namely 'leadership'. Planning is a pivotal aspect of leadership, and thus is also a constitutive element of ritual in the ritual economy.

We have also placed the cadre evaluation system into the larger context of the status order that is created by the nomenclature of the CCP. The nomenclature is a more stable and persistent feature of the CCP organization, compared to the annual rhythm of evaluations: it defines positions independent from the specific performance of incumbents. Similar to the plan, the nomenclature also defines a cognitive field that guides the actions of agents. One important effect of this is the derivative status of organizations relative to the rank of their leaders defined in the nomenclature. Organizations the leaders of which have a high rank relative to others will have a status advantage in bargaining processes with other organizations. So, the rank order sets up strategic fields of organizational interactions, which influence the implementation of outcome-related goals in the plan. These effects may be characterized as 'ritualistic' in nature, thus qualifying the CCP as a core element of the ritual economy. This is also recognized in the fundamental, even 'constitutional' difference between administration and leadership, or government and party in the Chinese state. This duality may be observed on many levels, such as in the organizational practice of establishing 'leading groups' which are chaired by the respective Party secretaries. So, we may also say that the CCP assumes the function of cognitive leadership, enabled by ritual as embodied in status orders. This is straightforward to observe, for example, in the strong motivating effects of public speeches by high-status party leaders which can trigger even nationwide instantaneous responses in terms of behaviour, without actually implementing administrative measures emanating from the formal position of the leader in government.

The disjunction between the output-oriented goal structure in the cadre system and the large leeway in the input structure of government is the major condition that enables two distinctive features of the Chinese economic style, namely territorial competition and experimentalism. This is because the tightness of the output goals incentivizes strong efforts in discovering ways to meet the goals. The connection between the cadre system and territorial competition has been theorized by the models of competition which have been developed by a number of economists in order to capture the peculiar dynamics of the Chinese economy analytically. Indeed, since success of regions has implications for cadre evaluation, the respective governments are led into a status competition, most explicitly visible in the ubiquitous use of rankings, reaching from rankings of townships or villages to the ranking of provinces in different dimensions. In other words, a fundamental feature of economic competition in China is the interplay between market competition and government competition across all levels of government. This is also the main difference between the developmental state paradigm and the Chinese case: Chinese market governmentality is shaped by government competition. Government competition is in turn embedded in the status order emanating from CCP organization.

This pervasive role of competition is not sufficiently covered by common notions of 'decentralization'. In addition, the notion of regional decentralization is insufficient, since it does not cover the *tiao kuai* dualism, as we have seen. This dualism is another important aspect of an entirely new organizational routine that does not tie up with historical legacies, and which relates to the structure of government, thus highlighting the role of 'systems' as opposed to 'regions' in the administration. The most glaring example of the resulting misunderstandings happened in the contemporary interpretations of the fiscal crisis of the mid-1990s, which only saw the regional decentralization and overlooked the capacity of the central government to reshuffle the relative power of systems, in this case the central fiscal and tax administration. Within just one year, the central government was able to redirect fiscal flows in favour of the centre by means of changing organizational structures and rules of tax assignments. This was of course also enabled via the centralized control of the nomenclature. In conclusion, it is necessary to employ a different paradigm in order to understand and analyse government in China in terms of a structure that is 'compound'. This means that government is dissected into a large number of units that are partly defined regionally, partly functionally, and which have different degrees of decision autonomy and pursue partly independent goals and interests. In this compound structure, I argue, the internal relations are structured by ritual, or, more specifically, by the status order that mainly emanates from the CCP organizational structure. In other words, given the infrastructural challenges of state building in China, mere decentralization of government would cause the rapid accumulation of informational asymmetries and principal–agent conflicts between the different constituent units of compound government. From that perspective, the CCP and its ritual order is an institutional means to contain these dysfunctions.

As we have seen, the relative status of the units in compound government is also influenced by other factors which partly reflect the economic status of a region or the economic significance of a sector. For example, power companies and the related government organizations have an elevated status owing to the centrality of power supply for economic growth on every level of government. Or, peripheral regions have lower status than economic centres. One particularly interesting determinant of relative status is the role of locations in the context of experimentalism, which is reflected in their identification as a 'model'. The notion of 'model' directly ties in with the cognitive mechanisms of ritual, as it establishes common knowledge of actors at the government/market interface about future institutional and organizational changes, thus stabilizing expectations in a complex and uncertain environment. We have met one conspicuous example, namely the initiative of 'Building a New Socialist Countryside' which is not just a developmental effort but aims to contain and even eliminate the forces of government involution in the local states.

Experimentalism is the second major feature of the Chinese economic system, as is reflected in the scholarly literature. However, this is often only seen as being a transitory phenomenon. In my approach, experimentalism is a systematic and enduring feature of economic style, again reflecting unique patterns of governmentality. This partly relates to the aforementioned gap between output goals and input autonomy which can only be factually closed by a local trial-and-error process, also building on collective learning across localities, mediated by 'models', among many other mechanisms. As we have seen, the cadre evaluation system imposes a peculiar dynamic upon the system, which may best be covered by introducing the theoretical notion of the political entrepreneur. Political entrepreneurs launch experiments, and in case of success there is a large number of imitators which shun the risks of experimentation or lack opportunity. This results in a campaign-style implementation of economic policies. We have seen that this creates certain patterns which we can compare with the role of political entrepreneurship in democratic countries, where the electoral cycle looms large and motivates incumbents and competitors to launch new projects, ideas or policies in order to gain majorities. In China, the cycles in the nomenclature system focus the initiatives of political entrepreneurs. Therefore, we can also speak of different institutional regimes for political competition. This is important to note because the standard approach to authoritarianism emphasizes the strong position of the incumbent and often defines competition in terms of extra-institutional power struggles. In the Chinese case, competition is highly structured, but also highly diverse and open-ended, because it occurs on every level and dimension of compound government, and institutionalizes political entrepreneurship.[72]

I have also referred experimentalism to the feature of cognitive field dependence, which relates experimentalism to the pervasive role of localism. This is the belief that successful action is only possible if it takes full account of local contexts, which always requires pragmatic experiments in order to make these contextual determinants explicit. As a result, we observe a sometimes paradoxical mix of local diversity and uniformity of movements in the process of imitation, which eventually even violate the principle of contextualization. Against this background, I argue that we can reconstruct experimentalism in terms of the Aoki model as a permanent institution in the Chinese economic system, hence of its economic style. This is mediated by a number of rituals that channel experimental actions, such as the criteria by which certain locations are designated as 'models'. Experimentalism also comes along with the institutionalization of political entrepreneurship.

Thus far, it appears that many of the characteristic features of economic style relate to the modern organizations of party and government. However, these modernizing institutions play a central role in the process of state building which started out from the structures of the Imperial state, and was relaunched under the conditions of late Maoism, in particular cellularization. Maoism played an ambiguous role in state building, because on the one hand it extended the grip of the CCP down to the village level, but at the same time reinstated the traditional boundary between the rural areas and the state even in constitutional terms, identifying the People's Communes as the domain of self-government and self-reliance, together with the revival of atavistic forms of taxation, even against the backdrop of the conditions of late Qing China, namely relying on corvée labour and taxes in kind. In other words, Maoist cellularization modified, but reinstated the duality of local state versus central state. This created very strong path dependencies of institutional change, with the highly suggestive symbolism of abolishing the agricultural tax in 2006, which was perhaps the longest existing tax regime in world history, with a continuity of more than 2500 years. This is also reflected in the many family resemblances between the local tax system in Republican times and in reform-era China, such as the role of irregular levies and fees.

If we ask for the determinants of these path dependencies, the functional equivalences to 'brokerage' in the traditional system loom large, as does the role of local elites. The Communist revolution was accompanied by a radical destruction of traditional elites, often even physically. In addition, the ideological basis for traditional elite identity was eroded. Yet, following the demise of Maoist radicalism we also observe the reinstatement of functional equivalences. However, the developments are very complex and therefore difficult to assess.

To begin with, if we directly compare the county level past and present, there is a stunning similarity in defining the county as the fundamental unit of the local state. Yet, the modern local state extends downward to the village level, and there is a strong trend of fiscal centralization and formalization of government. The forces of government involution partly work against this trend and appear to revive certain structures which relate to the operation of similar fiscal constraints both past and present. In other words, we can posit that the path dependencies are partly the consequences of the resilience of certain constraints resulting from the costs of governing a large territory and population. Indeed, the commercialization of public finance amounts to the self-funding of government functions and personnel in the past, including the aspect of widespread corruption. Given the huge variety of local states in China today, it is impossible to generalize over this observation. However, we may safely say that it is the general constraint of the costs of government which seems to create the family resemblances between past and present. These costs evolve via the innovation of certain organizational measures, communication technologies and so forth. But at the same time society has become increasingly complex, thus resulting in an arms race between state building and societal evolution. In the end, the confluence of all of these forces reproduces a pattern of governance that still maintains features such as culturalism, though in a modern shape.

Therefore, we may also reflect upon certain functional similarities between the roles of the local elites, both past and present. We have seen that the duality of local and central state is also reflected in the glass ceiling between the county level and higher level of governments as far as the political careers of party members are concerned. To a certain extent, this even creates a stronger line of separation between the local and the central state today, as in Imperial times assuming the position of a county magistrate was the first step in an upwardly mobile career pattern. Yet, this comparison would only apply to the top position of the Party secretary. For all other members of the party and government organizations in the local state we can draw a limited comparison between degree holders in the past and grassroots-level cadres in the present. There are many interesting parallels here, such as the strong involvement of the gentry in merchant activities as compared to the business activities of local state-affiliated Party members nowadays. We also observe the increasing penetration of the political elite by business representatives.

I do not wish to overemphasize these comparisons, but one point seems central in theoretical terms, namely the role of social capital in establishing the status of local elites which is based on the relationship with the institutions of the state, both Imperial and modern. In the current Chinese political system, connections with political elites are an essential part of individual social capital, even more so membership in them. In order to understand these mechanisms better, we need to investigate more deeply the mechanisms of social networks in China. This is one task of Chapter 5.

Notes

1 One of the most influential conceptualizations of the 'local state' was Oi (1992, 1996); see also Blecher and Shue (2001). Oi put this notion in the theoretical context of corporatism, to which I come back in the final section of this chapter. Corporatism refers to the more specific concept of 'state corporatism', which means that corporatist embeddedness of the economy is designed and orchestrated by the government and is not emerging from autonomous and spontaneous civil society processes. Oi therefore speaks of 'local state corporatism'. Local state corporatism means essentially two things. One is that local governments pursue an active role in setting up and developing own economic projects, sometimes even in the context of local government holding structures. This model was most prevalent in the high point of the development of township and village enterprises, which was also the empirical background of Oi's studies. The second meaning is that local governments actively support and guide private business development, for example, via the posting of officials in local business associations and Chambers of Commerce (see, for a case study, Foster 2002). With the decline of the TVE sector, the second model is becoming more prevalent.

2 In his magisterial analysis of the institutional structures of Chinese economic reforms, Xu (2011) also elaborates on the historical continuities between Imperial and contemporary China, especially with regard to the levels of the provinces and the county. These continuities are seen as underlying the emergence of what he calls the 'regional decentralized authoritarianism' (RDA) model of governance in China's economic system. The special role of the county is highlighted in Zhou Qingzhi (2014), who also refers to the state (government)

involution paradigm that I introduced in Chapter 3. Zhou accentuates the differences between the dualistic model of governance in Imperial times, without bureaucratic penetration at the local level, and the situation in contemporary China in which this has been partially achieved. However, at the same time, against the background of the state involution paradigm, he argues that this penetration is still driven by the traditional motivation, namely fiscal appropriation of resources, which fails to match the growing complexity of local-level economic and social conditions. This leads to many dysfunctional phenomena which still bear the marks of state involution. In Xu's account the complex relationship between the different levels of government is not made explicit, however, because he relies mainly on the logic of the economic competition models, in which all levels in 'difang zhengfu' are also being conflated on an abstract level. I come back to these models below.

3 As we have seen in concluding Chapter 2, in late nineteenth-century China notions of federalism loomed large, as Min Tu-ki (1989) has shown in great detail. These ideas were partly rooted in traditional notions of *fengjian*, the term that has also been appropriated linguistically to designate 'feudalism'. In fact, this referred to modernist claims of Confucian local elites and thus reflected the historical tensions between the gentry and the Imperial state, without actually referring to 'feudal' structures in the genuine sense, hence a strong nobility with military functions. The notion of *fengjian* referred to the idea of local self-government and thus to the formalization of what I have designated as culturalistic governance of the Imperial local state. In urbanizing nineteenth-century China, this idea was interpreted in giving a stronger formal role especially to economic interest groups, often organized in traditional guilds or, in the modernist context, as Chambers of Commerce. These groups were no longer presenting the gentry in social-structural terms, but were still influenced by traditional Confucian ideas and values, and were mostly led by degree holders with official status. In this sense, the provincial self-strengthening movements were distinctly urban phenomena, thus reflecting the emergence of a 'bourgeoisie' (see the classical studies by Bergère, summarized in Bergère 1983). This has to be neatly distinguished from the strengthening of the role of the provinces as administrative units in contemporary China, which is a phenomenon emerging from the internal dynamics of the central state. Therefore, provincial autonomy has no social-structural roots in urban society today. This is a central question in future developments.

4 In the context of discussing the modern Chinese consumer society, I have already pointed to Tomba's (2004) research (Chapter 3, n. 34), which showed how the privatization of urban housing may be seen as a direct 'social engineering' of the CCP in creating an urban middle class that is a stakeholder of CCP rule.The function of provinces in imposing central control of Chinese territory is a constant in Chinese history which has been documented in detail by Skinner (1977c), who showed that the design of provinces, though reflecting natural geographic conditions, was also clearly influenced by criteria of optimizing political control in the vast territory of China, especially with regard to taxation and the military (see Chapter 2, n. 65). This is especially visible in the fact that provincial boundaries were sometimes designed to separate natural economic and social territories, simultaneously assigning the role of administrative centres to places which were not necessarily also economic centres. By means of this approach, the Imperial state aimed to suppress centrifugal tendencies that might arise from the convergence of economic and political power in certain places. This has to be seen against the backdrop that Chinese provinces are very large administrative units which often correspond to large countries in comparison. The political function of provinces clearly is also prevalent

in contemporary China, in spite of many phenomena of decentralization of policy functions and initiatives, such as in lawmaking (see overview in Donaldson 2010). The weakening of the central fiscal state in the early 1990s was interpreted by many observers as a direct expression of the growing power of the provinces, thus giving rise to the ideas of 'quasi-federalism'. However, as Tsui and Wang (2004) have convincingly shown, this is a very misleading interpretation of the real conditions: decentralization measures are always under tight control of the central government.

5 These cases are especially visible in what has been the Jiangnan region in Imperial times, such as Jiangsu province, the homeland of the phenomenal TVE growth in the 1980s. A classical case is the city of Kunshan which, within only two decades, experienced explosive economic growth into a modern urban place, starting out from being a rural county (for illuminating descriptions and analyses of this case, see Keng 2010 and Kirby *et al.* 2013). This development was also reflected in administrative upgrading: many urbanizing counties today have the designation of 'county-level cities' for that reason. The Kunshan case illustrates the role of the local state in ideal-typical fashion. For example, the Kunshan local government took autonomous and illegal action in setting up an industrial development zone, actively attracting Taiwanese investment in particular. Up until today, the local leaders have pursued autonomous industrial policies, for example, in the context of upgrading the local industrial structure. Kunshan also demonstrates the role of 'local state corporatism' as envisaged by Oi (see n. 1 above). This even applies to the strong group of Taiwanese investors which is organized in an independent business association. For example, Taiwanese business associations publish rankings of locations in Mainland China for investment opportunities and conditions. In the first two decades, Kunshan government closely followed the interests of Taiwanese investors. When the growing economic strength of the local government also led to a weakening of these corporatist connections, there was an immediate response by the Taiwan business interests, leading to a renewed intensification of bilateral consultations. Governments in newly emerging urban places such as Dongguan in the Pearl River Delta discuss the question of citizenship and civil society expressively, because they face the problem of how to create stable and 'harmonious' social structures facing huge migrant inflows within just two decades, exploding from a rural community into a multi-million metropolis. So, the Dongguan government adopted a strategy of fostering the emergence of a 'New Dongguan Man' ('xin Dongguan ren'), for example, by means of setting up mixed residential districts or actively involving local associations, including native place associations (cf. Ngok and Zhuang 2013). For an overview of the role of cities in the first two decades of Chinese reforms, see Chung (1999).

6 In Western media, the Chongqing case has attracted much attention owing to the Bo Xilai affair, which put an abrupt end to the stellar career of a 'princeling'. On the one hand, Bo was presumably quite successful in fighting against emerging local mafias, but he also created a corrupt personal network of his own which was exposed to the public in a murder case involving a foreign businessman and his wife. Much media attention was also drawn to Bo's 'retro-Maoism', such as promoting public activities with performances of Cultural Revolution songs, etc. (for a summary of the events, see Osnos 2014: 253ff.). However, these images do not sufficiently reflect the substantial local reforms which have been overviewed by Huang (2011a) and positively evaluated by the World Bank (2014: 234ff.) with special reference to the system of landownership. So, the Chongqing case clearly shows the two faces of a metropolitan 'local state'. Regarding economic and social policies, Chongqing is special in being the testing ground for more 'leftist' approaches which emphasize social

justice and equal opportunity by maintaining basic structures of public ownership, both with regard to state-owned companies and land. This approach is strongly influenced by theoretical and conceptual work of leading Chinese scholars, in particular Cui (2011), who builds on the economic theory of socialist market economics championed by the economics Nobel laureate James Meade. These theories argue that public ownership of land should be maintained while creating markets for land-use rights. In practice, as the World Bank study affirms, this has considerably improved the income position of farmers in the Chongqing region, partly because they could participate in the economic valorization of land during urbanization.

7 For a recent overview, see World Bank (2013: 95ff.). A comprehensive study with analytical depth is Wong and Bird (2008).

8 On this development, see Wong (2009). For example, between 1986 and 2003 the share of budgetary resources in education funding dropped from 75 per cent to about 55 per cent. Almost all public services, especially in less developed regions with a weak tax base, are provided with charging users directly, reaching from education to agricultural extension to healthcare. There is a direct statistical correlation between the level of salaries in such public service units and the extent of user charges and fees, which establishes a direct motivation for employees in these units in setting up such schemes. For example, rural schools may even set up workshops and factories to earn additional income. It should be noted, as Zhu (2010: 192ff.) reports in the case of Shanghai, that these developments also took place in urban areas. The grassroots-level government organizations, the neighbourhood committees, had increasingly to fund themselves via the commercialization of services.

9 The so-called 'tax-for-fee reforms' have been the object of numerous studies, such as Kennedy (2007), Li (2007) or Göbel (2011a, 2011b). Göbel emphasizes that the actual policies which resulted in even the wholesale abolishment of the agricultural tax were actually a complex composite of intended and unintended effects. The original idea of the reforms was to abolish irregular fees in the countryside which had been exploding in the aftermath of the centralizing tax reforms of 1994, even though they had always been a constitutive element in the local tax system. The approach was to integrate those fees into the regular agricultural tax. However, this had immediate consequences for the scale and quality of local public services which deteriorated substantially, since funding was drying up. In particular, the reforms resulted in a fiscal crisis at the township level (cf. Chen 2014). Since the reforms did not produce the desired aim to improve the conditions in the rural areas, finally even the agricultural tax was abolished in the context of the campaign of 'Building a New Socialist Countryside'. This amounted to a final centralization of budgetary responsibilities at the county level since there was no longer a specifically 'rural' tax base. This partly reflected the urbanization dynamics, with towns assuming a stronger role in mediating county-level governance and budgeting. At the same time, however, township-level cadres increasingly work in the villages as so-called 'sent down cadres', often in the context of implementing centrally defined policies. Since the townships cannot fund these activities, these positions are factually pulled into the orbit of higher level budgets, which therefore increasingly depend on intergovernmental transfers. These patterns indeed show the mark of 'government involution', as is evident in studies such as Smith (2010), who speaks of the 'hollowing out' at the township level. Chen (2014) is especially vocal in arguing that the fiscal reforms eventually led to disconnecting the local populace from government, in both the case of fiscal weakness and strength, paradoxically. Places with strong economic dynamics manifest the concentration of cadres on business activities, and the local population is able to finance

commercialized services anyway. In the end, this pattern also undermines the relevance of local elections.

10 The evolution of the Chinese fiscal system has been overviewed and analysed in many studies, such as Wong and Bird (2008), who also point to the pivotal role of the 1994 reforms. In 1993, the share of fiscal revenues in GDP had declined to about 15 per cent. Of this, the share of central government had fallen to about 13 per cent, so that the central government actually only controlled 3 per cent of GDP through fiscal measures, which is extremely low even for capitalist countries. This picture does not even fully reflect the redistribution of fiscal powers to the local states, as extra-budgetary revenues was largely not included in the data at that time. This development created a sense of crisis not only on the part of party leaders but also influential Chinese intellectuals, with the famous analysis by Hu Angang and Wang Shaoguang (Wang and Hu 1995) taking the lead. These developments were seen together with centrifugal tendencies in economic reforms, especially with regard to the regionalization of development dynamics in the coastal areas, leading to distinct developmental trajectories in Guangdong, the former Jiangnan region or the northeastern regions. Contemporary observers therefore diagnosed the potential for China falling apart along macro-regions; see the volume edited by Goodman and Segal (1994). For example, given the huge inflow of FDI into Guangdong province already in the 1980s and early 1990s, mainly via Hong Kong, Guangdong was actually autonomous in fiscal terms. However, from hindsight these views tended to overlook the degree of political integration not only in administrative structure (see the previous discussion of provinces in n. 4 above) but also via the CCP (for an assessment see Goodman 2000).

11 The pivotal role of extra-budgetary funds in the Chinese fiscal system has been scrutinized and theorized so early by Chinese authors such as Deng Yingtao that I have relied on in my own analysis in Herrmann-Pillath (1991: 545ff.). This has been only slowly recognized also in the international literature; for a survey see Wong and Bird (2008). Extra-budgetary funds amount to approximately two-thirds of the official budget, but mainly accumulate at the level of the local state, although there are also ministerial-level extra-budgetary funds. The picture is complex because there is also the distinction between 'within-system' and 'extra-system' funds. A general direction of reforms after the mid-1990s was to transform as many funds as possible into within-system funds. In other words, there is a formal legitimization for raising the corresponding revenues, and these are part of official budgeting procedures, although the entitlements of the respective local governments are protected. Beyond these structures, there have also been 'black accounts' held at banks, which was later also prohibited. However, there are many ways in which government-related companies or service units can actually park hidden revenues outside the budget. The resilience of this system reflects the ritual nature of the entitlements.

12 Roughly, the 1994 reforms created a funding gap of 30 to 40 per cent on the level of local governments in the Chinese definition, i.e. including all non-central levels. This means that, whereas local governments obtain only about 40 per cent of revenues they have to fund about 70 to 80 per cent of all expenditures. About 50 per cent of budgets are funded via fiscal redistribution; again, a concise overview is in Wong and Bird (2008). However, in more detail this imbalance is most pronounced at the county level, where the aggregate deficit amounts to about 5 per cent of GDP as compared to much lower shares at the provincial level (about 1.5 per cent). This reflects the fact that there is also a centralization process at the provincial level, with provinces increasingly controlling revenues of lower levels, with the corresponding need for intra-provincial fiscal redistribution.

13 According to the data analysed in OECD (2013: 46), at the end of the 2000s the surplus on the central level amounted to 6.1 per cent of GDP, whereas the consolidated deficit of the subnational budgets amounted to 7.8 per cent. In the distribution of the latter, the county level stands out, with 4.9 per cent deficit. In comparison, the township-level deficit is minuscule, with only 0.1 per cent. It is also important that after fiscal transfers, the bulk of national borrowing is with the central government (2 per cent of GDP), and the county level even has a surplus 0.6 per cent, receiving a whopping 5.5 per cent in transfers. Regarding the degree of central control of the budget, I have already pointed to the analysis offered by Tsui and Wang (2004). More specifically, the authors point to the intentional proliferation of non-funded mandates and legal stipulations in reducing the autonomy of local governments which evidently cannot be countervailed by the local governments. Yet, this also creates the pressure to find alternative sources of revenue and income, especially also of running formal or informal deficits. Further, the authors stress the role of the cadre management system that I will analyse in the following two sections. Imposing targets upon cadres is a major channel of controlling lower level government behaviour apart from the administrative directives. The two elements combine if the non-funded mandates are also translated into performance targets.

14 For example, local authorities may request special conditions in procuring goods and services from the SOE or demand for employment guarantees (see Lin and Chen 2013). Other measures include co-financing of local infrastructure, such as building roads in the neighbourhood of the SOE, etc.

15 Especially after the financial crisis of 2008, the amount of local government debt has grown tremendously; in 2009 local borrowing amounted to more than 30 per cent of GDP. According to the meticulous calculations by Feng (2013), the local debt in 2012 was about 25 trillion RMB, compared to 8 trillion at the central level. The entire status is non-transparent and therefore became the object of a national audit at the end of 2013. This audit showed that the local debt is distributed unequally across the provinces, with the general pattern that less developed provinces are more indebted because the local tax base is weak (*The Economist*, 22 February 2014, 43f.). OECD (2013: 17) reveals that one-third of off-budget borrowing is via the investment platforms, and other major organizations include the so-called 'service units' which are spin-offs of local government with semi-private status. The LGIVs may also issue bonds, however, which are by far the largest source of funding in direct bank loans.

16 Schurmann (1966: 188ff.) is the *locus classicus* of analysing the *tiao kuai* distinction, which remains valid today. The important implication is that the notion of 'decentralization versus centralization' is seriously misguided if it is interpreted in a single dimension, which is often the case. If we add the dual distinction of administrative modes, we actually have to consider a complex four-dimensional organizational structure. So, decentralization and centralization can proceed in many different forms and simultaneously. For example, there is often decentralization of regulatory competences in the context of local experiments which, however, does not necessarily imply that the administrative control is also being decentralized, if experiments are actually triggered by central-level decisions. Decentralization can proceed along both the *tiao* and the *kuai* dimension as well: thus, in the early stages of reforms, there was decentralization in the *tiao* dimension when the administrative powers of branch ministries were curtailed, but that did not necessarily imply territorial decentralization. An important criterion for determining the relative role of the dimensions is the assignment of personnel management authority and the corresponding budgetary responsibility. A strong factual role of the *kuai* dimension typically results if it refers to the territorial administrations and not to the

higher level *tiao* organizations. It is important to note that these distinctions play a significant role at every level of government, down to the grassroots level (see e.g. Zhu 2010). For example, Kennedy (2007) points out that functions are often not assigned separately and unequivocally (which is called *tiaotiao* vs. *kuaikuai*), but are assigned to both the *tiao* and the *kuai* dimensions even in terms of budgeting. An example is rural education where the salaries of elementary schoolteachers are paid by the county government and the subsidies for living expenses by the township government. These mixed assignments create constant tensions and struggles over the allocation of final decision rights.

17 The complexity of intergovernmental relations in China across different jurisdictional levels has also been emphasized by Li (2007) who therefore rejects unidimensional conceptualizations of 'decentralization'. Central and local agents are embedded in complex networks of relationships and constantly bargain over the allocation of decisions rights in particular contexts. It is interesting to note that constitutional lawyers in China have begun to explicitly recognize these phenomena, such as the influential scholar Jiang (2010). Jiang argues that the formal Constitution needs to be seen as being complemented by certain principles that guide the interpretation of the Constitution or undergird its implementation. In this context, the Communist Party and its organizational structure attains the status of a constitutional principle. This relates to the explicit recognition of the central/local dynamics as a principle of policy-making. In the current context, and as elucidated in Chapter 5, this means that the CCP is a pillar of the principle of centralization, as emphasized also by authors such as Tsui and Wang (2004) or Naughton (2009).

18 For a detailed analysis of these reforms in terms of the *tiao kuai* pattern, see Mertha (2005), who speaks of 'soft centralization'. Mertha distinguishes between three levers through which centralization measures can work. First, the personnel and budget allocation mechanism, the so-called 'bianzhi' (编制); second, the nomenclature system of assigning positions to particular people, and third, the fee-collection procedures. The *bianzhi* is the most immediate instrument, since it decides which resources are effectively available to lower level administrations: centralization means that the *bianzhi* authority was centralized at the provincial level. This is controlled by a government body, whereas the nomenclature is under the control of the CCP organization department. Again, the question is whether the CCP organization department of the same territorial level controls assignments in functional departments on the same level, or whether the organization department of the next higher level, though within the same functional line, makes these decisions. Centralization means the latter. Taking both levers together, centralization means to strengthen the functional dimensions vis-à-vis lower level territorial units, but also implies a stronger position at the provincial level, in the territorial meaning. Regarding fee collection, in the decentralized system remittances would be made directly to the government bureau responsible for the policy domain (such as a fee for environmental damages); this money should have been transferred to the local finance bureau which theoretically would have been under higher level control. But effectively the fees remained within the control of the bureau, thus constituting extra-budgetary funds even outside the system of financial supervision. Centralization means that the bureaus only issue the payment notice, with the payment directly made to the local finance bureau. Then, it depends on bargaining between local government and the finance system how much of this money is actually submitted to the higher level finance bureau.

19 For an overview of these reforms, see World Bank (2014b). They were an important element in the reform agenda announced by the third plenum of

the eighteenth Central Committee in October 2013. The agenda was immediately implemented in promulgating a revision of the Budget Law in August 2014.

20 For a detailed study of these local variations, see Ong (2011); cf Chen (2014). The full picture includes the role of the Rural Credit Cooperatives which in most regions were simply extensions of the Agricultural Bank in receiving deposits and savings from the farmers. In regions with high potential for TVE development, grassroots-level governments could rely on loans in order to set up and support TVEs which eventually also created revenue enabling them to pay back the loans and funding further extensions of government investments. These successful examples were copied also in regions with less potential, only resulting in growing indebtedness of local governments. In regions that successfully develop endogenous business potential, there are many ways in which grassroots-level cadres can maintain control of funds via spinning off business entities from public administration or directly participating in company profits. A most simple way is to distinguish between taxes and profits after tax and giving claims to the local population and managers to the latter. In a shareholding structure as described in the context of land management, this arrangement would shelter local business incomes from higher level taxation.

21 For a detailed model of these interdependencies, see Che and Qian (1998a, 1998b). It is important to realize that this includes the cultural dimension, as has been clarified by Smyth (1997), referring to network structures that I scrutinize in Chapter 5. This also means that as an outcome of the bargaining game, it is not only the partial autonomy of the local state that is being reproduced, but also the relative private property rights of business, since the same argument applies for the relationship between local state and business. One important aspect of this relationship is that the local government is also acting as a stakeholder (as I detail in Chapter 6), with implicit claims on residual profits that are implemented via fees and other contributions of business to the local community (or, in the negative version, outright corruption).

22 For recent studies of the reforms regarding the county-level administration, see Tan *et al.* (2015), who also survey the literature. In earlier phases of reforms, the approach was to place counties under the supervision and direction of cities,'shi dao xian' (市导县); see Lam (2010). The general idea was that the regional economic interdependencies should be strengthened, especially with regard to rural–urban division of labour, such as in fostering cooperation between TVEs and urban industry. However, in many cases, this resulted in weakening the position of counties relative to the municipalities, often the prefectural level. Thus, the next step of reforms was to place counties under the direct control of provinces, while simultaneously implementing new mechanisms of budget allocation. This was launched as an experiment during the Eleventh Five-year Plan, starting in Zhejiang province, a region with strong local development and decentralized urbanization dynamics. The policies followed the same pattern, establishing direct budgetary relations between county and province and prohibiting any budgetary appropriations or subsidization by the municipal level vis-à-vis the counties, including the delegation of tasks. At the same time, the provincial level was obliged to enhance the budgetary provisions at the county level in an effort to resolve the widespread problem of county-level debts. According to the econometric analysis by Tan *et al.* (2015), these measures indeed redistributed budgetary resources from the municipal to the county level, with strong effects on the rural provision of public goods such as education, and decreasing the rural–urban income gap.

23 This example is based on the detailed case study by Zhou Xuegang (2012). This refers to a special element in the initiative 'Building a New Socialist

Countryside' with the slogan 'Every village with a road'. As is generally the case, such central-level initiatives are only sparsely supported by budgetary allocations. Yet, county-level cadres are evaluated in terms of succeeding in implementing the policy. So, they put pressure on grassroots-level cadres to raise funds. The central instrument is the so-called 'she' (赊), basically a form of supplier credit. The ritual character of this type of loan is visible in its highly personalized nature, thus being a personal obligation of the responsible cadres, such as the Party secretaries. For example, repayment is expected on New Year's Eve, according to Chinese custom. These phenomena play a major role in rural infrastructure projects. If repayment is actually made via network favours, such as opening up new business opportunities, the grey area bordering outright corruption narrows down. Then, what is originally a fiscal phenomenon translates into a collusion between local cadres and especially local construction companies. A case study of such corrupt networks is Yao (2013).

24 According to the data analysed by the World Bank (2014: 206f.), approximately 10 per cent of land devoted to urbanization projects was appropriated illegally in 2011. In 2013, there were roughly 100,000 incidents of local protests, of which 60 per cent were caused by perceived injustice in land appropriations.

25 This figure is a modified version of the original diagram in Heberer and Schubert (2012). In this seminal work the authors argue that county-level leading cadres are a 'strategic group' in the sense of the so-called 'Bielefeld approach' to development policy. Strategic groups differ from interest groups in sharing an identity but having no shared formal organization in order to pursue their collective interests. Yet, they pursue similar goals, share values and also have a strong propensity to cooperate in certain contexts. Strategic groups define their interests relative to the political system, so that these also transcend the economic domain, as in the interest group paradigm.

26 For a detailed case study of the career patterns of county-level cadres, see Feng Junqi (2010). The principle of the systematic alternation between government and party tracks is described there (ibid.: 100f.). Feng's analysis basically supports Heberer and Schubert's (2012) views; see also Schubert and Ahlers (2012) on the role of leading cadres in the policy process. On the 'glass ceiling' between the county level and the municipal level, see Kostka and Yu (2015), who study the Party secretaries on the municipal level and notice that they rarely rise from the county level. This is a further confirmation of Heberer and Schubert's view that these cadres form a distinct strategic group within the CCP apparatus. One factor which constrains the upward mobility of county-level leaders is education, since higher level jobs often require a university degree. For local leaders, studying at a university is mostly not the typical part of their individual career. This plays together with age requirements, because most county-level leaders only reach this position when already entering the age bracket which also limits access to upper level leading positions.

27 In the case study by Feng (2010: 39ff.), leading cadres recruited before 1967 all stemmed from other provinces, and after that year all came from the same province. In the 2000s, about 30 per cent of leading cadres came from their native county. However, top positions may be recruited from other counties. Interestingly, the author notices that even if the cadres come from other areas, there may be a strong bias towards certain places of origin. This partly reflects certain locational advantages in terms of levels of education or economic development, which obviously also improve individual career prospects. Beyond that, there are idiosyncratic factors, since some places are renowned for their special *esprit de corps*. These phenomena contribute to create a certain elite consciousness of the leading cadres. On similar observations, see Pieke (2004).

28 Heberer and Schubert (2012: 231) quote a fascinating comment by a county leader who argues that the county is a miniature of the country. This was also the conviction in Imperial times; see Watt (1972: 17).

29 For a detailed study of the relationship between township- and county-level cadres' administration and budgetary relations, see Oi *et al.* (2012). The authors argue that the abolition of the agricultural tax was the watershed event that triggered a fast centralization of fiscal administration at the county level. This effect was bolstered by the fact that corvée labour was also restricted, which reportedly still made up for more than 50 per cent of village-level infrastructure investment in the 1990s. Therefore, the villages now rely much more on direct budgetary allocations from the township level, which also applies to the latters' relationship to the county level. In addition, village-level cadres have been put on the payroll of the government, with township-level cadres also being present at the village level. The authors conclude that within a few years, the entire rural fiscal system has now been included in the national budget and supervision mechanisms, with the county as the pivotal unit. However, it is straightforward to recognize that this does not fundamentally change the relationship between the local state and the central state. Interestingly, Wang (2012) argues that this fiscal centralization has also had the effect that township and village cadres increasingly perceive themselves as representatives of their local communities, thus adopting the stance of 'protective state brokerage'. This is visible in the increasing number of local cadres who support petitions to the government.

30 On these phenomena, see again the case study by Feng (2010: 63ff., 142ff.). The author distinguishes between 'large' and 'small' political families, the former referring to dynasties with a network of relatives in leading positions across different departments and places. Smaller families count four or fewer positions. He also notices that the one-child policy has tended to suppress this pattern recently. Further, there is more upward mobility of cadres' children, especially if they enjoy a good education. They may prefer to work with a metropolitan organization once having studied at a city university, for example.

31 For example, as Zhang (2015) reports about the regulatory framework in electricity generation, which is determined by the interplay of four organizations – the NDRC, the State Electricity Regulatory Commission (SERC), the SASAC and the Ministry of Environmental Protection – so far as renewable energies are concerned. The SERC was created in response to the unbundling of the monopolistic electricity sector into five power companies and two grid companies. However, the NDRC as the top-level strategic institution of the CCP remained in control of important regulatory parameters, such as pricing. Even when in 2008 also a National Energy Administration was created, this happened under the auspices of the NDRC. These arrangements clearly reflect the status difference between the NDRC and the other organizations. However, this does not mean that decision-making is highly centralized. This is because the *tiao kuai* mechanism fully applies to the NDRC, since lower level NDRC bureaux are under the budgetary control of the respective jurisdictions. The regulatory commission also relies on local staff. Then, the central-level status difference is replicated at the lower level, but also against the background of limits to direct central control of lower level NDRC decisions. Therefore, local government interests strongly impact upon the implementation of local-level policies. In particular, concerns for cheap energy supply fostering economic growth loom large, thus eventually limiting the role of the regulatory commission in pursuing consumer interests and environmental goals. As an example of local autonomy in creating strategies for the energy sector, see Kostka and Hobbs (2012).

32 In her classical characterization, Shirk (1984) called the social order in Maoist China a 'virtuocracy' as compared to a 'meritocracy'. In this virtuocracy, ritualistic expressions of proper moral behaviour, as defined by Maoist ideology, were of prime importance in assigning people to positions. The resulting moral conflicts and struggles have been magisterially analysed in Madsen's (1984) study of a Cantonese village, and are also reflected in the recently flourishing Chinese literature on village histories, such as Tan (2010: 131, 399), who emphasizes the resilience of traditional moral notions which he refers to explicitly as the 'five relationships', 'lunchang' (伦常). Madsen elaborates on the dynamics of moral tensions which work out in a bipolar spectrum, defined by Maoist universalist ethics and traditional moral norms which bear the strong influence of Confucianism, without being explicitly referred to it. These conflicts were complicated by the fact that Maoist morality was interpreted partly in terms of the latter, and here allowed for different interpretation. Madsen argues that Confucian morality is particularistic and contextualized, with the most general norm of displaying 'human feelings', which means that certain particularistic behaviours and adaptive strategies are recognized as proper moral forms. So, for example, if cadres give special favours to family members, this is morally acceptable or even expected in the light of Confucian morality, whereas it is condemned by the Maoist view. Yet, as Madsen explains, the dynamics of struggle emerged because particularism may be interpreted in different ways, depending on where the borders of the reference group are defined. This corresponds to Fei Xiaotong's views on the 'circles' in Chinese society. So, the village or the collective may also become the reference group, which creates the tricky possibility of casting particularism in Maoist terms, since the collective is certainly intrinsically of high moral value. These interpretive difficulties popped up in the long series of ritualized moral struggles, triggered largely by campaigns and more specifically by interventions of external work teams who represented the universalist Maoist morality. However, since these could never be resolved, the village fell back on what Madsen calls a 'Liuist' morality which explicitly recognizes self-interest and appears as a merger between a realist Communist morality and Confucian ideas.

33 See Chapter 2, n. 28 and n. 69. For a comprehensive evaluation of the recent CCP recruitment approach, see Dickson (2014). Dickson reports that a clear trend has been emerging in focusing on urban areas and the highly educated strata of the population. More than two-thirds of new members are male and have at least high school or college degree. At the universities, the majority of students often apply for membership, so that competition is tight, and there is even a cap on the total number of acceptances per university. Since even private businesses prefer to hire party members, the motivation is obvious, of course. But at the same time, the tight competition implies that extra-curricular political or civic activities play a central role in successful application. Party members are consistently more active in civil society engagements, elections or donations, thus displaying civic and moral leadership. One surprising result of Dickson's research is that Party members display stronger loyalty to the central state than non-members, but not to the local state, even if local economic development is strong. It is important to note that criteria relating to moral and ideological probity continue to play a role in the ongoing valuation of cadres and professionals, for example, in SOEs; for a case study of CNOOC, see Bower *et al.* (2012). Therefore, I surmise that an important cultural category of assessing individual behaviour persists as a behavioural standard, which is biaoxian (表现), the 'displaying' of certain behaviours. For example, Gossaert and Palmer (2011: 190) point to the quasi-religious status of this criterion in the Maoist 'virtuocracy' (see Chapter 1, n.32), which I interpret as a ritual notion.

34 For a brief survey of the Party school system see Shambaugh (2008a: 143ff.; 2008b). There are approximately seven million party cadres and 34 million government cadres, compared with a total membership of the CCP of around 80 million. Therefore, the Party school system is pivotal to controlling the group of core cadres. It is basically divided between the central and the provincial system, with the Central Party School playing an essential role in defining ideology and designing and communicating strategic orientations of the CCP, which is also reflected in the fact that the head is always a member of the Politbureau (for example, Hu Jintao occupied this position). The system continues on the lower level, with substantial differences in quality and equipment; see Pieke (2009). Further, there are also innovations in the shape of special leadership academies for top-ranking cadres that more closely reflect modernist aspirations, whereas the Central Party School stresses ideological content (Chin 2011). This is supplemented by special study abroad programmes for leading cadres, such as in cooperation with Harvard Kennedy School. For government cadres, there is also the National School of Administration with its many local branches. In recent years there has been a lot of administrative streamlining in the system, with a substantial reduction in the number of party schools, thus reinforcing the elitist character. The cadre training institutions also offer academic degree programmes. Pieke (2009) presents the argument that the growing qualitative gap between national and local party schools widens the status differences between economically advanced regions and less developed ones.

35 On 'civilization', see Chapter 3, n.3.

36 This assessment follows the comprehensive study by Wedeman (2012). Most Western observers claim that corruption in China is systemic and reflects the institutional conditions of the one-party state (see e.g. McGregor 2012). However, even if one accepts this interpretation, the distinction between local and central state remains essential in shaping public perceptions of corruption, which eventually also impacts upon its actual practice. This picture has recently become flawed, when the anti-corruption campaign also involved the highest level political figures such as Zhou Yongkang.

37 For a survey of the security system and its evolution, see Wang and Minzner (2015). The authors show that the extension of the system goes back to the Tiananmen incident, and they argue that this is not simply tantamount to creating a 'police state'. Interestingly, the authors point out that these approaches to the 'comprehensive management of public security' bear strong resemblance to Imperial times in two respects. First, local cadres are strictly assessed in terms of their handling of local security issues and are therefore forced to adopt preventive measures, because any open manifestation of deviance would already impact negatively upon their evaluation; and second, grassroots-level units are collectively made responsible for failures in regulating and containing social tensions, such as schools and universities. The latter resembles the traditional 'baojia' (保甲) systems which for centuries have been recommended by Confucian scholars as the best way to maintain social order. These measures were accompanied by a reshuffling of nomenclature ranks, putting chiefs of public security departments above the rank of local government representatives, another example of using rank as a strategic lever. Detailed examples of the security policies on the county level may be found in Zhou Qingzhi (2014: 200ff., 225ff.), who distinguishes between different models. Local governments have created a strong capacity in surveying and intervening in grassroots-level tensions and conflicts, for example, via directly assigning township cadres to part-time jobs in the villages. This has created a certain pattern of interplay between citizens and authorities, for example, in the context of petitions,

'shang feng' (上访) (cf. Li *et al.* 2012): Especially in the 2000s, there was an explosion of petitions, often even reaching Beijing, and for local governments it became an essential task to keep the number of petitions low. This might imply outright suppression, often highlighted in Western media, but often also instigates constructive or even desperate attempts in addressing local grievances. The approaches differ across the localities, reaching from strengthening and increasing the number of grassroots-level party organizations to the development of more formal structures of citizens' involvement in village and district government. One famous model is the Taicang model of 'mutual interaction between government and society', 'zheng she hudong' (政社互动), which gives more rights but also responsibilities to village and district councils.

38 For a short general overview of the state of civil society in China see *The Economist*, 12 April 2014. According to Hsu and Jiang (2015), there were about 500,000 social organizations registered with the Ministry of Civil Affairs, but probably up to eight million unregistered NGOs in China in 2013. As the case study of Shenzhen shows (Ma Hong *et al.* 2013), this huge gap results from the often slow responses of the public administration to the rapidly changing social landscape. Even in Shenzhen in 2012, only approximately 10 per cent of social organizations were registered, even though the municipal government had launched an initiative of registration. Certainly this also reflects the fact that many of these organizations do not have a very elevated status and range of activities, including, for example, a large number of pensioners' associations, 'laoren xiehui' (老人协会). Hsu and Jiang argue that there are different types of NGOs and that the entire field is still in transition and dynamic shape, depending on the individual background of founders and government policies, without having yet coalesced into an established set of routines and norms. For example, NGOs founded by middle-aged ex-government cadres largely maintain close cooperation with government agencies, whereas those founded by young people without any previous experience of government tend to shun close relationships with government authorities. However, generally speaking, it remains important to emphasize that the expansion of the NGO sector has been clearly announced as a policy strategy, especially at the level of the local state.

39 The term 'responsive authoritarianism' has been coined by Fukuyama (2011), and the term 'consultative auhoritarianism' is used by Teets (2013). The case studies analysed by Teets show how the CCP allows more room for civil society, even if this touches on sensitive issues, but contributes to the resolution of social tensions. One example is the many initiatives devoted to migrant children. As long as those organizations do not engage in activities that challenge the Party state in a systematic way, they are given relatively large autonomy. This may also be usurped for independent goals, as is most obvious in the case of religious charities (see e.g. McCarthy 2013). Religious charities often use welfare activities as a vehicle to realize their religious goals, both individually as well as with regard to attracting new followers. This is also an example were tensions with the Party state can erupt. The other model is analysed by Thornton (2013), who created the acronym PONGO ('Party-organized NGOs'). This is a clear example of state corporatism in the variant of a Party-led corporatism.

40 The notion of the 'quadripartite system' has been proposed by Chen (2010). China formally signed the ILO standard on the 'tripartite system'. The 'quadripartite' reality is not simply a dysfunctional deviance, as certain forms of public resistance are also recognized as a legitimate form of expressing grievances, and since the avoidance of these incidents is a formal element in assessing cadre performance. Thus, wildcat strikes are a form of symbolic communication that is consciously performed with the aim of attracting the attention of

higher level authorities. One of the most famous cases (which was not a labour conflict) is the Wukan incident also analysed in Zhou Qingzhi (2014: 239ff.), when an entire village was eventually encircled by security troops, and finally even the provincial governor intervened. Generally speaking, the social capacities of migrant workers in organizing collective action are relatively weak, also because working conditions often deliberately curtail their emergence. Often, workers rely mainly on traditional forms of association, such as native–place associations, or even deviant structures such as gangs (see Wang *et al.* 2015); however, there is also the increasing activity of supporting organizations, such as NGOs, even including international ones, as an example (see Hofman *et al.* 2014). This sometimes meets with positive responses by employers, who want to improve labour relations, for instance, in containing high rates of labour turnover. Further, it needs to be recognized that not only workers but also employers are often only weakly organized, which exacerbates coordination problems especially in raising wages individually, since this is seen as losing competitive advantage against competitors. Thus, both sides would tend to perceive the local government as the ultimate arbiter in disputes over wages. Indeed, against the backdrop of the widespread belief that China has reached the 'Lewis turning point', there is no automatism in markets driving the rise of the wage rate. This became most obvious following the financial crisis of 2008, when the fall of foreign demand put great pressure on South Chinese exporters. In spite of complaints about wage pressures, local governments colluded with business in sustaining the prevailing regime of wages (see Lüthje 2013).

41 The new Labour Law of 2008 only recognizes individual rights of employees towards employers and does not formally regulate collective action, such as the right to strike. In many instances, conflict resolution is exercised via the courts in a mediatory role, thus partially obviating the need for collective action (see Chen and Xu 2012). This partly recognizes the legality of complaints, but remains a state-led solution that is mainly driven by security concerns. This pattern is called 'grand mediation' and is supervised by the 'comprehensive centres' for managing public security mentioned earlier (see n. 37 above); for a comprehensive overview see Zhuang and Chen (2015). There is also a stepwise leveraging of mediation mechanisms reaching from mediation by grassroots-level organizations to the courts. Chan and Hui (2014) report on new forms of 'consultations' between workers and employers which can be mediated by representatives who do not formally belong to the unions, thus formalizing the 'quadripartite' pattern. Most recently, there have been local experiments with formally establishing collective bargaining, such as in Ningbo (www.chinese-workers.com.cn/_d276712700.htm, accessed 13 June 2015). These cases are an example of the 'big party, small government, big society' model. The background is the conditions in industry clusters with a high share of private businesses which are also only loosely organized collectively. So, the local party committee takes the lead in creating an employers' association and actively assigns the task of collective bargaining to the local union and this newly established organization. The result is a comprehensive agreement not only on wages, but also on other aspects of working conditions, such as workplace safety. So, a tripartite system emerges, but with the Party as an element instead of the government. In this process, the party leaders can exert strong moral suasion on the two other parties, referring to notions such as 'harmonious society'. This is what constitutes a ritual order of the local labour market.

42 The use of 'models' in propagating rural reforms has a long tradition leading back at least to Republican times (see Thøgerson 2011). On the structures and processes of policy-making and implementation in the context of 'Building a New Socialist Countryside', see the papers by Ahlers and Schubert (2009,

2013). Their work is interesting, since it stands against the dominant trend in current studies on Chinese policy implementation that emphasizes its failures, especially in terms of local deviance and outright subversion and, eventually, the 'hollowing out' of local institutions (see Smith 2010). Instead, the authors analyse the ways in which higher level authorities activate local potential via the communication of policy guidelines and the propagation of models, together with the identification of change agents in particular localities. This also means adapting general policies to local circumstances, thus applying regulations in a flexible way. For example, the central policy requires the matching of funds in mobilizing local resources, which is often substantially softened for poor communities. Another way of adaptation is to even change mandatory targets in cadre evaluation, thus linking local strategy with contextualized performance assessment. An essential element of success is the establishment of so-called 'leading groups' which represent the strategic importance and activate the rank of members in implementing strategic priorities. I have already detailed the role of Party secretaries in the previous section and have also mentioned the specific routine expressions that describe this policy process, such as the relationship between 'thinking' and a 'model' (see Schubert and Ahlers 2012).

43 Heilmann (2008) has explored the different dimensions of this distinct policy process and has pointed out that it may have been influenced by American pragmatism, especially by James Dewey, who delivered lectures in China in the 1920s and attracted lots of attention. Mao Zedong himself is said to have attended some of these events. Pragmatism certainly harmonizes with traditional Chinese thinking, and is even more explicit in Confucian pragmatism (see Chapter 2, n. 86), but also in terms of the emphasis on situational logics and complexities in Daoism. The role of local forces in constituting frameworks for action is also explicit in one central term of traditional popular religion, 'efficacy', 'ling' (灵) (see Dean 2003). Religious practices can only be effective in activating such local confluences of cosmic forces, thus establishing also the ritual places and spaces, such as positions of temples or graves. Heilmann also describes the distinct routines that define the policy process in special terms. These are the experiments that may be seen as 'typical' for a certain situation, 'dianxing shiyan' (典型试验) and which trigger a process 'unfolding from a point to the surface', 'yi dian dai mian' (以点带面) or integrate point and surface, 'dian mian jiehe' (点面结合). These expressions reflect a peculiar attitude towards the notion of a 'typical situation' which is strongly imbued by normative aspects. This means that the 'typical' situation is not simply an 'average' in descriptive terms, but refers to potentialities that are 'typical' but which need to be activated by action, which is the experiment. Accordingly, a model can only be transferred when it is contextualized. In policy terms, this means that experiments are often conducted in a subversive way, such as in the famous Wenzhou case (see Parris 1993). Parris traces the debates about the proper designation of the Wenzhou case in the 1980s, where the term 'model', 'moshi' (模式), was avoided because of its normative implications, and instead 'pattern', 'geju' (格局) was used. An intermediate term was 'pilot project', 'shidian' (试点), used by the then premier Zhao Ziyang. The debate was only settled when Wenzhou was finally recognized as an experimental zone.

44 Heilmann *et al.* (2013) report the interesting case of the national 'Torch programme', 'huoju jihua' (火炬计划), one of the core elements in China's innovation policy. The programme was launched in 1988 and is devoted to the commercialization of high technology. It includes 83 'high-technology zones' which have been established by local governments nationwide. Interestingly, this programme was created under the direct responsibility of the then Chairman of the State Science and Technology Commission, Song Jian, who was not

satisfied about the growing clout of the National Planning Commission. Since he could not directly rely on central government budgetary resources, the programme was designed to be built exclusively on local resources. This resulted in certain developments that might be interpreted as failures in plan implementation, since commercial ventures often dominated the scene. On the other hand, this could also be interpreted as optimal adaptation to local conditions. Tsai and Dean (2014) develop an explanatory framework for analysing successful launches of local experiments and their specific context in the sensitive case of political reforms. They combine economic factors with specific political conditions, which include a 'factional mechanism' that is rooted in personal relationships between the provincial and the general Party secretary. Provincial Party secretaries in turn rely on the initiative of grassroots-level Party secretaries. Allowing for grassroots-level experiments is a low-risk strategy for both sides, because the provincial Party secretary may not need to assume responsibility for local actions. Since grassroots-level actions are often also under direct scrutiny of the central authority, central support may encourage the provincial secretary to go ahead. For this interaction, personal relations are important.

45 On the unique institutional dynamics of the double-track system, see Naughton (2007: 91ff.). The earliest comprehensive analysis of the double-track system was Byrd (1987, 1989), who had already shown that this system allows the achievement of efficient equilibria with the standard marginal conditions, leaving infra-marginal rents open for distribution however, which sets incentives for rent seeking and corruption. One could argue that these rents are side payments to the incumbents of the old system, thus lowering the political transaction costs of reforms.

46 Looking at the conditions at the county level, again Feng (2010: 131ff.) is a very valuable case study. In the year 2008, economy-related categories constituted an important part of the total of 1000 performance points that cadres could accumulate, such as GDP 60 points, urbanization 30 points, key projects 50 points and so on. In comparison, spiritual civilization received 30 points maximum. The only 'veto' targets were population policy and societal governance. Every year, the county government issues awards and a ranking of the most successful townships, and there is a clear impact of positioning for the subsequent careers of the respective leaders. However, Feng also argues that there is no automatism between high economic performance and advancement, and that the overall assessment matters significantly. One reason is that career patterns include a double step, first moving from more peripheral to central townships, and only then up to the county level. For similar information about other cases, see e.g. Chen An (2014: 727) where the rubric 'economic construction' makes up more than 50 per cent of the performance points. Schubert and Ahlers (2012: 82ff.) describe the cadre evaluation system at the county level and also point out that the results of evaluations are always made public.

47 On the structure of competition models, see Xu (2011); they often build on the generic theoretical model by Maskin *et al.* (2000). These models are based on a number of assumptions, in particular similarity of economic structures, since otherwise the behaviour–performance link cannot be compared across different cases; further, this structural similarity also keeps externalities across the different cases low. Only then can the competition models also operate efficiently. As was reported in n.46, however, these models exaggerate the role of GDP performance targets as a result of the necessary abstraction. In reality, the empirical literature has partly shown that the career prospects of cadres on all levels are only partly determined by economic success; for an early contribution

see Landry (2003). In a more recent econometric investigation, Luo *et al.* (2015) survey the literature and show that on the municipal and the county level, there is a strong impact of TFP growth on the probability of promotion; that may fit the observation that 'specialized' cadres or 'managerial cadres' (such as cadres transferred from leading positions in SOEs) also enjoy better chances. This means that the cadre evaluation system would indeed value economic leadership qualities. On the example of environmental policy see the case studies by Eaton and Kostka (2014) and Kostka and Hobbs (2012), which show how the leaders' time horizon affects the choice of policy priorities. This relates to the practice of rotation: every newly arriving leader has to design projects that are clearly linked with his person and can be finished within the time period of incumbency so that performance may be clearly assigned. Further, what matters is not so much the absolute record, but the comparison with the performance of predecessors and peers in neighbouring units at the same administrative level.

48 This system has evolved out of the general concept of 'responsibility systems', 'zeren zhi' (责任制), which have been applied across all economic and political domains since the 1980s. On the cultural roots of this system, related to the term *bao*, see Faure (2006: 73ff.), and Chapter 2, n. 32. The common feature of those systems is the contract which is concluded between a responsible person and the supervising agency. In the context of the local state, these systems are embedded in a comprehensive organizational structure of cadre evaluation (see e.g. Edin 2003; Ahlers and Schubert 2012). In this case, the evaluation is not simply conducted by the superordinate agency but by the organization department of the CCP. As we have seen previously (n. 46 above), there are a large number of specific tasks included in the obligations of cadres and which are all covered by a point system.

49 On the example of rural industrialization and TVEs, see the aforementioned study by Ong (2012), and n. 20 above. Chen An (2014) argues that these mechanisms contribute to an increasing gap between cadres and villagers as citizens, thus confirming Zhou's (2014: 168) assessment that the emphasis of economic performance criteria does not necessarily imply that the interests and concerns of the people are given stronger weight.

50 The continuing gap between subnational GDP and national data has been noted by many observers; see e.g. www.nzcta.co.nz/chinanow-general/1592/china%E2%80%99s-provincial-gdp-figures/ (accessed 7 November 2015). Often the national GDP data directly appear to define the lower bound for the dispersion of the provincial-level data, which is impossible. On the reliability of Chinese statistics in general, see Holz (2003). Holz argues that already in the early 2000s, the NBS had emerged as a professional organization that is certainly not falsifying data but rigorously strives to control such activities at the local level. Contradictions between GDP data and control data often result from the fact that coverage is not fully identical; for example, energy use data may not include all industrial enterprises. There is little direct empirical evidence on the local falsification of statistics. One empirical study is Tsai (2008), which shows that in a sample of villages, income data are on average inflated by about 50 per cent, with extreme cases up to more than 400 per cent. Tsai shows, among other aspects, that falsification is more probable when there are close relationships between township and village cadres, which implies that falsification can help improve the performance of the former. If villages leaders are elected and chosen from the business field, which happens increasingly, there is much less tendency to falsify. Another recent study by Jie (2015) offers a typology of different gaming behaviours, distinguishing between 'benign' and 'pernicious gaming', and in the latter between 'coping compliance' and

'malicious deviance'. In all these types the problem is central that performance targets may not match the local conditions and therefore cause adaptive behaviours with different degrees of deviance, aiming at fulfilling performance targets, both individually and with reference to domain of responsibility.

51 Zhou *et al.* (2013) show how in the field of environmental protection upper level authorities try to flatten out the differences in performance in their jurisdiction. For example, if a township experiences rapid economic growth at the cost of the environment, environmental indicators may be shifted to another township that still has leeway in meeting the minimum standards. Obviously, this may lead to strong distortions of grassroots-level statistics, but these may possibly average out on the higher level so that the aggregate data reported are close to accurate. I proposed a cultural interpretation of Chinese statistics in Herrmann-Pillath (2000b).

52 For the example of banking, see Yazar (2015). Yazar studies the Chinese Banking Regulatory Commission, which is also formally an independent regulator. One essential task is to supervise the safety of the banking system, such as monitoring and constraining the status of non-performing loans. This can stay in tension with the general aim of economic policy to maintain growth and employment, as in the aftermath of the financial crisis in 2008. Yasar argues that there is a three-level system consisting of principal (central government), supervisor and agents (industry) which opens up the possibility that principal and agents collude, thus weakening the position of the supervisor. This may involve extreme actions, such as in the reported case of the post-2008 crisis in Wenzhou, when the implosion of international demand put pressure on private industry. Since Wenzhou is a 'model' region, eventually even Premier Wen Jiabao paid a visit and made a statement that one should flexibly show more tolerance in the NPL issue. Therefore, within few years the NPL ratio had surged upward.

53 The structure of the Maoist planning system was scrutinized formally by Lyons in a number of articles (1985, 1986, 1990) which were devoted to testing Donnithorne's (1970) cellularization hypothesis. Ishihara (1993: 11) gives a concise overview about the diverse waves of decentralization and recentralization. In 1957, about 18 per cent of industrial enterprises were under direct control of the central government which amounted to about 40 per cent of output, thus indicating the general rule which still applies today that central enterprises are on average larger than lower level enterprises. In 1970, these numbers had dropped to only 0.2 per cent of enterprises under central control with just 8 per cent of output. Accordingly, the reforms were initiated with a recentralization that concentrated on the very large enterprises, so that the numbers were 2.8 per cent and 30 per cent, respectively.

54 Therefore, in analysing the effects of economic reforms and marketization one important indicator is the degree of regional specialization; declining regional specialization would indicate cellularization, increasing specialization would indicate marketization; see the discussion in Naughton (2003) or Bai *et al.* (2004). Therefore, this indicator also played a pivotal role in Young's (2000) provocative analysis claiming to show that in the first two decades of Chinese reforms the planning system has not really been dismantled but only decentralized regionally. However, the indicator is problematic, as is well known from the theory of international trade, because it does not take into account the possibility of market-driven intra-industry trade, which would not affect the specialization above a certain level of aggregation. For example, Young's indicator is highly aggregate and would therefore not allow one to distinguish these two possibilities.

55 As I mentioned previously, this argument goes back to Young (2000). Holz (2009) is a concise critique of Young's approach. As I discussed in n. 54, the

problem is that all possible indicators of regional specialization are theoretically loaded and therefore open to interpretation. So, there is always a tension between specific information about the effects of government intervention and the extrapolation to national-level aggregate phenomena; for example, the automotive industry has long been an example of the resilience of planning and industrial policy on the local level, since the industry was highly fragmented (for an overview, see Herrmann-Pillath 2008a). Industrial restructuring was intended to reduce parallel investment across regions, for example, by means of transforming former car producers into suppliers of parts. However, PriceWaterhouse Coopers (2011: 60ff.) still report that the Chinese supplier industry operates on individual factory scales that are far smaller than the international average. This indicates the persistence of inefficient parallel structures, presumably because of the intervention by local governments. Generally speaking, the literature on local protectionism has argued that the phenomenon was still strong in the 1990s but has been retreating in the wake of the 2001 WTO entry (see e.g. Poncet 2005; Barthélemy and Poncet 2008). In Herrmann-Pillath *et al.* (2014) an approach is used that builds on a largely atheoretic model which focuses on growth spillovers across territories and formulates an internal measure comparing the scope of spillovers among prefecture-level units, distinguishing between prefectures that are neighbours with and without a provincial border. The results show that there is strong market integration within provinces, but relatively less integration across provincial borders. Interestingly, this is most pronounced for the southeastern coastal provinces which are normally seen as being most advanced in marketization.

56 The classical work on this is Blecher and Shue (2001), who follow up on Oi's (1992, 1996) work on 'local state corporatism' that I considered previously. The authors reinforce the idea that local state interventionism was essential in overcoming limitations to development which are inherent in market dynamics. This argument is akin to Huang's (1990) analysis of the role of rural industries in overcoming economic involution. As I outlined previously, Huang argued that Maoist collectivization actually reinstated the involutionary dynamics of the family-based traditional economy, and that therefore marketization as such could not change this pattern. So, we meet a 'big push' argument familiar from development economics, though modified in referring to the role of local governments.

57 Greenhalgh and Winckler (2005) present a detailed account of the evolution of Chinese population policy, which underwent almost yearly changes and corrective measures in both directions of liberalization and strengthening. The policy is therefore an excellent case study for understanding the role of planning in the larger context of Chinese governmentality. The authors distinguish between three basic modes – 'revolutionary mobilization', 'bureaucratic professionalism' and 'socialist marketization' – with the direction taken towards the third, which was enshrined in the Population Law of 2001. Prior to that, birth control had no separate legal basis. Mobilization approaches were dominant in the initial years, such as in 1983, when the number of forced sterilizations exploded. New information about population data and techniques recurrently resulted in adaptations of policies, with the general trend moving away from 'birth control' to 'population policy' in the sense of a comprehensive 'biopolitical approach' that also emphasizes population quality, as I have elucidated in Chapter 3. It is also important to emphasize Greenhalgh and Winckler's observation that the policy was increasingly informed by international expertise, such as importing notions of public participation, practically included in the extension of programmes that emphasize general advice on sexuality and

family planning. This transition was accompanied by the fact that increasingly economic conditions and the resulting individual incentives shifted preferences about family size anyway, even in the rural regions. The cost of raising children exploded all over China, thus reducing decisively the individual aspirations to larger families.

58 Naughton (2009) presents the clearest case for including the nomenclature system and the cadre evaluation system as one of the essential distinctive features of China in the comparison with other transition economies, especially Russia. There are two general effects of this system. One is that the CCP can retain control over regional power holders in the economic domain, thus containing the centrifugal tendencies that erupted in Russia following the dissolution of the Soviet Union, which could only be held at bay by creating Putinism as a distinct form of authoritarianism based on the collusion with parts of the new oligarchy. The second is that the cadre evaluation system, as I will also argue, allows for retaining elements of planning even if these are only formulated as indicative plans or even 'forecasts'. This analysis is also supported by Chung's (2016) overview of central government instruments in governing the local states. For example, the CCP abolished the dual *tiao kuai* leadership of the discipline inspection commissions in 2004, thus vastly enhancing central control in a very sensitive part of the nomenclature system.

59 On this example, see Kostka and Hobbs (2012) and Eaton and Kostka (2014). One interesting aspect is the complex intertwinement of temporal structures that patterns the planning process and the cadre evaluation process. For both, typically a period of about three to five years is the fundamental unit, but they do not coincide, of course. This means, however, that the rhythm of Five-year Plans no longer dominates the political-economic dynamics of economic processes. Cadres will concentrate on their individual career rhythms, which means that they would aim at success in their mid-term, which is recognizable for superiors who decide on further advancement after term completion. This also implies, however, that the intensive processes of consultations and internal discussions of the Five-year Plans impact also upon the individual-level dynamics. For example, leaders who are able to perceive policy shifts via early signals emerging from these interactive communications may successfully launch initiatives that may later be identified as 'models' when the policy is adopted officially. This means that planning and experimention work together in creating a kind of 'anticipatory planning' at the local level.

60 Thus, for example, President Xi Jinping created a 'Leading Small Group for the Comprehensive Deepening of Reform', 'Zhongyang quanmian shenhua gaige lingdao xiaozu' (中央全面深化改革领导小组), which reflects the strategic decision of the thirteenth Party Congress to install the market as the guiding principle of economic policy. This approach percolates down to the lowest level. For example, in their analysis of the 'Building a New Socialist Countryside' initiative, Schubert and Ahlers (2012) show how county-level cadres create corresponding 'leading groups' which assume strategic leadership in designing and pushing initiatives without actually deciding on them in detail.

61 The early reform economists such as Sun Yefang developed the idea that marketization may be combined with planning in a way that is very close to Keynesian thinking, especially in its more interventionist forms that were also dominant in Europe in the 1950s and 1960s, such as 'planification' in France. Keynesianism was familiar to Chinese economists, since there was small number of economists who had studied economics abroad, such as Ma Yinchu (see Chapter 3, n. 8 and n. 12) or the development economist Zhang Peigang. I have reviewed these ideas in great detail in Herrmann-Pillath (1991: 131ff.).

Chinese economics has rarely been scrutinized as an independent ideational source of the policy process; exceptions include Hsu (2005).

62 Heilmann and Melton (2013) give a comprehensive overview of the current Chinese planning system and present the disputed view (see Naughton 2013), namely that it is a new approach to development planning which they characterize as 'controlled multiple advocacy'. They distinguish between national plans, regional plans and special plans. As for the national Five-year Plan, they note that there are still a number of binding targets, in spite of the fact that the plan has been renamed. These binding targets serve to communicate and enforce the CCPs strategic goals, such as in environmental and energy policy. Correspondingly, there is also a special plan in the energy domain which has driven the fast expansion of renewable energies, with many mandatory targets and also explicit mechanisms of intervention. However, the authors emphasize that plans largely address the government bureaucracy, and not the actors in the economy directly. This establishes the link with the cadre evaluation system and the nomenclature. There is also the notion that large-scale investment projects on the local level must be included in higher level plans, which applies especially to the macro-regional plans, since they are intended to coordinate the individual development strategies of local governments, such as the 'Pearl River Delta Programme' adopted in 2009.

63 Heilmann and Melton (2013) describe all those processes in detail. In case of the Eleventh Five-year Plan preparations started in 2003, but the final plan was only released at the NPC session in March 2006, after a final round of expert and public consultation under the leadership of the NDRC. Prior to that, an intensive process of discussing and drafting parts of the plan took place, with a number of distinct activities that are embodied in different types of documents, as the authors list: decisions, 'jueding' (决定), opinions, 'yijian' (意见), programmes, 'fang'an' (方案), explanations, 'shuoming' (说明) and methods, 'fangfa' (方法). In drafting such documents, many different levels and branches of government are involved. This is what the authors call a 'five-year policy cycle' instead of a 'Five-year Plan'. It is important to note that these cycles cut across transitions in government offices, so that policy continuity is guaranteed.

64 As an interesting example, see Yeo (2009) on the telecommunications industry. This also shows the partial recognition of the limitations of the concept of independent regulation in the Chinese context; see the discussion in Tsai (2014). Even though it has been argued recurrently that an independent regulator should be established for the telecommunications industry, Tsai argues that the experience with the weak performance of the power industry regulator has led to favouring the establishment of a 'super-ministry' in the telecommunications and information industry, the Ministry of Industry and Information Technology (MIIT). The MIIT, however, remains under the supervision of the NDRC, which, similar to the previously considered case of electricity (see n. 31 above), also keeps certain decision rights. On the other hand, there is the SASAC which directly exerts partial ownership rights regarding the telecoms companies. These mainly affect issues in industrial restructuring, which would therefore overlap with the MIIT regulatory competences. Yet, at the same time the SASAC rights are also contained, especially because financial flows directly connect the companies with the Ministry of Finance, so that the SASAC cannot exert autonomous ownership functions over residual profits, and, even more importantly, the top positions in the companies are under the control of the CCP nomenclature. Since NDRC also has a line of authority connecting with the SASAC, this implies that the regulatory role of the MIIT is relatively weak. The result of this constellation thus far seems to be that the telecoms

companies may collude with their formal owner, the SASAC, in protecting industry interests. One sensitive issue is pricing, which would directly affect consumer interests, and which should be represented by the regulator, the MIIT. However, 'excessive price competition' was actively restrained by interventions of the NDRC and MIIT in the 2000s, thus protecting the profitability of telecoms companies.

65 For an assessment of these early developments, see Pearson (1997). During this period, industry associations emphasized vertical connectivity and less horizontal connectivity, thus only operating weakly as an interest group of business. For an illuminating case study on business associations in the local state, see Foster (2002). In more recent times, one should also emphasize the desire of even private entrepreneurs to stay in close touch with official authorities, which certainly results from the uncertainty that the planning process creates for private businesses, as long as there is no direct access to the internal consultations. This is achieved by becoming a member of local political bodies or statist associations. Unirule Institute (2015) reports that the vast majority of entrepreneurs believe that becoming a member of local political bodies is crucial, reflecting also the belief of two-thirds of respondents that they are dependent on political authorities.

66 Even in an advanced region such as Shenzhen, however, the dynamics of civil society organizations appears to overwhelm the administrative system, as the vast majority of associations operates without official registration (see Ma Hong *et al.* 2013); one reason is that the 'villages within the cities' are especially vibrant places that are difficult to supervise. One lever to incentivize registration is the tax law, because associations would need to register in order to receive tax privileges as NGOs. If they fail to register, they may violate tax law. However, among the large number of local associations there are few business-related ones, with most being established by pensioners to organize collective activities. Local economic associations are established even at the neighbourhood level, thus remaining small in size, though pursuing the function of representing business interests vis-à-vis the local government. Other associations focus on particular industries which may be concentrated in a particular location.

67 I am not aware of more detailed research on these developments. As an interesting case (reported by the founder in a collection of articles; see Wu Jiyan 2014), I refer to the Hunan Chamber of Commerce (湘商商会) which was established in 2003 in Chongqing and rapidly evolved into a national phenomenon, with many Hunan Chambers founded in various locations. The first national convent of these Chambers was held in 2007, and in 2009 the largest regional Chambers co-organized a joint national meeting. Obviously, this took place independently of the National Federation of Industries. In 2010, the CCP Party Committee of Hunan province issued an 'opinion' on these developments, strongly encouraging their development. These Chambers have the standard functions such as mutual information, support, sometimes also coordinating projects such as the establishment of industrial parks for their members and so forth. However, the founder Wu Jiyan also instils the Chambers with a unique cultural spirit, both in the sense of tradition and modernity, which transpires in the frequent use of the traditional term 'shangbang' (商帮). The traditional aspect relates to the historical identity of Hunan province, which is a famous place of origin of military leaders (most importantly, of course, of Mao Zedong) but is less well known for business (indeed, Hunan became more densely populated only during the Qing dynasty, mainly by migrants from Jiangxi province who assumed a more active role in trade; see Perdue 1987: ch. 4). So, Wu constructs a 'business culture' of modern Hunan (also referring to

Mao Zedong, his strategic thoughts, and even to the fact that Mao's father was a rice merchant). The modernist aspect looms large in the emphasis on national spirit and civic responsibility on the one hand, and globalization and openness on the other. Thus, for example, Wu explicitly rejects the idea of 'Confucian merchants', 'rushang' (儒商). These ideas are enshrined in solemn declarations and mission statements of the Chambers. Wu also clearly puts the Chambers in the context of civil society developments in referring to the expression 'small government, big society'. So we may say that, on the one hand, the Chambers commit themselves to national goals, such as pursuing a 'harmonious society', thus apparently reflecting a 'state corporatist' dimension; yet, at the same time, they are grassroots-level initiatives with a distinct approach and identity.

68 For an illuminating study of the role of CEOs in national-level CCP institutions, see the study by Brødsgaard reported in Chapter 3, n. 73.

69 Even in core industries, such as telecommunications and automotives, the central government has accepted the rise and establishment of private industry competitors, even when SOE incumbents failed to be successful, in spite of having received the full support of the central government; for the case of telecommunications, see Harwitt (2007). Interestingly, the most successful companies are one private (Huawei) and one state-owned (ZTE), and even the state-owned company was actually not the focus of central government policy-makers, as it was an autonomous initiative originating in the Ministry of Aerospace and adopted the approach early on to raise funds on the newly established stock markets. Since the ownership status of Huawei is also opaque, we meet examples of hybrid companies here with close connections to political circles. Similar developments occurred in automotives, with the rise of companies such as BYD and Geely, where the direct support of local governments was also crucial in their early expansion (see Thun 2006; Conlé 2015). Conlé emphasizes the fact that the emergence of new production architectures also influenced the institutional patterns. In automotive industries, market entry has been facilitated by the modularization of components and platforms which reduced fixed costs of product development and enabled flexible supplier structures. This also enabled independent industrial policies at the local level.

70 The economic literature is aptly summarized in Xu (2011), and goes back to the seminal analysis of the 'regional property rights system' by Granick (1990), among others (see Chapter 3, n. 69). There is also a distinct and related intellectual tradition in China which started with early contributions such as Fan Gang's notion of 'brothers' competition' reviewed in Herrmann-Pillath (1991). The political science literature on 'fragmented authoritarianism' was launched in the seminal volume by Lieberthal and Lampton (1992) and has engendered a broad discussion in which there has been an ongoing generation of alternative views, such as the research on 'state capacity' in China. Generally speaking, the economic approaches tend towards oversimplifying the political structure, as my discussion of the 'quasi-federalism' paradigm has shown. In Herrmann-Pillath and Feng (2004), we have tried to achieve a theoretical integration by means of Breton's (1996) concept of 'compound government' which explicitly includes the notion of competition in the generic analysis of public institutions.

71 The notion of 'routines' has been given a prominent place in approaching economic systems and organizations in evolutionary economics, beginning with the classic by Nelson and Winter (1982); for a survey of more recent developments, see Lazaric (2011). The notion originated in the 'Carnegie School' in organization studies of the 1950s. In evolutionary economics, the notion

combines with a comprehensive view on the economic process, in particular innovation, thus combining micro- and macro-perspectives. The general idea is that market competition selects firms as carriers of routines, thus effectively channeling the diffusion of routines in a population of economic agents (cf., among others, Hodgson and Knudsen 2004).

72 For an overview of the approaches to political competition under authoritarianism, see Razo (2013). Political entrepreneurship is an important notion in applying evolutionary principles to politics from the perspective of economic theory (see e.g. Wohlgemuth 2000, 2002). This is very different from conventional approaches to political economy which are dominated by the Public Choice paradigm, reflecting the basic conceptual underpinnings in equilibrium theory. The theory of political entrepreneurship is inspired by Schumpeterian thinking, thus emphasizing uncertainty and innovation in political action.

5 The ritual foundations of markets

Chinese networks and the ritual embeddedness of economic action

In this chapter I want to look again at the 'other side' of market governmentality in China: markets. However, I will only marginally describe and analyse the particular mechanisms of markets, such as markets for grain or stock markets, but I investigate the normative and institutional foundations of markets, or, in other words, I look at the ritual aspects of markets. This involves two more specific questions. The first is how markets root in basic normative concepts and ethical values. I put this question in the context of the modernism component of ritual and relate it to the much-debated issue of whether 'modernization' also means the transition to a particular set of values which are largely associated with 'Western' values. In this view, markets are not simply economic technologies governing the allocation of goods in society, but also go along with certain values that have been characterized, for example, by Max Weber as 'rationalization'. This also ties in with the question of how far the Chinese economy gyrates towards capitalism, thus also adopting a particular value system that is often seen as undergirding capitalism.

One core topic here is 'individualism', standing in opposition to 'collectivism'. As we have seen, markets have been a pervasive element in the traditional ritual economy, so any belief that traditional culture and markets may stay in tension can be easily refuted by empirical facts. Yet, there remains some doubt about whether 'capitalism', in whatever form, still makes a difference in terms of the necessity to transform the value basis of Chinese society. In practical terms these issues pop up in more specific shape; for example, when the issue of the 'middle-income trap' is currently raised, and some observers would argue that China still faces obstacles to the transition to a truly innovative and liberal society which is deemed necessary to break through the trap. In these views, and similar to explanations of failure in Imperial China, Chinese ritual would be seen as an obstacle to market modernization. In the context of economics, this boils down to the philosophical question whether markets can be approached in an instrumental view only, which is dominant in China today, or whether they also embody a distinct value system of their own that also constrains political action and hence market instrumentalism.[1]

Another question I will deal with in this chapter is how markets are rooted in particular behavioural norms and the resulting interaction patterns. To a certain extent these connect with the more foundational value issues. I concentrate on one specific aspect that ties up with one of the general analytical categories I introduced in Chapter 1, namely social capital. In this view, markets are seen as being embedded in social structure, in particular in networks. This perspective reflects the pivotal role social capital has achieved in development economics and the theory of growth in the 1990s, on different levels of analysis, reaching from the explanation of differential success of micro-entrepreneurs in rural areas to the analysis of large-scale divergences across regions in developed economies such as Italy. In these views, markets may be economic technologies in the first place, but they need to be embedded in social structures that enable successful agency in markets. This question boils down to the analysis of social networks as media of market transactions.

These two questions are related in many ways, as the behaviour in social networks is guided by values that shape the mutual expectations of actors. Here, we meet a direct conceptual relation between the analysis of traditional Chinese culture and the explanation of social behaviour which has been the object of a large number of Western and also increasingly indigenous scholarly contributions. This is because Confucianism in particular propagates a certain set of values that is directly relevant for establishing and maintaining social interactions, such as the value of 'trust', 'xin' (信) (in modern Chinese complemented as 'xinren' (信任)). So, on the one hand, there is the empirical issue of how far real-world social interactions are driven by certain behavioural norms that may be related to values like this one, even without explicitly referring to the corresponding ideological background or written cultural tradition; on the other hand, we notice that in indigenous discussions these values are often factually invoked when reflecting upon these empirical patterns of interaction. The latter occurs in different shapes: one is the level of the 'participating internal observers' in the 'mirror of culture', such as when entrepreneurs consciously identify themselves as 'Confucian entrepreneurs', 'rushang' (儒商). This is what I will discuss in the next chapter. The other is that 'internal reflecting observers' work on the indigenization of social theory. This is what I will touch upon in this chapter. In this case, contributors to the debate argue that Western social theory is insufficient in dealing with Chinese social behaviour, since its theoretical terms are themselves culturally biased. We have already seen in Chapter 1 that this argument can claim plausibility, especially with reference to foundational concepts such as 'individualism'. Then, it is important to investigate the potential theoretical significance of indigenous terms in describing Chinese social interactions as opposed to 'Western' ones.[2]

This kind of research also gains in significance if we recognize the simple fact that social interactions and networks are, of course, not only confined to markets but are also universal in human life. Therefore, they also encompass the political domain. This raises additional fruitful questions. One is how values and social interactions shape the behaviour of political agents as well, so that we can identify certain similarities across the domains. The other is whether such similarities also impact upon the specific forms of cross-domain interactions (i.e. shape the interface between state and market). Thus, we gain additional insights into market governmentality. One important illustration of this is the cultural dimension of corruption, which I therefore choose as one empirical reference in this chapter. It is highly significant, in this context, that in traditional Chinese conceptions of society, this assumption of the homologous structure across domains is explicitly made in envisaging the state as being structured like a family, thus highlighting a common pattern of authoritarian paternalism. This idea has also often been received in scholarly research.[3]

According to standard economic theory, markets centre on individual actions: economics follows both normative and descriptive individualism.[4] However, as I have already clarified in Chapter 1, this is also a cultural conceptualization. The 'under-socialized' view on markets has been corrected recently by the deployment of analytical tools of economic sociology. In this view, markets are always and everywhere socially embedded. This means that markets can only be properly analysed in considering their underlying network structure. However, this insight is only slowly gaining ground in economics. The reason is that the analytical tools of economics and network analysis do not easily match up, even in terms of the basic ontological assumptions. Network analysis is structural, whereas economic analysis is reductionist in terms of the programme of methodological individualism.[5] These analytical problems are reflected in a sometimes hidden, sometimes explicitly stated presumption that the proper functioning of markets also presupposes individualism as a normative framework, both in the sense of providing legitimacy to certain institutions of markets that protect individual rights, but also in the sense of emphasizing certain behavioural standards. For example, the conceptualization of modern markets often relates to the 'heroic' view on entrepreneurship, with individuals taking risks and breaking with established norms and conditions. Innovation is seen as being launched initially by audacious individuals; therefore individualism is a precondition for maintaining innovative potential in any society. Indeed, one of the founding fathers of the modern economic theory of entrepreneurship, Schumpeter, also believed that capitalism will finally succumb to the forces of bureaucratization in the modern economy, increasingly favouring the emergence of large-scale organizations which no longer give a central place to the heroic individual. In his view, the transition to socialism was not a revolutionary necessity, but a side product of economic modernization.[6]

The visitor to China today will easily realize that the heroic view on entrepreneurship is widely accepted. Bookstores abound with biographies of famous entrepreneurs and political leaders. Large companies are often seen as being creations of individual founders who continue to play an essential role as a leader even after growing to a substantial size. At the same time, the individual motivation to assume the entrepreneurial role is widespread, with many Chinese eventually aspiring to set up their own business. This reflects a general inclination to highlight the role of leaders, which is also bolstered by CCP routines, especially more recently, where leaders such as Xi Jinping assume a very elevated position in public perception, again also in the sense of pushing change in society and politics.

The individualistic view on entrepreneurship has been questioned in many ways, especially in the context of considering full cycles of innovation, which include market penetration that normally has to rely on larger scale organization capacities. One aspect looms large in the context of this chapter. This is the role of social capital in enabling entrepreneurship. Individual entrepreneurs typically need to rely on personal networks, because they often lack access to more formal sources of resources for launching their projects. From that point of view, the heroic picture leaves out important determinants of entrepreneurial success and appears to be another instance of the 'under-socialized' view of markets.

These methodological issues are important in the context of Chinese studies, since one of the most influential concepts of Chinese studies in the past 40 years is certainly the concept of *guanxi* as far as imports of indigenous conceptualizations into international research are concerned.[7] This is a methodological phenomenon *sui generis* in the mirror of culture, as it is most salient in recognizing that the term is still used in Chinese in order to describe a phenomenon which appears at the same time to be universal if considered from the angle of social network theory. *Guanxi* as a term is simply 'connection', and social network theory describes exactly what is referred to as network activity in social network thinking. For example, building *guanxi* means to bridge structural holes in social networks that help increase influence and improve economic outcomes.[8]

So, from one perspective we could simply say that the focus on *guanxi* in Chinese studies actually exposes the neglect of networks in understanding Western society and markets in particular, and does not make any more specific statement about the nature of Chinese society or culture. In other words, in the mirror of culture, the neglect of networks in Western economics is a cultural phenomenon *sui generis*, and the Chinese case would actually emerge as the universal and generic one. In other words, modern social network analysis would appear to be the study of *guanxi* as a generic phenomenon, and there is nothing special to add in the case of China. The neglect of *guanxi* in Western societies would be seen as reflecting a cultural narrative that emphasizes modernization, rationalization and formalization as achievements of modernity and which hence imposes an implicit normative constraint upon the proper recognition of networks. This is straightforward to observe in economics, where the idea is often presented that modern markets are anonymous and build on abstract formal rules, thus overcoming the limitations of traditional markets that build on particularistic ties. Therefore, the rediscovery of networks as a medium of market organization was orchestrated in sociology, but not in economics, beyond certain more specific concepts such as 'relational contracts'; however, in economics these were only seen as being efficient under certain conditions, and did not count as universal constituents of markets.[9]

Methodologically, these considerations would imply that we approach *guanxi* as a generic phenomenon that provides the social foundations for markets, and just treat China as a case study. However, this view is not the prevailing one in China studies. Here, we observe basically two positions:

- One view points to the role of networks under the conditions of institutional uncertainty resulting from the transition from planned economy to markets. This view may be reconciled with general economic reasoning, insofar as the weakness of formal institutions is seen as propelling the use of relational contracts in arranging market transactions. In a relational contract, the involved parties rely on secondary properties of market agents such as personal relations in order to reduce uncertainty. They also use certain mechanisms to contain deviant behaviour. For example, even phenomena such as corruption may be seen as a mutual exchange of 'hostages', in this case reputation, that stabilize the relationship. The upshot of this view, however, is that once the quality of formal institutions improves, *guanxi* practices will lose their functional value and wither away. This view may also explain the persistence of *guanxi* practices through historical times, since institutional uncertainty and weakness of formal institutions can also be diagnosed for Imperial times. Thus, persistence of *guanxi* is not following on from cultural tradition, but reflects similar institutional conditions, both past and present. However, this argument may justify the assumption of a long-term persistence if the widespread use of *guanxi* undermines the emergence of strong formal institutions, both for the reason of lowering the demand or the need for them, and of eroding their quality. In other words, this approach does not preclude the working of strong path dependencies in explaining even the persistence of *guanxi*. However, the argument would also entail the hypothesis that the inefficiencies of the resulting institutional set-up would be discernible in systems-level comparisons of economic performance. The case in point explains the high levels of corruption as expressions of *guanxi* practices.[10]
- The other view approaches *guanxi* as a cultural phenomenon. This view does not question the homology between *guanxi* and generic

> networks, but would assert that there are phenomena of network construction that are unique to China. This also applies to the relational contract explanation. However, the cultural approach to *guanxi* implies that *guanxi* will retain their importance also under a regime of improved formal institutions. There is even the possibility that the direction of reasoning is reversed: the weakness of formal institutions may be explained by the strength of functionally equivalent informal institutions. As a consequence, strengthening formal institutions would not be seen as a necessary step towards improving the workings of markets. In other words, different institutional set-ups, one with *guanxi* and another without, would possibly show the same levels of performance. The persistence of *guanxi* through history would be explained as an expression of more fundamental cultural determinants which are specific to China. In this chapter I mainly explore this position, but I specify the term 'cultural' in terms of the intermediate theoretical term of 'ritual'.[11]

I think that these two interpretations do not really exclude each other, since the functional approach only predicts the decline of *guanxi* if formal institutions are seen as dominant frames of markets, which is even in doubt for advanced market economies if we follow generic social network analysis. There is also the possibility that informal institutions operate under the shadow of the law, which means that formal institutions are largely observed by market actors, although they arrange their transactions without fully relying on them. In fact, this is often the standard, especially in transactions that cross different jurisdictions. In this case, commercial codes and business practices interact with formal institutions, but the actual use of the latter can be very costly, such that the actors rely largely on the informal institutions. Formal institutions are only invoked when conflicts erupt that cannot be resolved by other means. Interestingly, as we have seen in Chapter 2, this practice was part and parcel of legal procedures in Imperial China, when the Magistrate's Court recognized diverse local customs in their judicative activity, and local inhabitants could opt for official recognition of contracts depending on need and interest.[12]

In other words, there is the general assumption that in the course of societal modernization, formal and informal institutions can evolve towards functional equivalence, such that we cannot simply say that functional improvements make informal institutions obsolete. There is also the possibility of cohabitation of formal and informal institutions even if they do not converge, which would be an expression of normative pluralism. In the context of legal studies on China, this view has been expounded in recent ideas about the role of networks in informal governance structures and even regulation of markets, and the explicit use of network structures in enforcing the law and the resolution of conflicts. I argue that the concept of 'ritual' is the proper framework to grasp these complex relationships, especially in making the distinction between formal and informal institutions obsolete or at least putting it in the secondary position. For example, if the value of *guanxi* is also determined by the relationship with persons on a particular formal position in government, *guanxi* include the essential reference to the status order emanating from the nomenclature, which is itself a formal institution.[13]

These observations point towards the general idea that *guanxi* may be conceived of as a specific manifestation of the ritual economy. This interpretation makes sense, but stays in a certain tension with those indigenous interpretations which may view *guanxi* as a deviant or even illicit form of relationship, thus actually making a distinction between proper relationships and *guanxi*. Partly, this reflects different cultural contexts in rural and urban society, with the latter often seeing *guanxi* as a remnant of traditional behaviour, thus defining proper behaviour in terms of modernist conceptions, such as professionalism. Yet, this also goes hand in hand with the introduction of new terms that often appear to designate similar behavioural patterns. I come back to this point in the section on corruption below. Right now, I therefore argue that the analytical primacy belongs to the term 'ritual', and *guanxi* is therefore only one manifestation of ritual.[14]

What is the 'Chineseness' of *guanxi*? There is some confusion about the term because certain authors tend to enlarge it to refer to social relations in general, including even kinship into the notion. However, this is seriously misleading and also does not match most of the actual indigenous uses. What is especially problematic with the extensions is mixing up social relations that cannot be shaped by the individual with ones which can: kinship belongs to the former, *guanxi* to the latter. It is an essential feature of *guanxi* that individuals are free to choose their activation, even though, once they exist, social pressure may emerge that makes avoidance difficult. In other words, there is a distinction between actively choosing, designing and establishing *guanxi* and acting within a certain set of given *guanxi*. One of the central instrumental variables in this process is the monitoring and management of reciprocity. A defining feature of *guanxi* is the existence of long-term reciprocity which is sustained by imbalances in the current interactions. This distinction defines the difference between genuine *guanxi* and ordinary social interactions. In *guanxi* relations, individuals deliberately create and maintain imbalances in reciprocal interactions and thereby maintain their relationship.[15]

The most essential features that may be extracted from *guanxi* research are as follows:

- *guanxi* are built on shared and constructed ascriptive similarities between individuals;
- they are maintained by keeping imbalances in long-term reciprocity;
- they combine an instrumentalist orientation with an affective anchoring.

To begin with the first point, *guanxi* can be creative in terms of assigning social markers to members and non-members. In other words, *guanxi* build on shared characteristics of individuals that are not necessarily given by pre-fixed identities such as kinship. These have been called *guanxi* bases, and may refer to certain shared experiences of earlier assignments. For example, a *guanxi* basis may be the classmate relationship or the same native place. In the latter case, it is most evident that the basis does not necessarily presuppose previous acquaintance. This is why the basis can be socially creative in establishing an entirely new relationship. Obviously, the feature that is being mobilized does not give any information about the a priori quality of the individuals. Hence, *guanxi* can only be sustained if a chain of positive experiences follows up. Therefore, in the end we may also say that all kinds of past successful interactions can become a *guanxi* basis, as long as there is an emergent criterion of categorization. This turns *guanxi* into an open network in terms of membership criteria.[16]

In business folklore this is reflected in the importance of events that are explicitly designed in order to create those shared experiences. So, practitioners emphasize the role of relationship building in finally establishing a functional relationship, such as repeated meetings in relaxed contexts, for example, restaurants. Thus, in analysing *guanxi* it is important to refer back to Fei Xiaotong's analysis of 'circles' in Chinese society. *Guanxi* bases should not be misperceived as fixed assignments to categorial groups, such that membership would automatically confer certain rights and obligations upon other members. This implies, most significantly, that *guanxi* are strictly individualistic. Strictly speaking, all *guanxi* are ego-centred networks, not only from the perspective of the ego, but also from the perspective of an external observer, since the ultimate criterion of membership is the relationship with the ego. In this sense, *guanxi* would actually appear as ephemeral phenomena that are continuously changing and morphing into new patterns, since every member of a network has her or his own ego-centred network, the entirety of which emerges from the interferences of these.

So, we can put forward the hypothesis that a fundamental difference between Western and Chinese networks is cognitive in nature, namely referring to the general feature of field dependence. Networks always impact upon agency via structure, but the question remains how networks are perceived by the actors. *Guanxi* individualism also means that network structure becomes contingent, and network formation is guided by field-dependent cognition. The core phenomenon is the contextuality of identifying *guanxi* bases. We have already outlined the basics of this distinction when introducing Fei Xiaotong's conceptualization of networks. The important methodological consequence is that we cannot approach *guanxi* as a structural phenomenon of Chinese society that may be ascertained and analysed from the viewpoint of an external observer, even adopting an etic perspective. In spite of the fact that *guanxi* are constitutive of the distribution of social capital in society, and hence ultimately also the distribution of agency powers, we cannot relate this to fixed structural properties.[17]

Indeed, we cannot interpret *guanxi* as expressions of group orientation, but as manifestations of individualism, corresponding to Fei's image of the expanding circles as wave-like patterns centred on the individual, and denoted as 'egocentric'. Every web of *guanxi* is unique in the sense of being the ego's web, and can mobilize an open and unconstrained number of *guanxi* bases. This also means that the effort of building *guanxi* is an investment in social capital. If we relate this observation to the social capital literature, clearly *guanxi* are a manifestation of Burt-style social capital; that is, they are network structures that are created by individuals in order to achieve individual advantage. Then, we also realize that *guanxi* bases are not necessarily a defining feature of individual identity. This means that, in spite of the shared feature, individuals may differ in many other respects. For example, *guanxi* based on native place can bridge status distinctions. This means that a *guanxi* network is actually a network that is potentially heterophyllous, in spite of building on a shared feature. In fact, many of those shared features are ephemeral, such as being born in the same lunar month, and thus almost work as a randomizer in creating social relationships among people who would be different in many other respects. This is a most important property that undergirds market transactions and determines their performance. As is established in social capital theory, heterophylous relations manifest a higher probability of opening up new opportunities for gaining individual advantage.[18]

The fact that *guanxi* are potentially heterophylous is most salient in analysing the role of emotions in making *guanxi* sustainable. This relates the notion to the classical distinction of network analysis between 'strong' and 'weak' ties. *Guanxi* appear to be a specific form of organizing weak ties. Accordingly, the 'Chineseness' of social networks rests upon a unique structuration and activation of weak ties. This is important in understanding the relationship between *guanxi* and market dynamics: in the general argument about weak ties and heterophylous relations the idea looms large that these relationships are particularly prone to generate new information for market actors. The more encompassing and far-reaching weak ties, the higher the probability of improving economic performance, especially in the context of markets. In the distinction between strong and weak ties, the notion of emotions plays an important role, as strong ties by definition are shaped by strong and deep emotional commitments, such as friendship ties. This implies that in reflecting upon the cultural specificity of *guanxi*, we need to consider the specific way in which emotions are handled in these relationships. In established theory, weak ties are defined by the absence of emotional commitments. In the Chinese case, however, emotions have specific functions in maintaining *guanxi*. Therefore, the essential difference between Chinese *guanxi* and the common notion of social networks lies in the apparently paradoxical combination between weak ties and emotional components.[19]

In indigenous terminology there are two different terms that come into play here, namely 'renqing' (人情) and 'ganqing' (感情), which both relate to the generic term for emotions, 'qing' (情). The term *renqing* refers specifically to ritual in the sense that *renqing* is the moral commitment to norms of reciprocity in social relations. For example, *renqing* refers to the norms of gift-giving in traditional rural society. Then, *renqing* can also become reified and refer to the gift itself, even including money in 'red envelopes'. The term appears also in many combinations, with a most important one which relates to the long-term reciprocity in social interactions, the 'debt of renqing', 'renqingzhai' (人情债). So, *renqing* is the ritualistic aspect of *guanxi*, and in this sense an externalist-expressive notion, which explains also the reifications. This also means that the emotional display is mediated via those embodiments, and less via direct bodily expressions.[20]

Therefore, in spite of using the term *qing*, *renqing* is not an emotional category in the standard sense, which tends to be internalist, in the sense of referring to internal states, although it refers to emotional commitments, and, in particular, to the notion of 'face' which comes into play if norms of *renqing* are violated. Loss of face triggers a set of inner emotional states which have been particularly relevant in Chinese tradition up until today, namely shame and embarrassment. These emotions relate to the failure in fulfilling the social role, in the sense of the persona, in the ego-centred webs of relationships. It is well recognized that the Chinese language distinguishes between two kinds of face, which reflects the ambivalence of *guanxi* as well: 'lian' (脸) is the 'moral face', whereas 'mianzi' (面子) is the reputation in terms of signalling social status. Face is also the object of reciprocity, as individuals not only care for their own face but also the face of others: this means that they 'give face' to the other. In this sense, face is a kind of universal and abstract embodiment of *renqing*, and is the object of ritualistic exchange.

There have been many debates over the proper translation and meaning of these different terms. Therefore, I can only posit one possible interpretation. This is that the two meanings of face relate to the individual (*lian*) and the social network (*mianzi*), respectively, thus placing less emphasis on the distinction between 'moral' and 'social' reputation. Reference to morality is actually pointing towards universalistic moral norms, which enable the individual also to assign 'face' as *lian* to himself, whereas 'face' as *mianzi* can only be given to an individual by others (i.e. it is an emergent network property). As such, however, it is also moral in essence and does not simply refer to social status as measured by wealth or position. This is also obvious from considering *renqing*. *Renqing* is not simply an 'emotion' that is assigned to the individual, but is a socially approved, externalized emotion that is fundamentally moral in nature.[21]

This moral nature becomes salient when considering the related notion of reciprocity. Again, we face problems of translation, as the central Chinese term 'bao' (报) has a meaning that combines instrumental reciprocity with even transcendent meanings, thus highlighting the moral dimension. The term 'reciprocity' may falsely suggest that the standard of evaluating reciprocity is the individual valuation, whereas in fact the standard is a socially recognized and ultimately an ethical valuation. This ambiguity is evident in different relevant ideational frames. In rural China, reciprocity is the flow of gifts that is observable to everyone, such as the chains of mutual exchange that occur during the sequence of life cycle events that alternate between families. However, reciprocity occurs under the shadow of the afterworld, an idea that was partly shaped by Buddhism and the notion of universal retribution. In popular religion, this means that all actions will come up against a compromise, both rewards and punishments, at any time in the future, including the afterlife. In Imperial China, this belief was articulated in certain customs such as moral bookkeeping. In other words, individuals maintained regular accounts of the deeds in order to calculate the balance which they would have to confront in later times and in the afterworld. This may be distinguished from the Christian belief in original sin, which can never be bargained away by any amount of doing good deeds. This means that reciprocity also establishes moral commitments which may be balanced even in the transcendental domain. Therefore, *renqing* may best be named as 'moral sentiments' in the sense of Adam Smith.[22]

The notion of *renqing*, as is evident from the previously mentioned term *renqingzhai*, ties in directly with the notion of long-term imbalances in social relations. Without current imbalances, no *renqing* would emerge that could stabilize the relationship and activate face as a mechanism that governs individual behaviour. As I showed in Chapter 1 when discussing the Hofstede approach, one reason why this value standard was modified to include 'long-term orientation' was the strong role played by this value in Chinese contexts. So we can venture the hypothesis that this is rooted in the unique dynamics of *guanxi* and the resulting emotional structures, which then show up in responses to value questionnaires.

We may therefore also say that *renqing* is a ritualized form of emotions governing social exchange. One possibility of catching the specificity of this notion is to differentiate between 'affect' and 'emotion'. This relates to an ongoing discussion about the specific forms of emotion expression in China, at least so far as traditional patterns are concerned. In this context, it is important to distinguish neatly between the expression and its evaluation. Social psychology has established that, basically, there are no substantial differences between Chinese and Western individuals in identifying and expressing emotions, but also that Chinese individuals evaluate these emotions differently. Western individuals appreciate emotional states that are affectively loaded, whereas Chinese individuals appreciate states that are more balanced and neutral. This matches ethnographic accounts that traditional social behaviour allows for a split between expressing and evaluating individual affects. Individual affects may be expressed freely, even violently, but they are simply seen as irrelevant to social interaction, just like natural events. Emotions that count are the socially approved and externalized emotions which have a ritual meaning. Accordingly, individual emotions weigh more strongly in social interactions that relate to ritual, such as shame.[23]

The underlying mechanism is the relationship between face and shame. The role of shame in Chinese culture is intricate and important, because it is a culturally evolved emotion that actually has the function to contain the expressions of other emotions in their direct impact upon those roles.[24] This means, in particular, that shame relates to orthopraxy and hence to ritual. Shame directly assigns responsibility for any kind of behaviour towards the individual, and hence is strongly individualistic. Yet, at the same time, it also subordinates any other emotional commitments to the social role which is regulated by the emotion of shame. This relates to the role of shame in the socialization process. So, expressing emotions such as anger is possible, but remains without impact upon role fulfilment. Orthopraxy is role fulfilment without any necessary connection to other 'inner' emotional states. So, this peculiar relationship between shame and other emotions is an important feature of the ritualistic nature of *guanxi* as a form of organizing and stabilizing weak ties.[25]

'Giving face' includes the avoidance of any kind of action that may embarrass the other side. Thus, concern for face is the reason why communication is often indirect, avoiding direct confrontation about controversial issues. However, indirectedness does not imply avoiding the sensitive issues at all, since the *guanxi* network is also a web of communication that disseminates information about the behaviour of its members. This sort of 'rumour', 'yilun' (议论), directly influences the perception of face in the network and is therefore a strong lever of reputational sanctions of which all individuals are aware. In this unique network structure, triadic patterns are the core unit. This is a major difference to standard economic conceptualizations of transactions which are dyadic. Triadic patterns have always been a central phenomenon in the organization of markets in the Chinese tradition, in the shape of the middleman and guarantor. The middleman is a person with a high reputation and face. If the middleman agrees to mediate in a transaction, he is running a high risk of losing face. This is a guarantee for the other two parties that the information he mediates is genuine. So triadic intermediation is an important way in which *guanxi* also undergird market transactions.[26]

To summarize the discussion thus far, *guanxi* involve a number of peculiar emotional structures which I denote as 'moral sentiments' and which are not individualized inner states of individuals, but manifest the emotional anchoring of *guanxi* and its expression in proper actions that maintain the *guanxi*. However, *guanxi* also involve such individualized emotional states, namely the *ganqing*. *Ganqing* is an individual emotional commitment to the relationship, in the sense of an affectual binding. Whereas *renqing* covers the ritual dimension, *ganqing* relates to the personal dimension of the relationship. This is another reason why *guanxi* require the investment in generic relationship building by means of frequent non-functional interactions. This emotional commitment makes *guanxi* ambivalent with regard to markets. In fact, in many circumstances it appears to be reasonable to avoid *guanxi* in market relationships because the emotional commitments may block access to the most profitable alternatives. So, we cannot simply say that *guanxi* and markets always go hand in hand, even under conditions of institutional uncertainty. There is also the phenomenon of *guanxi* avoidance in market contexts. As I have already emphasized, this is further evidence of the individualistic nature of *guanxi*. *Guanxi* are not simply forced on to the individual in the same way as kinship obligations are enforced by social norms, but the individual is in charge when handling, activating or avoiding *guanxi*. Therefore, in *guanxi* relations the functional aspect always looms large, in spite of the emotional commitments.

Actually, emotional commitment and instrumental relevance are mutually supporting features of *guanxi*. This is a very important difference to the handling of emotions in Western contexts, where the emphasis on instrumental goals aspects may destroy the emotional commitment. In this sense, we may even say that in the Chinese context, emotions are rational. This is sometimes perceived as opportunism by Western individuals interacting with Chinese individuals, sometimes misperceiving emotional commitments as indicators of non-instrumental relationships such as friendship. However, in the indigenous view, these non-instrumental relations are clearly different from *guanxi* relations, even though the latter also manifest emotional commitments. Therefore, one of the peculiar cultural features of *guanxi* is instrumentalism with regard to emotional commitments. The most fundamental function of emotions is the creation and maintenance of trust between the interactive partners. This is what the rationality of emotions resides upon.[27]

Thus, we can finally relate the notion of *guanxi* to the phenomenon of trust, which is also widely recognized by economists as an essential element of well-functioning markets. Trust emerges owing to the confluence of the two kinds of emotions that undergird *guanxi*: *renqing* and *ganqing*. In this sense, we can indeed argue that *guanxi* are a universal medium of markets in China, in the moment when issues of trust are involved. This also implies that the ritual order of *guanxi* impacts upon market performance.

To summarize my analysis of *guanxi* thus far, three features of social networks appear to be specific to China:

- field dependence of network boundaries;

- instrumentalism of emotional commitments;
- long-term reciprocity as stabilizer.

However, this characterization also shows that it would be misleading to approach *guanxi* as the central social phenomenon. *Guanxi* is simply a mechanism of establishing social relations that is itself embedded in the larger patterns of ritual. This also explains why the term often has ambivalent meanings, as there are also improper ways of 'pulling *guanxi*'. Only in the larger semantic canvas that is spanned by terms such as *mianzi, renqing* or *bao* can we properly assign a meaning to phenomena of *guanxi.* One particularly important aspect of *guanxi* and face is that, accordingly, *guanxi* are deeply integrated with the status order, thus reflecting Fei Xiaotong's emphasis on hierarchical relations. These are not simply related to formal status order, such as political status, but to reputation in general, hence positioning in the ritual economy. One of the clearest pieces of evidence for this is the rise of what economists call 'positional spending'; that is, the rapid growth of expenditures devoted to gift-giving, with the more specific form of spending on the occasion of life cycle events, thus actually reviving a central aspect of relationship management in traditional China. So, the semantic ambivalence of the term 'ritual', *li*, becomes fully evident, as *li* originally also related to 'gift' (as today in 'liwu' (礼物), gift). Again, we have to consider the two sides of gift-giving, expressing one's own position and recognizing the position of the other. So, the status order is directly expressed in the value of the gifts, such as in 'giving face' to a person with high status in sending the appropriate gift.[28]

Taken together, we may say that *guanxi* is a particular cultural pattern of the formation of social capital in building and maintaining weak ties. The most condensed expression of this phenomenon is the creation of trust among individuals who are only loosely related otherwise. Trust, *xin*, is a core value of the Confucian canon of virtues. One of the intricate issues in dealing with Chinese culture is the role of trust in social relations that go beyond the borders of the 'familiar', 'shu' (熟) if understood as the existence of strong ties. This is where *guanxi* come into play. Indeed, we may surmise that the ultimate instrumentality of *guanxi* does not rest in the value of the opportunities that may be reaped by utilizing them, but in the value of the information that may be gained via them.[29]

Trust, corruption and social order

I have already stated that the concept of *guanxi* is ambivalent in indigenous views, especially in the urban context. Often, *guanxi* appear to be hotbeds of illicit relationships, if not outright corruption. This stays in contrast with other claims that propagate *guanxi* as a specifically Chinese cultural capacity in managing social relations, thus conceiving them as a major element of social order. This ambiguity may be condensed to the question how far *guanxi* are an independent basis for trust, as seen not only as a particularistic, but also as a universal social and moral value. The question of trust is a crucial one for understanding Chinese society, past and present, according to many observers.

For one, this refers to the standard view on circles of trustworthy relationships which normally would not extend to strangers.[30] In this view, kinship is the strongest foundation for mutual trust, and other personal relations follow with decreasing strength. Among strangers, mistrust would be endemic. Although this is largely explained as reflecting Confucian moral convictions that allegedly emphasize ethical particularism, probably empirically more convincing is referring to the Chinese tradition of migration and travel, which often led people into completely unfamiliar environments, thus turning them into strangers in an unfamiliar place. So, endemic mistrust may be a feature especially of the frontier and migrant societies which were widespread in late Qing China, for example, when coastal people visited interior provinces such as Hunan or Sichuan. To this, one might add the fact that Qing China was under foreign rule, thus also highlighting ethnic discrimination. Interestingly, this argument may also apply in modern contexts, *mutatis mutandis*, as in the special case of Taiwan with the tensions between native Taiwanese and Mainlanders after 1948. These conditions were further accentuated in the historical experiences following the collapse of the Empire, which for most Chinese meant chaos, violence and dislocation. As I have argued previously, this certainly also applies to the most recent times, especially during the Cultural Revolution, when political campaigns led to a very high level of individual insecurity. In this sense, the Cultural Revolution may be seen as a watershed event in China's psycho-cultural history, leading to the collapse of any kind of traditional moral order, and thus accentuating the loneliness of the individual in a hostile social environment.[31]

However, this standard view on traditional China stands in tension with two other observations. One is the central role trust, *xin*, plays in the Confucian canon of virtues, both in popular and elite versions. We can relate this to the notion of ritual and the related concept of sincerity, *cheng*, which may also be translated as 'authenticity'. These values are clearly promoted as universalistic moral norms, especially in the sense of individual character features: the morally perfect person is someone who is absolutely trustworthy in relation to everyone, not only his kin and peers. In reality, these ideas exerted a strong impact on practices among merchants, who often relied on ritualized codes of conduct that referred to these values. The other observation is the factual resilience and growth of markets in traditional Chinese society far beyond the reach of 'strong ties'. This matches the previous analysis that treats *guanxi* as organizing principles of 'weak ties'. Then, we notice that the standard view on concentric circles of trust with declining reliability entirely blanks out the role of non-kin organizations in providing for the establishment and maintenance of *guanxi*, as I elaborated in Chapter 2. For example, native place associations were based on a criterion of similarity that certainly also gathered strangers together, yet from the same places of origin. They operated as an arena in which *guanxi* relationships could flourish, to be explained easily through standard hypotheses about the role of reputation and reciprocity in maintaining reliable interactions and containing cheating even among strangers. Chinese traditional social structure was far richer than the standard view recognizes, and this social structure enabled trustworthy interactions with a very wide range and complexity. That being said, we certainly also need to take into consideration the different meanings of kinship in these contexts, as extended agnatic and affinal kin relations could achieve considerable scale and reach, covering thousands of individuals living in different locations, and stretching those relations geographically when travelling.

On the other hand, if we consider the conditions in contemporary China, there is the widespread perception of a fundamental and worsening 'crisis of confidence', implying a pervasive erosion of trust in society, thus apparently compressing trusting relationships into a shrinking circle of relatives and friends. This crisis of trust seems to be driven by systemic phenomena, especially corruption and the many occurrences of regulatory failure that tie in with the former. One especially conspicuous example is the series of food scandals in China, since food is certainly a major concern in the Chinese lifeworld in terms of enjoyment but also and particularly as a determinant of health. Therefore, if food proves to be of unreliable and even harmful quality, this has strong effects on the individual's trust in the system. Both experiences match the more general trend in public opinion that diagnoses a decline in morality as a consequence of rampant marketization, competition and hedonism, a picture that is currently reinforced by the campaign against corruption which made public many instances of high-level corruption involving serious personal misbehaviours, such as high-ranking CCP functionaries maintaining luxury lifestyles, many mistresses and expensive mansions.[32]

So, with the launch of the anti-corruption campaign, a growing number of Chinese see Chinese society as being trapped in a political system that systematically enables political elites for personal enrichment. However, there is also the fact that corruption does not seem to endanger economic growth and entrepreneurial success. There is another fact that may appear even more astonishing, namely the generally high level of confidence that Chinese individuals express in their political institutions. This matches with the general characterization of China as a 'high-trust society' that transpires even in the most recent surveys about values, but which is a stable characteristic throughout the years. We can relate this paradox to a similar observation we have just made regarding traditional China. As I briefly surveyed in Chapter 4, we observe a vibrant and rapidly growing civil society in China, with hundreds of thousands of local initiatives added every year, in almost all social domains, with the only limitation imposed by the political control and sometimes suppression of the CCP. Many of these initiatives expressively invoke civic values, and some also relate these to traditional Chinese values. From that perspective there is a crisis of trust, but there is also a vigorous response to that, which in turn builds on a shared basis of trust, the lack of which is otherwise deplored.[33]

We can substantiate these observations by glancing at recent international value surveys. Indeed, one surprising fact about China is that in the recent waves of the World Value Survey China scores very high (close to Scandinavian countries; I give the example of Sweden in Figure 5.1) on the 'general trust' question (Can most people be trusted?).[34] I compare China with other large countries in the world, featuring different political systems and cultural backgrounds, and include Sweden as reference for a 'high-trust society'. China stands out, especially against the other so-called emerging economies in the sample, Brazil and Russia, both known for rampant corruption. The WVS allows a comparison of the results through time, though with varying coverage of countries and certainly with different statistical quality of local implementation. Yet we can clearly say that the performance of China is stable through time, always showing a share of people who 'generally trust' above the 50 per cent line. In comparison, Russia has been deteriorating over the same time period. There is another WVS question which confirms this result, asking whether people think that most others will take advantages of them or will be fair. This allows for choice among degrees. Again, China's profile is similar to the Swedish

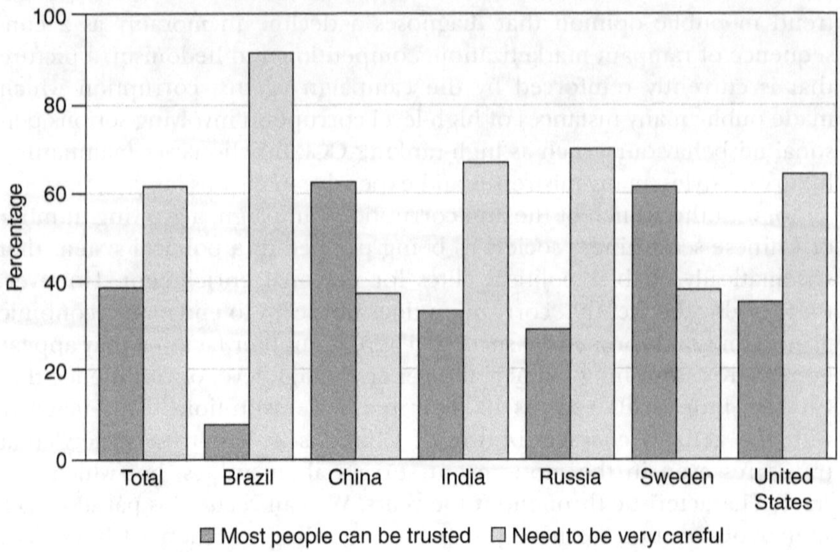

Figure 5.1 General trust.

one. Hence, according to this result, China is among the small number of 'high-trust' societies in the world.

The 'general trust' question is very important in the context of economics, since in most research on the relationship between values and economic performance this question is used as a proxy of social capital. However, upon closer examination we need to be analytically precise here, as social capital is a source of trust but should not be conflated with it. On the other hand, trustful interactions are a breeding ground for social capital. By implication, if it were claimed that the exceptional Chinese data are biased, other research in this area may have been on the wrong tracks. Indeed, China is also a regular outlier in social capital research. The trust question is so important, since economic theory suggests that a high level of trust is conducive to the growth of markets because it contributes to a low level of transaction costs. This is especially relevant in the context of the 'anonymous markets' paradigm, because otherwise market actors could only rely on legal enforcement in order to protect their interests. If 'most people can be trusted', that includes strangers on the marketplace. So, the results would suggest that China offers good conditions for market development, and that, obviously, even widespread corruption does not countervail this tendency. The latter observation raises the tricky question that I discuss in a later section: namely whether corruption itself builds on trust or is a means to create predictable environments.[35]

If one checks for the external validity of this survey result, it evidently runs against a widely cited assumption about Chinese culture that we have already discussed at the beginning of this section. This states that Chinese in general express very low trust in strangers. Fortunately, the WVS allows for assessing this apparent contradiction with another question: China no longer seems to be that exceptional. Asked whether they trust people whom they meet for the first time, China is still far above Russia, but is now clearly below the values for advanced Western economies, thus matching expectations (Figure 5.2). Is there any way to reconcile the two results?[36]

I argue that the special dynamics of *guanxi* can explain the peculiar Chinese results, which leads us back to the analysis of social structure by Fei Xiaotong. The simple question is what people have in mind when they refer to 'most other people': if they think of 'most other people' with whom they actually interact in everyday life, the response will be different from people who would consider this question in the abstract way, namely thinking of all people who they may possibly meet within a certain arena of potential social interactions. So, the cognitive framework matters that guides the responses: if the question is viewed in a field-dependent context, people will adopt the first perspective; if it is viewed field independently, people will adopt the second, viewing their society as an abstract category. More specifically, we can relate this to the *guanxi* analysis. The *guanxi* network is not a network of people who are connected via primordial emotional bondings, such as kinship or friendship. *Guanxi*

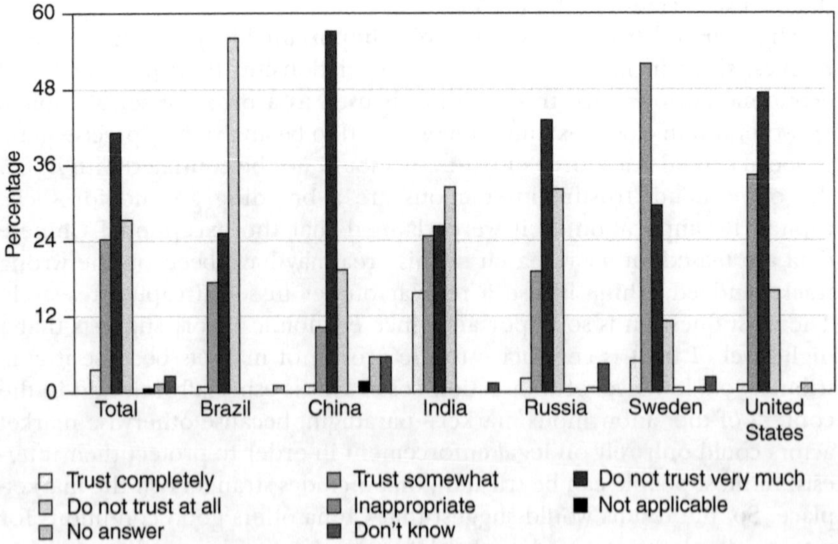

Figure 5.2 Trust towards strangers.

extend far beyond that and mostly include semi-strangers, as I have argued in relating *guanxi* with weak ties. *Guanxi* are a mechanism that turns strangers into familiar people, yet still beyond the reach of close relationships. So, if a person perceives society via the lenses of her individual *guanxi*, then the general level of trust is high. However, *guanxi* do not include people who one meets for the first time. So, trust is low without *guanxi*. Yet, if most interactions happen between members of ego-centred networks, this does not affect the general trust in society. In other words, in a society of 'circles', social relationships can be open and extensive, approaching the reach of so-called 'anonymous' networks, yet the particular relationships are not anonymous, especially if we take the triadic patterns into consideration and the role of face. As a result, China emerges as a 'high-trust society' in the surveys, even though many Chinese would even expressively deplore a 'crisis of trust'.[37]

Indeed, we have already noted the widespread discourse about the crisis of confidence in China. This is largely related to the phenomenon of corruption, and more specifically to certain phenomena in the marketplace. As mentioned already, an especially sensitive area is food safety, given the high cultural value of food consumption in China. In this case, we have a special constellation which results from the modernization context and the expansion of markets. The relationship between a customer and a large corporation cannot be arranged in a *guanxi* network, but builds on confidence in brands and regulatory supervision. So, after the milk powder scandal, confidence in Chinese products has been seriously damaged up until today. Thus we need to distinguish between personal trust and institutional or system trust, as is regularly done in theoretical treatments of the trust issue.[38] Then, one would argue that China has an especially powerful social structure generating personal trust with large range and scope, but is deficient in system trust.

However, if we go back to the WVS survey, again this cannot be confirmed. The results could only be explained away in arguing that Chinese respondents just give 'politically correct' responses. For example, there are questions asking about confidence in the police, the civil service, the courts and the press, allowing for gradual differentiation. Some results are extreme: for example, only about 23 per cent of US respondents express confidence in the press against about 60 per cent of Chinese. In the case of the police, the two countries both approximate the 60 per cent overall confidence level, clearly differing from Russia where about 55 per cent of respondents express no confidence.

One explanation of this apparent contradiction refers to the dichotomy of local state versus central state, thus relating the survey results to one of the essential defining features of Chinese governmentality. This transpires in the question about confidence in central government, which I give as an illustration in Figure 5.3. In this case, China leads the pack with up to 85 per cent of respondents expressing confidence, whereas the majority of US respondents express no confidence. This question clearly needs contextualization, if one considers that the opinion in Russia is roughly divided, and that in Brazil the majority is in the negative, in India in the positive. In democratic systems, certainly the question is influenced by the

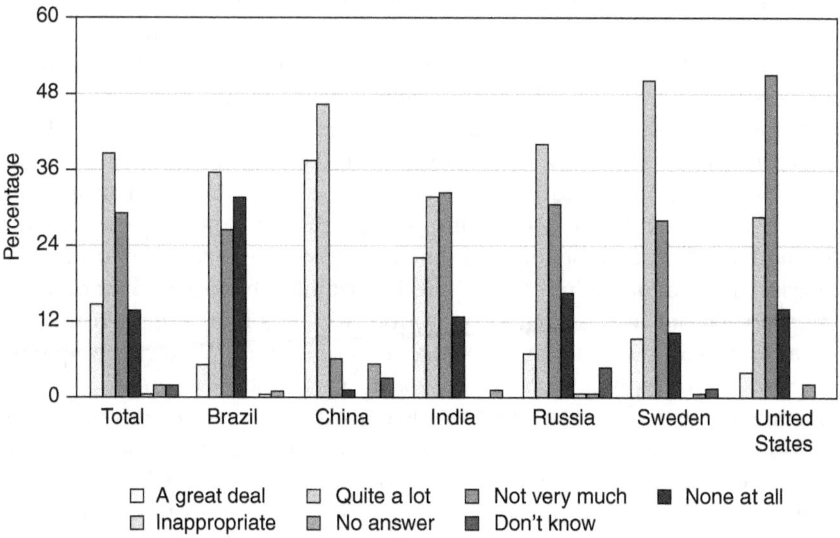

Figure 5.3 Confidence in national (central) government.

perception of the incumbent government at the time of the survey, and thus may be a partly transient phenomenon. On the other hand, this also means that in the case of China we might observe a more stable perception. In most discourses about corruption, criminal corporate behaviour or abuse of power in land transactions, responsibility is assigned to the local state and its representatives. This separation between the local state and the central state is certainly also a persistent message of anti-corruption campaigns in China, although a remarkable feature of the recent campaign is that it also targets highest level politicians or even army leaders. But generally speaking, the central government assumes the position of moral leadership vis-à-vis the local state in these campaigns. Therefore, even though the explicit naming of widespread corruption in campaigns confirms societal perceptions of the issue, this does not necessarily affect confidence in central government. So, campaigns can even lead to higher levels of legitimacy of the government, even though possibly eroding the legitimacy of the local state. But since local states differ across China, this does not automatically entail a national crisis of legitimacy. This is also evident from another question in the WVS related to confidence in the civil service, which largely encounters citizens on the local level. Here, levels of confidence are generally higher across most countries (with especially weak performance of the US), but China is again on top, together with Sweden and India.[39]

Interestingly, the interpretation of these results in terms of the central/local duality also makes sense in terms of Fei's general model of 'circles'. If corruption is seen as being organized in *guanxi* networks, these do not have systemic-level properties, but are fragmented into local phenomena. Relative to these local processes, the central government assumes the role of moral leadership. Hence, the fight against corruption is another expression of ritual, as I argued in Chapter 5. We can say that this ritualistic leadership is a means to channel *guanxi* interactions into proper ways. So, the question indeed looms large how far *guanxi* are part and parcel of corruption, in the sense that *guanxi*-based markets would necessarily entail high levels of corruption. This hypothesis can be made in a straightforward manner, since *guanxi* imply a recurrent flow of gifts and the exchange of mutual benefits which may accompany or even undergird market transactions. Therefore, there is certainly a huge grey area between *guanxi* relations and outright corruption, which is most salient if we consider the cross-cultural tensions that emerge when Western companies impose international business standards upon Chinese employees and partners.[40] Of course, we need to distinguish neatly between corruption among market actors and corruption between market actors and holders of office. However, given the strong overlap between business and the public sector in the Chinese system, this distinction is often difficult to make, especially in the case of state-owned companies, but also in local business which may be controlled by former cadres.

In the general taxonomy of corruption, we can differentiate between the various degrees of corruption and its systemic roots. Often the public image of political corruption is shaped by the image of kleptocratic regimes which are dominated by a political leader. In the most extreme form, this means that a hierarchic network of patronage relations is established which encompasses almost the entire society. This may also be reflected in the standard corruption indices. For example, the Transparency International Corruption Perception Index puts China at the rank of 100 (of 175 countries), Russia at 136, Indonesia at 107, India at rank 85, and Brazil and Italy at rank 69. In 2010, China stood at rank 78 (of 178 countries), so we may conclude that the anti-corruption campaign launched in 2013 also influenced public perception, since, after all, we may assume that the campaign as such may have even reduced the actual incidence of corruption. Overall, China lingers in the middle ground across the years, together with many democracies of the developed world.[41]

Against this image, we need to recognize that *guanxi*-based corruption manifests a different structure. *Guanxi*-based corruption centres on particular individuals as well; however, egocentric *guanxi* networks stay in a competitive relationship with each other. There is no necessary trend towards complete integration into one single network. This is certainly also determined by the size of China and the dichotomy between local and central state. In the local state, extreme forms of patronage hierarchies may come into existence, hence establishing local kleptocracies (the so-called 'predatory states'); yet, this is still far away from a national kleptocracy. Even if a patronage network is created by central-level patrons, this remains limited in scope and certainly does not achieve national scale. This implies that even if corruption is prevalent, it does not necessarily obtain systemic status.[42]

Network competition may even explain what many practitioners have referred to as the 'efficiency' of corruption in China. This means that corruption is perceived as compensation for a service that pays off for both sides. This observation is relevant in understanding the changing nature of corruption in the course of reforms. Generally speaking, we can distinguish between two stages. The first stage was the period of market liberalization up until 2000 generally speaking, and the second period is between 2000 and the present. In the first period, most corruption occurred in the context of the double-track system. This means that there were strong incentives to exploit regulatory loopholes between administrative allocation and market allocation of goods. For this form of corruption, we can indeed state that it is 'efficient' in the sense of channelling economic activity into markets, thus creating a tendency to realize optimality conditions. The effects of corruption mainly show up in the distribution of results, with rents even being dissipated via the competition for opportunities of corruption. In this context corruption is widespread but also dispersed, and rarely involves huge transfers of wealth.

In the second period, we observe another pattern of corruption that appears to be a shift towards pure cases of bribery, which is also evident from the recent anti-corruption campaign. A major impetus for this change was the role of land transactions and real estate development in the local state, as we have analysed in Chapter 4. These transactions involve much larger single values of corrupt actions and therefore have a much bigger impact on the distribution of wealth at the top of the income distribution.[43]

So, we can venture the hypothesis that the pattern of corruption in China is driven by the interaction between network dynamics and the trajectory of institutional change. This implies that the economic consequences also differ through time and in comparative terms. Yet, one general feature of Chinese corruption is that it is not systemic but individual and local in nature. This corresponds to the previous analysis of the impact of the local state/central state dualism. Correspondingly, even a relatively high incidence of corruption would not imply that corruption blocks access to individual opportunities for the majority of individuals. Interestingly, the WVS also allows support of this hypothesis by some its results. One question is about the perception of the factors that determine individual success, personal effort or luck and connections. The Chinese pattern most closely approximates the US pattern, clearly geared towards the majority of respondents who believe that 'hard work brings success' (Figure 5.4). In comparison, in Russia and India the distribution is much more biased towards the other pole. In other words, corruption does not affect the general belief of people in the openness and possibly even fairness of the distribution of economic opportunities in society. This is also reflected in several other results. One remarkable result reflecting the openness of opportunity is the question whether 'people can only get rich at the expense of others', where, on a nine-grade scale, only a small minority of Chinese tend towards this pole; the distribution is geared towards the pole 'there is enough for everyone'. This compares, for example, with a majority of Indians who tend to support the former statement. Chinese also largely believe that competition is good for society, an opinion regarding which countries show a more convergent trend.[44]

One of the important expressions of this basic attitude is the acceptance of disparities resulting from individual effort and success. Certainly over recent decades the general concern about growing disparities in Chinese society has heightened. However, these concerns are mainly driven by the perception of abuse of political privilege. Reliable data on public opinion are difficult to gather. Generally speaking, it appears that the Chinese are ready to accept disparities that reflect individual success, as long as the access to opportunity is open to everyone. This is indeed a Chinese version of the 'American dream'. For example, there is widespread agreement that the *hukou* system results in unfair discrimination of rural dwellers in terms of opportunities. At the same time, many rural

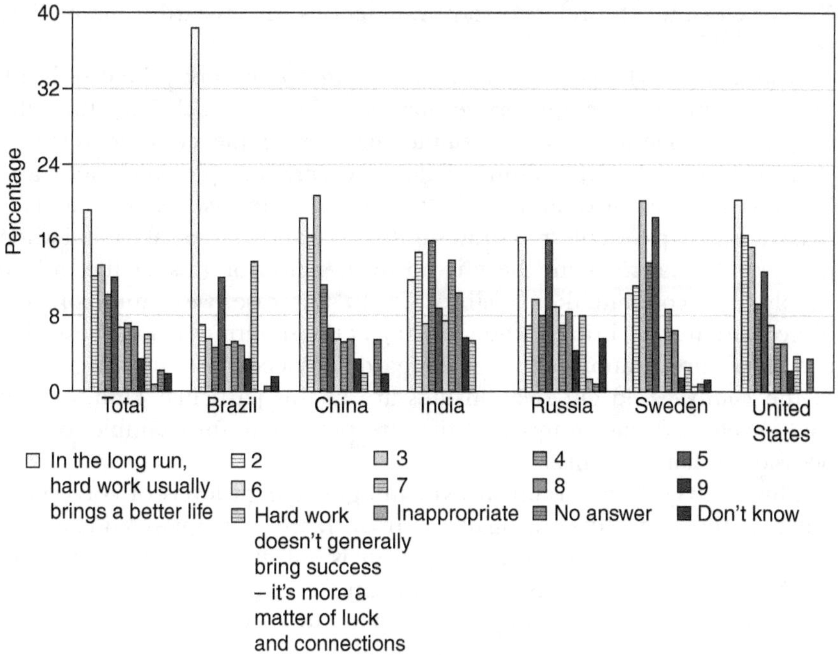

Figure 5.4 Hard work brings success.

people show a positive attitude towards the gradual opening up of opportunities. This may be partly explained by the different reference groups which count for the self-assessment, and thus points again to the strong role of local contexts.[45]

So, the paradox of corruption in China is not easy to resolve. As a final point, we need to consider another aspect of *guanxi* that may impact upon patterns of corruption. This is the long-term horizon of reciprocity. Thus, we distinguish between spot transactions and delayed reciprocity. A typical spot transaction is to pay a bribe to a policeman in order to avoid a fine. This type of corruption is also widespread in China, but is probably confined to certain areas as far as systemic aspects are concerned. One example is the healthcare sector, where 'red envelopes' are a systematic phenomenon in the relationship between doctors and patients. Yet, here we also observe the grey areas between 'gift-giving' in establishing *guanxi* and outright bribery. The point is whether the gift results in privileged treatment, though not necessarily in substandard treatment of patients who do not offer a gift. Here, prior relations between related patients and doctors also come into play, such as when a relative introduces a patient to a doctor, referring to earlier interactions, and supports this with a gift. So, bribery embedded in existing *guanxi* is regarded as morally different from bribery in an anonymous setting, such as in the case of the policeman. Nevertheless, we still refer to spot transactions with regard to immediate reciprocity.[46]

If we consider long-term reciprocity in *guanxi* networks, the case is different. Then, the corrupt service may be delivered much later than the original compensation. For example, businesspeople cultivate relationships with officials without immediately receiving compensation such as a business licence 'next morning'. If they cultivate *guanxi*, they actually make advance payments and draw on this accumulated social capital when in need. At that moment there is no further flow of gifts, as the official simply feels committed to reciprocate. In this case, we cannot provide direct evidence for bribery when looking at the spot transaction. Nevertheless, the entire relationship may be regarded as a corrupt one. Large parts of the *guanxi*-based gift relationships are of this particular kind, even if 'red envelopes' may be involved that are presented, for example, on the occasion of family events.

This analysis is important in explaining why high levels of corruption are not necessarily destroying trust. In fact, the corrupt relationship is based on trust, since long-term reciprocity is not sustainable without trust. At the same time, fulfilling norms of long-term reciprocity creates and confirms trust. This certainly only applies to members of the corrupt network, but, as I have stated previously, if those networks are competitive there is even the possibility of opting out of one network and exploiting another. This means that in a competitive network structure trust is also maintained via reputational sanctions that operate in a corrupt environment. In fact, the 'advance payments' may even be seen as an element of competitive strategies involving the buildup of a diverse social capital basis which is only activated later, depending on the current assessment of the actual value of particular relationships.

If we move to a more abstract level, we can relate corruption to the notion of the status order. In this status order, *guanxi* are mainly activated and reproduced by 'giving face' to other people, especially individuals with higher status. Thus, a businessman may feel obliged to 'give face' to an official with high status. Face-giving needs to rely on vehicles, which can be invitations to exclusive restaurants, and leaving a bottle of expensive cognac afterwards for the official as a 'leftover'. So, a substantial share of the luxury goods and services market in China may relate to these *guanxi* activities, which was evident from the sudden collapse of sales when the Xi anti-corruption campaign began. Yet, face-giving is not a spot transaction like simple bribery: face also implies the obligation to meet the role expectations afterwards. So, the high-status individual may need to display 'benevolent' behaviour to the low-status individual, acting as a paternalistic authority. In this particular sense, corruption is part of Chinese ritual. But this also reinstates the point made previously, namely that corruption, to a certain degree, even creates trust, at least among certain circles of participants. Without being able to prove this proposition, one may therefore suspect that the decline in the growth rate since 2013 is also related to the anti-corruption campaign which created increasing uncertainty about the reliability of social networks, especially in areas which were previously drivers of growth, such as infrastructure and real estate investment.

To summarize the argument in this section, we need to eschew the often cited image of Chinese society as being sharply divided between the circles of closely related people who maintain high trust in each other and the world of strangers in which mistrust is endemic. Following Fei Xiaotong's model of 'circles', I argue that *guanxi* relations mediate between these 'two worlds', thus actually transforming the lifeworld of individual Chinese in the larger society into a place of people whom one can trust. I claim that this is a major factor in explaining the rapid growth of markets over recent decades, following standard reasoning in economics.

Social values, individualism and marketization

In the first section, I advanced the claim that *guanxi* are a manifestation of individualism. This raises the question of whether Western ideas that markets are based on individualistic values can also be confirmed for China. Here, it is appropriate to consider value surveys again and to look at international comparisons directly on the level of the single items; subsequently I move on to more principled considerations.

Before I report some observations, I point to the fact that the issue of 'individualization' has received much attention in China studies recently. This is because the reforms have not only enhanced the space for the expression of individual interests, but also because they have pushed individuals into contexts in which they need to adopt individual initiative in order to safeguard their interests. This has to be seen against the background of the paradigm of 'communist neotraditionalism' which was influential in the 1980s, and which highlighted the 'organized dependence' of the individual under the Maoist institutional regime. This notion referred to the fact that in both the rural and the urban areas, mobility was severely curtailed even in the cross-organizational dimension. Members of People's Communes or state-owned companies rarely moved to other organizations. This lack of freedom created the conditions for dependence on the organizations and on superiors who control resources. Since the Maoist organizations were totalitarian in the sense of encompassing all aspects of individual life and its circumstances, individuals had to adapt to tight control and supervision. In the discussion of these peculiar conditions, however, the idea also loomed large that they continued with the patterns of authoritarian paternalism of the Confucian tradition.[47]

The dependence theory implies that individuals are not simply suppressed by superordinate authorities, but that they also adapt to this system in terms of individual values and aspirations. They internalize the institutional framework, partly because there is a pre-adaptation by other cultural traditions. Accordingly, market reforms and liberalization do not simply open up the channels of expressing individualistic interests, but are also a way of transforming individuals. In other words, we meet another example of the market as a form of governmentality. In a most extreme interpretation, individualism in China today would be conceived of as a state-orchestrated phenomenon. For example, migrant workers who move to the cities have to adopt individual initiative in all respects of their individual lives, and they do not have the choice of depending on the support of other social actors, especially the government. Interestingly, this implies that the most direct expressions of individualism in China today may be found in the social strata that are rooted in rural society, but which are in close interaction with the urbanization process. In comparison, urban society would be much slower in developing individualistic attitudes and lifestyles so long as organizational dependence on the state remains strong.[48]

Obviously, we face an intricate issue here if we relate this reasoning to the insights of the previous chapters in this book. We note that urban/rural duality would have a strong impact on the ways in which markets would be embedded in social values, with probably a different kind of market dynamism in the rural and urban areas, since the culture of dependence was mainly a phenomenon of the urban areas, whereas in the rural areas considerable local variety persisted, and the socio-psychological sedimentation of those alleged attitudinal stances was slow because of the disturbing effects of the waves of campaigns. Further, we would need to modify the picture of 'tradition' in the pre-adaptation argument, since we would have to highlight and also detail the impact of the Chinese 'little tradition' in rural areas on market dynamism, in distinction from the Confucian setting invoked in the dependence theory.

In particular, the analysis of dependence may misinterpret the role of the Cultural Revolution, which certainly affected particular groups in society differently, especially the cohort of the 'sent-down youths' as compared with other groups which were not transferred to rural areas, and also related to the wide variation in impact upon society across the country. For many of these Red Guard activists, the rural experience was already forcing them into a situation of independence and responsibility for their own fate, under conditions that were mostly very harsh for urbanites. They became involved in a number of ideological conflicts and local power struggles which ultimately deprived them of their original ideological zeal. So, the Cultural Revolution produced the opposite of what its instigators had intended: total ideological disillusionment and a loss of moral orientation. From this perspective, the market reforms after 1978 were also a measure that aimed at creating a new social consensus based on the individual interest in improving one's personal life. The market emerged as a moral consensus on a minimum level, partly reflecting individualistic values that almost paradoxically transpired from the struggles of the Cultural Revolution. This is a sort of default value if all other moral foundations crumble. This transition has to be seen against the background of the fact that in the areas most afflicted by the Cultural Revolution, many Chinese had to achieve a peaceful co-existence with others after a decade-long struggle with high levels of physical and psychological violence and abuse. Given the constraints upon migration, people could not simply leave the areas where they had these experiences. Therefore, falling back on the closest social circles or even their individual interests was a natural adaptation to these circumstances.[49]

If many social critics in China today deplore the rampant opportunism and egoistic pursuit of material wealth, this seems to reflect the fact that individualism in China is neither based in a set of individualistic belief systems that tie up individualism with other transcendental values, nor has it achieved the transition to reflexive modernization. With the latter term, observers refer to individualization as a reflexive project that explicitly considers the diversity and multiplicity of cultural identities, and opens up individual freedom in choosing from among those identities. This requires, above all, critical capacity. If we look at the current conditions of the educational system, it is interesting to note that often individualism is explicitly defined as an educational goal, but without the critical component. This means that individualism is defined as individual aspiration within the given social context, but does not question this context.[50]

The complexity of the situation comes to the fore if we look at data which show the appreciation of certain attitudes and values in educating children. The WVS asks respondents about choosing 'important child qualities' from a range of choices; so, the results are presented in the

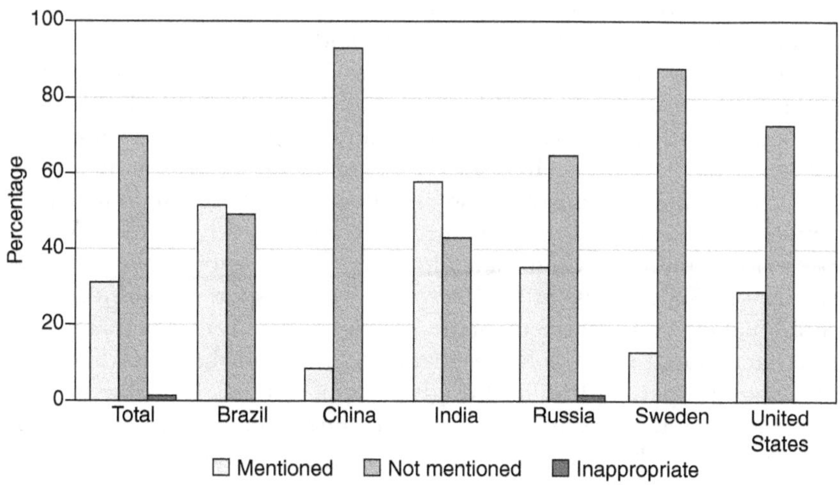

Figure 5.5 Obedience as the desired property of a child.

duality of 'mentioned/not mentioned'. One of the most surprising results, against the backdrop of previous considerations, is that in the most recent WVS wave, Chinese subjects score less than even American subjects in naming 'obedience' as an important child quality: just 7.5 per cent compared to 57 per cent of Indians and 35 per cent of Russians. The Chinese performance is consistent through time, even showing up in the first WVS wave. It is interesting to note that these results are distinctive against the background of results for other values in which the countries converge on high levels, such as 'feelings of responsibility' or 'tolerance and respect for other people'. So, we might surmise that a strong differential performance is an indicator for a significant cultural difference. In the Chinese case, this clearly speaks against the widely shared view that Chinese culture is authoritarian.[51]

This can be proven by looking at mirror results: 70 per cent of Chinese regard 'independence' as a value that should be instilled in children, compared to 53 per cent of US respondents, and 38 per cent of Brazilians and Russians. In the aggregate 'autonomy index', the distribution of the Chinese sample is more geared towards autonomy than the American one, and is clearly distinct from Brazil or Russia. There is also a more specific question related to autonomy: 57 per cent of Chinese subjects 'see themselves as an autonomous person', which tops all other countries considered here, including Sweden ('autonomous' is translated as 'zizhu' (自主), which differs from 'independent', 'duli' (独立)).

Now, and interestingly, Chinese subjects score much lower when considering creativity and imagination as personal properties or important child qualities. Only 17 per cent of Chinese regard 'imagination' as an important child quality to be nurtured by education, compared to 47 per cent of Swedes and 31 per cent of US respondents. 'Self-expression' also scores low (about 11 per cent), compared with more than 20 percentage points higher scores even in Russia, India and Sweden (unexpectedly, the US scores only 17 per cent). On the other hand, the WVS also confirms the standard clichés about China, emphasizing thrift and diligence. For example, thriftiness is regarded as an important child quality by more than 50 per cent of Chinese, Russians and Indians, whereas it is mentioned much less by Americans and Swedes. It is illuminating to relate these results with the traditional literature on children's education which has been proliferating in China since its inception by leading Neoconfucian scholars in Song times. In this literature, both respect for authority and individual effort in achievement are emphasized. This means that, on the one hand, social order is taken for granted, but on the other hand it is also seen as open and fluid, thus giving opportunities for those who are eager to take it. There is a clear gender dimension, of course, since this applies exclusively to males. Regarding male ideal types, however, there was also a strong emphasis on individualism, both in the image of the sophisticated literati and the roaming knights and even bandits who stay outside the social order. Traditional religious feasts explicitly recognize the role of marginal elements in society, and martial arts are also a ritual means to reintegrate them into society.[52]

The WVS originally aims at consolidating its survey results into a measure of 'modernity'. In this effort, the different results are statistically evaluated and condensed into a two-dimensional map which I show in Figure 5.6. One dimension of this map is the opposition between self-expression vs. survival values, the other between traditional values vs. secular-rational values. One can certainly argue about this analytical effort in many ways, but what counts in my view are the internal relationships which anyway would indicate some important factors working in the background.

One straightforward observation is that the dominance of survival values correlates strongly with the level of GDP. Yet, there are several cases which stand out in terms of what appears to be a delayed response to the growth of prosperity. All these cases belong to what is identified as the 'Confucian' group. Even Japan clearly falls back in comparison with all the other most advanced industrial nations. On the other hand, these countries belong to the leading group of countries in terms of the dominance of secular-rational values. China stands in the same league as Germany, the Netherlands and Denmark. In comparison, the 'English-speaking' world falls back, in particular what many would identify as the most advanced country in the world: the USA. According to this map, the

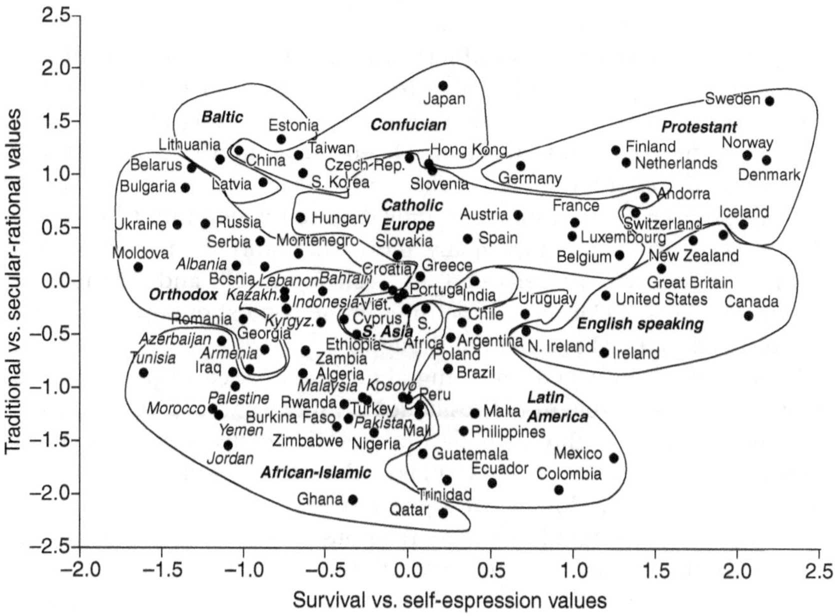

Figure 5.6 The WVS cultural map of the world.

most advanced countries in terms of overall 'modernity' are clearly marked by a particular religion, namely Protestantism of the European brand, and are located in Northern Europe.

This is not the place to discuss the methodological problems of modernization studies, but I think that these comparisons suggest some important ideas about the Chinese case and with reference to the ritual economy. One insight is that we have to take into consideration the possibility that 'modernization' in the sense of a particular Western European understanding of the term is not a unidirectional process but is obviously channelled by certain cultural factors, especially religion. This supports the Chinese theorists of indigenization of modernization theory that I mentioned in the first section of this chapter. It is also important to point out that economic development is not automatically related to certain value structures, such as was suggested in the famous Maslow hierarchy of needs. The opposite also applies: the dynamic potential of markets or capitalism does not presuppose only one particular cultural regime.

Regarding China, the WVS map motivates one to consider the possibility that what is regarded as a 'modern' worldview or value structure has actually always been a property of traditional culture. Interestingly, this idea has been discussed in the context of explaining the spectacular success of East Asia in industrial catch-up. Some authors argue that this was based on a pronounced head-start in human capital and cultural modernization, in this sense therefore a sort of cultural modernization actually pulling economic modernization.[53] In this context, we refer back to the results given in Chapter 2. However, there is one issue that relates to the interpretation of the term 'Confucian'. I have already pointed to the difficulties in judging the religious nature of Confucianism and the nature of Chinese religion. These are disjoint questions. Regarding the former, the rational nature of Confucianism has been recognized by many scholars, and certainly combines with 'This-worldliness' as a political ethics. However, this characterization certainly does not match with Chinese religion *in toto*, which includes many more traditions than Confucianism which may not even be regarded as a religion at all, and also may not reflect the status of Confucian doctrines in the context of popular religion as compared to the elite system of thought.

This is important when reflecting about the delayed response to prosperity that is observable in the resilience of 'survival values' in the 'Confucian' group. The duality actually opposes materialist orientations with individualistic aspirations that make themselves independent from material constraints. However, I argue that this distinction fails to grasp the important point that in Chinese religious tradition materialistic values play a central role, and that therefore the juxtaposition of 'material' and 'spiritual' is also misleading. On the other hand, a materialistic orientation may also undergird a secular orientation in behavioural stances, yet this orientation is itself grounded in a certain form of spirituality which actually denies the 'Western' duality of the material and the transcendent world. For example, when it comes to the role of wealth in society, the ubiquity of the wealth motive in popular religion is well known. Popular religion regards the pursuit of wealth as an activity that is essential for maintaining the family line. Money is a medium which also connects the living with the dead, and provisioning one's ancestors with the capabilities of a good life is the duty of the living. In other words, popular beliefs are imbued with this-worldly values, most importantly health and wealth. There is no negation of the material world in favour of transcendent salvation. Well-being is a central concern, which is not generally defined as other-worldly redemption and liberation. However, it would be entirely misleading to interpret this duality of material vs. spiritual in terms of Western religiosity. In fact, both categories are mutually encompassing.[54]

Considering the role of traditional religion, we can also add a few observations on individualism and instrumentalism here which build the bridge to more general observations about the individualism issue. This refers to the role of the household as the centre of religious activity, and hence what has been labelled the 'polytropic' nature of popular religion in China. The term 'polytropic' refers to the phenomenon that popular religion is not defined by different confessions but by different kinds of religious activities for which certain religious beliefs and the corresponding experts are seen as the best media to realize the resulting needs; for example, a need for spiritual enlightenment which can be best catered for by certain texts, or a need for help in case of suffering. This reflects practical distinctions in the popular lifeworld, such as regarding Buddhists as experts in the 'white' events of funerals and mourning. If we reflect upon these phenomena in the light of the individualism issue, it is straightforward to recognize that the traditional pattern of orthopraxy manifests the dominant role of the individual in choosing between these different modes of religious activity. Orthopraxy regulates certain aspects of ritual, but leaves much leeway for the individual in designing her or his (in the case of religion, both genders participate on the same footing but with different foci) own religious activity profile, and does not impose any particular interpretation.[55]

From this point of view, traditional popular religion was and still is thoroughly individualistic. This includes the dimension of 'family individualism' as far as the role of the household is concerned, especially in rites that explicitly refer to the family, but overall we may say that individual autonomy plays a systematic role in popular religion. This role can also be highlighted in understanding the institutional domain of popular religion as a 'religious market'. The notion of a 'religious market' is an analytical paradigm in applying economics to religion, but in the Chinese case we may also say that the term has an empirical meaning, in the sense that popular religion is practised as a market, as I have already outlined in Chapter 2. This means that there is a supply of religious services offered by a wide range of individuals and organizations, reaching from individual 'religious entrepreneurs' such as spirit media or independent Daoist priests to monasteries and large temples, which sometimes gather different suppliers at one location. These suppliers compete for the attention, recognition and eventually also material compensation of the believers, who therefore act as autonomous agents on the demand side. Although orthopractic ritual imposes certain collective standards upon their choices (e.g. in the important setting of funerals), in many other respects individuals are free to determine their own religious activities and beliefs, with the grey and varying borderline of 'illicit' beliefs as defined by the state.[56]

So, coming back to the WVS results, if we note a strong impact of religion upon the distribution of countries in the 'cultural map of the world', I posit that what the 'Confucian' group has in common is not 'Confucianism' per se, but the underlying values and attitudes embodied in the practices of popular religion. These include a strong component of individualism and materialism, however, themselves being part and parcel of religion and spirituality. In other words, I argue that individualism is a constant in Chinese cultural evolution.

The issue of individualism is one of the central categories that are conventionally used to distinguish between East Asian and Western societies, which are largely identified as being 'collectivistic'. As my discussion of the Hofstede approach in Chapter 1 has already highlighted, this dualism is highly problematic, since it lumps together a large number of countries that would all count as 'collectivistic', though being distinct in terms of shared cultural traditions. However, there are more principled issues here that have been raised in recent research in social psychology, and which question the assumption that 'individualism' and 'collectivism' belong to the same dimension, simply defining two poles between which the different societies vary. The problem is easy to see if we consider the reference of the terms 'individual' and 'collective': whereas this is almost naturally given for the former, the meaning of 'collective' is much more open. This has already been made clear by Fei Xiaotong's model of Chinese social networks: a 'group' can have different meanings, especially in the two senses of either referring to a particular pattern of recurrently interacting individuals or to a set of individuals who share a certain characteristic. The two meanings may be congruent, such as when we identify a set of individuals as being members of 'one family' who also interact recurrently. But if we look at the members of a large corporation, obviously the two possible definitions fall apart, with the corporation as a set of individuals sharing the property of membership, but actually being composed of a larger number of groups comprising recurrently interacting members. For example, top management is one group, the members of which would probably rarely stay in recurrent interaction with workers in a particular workshop, who form another group.

Fei Xiaotong's distinction of two different kinds of groups has been reinstated in recent social psychology as the distinction between 'relational collectivism' and 'categorial collectivism'.[57] Relational collectivism refers to recurrently interacting groups, categorial collectivism to abstract groups defined by shared properties. It is straightforward to refer this duality to the duality of field-dependent versus field-independent cognition. A field-independent cognitive stance would tend to highlight the abstract categorizations of groups independent from the specific local pattern of interactions, while a field-dependent stance would tend to accentuate the realized patterns of interactions. This observation is important in avoiding the analytical short cut that the two collectivisms may themselves be embodied in a set of individual values. It is sufficient to refer to the different cognitive stances in order to argue that the expression of 'collectivistic' orientations may be triggered by environmental cues that are then processed differently, depending on the prevailing stance.[58]

If we look at Chinese *guanxi* from this angle and apply Fei's analysis, *guanxi* clearly count as a manifestation of relational collectivism. This refers to two distinct phenomena. First, *guanxi* are not defined by abstract categories but by ongoing interactions. As we have seen, maintaining *guanxi* through recurrent interactions is traditionally seen as a necessary condition for their stability. Second, whether *guanxi* indeed trigger 'collectivistic' behaviour, however, depends on the specific incentives that inhere in a currently given structure, and which is indigenously defined via terms such as *renqing* or *mianzi*. This means that we do not need the assumption of 'collectivist' values embodied in the individual to explain certain 'collectivistic behaviours'. This matches the recognition of the individual's pivotal role in designing her or his egocentric networks.

These distinctions are exactly the ones also made in social psychology, with the important implication that individualism and collectivism can no longer be approached as two poles in the same dimension. Of course, this is also a definitional matter. But if we use the recent economic terminology here, the value dimension would relate to the polarity between 'individual vs. social preferences' which has been shown to be influenced by many factors. In social psychology, 'individualism' is related to notions of agency, whereas 'collectivism' is a notion of values. This means that in the agency dimension we might distinguish two poles which would alternatively assign agency to the individual or levels higher than the individual ('collectives'), and in the value dimensions we would distinguish between different degrees of egocentred or other-centred values. The economic distinction between individual and social preferences would fall into the second category. The two dimensions are combined in the sense of whether we consider the agency of choosing and maintaining values. This relates to autonomy, in the sense of whether the individual is autonomous in choosing values, or is heteronomous in adapting to external norms. As we see, this approach allows for interesting combinations; for example, an individual can be heteronomous in adopting egoistic values, or an individual can be autonomous in adopting other-oriented values. This opens up many degrees of freedom in explaining the relationship between values and behaviour.

If we consider the Chinese case from this angle, starting out from the previous discussion of religion, we can certainly say that there is a clear tendency to assign agency to the individual and not to a higher level collective. This is also reflected in the WVS results reported previously. In this sense, Chinese traditional culture, and in this respect also contemporary culture, would be diagnosed as being 'individualistic'. With regard to *guanxi*, we may also say that Chinese culture is 'relational collectivistic' in the sense of highlighting the role of recurrent social interactions in determining choices of action. At the same time, we might diagnose weak categorial collectivism. Interestingly, this characterization is reflected in a large number of popular characterizations of Chinese social behaviour over many decades, both from indigenous and Western observers. This has often been coined as the predominance of particularistic morality over universalistic morality. So, early twentieth-century reformers decried the lack of citizenship and nationalism among the Chinese (thus failing to identify themselves with the category of 'the nation'), or managers today complain about the lack of loyalty to the corporation. I come back to the latter aspect in Chapter 6.

However, it would be misleading to directly equate categorial collectivism with ethical universalism, since obviously categorial groups can normatively discriminate against others and thus follow a particularistic ethics. So, the social-psychological conceptual differentiation does not fully resolve a problem that has been discussed in Chinese studies for a long time, and which relates to the specific aspect of agency to which I referred above, namely the degree of autonomy of the individual in choosing values. This is partly covered by the distinction between 'particularism' and 'universalism', as in many views particularism is associated with the acceptance of local norms and values, thus a 'traditional morality', whereas universalism is associated with the idea that individuals autonomously submit themselves to universalistic norms. Although this connection is by no means a necessary one, it is illuminating in the Chinese case, since it refers to the contemporary discussion of reflexive modernization and individualization, which can be approached in the context of 'post-conventional ethics' as well. Both notions emphasize the autonomy of the individual in choosing values, and the awareness of this freedom of choice. If some scholars diagnose a lack of reflexive individualism in China, this would mean that individualism is actually emerging as a convention, thus factually expressing the lack of individual autonomy in choosing individual values. This is indeed surfacing in a number of empirical studies, such as about education.[59]

To summarize this part of the argument, we have to eschew the false polarity of individualism and collectivism and instead distinguish between different degrees of individualism in terms of assigning agency to the individual and the two different types of relational and categorial collectivism. The latter distinction may be traced back to deeper structures of cognition: field dependent versus field independent. To illustrate this argument, I present an ideal-typical and merely qualitative comparison between Chinese, Japanese and US-American culture in what are actually three dimensions if we also consider degrees of categorial and relational collectivism, respectively (Figure 5.7). Then, as we see, US-American culture may be characterized as highly individualistic and strong in categorial collectivism, but weak in relational collectivism, whereas China shows the combination of strong individualism with strong relational collectivism. Japan would emerge as the example of weak individualism and both strong relational and categorial collectivism, which is clearly reflected in common views about the 'Japanese corporation'.[60]

Yet, the complexity of the individualism vs. collectivism issue has not yet been fully explored, since another distinction emanating from social psychology has not been mentioned so far, which is the distinction between 'vertical' and 'horizontal' structures. This view still accepts the individualism–collectivism continuum, but posits that the vertical/horizontal duality is orthogonal to this. This means that both individualism and collectivism can appear in both vertical and horizontal variants. 'Verticality' means that social relationships are seen as being structured in hierarchies, whereas 'horizontal' means that individuals are seen as being located on the same level, in principle. More specifically, horizontal

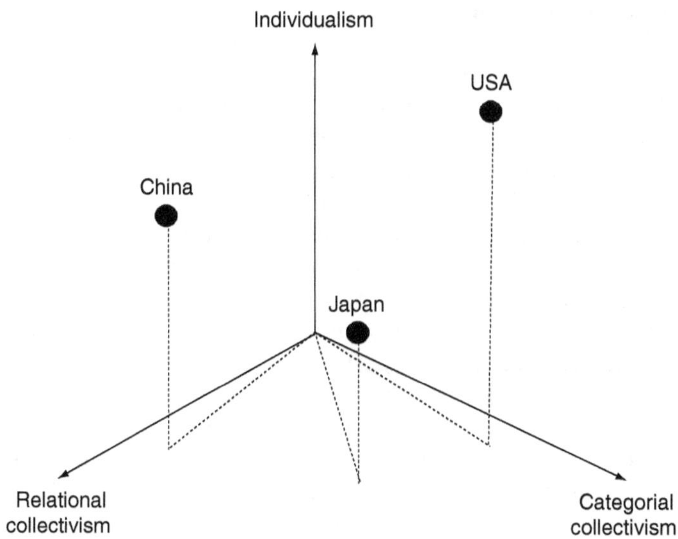

Figure 5.7 Individualism and collectivism: ideal-typical features of China, Japan and the USA.

societies emphasize mutual recognition, support and cooperation, whereas vertical societies emphasize rank distinctions, authority and competition. Combining this with the individualism–collectivism duality, we end up with the possibility that societies differ in terms of this dimension, but may share, for example, the verticality feature. One possible case in point is the comparison between the USA and China, if the two, as is often done, were assigned to the individualism and collectivism pole, respectively. However, both would share the property of verticality, in the sense that rank matters and competition for status, such as striving for wealth or elevated positions in society, so sharing a pattern of elitism and so forth. In comparison, Scandinavian countries might be classified as individualistic, also following the WVS categorization, but horizontal, which is reflected in stronger egalitarian values.[61]

Finally, the distinction between relational and categorial collectivism partly overlaps with the question of how far these classifications also relate to the institutional framework of societies. For example, relational collectivism as a characterization of traditional China would also go hand in hand with the institutionalization of this attitudinal stance, for example, in the lineage context. Legal traditions of Western countries emphasize categorial collectivism. Therefore, one could add the further aspect of the institutionalization of certain concepts of agency and values. One simple example is how far private ownership is established and protected by law, or how strongly redistributive values are embedded in certain institutions of the state such as the tax system. For example, Scandinavia in the 1970s may have been horizontal–individualistic, but with a strong institutional manifestation of collectivist values.[62]

If we now reflect upon the Chinese case and apply these ideas to the specific question of the relationship between the market and social values, we end up with a complex, though presumably realistic picture. The first observation is that there is a strong recognition of individual agency, reflected in the different results of the WVS that emphasize individual autonomy, potential for achievement and individual control of one's fate. This point is also manifest in the strong inclination towards entrepreneurship. In this sense, markets are undergirded by an individualistic stance. Further, we also note the predominance of relational collectivism relative to categorial collectivism. This matches an observation we made about the role of organizations vs. markets in Imperial China, namely that markets dominate formal organizations. In other words, relational collectivism bolsters the role of markets in coordinating economic interactions. More specifically, *guanxi* are a powerful medium embedding markets, which I look at in more detail in Chapter 6. There are important specific effects here, in particular the role of long-term reciprocity, which undergirds the strong performance of personal credit in financing private business ventures.

This picture needs further specification in terms of the verticality–horizontality distinction. We have noticed the pervasive role of rank and status in Chinese society, both past and present. Hence, there is a strong role of vertical relations in market patterns. Among other phenomena, this relates to the role of high-status individuals acting as third-party mediators of economic transactions. So, the triadic pattern of *guanxi* is strongly geared towards vertical relations. This has implications for the shape and content of social capital enabling individual economic agency: the network positions of related individuals are strong determinants. This also provides the social-structural basis for market governmentality as discussed above. Since the status order in society is partly and probably predominantly defined by the political status order, there is a direct impact of this status order upon the structuration and unfolding of market transactions. Again, we can see that this has been a permanent feature of Chinese society since late Imperial times, manifest in the symbiosis between the merchant and the scholar-official group, and the role of the CCP in today's economy. Finally, verticality is a strong driver of achievement motivation, in the sense of assuming higher positions in the status order defined by both wealth and power. Thus, for example, the co-optation of private businesspeople by the CCP is a two-way process, as the latter invest in high status reflecting their achievements in business. In terms of institutionalization, we can safely state that there is a strong trend towards the recognition of individual agency in Chinese civil and administrative law, and that there is also a relatively weak expression of redistributive modes in the political system. Summing up, we can therefore state that markets are firmly entrenched in the value system prevailing in China today.

Market instrumentalism and performing markets

In this section I relate the analysis of Chinese networks and values to the unique way in which markets perform. This is a vast topic, and I will only concentrate on certain basic principles which I briefly illustrate with a few examples. I have to begin with a couple of remarks on theory. Economists normally tend to separate markets from their institutional framework: institutions set up markets and define the rules of the game, and the market processes are the game. If we start out from the concept of performativity this is not sufficient, because we have to take into consideration the fact that markets need to be reproduced by the actions of the market agents, including their institutional framework. A standard way in which economists see the creation of markets is to establish private property rights and define rules how these may be exchanged among private actors. However, as we know from many instances, this may fail if market actors simply do not create sufficient supply and demand to maintain a certain market. In this sense, institutions created exogenously only define a potential market. This differs from the case of the endogenous emergence of markets where market participants simultaneously create the institutions which govern their interactions.

In addition, economists often overlook the material structure of markets, a topic that has been examined only recently by sociologists working on performativity. Material structures shape the way in which markets perform, for example, by relying on certain tools of transmitting information about market conditions. This essential role of materiality has become obvious for many observers in the rise of the digital economy where technological innovations, and less institutional innovations, have been the driving force of the emergence of entirely new forms of markets. However, this observation only heightens the awareness of what is a universal fact, namely that markets always build on market technologies, such as technologies transmitting information or technologies that render goods tradable. Technologies also impact upon markets via the market structures that emerge from the induced competition: this is, of course, well recognized by economists; however, if markets evolve endogenously, the impact upon institutions is normally blanked out. As we will see, this is particularly relevant for China today.[63]

As a consequence, market performativity at the same time applies to the institutions and the actual conditions of markets, which together I label 'market states'; I consider this theoretical point in more detail in the final section of this chapter. Market states include institutions, certain market conditions and the material structure that undergirds the interactions of actors that reproduce those states. This reproduction is called 'performativity' which is mediated via the embodiment of the aforementioned factors in the behavioural patterns of market actors. As I will show in the theoretical reprise, the material states of markets operate as public representations that mediate the reproduction of the entire institutional pattern. So, markets cannot be simply described in abstract terms, but have to be detailed as particular mechanisms with specific causal patterns. One aspect that is especially important in China is the interaction between market actors and regulators, with the latter not assuming an independent role, but mainly operating under the constraints of the goal structure imposed by the CCP as the avant-garde of modernization. This means that market performativity obtains a twofold meaning here, also including the aspect of the performance of markets, for example, in terms of growth or technological dynamism. Both the central and the local state interfere with markets in order to generate a certain performance, thus also becoming part and parcel of the mechanisms of market performance.

The concept of 'market states' is an important element in identifying an economic style. The standard economic approach disembeds markets from social, technological and institutional contexts, and therefore suggests that markets are neutral and describable in generic mathematical terms. This reflects an important insight: namely that markets are a social technology of their own status and significance. Interestingly, this is also how Chinese political leaders approached the notion of market under the auspices of Deng Xiaoping: institutions such as stock markets are neutral and may be used in different political contexts. But this cannot mean that a full description and explanation of markets can be done without tracing their embeddedness. The approach to economic styles disembeds and re-embeds markets in one analytical movement. Then, we immediately recognize that markets as cultural phenomena are also entangled in mirrors of culture, since this very movement is itself an expression of cultural assumptions and creations. This means, for example, that societies differ in accepting markets as social technologies in specific areas, such as markets for human bodies and body parts. Even though this also applies to modern Western societies, the idea of the separateness of markets is often maintained by economists, also in the normative sense (for example, when actually proposing to open up markets for goods and services which are conventionally seen as excluded from the scope of markets). This raises the question of whether and how far a certain cultural frame is also necessary for maintaining markets as a social technology, or, more specifically, whether there is a certain necessary relationship between markets and certain values, norms and beliefs. The *locus classicus* is certainly Max Weber's famous 'protestantism hypothesis' in explaining the rise of capitalism. Modern variants of this idea abound, such as the belief that markets need to combine with certain values of democracy in the long run. This is the analytical interface which connects this section with the previous ones.

To a large degree, the CCP has adopted the stance of market instrumentalism and market neutrality, and the Chinese state has played an active role in instituting markets. In the course of three decades of Chinese reforms, the emergence of markets was a central element in driving economic growth. Certainly, one part of the story is the creation of certain rights and entitlements that were increasingly allowed to become the object of market exchange. For example, when creating stock markets, initially a large part of the shares of SOEs were non-tradable and only transformed into tradable stocks gradually, thus contributing to the recent growth of stock markets and market capitalization. Similarly, markets for land-use rights were established gradually and experimentally, still with very different institutional frameworks across different locations, as we have seen. In these examples, the role of government is obvious, as the markets reflect certain legal innovations which define the underlying rights.

However, this is only one part of the story. If we look at the role of government, and in particular at the role of the local state, the much more common case is the creation of markets within a given institutional framework, which applies to the wide range of standard goods such as consumer goods or agricultural products. Local states often become active in creating markets physically, in the sense of establishing market sites, similar to the activities of traditional lineages in Imperial China. At the grassroots level, these activities often unfold in the context of the traditional market system, at least initially. So, for example, a county may become active in setting up a special wholesale market for a particular product group, aiming at achieving regional or even national significance, and also sometimes directly continuing with local business traditions. There are many examples when even rural backwaters may achieve national significance, such as the famous case of Yiwu, driven by the initiative of local states. The dynamics of these processes may be best understood as an interaction between endogenous network dynamics and public investments that lower barriers to entry. The latter relates to special local policies such as offering cheap market infrastructure, tax advantages and so forth, the former to the operations of *guanxi* mediated by leader–follower dynamics. This means that some entrepreneurs would open up the market as first movers, and others would follow as imitators, thus triggering a mutual ratchet of thickening supply which attracts a growing local concentration of demand. So, a pattern emerges that is also known from traditional China, namely the spatial concentration of markets from a certain branch of industry or even product line. This effect operates on every spatial level, thus also reproducing a Skinnerian-like market hierarchy, though being less influenced by purely geographic determinants.[64]

In this process, market development is a direct determinant of economic growth. Indeed, conventional GDP measures only encompass market-based interactions, and thus may also be interpreted as partial measures of marketization. This sheds a special light on high growth rates of GDP in China: these rates partially reflect the rapid expansion of markets as institutions. This is particularly important from the perspective of local states which focus on economic growth, reflecting the mechanisms of the cadre evaluation system, and therefore have an essential interest in developing local markets; that is, also attracting market transactions to their jurisdiction. This is independent from the question of whether these transactions are mainly mediated via private or public actors, though the fiscal system plays a role, as we have seen. This means that those features of economic systems that are conventionally regarded as defining elements become part of the activities of local states, in particular, in performing markets. For example, whether private or public ownership prevails in the local context becomes an instrumental variable for market development. If private actors withdraw economic activity from a certain area, local states would interfere by strengthening the role of public actors, or would alternatively establish special preferential regimes for chosen private actors. As a result, marketization does not imply the retreat of government from markets, but the opposite: local states may actually strengthen their interventions. This is also a question of local legitimacy of government, since maintaining a certain level of employment and achieving prosperity is a central goal recognized by all parties involved; so, if the local state fails in achieving this goal, legitimacy is in jeopardy. In other words, market development is also a political phenomenon. These patterns are heavily influenced by structural characteristics of a particular area, thus connecting geographic and industry features, and hence directly activating market materiality in the process of institutional transformation.[65]

In other words, market performativity is strongly contextualized, with the relationship between central and local state playing a pivotal role. As I have emphasized, the regional and sectoral variation is immense, so I just illustrate the performative dynamics with one ideal-typical pattern. In the course of reforms, the duality of the local state vs. the central state was often manifest in the fact that local states were also involved in the traditional procurement and distribution system, especially for those goods that remained under a certain degree of government control even when reforms speeded up, such as agricultural commodities (rice, cotton, etc.). This administrative structure created strong path dependencies of marketization, since local states could pursue different strategies of marketization, reaching from wholesale privatization to maintaining a local monopoly with a dominant trading organization sponsored by the local government. This structure was at the same time regulated at the central level, on the one hand via the general guidelines for reform and marketization, but also regarding regulations on product quality and product safety. These issues matter a great deal for agricultural products, especially if these also serve as inputs for industrial production, such as cotton for the textile industry. Interestingly, in many of these cases, there is also a direct relationship between the domestic and the international market which was being intensified via the liberalization of external trade, especially after the WTO entry in 2001. Quality issues could be sensitive in switching between domestic and international suppliers. These issues became even more salient when, as in agriculture, technological developments also created additional links between traditional sectors and modern industry. In the case of agriculture, biotechnology became increasingly important, which raised issues in regulating market access for domestic and international suppliers, and involved topics such as intellectual property rights and the monitoring of seed uses and seed qualities.

If we consider these regulatory issues in more detail, the duality of local vs. central state is often expressed in a modernist status order that encompasses the different market participants. This status order partly constrains their actions and leads to particular forms of market structure. A typical phenomenon is the duality of 'modern' and more 'traditional' actors. This relates to the transitional state of the Skinnerian market system. The opening up of the socialist distribution system allowed market access for a large number of small-scale businesses that engage in trading with agricultural products, such as seeds or products that are further processed by downstream industries. Although on the central level this system could be controlled via licensing procedures, the actual implementation occurs in the local states. Since traders are not restricted to a particular territory, regulatory differences tend to converge to the most liberal regime, thus also triggering competitive responses on the part of the local state.[66]

One of these responses is the creation of companies that assume the role of lead companies, for example, in the shape of so-called 'dragon head companies', 'longtou qiye' (龙头企业). So, a lead company in food processing may conclude direct supplier contracts with farmers, thus obviating the traditional marketing system as far as the lowest level is concerned. Yet, the company may actually be located on a higher level, thus also reinforcing links with the traditional structure, only changing the mechanisms of how the levels interact. A lead company is regarded to be of higher status than the ordinary traders, because the assumption holds (mostly justified) that it has better capacities in meeting the regulatory demands of higher level administrations or even of the central level. For example, a lead company may have received certain domestic of even international certifications such as ISO standards. Thus, the notion of the lead company expresses modernist distinctions of status, with immediate consequences for the financial structure and support on the part of local governments. For example, the lead company will have much better access to loans from the Agricultural Bank of China in order to further enhance technological potential, and may also have better access to industrial estates and so forth. In comparison, other private companies have to rely on traditional sources of loans, which I consider below. As a result, the local and regional market manifests a status order of different market participants, However, this status order rarely implies a complete dominance or even monopolization of the local market, because other actors may have specific advantages in terms of flexibility, speed or labour costs.[67]

In this context, it is important to realize that the simple juxtaposition between actors of different sizes is insufficient to categorize their organizational capabilities, though being more appropriate for judging certain technological capabilities because these depend on economies of scale. Regarding organizational capabilities, we need to explicitly include the network dimension in many different shapes, reaching from the traditional lineage to the activation of localistic identities. Again, one ideal-typical pattern may suffice. I have already pointed out the widespread phenomenon that certain villages may specialize in certain products. One developmental track is that in building on such traditional capacities, more complex enterprise structures may emerge endogenously which may transform local production patterns from parallel production to more complex supplier networks with a few leading companies that emerge endogenously. In addition, a typical phenomenon is the co-existence of more advanced companies and a large number of small-scale family-based production units that mainly cater to the needs of seasonal adjustments or unexpected market dynamics. Then, the lead company becomes a quality gateway for the entire local production system, again also obviating the role of lower level traders, which, however, continue to exert competitive pressure on it. There are many diverse structural features that impact upon these trajectories of marketization, such as particular technological bottlenecks (e.g. mills that process agricultural products according to certain quality standards) or the need to establish brands that reflect certain quality standards (as in textile production, where fashion labels are important in accessing certain consumer groups).[68]

In industries where scale economies loom less large, such as more traditional handicrafts, we can observe the advantages of network organization in purer form. One possible pattern is that traders and even workshops are spread out geographically, visible in other areas as only small-scale companies. Yet, this expansion keeps the localized network structure intact, which is only reflected in the local identities of the itinerant traders. This localized network structure continues to play important economic roles. For example, the native village may arrange special conditions with suppliers of inputs because they create sufficient scales of demand of the large number of small-scale producers. This also allows for quality control of inputs which in turn is crucial in maintaining the reputation associated with the local identity. The network is also operative in gathering and communicating business intelligence. In this context traditional customs play an important role, such as when travellers return home on New Year holidays.[69]

The important point in this example is that on the surface, such a pattern may be associated with a village that does not undergo significant structural changes *in situ*, even manifesting signs of demographic decline, as the majority of the workforce is itinerant. So, the pattern is also distinct from rural industrialization in the TVE model. Nevertheless, economic development may be visible in the advanced standard of living and the large number of new houses. Sojourners want to show off their success in business in the local community. We may conclude that network organization can be a powerful functional equivalence to organizational size. Yet, this is not necessarily recognized in the modernist status order, especially with regard to the accessibility of loans from the large banks.

If we want to further specify these patterns, we can refer to them as hybrid network-mediated symbiosis of markets and organizations, or as modularized networks. The notion of 'modularization' goes beyond the notion of 'hybridization' because the primary entity is the network and, based on market dynamics, the network crystallizes into organizational forms, which assume the shape of enterprises. This is a topic I will pursue further in Chapter 6, but at this point it is important to note that by implication market and firm are not opposite forms of organization in the sense of the 'markets vs. hierarchies' duality, but are manifestations of more fundamental network structures. For example, a kinship-based network structure can result in a flexible network of family firms that are coordinated via a flexible holding structure which focuses on financial transactions; or a political cadre network in the local state may venture to create a 'farmers' association' into which a lead company is inserted. In other words, market performativity is network driven, and may result in the creation of enterprises with different corporate forms. This interaction between market and firms I call network-mediated modularization. I put forward the hypotheses that this phenomenon is ultimately rooted in the fundamental patterns of field-dependent cognition, in this case also in the more specific sense of cognitive modularization.[70]

These different examples of possible trajectories of market performativity cannot claim to be representative, but illustrate the underlying mechanisms. So, in the aforementioned case of traditional handicrafts, local network structures actually expand geographically beyond the marketing structures of the Skinnerian type and create market dynamics in other places. They operate in the context of status orders, which may be referred to as 'niche economies'. This means that the migration of economic actors exploits markets niches in other places that are often embedded in the modernist status order. This was particularly important in the early stages of reforms, when state-owned companies often failed to meet the demand of local consumers. This created market niches in which low-status producers could expand. The modernist status order results in a particular shape of market performativity that creates a bias towards organizational bifurcations, with some actors growing in scale and others maintaining more diffuse and fragmented network organizations. However, the endogenous creation of larger scale companies also includes the possibility of mutual leveraging, which can be observable in the emergence of local clusters specializing in certain industries. In the first stage of the rise of the TVE sector, networks between urban SOEs and rural industries often played a crucial role in creating the niches into which the TVEs could expand.

More generally, this process of market expansion may therefore be mediated via many dimensions and forms of networks. The question is how their particular shape influences the direction of market development. In this regard, the traditional view of the differential reach of network types may become more relevant. For example, kinship networks may be more limited in scope and reach, and may also be strongly path dependent in the peculiar activities of kin, thus triggering unique clustering phenomena.[71] In the modernist view, this relates to the limited role of particularistic trust in expanding market relations, however powerful these may be. As we have seen in the discussion of the crisis of confidence, however, the assumption of expanded trust into corporate identities heavily depends on the confidence in regulatory authorities and on standards of corporate behaviour, which should go hand in hand with the promotion of organizational network structures. Then, market performativity directly emanates from the interactions between public representations and cognitive or behavioural stances of actors, even possibly entailing a failure of corporate structures. So, considering that status orders on markets are of universal relevance for information processing and quality signalling, the specific forms of the Chinese status order count in understanding market performativity. One is the co-existence of traditional and modernist market structures, which are maintained by different mechanisms of trust building, and the other is the reputational mechanisms that relate the market to the political status order and the CCP organization. The latter, as we have seen, partly drives the modernist corporate pattern, but, depending on context and locality, can also help overcome the limitations of traditional particularistic mechanisms of trust. In other words, I claim that it is the CCP status order which, in combination with the local vs. central state duality, also contributes to the resilience of dual market structures, and even opens up considerable potential for the endogenous emergence of modernist corporate forms. The central phenomenon in this regard and which I will discuss in Chapter 6 is the resurgence of the Chinese family firm.

As I have already argued, the particular trajectory of market performance partly depends on technological constraints. However, the modernist view may partly favour particular technological trajectories via standardization that do not necessarily cover all technological possibilities, and may also overlook the demand side. A case in point is *Shanzhai* production that I already introduced in Chapter 3. In the mobile phone industry of the Pearl River Delta we observe a neat case of market bifurcation that reflects a particular pattern of market performativity, which is another instance of dualism. On the one hand, there are the large-sized producers of mobile phones (and other devices) for the domestic and the international market, such as Foxconn. These producers rely on the labour market, and in particular on migrant labour, in order to create competitive advantages. On the other hand, the emergence of these industries went along with the commodification and standardization of components of mobile phones, mostly produced by Taiwanese companies such as MediaTek. A significant share of their production entered the open local market, often as 'grey' transactions, for example, when large-scale producers ordered volumes of chips which were larger than their needs and so channelled surplus orders to the open market. This availability of components offered opportunities to access the mobile phone market for small-scale producers. The technological standardization lowered the standards for technological capacities in producing mobile phones, because the standardized components could be combined via software interfaces which are much easier to modify. As a result, a large number of small-scale producers entered the market, creating the *Shanzhai* phenomenon. As I have already outlined, *Shanzhai* producers utilized market niches in the low-price low-status segment that, however, also offered a huge potential in terms of total volume. The producers accessed this market with a highly individualized production that matched their small scale, but met with the demand of consumers for individualization and originality of design features and functionality. So, an entire industrial ecosystem has emerged in the Pearl River Delta in which large- and small-scale producers co-exist in different market niches.

The *Shanzhai* case also illustrates how the interaction between local states and central states shapes market performativity. One particularly important aspect here is the regulation and enforcement of intellectual property rights, also illustrating the tight connection between domestic and international markets, which has affected almost all markets in China following the WTO entry in 2001. *Shanzhai* producers often violate intellectual property rights of international companies, yet the local state may be reluctant to enforce those rights. One reason is that the *Shanzhai* producers create market growth, and hence local employment and income. But another reason is that the status order of producers creates high costs of enforcement, since the low-end and small-scale producers are far too numerous and flexible.[72]

I submit to generalize the observations made thus far in stating that market performativity in China maintains basic structures of the economic style of commercial capitalism mediated via networks and based on the family as the basic production unit. Clearly, this also implies that the small-scale producers face serious constraints in technological capacities. Yet, as the example of *Shanzhai* producers shows, these may be overcome if technology is generated from exogenous sources. This is partly reflected in the phenomenon of IPR violations: copying of foreign technologies feeds the dynamics of commercial capitalism in China.

If we go back to the example of the rural areas, the resilience of the family as a basic economic unit may be regarded as a fundamental phenomenon of the ritual economy that is reproduced by the specific interaction between institutions, organizations and markets. Interestingly, one institutional precondition is the continuity of the collective ownership of land. This creates the possibility for directly linking the family with downstream industries via specific forms of market organization. Going back to the example of 'dragon head companies', one pattern is that a county government may launch such a company and then also lend special support in establishing supplier networks that transform the early reform 'responsibility contracts' of farmers into supplier contracts. So, for example, a food-processing company may set up contracts with potato growers, which on the one hand keep the original land-use rights but effectively result in a vertical integration with the company. Thus, what was traditionally a Skinnerian market structure becomes a more stable organizational pattern. However, this remains market- and family-based, since farmers do not become full-time employees and give up their land-use rights. So, a particular existing arrangement regarding property rights on land, hence the land market, interacts with network dynamics, partly based also on the status orders in the local state, resulting in a modularized technological pattern that possibly even overcomes the diseconomies of scale in traditional family production.[73]

So, an important feature of market performativity in China is the mutual penetration and symbiosis of markets and organizations that I call 'modularization'. The underlying more abstract concept is the network. Fundamental network relations basically include both private networks and the state. So, as in the example of a dragon head company, its establishment may be an element in the developmental strategy envisaged by the county Party secretary. Therefore, this strategy is also implemented via the CCP network structure, reaching down to the grassroots level where farmers need to be convinced to enter this new contractual model which may entail risks owing to the resulting specialization. The CCP network also reaches into the financial system and may therefore boost the growth potential of the dragon head company via easier access to loans. Other patterns involve the endogenous creation of lead companies, which may be adapted to by the political network, for example, when local business leaders are selected as Party secretaries, thus deepening the mutual penetration of business networks and political networks. So, marketization may mostly involve also a high degree of government intervention which aims at creating a specific pattern of market performance, such as generating local employment, entering certain trajectories of technological development and so forth. So, performance and performativity are closely related to each other.

The question is what this implies for the analysis and assessment of the entire economic system. In Chapter 3, I pointed to the dualism of the informal and formal economy. This allows one to quantitatively approximate the shape of the status order that is an important characteristic of the network structures. This is because the distinction between formal and informal is based on the status of the corporate organization in terms of the company and the labour law, thus also classifying the underlying employment relations. For example, a dragon head company as a high-status company may have full legal status as a limited liability company according to the Company Law. Thus, for full-time employees also the labour law would strictly apply. However, contractually integrated farmers are not counted as employees, as they remain owners of their land; so, the labour law does not apply to them and they remain a part of the informal sector. If we take this criterion as a standard, we can say that approximately 80 per cent of economic actors in China still operate in the context of commercial-capitalistic family production in the broader sense, hence covering all sectors. My example also shows that marketization can actually undergird mechanisms of reproducing informality, since the high-status companies can gain cost advantages in subcontracting to the informal sector. This means that the formal sector plays an active role in reproducing the informal economy which remains a dominant feature of the economic style.[74]

The two modes, namely markets vs. organization, may also be labelled with reference to the social capital term as duality of social capital vs. organizational capital. This allows one to establish a systematic approach to network structures in a more straightforward way, along the lines of the social capital framework outlined in Chapter 1. Thus, we can also lend further detail to the distinction between social capital and *guanxi* that I introduced in the first section of this chapter. *Guanxi* is a specific mode of creating network connectivity, and social capital extends beyond that in including the different network resources that are being mobilized via *guanxi*. So, for example, the formal network of the CCP is a resource that can be mobilized via *guanxi* and therefore can become social capital for individual entrepreneurs. Therefore, from the external perspective, the CCP organization itself embodies social capital, which, however, only remains a potential as long as it is not mobilized via *guanxi* relations.

One resource that is essential for economic activities is finance. From the viewpoint of performativity theory, finance is a means of performing markets, because it provides the channels through which sellers and buyers can actually implement their desired actions and coordinate them via money, the medium of exchange. In particular, this relates to the funding of entrepreneurial activity. We have already noted that the status order of markets in China also relates to differential access to loans. This raises the question of how the extremely dynamic private sector can finance its expansion. The central observation is the partial fungibility of social capital and finance. This means that networks can be activated in order to create access to financial means that are not accessible in the formal sector. However, the perspective on social capital always includes the dimension of power, and hence needs to consider the status order. There can be a strong interaction between social capital and market structure, mediated via power and status. This was already evident from the discussion of lead companies. For example, if market structure favours a strong role of certain downstream market actors, this can leverage the status order, putting them in a very strong position vis-à-vis the upstream producers. This has consequences for finance. So, for example, in these market structures farmers may be compelled to accept IOUs to bridge a certain production period, which also further heightens their financial constraints. This phenomenon has repercussions for the local state, however, also revealing the political side of the status order. Farmers' discontent may not only be directed at the companies, but also at the local government.[75]

There are different ways as to how this works out. The most direct expression is funding business ventures via loans that are raised in the extended family, reaching from narrow to larger circles. Other mechanisms include the so-called Rotating Credit Associations (ROSCAs), an institution that is familiar also from other developing countries, but which has a very long historical tradition in China. ROSCAs can be entrepreneurial projects on their own, in which case the personal relationships among ROSCA members matter less. If we look at these different channels, they vary in terms of the social capital involved. If an entrepreneur raises money in the context of her familiar networks, she relies on her own social capital. If an individual establishes a ROSCA, he relies on his social capital to provide access to loans to others who have insufficient social capital that they can independently mobilize. It is important to recognize the power of these traditional structures, which include a wide variety of forms, such as traditional pawn shops or varieties of underground banking. This is not the place to go into detail, but I highlight the co-existence between these forms of informal finance and the financial repression regime of the formal financial sector. There have been attempts in opening up or partially formalizing informal finance, such as in the 'Rural Cooperative Credit Foundations' movement of the 1990s, but they have not yet reached a systematic scale, together with the policy to open up more flexible forms of formal finance in the shape of municipal or rural banks. Yet, up until today, the dual structure of the Chinese economy has been maintained by the dual structure of finance.[76]

One major reason for the institutional resilience of this duality is that the central government is concerned about inherent financial instability of the informal sector. There have been many and recurrent cases of financial scams affecting large numbers of people, with even violent repercussions for local political stability, which triggered strong interventions by the responsible local states facing the disapprobation of the central government. However, we can say that at least in the past three decades, these phenomena have resulted in regulatory cycles. Regulation and suppression of certain firms of informal finance always create huge possibilities for reaping profits and rents by inventing new forms of informal finance. In other words, regulation incentivizes its own erosion. The local state often participates in these developments, as, most generally, informal finance is supportive of entrepreneurial activity and hence fosters local economic growth, and because there are many ways in which both cadres and the local state can profit from the informal financial sector, reaching from semi-official management fees that can be channelled into extra-budgetary funds, to outright corruption. So, regulatory supervision of newly emerging forms of informal finance weakens. As long as there are no publicly visible dysfunctions, informal finance will expand until new troubles emerge. Following interventions can counterproductively trigger a local financial crash if the public suddenly loses trust in the respective informal financial organizations, with resulting runs leading towards local contagion. This triggers re-regulation, and a new cycle begins.[77]

Larger scale business ventures often rely on social capital that creates idiosyncratic connections in the local state, thus eventually even enabling access to the official financial sector. In rural areas this may be access to the Rural Credit Cooperatives, which in turn can mediate loans of the Agricultural Bank. In these cases, social capital can be directly converted into loans. The advantage lies in the scale: personalized social capital often only enables access to loans that are fragmented across different members of the network, such as a number of relatives. In comparison, loans mediated via the official financial sector can be much larger and thus may allow for qualitative transitions in business organization, such as endogenously creating a lead company. Thus, the differential availability of social capital and the corresponding patterns of fungibility explain the specific forms of bifurcation of market organization in a particular area or product branch.[78]

So, informal finance is an important example of the role of the local–central duality in driving market performativity, not only in the financial sector, but also in the local market structures that are shaped by the emerging patterns of financing business ventures, such as the effects on the achievable size of firms. Informal finance is also intrinsically local, although as such it is a nationwide phenomenon. Yet, the informal financial structures are only of local reach, but they can assume a leading role in private sector finance. In comparison, the evolution of the stock market is another case in point of the central–local duality, yet relates to an institutional phenomenon that has rapidly achieved national-level scope. Stock markets were initially established only by local governments, with national regulation being instituted only in 1999 following the adoption of the Securities Law in 1998 and the creation of the China Securities Regulatory Commission. One reason for this delay in adapting national regulation to the factual emergence of stock markets were the ideological concerns in parts of the CCP leadership. However, as it was also seen as a way of SOE reforms without changing state ownership as a principle, eventually they received national-level recognition, initially with a number of special features such as a high proportion of non-tradable shares for SOEs, which was only tackled by launching further reforms in 2005. Right from the beginning, and similar to the development of informal finance, stock market performance was also seen in terms of political significance and legitimacy, since regulatory failures or other forms of stock market crises easily trigger strong public response, including riots and other forms of expressing dissatisfaction. Another dilemma was the need to tap international sources of capital for fuelling growth and structural change, at the same time maintaining control of a central sector by the CCP. So, until most recently, the institutional conditions of the Chinese stock market have been directly shaped by government interventions into safeguarding certain levels of market performance, thus also creating a unique form of market performativity. So, as the stock market received national recognition, a peculiar form of market governmentality was also established which clearly differentiates the role of the stock market in China from conditions under financial capitalism. One essential aspect is the control of the behaviour of top-level executives via the CCP nomenclature, which also allows for centralization measures when necessary, as after 1998. This example shows how the expansion and further marketization of the financial sector can be simultaneously accompanied by increasing CCP control. This means that understanding the regulatory environment without explicitly including this element would fail to recognize its nature.[79]

I want to conclude this section by briefly coming back to the issue of regulation and industrial policy that I examined in Chapter 4. We can approach the issue of regulation also as a way of market performativity. In this case, there is even the literal sense in which the government creates markets while explicitly aiming at a particular performance: hence, the government performs markets. This is what we also call 'market instrumentality' in the Chinese economic style. In this context, this mainly relates to the regulatory approaches of the central government with reference to the state-owned sector. However, as we have seen, market instrumentality also inheres in the approaches of local states in establishing markets as economic infrastructures, and which ties up with historical traditions.

In the state-owned sector, market instrumentality is salient in the structural reorganization of industries which emerged from reforms as highly monopolized, such as energy, aviation or telecommunications. There are industries which are traditionally established, such as electricity, and where markets are artificially created via industrial reorganization and the breakup of monopolistic structures. So, the result is a kind of politically orchestrated competition which is mainly fuelled by the cadre evaluation system. Even though the split-up companies remain state owned, even by the same level of government, such as being central-level SOEs, their CEOs are evaluated by their success in leading the particular company of which they are in charge. This means that competition in deregulated markets with the dominance of SOEs is partly a derivative of the competition system in cadre evaluation. This has implications for the regulatory framework, as top-level personnel management remains under control of the CCP organization department and is not left to what are the formal agencies that manage state-owned companies, namely the SASACs.

Against this background, an interesting case for understanding market performativity is when technological developments create the conditions for market entry for new competitors. In this case, the internal fragmentation of the Chinese state becomes an important determinant of market developments. This applies in particular to the duality of local vs. central governments. This may result in many tensions between central- and local-level actions, often in the context of central-level development plans which overlook the market potential of newly emerging industries. This opens up opportunities for new market entries, which, however, face many barriers because they operate outside the development plan and therefore cannot enjoy preferential conditions, such as in finance. This is when support by the local state can become crucial, so triggering market expansion outside the plan, which typically may result in a renewed regulatory effort by the central government. For example, in the energy sector this has created strong path dependencies with complex interactions between market performativity and the political status order, such as in launching alternatives to carbon fuels. This has resulted in a highly diversified national map of technological trajectories, driven by interactions among business and political actors on the different levels, and an increasingly autonomous role of SOEs in influencing policies adopted by the central state. In understanding such complex situations, it is important not only to look at the formal regulatory institutions, but also at the concrete network structures that are shaped by the status order and that may enable even single private entrepreneurs to navigate the structures of the local and central state.[80]

To summarize, market instrumentality introduces a substantial modification of the notion of the 'regulatory state' in the Chinese context. If we refer back to the more general background of modernism and the growth model, market instrumentalism means that markets are created or allowed to emerge spontaneously because they are seen as social-technological devices that incentivize entrepreneurial responses which eventually result in growth. This is indeed the Dengist philosophy of economic policy and means that regulation and deregulation are actually means of steering economic performance in general and market performance in particular. In this approach, the market is not seen as an autonomous domain in society but as a policy instrument that is often used to respond to economic developments even in the short term. This policy stance is bolstered by the principle of experimentalism. Western observers tend to see this as deficient, because they argue that expectations of economic actors may be destabilized because of the lack of a stable regulatory framework. However, this interpretation may fail to recognize the role of field-dependent cognition in responding to this peculiar regulatory pattern. The simple reason is that for many entrepreneurs, in considering the structural conditions of the Chinese economy, the horizon for forming expectations about business opportunities is relatively short term. For example, an entrepreneur in informal finance can reap substantial profits within a couple of years, during which the relevant regulatory framework is stable and social capital is crucial, which is also independent from regulatory changes. This means that regulatory changes may often not destabilize expectations but, on the contrary, create a sense of recurrent opportunity. So, market instrumentalism and market dynamism do not appear to be contradictory.

Theoretical reprise

In this chapter I have explored the cultural foundations of markets, focusing on certain selected aspects: the embeddedness aspect that relates markets to networks, the value aspect that looks at the behavioural foundations of markets, and the performativity aspect that investigates the specific market mechanisms. These aspects may be directly related to the central theoretical categories I developed in Chapter 1.

To begin with the performativity aspect, which appears to be the more fundamental one, we have seen how markets are actually created and operated via the implementation of particular mechanisms that are triggered by actions of market actors and enabled by certain structural features. We can generalize and say that these structural features are networks, institutions and technologies. The role of technologies is complex because this refers first to the market devices that enact markets, such as certain technologies of exchange, but also to the technological conditions that incentivize certain actions via the effects of economic data on actors' decisions. This effect is well known, though rarely explicitly recognized in the abstract definition of markets; for example, the fact that digital technologies often manifest strong network externalities is an important driver of corporate strategies in these markets and determines the evolution of market structure, eventually also affecting the diffusion of standards, possibly interacting with political decisions about their content, and so on. We have seen that these interdependencies are important in China, even for the case of traditional sectors such as agriculture, as in the role of modern food processing in reshaping traditional market structures. The use of technologies is partly determined by the institutional framework. In the example of digital technologies, the exploitation of network externalities was also enabled by the change of regulations on the US capital market, greatly easing venture capital funds and access to capital markets for new internet companies. Again, we saw that this also applies to traditional industries in China: the current institutional framework on land property rights is a factor in retaining the family as a production unit, thus supporting the emergence of specific combinations of markets and organizations in the food industry. Finally, if we look at the concrete chain of events that leads towards certain market outcomes, we see that market actions are enabled and materialized in networks of actors, such as when the contractual relations between food-processing companies and farmers are mediated by township cadres.

We can capture these different interdependencies in the notion of a 'market state' which is an extension of the Aoki model of institutions. By this analytical step, we overcome the separation between markets and institutions. Conventionally, as I mentioned at the beginning of this chapter, markets are the games that are played according to certain rules, the institutions. If this is complemented by the perspective of political economy, we would question the actions by which the market actors try to influence the institutions. However, even then, the two notions, namely markets and institutions, are seen as being separate. In the notion of a market state, we follow the idea of 'institutionally guided behavioural patterns' and therefore endogenize the institutions in the sense that the market processes and states are themselves seen as embodiments of the institutions. But this implies, vice versa, that we have to include behavioural and structural aspects of markets in our view of institutions. So, the market state as an institution in the sense of Aoki's model refers to institutional patterns that are embodied in the recurrent actions of actors, and recognizes that this recurrent nature of the actions is determined by the three aspects of networks, institutions and technologies. In this use, of course, a certain confusion may emerge about the double meaning of institutions, as we need to pay attention to the conventional use of the term 'institutions' as well in order to understand the relationship between the three aspects. For example, the arrangement of land property rights in China is an institution in this sense. However, with reference to markets, we cannot simply say that market states directly reflect this institution. In fact, the land property rights institution is just one of the various public representations that influences the emergence of certain market states as institutions.

In the Aoki framework, a market state is an equilibrium that includes both institutionalized behavioural patterns and a certain market performance. Public representations play an important role in stabilizing these states. For example, in the Chinese context, government policies and plans assume this role in supporting certain expectations about future market performance. This includes expectations about institutional settings, such as land property rights. But there are also other public representations which relate to the legitimacy and the accepted forms of behaviour in certain markets.[81] This is where the role of networks comes into play, because as long as there is no strong intervention by central-level legal design, these expectations evolve endogenously in networks of interactions. This is how the status order directly affects market performativity; for example, high-level support by certain political leaders (their 'thinking'), both in the local and the central state, can trigger the diffusion of certain market practices and business strategies, resulting in a certain market performance.

We can put more flesh on the bones of this abstract reasoning when we add the elements–patterns–processes–states perspective. In this general framework, we can specify particular mechanisms to approach as manifestations of the specific Chinese economic style. One foremost example of this is the notion of the modularization of markets and organizations. If we continue with the example of agriculture and food-processing industries, modularization is manifest in particular transaction patterns between farmers and food companies in which farmers maintain their partly autonomous role as production units and do not become employees of the company, yet the relationship is constrained by certain contractual features that are not simply the result of bargaining between the two sides, but have also been designed by interventions of local cadres. This intervention reflects the peculiar structure of land property rights, since farmers control the use rights, but cadres represent the collective as the ultimate owner of land. The role of cadres is ambivalent, depending on the specific goals they pursue, and can be traced only in case studies and their comparisons. But on an abstract level we can generalize regarding the impact of the differential distribution of social capital among the various parties involved. If we only look at the relationship between farmers and companies, the relative bargaining position of the company is partly determined by the market structure that reflects current economic and technological conditions, such as the degree of local monopoly power. Once we include the cadres here, this relationship can be fundamentally transformed, depending on how the cadres evaluate the roles of the other parties. This can lead to instances of corruption and profiteering in supporting the company in imposing bad deals upon the farmers, but can also result in a developmentalist approach which favours farmers' interests. One important point holds generally. The different network position of cadres allows for making opportunities accessible also for the other parties that would not be available without them, with direct impact upon the realized market states. Cadres may actively support the relationship between farmers and companies, thus reducing transaction costs and resolving problems of information asymmetries, they can influence the result of the bargaining in supporting outcomes which are stable in the longer run (such as agreements on minimum purchasing prices), or they can open up access to certain opportunities, such as supporting a company in obtaining a loan from the local branch of the agricultural bank.

As this example clearly shows, one important aspect in the interaction between networks, technologies and institutions is the role of the state in acting as a third party or intermediator in establishing market states. If we referred to this previously as 'local state corporatism' or 'localism', we can now move to the micro-analytical foundations and relate this to the network structures and the distribution of social capital among the different parties in evolving market states. In the positive case, for example, a leading cadre at the township level is able to establish network connectivities which reach much further than the connectivities that farmers can establish, thus substantially enhancing their social capital in undergirding entrepreneurial actions. Only if we move to the micro level can we adequately evaluate the general role of the state in relation to markets. The methodological difficulty that results from this step, however, is that we can only rely on case studies, and may reach the wrong conclusion if we generalize over single case studies for assessing the situation in China. Yet, we can certainly say that the duality of local and central state is essential for market performativity in China in the sense that, depending on the industry and sector, the local state is deeply involved in market performativity in at least two ways. One is the specific shape of social networks that undergird market states, the other is the contextualization of certain institutions, such as legal prescriptions, which we have denoted as 'localism' and 'experimentalism' in Chapter 4.

So, in the more detailed Aoki model, we consider different elements, such as local networks between cadres and business, national regulatory schemes, or entrepreneurial strategies, which work together to create a pattern, such as in the *Shanzhai* industries. That pattern triggers processes of growth, i.e. market performance. Growing markets coalesce into certain states with recurrent patterns of interactions, namely market states, which are recognized by the actors as stable reference frames for their further actions. In these market states, the relationship between the different elements assumes a sustainable pattern, resulting in a highly diverse ecology of markets in China.

It is only by taking this micro-level perspective that we will properly understand a number of phenomena reported in this chapter, in particular the relationship between networks and trust in society and markets. There is substantial literature in economics that highlights the central role of trust in the expansion of markets. Many observers have also pointed out that this creates certain difficulties in dealing with the Chinese case, as in the public perception corruption is widespread and a crisis of confidence has been smouldering for years. I have proposed a solution to this puzzle in arguing that the specific construction of social networks in China, together with the fundamental cognitive stance of field dependence, is a basis for societal-level trust in the flow of particular transactions, even if there is a crisis of confidence in certain respects. So, for example, whereas there may be a crisis of confidence in corporate actors, in the everyday lifeworld people still interact in wide-ranging *guanxi* networks that are fertile grounds for general trust.

This allows for identifying certain mechanisms that may be regarded as elements in defining the Chinese economic style as ritual economy. The relationship between ritual and networks has been emphasized by many authors. For market performativity, there are two aspects which deserve most attention, and which we can see as Chinese special features against the backdrop of the general theory of social networks. The first is the role of long-term reciprocity and the corresponding norm to maintain short-term imbalances of reciprocity. Clearly, this creates a risk of cheating and failure to meet the expectations of long-term reciprocity. In traditional China, these beliefs were deeply embedded in religious notions of reciprocity, especially in Daoism, but also in Buddhism, which therefore undergirded universalistic Confucian norms of 'sincerity'. These religious foundations actually resulted in what one might call a 'field-dependent universalization of particularistic relational ethics'. Thus, long-term reciprocity becomes a strong foundation of trust in social interactions, which is partly directly relevant also for market transactions. As we know, in the market context Chinese actors carefully judge and evaluate the activation of *guanxi*, and would often even try to avoid the direct intermingling of *guanxi* with actual market exchange in order to preserve market reciprocity. On the other hand, for opening up market opportunities, long-term reciprocity can play a crucial role, and thus contributes to the stabilization of entrepreneurial expectations.

Certainly, we cannot argue that these behaviours are today directly embedded in religious beliefs, but at the same time we can also say that there is still a strong legacy of traditional religion in the rural areas, and that religious beliefs are partly immanent to more general notions of ritual and accepted social norms. In this context, we need to take note that there is a burgeoning popular literature on *guanxi* and corresponding ritual, and that traditional Confucian notions of trust and sincerity are central ideas in a growing number of grassroots-level popular movements aiming at the moral transformation or a moral revival of the Chinese people. In other words, I argue that a popular culture of trust still survives in China. Theoretically, this means that there are many transitional forms between social capital in terms of network structures and social capital in terms of more formal organizations, such as the burgeoning native place associations in areas with a high share of migrants in the local population. This reflects deep structural tendencies in social complexity in the *longue durée*, as we saw in Chapter 2.

The second specificity of *guanxi* is the complex emotional patterns that are also the object of continuous reflection and evaluation of *guanxi*. This refers to two different dimensions. One is the role of moral sentiments, a term coined by Adam Smith that I introduce as a translation of *renqing*. Moral sentiments are socially approved and ethically grounded expressions of emotions that match behavioural expectations created by ritual. Against this background the concept of *guanxi* appears to be overly narrow, and reference to the more general notion of *li shang wanglai* may be more appropriate. The other dimension is that of personal affections, labelled *ganqing*, which result in a peculiar combination of emotional and instrumental aspects of social interactions. I argue that both are supporting features of market operations, and also introduce Chinese peculiarities in economic style.

Regarding *renqing*, there is a strong activation of reputational concerns, mostly referred to as 'face'. As is well known from game theory, reputation can be a cause of commitment and endogenous stabilization of institutions independent from third-party enforcement. So, I argue that there is a strong background factor in driving a particular form of market governmentality. Some authors have generalized over this as a form of relational governance. What distinguishes this form of governance from general reputation effects is that apart from the explicit norms that govern expectations about reciprocity, in China the intermingling of political and market networks matters a great deal. In this regard, Western observers tend to overemphasize the resulting possibility of corruption. As I have argued, even when taking corruption into consideration, the impact of long-term reciprocity can have the counter-intuitive effect that corrupt networks even increase trust in business. But beyond this special argument, which is certainly difficult to evaluate against the weight of eroding effects of corruption, we have to consider the pervasive role of reputation in the CCP-related social networks that connect business and politics. Reputation is also a major political criterion in the cadre assessment system, and the success of business projects in the area of a cadre's competence matters a great deal. So, relational governance would mean that cadres are often involved in business transactions, such as playing the role of intermediaries, and then actively contribute to their success, with a large grey area between legitimate *guanxi* practices and corruption. This means that we cannot only examine reputational effects in the market domain; we also need to consider reputational effects in the status order, which is politically shaped. The latter can leverage the former, an effect that was certainly very important in driving the marketization and industrialization of many rural areas in China. For example, when high-ranking cadres act as intermediaries for business relations, they risk their face in their personal cadre networks. Hence, business actors may place more trust in information about business opportunities that is transmitted via cadre networks. As we have seen, generally speaking, the political rank order also seems to reflect a rank order of levels of confidence, with central state actors receiving the most trust. This may also reflect trust in their organizational capabilities, social capital and other resources that they can mobilize. This argument allows one to specify the generic argument about status in markets as a mediator of quality signals in such a way that we identify a peculiar form of market governmentality as an element of economic style.

The effect of *ganqing* differs from this, as it directly relates to the personal relations that people maintain, so cannot be seen in the light of systemic institutional features. However, the fusion of instrumental and emotional aspects introduces a component that is conducive to market dynamics in the sense that instrumental market relations can be emotionally loaded, hence at the same time creating emotional satisfaction, but also undergirding mutual commitments of market actors. We can generalize this in positing that business is a form of life. This is what is often highlighted in the popular folklore about Chinese businesspeople, where, for example, in a typical Chinese family business, business issues permeate the entire lives of individuals, making distinctions between working days and holidays or between working time and spare time obsolete. I think we can make theoretical sense of these observations in arguing that the separation between 'work' or 'professional life' and the private sphere of emotions is overcome in the Chinese cultural context, with obvious effects on work effort or ease of entrepreneurial activity. This matches our observation on values, such as optimism regarding opportunities in society. These values foster a positive stance towards markets as media of opportunity, thus certainly driving their dynamics. Clearly, this also has effects on the organization of economic activity in firms. This is the topic of Chapter 6.

Notes

1 Interestingly, this issue is not only relevant in the context of Mainland China; it is also being discussed with reference to Singapore. In the past, Singapore has adopted a value system guiding politics that comes very close to traditional conceptualizations of Chinese culture as being 'Confucian'. This includes tight constraints upon certain 'liberal' attitudes in social life. Thus, we may say that Singapore is another instance of a Chinese ritual economy. Yet, with the achieved high standards of living, Singapore today also faces the challenge of liberalization, since maintaining competitive advantages may require liberalizing society, such as opening up in the area of sexual norms (cf. the survey in *The Economist*, 18 July 2015).

2 I have already briefly touched upon the issue of indigenization in Chapter 1, n. 15. In the current context, this refers to both the value and the interaction dimension. The indigenization issue was seminally raised by Taiwanese researchers for the first time, in particular Yang (1989: 457ff., 1996). Yang argued against radical indigenization theories, and is in favour of more detailed contextualization, especially in considering values which appear to be specifically Chinese. One conspicuous example is 'xiao' (孝), 'filial piety', which is central in the Confucian philosophy, also with regard to popular culture, but it is difficult to translate and certainly difficult to relate to other values emphasized in the Western tradition. Yet, Yang argued that a general 'modernization' framework still applies. Another influential author, Hwang (2006a), adopts a much more radical indigenization approach. In the past two decades, these debates have also been picked up in Mainland China, as aptly surveyed by Kulich and Zhang (2010). One simple approach is to directly modify or enhance standard value lists by specifically Chinese ones, thus adding 'filial piety' or 'harmony'. More sophisticated approaches, also adopted by leading Western researchers such as Schwartz, would still rely on etic questionnaires but would try to relate observed patterns with emic categories. In all of these approaches, the hypothesis of distinctly Chinese values, also in the context of modernization, is largely confirmed. This research tradition has to be distinguished from more general sociological research which tries to validate claims for cultural specificity of Chinese social behaviour. In the current context of network analysis, a leading scholar in Mainland China is Zhai (2013: 20ff.), who argues that one problem is that indigenous concepts cannot be clearly defined for principled reasons. The solution lies in adopting an indigenous analytical perspective based on empirical case work, which then results in more precise definitions. This is guided by universal theoretical concepts, but it is also sensitive to limitations that may partly result from hidden cultural assumptions, or simply from a certain limited focus of meaning which may not fully match Chinese data or terminologies.

3 The idea of similarities across domains was seminally developed by Aoki (1988) in his research on the Japanese economy. Aoki introduced a specific term to describe Japanese government organization, namely 'bureaupluralism', which manifests similar patterns as in corporate organization. In this regime, corporations, business associations and government organizations interact in a regular way to determine the policy framework of business, supported by institutionalized networking mechanisms such as the transfer of retired bureaucrats to associations and corporations. In Chinese studies, networks have always been of special interest also for political scientists aiming at understanding the internal dynamics of Chinese politics. A classical contribution was Pye (1981, 1988), who coined the term 'Confucian Leninism', and was one of the leading authors in the 'political culture' research on China originating in Solomon's (1971)

classic. Pye developed the analysis of Chinese politics in terms of factional dynamics, with factions being a culturally specific network formation within the CCP that builds on personal relations that are largely devoid of specific political ideas or programmes, and in which mutual trust in a status hierarchy plays an essential role. At that time, these ideas were not applied to the economy, which was mainly under the regime of planning. Regarding the homologies between family and state in the traditional view, suffice it to consult Baker (1979) for an overview. This refers to the notion of the 'wu lun' (五伦), the five relations, which is often referred to when analysing Chinese social networks.

4 On this distinction, see Ross (2011) with reference to Hayek. Hayek is an interesting case showing that the two need not necessarily coincide, as Hayek is certainly normatively individualistic but not descriptively, for example, when highlighting the role of group competition and the role of culture in accumulating tacit knowledge. Yet, this tension was never systematically resolved (see e.g. Vanberg 1994: 77ff.). Economics in general adheres to both assumptions, with descriptive individualism being enshrined in methodological individualism. Ross shows that normative individualism does not entail descriptive individualism, because independent from the specific empirical analysis of agency we can maintain the normative standard that only individual interests would count in evaluating social states.

5 On these methodological tensions, see Jackson (2014), who, however, tends to introduce networks only in the context of specific aspects of economic behaviour, such as the diffusion of certain innovations. I have already pointed to background literature in Chapter 1, n. 60. The approach of social network theory is more radical methodologically and claims universal coverage, including any kind of economic process. For example, this even affects the sorts of data that are seen as fundamental for empirical research (see Knoke and Song 2008: 15ff.). Whereas economists normal use data that classify agents into certain categories (such as people with the same level of income), social network analysis strictly focuses on relational data. This means that the database consists of particular kinds of events in which at least two individuals are connected.

6 The heroic view on entrepreneurship is systematically explored in the so-called 'Austrian' tradition in economics, such as the review by Kirzner (1997). Schumpeter's (1950) classical contribution argued that innovation would increasingly have to rely on large-scale research and development, thus eroding the role of the individual entrepreneur. However, the 'heroic' view also needs to be confronted with a network-based view if we want a remedy to under-socialization. In economics, this perspective has been taken, among others, by evolutionary theorists such as Aldrich (1999), who considers the social resources on which individual entrepreneurs have to build in order to achieve market entry. Of course, this is a view mainly prevailing in sociology, such as in more specific contexts of development economics (see e.g. Portes and Sensenbrenner 1993). Recently, similar views have been also developed in the context of the digital economy, where increasingly innovation is seen as emerging in interactive networks joining producers and users (see e.g. Hartley 2009).

7 On the intellectual history of the *guanxi* notion in Chinese studies, see Gold *et al.* (2002: 3ff.). The authors emphasize that the term was not especially prominent in the 1980s, because most Chinese interview partners avoided the term (see e.g. Pye 1988), as it was seen as partly illicit. However, the term rapidly underwent a strong career in various respects. In Chinese studies, there were seminal works such as Yang (1994) which established *guanxi* as an elementary analytical framework in understanding social interactions in China. This coincided with a re-evaluation of the term in indigenous conceptualizations, especially also in publications directed at a broader audience. The 'guanxixue'

(关系学) emerged as an essential part of the Chinese cultural legacy, included the larger framework of Confucian doctrines about social behaviour (see e.g. Dong 1999). However, this career was also criticized as over-inflating the meaning of the term, especially in the sense of overlooking the more general and comprehensive frameworks related to ritual as an encompassing framework, such as the *li shang wanglai* framework that we have already met (see Chang 2010). There is also a strong belief in the *guanxi* concept in management science; see Chen *et al.* (2013), who review a stock of contributions in the four-digit scale of the number of pertinent papers. Interestingly, these contributions often come from ethnically Chinese researchers in Western academia, such as Li (2007), thus clearly evoking the framework of the 'mirror of culture'.

8 On the affinity between *guanxi* and social network analysis, see Wellman *et al.* (2002). Interestingly, the authors paint an image in which both the Western and the Chinese perceptions of society move to a network-focused view, and argue in favour of a universalistic network concept that is contextualized for China in terms of *guanxi*. The similarities apply to important specific aspects, and hence go beyond the general and obvious ones in terms of universal network notions. For example, in his treatment of *guanxi*, Zhai (2013: 121ff.) emphasizes the triadic notion of balance, which matches the notion of the triad in balance theory (see Wasserman and Faust 1994: 225ff.). Balance theory explains single interactions as reflecting balances of social exchange or valued relationships in the larger embedding network structure, which is exactly what Zhai claims is a specific feature of Chinese *guanxi*.

9 One influential model of institutional development is North (1990), who speaks of traditional network economies as 'bazaar economies'. Although North recognizes the interaction between informal and formal institutions in economic systems, he also maintains the idea that with growing reach and scope of markets, formal institutions obtain priority. This is also maintained by other influential authors such as Greif (1994) who, on the one hand, demonstrates the functional equivalence of networks with legal regimes, but also points out that the former impose constraints upon the sustainable growth and expansion of market relations. The concept of relational contracts is a central notion in Williamson's (1985) transaction cost economics, but is mainly a microeconomic notion in the sense of applying to the level of single transactions, distinguishing an alternative regime between markets and hierarchies. This does not necessarily have implications for the systemic level.

10 The position of the transient nature of *guanxi* was clearly formulated by Guthrie (1998), who argued that internationalization and professionalization will inevitably lead towards their erosion. This matches the view that *guanxi* have a different context in rural and urban areas, which was already posited by Yang (1994). In the modernizing urban context, the dysfunctional aspects of *guanxi* are often emphasized. Yet, Yang (2002) maintains that the erosion hypothesis does not hold, and points to contradicting evidence. She also highlights the gender dimension, which contributes to resilience, since *guanxi* are especially pronounced in male interactions. Wank (2002) argues that the *guanxi* practices also undergo changes, including linguistic practices which may relate to similar underlying phenomena but avoid the stigma of the term *guanxi* as being associated with corruption. The relational contract explanation has been seminally explored by Solinger (1989). This explanation differs from cultural approaches in highlighting the special conditions of a transitional economy where market relations expand within a still incomplete legal framework and high uncertainty of market dynamics; therefore, market actors rely on personal relations, especially including political actors, in order to reduce uncertainty.

11 Interestingly, the functional role of *guanxi* in shaping the legal order has been emphasized by legal scholars recently; see Potter (2002) or Liebman and Wu (2013), who even introduce the notion of 'network justice'. This refers to phenomena such as the activation of social networks in mediation or the collection of information for judicial decisions via social networks, more specifically also social media. Interestingly, this may also relate traditional *guanxi* to modern information technology, as network connections are more easy to access via modern means of communication. The term 'network justice' refers to this confluence of modern technology and social networks.

12 On Chinese practices, see Chapter 2, n. 38. In European history, this corresponds to the emergence of the *lex mercatoria* (see e.g. Milgrom *et al.* 1990). To be sure, the *lex mercatoria* also includes a set of written rules, and certainly relies on formal institutions in its modern shapes, such as International Courts of Arbitration. However, as Schmidt-Trenz (1990) has rigorously shown, these institutions formalize what evolves endogenously as a body of rules that is not enforced by any kind of governmental organization, thus requiring mechanisms of commitment and self-enforcement.

13 Legal scholars such as Clarke (2010) tend to emphasize the dysfunctional effects of informal practices, for example, in the context of corporate governance, which is also often highlighted for the Japanese case. Status distinctions may influence the relationship between different shareholders, thus undermining their role in monitoring management. Or, concerns for face may stifle open and productive discussion in the boardroom (cf. Smith 2012). On the other hand, Liebman and Milhaupt (2007) have shown that regulatory authorities often use appeals to 'face' in enforcing corporate governance standards upon companies, thus directly activating *guanxi* dynamics. Lau and Young (2013) believe that China manifests a distinct model of 'relational governance' in which reputation, face and trust as central parameters may be institutionally enhanced, for example, via voluntary codes of conduct in associations. They also include paternalistic guidance by government agencies in this pattern.

14 This is the position developed by Chang (2010) in the *li shang wanglai* model (see Chapter 2, n. 22).

15 De Glopper (1972) pointed out that Chinese businessmen often try to avoid *guanxi* because of the involved obligations to reciprocate and because of the emotional component. Therefore, one cannot simply say that *guanxi* stay at the core of traditional Chinese business organization; on this important point, see also Yang (1994: 143ff.). Many business transactions cannot be regarded as being manifestations of *guanxi* because they entail immediate and balanced reciprocity. This also applies to interpersonal relations in general. Kipnis (2002) therefore even highlights the phenomenon of '*guanxi* avoidance'. The notion of long-term reciprocity and imbalance is wonderfully illustrated in the biography of the Ming-Dynasty painter and poet Wen Zhengming by Clunas (2004). Clunas refers to modern research about *guanxi* in order to analyse one essential phenomenon in the social organization of art in traditional China, namely that many paintings were actually gifts sent to other people. Some of these gifts would even circulate among the same people, which is visible in adding epigraphs and poems to the original. Clunas therefore argues that the flow of gifts, as in traditional rural society (for contemporary analyses see Yan 1996a, 1996b) serves to maintain stable personal relationships among members of the scholar-elite. However, he also gives examples of how Wen Zhengming actually avoided mutual obligations. This is possible when directly reciprocating a certain favour which may establish obligations to reciprocate at a later date. So, if a favour is immediately reciprocated by a gift, this actually destroys the buildup of *guanxi*. I come back on this point below.

16 The seminal contribution to building a *guanxi* model of the kind I summarized is Jacobs (1982). None of the components should be missed; otherwise the *guanxi* will unravel. For example, if *guanxi* are not maintained by recurrent interactions which entail also the mutual flow of favours and support, the instrumentalist basis will erode, and cannot be substituted by merely expressing affective closeness (cf. Chen and Chen 2004). This implies that, at odds with social network analysis, it is possible and actually often done to evaluate *guanxi* in terms of different degrees of 'strength'; so, one cannot simply distinguish between 'weak' and 'strong ties'. This is probably the reason why *guanxi* are often falsely extended to include kin relations, since 'strong *guanxi*' may resemble these relations in terms of the implicit reciprocity of the long-term relation. Indeed, if Chinese 'pull *guanxi*', they are very sensitive in assessing the strength and reliability of *guanxi* and evaluate how far they can be actually relied on without making demands that are socially unacceptable. The *guanxi* basis should not be confused with a categorial assignment, but only serves as a trigger for creating *guanxi*. In what is also a classical contribution, King (1994) therefore refers the Nakana Chie's distinction between 'attributes' and 'frames' as ways to assign individuals to groups; this distinction comes close to Fei Xiaotong's distinctions discussed previously. So, a 'frame' is a fixed group with clearly defined boundaries and membership criteria, whereas group assignment via attributes implies that individuals can share a number of attributes on which relationships are built. In this case, what matters is whether attributes are obtained by birth or other mechanisms of fixed attribution, or whether attributes can be achieved via certain social practices and efforts. The latter applies to China. This means that the *guanxi* basis may be interpreted in a flexible way. For example, when I recently attended an alumni meeting at a top Chinese university, I realized that there were also non-alumni members. The manager explained to me that the alumni association serves as an arena for building relationships, and therefore the association would be open to non-members who are introduced by members.

17 In his indigenous theoretical approach, Zhai (2013: 35, 47) speaks of the special feature of 'lianxu xing' (连续性) (i.e. 'continuity'), which characterizes Chinese social structure, which in his account means that, for example, there is no clear distinction between 'micro' and 'macro' or across certain social categories. Zhai (2011: 127ff.) therefore introduces the distinction between 'authority' and 'ordinary life authority' (日常权威). The former emanates from fixed structural positions of individuals, the latter from *guanxi* relations. For example, there may be a structural authority of *A* over *B* and *C*, but if *B* maintains a *guanxi* with *D* who exerts structural authority over *A*, this results in ordinary life authority of *B* over *A*. The fluid and decentred nature of *guanxi* has been highlighted in Yang's (1994) term 'rhizomatic networks' which compares with hierarchical 'arborean' networks. The individualistic nature of *guanxi* has also been elaborated upon in King's (1994) classical paper. King describes the individual as the 'architect' of social relations and relates this to the traditional Confucian notion of the 'self', 'ji' (己).

18 Social capital theory is multifaceted. One common distinction is between 'Burt' and 'Coleman' social capital, which relates to two different conceptualizations common in the literature, but which are often labelled differently, such as 'bridging' and 'bonding' (see Burt 2002). The 'Burt' approach is about bridging, following Burt's (1992) classical work on 'structural holes'. This matches individualistic theories such as Nan Lin's (2001), which emphasize the instrumental role of social capital for individual advantage. This perspective comes close to *guanxi*, which is also evident from Zhai's indigenous discussion of the difference between *guanxi* and social capital. Zhai (2011: 79ff.) argues that

social capital is a more structured notion and refers to public patterns that are embodied also in organizational or institutional features, whereas *guanxi* are ephemeral, dynamic and contextual. This distinction actually takes the Coleman version as a reference, which treats social capital as a public good that resides in groups of actors and enables collective action. This view is consistent with Putnam's (2000) approach in political science, which stresses even more strongly the institutional aspects of social capital, such as being embodied in civil society structures. Zhai's notion of *guanxi* and of social capital can be reconciled if we treat *guanxi* as a Chinese manifestation of 'bridging' or 'Burt' social capital (for a related discussion, see Li 2007).

19 This distinction also underlies the 'Burt' vs. 'Coleman' duality. 'Bonding' emerges from strong emotional commitments, thus creating tendencies for sharing, trusting and altruism, which are all conducive for collective action. Heterophilous relations would build on instrumental rationality, so being emotionally neutral. Accordingly, the 'Burt' perspective is more congenial to an economic approach to networks. However, as Burt (2000) argues, for many economic activities a combination of both bridging and bonding may be the optimal pattern. Generally, bridging facilitates access to new information, but bonding facilitates the sharing of information which is important in arranging cooperative relations.

20 The central role of *renqing* has been highlighted in ethnographic studies of rural society, such as Yan (1996a,1996b) or Kipnis (1996). The term is sometimes written erroneously using 'ren' (仁), thus falsely suggesting a direct relationship to the central Confucian virtue (see e.g. Gold *et al.* 2002: 10). In urban society, another term is often used, namely 'jiaoqing' (交情) (see Chen and Chen 2004). *Jiaoqing* refers to established standards of business behaviour. Yang (1994: 67ff.) discusses *renqing* in contrast to *guanxi*, in the sense that morally proper *guanxi* are based on *renqing*, whereas *guanxi* without *renqing* may often be of suspect moral value. *Renqing* is often also used as an umbrella term covering the entire set of socially appropriate interpersonal emotions.

21 One of the most influential authors in English-language research on face is Hwang (2006b), and Hwang and Han (2010). Presumably, the semantic ambiguities also result from the fact that *lian* is a term that is more often used in north China, whereas *mianzi* is the dominant term in south China. My analysis closely follows the indigenous approach by Zhai (2013: 158ff.). For a classical treatment on face in traditional Chinese society, see Stover (1974).

22 I have proposed this translation of the term *renqing* in Herrmann-Pillath (2015). As Zhai (2011: 201ff.) notes, the concept of *bao* (reciprocity, retribution) is curiously underdeveloped in research about social relations in China. The classical work on the history and contemporary relevance of the notion is Yang (1957), who especially explores the religious meaning, thus also showing that notions of social reciprocity are embedded in popular religion. On the contemporary relevance of the *bao* notion, see Leung (2010: 234). On the widespread practices of moral book-keeping see Bauer (1990: 212ff., 666ff.). These played a particularly important role in Daoism and were also an element in popular conceptions of education. A person would be exhorted to write down a daily balance of good and bad deeds, based also on some publicly recognized standards, and thus would be aware of the chances of salvation from hell. Bauer argues that this tradition was transformed in modern times into educational practices such as writing journals which would not be seen as private but as 'public', for example, shown to the teacher.

23 One influential contribution to the debate about emotions in China was Potter and Potter (1990: 180ff.) with reference to rural society; see also Russell and Yik (1996). Potter and Potter also argued that sincere emotions would therefore

mainly be seen as being expressed in work, as effort. This matches my notion of ritual labour, thus implying that it is not inner states of individuals which count but socially relevant facts that are being expressed in emotions. There is substantial psychological evidence in the framework of so-called 'affect valuation theory' (see Tsai *et al.* 2006) which distinguishes between 'ideal' and 'actual' affect and hence between valence and arousal. This sheds new light on the values discussion, as one distinguishes between the occurrence of certain states and their evaluation. So, US Americans typically value arousal positively, whereas Chinese subjects do not do so to the same extent; they prefer calmness (low-affect arousal positive). This affect valuation has behavioural consequences, of course, but it does not imply differences in the emotional structures as such. On the convergence of Chinese and non-Chinese patterns of emotions, see Yik (2010). On the aforementioned distinction, she notices that there are still problems of interpretation, such as whether people see certain emotions as appropriate or whether they like to experience these emotions. Another aspect that also touches upon the Potter and Potter thesis is the role of emotional display rules (Matsumoto and Hwang 2011). Here, Chinese actually value open display of emotions more than even Italians. This may relate to the view that these expressions are factually irrelevant in governing social interactions.

24 On the uniquely rich lexicon of shame in Chinese, see Li *et al.* (2004). Shame is most strongly associated with the term 'face', and thus is an emotion that is mainly triggered by 'loss of face'. The term has received much prominence in anthropology when Ruth Benedict introduced the distinction between cultures of shame and cultures of guilt, with the latter referring to the individualization of moral responsibility in Western societies. However, modern psychology cannot confirm this sharp dichotomy, at least in the Chinese case (see Yik 2010). This being said, the notion of shame is certainly one of the oldest Chinese ethical notions, beginning with Confucius, who thought that shame is an essential feature of humanity, thus also directly relating it the virtue of *ren*. So, shame is central to moral education (see Roetz 1992: 289ff.).

25 In Lin's (2011) study of shame in contemporary China, this individualization of responsibility becomes most obvious in her example of disabled people. Shame relates to established standards of proper human behaviour and appearance. So, the disabled person should actually feel shame about his state. This clearly demonstrates a difference between shame and guilt, since the disabled person is not responsible in terms of guilt. But from the perspective of shame, it is the disabled person who bears responsibility to change her state in order to meet the standards of propriety. So, shame triggers individual efforts in overcoming the state of being disabled. Accordingly, responsibility does not lie with society. So, the notion of shame also closely relates to the term *suzhi*.

26 On the role of *guanxi* as public arenas, see Gao *et al.* (1996: 289f.) and as an example of *yilun* as gossip see Farrer (2002). Zhai (2013: 133ff.) argues that in Chinese *guanxi* the issue of verifying information looms large, so that the most valuable information is not attainable in 'weak tie' relationships, which cannot resolve the problem of the trustworthiness of informants. I have already mentioned the correspondence between the triadic nature of *guanxi* and the triad as a basic unit in social network analysis. Indeed, economists normally see transactions as dyadic, thus generalizing the simple supply/demand dualism. Transaction cost economics is a case in point. The triadic approach in social network theory goes back to Simmel, who seminally argued that 'society' only emerges among at least three individuals (see Nooteboom 2006).

27 There is much evidence on the cultural distinctiveness of Chinese in this respect. Chua *et al.* (2009) distinguish between 'affective trust' and 'cognitive

trust', and show how these two forms of trust relate to social relations, comparing US Americans and Chinese. In the Chinese case, both forms of trust strongly interact, especially in the sense that economic interactions, hence instrumental relations, also enhance affective trust, which is exactly opposite in the US case. On the other hand, social relations also enhance cognitive trust among Chinese. This matches other results about comparative corporate cultures; for example, Sanchez-Burks *et al.* (2003) show that in US companies a 'protestant' work culture reigns which sees affective relations as a potential disturbance, whereas for Chinese the affective dimension is essential also in order to enable successful instrumental action. Interestingly, Chua *et al.* (2009) argue that the modern Chinese term for trust, *xinren*, actually reflects this interaction between affect-based and cognitive trust, as *xin* is the emotional component, and *ren* refers to a particular competence, hence an instrumental aspect.

28 On the strong resurgence of positional spending in rural China, see Brown *et al.* (2010) and the journalistic account in *The Economist*, 30 November 2013. Brown *et al.* try to explain the observation that spending on funerals, weddings, etc. rises much more rapidly than the level of income, especially in poor areas. At a closer look, the behaviour seems different for different income brackets, which may partly reflect a different setting for reputational competition. As has also been shown for other countries (see e.g. Moav and Neeman (2012) for the case of India), positional spending becomes particularly important once other status indicators such as education are weak. In China, it is often the rural poor who spend disproportionally on family events for reputational reasons, whereas higher income groups mainly appear to follow social trends. However, generally speaking, this reflects the revival of ritual concerns, in the sense of face driving the flow of gifts in society.

29 As I mentioned in n. 26 above, this is a central thesis in Zhai's (2013: 132ff.) analysis of *guanxi* in relation to the distinction between 'strong' and 'weak' ties. He argues that the major function of *guanxi* is not to transmit information but to assert the quality, the trustworthiness of that information. Therefore, the Granovetter argument on the high informational value of 'weak ties' would need substantial modification, since the emotional factor is essential in creating trust.

30 This view is most clearly and systematically expounded by Landa (1994: 102ff.); see also other standard expositions, such as Gabrenya and Hwang (1996). Landa approaches Chinese trading networks as concentric cycles which are based on the von Thünen model of central versus peripheral locations, supposing a precise rank order of relationships of different closeness, such as the distinction between family members and clan members. Interestingly, this model of circles is in stark contrast to Fei Xiaotong's image of circles which are seen as dynamically overlapping and interfering. Hence, we may say that this conceptualization actually operates in a field-independent cognitive mode, thus unequivocally assigning particular individuals to particular categories which relate to ego, yet may be identified independently from the egocentred network, such as sharing the property of the same native place. This shows that an important aspect of *guanxi* dynamics gets lost, since such categories are only *guanxi* bases, and thus do not automatically imply certain levels of trust.

31 As an illustration of the culture of endemic mistrust in Qing dynasty China, Kuhn's (1990) detailed study of a 'witch-hunt' is impressive. This was triggered by the panic resulting from the belief that evil ghosts would roam the country and cut the queues of Chinese, which would immediately result in cruel persecution as Ming loyalists and enemies of the Manchu state. Kuhn argues that these socio-psychological tensions reflect the growing pressure in an increasingly competitive society facing overpopulation and ecological distress. The

waves of migration and emigration triggered by catastrophes such as the Taiping rebellion only heightened these conditions. The East Asia Analytical Unit (1995: 123) reports that in Chinese communities in Southeast Asia, 90 per cent of first-generation emigrant respondents report that they had experienced the conditions of civil war and other forms of extreme distress. Forty per cent of younger generation immigrants report experiencing violence during the Cultural Revolution. Regarding the Cultural Revolution, beyond ethnographic reports there is survey research that highlights the distinctiveness of values of the generation which were active agents (Red Guards, etc.) (see Egri and Ralston 2004). For example, in terms of materialistic orientation and openness, this generation corresponds with the youngest reform-era generation.

32 On the food scandals, see Chapter 3, n. 38. The milk powder scandal was particularly sensitive against the background of the one-child policy: poisoned food might put the life of the only child in jeopardy. I have emphasized that the food scandals are largely interpreted in moral terms, especially with reference to the government as the responsible regulatory authority. This public concern about declining morality as a consequence of marketization has been gaining strength in the past two decades (see e.g. Wang 2002). However, as Kipnis (2016) notes, we have to make a clear distinction between public and intellectual reflections about perceived moral crises and the factual behaviour in everyday life, which is presumably reflected in the value surveys I examine below.

33 As one example, I would like to introduce the *Yidan xuetang* studied by Billioud (2011; for the website of the organization see www.yidan.net/). The *Yidan xuetang* builds on Confucian values and is a grassroots-level movement that mobilizes people to do 'righteous works', 'yigong' (义工). The movement has a strong following and focuses mainly on joint reading and educational activities, referring explicitly to the *jiaohua* notion. One core value is trust: people are called to trust each other and to be trustworthy. This needs to become manifest in the 'righteous work'. Hence, we meet an interesting variant of what I call 'ritual labour': being righteous is less a question of inner belief, but requires work and effort which on the one hand manifests one's values but also helps enable continuous moral development and improvement. Palmer (2011a) approaches these phenomena in the context of the aforementioned 'religious market model' and emphasizes that in spite of the widespread commercialization of religion, there are also strong countermovements that emphasize authenticity and deliberately keep their distance from commercialization.

34 The World Value Survey is an international project launched by the political scientist Ronald Inglehart in order to establish benchmarks for assessing modernization worldwide. Today, it is one of the most important sources in comparative value studies that allows for easy data access and customized uses that I also rely on in this section (www.worldvaluessurvey.org/wvs.jsp). The organization coordinates the work of dozens of local research teams which basically follow the same methodology and use the same questionnaires. The website allows one to compare data over several so-called 'waves' that collect the global data every four to six years. I generally use the data from the most recent survey, published in 2014. The methodology is fully documented at www.worldvaluessurvey.org/WVSDocumentationWV6.jsp. Research in China was conducted by the renowned Research Center for Contemporary China (RCCC) at Peking University under the leadership of Professor Shen Mingming, including international cooperation with US and Taiwan scholars. The sample was constructed by using one of the most advanced GPS sampling procedures which start out from a geographical decomposition of China into so-called primary sampling units which are then further processed. The final sample of returned

questionnaires was 2300, covering the entire area of China. So, data quality and representativeness reflect the state of the art and certainly allow reliable comparisons between China and the rest of the world.

35 Since Glaeser *et al.* (2000) there has been a debate about what the 'general trust' question really measures. The authors argued that it might reflect 'trustworthiness'; the ambiguities result from the difficulty in distinguishing between the beliefs about other people and the preferences about one's own behaviour. In one of the most recent evaluations, Sapienza *et al.* (2013) argue that the question is about the trustworthiness of others, though extrapolating beliefs about one's own trustworthiness on others, based on perceived similarities. This may explain an interesting difference between Chinese and North Europeans or Americans in the question whether one trusts people of another nationality. The Chinese express considerably less trust compared with the strong response when implicitly assuming that reference is a context dominated by other Chinese. The ambiguities of trust vs. social capital are discussed extensively by Beugelsdijk (2006b) and Bjørnskov (2006). Beugelsdijk argues that empirical research about social capital using data on trust does not sufficiently distinguish between trust on the micro-level, which is built into social networks, and the macro-level, where it is mainly institutional trust. In aggregate analyses, therefore, trust often reflects the quality of institutions. So, for example, if only advanced industrial countries are considered, the statistical correlation between trust and growth vanishes. Bergren *et al.* (2008) demonstrate the strong impact of including China in samples testing for the relationship between trust and growth: China drives the result confirming the relation, but her exclusion makes it much less robust.

36 The huge difference between the two results allows for easy manipulation of the analysis. As I have already mentioned, China is often an outlier in social capital research. However, this can be changed once one refers to the other trust question. So, for example, Greif and Tabellini (2010) use this question because, in their general argument comparing Western and Chinese long-run economic development, they need supporting evidence that China is a low-trust society. They do not mention the 'general trust' question, although this is the standard question used by economists.

37 I have already mentioned Zhai's (2013) notion of Chinese society as having the property of *lianxuxing*, 'continuity' (see n. 17 above). The current discussion confirms this view. The 'general trust' question falsely suggests an analytical separation between 'society' as an abstract category and 'society' as a set of factual social relationships, including potential ones that emerge from existing relationships. Continuity applies for the latter.

38 For pertinent surveys, see Nooteboom (2002) or Beugelsdijk and Maseland (2011: ch. 7).

39 Indeed, this split perception may even be shown to hold for party members, as Dickson (2014) reports. Party members show a higher level of confidence in the central government compared to the general population, but they converge when assessing local government. This split between local and central is an excellent example of Schubert's (2008) general discussion of the notion of legitimacy in China. He argues that macro-level aggregate notions of legitimacy may fail to grasp the important micro-level mechanisms that create legitimacy. The duality of local and central state is a pertinent example, as is also discussed by Pieke (2004), who refers to the ambivalent relationship between corruption and the quality of government institutions and governance structures. Pieke elaborates on the role of 'leading cadres' in establishing workable and efficacious governance structures in spite of deeply entrenched localism, resulting in a multi-dimensional but strong integration of the state. This is one factor that

may explain the results of the WVS. In related research on political participation, Ng (2010) reports that compared to Taiwan and Hong Kong, Mainland Chinese appear to express relatively high levels of political participation and also perceive the government as responsive, which would support the WVS results. This may reflect the efficacy of certain channels of influence, such as the use of petitions, which often also happens in the field that spans local and central governments. Similarly, Manion (2014) identifies patterns of 'pork barrel politics' in local People's Congresses, where delegates certainly do not represent different strands of political approaches or programmes, but look after the specific interests of their 'electorate'.

40 For an interesting business case, see Xin and Wang (2011). One pervasive problem in sales management is the use of gifts, commissions and kick-backs, which are often portrayed as regular elements in Chinese business practice. This can lead to serious tensions with corporate codes established by international companies, resulting in open conflicts between foreign and Chinese managers. After all, competition is tight, and the Chinese managers work under high performance pressure. Interestingly, the professional Chinese commentators on this case tend towards imposing the standards, but also emphasize the need for mutual recognition and reconciliation. Chua (2012) points out that Western businesspeople often falsely interpret certain ways of gift giving as kick-backs and therefore apply direct tactics which then violate the sensitive etiquette underlying gift giving. In other words, gift giving in *guanxi* building is different from outright kick-backs.

41 The data are taken from the Transparency International website, www.transparency.org/research/cpi/overview (accessed 2 August 2015).

42 This is the argument deployed by Li and Wu (2007) who compare China with Southeast Asian clientilist states. Wedeman (2012) reaches a similar conclusion, though not based explicitly on the argument about network structures. In his analysis, efforts of the CCP to contain corruption are the major explanation for the limited scope of corruption. On the different forms of local states, of which the predatory ones are only one type, see Baum and Shevchenko (1999).

43 The shift in patterns of corruption has been empirically identified by Ko and Weng (2012), who show that in the first stage violations of administrative regulations were the dominant form, but in the second stage cases of bribery predominated. One problem in assessing corruption in China, as Guo (2008) argues, is that the institutional framework has been constantly changing, thus recurrently creating new incentives and new forms of corruption. The legal system and law enforcement procedures have only a delayed response to these rapid developments, so that even statistical data may not be reliable in earlier phases of change. So, there will be many cases of unreported corruption. The two-stage distinction is also made in the authoritative and comprehensive work on Chinese corruption by Wedeman (2012). Wedeman also distinguishes between 'developmental corruption' and 'degenerative corruption'. The former is characteristic for countries such as South Korea and Taiwan in their stages of industrial transformation. Developmental corruption is manifest in close relationships between authoritarian rulers and corporate elites, but partly builds on shared interests in corporate and national development. Kleptocratic regimes such as those in many African states and successor states of the Soviet Union simply redistribute wealth, ultimately even jeopardizing national development. China assumes a unique position as she features one-Party rule, which certainly provides many opportunities for corruption. Yet, since there is also a formidable disciplinary apparatus, and because of the huge size of the country and the corresponding fragmentation of the corruption networks, corruption does not evolve into a wholesale kleptocratic regime.

44 These results of the most recent WVS therefore confirm the results reported and analysed extensively by Whyte (2010). Based on the same state-of-the-art sampling procedure as used in the WVS, this book reports results of a national survey of the perception of income inequalities in China, a snapshot of the conditions in the mid-2000s; its conclusions are basically confirmed by follow-up research reported by Whyte (2016). So, this reflects the period of heightened national attention to this issue under the Hu and Wen leadership emphasizing a 'harmonious society'. As reported in Li and Sicular (2014: 14), this also means that the relative improvements in rural incomes versus urban incomes did not yet count which mostly occurred after that time, though with continuous absolute improvements, yet with still stronger growth of urban incomes, since the end of the 1990s. The survey shows that the majority of Chinese citizens are highly aware of the real reasons for the inequalities. So, the majority of respondents accept inequalities resulting from merit and entrepreneurial success, and they also respect the right of wealthy people to enjoy better conditions of living for themselves and their families. At the same time, they see disparities resulting from political privilege as extremely negative. Interestingly, urban citizens even recognize that the *hukou* system is working to the detriment of the relative position of rural citizens, whereas the rural respondents generally tend to believe that there are enough opportunities for improvement and that discrimination does not matter very much.

45 Actually, in the aforementioned Whyte (2010) survey, the rural respondents were quite satisfied with the achievements of recent years. The group that expressed most dissatisfaction were the low-skilled urban workers in the interior provinces. These differences clearly reflect reference point effects, as is also emphasized in Han's (2012) assessment. Han argues that rural people are aware of discriminations, but do not translate this into assessments of their living conditions in terms of personal satisfaction. In this sense, they have internalized the status order and regard other rural people and their own previous positions as reference points, and not urban people. So, even migrants appear to be more satisfied with the personal outcomes of reforms than urban respondents.

46 On this social acceptance of certain ways to exploit social positions for personal gain, see Stafford (2006); this was also one of the central moral tensions that erupted in Chinese rural society during the Maoist regime (see Madsen 1984). The important point is that these notions are related to certain moral convictions about the 'human' nature of such behaviours. For example, a cadre may feel obliged to engage in such activities because this supports his family, or because it is a matter of face, which is also recognized by the local community, in spite of everyone being aware of the partly illicit nature of the behaviours. Zhai (2013: 113ff.) discusses the example of gift giving in hospitals against the background of the *guanxi* notion. In fact, gift giving is explicitly prohibited (which may even include simple items such as cold beverages before a surgery). In his case study, a patient first did not send a gift, but decided to do so after the surgery. Zhai argues that this shows how gift giving is seen as part of a larger ritualistic network in which imbalances or damage to one's face would otherwise occur. So, the gift gives face to both the patient and the doctor, and as such is not directly interpreted as outright bribery in achieving a certain result.

47 The seminal contribution was made by Walder (1983, 1986) also tying in with work such as Parish and Whyte (1984) on Maoist urban society. This work is different from the 'political culture' research that I mentioned earlier (see Chapter 2, n. 28) in emphasizing the role of institutional factors independent from cultural tradition. For example, the earlier work also included research on traditional socialization practices. The 'neotraditionalism' research focuses

on institutionalized political socialization instead. Interestingly, this research has also been vindicated in value studies, such as Inkeles *et al.* (1997). Similar to the WVS, these studies aimed at ascertaining degrees of 'modernization' as reflected in values such as individual autonomy. In the 1990s, urban people actually proved to be more 'traditional' than rural inhabitants living close to the cities. Evidently, the latter were facing a range of opportunities in interacting with the urban areas and responded with individual initiative, whereas many urban individuals still remained attached to the safe organizational structures inherited from the urban *danwei* system.

48 This relates to the research cited in n.47 above. The notion of 'state-led' individualization is proposed by Yan Yunxiang (2010). This relates to the *suzhi* notion discussed in Chapter 3. Individualization is therefore also related to the idea that the market is a 'civilizing' device and therefore a part of governing society, such as when officials claim that labour migration actually contributes to the personal enhancement of migrants (cf. Yan Hairong 2003).

49 This analysis follows Madsen's (1984) seminal analysis of the famous case of 'Chen village', with the addendum of Chan *et al.* (2009). I have already pointed to value surveys which confirm this picture (see n. 34 above). Interestingly, Metzger (1977) predicted this transition to a more market-based and utilitarian morality as a backlash against radical Maoism, using the reference to Confucianism in its historical transformations. So, market morality may also be seen as a modern transformation of Confucian pragmatism.

50 The theory of reflexive modernization was developed by the sociologist Ulrich Beck and received some attention in China studies; see the volume edited by Hansen and Svarverud (2010). In the Foreword by Beck and Beck-Gernsheim, the authors argue that the Chinese case is a unique combination of modernity and individualization, because 'neoliberal deregulation' happened before individualization took place, as in Europe. 'Reflexive modernization' is coined the 'second modernity' in the sense that the postcolonial world enhanced the cultural diversity of modernity and entrenched cosmopolitanism, which requires reflexive capacities in shaping one's identity as a subject. In my analysis, this view does not recognize the specific forms of individualization inherent in the Chinese tradition, especially with regard to economic action in the context of markets. So, the account of the 'neoliberal transformation' is certainly wrong as far as the relationship with individualization is concerned.

51 In political science, the preference for obedience in childhood education is regarded as one of the most reliable predictors of political authoritarianism (see Stenner 2005). This especially holds for the comparison with the power–distance measure that is prominent in leading values surveys such as Hofstede's or GLOBE. This aggregate indicator may reflect many different attitudinal stances, such as conservatism, and is therefore ambigious on authoritarianism.

52 The WVS results can be supported by many other studies using different methodologies, such as reported in Kulich (2010: ch. 8). One method is to consider preferences for proverbs. Chinese respondents often tend to choose proverbs which relate to effort, personal advancement and success, and much less to what is normally regarded as standard 'Confucian' values. On the Confucian classics on children education, see Chen Lai (1994, 1995). There was a clear idea that the individual is responsible for his own fate and that effort will bring success, encompassing both moral goals and material advancement. This reflects what he calls 'secularized Confucianism'. On the significance of male ideal types and heroes, see Saari (1982) and Boretz (2011: 40ff., 115ff.).

53 The idea that 'social capabilities' represent a potential for growth especially in the context of catch-up processes has been seminally expounded by Abramovitz (1989: 43ff.). It broadened the standard economic growth theory to include

social and cultural factors. In the Chinese context, this has been applied by Wade (1990) in explaining the rapid development of Taiwan following the Second World War. This reflected the legacies of Japanese colonial rule, which had not only created infrastructure and basic industries, but also raised the educational level of the population.

54 I discussed the role of money in Chinese tradition in Chapter 2, n. 67 and n. 68. To add some detail, one essential aspect is the role of the body in Chinese religious practices (see Palmer 2011b). In contrast to European traditions which separate body and soul and even derogate the body, in Chinese tradition the body is seen as sacred, and bodily experiences reflect cosmic forces which may be the object of religious activities. For this reason, practices such as nourishment for health purposes may be deeply imbued by religious meanings. One interesting example of this aspect of Chinese religiosity is the failed attempt of Communist authorities to neutralize related religious practices by artificially creating the Qigong tradition as a way of bodily perfection and exercise. Qigong was even sponsored by Mao Zedong, with interesting mixtures of magic that were also inherent in Maoism at that time, so already leaking the religious potential. Qigong proved to be the origin of many new religious movements, the most important being the Falun Gong, which the CCP regards as a major threat today. So, in 1999, Qigong was forbidden to be practised in China (for a survey of developments, see Chen 2003). This example clearly shows how the material world is 'spiritualized'.

55 This account follows the seminal work of Chau (2011, 2012). Chau distinguishes five modalities: Discursive/scriptural; personal-cultivational; liturgical; immediate-practical; and relational. The religious subject can relate to many different providers of services in these various modalities. In this context, 'efficacy' assumes a central role in determining individual choices. Actually, although this is seen as an objective phenomenon ascribed to certain persons or places, such as a temple, ultimately the arbiter of efficacy is the individual and her experience of relief, salvation or happiness. Regarding the central role of the household, Chau (2014) argues that in Christianity, the rite of sacrament means that God hosts the believers, who congregate at a certain sacred location, the church. In China, temples are not identified as exclusive sanctuaries, and the household is actually the elementary sanctuary, keeping altars and conducting elementary religious activities. So, the household is the host. It is illuminating to compare this with Foucault's (2004b: 177ff., 187) analysis of the image of the 'shepherd' in medieval Christianity. Here, the community is seen as staying under the absolute spiritual control of the leader, the shepherd, and total submission is required to manifest true belief, even permeating the inner self. In comparison, Chinese orthopraxy allowed for much freedom for the individual in determining her or his beliefs.

56 Chau (2011) also refers the modalities perspective to the 'religious markets' model. For other applications of the model in Chinese contexts, see Yang (2006) or Lu *et al.* (2008). For Taiwan, Lu *et al.* show, among other interesting observations, that 'efficacy' drives the differentiation of the religious market and also the growth of organizational complexity. One prediction of the religious market model is that monopolization and strong regulation stifle religious activities, and that liberalization and deregulation increase the level of religiosity in society, with the USA as a prime example. Thus, the religious markets model makes a different prediction than ordinary modernization theories, including the WVS, thus possibly explaining the special position of the USA on the WVS world map. For China, this prediction also seems to hold, as Yang argues, with the emergence also of 'grey' and 'black' markets of religion that undermine government regulation. Chau's point is that the religious

markets model is not simply an analytical model, but is also empirically valid for religious practice as such. In this view, religion is actually a model for markets in general. Whether the religious market model directly implies individualism is an open question: the answer depends on how one interprets the role of the household. Tan (2010: 291, 449) argues that the recent social changes in China have drastically reduced the scope of moral obligations to the family, but not to the individual. However, as my discussion in Chapter 2 has shown, one could argue that this 'family individualism' also stood at the centre of traditional ritual.

57 This distinction is based on the literature review by Brewer and Chen (2007), but alters the wording for the two 'collectivisms'. The authors refer to categorial collectivism as 'group collectivism' which I deem less appropriate because the term 'group' is not sufficiently specific. Groups can be categorial and relational. Terminologies are messy in this field, since psychologists often refer to another duality, 'ideocentric' versus 'allocentric', which might be compared to the economic distinction between 'individual' and 'social preferences' (Bowles and Polanía-Reyes 2012). The psychological distinction is often seen as referring to individual behavioural stances, whereas 'collectivism' is seen more as a group property, hence a cultural category. For an application of this duality on China, see Liu *et al.* (2010: 581).

58 This is the view of the 'ecological' approach to culture championed by Yamagishi (2012) that I introduced in Chapter 1 (see n. 22), also reporting on his experimental results which show that Japanese and US Americans do not differ in terms of individualism in decontextualized situations. There is also evidence on the Chinese that matches this view. For example, Chen *et al.* (2007) also experimentally test a public goods game and show that the major difference between 'idiocentric' and 'allocentric' individuals may not be their internalized values but the different ways in which they respond to behavioural clues in the environment. The authors distinguish between 'group norm' and 'group identity' and show that, when it comes to the degree of cooperation, the two orientations do not differ with reference to group identity but to group norms. Idiocentric individuals would cooperate less when there is a cooperative group norm, while allocentric individuals cooperate more. All in all, psychological research has only produced mixed and inconclusive evidence on the hypothesis that the Chinese have internalized collectivist values, such as interpreting their own self in terms of the collective (for a survey see Leung 2010).

59 On the discussion about post-conventional ethics, see Roetz (1992) and Wilson (1981). In this early literature, reference is often made to Kohlberg's stages of moral development (see Roetz 1992: 51ff.) who is also a critic of standard applications in the Chinese context. Kohlberg developed a sequence of stages of moral development, in which the 'conventional' ethic is defined as adherence to tradition and group standards, whereas the post-conventional stages include protest ethics, social contract and relativistic ethics, and rule-based, reflexive and universalistic ethics as the pinnacle. Roetz argues that classical Confucian thought already showed the transition to post-conventional ethics. Regarding the relevance of these categories in China today, it is probably interesting to note that current educational styles indeed struggle with this transition. In particular, when it comes to individualism, there is often a very strong emphasis on the individual as being fully responsible for her or his own fate, which resonates with the Confucian educational tradition, even including the activation of individual initiative and creativity, but at the same time these orientations are being fostered by authoritarian approaches, such as exhortations, regular memorization of slogans, or public rallies that raise the collective 'individualistic stance'. On pertinent case studies, see Hansen (2013) or Lin (2011).

60 In the 1980s, cultural approaches to the Japanese corporation were popular, which emphasized the unique relationship between employees and the corporation (for a concise contemporary summary see Iwata 1992). These were traced back to the corporate structure of the Japanese family and family firms. One of the characteristics was seen as combining formal ascription to the company with a strong emotional basis for loyalty and commitment.

61 Shavitt *et al.* (2011) give an overview of this distinction, which originates from Triandis' (1995) work on collectivism vs. individualism. The distinction leads to a fourfold typology of societies with a number of particular predictions, such as regarding attitudes towards competition, cooperation or expressions of power. As with other value models, one problem is whether these are psychological or cultural distinctions. For example, there is a gender dimension that seems to be orthogonal to cultural groupings, as tendencies towards vertical individualism are stronger among males than among females.

62 This aspect is reflected in the large-scale survey on leadership styles, GLOBE (see Gelfland *et al.* 2004). The GLOBE survey distinguishes between 'in-group collectivism' and 'institutional collectivism'. This duality does not fully converge with the distinction between relational and categorial collectivism, but comes close to it. Further, as I have discussed previously (see Chapter 1, n. 16), the GLOBE survey also distinguishes between 'values' ('should be') and 'practices' ('as is'). Regarding institutional collectivism, China scores high in the 'practices' dimension, where it compares with countries such as Sweden or Ireland. China's 'values' score is close to the practices score, yet this has to be seen in the context of the other countries. In fact, China does not belong to the group with the highest 'values' scores, which includes many Latin American and South European countries. Of the so-called 'Confucian' countries, only Taiwan joins this group (score 5.15, compared with Mainland China's 4.56). China is together not only with Germany, but even with the Netherlands (score 4.55) which is the prototypical 'individualistic' country in the Hofstede account. So, we cannot clearly relate the results on institutional collectivism with the standard divisions of countries along the 'individualism/collectivism' duality. This is even more pronounced for the 'in-group collectivism values' score: all countries locate on a relatively high level of scores, but China is actually the third lowest value in the entire set (5.09), which would nevertheless imply an appreciation against the 'practices' score. The group with the lowest scores includes Germany, the Netherlands and South Africa, whereas the countries with the highest scores are mostly Latin American ones. So, we face a pattern that by no means supports the standard classification of China in the Hofstede framework, especially in terms of the international comparison.

63 These questions have been taken up in Chinese studies by authors such as Augustin-Jean (2010), drawing upon the sociological literature on performativity and materiality of markets, such as MacKenzie (2007), Callon (2007) and Çalışkan (2007). Partly, this perspective goes back to Actor–Network Theory as developed by Latour (2005), among others. Actor–Network Theory is fundamentally different from social network analysis that I have referred to thus far, as it sees technological artefacts as being constitutive of network structures, and approaches agency as an emergent property of these structures. This is called 'agencement'. As an interesting illustration from China, see Zhou's (2011) comparative analysis of three rural markets in one Chinese locality, for grapes, apples and corn, where the material characteristics of the products, the seasonality of production and the technologies of downstream users of the products shape the particular market structures. This can be partly explained also by standard economic reasoning, such as referring to technologies of quality monitoring of products which require different involvement of purchasing agents, etc.

64 As one example, see Zhou and Ai (2014), comparing the two cases of a local market for grapes and another one for almonds. In comparison to the traditional Skinnerian model, in the case of grapes local producers tie up directly with national wine producers, often even SOEs, which therefore cross-cut the regional hierarchy. The regional hierarchy remains much more intact if market transactions are mediated via small-scale petty traders who travel around the region. Carrillo (2011: 56ff.) reports a case in detail where county- and township-level governments actively establish specialized retail and wholesale markets that partly revive traditional marketing structures.

65 As an example, see the analysis of the sugar market by Augustin-Jean (2010). Sugar is an interesting case, as it has been regulated in many countries in the past, so that international regimes also have liberalized only slowly under the auspices of the WTO. Sugar is an essential input for the food industry. In China, sugar production is concentrated in Guangxi province, one of the poorest provinces, implying that sugar plays a central role in the regional development strategy (up to 40 per cent of provincial employment is directly or indirectly linked to sugar production, trade and processing). The liberalization of the industry was a goal of the central government, but the local governments also heavily depended on the taxes that sugar mills would pay, which created their interest in keeping the purchasing prices paid to farmers low. This constellation unfolded against the background of increasing international competition with downward pressure on prices, especially after WTO entry. In the 1990s, one particular problem also typical for other products was the widespread use of IOUs to pay the farmers, which created pressure towards industrial restructuring in order to enhance the competitiveness of the downstream industries, which would be able to pay the farmers properly. There is also tough inter-regional competition, since the modernized mills often run below capacity, yet local governments want to protect their revenues. Further, the entire system relies on a large number of local agents who actually connect with the farmers and who are often former cadres. These agents build on their personal networks to organize the trade in sugar cane. So, this example shows how technological conditions (the co-existence of traditional family farming and modern sugar mills) and institutional determinants (e.g. deregulation) result in a complex interplay of actions of the different parties that ultimately run the sugar market. As Augustin-Jean emphasizes, this certainly does not imply a retreat of government from markets; on the contrary, markets and government remain deeply enmeshed with each other.

66 For the example of the cotton market, see the detailed analysis by Alpermann (2014). Alpermann refers to Fligstein and Adam's (2012) theory of 'strategic fields' to explain market evolution. As in the aforementioned example of sugar, market liberalization has immediate consequences for technological structures, and vice versa. In the seed business, international companies like Monsanto aimed at penetrating the China market, but at the same time liberalization led to the market entry of literally thousands of small-scale family firms operating in seed production and trading. This combination rendered regulation and quality supervision a daunting task, including the enforcement of laws against fraud and IPR theft. These regulatory goals, however, are always put into perspective by the developmentalism which is adopted by both the central and the local governments, not necessarily without tension. Local states would often foster companies and business activities that do not match the modernist standards of the central government. One conspicuous phenomenon resulting from this constellation, which I will examine further below, is regarding larger companies as being more advanced. In the case of cotton, there is also an interesting impact of international regulation, as these standards are biased against

small-scale traditional cotton growing (more specifically against hand-picked cotton). In practice, this means that the larger producers and traders, partly emerging from the old socialist planned distribution system, co-exist with the Skinnerian petty traders which also help to sustain traditional production technologies. On the side of the central government this is seen as 'excessive competition', leading towards quality issues pervading the system. So, the national cotton market has evolved into a bifurcated system along the fault lines between the local states and the central state.

67 Lingohr (2007) details this referral to the example of sweet potatoes in Sichuan province. China is by far the largest producer of sweet potatoes in the world. A main use of potatoes is the production of starch which is used, among other purposes, for the production of instant noodles. The central government actively supports the creation of 'dragon head companies' which are defined according to certain criteria (size, technology, financial power, etc.) and which receive special support. However, the 'dragon head' approach is also adopted by the local states, so that there is a vigorous competition between companies on different levels. These companies enter a contractual relationship with farmers using different models, even including the leasing of the land so that production is directly steered by the company. One attractive aspect for the farmers are guaranteed minimum prices. The local state is always involved, as townships arrange the selection of farmers, establish procedures for quality control, etc. There is also an alternative approach, the so-called 'rural associations', which are largely set up by local entrepreneurs who have good a relationship with the local state, perhaps even former cadres. These associations adopt similar technological models, such as entering the production of instant noodles, and partly adopting a cooperative framework, with farmers becoming members.

68 Brown and Hagel III (2005) argue that these network structures have evolved into a new model of innovation, thus even feeding back on technological structure. They analyse the rise of domestic motorcycle producers with international reach. This example is also illuminating because it shows the potential impact of foreign direct investment. In this case, Japanese motorcycle producers have set up joint ventures in China, which actually operate as 'lead companies'. Also responding to domestic regulations, they built up a local supplier network. However, this network started to evolve endogenously, when these suppliers in turn built networks with subcontractors. In doing this, the Chinese main suppliers developed a modularized technology in which subcontractors would only meet certain broad standards, and could also implement their own innovation strategies. This network is mainly market based, so the modularization also lowered transaction costs that might result from hold-up problems. On this modularization pattern see also Fujimoto (2002).

69 This description is based on the extensive village study by Wu (2014); for a concise summary see Wu (2015). The village specializes in jewellery. The goldsmiths travel to other places in the countrywide and rely on their network in order to procure inputs with economies of scale. Wu calls this model 'one village, one profession', 'tongxiang tongye' (同乡同业). Interestingly, the sojourners do not set up their own organizations at the places where they are active but rely exclusively on the network mediated via their native village. This includes a regular long-distance bus service that connects people and transports materials. The network is partly supported by kinship relations, which are particularly important for funding new businesses by the younger generation of villagers. The entire system is deeply embedded in traditional practices, such as when the goldsmith community also contributes to rebuilding local temples.

70 The term 'modularization' plays an important role in studies of industrial organization and technology; see Sanchez and Mahoney (2013) for an overview. I come back to this later in more detail; at this point suffice it to mention that modularization in this context refers to the different architectures of firm organization emerging from the interaction between market and technology. As Fujimoto (2007) argues, this is rooted in specific design approaches to products and production technologies; design is an activity that is certainly shaped by cognitive processes and dynamics. It is interesting to note that this analytical approach is often used by Japanese researchers, also with a specific conceptual framework informed by Japanese language research on Japanese industry.

71 As an example of market expansion undergirded by traditional network structures I give the case of the Luo (罗) in Fengshun (丰顺) county, Guangdong, Meizhou Prefecture, as reported in Zhou (2003). The Luo are a very large lineage which in their native place Tangnan (汤南镇) constitute 90 per cent of the local population and factually control the township government via their 'Seniors' club', 'laoren hui' (老人会), which is the lineage elder council. They have a vast business network, in which entrepreneurial leaders attract followers often in a systematic way. For example, a Luo entrepreneur moved to Shenzhen and opened up a hotel. Gradually, he attracted many other Luo to the site, who thus dominate the local service industry there. The limitations of these traditional structures for market expansion are analysed by Ruan and Zheng (2012). The authors demonstrate econometrically that lineage-based market structures show less spatial reach and also result in a lower number of TVEs in the rural areas.

72 On the peculiar interaction between technological opportunities, entrepreneurial dynamics and market development in the *Shanzhai* case see Shih *et al.* (2010). It is important to note that the *Shanzhai* model has a generic status in the Chinese innovation system, as detailed by Booz&Co (2009). This relates to the modularization paradigm in supplier networks that I mentioned previously. So, for example, leading private car makers in China emerged from *Shanzhai* production patterns, which was salient in the many early stage disputes about brands and IPR. A typical phenomenon was that those producers combined design features of established brands into new designs, though keeping reference to the original brands clearly visible. However, some of these *Shanzhai* companies later went 'mainstream' in gradually developing their own brand identities and product portfolio. The specific nature of the *Shanzhai* market was indirectly recognized by the WTO case examined by Yu (2011). The USA filed a complaint against the Chinese government claiming that the Chinese authorities would have to apply criminal law procedures against counterfeiting in the *Shanzhai* system, and not only administrative measures. The Panel decided that the *Shanzhai* production did not match the TRIPS criterion of 'commercial scale'. Obviously, this did not take into consideration the total size of the market but the fact that the producers are all small-scale workshops, so that single batches of products which may violate IPR remain below 'commercial scale'. This also recognized the adequacy of measures against counterfeiting in terms of governance costs. Given the structure of the sector, applying criminal law would be extremely demanding.

73 We met the example of sweet potatoes in n. 67 above. This argument has been fully elaborated by Huang (2011c), who also explicitly relates these phenomena to the traditional form of family production in Imperial China. His point is that network organization creates economies of scale that go beyond the production patterns of conventional agricultural technology. On the specific impact of the land property rights regime see Zhang and Donaldson (2008) and their analysis of the different contractual variants. For example, a farmer may just

enter into a supplier relationship to a lead company without changing the status of his land-use rights. However, as we have seen previously, in principle the land lease contracts could include many specific regulations. So, they leave much leeway for further specifying the rights, including certain task patterns. For example, the farmer may agree to fully specialize in a particular crop, with guaranteed minimum prices as compensation. All variants are possible, including the extreme form of subcontracting the land-use rights to a company and assuming the role of a wage earner. In all of these cases, the underlying land property rights remain with the collective, such as the village or the township. Hence, the local status order shapes the specific trajectories. Much depends on whether the local cadres tend to represent the interests of the farmers, or to exploit the business opportunities also for their own advantage.

74 I have already referred to the work by Huang (2009, 2013) estimating the size of the informal economy (see Chapter 3, n. 18). The argument that the formal economy actually undergirds the informal economy is relevant for evaluating the prediction that *guanxi*, hence traditional forms of network organization, will wither away as a result of globalization. One case in point is Walmart (see Xue 2009; Yu and Pun 2009). In contrast to the original intentions of Sam Walton (see Appelbaum 2009), Walmart in China maintains relationships with intermediary traders, which replicates an interesting historical pattern. The cost advantages of producing in China rely mainly on the competitiveness of the family-based economy; however, transaction costs are too high to establish direct relations between Walmart and those suppliers. This creates the conditions for subcontracting networks. Walmart has strict corporate CSR guidelines which would prohibit the inclusion of 'sweatshops' in its supplier network, but in fact the intermediaries and their subcontractors cannot be sufficiently monitored. So, Walmart actually reinforces the traditional symbiosis between networks and family production, for example, as in many consumer goods, the revival of single product villages that focus on one particular product group, such as socks or particular toys. In these clusters, family firms achieve economies of scale beyond the single unit, while at the same time keeping labour costs low. This pattern is further supported by the employment of migrant workers.

75 The notion of fungibility is deployed in detail by Zhou and Ai (2014) in their analysis of rural finance and market structure. They compare grape and almond production. In grape production demand is highly concentrated, often with high-status SOEs as wine producers. Because of the tight time constraints during harvest, farmers are systematically put into a weak position. This is also bolstered by the differential distribution of social capital between farmers and cadres, who often act as local agents in the grape-trading system. So, the downstream producers can impose what Zhou and Ai call 'credit taking' (as opposed to credit lending) upon the farmers in the shape of IOUs that are repaid only once the producers have sold their product. The almond market is organized very differently because the crop area is much more decentralized and larger. Here, small-scale peddlers roam the area, competing against each other, so that farmers are in the position to demand cash payment. The peddlers, however, are often forced into credit taking by the middlemen who sell the almonds to the end-buyers. The different positions of middlemen and traders result in differential barriers to market access: since middlemen need to fund what can be a large gap between momentous expenses for buying the product and receiving payment by end-users, entering the business requires considerable funds, which presupposes social capital. These conditions are characteristic of many agricultural products and industrial raw materials, as we have seen already in the example of sugar.

76 The classical and comprehensive study of these phenomena is Tsai (2002); on ROSCAS in particular, see Hu (2007). The essential role of informal finance in the Chinese economy has been driven by the rapid growth of the private sector, especially in what was historically the most advanced economic area, the Jiangnan region, which also has a strong historical tradition of informal finance. Tsai argues that the structures are very complex, highly diverse around different localities, and their evolution is strongly path dependent. The local–central duality matters crucially, because the growth of informal finance is mainly under the supervision of local states. Local states turn a blind eye or even support it, because it contributes to local economic growth, and because the local state can participate in its profits, for example, via imposing fees and other forms of contributions. So, we have a typical example of how experimentalism shapes an important sector in the Chinese economy, since in this case many forms of informal finance are explicitly illegal, given central-level national laws. Interestingly, we also observe an analogue to the *Shanzhai* dynamics, because, over the years, in many cases some of the underground activities have morphed into regular formal organizations, such as urban cooperative banks emerging from the private 'money houses' of the 1980s. This occurs largely via entrepreneurial strategies that aim at co-opting formal political structures of the local state. Some outright forms of this are 'red hat' companies which are camouflaged as 'collectives' in the industrial sector, but which actually conduct financial operations. In the case of urban cooperative banks, they may have emerged from stabilization efforts of local governments which also invest in the money houses in order to become shareholders and thus also assume internal controlling roles. Local states may also pursue independent strategies for formalization, such as in the Rural Cooperative Credit Foundations, which were curbed by central regulatory intervention (for a detailed case study, see Lux 1998). In all of these activities, social networks, reputation and trust created by reciprocal exchange across different dimensions of the local status order are essential in stabilizing the institutional structures of the financial market.

77 An example is the decision of the State Council in 2012 to declare Wenzhou a 'Pilot Zone' in financial reform (see Feng and Herrmann-Pillath 2013). This was in response to a highly problematic situation of private business development following the financial crisis of 2008, which even endangered the stability of so-called 'dragon head companies'. This partly resulted from the external shock of shrinking demand for exports, but also the growing instability of the informal financial sector. The rising number of souring loans was widely noticed by the public, with the consequence of declining confidence, already triggering runs on particular institutions. Since this had happened repeatedly in the past, this time the central government interfered (even with Premier Wen Jiabao visiting the area) and announced a reform policy that was also bolstered by expanding the local credit supply. This policy included the establishment of a central regulatory authority at the level of the local state. As Tsai (2002) has argued, one problem in regulating local finance is that different government agencies have conflicting interests; for example, local finance stays in competition with the formal financial sector, but is more positively appreciated by the fiscal and industrial administration. In these attempts, new organizational forms such as 'micro-credit organizations' often serve as new bottles for the old wine of informal finance.

78 As Tsai (2002) notes, there are many intriguing aspects here that relate to the specific distribution of social capital and network formations. For example, there is a gender dimension, which is also familiar from the performance of micro-credit organizations worldwide. The strong expansion of ROSCAs was

often driven by the participation of women in business, both as independent entrepreneurs and as traditional managers of the family purse. One explanation offered by Tsai is that relying on informal finance in case of need may be seen as threating face for male entrepreneurs, so women assume the role of a lender. At the same time, women develop stronger relations of trust and can maintain their reputation, for example, because all participants in these schemes are more confident that the women will also stay in the local community. At the same time, the ROSCAs created by women are smaller in size and hence inherently more stable. This compares to pyramidal schemes that have been created in several regions of China with devastating consequences, where loans taken from ROSCAs were used in order to create even bigger ROSCAs, ultimately leading to sudden domino effects and financial collapse.

79 For example, Clarke's (2010) analysis of corporate governance in the context of capital markets does not include more detailed information about the role of the CCP organization. Other authors, such as Heilmann (2005) or Gottwald and Collins (2012), highlight this aspect, speaking of a Leninist regulatory regime. For an illuminating analysis of the political dimension of Chinese stock markets, see Wang Jiangyu (2010). Wang argues that the regulation of stock markets is guided by concerns about political legitimacy and stability, which certainly proved to be true in the crisis of summer 2015, when international observers raised eyebrows over the methods that were applied to stabilize the situation. However, these stood in line with the general Chinese understanding of the role of stock markets, so only brought into the limelight what was a principled approach anyway. Interestingly, this includes the important feature that even further steps towards liberalization, such as allowing pension funds to be invested in stocks, were taken as a stabilization measure at this point. In other words, stock market performance is interpreted as a political state, which requires supervision and monitoring. Wang argues that this also explains certain more particular features of governance, such as the tight controls of the IPO process on the one hand, but the much more lenient approach to insider trading or manipulation on the other hand. In fact, both patterns reflect the Leninist regulatory style, with a modernist stance. Access to the most advanced form of corporate finance should be controlled by the CCP, also in order to safeguard the quality of market participants; at the same time, market operations should be supported, avoiding instances of 'regulatory chill' as in the case of informal finance. Control of fraudulent behaviour is therefore mainly implemented via CCP network structures and its formal disciplinary apparatus.

80 In relation to the aforementioned example of energy, this may be observed in environmental and energy policies in recent years, where often the factual market dynamics did not match the original developmental plans adopted by the central government. This applies at both the central and the local level. At the central level solar energy is a case in point, which was initially only aiming at global markets and was not seen as a major element in national strategies towards sustainable growth (on this case see Fischer 2014). When the global strategy ran into difficulties, national priorities adapted, also reflecting strong interest group politics. These faced a number of external shocks: first, the financial crisis of 2008, then the regulatory and protectionist interventions especially on the part of the USA. These triggered responses both by local and central governments, resulting in the adoption of a long-term development plan. This changed the field of interests in the industry, because so long as the solar industry was only export oriented the dominant players were private businesses and local governments. In assuming a role in the national-level energy plan, new players emerged, especially SOEs that also received preferential policies. Competition between renewable energies and traditional energies with

powerful and large SOEs grew stronger. For example, the State Grid Corporation also became actively involved. These complex interactions in creating sustainable markets and achieving a certain market performance may be observed also in more special cases. One is methanol (reported by Kostka and Hobbs 2012), where certain local governments used their own strategies in trying to open up market opportunities together with affiliated business interests. In this case, local governments directly challenged the interests of very influential central-level SOEs, such as Sinopec. Interestingly, in this case even provincial governments actively colluded with local governments in pursuing methanol strategies independent from national regulation. One factor is different time horizons in responding to challenges such as pollution; for example, the central government represents more long-term interests, such as developing electric cars also as a part of positioning China in the automotive industry, whereas provinces without a stake in automotive industries were more concerned about quick improvements in pollution control. Lower down the administrative hierarchy, local states would seize market opportunities created by provincial-level policy and regulatory environments.

81 This observation has been systematically and theoretically grounded in Carroll and Hannan (2000) and Hannan *et al.* (2007); for a concise summary see also Hsu and Hannan (2005). These authors develop a sociological approach to the use of 'labels' which denote certain default forms of organizations that come along with expectations about certain organizational patterns, interactional forms or social practices which are held in an audience and which provide the settings in which the organizations operate. The labels correlate with certain niches in the market, thus also structure market processes. This also implies that there may be niches which are not occupied by certain organizations, thus representing market opportunities. However, since there are not yet clearly specified labels identifying those niches, entrepreneurial action has to overcome many difficulties in communicating with its audience. One much-cited example is the rise of craft breweries in the beer market which has been dominated by large breweries in the USA. These small breweries take off once the label has been established, such that, for example, banks recognize these types of business and know how to assess the risks.

6 Chinese enterprise, organization and ritual

The Chinese enterprise as a network organization

In this chapter I develop the idea that in China's ritual economy the notion of the 'corporation' remains weak. Whereas in the previous two chapters I dealt with the interface between markets and the state based on my analysis of market governmentality, I now look at the interface between market and organization in the context of the phenomenon of modularization introduced in Chapter 5. So, the topic also ties up with the analysis of the *longue durée* of the market system in China, and asks how far the forces of market involution in traditional China cast a shadow over more recent developments. As we saw, these forces created a trajectory of market development which suppressed the emergence of more complex organizations, in particular of what we identify as 'modern corporations'. I argue that in the context of modularization, and reflecting the specific form of market governmentality, the role of the corporation in the contemporary Chinese economy remains fragile and is unfinished business in the agenda of modernization. In this argument, I do not claim that this is a permanent feature of Chinese economic style, but that it has been a hallmark of market transition thus far, and that it is only gradually changing, especially in response to the growing integration of the Chinese economy with the global economy. However, as I will argue, the impact of globalization upon the Chinese economy is not unequivocal with regard to corporatization, and even appears to partly leverage the forces of market involution which have hampered corporatization in the past.

That being said, we should avoid false normative assessments of Chinese developments, since the historical model of corporatization in the West is also under pressure of change in the global economy. This is not the place to delve into these discussions proceeding both in academia and the media, but suffice it to note certain highlights. One argument that has held sway for many years now is that the emergence of the internet will erode the traditional notion of the corporation as it opens up new ways of organizational hybridization, thus rendering the borders between the corporation and the market obsolete, for both technological and organizational reasons. The most recent version of this argument is the notion of 'platform capitalism', in which corporations mainly organize networks of loosely affiliated independent workers or suppliers of services, thus not only undermining the traditional organizational structures, but, most interestingly in comparison to China, also erode the institutions of the formal social security system, thus partly also driving the growth of an 'informal economy'. If this trend persists in the global context, the very adoption of the most advanced forms of capitalist organization will actually bolster the resilience of 'traditional' structures of market governmentality in China. Another example is the resilience if not resurgence of family business worldwide. This has clearly disproved earlier assumptions about the necessary withering away of these 'traditional' forms of organization in favour of the modern public corporation. In these earlier opinions, there was evidently a bias towards emphasizing the costs of family organization (such as, typically, the intermingling of family affairs with business), underestimating the many advantages of family organization in terms of commitment, long-term decision-making and so on. Again, this observation calls for great care in evaluating the Chinese situation, where traditionally family business has played a pivotal role.

In other words, we need to disentangle the analysis of the Chinese enterprise from modernist accounts of Western development, thus for another time explicitly reflecting on the 'mirror of culture'. This is extremely important in avoiding the creeping in of normative judgements in assessing the specific patterns of business organization in China. For example, in recent decades there has been intensive international cooperation between China and organizations such as the OECD with regard to the buildup of modern corporate governance structures. In these efforts, often the Company Law together with associated laws is treated as the reference framework for assessing the Chinese situation, which leads to overlooking certain essential elements of corporate governance as it is actually practised. In the state-owned sector, this mainly refers to the role of the CCP in shaping the 'market for managers' via the nomenclature system. This shows that standard approaches to corporate governance tend to concentrate on the capital markets and the shareholder perspective, but neglect the market for managers as an important embedding element. This becomes partly evident when considering the role of corporate bodies in determining the role of leading positions such as the CEO, which are also included in the CCP nomenclature. If this is considered at all, it is mostly in terms of a factor of disturbance in the mainstream model of corporate governance, and there is no systematic view on CCP impact in terms of a potentially alternative model of corporate governance.[1]

In this sense, this chapter pursues a 'deconstructionist' account of the Chinese enterprise. I oppose the term 'corporation', in Chinese 'gongsi' (公司), with the term 'enterprise' in Chinese 'qiye' (企业). I claim that

Chinese firms are mainly organized as enterprises, and that they are external manifestations of underlying entrepreneurial networks. In this sense, I present the thesis of the primacy of the entrepreneurial function in Chinese business enterprise, in comparison to the organizational function. Analytically, this means that I take the notion of network as being fundamental, and then look at two different, ideal-typical modes of network formation in the economy, markets and organizations; the question is how these two relate to each other, especially in the context of modularization. Obviously, this question leads us back to fundamentals, especially with regard to Fei Xiaotong's distinction of two kinds of basic network structures, which, as we saw, corresponds to the distinction between two forms of collectivism, namely relational and categorial. Then, we can relate the weakness of the corporate form of network organization in the *longue durée* also to the dominance of relational collectivism, or, in Fei's parlance, to open and flexible circles in the organization of enterprise. The emphasis on these network forms also implies egocentrism, which I relate to the primacy of the entrepreneurial function. In this sense, the weakness of the corporate form also reflects entrepreneurial individualism. This corresponds to the 'heroic' model of innovation that I discussed in Chapter 5, and is indeed most visible in the huge public attention that individual entrepreneurs attract in China. However, I emphasize right from the beginning that another misunderstanding in the 'mirror of culture' should be avoided; that is, the equation of entrepreneurship with private ownership. As we saw in Chapter 4, a fundamental principle in CCP organization is strategic leadership, and this implies that 'leading cadres' also assume an entrepreneurial function in their domain of competence. This means that, in considering the role of entrepreneurship in networks, we need to distinguish different entrepreneurial functions, and strategic leadership is certainly a core function.

There are two aspects of networks that we need to distinguish against the backdrop of our analysis of market governmentality: private and public or political. Under current conditions of the political system, this by and large means interpreting 'state ownership' as a manifestation of the network structure of the CCP. So, my typology of companies in China is mainly sociological and corresponds to the approach in social network analysis that focuses on the power structure in the corporate sector, shifting attention away from the formal features of the corporate governance institutions. This research is congenial to the analysis of the Chinese situation, thus reflecting the affinity between the concept of *guanxi* and the concept of social network. Generally, this means looking behind the structure of formal corporate governance institutions and highlighting the network structures that connect individuals beyond organizational boundaries. In the context of Western industrial economies, these network structures match a particular aspect of market performativity, which is the role of finance in structuring business. So, social network theorists would claim that corporate control is at least partly diffused across social networks of individuals who are in turn formal members in financial organizations, such as banks. This view highlights specific network aspects of financial capitalism, thus pointing towards analysing the role of alternative social networks in China, especially the CCP network. Interestingly, status also plays a significant role in the organization of Western corporate networks, both at the individual and the organizational level, thus also establishing a conceptual bridge to the notion of ritual economy.[2]

For taxonomic clarity, I simply distinguish between two poles of network, private and political, and there is also a large domain of hybrid forms. The 'political' pole is manifest in organizational terms such as 'public' so far as the corporate form is concerned. This duality also relates to the distinction between market and state, and so immediately establishes the conceptual bridge to market governmentality. So, in fact, we immediately realize that the distinction of the poles is just a heuristic device, as in reality the two aspects, the private and the political, always intermingle.

With regard to the phenomenology of business enterprise, this means that we distinguish the following:

- Private companies are family businesses or investor-managed firms, with the latter divided into owner-managed firms or investor-controlled companies; the latter category is relatively small and largely overlaps with the third category of hybrid organizations.
- Public companies are state-owned companies on the different levels of territorial administration and with multiple public owners; I approach these as 'stakeholder organizations', since public investors pursue a multiplicity of goals beyond mere financial considerations.

Hybrid companies display a large range of variations, reaching from private companies that are closely aligned to the government via personal connections, to state-owned units that have large stakes of private investors who actively partake in decision-making; for these companies, the notion of 'stakeholder companies' may also be applied, so that this notion becomes an umbrella term, resulting in a more basic distinction between private companies and stakeholder organizations.

Whereas the standard approach to corporate governance focuses on ownership and control, my approach would emphasize two economic functions: investment and entrepreneurship. For example, in a private company the investor and the entrepreneur may be one single person. In a family business, the entrepreneur may remain a single person, but the investment, hence finance, may be raised in narrower or wider circles of kin. Or, in a public company, investors may include both government and private organizations, but the entrepreneurial function may be dispersed in CCP networks that define its strategic leadership. So, I argue that the conventional approach to corporate governance, which is mainly based on analysing the legal framework, needs to be changed in the Chinese context in focusing on the factual network relations that are manifest in the two business functions of investment and entrepreneurship. This perspective is also the most appropriate one, as the 'hybridization' of the SOE sector is the official policy of the Chinese government today. Together with the co-optation of private business, this means that the third type of corporation will certainly increase in significance, and for this case the legal perspective is especially deficient. This theoretical perspective matches recent developments in the theory of industrial organization, contextualized in institutional analysis, and emerging from the 'varieties of capitalism' literature. Here, ownership is only one aspect of analysing so-called 'architectures' of economic processes and structures, which combine certain technological conditions with specific forms of coordination. This approach directly ties in with the concept of 'modularization' that I have already deployed, and fits especially well with the phenomenon of hybridization of ownership.[3]

In terms of numbers, Chinese statistics do not provide a clear picture on the distribution of corporate forms in the economy. Generally speaking, the number of SOEs has reduced dramatically over the past two decades, and private business has become the numerically dominant form; for example, in 2012 there were about 7000 industrial SOEs and about 190,000 private industrial firms. At the same time, and categorically independent, there were about 67,000 industrial companies with limited liability and about 9000 shareholding companies, which are separate from about 7000 private shareholding companies. These numbers need contextualization in considering the size of the companies. Generally, an average SOE is one order of magnitude larger than the average private firm, especially with regard to capital stock. This size difference is also visible when comparing the two kinds of shareholding companies. Given the complexity of reforms in corporate structures, it is no wonder that the official statistics do not really allow one to identify the quantitative significance of different kinds of companies, even if we only look at the proportions of different legal types. These difficulties also include the fact that different statistical categories may refer to different definitions of the entire set of corporations. The reason is that the two basic legal categories according to the Company Law, namely the limited liability company and the publicly listed company, are both indifferent with regard to the ownership structure that is reflected in the listed capital shares. In spite of the fact that there are shareholding companies which are explicitly designated as 'private', we cannot conclude that all other shareholding companies are state owned, but refer all of them to the hybrid category. This is important in gauging the influence of the government on the economy. All publicly listed companies apart from the formally purely private firms include government units or government-related organizations such as investment trusts as shareholders. This means that the category of the listed company actually also reflects the underlying network structure between public and private actors in the economy. So, all in all, we note a paradox in the modernization of corporate structures. The new legal forms actually make it much more difficult to ascertain the structures of ownership and control in the Chinese economy, compared with the traditional distinctions directly reflecting ownership.[4]

One also has to pay attention to the special role of conglomerates, 'qiye jituan' (企业集团), which include many companies as independent legal persons which can have different status in terms of ownership, even extending into the private sector. These conglomerates are integrated via cross-shareholdings in which the original owners no longer appear as investors, thus obfuscating the factual impact of ownership. Cross-shareholdings are also important beyond the formal framework of conglomerates and are often essential in identifying the hybrid nature of even a formally private firm; for example, a shareholding company under government control may no longer be explicitly designated as 'state owned' in the official statistics, but just as a listed company according to the Company Law, and then appears as an investor in a private company as a limited liability company. But in fact, this investment may be directly driven by underlying entrepreneurial networks involving cooperation between private entrepreneurs and government officials.

So, what may be regarded as a major step towards the modernization of corporate governance in China is effectively masking the resilience of the ritual economy in the sense of a network-based organization of enterprise. For example, in the transition of township and village industries towards independent companies, the limited liability legal form is an appropriate means, but the different capital shares may be owned by the private actors in an MBO scheme which also retains a share of the local government, often hidden by the intermediation of a local investment company that is owned by the government. Considering that the MBO often involves the incumbent management which in turn may have been recruited from the cadre stratum in the past, obviously the new corporate form of limited liability covers many hybrid companies which are manifestations of social networks among local elites. In other words, the corporate form is a legal means to organize this network-based entrepreneurial activity and does not constitute a corporate actor in the strict sense of the term.

So, the difference between the corporation and the enterprise, in my use of the terms, is one of social ontology. As already discussed in Chapter 2, one conspicuous feature of the Chinese economy in Imperial times was the absence of corporate organizations in the context of the market system. There are two different ways to look at this phenomenon. One view would emphasize the weakness of the legal system which was lacking the notion of a corporate social identity, which had emerged in Europe in early times in the context of ecclesiastical law, and which was then extended into non-religious domains. In this view, the corporation was a legal invention that did not occur in China, thus limiting the evolution of modern capitalism. As I have already shown, this view fails to take note of functional equivalents, since lineage organizations in particular may be seen as perpetual organizations that are often even established separate organizational entities with a governance and shareholding structure. Further, we face another difficulty in the mirror of culture, as we need to take note of the fact that, in the transition to capitalism in Europe, most companies remained family-based organizations and did not assume the corporate form. So, the corporation is a phenomenon of mature capitalism, but was not a necessary element of the emergence of capitalism. The alternative view may be more relevant, since it emphasizes the competitive advantage of loose network-based organizations in the context of the market system.[5]

This second way of reasoning may be supported by the evidence that following the first introduction of the Company Law in 1904, with several successors in Republican China, corporations did not emerge as significant players in the Chinese economy. Indeed, the legal form of the corporation was largely used for setting up government-controlled companies or for foreign investments. The indigenous companies almost entirely relied on the pattern of partnerships when organizing joint investments, thus also including full liability. This preference may be explained by the severe political uncertainty of Republican times. If we look at Overseas Chinese business, the same argument largely applies: many Overseas Chinese businesses have used a manifold of legal forms in different countries to organize the family business as a multinational conglomerate in which risk diversification is pursued. This means that there are difficulties in separating cultural from institutional factors. Yet, independent from the explanation, the descriptive account remains the same: in much of the twentieth century the corporate form remained very weak in Chinese economic contexts, largely reflecting the role of the government in the economy, such as Guomindang-owned companies in Taiwan following the Second World War. In the private sector, the corporate form was simply a legal instrument used in making entrepreneurial projects operational, with a continuous effort to keep external interventions into entrepreneurial networks at a minimum that might result from choosing a particular legal form.[6]

If we look at the situation in Mainland China today, we have to recognize that the institutional limbo continued until recently. The new Company Law only obtained full legal force for private companies in 1994, and the new version of 2005 regulates the limited liability companies and the public corporation, thus concluding a decade-long effort in the 'corporatization' of state-owned enterprises (under the slogan of 'creating a modern enterprise system'). This means that throughout most of the period of market transition, private companies and state-owned companies were also transforming into the new forms of corporation, with a large number of transitory organizational hybrids, such as the Township and Village Enterprises in the 1980s and 1990s. As I have already pointed out, therefore, we cannot assume that the evolution of corporate forms has already achieved a final state, in spite of the rigidity of the legal framework. But I will also argue that in the context of transition, certain features have emerged and will prove to be resilient, which are manifestations of the ritual economy, and therefore may be a stable feature in the years to come. It is extremely important to recognize that the evolution of corporate forms was stalled throughout most of the twentieth century, and that the creation of formal institutions only took place over two decades. If we compare this with the requirements for a workable corporate governance framework according to Western-style institutions, it is straightforward to see that this is a utopian benchmark, as this presupposes a strong infrastructure with regard to specialized lawyers, courts, independent financial media and so on. So, what we see is a co-evolution of this infrastructure, formal institutions and actual practices. This co-evolution is, in my view, shaped by the more fundamental structures of the ritual economy.

It is illuminating to look at the development in Taiwan during the past decades. Here, in the 1980s, a distinct term was used to refer to the fact that entrepreneurial activity was organized in the context of networks of entrepreneurs who opted for particular legal forms to implement particular projects. Nevertheless, the basic organizational unit remained the network of related entrepreneurial projects, which were manifest in supplier relations, mutual investments or other forms of close cooperation. These networks were called 'guanxi qiye' (关系企业), 'related enterprises'. The term *guanxi* is here used in the generic sense; however, if we look at the emergence of certain large-scale businesses, *guanxi* practices in the traditional sense also played a role. The *guanxi qiye* was a proposition in social ontology in the sense that one did not simply refer to networks as such, but assigned a separate status to certain networks, for example, by identifying boundaries in listing the members or by assuming mutual liability of members for business outcomes. So, in spite of the fact that the *guanxi qiye* was not a legal entity (but could become one as a conglomerate), it was perceived as a quasi-corporate unit in organizing entrepreneurial activity. In more detail, for example, a typical pattern in creating entrepreneurial networks is that the owner of a company may financially support entrepreneurial projects of employees who set up their own business. The two businesses might then continue to cooperate in supplier networks or other respects.[7]

It is interesting to note that if we consider extended kinship, the distinction with *guanxi* may become blurred, because, within larger circles of extended kin, the emotional commitments of members may thin out, so that, for example, lineage membership may approach the function of a *guanxi* basis. This is a form of modularization of market and organization characteristically prevailing in historical times, as we saw in Chapter 2. In this case, network relations also begin to transcend the conceptual borders of a corporate organization, as in the case of the Taiwanese *guanxi qiye*, in which observers in society and business started to recognize the implications of this and transformed a hidden social ontology into a public one, if not in legal terms, so in terms of public representations and practices. In other words, as we have already seen when discussing market modularization in Chapter 5, there are fluid boundaries between tighter and looser network organization, such as when, in South China today, migration of entrepreneurs might be organized in lineage contexts, with some individuals and their companies assuming a lead role. If we consider the social transformation of kinship during modernization, this pattern may lose its explicit reference to lineage symbols and rituals, yet continue with activating the connections to more distant kin. In this sense, some entrepreneurial networks may still be seen as kin-based *guanxi* networks, even under conditions of social modernization. Indeed, this remains true for Taiwan today, since the large majority of publicly listed companies are factually controlled by networks of extended kin.[8] So, the family and kinship organization is the more basic organizational unit as compared to the legal corporate firm, even understood with reference to the traditional notions of extended family.

In this context, we have to consider one essential aspect of market performativity that we analysed in the Chapter 5, namely the role of finance and financial repression in shaping business networks. As in the Taiwanese case, this link certainly mattered greatly in maintaining the strength of kinship relations in business organization. As long as the formal financial sector discriminates against small and medium-scale enterprises, there is a strong need for activating kin-mediated investor relations, especially in the early stages of company development. As is also well known from many other countries, if certain regulations only start to hold beyond a certain size, many owners keep the size of their business below that threshold. This, however, at the same time makes access to the formal financial sector more difficult. Yet, one cannot simply argue that this has to be blamed on government intervention exclusively: lack of access for SME to the financial sector is a problem even in countries where this is actively promoted by the government. So, in fact, we observe a unique impact of market-induced status orders, which can be bolstered by government interventions but also emerge endogenously. This status order implies that high-quality financial services are mainly provided to high-quality clients, and that low-quality clients are partly excluded from access. 'Low quality' is not necessarily related to objectively higher risks, but perceived risks owing to asymmetric information or, generally, lack of the necessary contextualized knowledge in order to assess the quality of local small-scale companies. Therefore, the resilience of traditional forms of informal finance is also endogenous to markets. This is also evident from the fact that often entrepreneurs even avoid accessing formal financial services. So, in the resilience of traditional network structures, we observe a peculiar interaction between the two functions of investing and entrepreneurship. The Chinese networked business is a unique manifestation.

Beyond this special impact of finance, the examples discussed thus far show that there is a close interaction between industrial ecology and network formation. If an employee turns independent supplier in an entrepreneurial network, this is also determined by the technological opportunities and the forces of optimizing processes. In the case of China, one of the most significant developments in recent decades was the coincidence between market liberalization and the globalization of supply chains, together with industrial restructuring in the more advanced industrial economies. This development has triggered the so-called 'fragmentation' of the global economy, which refers to a unique pattern of exploiting comparative advantage. It means that international trade is increasingly taking place as the trade of intermediary products. Producers in different countries specialize in certain parts of the final product according to their comparative advantage, and these products are then assembled in one country which therefore cannot be regarded as the 'producer' of the item. The producer is the network of suppliers of intermediate products that is often orchestrated by the owner of the brand and the technological knowledge embodied in the final product.[9] This means that even the producer of the final product may not be the one who is the designer of the global production chain. This is important to note because it implies that, to a certain extent, the final owner mainly obtains the position of a commercial agent that optimizes business designs, or in addition as the creator of the knowledge that is embodied in the final product. The former example may be typically found in more traditional consumer goods industries such as textiles or toys, where international trading houses often specialize in managing global production chains, or where global retailers such as Walmart directly manage them. As for the latter, Apple is one of the most famous representatives.[10]

For China, these trends proved to be a unique opportunity for development, as Chinese producers could integrate into those networks in order to gain market access based on their comparative advantage. So, for example, compared to the development in some of the tiger economies of the past, especially newly invested companies could rely on the design, quality control, marketing and logistics of lead companies in order to gain access to foreign markets, thus fuelling the fulminant expansion of Chinese exports. This meant that the international design of production chains and the mechanisms of network formation in China worked together in creating the industrial and social ecology in which Chinese entrepreneurial ventures flourished. Considering this important role of networks in organizing entrepreneurship, I posit a distinct hypothesis. I claim that the contemporary forms of supply chains in the global economy are an organizational correspondence to the traditional commercial capitalism that was rooted in the ritual economy. This hypothesis is not only based on the observation that Chinese networks are pre-adapted to the functional requirements of supply chain organization, but also that the distinct competitive advantage of the Chinese family in traditional times is reinstated in the context of supply chains. In other words, I argue that the emergence of fragmentation in the global economy and the capacity of network modularization in China came together, thus leveraging certain mechanisms of the traditional economy that have been designated as 'commercial capitalism'.[11]

Interestingly, we meet two distinct patterns in Chinese supply chains. One is epitomized in the Foxconn model which is based on the organizational structure of the corporation and which involves the creation of huge production units with distinct organizational features (see below). This structure is often necessary if very high quality of the final products needs to be achieved, such as in the production of Apple products. The other is the network structure of a large number of mostly small-scale family businesses which operate in a similar industry or product category, such as toys or textiles. This is particularly efficient in industries with very high pressure on costs, strong seasonal fluctuations and rapid change of product designs. Both network structures are organizationally resilient because they ultimately exploit the cost advantages of the family in two senses. One is the self-exploitation of the members of the family in small-scale businesses, the other is the exploitation of migrant labour which is often embedded in family structures as well, be this that entire families migrate, or that workers remain connected to their families in their rural native areas. As in earlier Taiwanese developments, there is a strong gender component here as well, since female migrant workers are often employed who plan to get married after working for a number of years in order to contribute to the accumulation of family savings.

The large number of small-scale family businesses is often organized into supply chains by certain lead companies which are mainly family owned, as we have seen in Chapter 5. For example, many companies in an urban district may be connected with a major textile producer who also owns brands. The network is used to keep costs low and to better adapt to seasonal variations of demand. This means that we cannot understand the structure of business if we only look at the corporate unit of the lead company. Actually, the business unit, even in the sense of the production unit, is the network of family firms. In organizing these networks, leadership comes into play which is partly a manifestation of the ritual economy. This means, for example, that the entrepreneur owning the lead company also assumes roles in the local civil society, such as in organizing business associations. Business associations can become active in regulating conflicts between labour and capital, thus contributing to network development and resilience. One particularly powerful mechanism is the adoption of intermediary financial functions of the lead company, such as when the owner is also active in investment companies or similar enterprises in which he acts as an intermediator in creating networks of entrepreneurial activity in a region of his reach.

In the exporting areas of south China, such as Dongguan, these network patterns also include the activity of local governments behind which the social structure of the original villages looms large, as we have seen in earlier chapters. Local elites dominating the village or district administration contribute to entrepreneurial ventures or even partake financially in giving access to land, sometimes providing access to funding via local government investment bodies, or even organizing the supply of a workforce. Therefore, in these cases, the entrepreneurial networks even assume a hybrid nature, thus being another instance of localism in the ritual economy.

In arguing that this model is a transformation of the commercial capitalism model of the traditional ritual economy, I highlight the fact that the single firms in the network remain only superficial expressions of what is basically a commercial or trading pattern. This means, on the other hand, that technological development is not a basic feature, as there is only weak independent capacity to accumulate specific skills and knowledge pertaining to production. This is reflected in the very low share of value added that actually remains with the Chinese part in the global production chains, mainly wages and land rents, and entrepreneurs always working at the edge of profitability in the long run. This is what currently puts the companies in the traditional export areas under very high pressure, since they often lack the capacities for industrial upgrading. In other words, we can see firms in these contexts as specific combinations of the entrepreneurial function and network formation, with the entrepreneurial function reduced to its core component, namely the profit-oriented combination of production factors in order to create a marketable output. Depending on technological conditions, these combinations can happen in a very flexible and transient way, so that the entrepreneur actually concentrates on the trading function, with the firm becoming only an indirect tool to connect supply and demand. This is why I propose to use the term 'enterprise' as opposed to 'corporation' to refer to the Chinese firm.[12]

However, the network model may be observed in many different shapes, sometimes involving also technological engineering of the network relationships. An interesting variant is the dissolution of the innovation process into network structures. In this case, the lead company sets incentives for suppliers to implement product innovations, but at the same time only defines relatively broad standards for bringing decentralized production together. This network pattern has been designated as 'local modularization' by some observers. The interesting aspect is that as opposed to the aforementioned highly integrated knowledge-intensive global production chain, the lead company does not monopolize the necessary technological knowledge in producing the different parts of the product, but allows for the dispersion of the knowledge in the network. However, this also implies that the entrepreneurial risk is not shared. So, we can say that the 'commercial capitalism' patterns combine together with technological conditions in creating what has been called in industrial organization literature an 'open modular' structure which compares especially with closed integral structures typical for many large corporations in the Fordist tradition of production organization and innovation management by in-house units.[13]

Modularization implies that certain knowledge remains exclusive to the producers of single modules. This is also valid for global production chains, with an important twist. Supplier networks are networks with a downstream lead firm. We also observe networks with upstream lead firms, especially in innovation-intensive industries such as electronics. These models come very close to the traditional organization of the market system, where larger scale merchant enterprises often simultaneously provided the grassroots-level families as production units with inputs and credit.[14] In considering these historical roots, there are two polar variants of this pattern, depending on whether there is also a final buyer of the end-product who also exerts control over design, quality and so forth, or whether the network members themselves take autonomous decisions on the final products.

The salient modern example for the latter case is the *Shanzhai* model introduced in previous chapters. In the *Shanzhai* model, providers of certain basic modules of electronic products such as mobile phones allow (often willy-nilly) for the free diffusion of those modules in a vast population of small-scale family firms. This hardware can be easily put into different uses by manipulating the software, which does not require production units for the modules, but only the technological capacity to put the modules together. This enables small-scale production of a huge variety of products, such as mobile phones with various designs and various combinations of functions, thus meeting the specific demands of consumers more effectively than formalized production in larger corporate units. The basic organization of family firms is extremely weak and flexible, which makes enforcement of IPR very difficult, and thus releases creative productivity from legal constraints. However, considering the sources of the competitiveness of the family firms, these lie in the local network structure in which the huge variety of modular inputs can be provided, including customized items such as specially designed cases for mobile phones.

As we can see, these principles of network organization also reflect the fundamental cognitive patterns of modularization examined in Chapter 2. For example, a *Shanzhai* mobile phone as an artefact is similar to a Chinese character in arranging a large number of elements into a coherent pattern. This principle is also currently emerging in the use of 3D printing for creating customized artefacts.[15] Then, we may say that the modularization of technological elements in the final product matches the modular structure of the small-scale businesses that flexibly emerge and adapt to market needs and demand. This means that social organization and artefactual structures converge on the same fundamental cognitive principles.

On the one hand, this model certainly cannot be fully covered by standard concepts about corporations, which is instructively reflected in the difficulties of the international legal system and trade law in categorizing these phenomena. On the other hand, *Shanzhai* ecologies also provide the ground on which more standard corporate structures can emerge, if a company starts to move on to higher levels of complexity in the value chain and to adopt the role of a lead firm in arranging a network of suppliers into a more coherent pattern. For example, leading companies in the Chinese automotive industry emerged in this way, after going through a stage of rampant copying combined with free variation of designs and technological elements.[16]

An interesting variant of this network model may be observed in the rural areas and is directly connected with the institutional regulation of landownership. As I have shown in Chapter 3, landownership in the rural areas remains collective, but land-use rights belong to the family. In this legal construct, the collective imbues the group of families that possess the usufructuary rights with a corporate identity. This construct implies that the family is constituted as a unit of economic decision-making, and that it is even stabilized by the ownership institutions. These special conditions create the possibility of arranging entrepreneurial network structures which build on the family as a unit, if the collective-level organization aims at consolidating the technology of land-use and building supply chains connecting up with the food industry. For example, a typical pattern is that a village might enter into a contractual relationship with a lead company in the food industry. The lead company will determine the pattern of land use, such as which crops are chosen, which quality standards need to be observed and so forth. However, this does not imply that the farming families give up their land-use rights. Further, the subordination to the lead company may also include the provision of jobs to family members, so that some of them may be able to leave agricultural production. So, also in these models, we observe the resilience of traditional network structures which is partly caused by the socialist land institutions, thus paradoxically bolstering the role of the family in the networks.[17]

All of these different patterns relate to a phenomenon that has been the object of intensive research especially in Europe in the 1980s and 1990s, namely the role of industrial districts or clusters in creating competitive advantages of countries. So, we can connect the analysis of Chinese business networks with the phenomenon of localism. In Europe, this discussion was also triggered by the observation that in regional clusters, small and medium-sized companies could establish complex networks, partly also with lead companies owning strong brands, that made up for lack of economies of scale in terms of flexibility, agility and adaptation to customers' demand, such as in the fashion industry. In hindsight we have learned that this enthusiasm was partly exaggerated, as some of the model cases later entered troubled times in industrial restructuring.

Yet, one important theoretical point in this literature remains true when considering the Chinese case. This is that in regionalized contexts, specific forms of social capital and accumulated human capital, both individual and shared, may support strong networks of cooperation between companies that allow for alternative forms of investment and industrial organization. There is strong evidence that this also applies in the Chinese case, as local clusters have a long historical tradition. Examples abound, with villages specializing in certain products or product categories, thus building on the transmission of certain skills and business know-how between both generations and entrepreneurs. As in the European case, these localized clusters may become the object of local government intervention, such as in creating certain lead companies, or other forms of support, such as in marketing and brand building, or training programmes for workers. Generally speaking, local governments can create the conditions for flexible access to resources, including, as we have seen in another context, the governance of migrant labour and labour conflicts.[18]

Family and ritual in Chinese business

In this section I will take a closer look at the impact of the family upon business organization. Obviously this refers to the domain of private business in the first place, but if we treat the family in the context of the ritual economy it is also important in considering the traditional role of the family as an ideal type of ordering social relations. Even in contemporary China we find many examples where entrepreneurs refer explicitly to the company as a 'family', in this case without suggesting that the company is a family business, but that corporate culture and organizational measures reflect familistic ideals. In research on Chinese business, this reference to the family as an ideal type is largely implicit in the notion of 'paternalism' which is often seen as an essential ingredient of Chinese management. Therefore, in this section I not only deal with family business as a form of private business, but with the more encompassing role of the family in modern China's ritual economy. This ties in with a strong strand of research on Chinese entrepreneurship and leadership in organizations, where we can identify a particular style of leadership as an expression of ritual. In this literature, the notion of leadership is actually a generic one. Therefore, studying family and ritual would also have implications for understanding leadership in any kind of organization. Thus, there are cross-connections with previous treatments of the leadership topic, especially in the context of the Communist Party.

At first sight, we might suppose that all private business is family business, especially in the Chinese context. However, the scholarly literature on family business clearly establishes a distinction between the owner-managed firm and the family firm, the latter coming into existence, for example, when the company retains its identity as being family owned across at least two generations. In other words, a company managed by the conjugal unit would not count as a family business, contrary to the pre-scientific notion.[19] This criterion creates serious difficulties in understanding family enterprises in contemporary China, however.

The reason is that as a reflection of the tumultuous economic history of the PRC, the vast majority of family businesses were only created in the 1980s at the earliest, with a considerable share in the rural areas. This means that so far they can only count as owner-managed firms and not necessarily as family businesses. Because of the synchronization of the creation of enterprises after 1978, the large majority of owner-managed firms is now approaching the time when the generational transition is at stake. This also implies that we now observe whether and to which extent genuine family businesses are emerging in Mainland China. This is in fact not only a phenomenon at the micro-level, but it also affects the structural and aggregate level owing to the synchronization of the life cycle of private businesses. Yet, we have to take note that this phenomenon has only recently attracted the attention of policy-makers and academia in China. In spite of the centrality of the family in Chinese tradition, most research has thus far been defined in terms of 'private business', thus blanking out the specific issues involved in the possible status of a family business. This also applies for Western research, so that, all in all, our picture of Chinese family business in Mainland China is highly deficient. This compares to the research on Southeast Asia, Hong Kong, and partly Taiwan, where the family is seen as the pivot of Chinese business structures and has thus attracted much attention, especially with regard to issues specific to the family, such as the generational transition. Yet, even in this context, some of these aspects have not attracted the necessary attention because, also in these areas, the majority of Chinese family business is relatively young, largely established after the Second World War.[20]

Correspondingly, it is difficult to assess the quantitative significance of family business in China. There are no statistical data that distinguish between private business in general and family business in particular. The Chinese business media tend to focus on the family firms attracting wide public attention, and thus the wealthy families and listed companies. This reflects the increasing self-confidence of affluent families, and also the rapidly growing market for specialized consultancies. For these kinds of companies, the most recent surveys present a mixed picture. Generally speaking, family business tends towards including more various kin into the management structure, with the husband and wife axis as a centre. On the other hand, according to the most detailed data of companies that are listed at the Hong Kong stock exchange, the share of companies where the CEO is also a family member is slowly retreating. However, such observations only cover a minuscule – though in terms of economic impact – significant share of family businesses in China. Yet, we notice the transitional dynamics, in particular observations such as that the role of affinal kin seems to increase, often formally included as investors, i.e. shareholders. These are phenomena that may reflect traditions of the ritual economy, but are difficult to assess empirically for the time being. So, what we lack is actual information about the intentions that drive entrepreneurs and their families in continuing their business, with the important distinction between family wealth in terms of assets and the entrepreneurial dimension of the specific business venture. This refers to the identity of the family business as a going concern across generations.[21]

What the data also consistently show is that companies which limit the role of non-kin in top-level decision-making seem to perform worse. So, it is of the utmost significance to recognize the current succession crisis in the Chinese economy which is partly driven by elements of ritual, here in the sense of traditional beliefs and attitudes. This is most evident in considering their impact upon business succession. In a nutshell, this refers to the norms that only male descendants should inherit the family estate; that in principle all male descendants have a claim on this estate and that it should be divided equally; and that the situation should be avoided where non-family members may gain control over essential decisions in the business unit. These norms have various consequences for the succession event, and are currently followed in different ways. These observations cast an interesting light upon the factual role of ritual in organizing economic activities, but also lead us to consider the diversity of Chinese family businesses.[22]

The instability of the Chinese family enterprise is a well-recognized fact in the literature about Overseas Chinese, Hong Kong and Taiwan businesses, and is rooted in the developmental cycle of the traditional family. In simple terms, this means that the traditional family will enter into a stage of division even before the patriarch passes away ('fen jia' (分家); cf. Chapter 2). This is partly an expression of custom, but it also results from tensions in the kinship architecture, especially with regard to the role of wives and gender relations. Once the wife becomes a mother, the inherently strained relationship between the husband's mother and the daughter-in-law may be resolved by imposing the interest of the 'uterine family', hence 'dividing the hearths' and setting up an independent nuclear family. Although this is certainly a sign of instability, one should also realize that in traditional rural society, the arrangements for family division were also regulated in a formal way, often based on contractual terms, in which not only the handover of assets was determined but also the obligations of children to provide regular assistance and support to their parents. This shows that the normative framework of the *jia* has always allowed for rational arrangements of the economic relationships within the family. Yet, the implication of the traditional rules of family division is that the property of the family has to be divided among the male children, including daughters today if the legal norms are applied correctly (which is often not the case). From this point of view, Chinese family businesses may be especially prone to dissolution, compared to other cultural contexts where, for example, more flexible arrangements would be accepted, and the stability of the business as a going concern might be supported by rules such as primogeniture (as in the important historical case of comparison, namely Japan).[23]

Family division does not necessarily mean that the family as an economic unit is dissolved. This relates to the flexibility of the *jia*, discussed extensively in Chapter 2. In the agricultural economy, family division is largely simply the division of land among brothers, which was a major determinant of the fragmentation of land holdings. This may also apply under modern conditions, such as in real estate. In the context of more complex business ventures as in manufacturing, family division can take place in the context of creating conglomerates of firms, with the family and its patriarch actually adopting the role of a financial holding, and assigning the executive positions in the different companies of the group to different family members. If the family can maintain its unity, this structure is also an arena in which the brothers may undergo entrepreneurial education, so that in the end the most capable would assume the position of the leader and new patriarch. However, this ideal-typical model rarely materializes. In particular, in the third generation, when cousins may also have claims on the second-generation brothers' estates, instability increases and many conglomerates fall apart. This tendency is difficult to contain, since most family businesses traditionally keep professional managers out of the leading echelons of the firm, so that the formal organizational structure is too weak to maintain integration. Apparently, the resilience of corporate organization in Overseas Chinese business often depends on idiosyncrasies of family history and on the particular domain of business. For example, there is the possibility that certain products have won a strong brand identity in the past, such that it also becomes a matter of family reputation to maintain this public image. Then, family members may be able to overcome centrifugal tendencies and find solutions for arranging the relationship between family and business while actually giving priority to the corporate identity.[24]

In this standard model of the Chinese family business, there is a clear differentiation between the two functions of entrepreneurship and investment. The ritual constraints upon business organization mainly relate to the entrepreneurial function, thus creating the instability of the business as a going concern, but affect the investment function to a lesser extent.

So, Chinese family business tends towards being most stable in the context of investment activities that are coordinated within the extended family, which does not necessarily imply the existence of a formal holding company. So, we can speak of kinship-mediated partnerships of a traditional type. As we have seen in the previous section, this was the most common way in which *guanxi qiye* emerged in Taiwan.

Under the current conditions of Mainland China, there is the special impact of the one-child policy, which often leaves the family with only one person who may take over the company. This has diverse effects, which put ritual concepts under pressure. One is that gender roles will change, since single daughters would inherit the family estate. However, the break with tradition is not as strong as it might appear, since in the separation of roles between the *jiazhang* and the *dangjia* it was always accepted that under certain conditions females might assume the role of the *dangjia*. Indeed, in many contemporary family firms in Mainland China, the handover to daughters is considered to be an acceptable option, and the share of women in top executive positions is increasing. In this context, general value change in society impacts directly upon business behaviour.[25]

This range of flexibility also applies to the employment of non-family members in top management. Here, we can apply the *guanxi* logic in the sense that the buildup of emotional relationships with non-family individuals may create a relationship that converges with a family-type close bonding. This shows again that for understanding family business in China it is important to distinguish between the different functions of entrepreneurship, investment and management. The traditional division of the *jiazhang* and *dangjia* roles allows for the diversification of the entrepreneurial and the managerial functions, while maintaining full family control of the investment function, and hence the financial wealth of the family.[26]

So, probably the major challenge for family companies is that the successor generation is often not willing to continue with the business. These are standard problems in family business worldwide. In China, rapid value change exacerbates the difficulties. A typical constellation is that many families send their children abroad to receive better education, often in management. So, they stay abroad for years and return not only equipped with new knowledge but also with the experience of different lifestyles. This leads to tensions with the patriarch, who wants to raise a successor but is at the same time reluctant to cede control. So, issues emerge such as that the young generation may prefer to move to another area of business, or would like to change the structure of the company, if not outrightly refusing to take over the company. Again, in these cases falling back on the financial holding model can help, thus actually allowing the younger generation much entrepreneurial leeway. In fact, we can observe in China today that the current challenges in industrial restructuring and upgrading, especially in the export-oriented regions in the Pearl River Delta and

Zhejiang province, actually ease this model of generational transition, since the founder's business is often in trouble. New entrepreneurial initiatives by the younger generation may therefore be very welcome. Therefore, generational transition can help resolve these challenges of restructuring, and at the same time may result in the survival of the family enterprise. Further, value change does not necessarily imply that traditional aspects of ritual lose their force; in fact, ritual can also serve as a repository of cultural creativity in creating new forms of business organization and corporate culture.[27]

This brief outline of the current situation of family businesses in China shows the importance of the family as a ritual phenomenon in business organization, even affecting the aggregate level in terms of structural change and business dynamics. One immediate expression of this is the relatively weak position of family business in terms of technological competitiveness. If, as we have seen, the investor function dominates the entrepreneurial function, this reinstates the role of the family along the lines of commercial capitalism. So, the specific business venture is not necessarily seen as a long-run going concern, but as a medium-term investment in order to reap profits. Therefore, the family business typically manifests a much lower investment into research and developing new products than other types of business. This means that challenges of structural change are mostly met by withdrawing from a certain area of business, and not in terms of building long-term sustainable capacities in technological transformation.

As I have stated in the introductory paragraph, the significance of the family business in understanding the ritual economy not only lies in the organizational pattern per se, but also in the specific leadership style associated with it. This leadership style plays a major role in defining the specific 'Chineseness' of family business, according to the most influential paradigms in the literature. Here, the ritual dimension is most visible, as leadership is inextricably enmeshed with the notion of hierarchy. The term largely used is 'paternalistic leadership'.

This notion directly ties up with the notion of ritual in the traditional meaning, as it is mostly seen as being an expression of Confucian values. This has resulted in a large strand of literature claiming the cultural uniqueness of Chinese business, such as in the conceptual shape of 'Confucian capitalism'. These notions largely refer to two different aspects of Chinese business. One is the networking perspective examined in the previous chapter; the other is the leadership perspective. In referring to this characterization, however, we need to draw attention to the intricacies of the mirror of culture, as this ideal type has been questioned by many scholars, mainly for two reasons. The first is that the traditional family already allows for many variations, so that there is much more potential for frictionless adaptation than a rigid categorization into ideal types would suggest. The second points to the ideological frame of this characterization, which merely hides the functional and opportunistic basis of leadership practices under the conditions of harsh capitalist competition; this view would also imply that the capacity for change is high, since cultural or ritual constraints are actually weak. If we put the two criticisms together, we may conclude that ritual constraints upon the transformation of family business would actually be much weaker than is normally suggested, but also that the potential cultural impact must occur on a deeper level, allowing for much more diversity on the level of external manifestations. One problem that also becomes salient here, and one which I will further explore in the final section, is the exclusive focus on Confucianism in defining the paternalistic leadership style as a core feature of Chinese enterprise. As I have argued consistently throughout this book, the notion of ritual reaches far beyond this. With regard to family business and paternalistic leadership in general, this means that the impact of tradition can be multifaceted, including also many non-Confucian elements.[28]

Keeping these caveats in mind, the paternalistic leadership pattern refers to a 'Confucian' model in the sense that the leader is expected to assume the position of a teacher and a moral example vis-à-vis members of the organization. In this sense, leadership is explicitly related to followership. Employees would approach the leader as a source of advice, orientation and also support. On the one hand, this implies an authoritarian relationship, which is manifest in many phenomena, in particular the strong tendency to monopolize access to knowledge. This is a major limiting factor in adopting modern management practices in Chinese family companies, because the owners prefer to keep sensitive and important information secret, such as financial data or market intelligence. So, it also fosters the practices to assign other leading positions to trusted family members.[29]

However, followership also implies a special responsibility for the leader to take care of employees' concerns. This leads to a particular pattern that certainly cannot be found in every family business, but is evident in many reported cases. There are no formal mechanisms regulating employees' participation in decision-making, but the leader is expected to express concern and pay attention to employees' opinions. This is enabled in particular management styles, such as the campaign-style mobilization of effort and problem-solving activities. Here, the leader does not impose detailed controls, but triggers the activism of the employees and assumes the role of the final evaluator of the results. In other words, the paternalistic model builds on the expectation that the leader is recognized by the followers. This recognition is largely incited by moral leadership. This is expressed mainly in two ways. One is that the leader has to set a moral example, especially with regard to work effort, sincerity and reliability; the other is paying attention to the private matters of the employees, such as extending help in case of family emergencies or sending gifts on occasion of special family events. One negative side effect of this can be the rise of informal groups in the organization, encompassing people with good personal relations with the leader and his trusted colleagues. Here, we see one example of the necessary distinction between 'Confucian' aspects and ritual in general: the formation of informal groups in the organization reflects the *guanxi* logic of reciprocity, and less the paternalistic hierarchy. This also distinguishes between particularistic groups in general and nepotism. So, the generic ritual aspect in leadership is the peculiar leader–follower dynamics, and not the 'paterfamilias' structure.[30]

This ideal-typical model of Chinese leadership has certainly changed under the conditions of modernization, but researchers still present a modified version of it which retains the emphasis on the elements of authority, care and morality. Modernization appears to further highlight the participatory elements of the model, which is expressed in the stronger need to win legitimacy as a leader. Yet, authority also means that centralization of decision-making and strict discipline are sustained as central organizational patterns. So, it has been suggested that the 'authoritarian' model of paternalism is shifting towards an 'authoritative' one. This kind of research is explicitly aiming at an indigenous perspective on leadership. It includes as central aspects the elements of authoritarianism, morality and benevolence. This extends to the Confucian framing, but also moves beyond the context of the family. In empirical studies, what emerges is that authoritarian structures as such do not necessarily create compliance on the part of employees, but the other two elements; in fact, there is evidence that one-sided emphasis on authoritarian leadership can reduce the commitment of employees. Benevolence relates mainly to the traditional notion of *bao*, hence reciprocity. So, we meet another instance of the *guanxi* logic, which means that 'benevolence' is not simply altruism, but is seen as the exchange of favours instigated by the leader. So, the leader has to offer 'gifts' of attention and care to the employees who therefore develop commitment in terms of gratitude and feelings of obligation. However, what is even more influential in this model is morality, meaning that the leader must be a moral exemplar. Evidently, morality is closely connected to respect, hence issues of face, and creates legitimate claims on authority which are recognized by the followers. Taken together, we can clearly identify this model of leadership as a ritual one, thus appearing as an important building block of the ritual economy.[31]

When discussing these meanings and possible transformations of paternalism in China it is important to keep in mind more foundational aspects involving the mirror of culture, however. This refers to the possibility that Western researchers may tend to project their notion of 'paternal power' onto the Chinese social structure. In these Western notions, strongly influenced by Max Weber's views, the *patria potestas* is modelled according to the Roman model, in which it is clearly an individual right of the most senior person in the household and family. In the traditional Chinese concept of filial piety, however, there is a differentiation between the individual and the role it has in the cosmic order, thus always also opening up the possibility for distancing oneself from the individuals that actually control this power. This observation is also relevant for interpreting the meaning of 'family', as it would even imply that the father in the family is mainly defined in terms of his role, which also means that the real father may fail to meet the role expectations. This understanding would be the basis for the extension of the family paradigms into generic concepts of leadership.[32]

For this kind of extension there are different channels, with the one that is most deeply connected to traditional ritual, namely the extension of kin relations to non-kin contexts. On the one hand, this can simply refer to the inclusion of non-kin via personal relationships into the closer circle of leading management. But there is also the more generic use of the family metaphor in organizing the company. So, owner-managed firms may also be organized in using the family as a template without actually building on kinship as an organizational means. The family has always also been a template for arranging closer relationships among non-kin in rural society, with applying kin terms to non-kin. This pattern is also revived in a modern context, when close friends who set up a business together not only refer to each other with kin terms, but also pursue many practices that define relationships among family members.[33]

This matches the long historical tradition in China of using the family as a model for other organizations, even the Empire itself. This fundamental role of the family as a reference is rooted in the aforementioned universalization of the respective moral rules. Thus 'filial piety' is not simply a norm governing concrete family relations, but is a universal principle in organizing hierarchical relations. So, we may consider the extension of the notion of the family towards organizational forms that normally would not be subsumed among 'family business', strictly speaking. This question is important for different reasons, but is certainly relevant if observers argue that family business is also the context of a universal model of paternalistic leadership that transfers to other organizational contexts. Again, the question emerges whether this is mere ideological obfuscation of power structures, but we need to recognize many cases in which this reference is translated into very specific measures of organizational design.

We cannot make generalized statements about this point and only present case studies, but these are certainly illuminating. Interestingly, there is a convergence with organizational legacies of the Maoist system here and the *danwei* pattern. That is, I argue that in understanding the meaning of ritual in business organization today, it is again important to consider path dependencies that result from the confluence of traditional norms and ideas with the impact of institutional design and organizational interventions by the CCP. This point has been classically made in the research on political culture in the 1970s and 1980s, but only with reference to the pattern of authoritarianism and dependence. In the contemporary context, we can sketch a more complex picture that involves aspects such as the legitimacy of leadership in times of corporate restructuring and institutional change. The *danwei* concept played a central role in aforementioned theories about 'communist neo-traditionalism' that referred to the conditions of the 1980s. Meanwhile, industrial restructuring and ownership transformation have dissolved most of these traditional socialist work units.

Yet, we need to consider path dependencies of organizational change. Many private enterprises have emerged from existing enterprises with collective or state ownership. A case in point are the Township and Village Enterprises of the 1980s and 1990s. These enterprises often put the 'red hat' on, but were actually under the control of a private owner. Further, in the privatization wave of the late 1990s many hybrid companies were fully privatized via MBOs. This means, however, that the new owners actually retained many of the existing webs of organizational and personal relationships in the company. As a consequence, many of the role expectations related to the socialist model were translated into the new context, especially in the transformation of SOEs. The necessarily rising tensions with the stark realities of lay-offs and the trimming down of social services were mainly resolved in spinning off units of the company and focusing on the healthiest parts. For these, however, role expectations often proved to be resilient, thus driving further organizational development. So, considering this in the leader–follower dynamics, new private owners of formerly socialist companies would create legitimacy of their exertion of managerial power in mobilizing the dimensions of morality and benevolence. The latter highlights the role of reciprocity that was also important in the 'neo-traditionalist' setting.[34]

The role expectations in the leader–follower relationship were shaped by the *danwei* model, in particular with regard to the aspect of care. The *danwei* model was structurally based on the integration of the company with the lifeworld of employees in providing a full range of services, such as schooling, healthcare or public transport. In fact, many *danwei* units also assumed the role of a family-like organization, such as actively assuming the role of matchmakers or resolving conflicts in marriage. Since employees typically lived in company-owned compounds, private and organizational lives were deeply intermingled. Furthermore, companies often evolved into partly endogamous units, since until the 1990s the opportunities for free dating were still limited, and so many marriages were realized within the social context of the company. Still, in the 1980s, many companies also assumed direct responsibility for providing job placements for employees' children. By implication, in many SOEs the formal organizational structure was actually undergirded by an informal social structure in which families and kin played an essential role. We may therefore even speak of the 'familialization' of the *danwei*. In fact, the classical notion of socialist 'comradeship' was scarcely prevalent on the eve of the reforms, with circles of trust and mutual help concentrating almost exclusively on family members. In these relationships, traditional customs were vigorously maintained, such as the flow of gifts on important occasions of the life cycle.[35]

So, we may say that the *danwei* model was not only a pattern of socialist organizational modernization, but it also converged with notions of the family as a template for organizational design, and factually merged many elements of the family with organizational practices. If we now consider privatization processes, obviously there are many ways in which this legacy of *danwei* organizational culture can interplay with the traditional patterns of family business that might be introduced by private owners. In other words, we observe a cultural hybridization between organizational legacies of socialism and the traditional family business. Then, it happens that reference to the 'family' as an organizational template also means copying certain elements of the socialist company. This tendency is also bolstered by the fact that competition among companies on the labour market is strongly shaped by the status hierarchy between state-owned enterprises and private business. This means that, as long as SOEs retain features of privileges extended to employees, private business is forced to adopt equivalent measures if they want to attract highly qualified job applicants.

We can only refer to single cases in substantiating these observations, but at the same time these cases also serve as industry models that are widely discussed in the business media. Methodologically, it should be mentioned that the application of survey methods in order to achieve a more general picture may not be the adequate solution, because we can easily get entangled in the mirror of culture. For example, in assessing the degree of the traditional orientation of companies, one of the central litmus tests is the adoption of 'modern' human resources management. But in considering what the defining elements of this are, one easily realizes that some categories may be interpreted both in terms of a modern and a traditional approach. One conspicuous example is the adoption of formal approaches to skill development and training, which may also be seen as expressions of the Confucian emphasis on learning and self-improvement.[36]

Then, family-style business typically refers to the 'care' dimension, such as providing affordable housing to employees or giving support for health insurance or in case of emergencies. However, there are also more specific measures that reflect even traditional notions of the family. For example, the company may send a specific amount of salary or bonus payments directly to the parents of young migrant workers in order to express the leaders' concern for filial piety. Or, the company may explicitly invite employees to recommend kin for open positions, while at the same time controlling the allocation of kin within the company in order to keep nepotism at bay. The latter example is also interesting in pointing towards a tendency among younger generation successors to avoid kinship as an organizational means. However, this does not preclude using the template of the family as a framework for designing the organization.[37]

To summarize this section, I claim that the family retains its role as a central element of China's ritual economy, independent from the fact that organization hybridization also means that the extended family in terms of the kinship structure may be withering away as a consequence of the one-child policy. However, in the current situation there are complex forces working towards different directions. One long-term trend is the reinstatement of the family in the context of the family business. In this regard, one observation attracts attention, namely the fact that the rise of family business may be simply supported by the selection effect resulting from local and individual deviance from the rules of the one-child policy. In many areas with strong family traditions, successful businessmen could also afford to pay the heavy fines for violating birth control regulations, and *guanxi* with local officials could also help. As a result, market competition may actually give advantage to these strong families, so that eventually family business emerges as a more widespread pattern, especially in south-eastern coastal provinces.

State capitalism and stakeholder governance of SOEs

At the beginning of this chapter, I argued that the ritual economy of China is shaped by the fundamental dualism of private versus public enterprise, with a strong and possibly growing role of hybrid forms. The current model of the Chinese economic system maintained by the Communist Party places state ownership at the centre, regarding it as one of the defining differences of the capitalist market economies. In more recent times, the modernization effort in the SOE sector has also revived the traditional position of modernism as it was already expressed in the mid-twentieth century. This position stated that private business was facing certain fundamental limitations for modernization, and that therefore the government had to adopt the role of the modernizing avant-garde. Accordingly, prior to the founding of the PRC, both main political forces, the Guomindang and the CCP, were strongly supportive of state-owned companies, going back to the tenets of Sunyatsenism. In the early decades of Taiwan economic development, this emphasis on national industries was largely reduced owing to the influence of American advisers. In Mainland China, the modernist position has been followed up until the present day. In this particular sense, modernism implies a status order of enterprise in China. We have already seen how this status order influences market organization, such as in finance, thus discriminating against private business. In this section, I look in more detail at how the status order influences the internal organization of public enterprise.[38]

The standard economic approach to SOEs is following the framework of property rights theory and corporate governance theory. Although this is certainly useful for understanding parts of the mechanisms that are operational in generating SOE performance in China, we have already seen that there are also unique conditions, especially the regional property rights system analysed in Chapter 3. In this chapter, I further explore these special conditions from the network perspective deployed in the first section. The difference between private and public enterprise is straightforward to establish: in the case of private enterprise, we mostly consider the role of personal networks in creating the operations under guidance of entrepreneurs. In the case of SOEs, there are personal networks and interorganizational networks. This means that networks operate on two levels: individuals and organizations. The two levels interact, as individuals are largely embedded in certain organizations when dealing with the SOE and its representatives, even if they pursue private interests. I propose to catch both levels with one term, namely the 'stakeholder'. Stakeholders in the SOE are both individuals and organizations, and, as in the opposition between 'shareholder' and 'stakeholder' when referring to the standard capitalist enterprise, stakeholders encompass many more groups than formally included in the formal organizational set-up of an SOE. This is the main reason why standard property rights analysis may reach limits in understanding the operations of SOEs in China. In addition, we have to consider the role of the CCP as a formal network organization. Since the organizational stakeholders of the SOE are government agencies, the CCP acts as a comprehensive higher level network that encompasses both individuals and organizations, the former in terms of their formal positions in the latter. This is the nomenclature system.

In order to understand this complex structure, it is necessary to look at its status at the origin of the reforms. In the regional property rights system, the different components of ownership were dispersed among a larger number of government units, which were proverbially known in Chinese as 'many mothers-in-law'. By this term, observers referred to the lack of centralization in the planning system, such that an SOE was factually meeting with demands and goals coming from different parts of the government bureaucracy, such as regarding production from the industry ministry or financial flows from the finance ministry. These different branches of the administration were not integrated into one single line of command. This is especially true if we consider the situation in a traditional SOE on a lower level of the territorial hierarchy, because in this case also the *tiao kuai* dualism applied. So, apart from the role of the territorial administration, higher level administrations might impact upon the SOE via the line authority.[39]

This particular constellation was manifest in the slack of the plan, because the different demands of different authorities had to be reconciled by way of compromise. Allowing for leeway in plan fulfilment enabled the SOE to flexibly adapt to these demands and strike a balance. As we have seen, slack was a precondition of the successful deployment of the double-track system in the 1980s and early 1990s, because it enabled companies to activate unused capacities in order to enter the newly liberated market domain in the Chinese economy. So, characterizing the transition to the market as starting out from a centrally planned economy would be a misperception. The starting point of reforms was a bargaining system in which the SOE already played an active role in reconciling diverse demands of related authorities and even maintained a number of additional transactional channels in order to gain access to the required resources. In particular, SOEs developed their own networks of related firms in the territory of their location early on, even by means of setting up collective enterprises, but mostly in maintaining supplier relations, for example, with rural industries. In other words, if we consider the differentiation between the entrepreneurial function and the investment function, in terms of the latter the standard SOE was constituted by investment relations with different governmental organizations, hence an organizational network, whereas the entrepreneurial function was partly decentralized to the individual level, namely the director, 'changzhang' (厂长). Often, the director was also the Party secretary, so that we can say, for simplicity, that the entrepreneurial function was also dispersed in the Party network.

So, as a first approximation, we may say that the traditional SOE was an epiphenomenon of the bureaucratic network of the Chinese state, which was in turn embedded in the political network of the CCP. The network of the CCP became dominant in the Maoist era, when even state institutions were weakened in favour of political mobilization that was orchestrated via the Party. This found expression in the massive administrative decentralization of the 1960s and 1970s. In this decentralization, the local governments formally assumed many functions of ownership, but, given the political conditions, this meant that the CCP structures largely exerted control, thus strengthening the dilution of the entrepreneurial function in the CCP network, while at the same time keeping the investment function with the government units, which were, however, controlled by the CCP. Against this backdrop, it is essential to recognize that the early reforms of the 1980s were at the same time an incipient process of marketization and a process of centralization, in other words strengthening the government administration vis-à-vis the SOE. This fact is often overlooked when considering the issue of 'marketization' in China. Approaches to centralization included in particular the imposition of systems in which detailed goals were defined by upper level authorities and cast into contracts between SOE management and the administration. The contractual schemes made the bargaining process more transparent and binding, and simultaneously allowed for a tighter professional supervision of SOE directors. At the same time, reform schemes also always expressed the demand to separate the Party organization from the corporate organization. So, in fact, the early phase of reforms would have implied a shift of the entrepreneurial function to the organizational network of the government. This is the 'factory director responsibility system' ('changzhang zerenzhi'). This system formally recognized the autonomous entrepreneurial function of the director, within the limits of goal fulfilment imposed by the contracts that were concluded between director and administration.[40]

Centralization of control and supervision of SOE is a consistent trend in the entire reform era, and reveals the important insight that SOE reforms were driven by the evolving relationship between central and local state. There are two aspects where this is most salient. The first refers to what we have already analysed in Chapter 4, namely that the privatization policy of the late 1990s was mainly a policy that aimed at stripping the local state of its assets, with the result that the higher level entities would assert their leading role in the public economy. The second is that this was often accompanied by a policy of restructuring and mergers that would also lead to a concentration of ownership at higher levels of the administration.

The latter policy is an explicit network strategy and goes back on early ideas regarding the role of 'trusts' in the modern economy. In the 1980s and 1990s this was realized under the heading of 'qiye jituan' (企业集团) conglomerates which meant that certain lead companies would merge with other companies dispersed among the administrative structure in order to build larger and more efficient corporations. For example, this kind of restructuring was pursued in the automotive industries where Maoist development had created a highly fragmented industry structure in which most production units were operating far below minimum capacity in obtaining scale economies. However, although in principle higher level authorities had the power to impose such restructuring upon other administrative units, they had to cope with the established rights in the regional property rights system. For example, local authorities were keen to protect jobs and revenue claims in the restructuring. Therefore, in this regard Chinese gradualism cannot be interpreted as an intentional approach but reflects the complexity of the bargaining dynamics in the network of bureaucratic organizations. The result of such a process is the transformation of direct bureaucratic control into a system of network governance. If we look at the automotive industry as an example, this process has not yet been completed. One measure was to transform independent producers into suppliers in larger conglomerate networks. Yet, the Chinese suppliers still largely operate below the optimum size, thus manifesting the impact of competing interests in the governing bureaucratic network structure.[41]

Looking at this constellation in more detail, there is a tension between the entrepreneurial and the investment function, both by and large aligned with the two networks of the Party and the government. The latter controls investment functions and also rights to receive revenue and residual profits via mechanisms that include both formal means, such as taxation, and informal means, such as irregular fees or other contributions to the local state. Considering the position of the leadership of the SOE, these demands partly stood in tension with the entrepreneurial function, which, for example, would favour reinvestment in business projects of the partly autonomous SOE. This tension also puts the Party network and the government network into a possibly strained relationship, as the Party network is the means by which strategic economic decisions of higher level authorities would be imposed upon lower levels. This means, for example, that the director of an SOE may face the decision of higher level authorities that this SOE should undergo restructuring by becoming part of a conglomerate led by another government unit than the original unit responsible for this SOE. As a member of the nomenclature system, the director would have to enter negotiations with the potential partners, with the Party creating the arena in which the different stakeholders would come together and realize the bargaining process. So, the entrepreneurial function remains diluted in the CCP network, with the director, after corporatization named the 'CEO', in a pivotal position. His success in the bargaining process is mainly measured according to the goals defined by the higher level Party bodies that formulate strategic development plans.

As we know, this process of reforming SOEs has been an extremely arduous one, creating many conflicts and tensions at the local level where SOEs were actually located, independent from the question of which government level is representing the investment function. This belies ideas that Chinese 'gradualism' was a process with fewer social costs than the 'big-bang' strategy pursued by East European countries. On the contrary, SOE restructuring led to rapidly rising local unemployment rates and many other disadvantages for the places where SOEs were located.[42] This means that SOE reforms have always been an immensely political process, involving the different stakeholders of the corporation, reaching far beyond the formal 'shareholders', that is, owners, in terms of the investment function. This implies that the entrepreneurial function is a highly politicized one, in distinction to the conditions in the private enterprise. Whereas the private entrepreneur needs to develop network relations also with many government agencies in order to pursue his independent entrepreneurial goals, the CEO of an SOE is directly involved in complex political bargaining among the stakeholders in the organizational network in which the SOE is embedded. This is shaped by the fundamental difference to private enterprise, namely that the career of the incumbent CEO is determined by the nomenclature system. This implies that the CEO represents an entrepreneurial function that is not necessarily fully congruent with the ascribed 'interests' of the corporation, but is partly determined by higher level CCP authorities.

The process of industrial restructuring was accompanied by a set of policies that were difficult to coordinate. One was the gradual scaling back of the size and number of economic planning agencies in the government administration, epitomized in the reduction of the number of ministries and the creation of multi-functional ministries covering a larger number of industries that appear to be strategically interrelated. Another was the devolution of management rights to the company while creating a governance structure that would keep the ownership rights with the government. Measures like these were condensed into the formula of creating a 'modern corporate system' since the mid-1990s. This systemic change had to be complemented by changes to the internal structure of SOEs, especially in creating and expanding functions that allowed for autonomous strategy implementation and market operations.

These different policies were institutionally condensed in the unfolding of the shareholding system in China. The shareholding system is the means by which organizational and political networks can retain control over the SOE in spite of the many institutional changes via administrative reforms and industrial restructuring. This is a complex scenario, and I wish only to look at the principles in order to highlight the central point on the network structure and stakeholder governance.

Very early on in the reform process the idea was launched that state ownership could be reconciled with the creation of modern capital markets and the establishment of modern corporate structures, if the state increasingly adopts the role of an investor that controls assets which can be competitively invested in different corporate projects as a business enterprise. This is an idea which has slowly been implemented in the reforms and is institutionally manifest in the core organizational unit that controls SOEs today: the SASACs. This corresponds to the phenomenon that the state still retains control of a major part of non-traded shares in the SOE sector, or, if shares are turned into traded shares following further reforms lanched in the mid-2000s, retains a sufficiently large part of the shares in order to reach this goal. However, this does not necessarily mean that the government-controlled shares only belong to one single administrative unit. In fact, one of the essential advantages of the shareholding model was seen in the possibility that via the transformation of state ownership rights into shares, the tensions between conflicting claims of different administrative units could be resolved. This reflects an interpretation of ownership in the regional property rights system that treats government agencies as investors, hence assigning rights of ownership according to the relative share of past investments or other criteria for justifying claims. Therefore, in fact, a multiple group of administrative bodies may be involved behind the block of state-controlled shares, increasingly including intermediate public bodies such as local government investment vehicles. In this case, the link between the corporation and the state becomes mediated by hybrid organizations which operate between the market and the government. This is reflected in the growing diversity of actors in the capital market which assume the roles of investors, even though they remain public in legal terms, such as the government-owned investment companies.[43]

In other words, the corporatization and the transformation of SOEs into companies with a shareholding structure, both listed and limited liability corporations, is not implying the transition to a corporate governance mechanism which follows the shareholder-based model, especially in Anglo-Saxon capital market-based economies, but is actually the partial formalization of the stakeholder structure of an SOE. This structure is literally embodied in the composition of the boards which represent the different stakeholders-qua-shareholders. Nevertheless, this creates tensions with the formal model of shareholding which is actually legally implemented, especially with regard to minority shareholders, which today may include even international investors. These tensions surface when the corporate bodies that were formally the carriers of the entrepreneurial function would stay in tension with the Party network which is not directly represented as a 'shareholding stakeholder', yet remains the single most important stakeholder of the SOE, as it defines the strategic setting in which the entrepreneurial function of the SOE is realized. The impact of the CCP can be direct and indirect, as we have already seen in previous chapters. The direct impact results from the cadre evaluation system which may measure the performance of a CEO in different terms than an independent board would assess it (for example, profitability may matter less if certain non-economic strategic goals are pursued, such as gaining access to geopolitically critical resourses); the indirect impact results from the status order which puts different representatives of stakeholders into a hierarchical relationship, such as in the context of boardroom discussions.

These developments also tend to complicate the apparently simple approach to separating the role of SASACs and other administrative units. As already detailed in Chapter 4, this leads to a lack of clarity in assigning the ownership rights and the regulatory responsibilities among the different administrative units. Theoretically, in the shareholding approach, all other administrative units would lose their ownership rights which would be concentrated under the control of SASACs. However, this does not simply mean that multiple administrative claims on the SOE are reduced in number. For example, financial flows would still move via the Ministry of Finance which would therefore keep an interest that is independent from the SASAC as the unit that actually manages the ownership rights. On the other hand, since the SASAC controls assets of many companies in an industry, it also has interests that go far beyond managing the investments into single companies. Finally, the SASAC system still retains fundamental features of the regional property rights system; that is, there are SASACs on different levels of the hierarchy, which further complicates the relationship between state ownership and the role of the state as regulator.[44]

All in all, the trend is to enhance the position of the central level in managing state ownership, reflecting modernist views. Then, it is important to note that reforms of SOEs which use the shareholding system in order to modernize SOE management by means of including external investors and even international investors into the governance mechanism actually are a way to leverage the economic power of the government. This is most evident in the recent wave of SOE reforms that was promoted by the new leadership under Xi Jinping, where the notion of 'hybrid ownership economy', 'hunhe suoyouzhi jingji' (混合所有制经济) looms large. Basically, this approach aims at raising the funding capacities of SOE and improving the efficiency of SOE governance while at the same time retaining the dominant role of government in controlling ownership. So, as long as there is no fundamental strategic contradiction between the interests of international shareholders and the CCP, there is no reason why their inclusion should change the fundamental feature of corporate governance as a stakeholder system. After all, international shareholders can vote with their feet and sell their shares in order to express dissatisfaction with the situation. This means that, in spite of these ongoing reforms, the entrepreneurial function remains with the CCP, and only the investment function becomes more diversified.[45]

So, in sum, it seems appropriate to characterize the SOE system as a stakeholder arrangement that differs fundamentally from the shareholder structure of financial capitalism. On the one hand, the evolution of capital markets in China in principle allows for the inclusion of elements of financial capitalism. At the same time, however, the ownership arrangements not only reflect financial interests and motivations of the investors but include more encompassing interests as stakeholders. On the other hand, this stakeholder economy also differs from stakeholder economies in Western countries because certain stakeholders exert only a very weak impact upon the companies. The first observation in this regard is the lack of participation of employees in decision-making.

In principle, SOEs do have an organizational framework for employee participation, namely the workers' councils. Formally, under conditions of growing autonomy of SOEs, these councils could theoretically achieve a powerful position because they could even have a voice on strategic decisions such as major restructuring projects. But their role is actually limited to social welfare and spare-time activities, because the official trade unions largely control their agenda, whose role in turn is mostly limited to these issues. Furthermore, trade unions are also controlled by the Communist Party, which implies that in the internal power structure of the company, the Party secretary at the top of the corporate leadership team is also superordinate to the trade union representatives.

However, as we have already seen in the previous section, the SOE partly embodies the paternalistic leadership, which is rooted in the 'neo-traditionalist' *danwei* system of the past. Therefore, apart from the formal arrangements, corporate leaders need to maintain relationships of reciprocity with the employees of the corporation. This partly touches upon aspects of corporate culture that I discuss in the following section. At this point, suffice it to mention that the embeddedness of the SOE in the CCP network also has implications for the style of management, especially regarding the role of political and moral criteria in evaluating management personnel. Although this mainly appears to be an ideological ritual, yet there are also genuine ritualistic implications in terms of the relationships of reciprocity within the corporation, which may be reflected in certain concerns for the well-being of employees, the security of jobs and so forth. These relationships of reciprocity are also undergirded by the pervasive role of personal networks independent from the formal organizational structure of the SOE, and, at least in the recent past, even kinship networks, as we saw in the previous section. Both forms of informal embeddedness create specific expectations and commitments to reciprocity, or at least support the paternalistic dimension of the management style in SOEs. There are dimensions of management which may be particularly affected by these influences, such as performance evaluation schemes, or the management of lay-offs.[46]

At the same time, some external stakeholders are also weak, apart from the financial sector; that is, the banks. In spite of capital market growth, SOEs still rely mainly on bank credit for funding their activities, especially also running expenses. In the traditional planning system, banks only played a role as accounting agencies and mostly passively adapted to the demands of the production sphere. With the reforms since the 1990s, state banks could assume a more active role as actors in the governance of SOEs, especially regarding larger scale investment projects. But as state banks are themselves subject to the governance structure that I have outlined thus far, this means that they are controlled by other government agencies in turn, so that they may not act fully autonomously in their decisions vis-à-vis the companies. Further, the entire structure is embedded in the overarching CCP network. A typical mechanism is the role of 'leading groups' on different levels of government which are orchestrated by the top Party secretary in the jurisdiction. These leading groups are separate from the government hierarchy and may gather important stakeholders of the jurisdiction, including the banks. The leading group discusses and fixes strategic development goals, and therefore sends strong signals to the stakeholder network of SOEs. The nature of this relationship varies also with the policy environment. If the central government aims at cooling down the economy, banks can assume a more active role, whereas in periods such as the fiscal stimulus after 2008, the banks return to their accommodating role. By implication, the SOE sector manifests a relatively weak controlling role of the investor function, since the state banks do not play the role of an investor. In other words, investors (the government agencies) can leverage their capital by putting pressure on the banks for extending loans to the SOEs, thus creating a relatively soft budget constraint; this pressure is mediated via the CCP network. At the same time, as

I have already analysed in Chapter 3, a unique feature of the Chinese economy is the large share of corporate savings in the national savings rate. This means that SOEs retain a relatively large share of profits, which further enhances their independence from external investors as controlling entities.

In the standard property rights analysis of the SOE, this would imply that productivity and efficiency declines because incentives for maximizing profits would be diluted. However, this picture needs modification, owing to the impact of the CCP nomenclature and the cadre evaluation system which focuses on the entrepreneurial function, as I have outlined above. That is, the nomenclature structured 'managerial market' would seem to incentivize leadership behaviour that works in the opposite direction. Success in managing an SOE may include a number of elements that go beyond the immediate goal of business performance, but, on the other hand, the early reform measures of 'factory director responsibility systems' have also morphed into performance-based salary systems for top-level management. These incentive systems would leverage the competitive dynamics resulting from the nomenclature system. This means that, in spite of the weakness of formal corporate governance structures, the network structures governing the behaviour of individuals who are in charge of strategic decision-making partly make up for this deficiency.[47]

Of course, as we have seen, these incentive effects can be partly counterbalanced by the network effects on the competitive environment of SOEs. This has been analysed as the emergence of SOEs as a lobby group with its own status in the Chinese political economy. This partly reflects the much larger entrepreneurial leeway, which necessarily also implies that incumbents of managerial positions will try to improve their performance via playing the relational card, such as getting preferential access to loans, essential inputs or land; we have also seen that this involves close interaction with the regulatory agencies which partly control the competitive environment. Accordingly, there are estimates that the true performance of SOEs in the 2000s was much worse than the official data suggest, if one were to assume equal conditions for the SOE and the non-SOE sector.[48] In the current context, what is of greater interest is the fact that in these lobbying activities there is an immediate impact of the nomenclature status order upon the interactions between top SOE executives and government officials in their larger context. We have already met the unique conditions in the urban land market that result from this. For example, the CEO of a central-level SOE (*yang qi*) may have a higher rank than a local mayor, thus enabling him to influence decisions about local urban development.

This also points to the fact that, apart from the banks, the single most important external stakeholder of SOEs is the local governments, independent from their role of owners, as is evident in the context of the land management system. Generally speaking, local governments have a stake because SOEs contribute to local economic activity, thus being conducive to the goal fulfilment of cadres and to the creation of jobs, independent from whether the SOE is also controlled by the local state. This does not mean that local governments simply adapt to the needs of SOEs. In fact, as we have seen above, since SOEs have been undergoing very comprehensive restructuring measures recently, local governments often aim at imposing constraints upon SOE decisions because they fear negative consequences for the local economy. Since SOEs are often larger than the average company, stakes can be high, especially in areas that are structurally dominated by certain industries.

Other stakeholders are almost non-existent, as these would emerge in a civil society which remains tightly suppressed in China today. One exception is the role of suppliers and customers in the local economy. As we have already seen, product safety and quality concerns is an area where civil society is allowed relatively free rein, so even SOEs have to heed attention to these issues; this increasingly also involves environmental issues. Many SOEs also play an important role in local supplier networks, so that there are private companies which have stakes in the SOE. Yet, all these stakeholders still have only a weak impact upon SOE decision-making compared with the other groups considered thus far.

If we summarize the observations so far, the conclusion is that the large majority of stakeholders in the Chinese economy are government units or government-related actors. Therefore, we can define 'state capitalism' as a market-based stakeholder economy with government units as dominant actors, which differs from financial capitalism where private investors operating mainly in the context of capital markets are dominant. This notion connects with the ritual economy, as the relationship between stakeholders is status based and mediated by the organization of the CCP. I argue that these developments are more important than the formal changes of the governance system in defining the SOE as a corporate unit. This relates to a more general observation about governance in China. In spite of the fact that the formal institutions of governance are well established today, the existing network structure does not fully support their implementation along the lines of the financial capitalist model. What is lacking is a network structure in the legal and accounting domain that is strong enough to represent the interests of non-governmental actors, who in the SOE context remain minority shareholders, independent from whether or not government-owned shares are tradable.[49]

So far, we have discussed the stakeholder system only with reference to SOEs. However, if we relate this notion also to the duality of local vs. central state, we need to consider the growing association between the central state and the SOE sector on the one hand, and the local state and the private sctor on the other hand. The most important phenomenon in this regard was the rise and decline of the TVE sector in the 1980s and 1990s which also played an important role as driver of SOE reforms owing to the increasing competition. Initially, the TVE sector was also a part of the public sector because the local state assumed a guiding position in both the entrepreneurial and the investment functions. However, the entrepreneurial function was embedded in local networks on the individual level, thus defining an important difference to SOEs. This meant that leadership positions in TVEs were partly occupied by local cadres, but increasingly also by entrepreneurial individuals without direct party or government affiliation. These individuals would draw mainly upon their personal networks in devising strategic trajectories of TVE development, partly in coordination with the local state. As we have seen in discussing the fiscal system, this growing autonomy of the TVE sector was given much leeway also by central-level authorities because they implemented an implicit tax-sharing contract with the local state. The local state might assume a larger role in funding local development based on local taxes, thus relieving strain on central budgets, because the local state is better informed about the conditions of local business. Hence, there were strong incentives in both developing the TVE sector and exploiting it for fiscal advantage.[50]

The privatization of the TVE sector in the late 1990s and 2000s mainly worked via MBO schemes. This meant that the local state underwent the transformation from an investor to a stakeholder. Evidently, the immediate driver of this development was the fiscal straits of local governments; but there was also the growing pressure of private business in rearranging and clarifying ownership rights, which thus far were only secured in a network of personal relations. Yet, the local state retained a strong role as stakeholder. In economics, this relationship is often modelled along the lines of the 'grabbing hand' vs. 'helping hand' paradigm; however, in the stakeholder approach both aspects may co-exist, though not without tension. This is because the local state is supportive of private business as it contributes to local development goals, but at the same time individuals and organizations in the local state also aim at reaping particularistic advantages from the private sector. We may also say that the local state as a stakeholder maintains implicit claims on residual profit, which is normally the hallmark of a shareholder. These conflicting motivations and goals are negotiated in continuous bargaining processes mediated via *guanxi* networks. Therefore, in the local state we may say that stakeholder relations are embedded in *guanxi* networks, whereas in the central state the CCP network is the primordial medium of embeddedness.[51]

Hence the rise of the private economy is not necessarily challenging the foundations of state capitalism in China, if we were to use that term. The notion of hybridization of ownership is less apt in capturing the essential aspect of stakeholder governance. Ideal typically, we can distinguish between central state stakeholder governance and local state stakeholder governance, with the former focusing on SOEs and the latter on private business. Hybridization of ownership refers mainly to the opening up of the investment function, but less so the entrepreneurial function. Partly, hybridization means that certain stakeholder relations are transformed into shareholder status.

Corporate culture and the cultural creativity of Chinese enterprise

In this section, I will explore in more detail the cultural dimensions of Chinese enterprise, beyond the distinction between different legal forms and patterns of corporate governance. This effort focuses largely on the topic of corporate culture. In studies of corporate culture, there are different defnitions and understandings of the term, especially with regard to two aspects. One is whether corporate culture is the outcome of intentional design, or whether it is predominantly beyond the reach of management interventions, largely belonging to the realm of 'tacit' knowledge; the other is how far corporate culture is a reflection of national culture, and vice versa. Both aspects are connected, as aspects of corporate culture that are not amenable to managerial interventions may root in national culture. These issues are extremely important in approaching management and corporate culture in China. Traditionally, research on Chinese enterprise has clearly emphasized the idea that there is a strong impact of national culture upon corporate culture, thus assuming an 'ideal type' of the Chinese corporation; that is, a sort of average in the diversity of organizational variants. This has been justified by referring to a shared pool of traditions and the common frame of the Chinese family. However, this research also emphasized the impact of cultural hybridization. This raises the question, however, of what the implications for the statistical distribution of variants are; for example, hybridization may result in a multi-peaked distribution, so that empirical research would actually end up refuting the single ideal-type approach of the 'Chinese capitalism' hypothesis.[52] In Mainland China, hybridization is driven by many forces, such as: the role of socialist institutions and the CCP in creating organizational routines; the import and application of 'Western' management theories; the variety of regional historical traditions in organizational behaviour, and so on. From that point of view, great care is warranted in searching for an ideal-typical model of the 'Chineseness' of corporate culture.[53]

In fact, managerial design is an important force in formulating corporate culture today, which creates special difficulties in determining an 'ideal-typical' type of corporate culture, because individual entrepreneurial initiative and vision are often very powerful, thus possibly overcoming forces of tradition and of the environment. In addition, many of the corporations that are seen today as outstanding examples of corporate culture are only two or three decades old, so certainly bear the mark of the founders' visions. As we will see, this can complicate the matter further, as many founders also refer explicitly to Chinese traditions, both historical and most recent, when describing and legitimizing their individual visions. So, the issue of corporate culture stays in the midst of the 'mirror of culture', as there is a plethora of contributions from all sides, including also the participating internal observers (i.e. the entrepreneurs), who create corporate culture in order to maintain control of organizations which manifest a similarly spectacular growth as China's economy, growing from micro-enterprises of a handful of people into globally operating transnational corporations.

Indeed, the concept of corporate culture is currently very fashionable in China. Almost every company includes a page on corporate culture in their profile. Remarkably, there is often a significant difference between the English version and the Chinese version of these pages. This difference suggests that reference to corporate culture is a serious matter, and that cultural differences are perceived explicitly. This can be the result of opportunistic adaptation in designing the English pages as addressing a global audience, but I think that this does not automatically also apply to the Chinese pages. Yet, there are also complex aspects of national and global marketing and brand building, such that, for example, a leading Chinese company may explicitly create a 'Western' image in the domestic market in order to suggest advanced standards of quality and service. In other words, we need to be very careful in distinguishing between corporate culture as a means of communication, often related to the need to create strong national and global brands, and factual corporate culture in management and organizational design. The problem is that accessing the latter is very difficult, especially in those cases where leaders have explicit ideas about corporate culture. The same practices can be evaluated very differently depending on the position of the observer, and direct empirical ascertainment may be difficult to obtain or may be elusive.[54]

In this regard, I want to mention one aspect that I will neglect in my further treatment, for reasons of space. This is the impact of foreign companies upon corporate culture in China. Clearly, foreign companies serve as a model, be this as leaders in their respective business areas, but also via the competition for talents, who increasingly judge employers in terms of their individual aspirations. In the current context I want only to point to one special aspect, which is the indigenization of Western corporate culture, partly via the necessary translation of Western concepts that I just considered for the Chinese case. Similar to the Chinese case, this happens already in the very first step when certain propositions about corporate culture are translated into Chinese and are being adapted to cultural contexts in this process. In the next step, this refers to the merger of organizational practices with Chinese conceptualizations of work, effort or commitment. In this case, interesting variations on similar themes may emerge, such as the pre-adaptation of what is an organization-specific corporate culture of the Western company to contexts which are more generic for China, in the sense of possibly relating to a national corporate culture. In these cases we may therefore say that Western corporate culture becomes embedded in the Chinese ritual economy.[55]

Cultural mergers on the level of corporate culture also occur in the cross-organizational domain, the most important of which is certainly the role of the CCP as an organizational template for other organizations, especially SOEs. We have already seen how organizational features of the *danwei* can continue to survive in the context of other organizational forms, thus also contributing to the emergence of distinct corporate cultures. These effects can be very straightforward if we consider the fact that, even in formally private business, leaders may also be members of the CCP, even long-time members if they emerged from *xiahai* activities, and are therefore familiar with the specific methods of the CCP in order to create commitment and loyalty on the part of its members. As we will see below, these methods are especially powerful in creating identification of individuals with the corporation.

In this context, it is also important that corporate culture is also a part of the civilizational efforts of the CCP. In fact, many uses of the term actually refer to the 'soft' enforcement of socialist ideology on corporate practices. But the CCP also officially endorses and expects the inclusion of traditional Chinese values in corporate culture. This is especially true for state-owned companies, which still retain political criteria in the internal evaluation of personnel. Then, corporate culture appears as a modernist adaptation of socialist ideological standards, and corporations obtain the role not only as business organizations, but also as a constituent unit of social order. For example, until today, SOEs implement personal evaluation systems which also include general ideological criteria as a priority consideration, partly combined with the assessment of commitment and loyality. On the other hand, these approaches indeed match the paternalistic leadership paradigm as the SOE is also expected to display care and concern for employees, also beyond the corporation. Again, there are modernist accounts of this, such as the CSR discourse. Therefore, we may argue that the impact of CCP organizational culture partly runs via the transfer of elements of corporate culture (images, routines and so on), and partly via the direct design along formats and models following the Party line.[56]

So, what is remarkable about Chinese management today is that the notion of 'culture' or related notions such as 'values' indeed play a pivotal role, for many, if different reasons. I want to submit the thesis that this focus on culture is another manifestation of the ritual economy. In other words, I argue that one aspect of Chinese management is ritualization as different from formalization in terms of establishing formal bureaucratic regimes of corporate integration. As we will see, this is evident in a number of characteristics, such as the strong role of charismatic leadership in many of the most successful enterprises, which goes hand in hand with continuous efforts of restructuring the organization, thus implementing a regime of constant organizational change. In this regime, ritual is an important determinant of keeping the identity of the organization.

The 'mirror of culture' is omnipresent here, because there is also a strong movement towards the 'indigenization' (*bentuhua*) of Chinese management, which is by no means only taking place in Mainland China, but has been on the agenda in other Chinese contexts for many years. Indigenization is a fuzzy topic, since we already have a range of approaches, partly simply meaning to relate modern management to ancient Chinese philosophies (as in the case of the literature on strategy following Sun Zi filling bookshelves, also rich and fashionable in Western languages), partly also meaning to propose creative adaptations of Western management theories, which are, after all, also a highly diverse bunch of approaches, especially if we include the more practical versions that directly address management practitioners. All these different contributions are widely read in China, thus shaping the ongoing discourse about corporate culture. They also relate to the fundamental issue of defining 'Chineseness' across political borders. Included in these contributions is a list of main features of indigenous management that evidently reflects the conceptual frame of ritual, such as with the emphasis on moral leadership, the use of culture as a means of organizational integration and incentivization, or humanism, in the sense of emphasizing interpersonal relations and their role in individual gratification and recognition. These concepts are often condensed into specific Chinese terms, such as 'harmony', 'hexie' (和谐), 'sincerity', 'chengxin' (诚信) or 'perseverance under stress', 'chiku' (吃苦).[57]

To this, we might add the observation that slowly, but increasingly, Western management pundits are also discovering China as an independent intellectual domain of management theories, thus possibly repeating the history of the reception of Japanese management in the West, where we observed a similar complex interaction between Western and Japanese views and practices, which was reflected upon in constructing new theories about Japanese management. A driver of all these developments, as in the earlier Japanese case, is the perception of success, both in terms of China's economic performance in general, but also in terms of the growing global presence and visibility of leading Chinese corporations. A telling paradox in these developments are cases such as Huawei which is sold in the media as one of the lead examples of managerial success of a technology company which is a formally private business and partly shrouded in secrets; in fact, its transformation into a world leader in telecommunications technology was accompanied by a long-term consultancy by IBM and other Western consultants. Yet, in the Chinese discourse and also in the self-portrayals of the company, its 'Chineseness' is clearly emphasized.[58]

My major interest in this section, however, does not reside in these aspects but raises the question of how far corporate culture today may be interpreted as another manifestation of ritual. This is salient when the

CCP views corporate culture as an element in social order, and hence sees the nurturing of particular values in the company as a 'corporate social responsibility'. Accordingly, however, this 'ritual' may also appear to be mere window-dressing. At first sight this would lead us back to the 'Confucian' view of Chinese corporate culture, which is also immanent to the paternalistic leadership theories we have already scrutinized. However, considering the breadth of the meaning of 'ritual' as deployed in this book, this would obviously lead us astray. In order to highlight this point, I begin with one observation that is also familiar to many observers of the Chinese scene, namely the phenomenon of extremely tight and harsh labour discipline that may be observed in many Chinese companies. In the section on the family I argued that the family is still an organizational template for companies in China, which would certainly count as a very 'traditional' reference. However, this statement stays in stark contrast with organizational practices in many companies that are often referred to as 'militarization', 'junshihua' (军事化), and which have even attracted much attention of civil rights activists worldwide who criticize labour conditions in China, especially in the supply chains that have been built by multinational companies such as Apple or Walmart.

Militarization refers to the extremely tight discipline and supervision in these companies. What appears to be the provisioning of social services in the paternalistic paradigm can actually be an almost totalitarian means of control in the militaristic framework. This refers in particular to the organization of dormitories, with glaring examples such as the Taiwanese company Foxconn. These dormitories are not only crowded, but systematically apply organizational means to suppress private communications among workers, explicitly targeting subversive *guanxi* mechanisms. For example, workers from the same native area are not allowed to share rooms and are even assigned to different shifts in order to contain the buildup of collective capacities for action. The extreme psychological pressure resulting from isolation and loneliness in an anonymous crowd of workers toiling under a harsh labour regime typically results in many dysfunctional phenomena, even a high rate of suicides among workers.[59]

It is hard to reconcile these phenomena with 'benevolence' in the paternalistic leadership style; yet we may also argue that there is a direct link with ritual understood in the sense of a historical legacy. These management styles have to be seen against the background of the cultural dualism between Legalism and Confucianism in Chinese civilizational history. These two traditions reflect two opposing views on human nature, with Legalism adopting a pessimistic view of opportunism, egoism and amorality. Therefore, the Legalist view emphasizes the need for strict authoritarian discipline and reliance on detailed systems of supervision and punishment in order to achieve social cooperation. This philosophical stance is evidently reflected in the two organizational ideal types that may emerge from considering organizational practices in China. The so-called

'Confucian' enterprise co-exists with the 'Legalist' enterprise, and in fact, the former often absorbs many practices of the latter.

The Legalist organizational culture is most salient in the context of the employment of migrant workers, where it is also often justified by referring to civilizational drawbacks of the rural population, epitomized in a low assignment of *suzhi*. So, behavioural deficiencies are seen as being healed by often minute surveillance, such as the strict ordering of queues or tight management of schedules for toilet use, etc. Interestingly, the issue of militarization was raised early in Taiwan when considering the practices of Taiwan-invested companies in Mainland China, where similar arguments were made. So, we may generalize that Legalist organizational culture is a response to cultural cleavages in the workforce, such as distinctions of origin or social status in terms of rural vs. urban. In other words, there is a strong impact of in-group/out-group borders which are not mediated by the fact of shared organizational membership. These cleavages are also reflected in formal organizational structures. For example, the migrant workforce is largely employed in a different contractual status than the regular urban workforce, only with temporary contracts that do not provide formal access to special fringe benefits that the urban or local workforce enjoys. This may even be manifest in spatial separation, with very different working conditions for the two groups in different buildings. Thus, the societal status order is also reflected in the architectural and organizational design of the company. So, I posit that the dualism of organizational cultures is also an expression of the modernist status order in China's ritual economy.[60]

This interpretation is complex in the mirror of culture, as, right from the beginning, the tension between Confucianism and Legalism was also a tension between 'modernity' and 'tradition'. Confucian teachings explicitly defined themselves as a revival of traditional virtues, looking at the past for model states; Legalist teachings served as a philosophical legitimation of the totalitarian efforts of the First Emperor of China, which included a wide range of modernizing ventures, such as standardization or the buildup of a bureaucracy independent from traditional bondings. In fact, considering the historical legacy of China, the early Empire may be duly regarded as one step towards the creation of a modern state, and it is partly the Legalist legacy which effectively attracted the attention of Western observers under the *ancien régime* (which, however, was perceived and interpreted through the Confucian lenses provided by the scholar-officials with whom the Western visitors and travellers actually conversed). In this sense, the Legalist tradition also provides the ground for the modernist worldview of the present.

In this dualist view on organizational culture, Confucianism appears as the counter-pole to Legalism. However, in considering the philosophical roots of modern organizational culture, reference to Daoism is absolutely necessary. Whereas Legalism is mostly not mentioned explicitly as a background for militaristic management practices, Daoism plays an explicit role as a component of management philosophy in China today. This is important also against the backdrop that we may duly regard Daoism as that philosophical position which comes closest to basic values and beliefs in traditional Chinese popular culture. Whereas Confucianism and Legalism are clearly philosophies of leadership and governance, Daoism is a more comprehensive worldview which is deeply ingrained in many practical areas, such as food culture, medicine or the arts.

In distinguishing these different ideational sources of corporate culture, it is interesting to note that some indigenous observers refer them to geographic diversity across China, which also reflect differences in the expressions of traditional ideologies. These differences partly overlap with the differences in economic structure, however. For example, the salience of the Legalist organizational pattern in Guangdong may be related both to the fact that migrant workers are by far the largest share of the workforce, and that Neoconfucian orthodoxy had a strong impact upon lineage authority in the past, together with a long tradition of village self-defence in what was once a frontier region, also with sub-ethnic divisions (such as the Hakka population, who indeed were famous for military prowess). In indigenous conceptualizations, Daoism is mostly connected to private business of the Yangzi region, in particular Zhejiang province. A most common metaphor taken from the Daoist classic *Dao De Jing* is to compare Daoist management with properties of water: water is very flexible, yet hard in case of shocks, water permeates everything without being assertive, water is transparent, hence honest, and water is also supportive in relations with others. In indigenous views, this is the way in which private businesspeople can succeed, keeping low-key appearances but actually expanding their business worldwide; the Wenzhou business culture is seen as a case in point.[61] Yet, today, Daoism is mostly promoted as a universal ingredient of modern management philosophy in China. If we try to explain this against the background of more general considerations about Chinese values and practices, two points seem to be especially salient.

The first is that Daoism does not favour direct intervention into processes and rigid constructivistic design. Daoism even limits the scope for authoritarian leadership, as it emphasizes 'softness' and strategic thinking, as well as the ideal state of 'doing nothing', 'wu wei' (无为). This means that, in pursuing goals, a leader should concentrate on shaping the context of other relevant decision-makers without directly trying to intervene in their choices, such that their decisions also conform to those goals. One specific expression of this thinking is that management practices are adopted which establish direct connections between organizational units and the market, with short cuts in the organizational decision-making that directly align lower level decisions with the general goals of the company. This approach also matches external strategies of the company, which also emphasize the contextualization of measures taking local and global forces of change into consideration. I discuss this aspect in more detail below.

The second point is the active adoption of opposites in management, which is today even referred to explicitly as 'Yin–Yang' management in English-language research about Chinese management. This can be expressed in direct citations of classics such as the divination framework and inspires attempts at organizing the company in terms of polar opposites which, however, are expected to complement each other in their interaction. Again, this kind of Yin–Yang management also has strategic implications, since, for example, it implies that it is easier to combine apparently conflicting strategies (such as cost versus innovation leadership) in designing a flexible strategy. In this sense, Yin–Yang management has also recently been promoted as an alternative approach to management that is based on a distinct logic enshrined in the Chinese classics and representing a distinct cognitive style.[62]

Indeed, when considering Daoism, it is highly significant to relate this with the psychological and cognitive science approaches to field-dependent cognition discussed in Chapter 1. Here, what matter especially are the results regarding behaviour towards risk and uncertainty. Chinese subjects tend to give more accurate predictions of regression to the mean processes, such as in financial markets. Especially in the advent of adverse conditions, they tend to be more optimistic because they expect trend reversals that are already inhering in the current situation. In this sense, the Yin–Yang paradigm would be seen as reflecting the capability to recognize forces engendering the opposite in any kind of polar situation. Further, Chinese subjects also manifest different patterns of causal attribution. In particular, they emphasize contextual determinants in opposition to individual agency. So, the general feature of field-dependent cognition is directly reflected in empirically observable behavioural patterns.[63] Therefore, we can approach Daoism-inspired management theories also as explicit conceptualizations of these underlying cognitive structures. This particularly applies to the notion of 'shi' (势), which refers to contextual forces of developments across human and natural settings. This concept is also central to Sun Zi's military stratagems and means that decision-makers should observe the complex interplay of forces in order to determine, for example, the right time for action, and that they should try to influence these forces through appropriate actions.[64]

It is straightforward to recognize a fundamental principle of Chinese 'pragmatism' here, which may be seen as a more general aspect of Chinese ways of coping with challenges. This applies to the political domain as well, as the analysis of experimentalism and localism showed. The idea that successful action needs to be grounded in locally efficacious, confluent forces is a central notion in Chinese popular religion. So, we can treat this as a generic feature of not only corporate but also organizational culture in China, which bridges different domains, in particular the political and the economic. In the context of corporate culture, as I have noted, this creates a peculiar penchant to focus on market dynamics in order to implement strategies of organizational design.[65]

The distinct approach of Chinese companies to integrate market and organizational structure deserves attention in the context of the general analysis of ritual, for two reasons. One is that it questions the standard model of organizational hierarchy; the other that it emphasizes the role of the individual in organizational practices and dynamics. The former reason points towards the classical observation of the 'slim' pattern of Chinese family business with regard to the proportion of staff versus line personnel. This pattern has recently been pursued by Chinese companies explicitly, with the foremost example of the global leader in white goods, Haier Corporation.

As I mentioned previously, the focus on individual companies may fail to catch the average, which is certainly risky in this case, because of the towering role of the founder of Haier, Zhang Ruimin. Yet, on the other hand, cases like this are extremely influential in shaping the organizational strategies of other Chinese companies. So, let us look briefly at its main features, first of all noticing that the case also deserves attention as the founder explicitly claims to apply Daoist philosophy to management, thus illustrating what is treated as a hypothesis about background forces here, namely that there is an impact of ideas upon corporate culture. The first observation about Haier is that the corporation is undergoing a 'continuous revolution' of its organization throughout the time of its existence, thus recurrently disrupting organizational structure. The central idea in the most recent approach adopted in 2006 is minimizing the role of middle management in the company and implementing a fluid system of self-managing groups, the so-called 'zizhu jingjing ti' (自主经营体). In 2012, Haier Corporation consisted of 2233 units with an average number of members of 36, and a range of variations reaching from only one person to several dozen. Simultaneously, the company was divided into three levels: 'first line', 'yixian jingjingti' (线经营体), 'platform', 'pingtai jingyingti' (平台经营体) and 'strategy', 'zhanlüe jingyingti' (战略经营体) in order to minimize hierarchical structure, also abolishing completely the structure of fixed organizational positions. So, for example, platform units may provide 'accounting services' to first-line units.

This approach builds on earlier waves of organizational design which, among other measures, implemented a decentralized system of internal accounting by which every employee would have access to a personal data file that directly shows her daily contribution to the performance of her unit and of the entire company; correspondingly, she would also see how her flexible salary and bonuses would adapt to these performance data. Right from the beginning, the declared goal of this system was to enlarge the scope of individual decision-making in the company, later condensed into the slogan that 'Everyone is a CEO'. This was not interpreted as a system of tight individual control, but aimed at establishing a direct line of communication between the market and the employees most directly involved in creating the value of the company. Therefore, it was only consequential to extend the system in also redesigning the higher level of tasks in the company. This happened via the installation of 'self-organizing units' on different levels, from the shop-floor to top management. These units are defined as task-based, and leaders are selected in a company-wide call for applications; the leaders may in turn recruit their team members autonomously. This even includes the breakdown of corporate borders, because team leaders can also decide to outsource tasks and to conclude contracts with outside personnel.[66]

It is straightforward to see Daoist management philosophy at work here, as the general idea is minimizing hierarchical interference in what is basically a self-organized structure of local subsystems that would directly adapt and respond to the market. This is what is most expressively pursued by the founder and leader Zhang Ruimin, often with radical propositions. So, the claim is made that the system abolishes the leadership function as such, since the entire internal organization is based on a fluid structure of entrepreneurial units that build their relations via internal contracting. In this sense, the market becomes the overarching paradigm for corporate design. This ties up with the idea that a direct link should be established between customers and the elementary production units, also involving ideas that customers may become involved also as creators of products. That being said, at the same time we need to take note of the fact that, up until today, the founder of Haier has been directly involved in managing the company, with iron rules such as a weekly meeting with executives and invited participants from the grassroots level which aim at providing guidance to the organization down to the lowest level. This is certainly an example of charismatic leadership, but also includes a strong dose of Legalism, since the accounting system imposes a very tough discipline upon employees, with real threats of demotion or dismissal.

Indeed, interpreting the Haier system is ambivalent in the mirror of culture. On the one hand, the system seems to extend individual control in an extreme version of digital Taylorism, since the whole range of technological possibilities of modern information technology is exploited. On the other hand, in the Chinese discourse the system is hailed as a sort of ultimate liberation of the employee who would resume full control of herself as an intra-organizational entrepreneur.[67] This raises the interesting question of how far these management approaches may also be interpreted as an expression of individualism.

In this context, it is significant to observe that the combination of tight discipline and the appeal to individualistic notions often seems to be made in Chinese management discourses and practices. This largely happens in emphasizing the correspondence between individual freedom of action and responsibility, thus indeed activating Confucian legacies of thought. What emerges is the impression that individualistic notions are mobilized together with a strong emphasis on loyalty and sacrifice to the goals of the corporation. One famous metaphor that mirrors this linkage is the figure of the 'wolf'. Wolves have become a very loaded image of the combination of individualism and cooperation in the group, driven by a natural instinct for hunting. This combines with the idea that the task of management is also to transform the individuals, thus seeing strict organizational discipline as an aspect of an educational process by which the true potential of the individual may be actualized. We have noted this apparently paradoxical relationship between strict educational discipline and individualization also in other contexts, such as educational practices directed at migrant children.[68]

In this context, there is also a bridge to the widespread reference to Mao Zedong and Maoism in current management practices. One conspicuous example is the idea that individual progress has to be achieved through continuous critical reflection and public rituals of self-criticism. As I mentioned previously, these practices may in turn relate to similar practices of confessions in popular religion, especially in Daoism, thus representing a complex amalgam of tradition and different layers of modern developments. Yet, this idea also lends a particular twist to the notion of the individual, because it appears to be universally malleable according to the goals of the organization, if on its own free will. The mixture of Maoist and other traditional spiritual resources results in a strong moral dimension of leadership, thus also reinstating certain principles of the ideal-typical model of paternalistic leadership. A similar oscillation of traditional references and modern transmutations relates to managerial practices such as campaigns, which have been identified early as an ingredient of Chinese management practices. In Mainland China today, campaign-style management is often related to Maoist leadership techniques, yet we may also say that campaigns are an organizational means to contextualize individual and collective decisions in 'unfreezing' organizational structures, thus apparently being related to two different kinds of managerial leadership: one to implement organizational change, the other to create a corporate identity and impose this upon its employees.[69]

The issue of identity is of special interest here, as it relates to the distinction between the two forms of collectivism: relational and categorial. Corporate culture in China is emerging as a process that seems to create stronger behavioural foundations for categorial collectivism. This is most obvious in the more advanced technology companies, which represent the spearhead of corporate modernism in China. A typical feature of these companies is the very strong emphasis on corporate identity and a very rigorous internal screening of performance and behaviour in order to sort out employees with different degrees of individual commitment to the company.[70] In this sense, we may indeed speak of the mobilization of ritual means in order to integrate corporations that, on the other hand, pursue systematic strategies of decentralization and opening up organizational borders. This is also evident in the widespread explicit use of lists of criteria about proper attitudes and behaviour of employees, which are often communicated through corporate rituals. This results in the thesis that the tension between individualization and discipline is another expression of the phenomenon of 'ritual labour' that I introduced previously. Observing tight work disciplines is an expression of the sincerity of one's identification with the corporation, and is therefore also an expressive means.

In concluding this section, we realize that corporate culture obtains a similar role as in international comparative contexts of management: corporate culture is a means of organizational integration. In this sense, it is a ritual both in China and in other countries, so that we meet another generic ritualistic phenomenon. There are aspects that are specific to China which partly reflect the impact of ideas upon designing corporate culture, such as when traditional philosophies indeed inspire organizational design. However, there is also the question of how far corporate culture as a ritual also reflects more fundamental patterns of business organization in China, with the most central one being the relationship between networks and organization. I have discussed whether corporate culture may be a means to strengthen categorial collectivism in corporate organization, thus also defining more rigid and clearly identifiable borders between networks and organization, eventually turning the enterprise into a corporation. But this is by no means unequivocal when we consider actual practices. For example, corporate culture in SOEs clearly supports the stakeholder governance structures, as the SOE may adopt values that also open up channels of influence for the CCP network under the umbrella of CSR measures. On the other hand, in Chinese family business, corporate culture may indeed define an independent existence of the corporation relative to the family as the owner. Yet, in spite of these ambiguities, the fundamental point remains that corporate culture is emerging as an element of ritual in contemporary Chinese society.

One phenomenon that literally embodies this trend is the increasing permeability of borders between business networks and political networks, with many business leaders assuming positions in political organizations. This is a standard pattern in the career trajectories of higher ranked Party members, with SOE executives moving into provincial government, for example, but may also be observed at the grassroots level, where local businessmen may be assigned to the role of Party secretaries, with extreme cases where in fact the business organization 'overtakes' local structures. However, extremity does not imply rarity here. In fact, in the course of rural industrialization many entrepreneurs gradually turn into community leaders, especially if they follow the paternalistic model, which translates into assuming many functions in providing social services to employees, which may represent a majority of the local population anyway. In these cases, corporate culture and community culture merge. These role metamorphoses actually reflect the unity of ritual across social domains.[71]

Theoretical reprise

One core observation of this chapter is that market governmentality includes the role of business organizations. We can see this in the light of two different perspectives. One is the role of organizations in shaping markets, in the sense of modularization as a typical pattern. The other is the contribution of business organizations to the distinct Chinese form of governmentality in society. In my theoretical reprise I begin with the second point. This contribution is most directly visible in the role of corporations in governing the migrant population, especially in regions such as the Pearl River Delta. The specific amalgam of paternalistic leadership and Legalistic practices has emerged also as a frame for subjecting the migrant population to a form of para-governmental governance mechanisms, embodied, for example, in the separate compounds of factory dormitories, and realized via draconic forms of superveillance even reaching into the private lives of migrant workers.[72] However, there are many other aspects of which we can say that corporate organization has become a distinct setting for societal governance in the context of modernism.

I have already discussed the ritual aspects of professionalism in Chapter 3. The carriers of this culture of professionalism are mainly the business corporations which implement and enforce these standards. This is a domain with strong cross-cultural interactions, since most of those standards orginated in Western countries. This not only applies directly to HR systems, but also works via modern concepts of corporate identity and branding that also have implications for the behavioural standards to be applied within the organizations. Yet, as we have seen, these cross-cultural interactions by no means imply that the Chinese corporations simply adopt Western models. We can observe two channels by which hybridization, mergers and transformations proceed. One is the role of path dependencies, which is most explicit in the domain of private businesses emerging in the rural areas, largely taking the shape of owner-managed firms with a strong familistic orientation, also partly morphing into genuine family businesses. The other is the role of organizational design, which aims at creating corporate cultures which in turn are being influenced by ideas that tie up with Chinese intellectual and spiritual traditions. In this case we also considered more deep-structural influences of fundamental cognitive structures, such a field dependence and modularization.

With regard to societal governmentality, we may surmise that business organization becomes an important carrier of ritual. For example, in the family business, paternalistic leadership not only follows ritual precepts such as reciprocity and benevolence in the leader–follower relation, but also enforces ritual in activating traditional ideas in family-centred management. There are many examples of family businesses where leaders actually conceive of the company as a 'mini-state' where governing employees is seen as a civilizational process, partly even undergirded by adopting traditional rituals. These interactions are particularly important in many local states, such as when successful corporations also play a leading role in developing their local communities, also known from the patterns of 'factory towns' in European industrialization. Theoretically, this implies complex interactions among the company, the social environment and the local state. If we employ the notion of social capital here, we can say that the company evolves into social capital of the community, in the sense of representing developmental potential and a force of social order, but also community embeddedness turns into social capital of the entrepreneur, mediated via social networks among him, his close supporters and the political networks of the local state. I have already discussed the CCP policy of co-optation in Chapter 5; in the current context, this means that the societal status order also counts for emerging identities of entrepreneurs and their companies. Typically, this is being mediated in organizational forms such as leading roles in state-sponsored local business associations or membership in local political bodies. Ideal typically, the entrepreneur becomes a moral exemplar in the community, thus combining business success with local leadership.

By implication, private business beyond a certain size becomes part and parcel of the social order of the local state, thus evolving into a complement of SOEs on the central level. So, the theoretical notion of social capital also allows for a conceptual grounding of the stakeholder model of corporate governance that applies mainly to SOEs but may also encompass certain segments of private business. Certainly, these interactions can assume many different shapes, being embedded in the *guanxi* network structures, thus reaching from moral exemplar to corrupt impact. Thus, considering the diversity of local states in China in particular, the interaction between business and politics is of crucial significance in defining different types of social order, both functioning and legitimate or malfunctioning and illegitimate. Yet, we can conceive both as expressions of ritual in its different shapes.

So, in sum, I argue that the general hypothesis that markets are an integral part of governmentality in the ritual economy may be further detailed in approaching the Chinese enterprise as a pivotal element in reproducing this pattern. This extends to earlier conceptualizations of Chinese business in the literature on the Overseas Chinese. In this literature, the company is seen as an encompassing way of life for Chinese entrepreneurial families. In comparison to these diaspora settings which are defined by political exclusion, in Mainland China the political order gears this comprehensive form of life also towards a form of social order. There are many ramifications of this theme, which include the role of business in the larger project of modernism and national revival, which consequently means that successful business also has a political dimension. This applies to SOEs anyway, but also to many large-scale private businesses. What is CSR in modern parlance is the obligation of business to contribute to fulfilling the 'China dream' of achieving modernity and national greatness. So, modern ritual continues to represent the primacy of the political in creating social order, thus obviating ideas of separating different domains of society, in particular the economy.

Turning to the other aspect of market governmentality, the basic observation is about the primacy of networks as embedding both markets and organizations. In the context of modern internet technology, the idea of the breakdown of traditional concepts of corporate organization, especially corporate boundaries, has long been discussed. In China, these developments are also taking place in technology-intensive firms. Yet, I suggest also aspects that reflect the importance of determinants specific to the Chinese context. If we combine the results of the last two chapters, we can say that two forces work together in creating new forms of corporate organization. One force is the modularization of markets, which works via the creation of more stable network structures, reaching from loose supplier relations to more integrated schemes, such as in some models of 'dragon head companies'. The other is the many projects of corporate re-engineering that aim at endogenizing markets in the company, thus redesigning organizational structures along the lines of market relations. Evidently, both forces work together in creating a network-based corporate structure.

In this network structure, identity plays an important role in order to maintain a minimum level of integration. Here, I surmise that the general logic of *guanxi* applies in different shapes. This is partly a hypothesis that waits for further empirical confirmation. Yet, as we have seen, the *guanxi* logic creates special conditions for network formation in private business, such as when employees set up their own companies and maintain supplier relations with their original company, also having received a start-up loan or other forms of support. Here, long-term reciprocity in *guanxi* relations undergirds market transactions. The shared identity is emerging in these ongoing interactions, and it is not necessarily visible also in corporate identities such as brands. On the other hand, in tighter integrated corporate structures that move towards network organization, identity is an essential ingredient of designing corporate culture as a medium of integration. I argue that all these different shapes may be summarized as being expressions and uses of ritual in network organization.

In this context, it may be significant that in creating corporate cultures, the issue of 'Chineseness' looms large. So, this topic is deeply shaped by the 'mirror of culture', which creates enormous difficulties for empirical research. The field of Chinese management sciences is exploding, but there is widespread disagreement as to how far established management theories can adopt an etic stance, thus just transferring established 'Western' knowledge to the Chinese case, or whether there is the necessity to develop emic – that is, indigenous –approaches. This problem is further complicated because the business leaders themselves are often very active in developing their own syntheses of Western management teachings and Chinese traditions. These difficulties reiterate similar conundrums with earlier notions of 'Chineseness' in Overseas Chinese business organization. One possible reaction to this reinstates arguments raised in these earlier debates that simply look at 'Chineseness' as a means to obfuscate generic relations of power and market logic. However, this would certainly underestimate the role of cultural creativity in many cases where entrepreneurs indeed create new organizational models and 'make sense' of their business endeavours. Further, as a matter of fact, Western research also struggles with the meaning and empirical significance of even the most basic notions such as *guanxi.* Therefore, following my methodological precepts as developed in Chapter 1, I think that there is no way to escape from the 'mirror of culture'.

However, as we have seen in Chapter 2, there is an anchor for understanding the particular forces of network dynamics, as social networks are always interrelated with material networks, such as technological networks or infrastructural networks. This interaction was essential in explaining the decline and absence of large-scale complex organization in the traditional ritual economy. Since, for many reasons, we can argue that the instability of the corporation remained a feature of the Chinese economy until most recent times, we also need to consider the role of technology today.

As we have seen, the thesis of the primacy of the enterprise as a network organization is apparently still vindicated today. First, the most prominent form of stable corporate organization is the SOE. However, the SOE is also an epiphenomenon of the underlying multi-layered networks of individuals, government organizations and the CCP. This is immediately evident from the ease by which corporate restructuring can take place. In the past, this was mainly done in the context of reforms, thus apparently suggesting that the instability of the SOE as a corporate structure is mainly an expression of short- and medium-term policy initiatives. However, in my view this is a more permanent feature that results from the primacy of the network structures. In terms of ritual and economic style, the central phenomenon is the role of the CCP as the carrier of the strategic function, even dominating the investment function that undergirds the regional property rights structure.

Second, China is currently facing an economy-wide crisis of transition in family business. The question is how far private business in the owner-managed firm is just an entrepreneurial project driven by individual aspirations in social networks, or whether the resulting companies also obtain a corporate identity, thus actually emerging as an element in the social ontology in which traditional conceptions of the family are conceived. These issues are of immense practical relevance, as they influence, for example, the decisions of entrepreneurs about investing in research and development, new products and so on.

Now, it is important to realize that the Chinese development is strongly interacting with technological transformations that are currently taking place worldwide. We have seen that the emergence of global value chains also contributed to the resilience of commercial capitalism in China. Most recently, the pervasive role of the internet also in technologically transforming traditional sectors such as manufacturing actually undergirds the network organization of Chinese business. In other words, taking theoretical perspectives of the Actor–Network paradigm, there is a pre-adaptation between Chinese networks and emerging technological patterns in the global economy. One reference term is the notion of 'platforms' (such as in the notion of 'platform capitalism'), which neatly corresponds with my concept of modularization in the Chinese context. This potential pre-adaptation implies that we have to reconsider the standard model of economic or market involution. The central point in this thesis was that the Chinese ritual economy could not develop organizational structures out of endogenous market dynamics that would allow for the emergence of modern technology, thus ultimately failing to increase productivity in the long run. However, with the radically changing technological structures today, this argument may no longer hold. For example, platforms allow the organization of a large number of free-standing small-scale business units into one large corporate network with a strong brand and certain measures of integration. In Western countries, many observers look critically at these developments as they dissolve traditional forms of labour relations, actually reinstating the entrepreneurial role of the individual or the family. Clearly, the informal economy of China is easily adaptable to these conditions of platform capitalism. By implication, modern technology can resolve the dilemma of market involution while at the same time possibly reinforcing the role of traditional social structures in business organization.

Hence, I claim that the ritual economy may emerge as a competitive economic style in the context of most advanced forms of technology-mediated business. This possibility is already visible in the tremendous success of Chinese high-tech companies in global competition. This would imply that the historical failure of China to industrialize endogenously was actually the manifestation of a contingent mismatch between the ritual economy and technology at that time, with technological structures such as the steam engine or, more generally, centralized devices of power generation, also fostering what has been called the 'Fordist' regime of production. Today, internet-based technological transformations seem to create a match with the ritual economy, thus reinstating its relevance for constructing Chinese modernity.

Notes

1 For a critique of the standard approaches, see Wang Jiangyu (2014). Wang also points to the fact that the Chinese government even recommends these interpretations to international organizations, such as when endorsing the OECD Principles of Corporate Governance and also producing self-assessments on these terms. This creates the impression that China is in a process of 'transition' to these mainstream models. Accepting this interpretation means that one does not explore the question of why the Chinese government adopts this stance at all, given the undeniable fact that in CCP concepts of corporate governance the leading role of the party remains a pivotal principle. So, the question is still open as to what the real function of modern corporate forms actually is. As an example of this analytical bias, see the otherwise well-informed analysis by Clarke (2010).

2 For a survey on this aspect of social network analysis, see Carroll and Sapinski (2011). For example, for different 'varieties of capitalism' a shared feature is the role of board members in connecting up to a managerial elite that defines a power structure in the economy which transcends formal corporate structures. Overlapping directorates can be analysed by SNA tools in order to identify groups or even individuals with an especially strong position. The connection with analysing the role of the CCP in China may be to consider the role of networking platforms in Western economies, such as business associations, clubs or service organizations, as meeting grounds for networking. From that viewpoint, the CCP would be seen as an extraordinarily strong platform for organizing networks of corporate elites. Status considerations play a very important role in organizing corporate structures in Western countries, such as the involvement of investment banks in M&A procedures, which directly match partners of a particular status, or in the organization of closer cooperation networks (see Podolny 2005).

3 For a concise survey of the literature and an application to China, see Conlé (2015). This research also implies a much stronger emphasis on micro-level analysis and case studies, in the sense that over-generalizations are avoided that may often also be found in the 'varieties of capitalism' research (see Zhang and Peck 2014). Architectural analysis focuses on the interaction between firm organization and market organization, such as the question of whether certain production processes are organized in large and closed corporate systems, or whether they are decentralized and without fixed organizational borders. Seen in the context of the larger institutional setting, these structures also have implications for the interaction between government and market actors.

4 Redding and Witt (2008) argue that the Chinese economy may be characterized by the fundamental dualism between private and public sector. I think that this obfuscates the interaction and often intermingling of the two. On the problems of Chinese private sector statistics, see Rühle (2012: 298ff.). Especially for earlier decades estimates vary widely, for example, because many private businesses were camouflaged under the 'red hat' of collective entreprises. Yet, this camouflage also means that local governments might co-opt the private businesses, and so may also be seen as forms of network hybridization, as I argue below. Today, many statistical categories do not cover the entire private sector, because they may exclude companies below five million RMB turnover. Further, the group of 'ge ti hu' (i.e. companies with fewer than eight employees) is also often omitted. On the other hand, Huang (2008: 166ff.) points to the role of cross-shareholdings in larger corporate structures which may also distort our view of corporate types in terms of factual control. For the data mentioned about the proportions, see *China Statistical Yearbook* (2013: 121, 473), where we can also

add the data on employment for all sectors which confirm the picture for industry, where I considered capital stock. In terms of capital stock, private business only accounts for a share of approximately 20 per cent.

5 On these arguments, see my previous discussion in Chapter 2. Another factor is the specific interaction between technological development and corporatization in organizational terms which may have created path dependencies in the Western context. The centralization of energy generation by the steam engine favoured highly integrated organizational forms, compared to the labour-intensive technologies prevailing in China. Further, the invention of standardized mass production in US weapons manufacturing also strengthened this kind of organization, independent from the existing legal forms. Interestingly, these differences were also interpreted in another way by modern Marxist scholars who emphasized the resulting potential for the deskilling of workers. Deskilling shifts the power balance between capitalists and workers and so further strengthens the organizational form, in this view as an aspect of organizing social power.

6 In Chinese studies these phenomena are called the 'Kirby puzzle' (on the contemporary relevance of this historical analysis, see Goetzmann and Köll 2004). In his seminal paper, Kirby (1995) studied the observation that in spite of much legal progress in corporate law, the Chinese business sector failed to respond to these institutional innovations. Interestingly, Chinese political leaders seemed to share the opinion of modern institutional economists, arguing that the lack of legal instruments impeded the modernization of Chinese enterprise, so that the first Company Law was promulgated in Imperial times, on 21 January 1904, the 'gongsi lü' (公司律). After that, there was continuous legal progress, with detailed regulations following in 1914, adapting the German Commercial Law, and then a new Company Law of Republican China in 1929. The 'New Company Law' of 1946 introduced special categories for state-owned and foreign-invested companies, thus already reflecting the fact that the law was almost exclusively used in these contexts. In the PRC this law was annulled, yet the term 'corporation', *gongsi*, was only used for these two separate categories. According to Kirby, there were 1.3 million private companies in China in 1949, of which more than 99 per cent did not use the legal forms of the Company Law but operated as a family business of partnerships, 'hehuo' (合伙). This has to be seen against the background of the technological structure; in spite of ongoing industrialization, about 75 per cent of industry remained organized as 'traditional handicrafts' (Feuerwerker 1983: 50ff.). In particular, rural sideline production remained competitive until the 1930s in many branches (Feuerwerker 1980: 15ff.; Richardson 1999: 59ff.). The reasons for this delay of legal modernization are manifold, with many authors emphasizing mainstream arguments, especially on the dismal state of the fiscal system and corruption (see Bowen II and Rose 1998).

7 These structures have been studied in detail by Numazaki (1996). An illustrative case study is Uni-President Enterprises Corporation, which is today the biggest conglomerate in food industry in Asia. It was founded half a century ago as a member of the so-called Tainan clique, a group of entrepreneurs formed along classical *guanxi* lines. At the centre of this clique was a family business, Tainan Spinning. The founder of Uni-President was a second-degree cousin of the owner of Tainan Spinning and was also working in that company. In setting up his own company, he received financial support from his relative. The group further expanded, with thickening and growing network relations that were increasingly cast into the legal shape of the conglomerate.

8 Based on the Taiwanese and the Overseas Chinese case, Hamilton (1996a) has therefore ventured the hypothesis that the fundamental unit of business

organization in China is not the family firm but the network of family firms. Greenhalgh (1988) had shown that in shareholding companies shareholders with the same surname played a dominant role, which points more specifically to the extended family as network structure. Companies with a strong participation of extended kin also proved to be significantly larger and also economically more successful than other companies. Lee and Hsiao (2014) summarize the situation in Taiwan today and argue that the critical share of stockholdings for assuming a controlling position is only 15 per cent. According to the current legal prescriptions for transparency, only second-degree relatives need to be reported as shareholders, which, however, does not reflect the strength of extended kinship beyond this level. Therefore, Lee and Hsiao argue that about 80 per cent of publicly listed companies in Taiwan are controlled by families. Considering the situation in China today, this may point towards similar difficulties. According to a recent survey by Forbes China (www.forbeschina.com/review/201409/0037397.shtml, accessed 5 November 2015) of the two stock markets in Shanghai and Shenzhen, of 1485 private companies, 747 are family companies (out of a total of 2528 companies). The criterion is that the family must have controlling stakes (more than 25 per cent of shares) and that at least two family members are employed in top management. However, this definition does not make explicit where the boundaries of the 'family' are drawn. So, based on the Taiwan comparison, one may suspect that a much larger number of companies are actually family businesses. Götzmann and Köll (2004) argue that it has been a persistent cultural phenomenon in Chinese business up until today that elite families retain control of companies independent from formal shareholder arrangements, thus obviating the need for majority ownership.

9 'Fragmentation' is the term employed in the theory of international trade (see e.g. the surveys and analysis by Hanson 2012; Timmer *et al.* 2014). In sociology, the term used is 'global value chains' (see Gereffi 1996; Gibbon *et al.* 2008). The WTO (2014: 78ff.) combines the two terms. Sociologists are mostly interested in the forms of governance and the distributional implications, whereas economists mainly look at the resulting division of labour, however, also taking note of certain distributional effects that on first sight contradict established trade theories, such as the fact that in countries with a high share of unskilled labour relative to capital, the higher skilled workers and capital mostly benefit from fragmentation. Another term used more frequently recently, especially by the WTO (2013), is 'value-added trade', thus referring to the fact that in global value chains there is a large share of high-valued services originating in advanced industrialized countries that are traded implicitly, and so remain hidden in the official trade statistics. In the view of economics, fragmentation reinstates traditional theories of comparative advantage, as companies split up the production process into segments which are then allocated to countries with specific comparative advantages regarding this particular segment.

10 On these patterns, see Appelbaum (2009), among others. The peculiar dynamics of the Chinese case is most obvious in the role of intermediators for arranging the supply chains of global retailers, a point already touched upon in Chapter 5. One example is the trading company Li & Fung, headquartered in Hong Kong, with an annual turnover of nine billion. Li & Fung organize supply chains for other companies, but also maintain their own chain of retailers. They specialize in sensitive functions such as quality control and logistics. So, in the Chinese context, the balance between domestic traders and global retailers is different from in other countries, probably reflecting the strength of domestic network organization. Interestingly, this repeats the historical pattern analysed by Hao (1996), when Western economic imperialism actually triggered the rise of a class of Chinese intermediaries. With their involvement in

functions such as quality control, Li & Fung represent a transitional form towards fully integrated companies such as Foxconn which directly organize production in China. Yet, even these companies retain the function of traders in the sense that they serve as suppliers for a large number of clients. Their organizational structure is largely determined by controlling essential inputs (mainly produced in Taiwan and Japan) and the capability to safeguard quality.

11 This argument may be based on a possible extension of the formal model of 'networked equilibria' presented by Feenstra *et al.* (1999) and applied to the comparison between Taiwan, Korea and Japan. The authors show that there are different equilibria in combining vertical integration and market relations, thus actually analysing what I call 'modularization', tying up with the broader literature on this phenomenon in industrial organization studies (see Sanchez and Mahoney 2013). The core argument is that in general equilibrium models with vertical integration and product variety, there are multiple equilibria of industrial organization with regard to the degree of how large, vertically integrated business groups emerge. In a nutshell, this is based on an inherent positive feedback dynamic. If there are already larger business groups in the downstream sector, they would tend to vertically integrate in order to create more efficient production chains with larger batches, and hence lower product variety. If not, there is a tendency to organize more dispersed production networks with higher product variety. This ideal-typical situation may be found in Korea and Taiwan, respectively. The upshot is that political, cultural and historical conditions operate as selectors for particular equilibria. So, there are strong path dependencies which, however, result in equally efficient tracks. Yet, the resulting production pattern would differ. For example, the strongly integrated networks would concentrate on end-products with high brand visibility, whereas the loosely integrated networks would focus on market niches with wide variety.

12 The relentless pressure on costs is an enduring feature, especially in private business in China, which also results from the demands of Western customers such as the global retailers. Along the fragmented value chain, surplus is typically squeezed to virtually nothing for the end-suppliers. Interestingly, this may be a factor driving these companies into the sector of counterfeiting, since in this domain profit margins can be higher. Companies may simultaneously operate in both business domains, with the illegal business actually cross-subsidizing the regular business (see Midler 2008). It should be mentioned that my analysis of the Chinese firm matches with Casson's (1997) generic approach to the firm which emphasizes the 'market-making' function: firms are not mainly seen as companies that organize production processes but ones that enable market transactions. Recently, Watanabe (2014) has systematized the Chinese phenomena in a 'vigorous entry and low price' model of industrial organization, arguing that this is fostered by technological developments which allow entrepreneurs to rely on suppliers of fixed technological modules and platforms, so that the fixed costs of market entry are very low. This leads to a 'vertical disintegration' model in which production processes are mainly market mediated. Watanabe compares market structures in China with India, showing that in the same industries with similar technological conditions and market size, the number of firms is much larger than in China, resulting in the tight competitive conditions that all observers of the Chinese market emphasize.

13 I introduced the example of the motorcycle industry in Chapter 5, n. 68. As I discuss below, an important aspect of this knowledge sharing is that it is regionally clustered; on the motorcycle case see Sonobe *et al.* (2006). In the

mid-2000s, 30 per cent of motorcycle production in China was concentrated in the city of Chongqing. On the different types of modularity, see Fujimoto (2007). Modularity is a central aspect of the so-called 'architecture' of industrial organization and is also driven by technological developments which determine the nature of interfaces in production organization, as I have argued previously. An excellent example for this is the emergence of automotive firms from the motorcycle and supplier industry in China, such as Geely from motorcycles or BYD from batteries. As Conlé (2015) discusses in great detail, these firms carry over open-modular structures into the production of more complex cars in relying on the rich supplier industry in China which was created by the inflow of foreign investment in combination with local content regulations, which, however, collaborated over international standardization and certification (see Pesselhoy 2006). The open-modular firms even outsource essential components such as engines, and they try to integrate components which originally belonged to different platforms and models of different original producers, often struggling with frictions. However, there are also emerging markets such as for electric cars of micro-cars where such open-modular structures can be built from scratch.

14 See Chapter 2, n. 78.

15 It is interesting to observe that in this context international and Chinese patterns of organization intermingle. In this case, the model of the business incubator is often implemented with international investors (see *The Economist,* 18 January 2014. A prominent example is the Hax Accelerator in Shenzhen which has a partner organization in San Francisco (http://hax.co/). The basic idea is that the successful business model in fostering software startups of the past may also be applied to hardware. This builds on the availability of large numbers of flexible small-scale firms in Shenzhen which can produce prototypes and small batches of new products in an extremely short time.

16 On this model, see Booz&Co (2009). The authors develop a process model of Shanzhai that emphasizes the market opportunities of low-income consumers in the initial stage which can be most effectively exploited by small-scale and flexible private entrepreneurs. Initially, they rely exclusively on technology that is available on the market, including even design features, in order to save overheads. This results in a large number of IPR and trademark violations. The conditions in the Chinese mobile phone industry have been detailed in Imai and Shiu (2007) which point, for example, to the role of 'independent design houses' that were originally from Korea but were then followed by a large number of local firms. So, entrepreneurs in the handset market can even outsource these central functions in product development, which on the other hand fosters specialization and the diffusion of knowledge. Only a few of the entrepreneurial ventures grow to larger sizes and then start to invest in their own R&D and brand development, thus 'going mainstream'. In the automotive industry, companies such as BYD also own a large stock of own patents and converge with international practices in IPR management.

17 See Chapter 5, n. 70 and n. 75.

18 On the role of local governments in supporting cluster formation, see Watanabe (2014) or Conlé (2015). Tellingly, some of the original 'model clusters' in Northern Italy, especially the garment industry, are today overtaken by Chinese businesses which rely on the same competitive advantages as in their native areas; for example, many migrants from Fujian and Wenzhou are now active in those Italian clusters. Here, we see that two network patterns intermingle: the network organization of migration and the local network organization of production (for the case of Fujianese in Europe, see Pieke *et al.* 2004). In the 1980s and 1990s, the cluster model was hailed as a newly emerging model of

industrial organization, following seminal contributions such as by Charles F. Sabel (for a collection of pertinent papers, see Curzio and Fortis 2002). Theoretically, these views were based on evolutionary theories and the theory of complex adaptive systems, which therefore could also provide insight into the analysis of Chinese conditions. Another important source of conceptualization was the literature on national innovation systems adapted to regional development (see e.g. the volume edited by Braczyk *et al.* 1998). This literature emphasizes the role of local institutions and patterns of interactions in shaping collective learning processes and developing regional competitive advantages, and going back to classical contributions such as Storper (1995).

19 For a comprehensive discussion of the criteria for identifying a family business, see Felden and Hack (2014: 10ff.). In the majority of quantitative research, authors tend to employ the simpler 'components of involvement' approach which focuses on indicators such as the distribution of ownership rights. In comparison, the 'essence' approach emphasizes 'thick' criteria which define certain more specific characteristics of governance in family business and also highlight the specific competences and resources that are mobilized. The most advanced indicator, the F-PEC scale (power, experience and culture), uses a much larger number of indicators in those three dimensions in order to establish degrees of the strength of family characteristics. For example, this indicator encompasses the detailed analysis of the number of generations involved in different organizational structures of the company, or looks at the impact of family culture upon corporate culture. Such an approach is eventually necessary because the range of organizational variants of family business is very large, and also includes structures where the family focuses almost exclusively on financial returns, for example, by establishing a family foundation as the owner of the company, and rarely, if at all, interferes with business decisions.

20 According to the bibliometric study by Wei Zhihua *et al.* (2013), research on family business is only developing slowly in China, whereas it is exploding in the rest of the world. Moreover, the number of Chinese papers published on this issue has diminished over recent years. The field is still dominated by mostly normative studies, and by a small number of research centres in places where family business is very important, such as Zhejiang University and Sun Yatsen University in Guangzhou. Another unusual characteristic of Chinese research thus far is that it is mainly conducted in management science and economics, thus lacking interdisciplinary dimensions. This is significant in our context, because therefore anthropological or sociological aspects are neglected. On the contrary, in classical studies of Chinese business beyond Mainland China such as Redding (1990), the Chinese family stays at the centre of attention. However, there are many reasons why we may need to be careful in extrapolating knowledge about these family businesses on the situation in Mainland China, because, for example, there has not been political intervention into family structures as under Maoism and with the one-child policy.

21 Forbes China publishes an annual survey of family businesses listed in Hong Kong and Shanghai (www.forbeschina.com/review/201409/0037397_all.shtml). The criterion is that the family should have a controlling stake and that at least two family members should be involved in top management positions. So, this criterion does not match the scholarly definition cited in n. 19 above. According to the Forbes criterion, approximately 50 per cent of listed private businesses are family owned. However, if one takes the criterion of successful generational transition into account, only about 10 per cent of the companies would count as family businesses. So, what matters for the distinction is whether we count the intention to continue with the business as relevant for the classification as a family business. In the study by Chen and Dou (2014), based on a

sample of 284 family firms mostly from Guangdong, Sha'anxi and Jiangxi provinces, thus including many medium-sized companies which are more representative for the majority of family businesses in China, only 4 per cent of companies have completed the generational transmission, and 76 per cent have not yet taken any measure in this regard. There are clear behavioural differences between companies that identify themselves as 'family businesses' and those that do not, for example, in terms of commitment of the family to the business.

22 According to the Forbes data, the performance of second-generation family firms is particularly dismal on the Hong Kong stock market. Yet, also in Mainland China, family firms perform worse than non-family-owned private businesses, with the exception that second-generation companies perform better than first-generation companies. The problem with these sorts of data is that there may be a strong impact of the general economic environment, since family firms are also most prevalent in certain industries, such as machinery. So, exogenous shocks may actually explain differential performance that are not necessarily related to their nature as family firms. In Mainland China, the share of non-family CEOs is also much higher than in Hong Kong, which may already reflect the specific constraints upon family management resulting from the one-child policy. This results in particularly pronounced tensions between traditional Chinese ideas about inheritance and the pragmatic necessities, for example, regarding the handing over of the family business to the daughter (see below).

23 For a classic description of the inherent instability of the traditional Chinese family, see Baker (1979: 15ff.). This condition was projected into a model of Chinese family businesses which was very influential in the literature (Wong 1985). Wong distinguishes between four stages of family development – 'emergent', 'centralized', 'segmented' and 'disintegrative' – and between three functions – 'estate', 'management' and 'profit'. The distribution of profit is the first to be decentralized once children become involved in business management. If the children establish their own families, management will be decentralized next, resulting in the 'segmented' stage, which, however, still retains the unity of the estate. This also implies, however, that the different segments may operate businesses in many possibly disconnected areas, as in the highly diversified Overseas Chinese conglomerates. Disintegration means that the estate is also divided. Wong has already argued that under certain conditions cycles between segmentation and centralization could occur, when across the generations new leaders in the family emerge (see n. 24 below), thus explaining the resilience of Chinese family businesses across generations in a number of important cases. According to Wong, the essential factor in determining the transition to disintegration is the inclusion of first cousins in business organizations.

24 For an interesting and prominent case, see the Singaporean Eu Yan Sang Corporation (www.euyansang.com/), studied by Tung (2007), and Yeung (2002), who also directly applies that classical Wong model to Chinese family businesses. This corporation was created by a patriarch with 13 sons, resulting in irresolvable tensions during the third-generation transition. Many parts of the corporation were sold. However, in the fourth generation certain family members were able to stabilize the firm in concentrating on its core business, namely traditional Chinese medicine, adding strategic complements such as expansion into the hospital sector. The company is led by a professional management team which includes three family members in leading positions.

25 In the aforementioned survey by Chen and Dou (2014: 47), in discussing the different possibilities of handover, the highest share of respondents asserted

that the sex of the successor does not matter (81.43 per cent). Zhou Xibing (2014: 106ff.) presents a number of highly visible generational transitions involving daughters, such as the Wahaha Corporation which is still led by the founder, Zong Qinghou (宗庆后), who is preparing generational transition to his daughter who received a management education in the USA and then assumed the position of CEO of certain companies in the corporation. Zhou identifies three obstacles to the advancement of women to top positions in Chinese family business. First, women are often still seen as outsiders to the agnatic group, since they will marry into another group; this also relates to daughters-in-law who, however, may make up for the deficiencies of the single male heir. Second, there are many forms of gender discrimination in internal organizational routines, such as speaking at board meetings. Third, societal role expectations still emphasize the role of women as wives and daughters.

26 On the differentiation of functions, see Redding (1996b) who follows a model by Limlingan distinguishing between the entrepreneurial function, the managerial function and the custodial function. Only for the custodial function do the conventional assumptions on the role of trust in determining business relations hold, whereas the managerial function can be easily delegated to professionals, and the entrepreneurial function is allocated to selected members of the family according to their capabilities. As we have seen from the Forbes survey, in Mainland China about 50 per cent of CEOs in listed family firms are non-kin. Hang *et al.* (2013) conducted research on the factors that determine 'psychological ownership' on the part of professional managers in Chinese family businesses. They measure psychological ownership in the display of certain behavioural stances, such as stewardship, organizational citizenship behaviour and intention to stay. Interestingly, they find that kinship is less significant in determining psychological ownership than emotional commitments that arise in work contexts, which they call '*guanxi* closeness at work'. These commitments can be fostered by the owner by demonstrating paternalistic care for the employed manager, thus creating a quasi-family context, for example, in taking into consideration the personal circumstances of the employee. In Chapter 2, I outlined the extent to which traditional Chinese lineages were ready to employ professional managers on their estates.

27 For a book-length journalistic study of the problems with family business succession, see Zhou Xibing (2014). Tellingly, Zhou relates many of the troubles to problems of Imperial succession in traditional China, thus at the same time pointing towards the overcoming of traditional fetters (such as in the gender issue), but also activating this cultural repository. A highly visible example in the Chinese business media is the case of FOTILE Fangtai (方太) Corporation, today a high-end producer of kitchen equipment with international reach (http://en.fotile.com/; Fang 2013; actually, the case is also a leitmotiv in Zhou's aforementioned book, often citing its founder Mao Lixiang (茅理翔) who is himself a prolific writer on business issues). The son only agreed to continue in the family business under the condition that he might set up his own business in related areas, and would not be expected to employ relatives in high management positions. So, the entrepreneurial function has been separated, yet the family still controls the financial assets together, with the founder still being chairperson of the board of the group. However, at the same time the son employs many traditional motives in building corporate culture, such as reading circles of Confucian classics.

28 I discussed these issues in Chapter 1. On the factual flexibility of business organization in Taiwan, see Schak (2002). Schak studied Taiwanese investments in the Pearl River Delta and discovered that many phenomena contradict the 'Confucian' model. For example, family businesses were in a minority,

with most companies operating as partnerships, hence joint investments of non-kin, yet the owner and his core family, especially wives, may play a leading role. Intentions to achieve generational transition were there, but in a weak and minority position. There were also many professional managers; hence no preference for kin in organizing the business. However, Schak does not generally dismiss cultural explanations, as he points to the neglected friend–friend nexus even in the Confucian *wu lun* notion, which is certainly highly appreciated in popular culture, and to the widespread use of kin notions as metaphors for close relations between non-kin.

29 The classical model has been developed by Redding (1990) based on the study of Overseas and Hong Kong Chinese businesses. Embedded in a rich analysis of cultural, historical and fieldwork contexts, this study also employed a quantitative investigation based on a model framework of the 'Alston' approach in studying organizational structures (Redding 1990: 153ff.). The comparison between British and Chinese companies in Hong Kong was very clear: Chinese companies manifest a higher degree of centralization of decision-making, but a lower degree of role specialization and standardization. Interestingly, the degree of formalization was similar, yet there was a lower degree of configuration; the latter refers to the relationship between line and staff personnel. So, the typical picture of paternalistic leadership is reflected in organizational structure. The leader maintains much of the control over the company, including flexible arrangements of structure according to his perceived needs. In order to keep control, he relies on formalization (i.e. extensive written records), but he does not delegate this work to specialized staff management. Redding also observed that 'leadership' is more a question of 'followership', thus pointing towards generic aspects of ritual.

30 Many aspects of the Chinese leadership style have first been delineated in a remarkably detailed and comprehensive study of a large Taiwanese company by Silin (1976), which still retains much relevance today. This relates to specific aspects such as campaign-style leadership (*yundong*) and factionalism, and to the general model of paternalism. Redding's (1990) aforementioned work owes much to this early study, the relevance of which was later again confirmed by other Taiwanese scholars (see Chen and Farh 2010: 602). This research also established early that paternalism is not dependent on the family as a management frame but extends to all forms of corporate organization.

31 On this 'authoritative' model, see Farh *et al.* (2008) and Chen and Farh (2010). Farh *et al.* relate their model to other classifications of authoritarian leadership in the literature and show that in Taiwan, employees clearly preferred the 'selfless benefactor' (low in authoritarianism, but strong in morality and benevolence) and the authentic one (strong in all dimensions); they consistently degraded all combinations that would include low morality. Morality is a notion that emerges in most research on leadership which highlights indigenous concepts (see Zhang *et al.* 2014). The idea that there is a cultural inclination towards authoritarian leadership in China is clearly refuted by the GLOBE study on 'power distance' (Carl *et al.* 2004), which differs fundamentally from the much-cited Hofstede results in showing that for China there is a pronounced gap between 'as is' and 'should be' valuations. This reveals that the relationship between authoritarian leadership and modernist values is complex. For example, Hui *et al.* (2004) show that the emotional commitment to leaders is even more pronounced for employees with 'modern' individual values, becoming manifest in organizational citizenship behaviour. This means that they expect paternalistic reciprocity. Employees with more traditional values seem to expect less reciprocity. The authors suggest that the reason may be that traditional values foster a sense of moral commitment that does not require

reciprocity. Chow *et al.* (2008) show for Hong Kong and Taiwan companies in China that 'compliance-based' HR systems actually have a negative impact on company performance.

32 See Chapter 2, n. 98, referring to Hamilton (2014).

33 As a case study for this, see Zhang (2012). The Qingdao TGOOD Corporation is a typical *xiahai* project of former government employees in the electrical equipment industry. The entrepreneurial team of close friends is led by the founder who has created a family-style inner group, thus referring to a senior co-founder as 'elder brother'. This leadership style also includes the traditional role of women in maintaining smooth social relations in the company. So, the founder's wife is responsible for arranging reciprocal relations within the inner team, such as taking care of family events, etc. These activities actually create the 'family'-like environment. It is interesting to note that these arrangements often also serve to meet different requirements of leadership (Schak 2002). More expressive benevolence by the leader can also imply that formal lines of authority would be undermined because people are encouraged to address the leader directly in order to resolve certain issues. So, delegating the 'benevolent' tasks to the wife can resolve this contradiction.

34 This is the argument presented by Chan and Unger (2009). The authors distinguish between an 'American' and a 'Japanese' model of the corporation, with the latter emphasizing values such as community orientation, organizational commitment, etc. They argue that many restructuring efforts in SOEs follow the American model, aiming at higher efficiency and productivity. Yet, in cases of factual privatization, the resulting tensions between management and employees may result in constraints upon restructuring. In order to maintain legitimacy of these measures, new private companies may need to retain important features of the *danwei* model, thus actually creating a paternalistic organizational setting.

35 For a classical study of the social relations in the *danwei*, see Whyte and Parish (1984). The thesis of familialization is elaborated in the fascinating study by Zhang Yi (2002). Zhang studies one single case, but also contextualizes this while emphasizing regional differences. For example, in a multi-province comparison of 87 companies, about 40 per cernt of employees had relatives in the company. In his case study, in an SOE in the interior provinces set up as a 'third front' enterprise, almost all the employees had direct relatives in the company. The strongly endogamous structure emerged because the SOE was a modernist insertion into a traditional rural society; thus SOE employees kept separate from the local population. Apart from endogamous marriage, the expansion of kinship networks mainly occurred via the growing inclusion of relatives and children in the company, often via satellite companies with collective ownership. Affinal kinship and also the extension of kin relations to non-kin further thickened the kinship network as an informal structure actually underlying the formal structure. Family relations also determined the internal status order, with children often inheriting status from their parents.

36 The development of formal HR systems is often seen as a litmus test for the degree of modernization of traditional family businesses, as the traditional model is highly personalistic and strongly involves the owner in HR-related decisions such as promotions. There is a strong impact of size and branch which further complicates the analysis, because this may actually interfere with the impact of traditional values; for example, Zhu and Warner (2004) show that companies with a focus on the domestic market in traditional industries were less prone to establishing formal HR systems. More recently, as Liang *et al.* (2012) emphasize, the new Labour Law of 2008 gave a push towards formalization, which, as the authors argue, however, does not necessarily mean

eschewing traditional approaches. This relates to the problem mentioned in the text, and which is highlighted in Kim and Gao's (2012) study of 205 family firms in China. They clearly identify effects of scale in adopting modern HR systems, but argue that there is relative uniformity across the regions, which seems to preclude any effect of different levels of economic and societal modernization. So, they observe that formal personnel training systems are even more prevalent in the interior provinces, which may be explained by tighter competition for talents, but also as an expression of reciprocity along traditional lines. So, they see the emergence of a 'hybrid' system that combines modern and traditional aspects.

37 An example of this explicit approach to designing the company as a 'substitute family' for its employees is the restaurant chain Haidilao (海底捞) (see Zhongguo guanli moshi jieshu jiang lishihui 2012: 144ff.). The company offers the traditional 'Hot Pot', with more than 120 restaurants in China, also expanding internationally. The founder of the company mainly employs rural migrants and has established an internal mentorship system by which the migrants are trained and develop the personal skills to support a management style that allows for much autonomy in decision-making, especially towards customers. This is inspired by Daoist philosophies, a point I pick up on in the final section of this chapter. The company aspires to be a 'family' for the migrants, thus including housing arrangements and so forth. Bonus payments are partly directly transferred to the parents of the employees in order to foster the virtue of filial piety in the organization. Another company that explicitly strives to become a 'large family' (*da jia*) for its employees is the Jointown Pharmaceutical Group, one of the largest private companies in pharmaceuticals and healthcare (see Zhongguo guanli moshi jiechu jiang lishihui 2011: 138ff.). This company also invests heavily in *danwei*-type arrangements for employees, such as company-owned living compounds and special services such as free provision of canteen services. Beyond these generic characteristics of 'family-style' management, however, the company implements a special personnel management system. Employees are explicitly encouraged to introduce relatives to be hired by the company in order to enhance familistic bonding; yet, a special software system takes care of an 'avoidance rule', 'huibi' (回避), meaning that relatives are not allowed to work in the same organizational unit or become involved in decisions about promotions, etc. Another example of managerial 'familism' is the Dangle Corporation dealing in solar energy equipment, which regularly invites family members to company visits and offers educational programmes for employees' children (Zhongguo guanli moshi jiechu jiang lishihui 2014: 153ff.).

38 In the 1940s, the positions of the CCP and the Guomindang on economic policy did not differ substantially. Whereas the CCP aimed at establishing a mixed economy that would leave much space for markets and private businesses in the rural areas in particular, and searched for cooperation with industrialists who contributed to the national cause of liberation, Chiang Kai-shek adhered to the principles of Sun Yatsenism and opted for a leading role of government-controlled companies in the modernization process. As discussed in Chapter 3, these attitudes reflected a shared approach to modernization, which saw fundamental constraints working upon the family-based economy of traditional China. On the influence of American advisers on economic policy in Taiwan, see Wade (1990: 211ff.).

39 On this model and the pertinent literature, see Chapter 3, n. 69.

40 For a concise overview of these contractual systems, see Tenev and Zhang (2002: 13ff.) or Sheng and Zhao (2013: 10ff.). The contractual schemes remained a guiding approach in SOE reform until the mid-1990s, after which

the approach of corporatization was launched, together with the reforms of the tax system. Before, the contracts actually combined taxation and profit transfers to the owners of an SOE. There were actually two kinds of contracts, namely the enterprise-level contracts and the personal contracts with the director, which created messy and complex conditions. However, the contractual scheme also allowed for implementing gradual extensions of the rights of directors, such as regarding investment out of retained profits or hiring and firing. In particular, a system of competitive bids for the director position was gradually extended, and which therefore accentuated the entrepreneurial function of the director.

41 Faure (2006: 85f.) describes the case of Dongfeng Corporation which in the 1980s expanded its size considerably via the inclusion of a larger number of suppliers. It is interesting to note that this supplier structure existed before the onset of reforms, and that even at the beginning Dongfeng already had certain rights of control with some of the suppliers, such as nominating the directors. On inefficiencies in automotive supplier networks see Chapter 4, n. 56. For a comprehensive analysis of network structures in this earlier stage of group formation, see Keister (2000: 113ff.). Keister notes certain specific effects, such as closer exchange relations (e.g. interlocking directorates) when firms were located in the same region (which at that time could also be partly explained by lags in infrastructural development). She also notes clear status effects, which could be bolstered if a lead company also had a financial arm. Keister's results are confirmed and extended in Lee's (2007) analysis of 'clan'-like structures in automotive groups. These groups differ structurally, since some, such as the SAIC group, concentrate on narrower regions such as in this case Shanghai, and others continue to bear the imprint of the original ministerial structures to which they belonged, such as military industries that diversify into automotives. There are strong path dependencies in supplier relations, and also status effects of ownership type.

42 For an exemplary study of these policies, see Giles *et al.* (2006). If one traces labour market data in detail, the Chinese performance of transition does not differ substantially from the Eastern European one. In most large cities unemployment rates went up to two-digit levels, and labour market participation declined by almost 10 per cent, with mostly women and elderly workers withdrawing from the pool. Unemployment and changing employment was often accompanied by a substantial loss of benefits, especially health insurance. In addition, arrears in wages and pensions occurred frequently. So, these developments make it clear that there was and is substantial interest of local governments in stabilizing SOEs. As Hurst and O'Brien (2002) have shown, a particularly important group is pensioners who were increasingly showing willingness to act publicly, since they felt they were legitimate stakeholders in SOEs, for which they sacrificed their working lives.

43 Most treatments of the current governance structure of SOEs only look at the formal legal framework, as is also done by the Chinese regulatory bodies (see OECD 2011). This means that there is no substantial information about the real power structures that are behind formal roles as defined by the law. The cited OECD report is even less informative than other Chinese sources, such as the 2009 report by Zhongguo shehui kexueyuan *et al.* (2009). In this report, we find data about the ownership status of the largest three shareholders in the 100 top listed companies. The largest shareholder is 83 per cent state owned, and the second and third are still 32 and 23 per cent respectively; the share of private entities is larger for these positions. If one looks at the types of entities, however, only 10 per cent are government units for the largest shareholder, and close to 80 per cent for other corporations. For the next two positions, the

share of investment companies is rising substantially. Unfortunately, we cannot relate these numbers to each other, but it is evident that interlocking shareholdings play a major role in actualizing formal governance structures (as emphasized by Huang 2008). This also means that government units that stay behind another SOE which has shares in the original one can also exert indirect influence. Clarke (2010: 147) points to the resulting confusion, as many individual accounts on the stock market are actually held by investment funds which may legally be 'private', but which have a background in government entities. In other words, the more sophisticated the Chinese capital market becomes, the more diverse are the ways in which stakeholders can actualize their claims in financial relationships.

44 The structure of the SASAC system is concisely overviewed in Sheng and Zhao (2013: 37ff., 272ff.). Roughly speaking, the number of central-level SOEs is a little more than 100. Theoretically, there should be no further direct intervention of other government agencies into SOE management. Yet, as the Chinese term 'departmentalism', 'benwei zhuyi' (本位主义), suggests, the stakeholder claims are still being pursued (see Wang 2014: 641). As I outlined previously, for example, in interlocking shareholdings a SASAC may be the largest shareholder, but there are other corporations and investment companies which also hold substantial shares. Via their influence, 'departmental interests' can be represented. Compare my discussion of the regulatory state in Chapter 5.

45 This analysis follows the detailed study by Wang (2014). For an overview of these recent reform plans, see KPMG (2014).

46 Cf. n. 34 and n. 35 above.

47 This conclusion follows on from the recent study by Bryson *et al.* (2014). The authors analyse different aspects of the correlation between CEO remuneration and corporate performance features in order to determine differences in the corresponding patterns in Western countries. The result is that there are astonishing similarities, given the large differences in the factual corporate governance structure. There is a positive correlation between the size of the company and remuneration, a correlation between company performance and remuneration, and there are also steep gradients between the top-level positions in management that indicate tight competition for promotions. So, it seems that the combination between nomenclature competitions and incentive structure create similar conditions for corporate performance as in financial capitalism.

48 This emerges from the much-cited study by Sheng and Zhao (2013). According to the official statistics, the return on equity was about 8 to 9 per cent in the 2000s compared to about 13 per cent of private enterprises. The authors painstakingly analyse the impact of special conditions upon SOE performance. For example, based on the total area of land allocated to SOEs, they calculate the implicit land rent SOEs would have to pay if they were private entreprises, and subtract this from SOE profits. SOEs enjoy similar privileges for energy use. There is also a stark difference between the interest rates for loans that SOEs have to pay (about 2.6 per cent) and private business (about 4.5 per cent). Taking all these calculations together, the real returns on equity were calculated as being largely negative in the 2000s, with the exception of 2006 and 2007, when, however, the rates went only slightly above zero.

49 This is the central argument in Clarke (2010), who argues that in China probably the most important governance issue is the relationship between minority and majority shareholders, compared to the common focus on the principal–agent issue, or principal–principal conflict. Whereas principal–agent issues are rarely resolved by legal means, principal–principal issues would mostly involve disputes about violations of legal protections of minority shareholders' rights.

For this, a legal infrastructure is necessary, especially lawyers and accountants. However, their professional networks remain weak and, above all, lack sufficient autonomy.

50 I am referring here to the model developed by Che and Qian (1998a, 1998b) to which I have already alluded (Chapter 4, n.22).

51 Li and Rozelle (2003) analyse a sample of MBO procedures and their effect on the subsequent performance of privatized TVEs. There is a difference between companies where there is a discount and those where there is none: the former perform worse. One possible explanation for this is that in the former case there is still an implicit claim of residual profit on the part of local authorities, for example, in the shape of contributions to local infrastructure. Thus, the discounts reflect a strong stakeholder position of local government, which therefore also interferes with business decisions, thus causing lower levels of performance. I argue that in these cases the original model for TVE governance developed by Smyth (1997) still applies. The privatized TVE remains embedded in local networks of reciprocity that partly contribute to its entrepreneurial dynamics, but also imply that the TVE has to respond to local interests, which can be both legitimate (as in contribution to public goods) and illegitimate (corruption). However, at the same time these networks also create confidence in the environment for entrepreneurial activity, which, in earlier times, for example, would have been necessary to maintain the internal decision rights in spite of registering as a 'red hat' company.

52 Redding's (1990, 1996b) classical model of the Chinese enterprise is partly explicitly modelled as a hybrid, especially with regard to Hong Kong business. The Hong Kong case is of considerable interest, as on the one hand there is a long-run impact of British colonial rule upon local business practices, especially with regard to the legal system, and on the other hand there has been a constant flux of refugees from the Mainland to Hong Kong, with different backgrounds in business culture. For example, in the early stage of the Communist takeover many Shanghai large-scale businesses were transferred to Hong Kong, thus also transferring most advanced forms of industrial practices in the Mainland. Later, many refugees came from Guangdong province, so taking with them the traditions of small-scale and kinship-based business.

53 This transpires in attempts to project corporate culture onto an etic conceptual scheme of classifying corporate cultures, such as Tsui *et al.* (2006). They distinguish between a 'hierarchical', an 'integrative' (with two subgroups) and a 'market-oriented' type. Interestingly, the two legal types of SOEs and private companies show a relatively high share of 'hierarchical' and 'market-oriented' type, respectively, but both strongly overlap with the 'integrative type', which seems most essential for successful performance. Further, the SOEs show the largest variety of types, so that we can see the degree of adaptation of SOEs to the new competitive environments, and also that legal forms do not fully determine corporate culture.

54 As examples of the discrepancies between English and Chinese website presentations, I cite two world-leading companies. One is Huawei, in which 'self-criticism' plays a central role in leadership practices. As I discuss below, self-criticism is an essential part of CCP organizational practices. It is mentioned on the Chinese website as 'ziwo pipan'(自我批判). On the English website (with variations across different countries) we find 'continuous improvement', www.huawei.com/uk/about-huawei/corporate-info/vision-mission/index.htm (accessed 14 September 2015). Similarly, the Chinese 'arduous struggle', 'jianku fendou' (艰苦奋斗), reminiscent of military traditions of Maoism, is translated as 'dedication to the customer'. Another example is Haier Corporation, which, as I discuss below, follows Daoist management philosophy pursued by its

founder Zhang Ruimin. The Haier website has undergone substantial changes in recent years. Originally, the Chinese website contained many direct references to Daoism, including even the use of a phrase from *Dao De Jing* as a slogan for the corporate vision (天下万物生于有，有生于无, The Ten Thousand things emerge from Being, and Being emerges from Nothing; see www.cec1979.org.cn/jjh/view.php?id=75, accessed 15 September 2015). However, later both the Chinese and the international websites deleted these references and adopted more neutral, globally compatible wordings.

55 A fascinating case is Walmart as described and analysed by Davies (2007). Walmart is an important example, as the retailer sets up a large number of local branches which therefore manifest a much higher degree of localization than foreign investments that concentrate on a small number of large-scale organizational units which can be more directly controlled by Western management. In comparison, companies such as Walmart rely almost exclusively on local personnel, and hence are easily subject also to forces of contextualizing and localizing corporate culture. Walmart is known for imposing a strong corporate culture globally, based on management concepts of the founder himself, Sam Walton. These are enshrined in the 'Ten Commandments' which were translated into Chinese in a mode heavily geared towards Confucian values and terms. As Davies reports, Walmart employees on the one hand perceive their work environment as 'American' (such as regarding the encouragement of translocal mobility), but on the other hand there is a lot of convergence between Sam Walton's understanding of business and Chinese conceptions of morality. So, for example, the American 'associate' (which denotes a Walmart employee in order to suggest an egalitarian culture of commitment) is translated as 'tongren' (同仁), which suggests a strong moral identity in using the term *ren* and not 'tongshi' (同事). Walmart also invokes the image of the 'family', which is strongly received by employees, yet the 'family' is also perceived as being an 'American-style' one. Another aspect is leadership ideology, with even astonishing visual similarities between pictures of Sam Walton and Mao Zedong.

56 As an example, see the case of CNOOC (Bower *et al.* 2012). CNOOC is a petrochemical SOE with a strong global focus. Twenty-eight per cent of staff are party members and are thus directly subject to party discipline and the CCP personnel system. The wage system still pays homage to more egalitarian concerns. There is a strong emphasis on community values; for example, pensioners are still taking part in corporate profits. There is high investment in training and skill development. As such, CNOOC is not unique, as Farh *et al.* (2004) show in their analysis of organizational citizenship in China from a comparative point of view. Chinese companies emphasize values such as mutual help also beyond the professional context, and organize many group-related activities. For the role of corporate culture in CCP approaches to social control, see Hawes (2008). The CCP regards corporate culture as an important element in the modernist transformation of the economy, even explicitly emphasizing aspects of ritual. SOEs and large private businesses are expected to develop and implement concepts of corporate culture.

57 On the general characteristics of Chinese management and leadership as they emerged in the international literature, see Chen and Lee (2008). The other characteristics they include are 'dialecticism and holism', 'control mechanisms' and 'leadership agency'. For a related threefold classification of theories in the field of leadership, see Zhang *et al.* (2014), who discern context-free theories, modified theories including Chinese characteristics, and theories that build on indigenous concepts. For an overview of indigenization approaches in Mainland China, see Chen *et al.* (2014: 20ff., 77ff.). The authors distinguish between

four schools of thought. The first is interpreting traditional Chinese concepts in terms of modern theories, such as the *Yjing* in terms of fuzzy logic and complexity theory, which then allows for applications in management. The second is to start out from Western empirical management theories and to align traditional principles such as *jiaohua* or *xiushen* with their results. The third is to try out a new and creative combination of Western and Chinese core notions in order to create entirely new frameworks of management. One example is the so-called 'C-Theory' which explicitly builds on traditional cosmological thinking (the 'C' refers to China on the one hand, but also to central terms such as 'contingency', 'control' or 'creativity'). The fourth is to directly extract practical management wisdom from ancient Chinese philosophy, an approach that has also been fashionable in Taiwan for many years. One example is the co-called 'M-Theory', which refers to 'man', 'middle' and 'management', and explicitly picks up central ideas of Confucianism, such as putting human concerns at the centre of attention, striving at achieving balance and mediation, and so on.

58 On the role of foreign consultancies in the Huawei organizational change process, see Chen *et al.* (2014: 104ff.). IBM accompanied Huawei for one decade, beginning in 1999, after the founder Ren Zhengfei had visited IBM in 1997 for the first time and decided to introduce the IBM IPD process management to Huawei, but failed at the first attempt. Similarly, Huawei invited the global HR consultancy HAY to design the Key Performance Indicator system. These facts point to similar developments in the 1950s when Japanese managers avidly received the first works by Peter Drucker, who might have left a deep impact on what emerged as a 'Japanese management model'. Drucker is also widely received in China today, for example, regarding customer organization. One example of recent Western discoveries of a Chinese management model is Bouée (2011) under the auspices of Peter Berger Consultants. The author makes a strong point that Chinese management is coming back to its roots in activating Chinese spirituality. These are elements such as the flexibility and adaptivity of planning with the readiness to reduce planning in favour of keeping the organization open for facing contingencies; or a combination of reciprocity and authority, which also requires the search for consensus in the organization.

59 For a detailed study of the Foxconn case see Ngai and Chan (2012). The Foxconn CEO, Terry Gou, is explicitly quoted as imposing 'a dictatorship for the general good', 'ducai wei gong' (独裁为公). Foxconn maintains many production sites in China, with some achieving gigantic scales, operating as 'factory towns' with 400,000 employees. Many are employed as 'student interns' with the complicity of local governments which are keen to attract and keep Foxconn factories. Working hours are often overtime without clear regulation, and workers have to observe many rituals in the narrow sense, such as, even after 12-hour shifts, standing upright, reciting slogans and listening to exhortative speeches. In other words, many aspects of Foxconn management also resemble the mobilization approaches of the CCP during earlier periods, as in the Great Leap Forward.

60 Hwang (2008) speaks of a 'dialectical' relationship between Confucianism and Legalism throughout China's history, and reviews Taiwan's economic history in this light. However, this raises the question of how far both may relate to deeper cultural roots. This is evident when considering the relationship between Legalism and Daoism, which converge on a similar result via different tracks. This is self-regulation of social units without the interference of higher level hierarchies. In Legalist thinking, the system of punishments and incentives would be internalized through continuous education so that eventually

individuals would 'naturally' submit themselves to the institutional order. For practical matters, the distinctive role of Legalist management in containing disruptive effects of subcultural variety in Chinese organizations has been emphasized by many observers, such as Huang (2002) for the comparison between Taiwanese and Hong Kong companies in the Pearl River Delta; on 'militarization' of Taiwan-invested companies see Herrmann-Pillath (1994: 203ff.). I have already pointed to the study by Zhang *et al.* (2010) who describe the compartmentalized management in Mainland Chinese companies employing migrant workers. Since migrant workers are often employed via labour-leasing companies, they are also systematically shut off from many measures of 'benevolent' management, such as training measures for skill development.

61 On the 'water' metaphor in Daoism as applied to management and leadership, see Lee *et al.* (2008). On the regional interpretation, see Fang und Lin (2011a: 93ff., 2011b: 229ff.). They distinguish between three different business cultures in China: the Shanxi 'jin shang' (晋商) tradition, the Anhui 'hui shang' (徽商) tradition and the Zhejiang 'zhe shang' (浙商) tradition. These traditions differ in emphasizing different values, though being based on a shared frame of reference in Chinese culture. For example, the Shanxi tradition is mainly rural and agriculturally oriented, and hence emphasizes values such as frugality, the Anhui tradition is associated with Confucian philosophy in a more direct sense, so referring to values such as *ren*, and the Zhejiang tradition is Daoist. So, the authors even confront the 'Confucian merchant', 'rushang' (儒商) with the 'Daoist merchant', 'dao shang' (道商). Historically, they associate these differences also with different social orientations; for example, the Anhui tradition would also orient the merchant towards a scholarly career, whereas the Zhejiang tradition would praise ordinary life.

62 As an example of an explicit reference to the 'Yin–Yang' duality in management, see the educational company Huanqiu Tianxia (www.hqlsw.com/), which is one of the leading Chinese companies in English-language teaching and language proficiency tests (see Zhongguo guanli moshi jiechu jiang lishihui 2011: 120ff.). In a rich metaphorical language, the company identifies with the image of the 'German shepherd dog' which is seen as the synthesis of the 'wolf' and the 'sheep'. The 'Eight Trigrams', 'bagua' (八卦) of the *Yijing* are used to conceive of the management principles of the company in a set of Yin–Yang dualities, such as 'pragmatism', 'wushi' (务实) as 'yang' versus 'accuracy', 'xixin' (细心) as 'yin'. Practical consequences are, for example that the company mostly employs female managers but male teachers, thus also reflecting a Yin–Yang duality in the HR system. In the international context, the 'Yin–Yang' concept is based on the idea that in the Chinese cognitive style, opposites can co-exist without resulting in irresolvable conflicts. This is seen as being different from logical figures such as 'paradox' or 'dialectics' (for a critical Chinese view on this see Li Xin 2014). Peter Li (2014) relates this to the current discussion in management science about the 'ambidexterity' of organizations, which means that organizations can maintain a dynamic balance between strategic opposites, such as exploration versus exploitation.

63 For a concise summary of these results from psychology and cognitive science, see Ji *et al.* (2010). For example, Chinese subjects tend more than Western subjects to search for contextual explanations in understanding the reasons for a murder case or the failure of a sports team. Peter Li (2014) distinguishes between five types of cognitive frames regarding the treatment of polar opposites: 'neither/nor', 'either/or', 'both/and', 'both/or' and 'either/and', recognizing only the last one as representing the Yin–Yang logic. Many Chinese business leaders emphasize similar ideas about avoiding polar opposites in terms of mutually contradictory positions, such as the founder of Huawei, Ren

Zhengfei, who speaks of 'grey' approaches to management, avoiding simple conclusions that 'non-black is white' (Chen *et al.* 2014: 107).

64 For an interesting case study illustrating the principles of *shi*-oriented management, see Jing and Van de Ven (2014). The authors analyse successful change management at a large public enterprise, Chengdu Bus Company, which is a holding company of various sub-companies. Between the sub-companies there were divergent views about central issues of group management. For example, there was disagreement about the remuneration systems to be applied in the different groups. In order to resolve the conflicts, the chairman of the group simple reshuffled the leaders of the sub-companies so that they would be put into the context of the company that they perceived as representing the opposing view. This rapidly led to the resolution of the conflict and the adoption of a unified scheme. The point is that the holding company did not interfere in the process directly by imposing one solution, but changed the context for the different decision-makers in such a way that the conditions for decentralized agreement improved.

65 In their overview of psychological research on Chinese ways of addressing problems and coping with challenges, Cheng *et al.* (2010) refer to the aforementioned research on Chinese cognition and point out that the recognition of situational factors in attributing causes of performance also implies a 'passive' way of coping, which means a stronger readiness to adapt to circumstances, but also to properly identify opportunities in environmental changes. This also reflects the tendency to see low levels of personal control of the environment. They also directly establish connections with Chinese philosophies, in particular Daoism, in the context of dialectical thinking which fosters the recognition of factors of change in the environment and a concentration on dynamics.

66 These earlier stages of Haier organizational development are well documented also in the English-language literature; see, for example, the contributions by Lin (2005, 2009), who also provides translations of central documents and file samples of the Haier system. At that time, the so-called 'OEC' system stood at the centre of efforts, meaning 'Overall; Everyone, Everything, and Everyday; Control and Clear'. The precursor of the self-managed units was the 'strategic business units' (SBUs). This system mainly refers to the extremely detailed system of financial and operation control that introduced daily performance reviews based on weekly plans, and the fine-grained assignment of individual responsibilities for any kind of particular object and process. Every day, workers fill in forms documenting their performance and can calculate their daily wages, with the result being checked by their supervisor. The evaluation criteria are comprehensive and detailed, not only including quantitative production goals, but also, for example, criteria for assessing maintenance of equipment or work safety. The transition from this system to the new one was implemented as business process re-engineering, especially with regard to internal supply chains. My subsequent description of the more recent developments is based on the book-length study of Haier by Cao (2014).

67 This is the gist of the argument presented by Cao (2014). Cao starts out from the idea that Haier management is a pinnacle of developing humanistic management in the sense that the individual is seen as a 'whole world of her own' with many developmental potentialities. The open organizational structure is interpreted as a space for allowing individual entrepreneurial initiative, such as when opting for leadership of a self-organizing unit. This emphasis on the individual is characteristic also of other leading companies; see for the case of Huawei in Chen *et al.* (2014: 97). I noted earlier that 'individualization' is also an important aspect in ideas about the market as an educational arena for leveraging the *suzhi* of migrant workers.

68 The image of the wolf has been evoked by the Huawei founder Ren Zhengfei to describe the corporate culture of his company, http://wenku.baidu.com/view/7cc3ab2ead02de80d5d84002 (accessed 15 September 2015). The wolf has become popular in China following the fantastic success of a novel by Jiang Rong published in 2004, *Wolf Totem* (on this and the relevant context see Wedell-Wedellsborg 2010), which also led to a number of studies in the business literature on the 'Wolf's way', 'langdao' (狼道). The story is about a young Chinese in Mongolia who wants to tame a wolf, without success. Apart from the metaphors regarding individualism and group orientation, it is also an implicit reflection about the role of education and modernization relative to the primitive, even invoking themes of national identity (Han vs. Mongolian). On the educational practices in migrant children schools, see Hansen (2013), and Chapter 5, n. 59. These phenomena are widespread in Chinese society; for another example see the didactic approach of the famous English-language teacher Li Yang reported by Osnos (2014), who made a learning method popular which requires 'shouting' English sentences, thus inciting bodily expressiveness, together with a strong emphasis on self-confidence.

69 A famous example is the world-leading internet corporation Alibaba, which certainly does not count as a traditional enterprise, being founded by a single entrepreneur and a couple of close friends, Ma Yun (Jack Ma), who is today a global business celebrity. Ma explicitly refers to Mao Zedong's Yan'an rectification campaigns, Yan'an zhengfeng yundong (延安整风运动) in order to launch similar processes in the company. Alibaba also implements a system of self-appraisal based on a list of criteria which heavily emphasize the identification with Alibaba corporate culture (such as readiness for continuous change or sincerity) (see Chen *et al.* 2014: 130ff.). In Huawei Corporation, as mentioned previously, this system is most elaborate, with public sessions of self-criticism even of high-ranking managers (see Hawes 2008). Similar practices abound among Chinese companies. For example, Sangle corporation in solar energy focuses on the rural areas, explicitly following Mao Zedong's famous strategy of 'encircling the cities from the villages', and supplies equipment for Maoist memorial sites (Zhongguo guanli moshi jiechu jiang lishihui 2014: 172).

70 As an example, see Alibaba Corporation (Chen *et al.* 2014: 135f.). Although technological expertise, education and skills are essential criteria in the hiring process, in 2009 Alibaba introduced an additional stage in the recruitment process, the 'tasting the smell officer', 'wen wei guan' (闻味官). These are employees who have worked for at least five years with the corporation, and who are outstanding in terms of loyalty to the Alibaba values. The sole responsibility of these officers is to check for the compatibility of the applicant's personality and values with Alibaba.

71 On the increasing adoption of Party secretary positions by entrepreneurs in the rural areas, see Yan (2012). Yan shows that there is a strong role of traditional structures here, in particular lineages. Entrepreneurs who were also leading lineage networks in creating local business networks often gain sufficient authority as community leaders as well, and they also have substantial interests in safeguarding their social position. Hu (2007) recounts the model of 'integrating village with company' in a case study where a local entrepreneur built on local artisanal traditions (nail production out of scrap metal) and created a modern cable company which grew so strongly that even the village budget became partly funded by the company. The entrepreneur later assumed political positions on the provincial and even national level. Here, we can also see how a decidedly 'Confucian' corporate culture easily combines with political identities. A fascinating though certainly extreme and also rare case study is the career of the entrepreneur Sun Dawu of Hebai Dawu Group, a company in the

food industry (for detailed information, see Du 2011; Delman and Yin 2010). On the one hand, Sun created a corporate town which is also clearly recognized as such by the local people. Although originally a farmer, he perceives himself as a politician and philosopher. This works in both directions. On the one hand, he has created a unique approach to family business succession in designing a 'constitution' for the company which builds on political concepts such as 'constitutional monarchy' and the 'separation of powers'. This limits direct interventions of family members through the strong institutionalization of different corporate bodies, On the other hand, as a local leader he pursues 'republican' ideals and wants to strengthen civil society and local self-government. Sun has also established a Confucius temple, which thus lends a religious dimension to his efforts. He achieved national celebrity status after being gaoled on dubious grounds for a while, and later became very active in the media.

72 It is highly significant that there is also an explicit discourse about the potential drawback to this form of para-governmental governance, such as in Dongguan (see Ngok and Zhuang 2013). The barracking of migrant workers is detrimental to their integration into local society, thus even further accentuating cultural and social cleavages and tensions. So, local governments are also compelled to consider new forms of governing the migration process, such as developing housing schemes that are more open and allow for more regular interaction among different groups. These schemes would also challenge the corporate culture of comprehensive discipline. Thus, the relationship between the two springs to mind.

7 Conclusion: deciphering the Chinese economic style

One of the most common characterizations of the Chinese economy is the term 'state capitalism'. This notion lumps together countries as different as Brazil, Russia and China. The backdrop is a certain concept of and normative reference to the institutional setting in the majority of the OECD countries following the weakening of the standards of the Washington Consensus, which was partly also motivated by the phenomenal success of China. So, the notion of state capitalism appears to be a mainly negative characterization, namely pinpointing normative deviance. It is lacking specificity in identifying positive characteristics of 'state capitalism', especially with reference to the different countries involved, beyond simple observations on different forms of government intervention. In fact, given the differences between the countries that are included in this category, the methodological value of this category appears to be weak. This is especially deplorable because the notion vacillates between normative and positive functions. For many observers state capitalism is seen in a critical light, and is perceived as an oxymoron that carries within it the seeds of a necessary conversion to 'pure' systems.[1]

As we have seen, the notion of economic style is based on a very different methodological basis. This matches a different normative framework. Both the positive methodology and the normative foundations are rooted in adopting an evolutionary approach in economic analysis. Regarding the normative framework, the distinctiveness of the evolutionary approach may best be demonstrated by referring to Amartya Sen's seminal distinction between 'transcendental institutionalism' and 'realization-focused comparisons', with the latter being the normative companion to positive evolutionary analysis.[2]

Transcendental institutionalism is thus far the dominant normative perspective in economics. This means that economic science would allow for the identification of certain standards for institutions which are regarded as being 'optimal' according to certain theoretical criteria, though also supported by experience and empirical research. So, for example, most economists would accept the idea that free trade is an optimal institutional regime, supported by theoretical notions of comparative advantage and the related welfare economics, and also proven by the growth record of the world economy under the auspices of the Bretton Woods institutions that fostered the liberalization of world trade. Similarly, most economists would underwrite the idea that private ownership is a most efficient institutional regime, given theoretical notions of incentivization and information processing, and given the outcome of the politico-economic competition between socialist and capitalist systems during the Cold War. Then, these theoretical references are set as a benchmark according to which existing institutions are evaluated. The status quo is perceived and evaluated in terms of the distance to the benchmark, and policy recommendations would concentrate on ways and means of reducing this distance. So, for example, high levels of tariffs define the distance from the benchmark of free trade, and trade liberalization in terms of tariff reductions is the recommended policy to shorten this distance. One important consequence of transcendental institutionalism is that evaluations of institutions can be ascertained independently from the particular position of the observer, especially with reference to the distinction between internal and external observers. Accordingly, divergent evaluations by internal observers are typically identified as reflecting the positions of particular 'interests' which are affected by a certain policy. The policy adviser has to overcome these particularistic limitations of perspectives and set the right policies aiming at the transcendental benchmark. In other words, with regard to real-world political economy, the scientific observer assumes the role of an 'impartial third party' who is able to detach herself from the maze of special interests, and to identify the 'public good', though interpreted along the lines of individual welfare. This position also legitimizes the role of economists as advisers to governments.[3]

In comparison, realization-focused comparisons deny the relevance and even the possibility and feasibility of a transcendental benchmark for evaluating current and future institutions because they reject the idea that one can move beyond the normative reference frame of valuations that actually prevail in the particular society that is undergong institutional change. This is based on two observations: a positive and a normative one.

The first observation is that institutional change is always driven by the economic actors themselves, such that only their interests can be causally relevant, barring the utopian scenario where one 'benevolent dictator' would impose the transcendental benchmark institutions upon the society without any further distortions resulting from the response to this act on the part of the economic actors. So, under real-world conditions, even transcendental institutionalists have to design and recommend trajectories of institutional change that are compatible with the incentives governing the behaviour of the economic actors. Then, the question arises whether these apparently 'transitory' institutions may in fact be stable institutional states over a long period of time, considering the fact that the incentives that shape actors' behaviours are also changing recurrently. For example, a policy directed at the realization of free trade may need to be accompanied by establishing a strong welfare state as a sort of society-wide insurance against the risks of free trade in a world with rapidly changing patterns of comparative advantage. So, transcendental institutionalism falsely suggests possible trajectories of institutional change without establishing a proper causal approach to the sequence of actions that would result. For example, in the case of free trade one might argue that 'free trade' is a utopian state if there are no feasible sequences of actions that might lead towards it; actually, one can show that certain restrictions of free trade may be necessary conditions for maintaining an institutional state that approximates free trade to a certain degree.[4]

Obviously, this observation on positive analysis may also be interpreted in normative terms, which is our second observation. If only existing interests are causally relevant for institutional change, we are not allowed to refer to a transcendental regime as the foundation for normative judgements, where these interests are already imagined as having been processed in terms of a 'general interest'. Utopia is no reasonable basis for real-world evaluations, but this observation would only appear to be a negative critique, so needs to be rendered also in terms of explicit normative recommendations. These considerations would avoid referring to a transcendental desired state and would therefore pinpoint procedural aspects that directly relate to the actual interests of people who are affected by a certain policy. Here, it is important that the criterion for 'being affected' is not deduced from an external standpoint (which would re-introduce transcendental references), but is strictly oriented towards whether an individual perceives itself as being affected. Hence, a hallmark of realization-focused comparisons includes 'bystanders' in the process of evaluating institutions, as long as they perceive themselves as being affected. This leads towards an evaluative standard which emphasizes participation and inclusiveness. Current institutional change only meets foundational norms of justice and fairness if all relevant interests are properly represented and expressed in this process, without weighing them from the perspective of transcendental institutions. So, whether and how existing particular interests are actually included and respected in the process of institutional change is a major criterion of evaluation. If a benevolent dictator imposed free trade upon the world by fiat, this action would violate the normative benchmark of inclusion and participation, even if ex post this policy might increase social welfare for all. So, taking up the example of trade policy again, what matters is not whether trade policy approximates a transcendental benchmark of 'free trade', but whether and how in the process of determining trade policy all affected interests have a chance to partake in the process of institutional change, and whether they agree on whether a certain policy is indeed an improvement over the status quo.[5]

The approach of realization-focused comparisons is grounded in an evolutionary approach to economic analysis. The evolutionary approach is based on the general methodology of constitutive explanations and causal mechanisms as outlined in Chapter 1, and it eschews teleological references to transcendental institutional benchmarks in evaluating institutions. One dangerous methodological trap can be avoided that haunts much economic analysis of the 'transcendental kind'. This is the idea that the ideal-typical reference would go along with forces in the real-world economy that drive it towards the benchmark. This would compare with the biologist designing an 'ideal animal' and then claiming that real-world evolution would necessarily tend towards this benchmark. The intellectual blunder is most apparent, namely that the distance to the benchmark is implicitly seen as 'costs' that determine actual developments in the real world, thus suggesting that processes would eventually assume the direction of minimizing those costs. However, in the evolutionary perspective, 'costs' are only costs that are endogenous and immanent to the prevailing conditions of evolution, and which create the observed evolutionary trajectories. In fact, costs that relate to a utopian benchmark cannot impact upon decisions that are taken in the status quo, unless there is an alternative state already realized in the environment of decision-making which reveals these costs in terms of actual disadvantages that the current decision-maker is facing.[6]

Obviously, this discussion is highly relevant for China. Although the current assumption that China is 'in transition' is shared among many Chinese and 'external observers' such as many economists, there are principled differences between those two alternative positions; these directly relate to the differences between the two alternative ways of evaluating institutions. In the eyes of most economists, Chinese 'state capitalism' would be a transitory phenomenon, and there are forces that drive China further along the track towards 'mainstream' institutional patterns, such as privatizing SOEs. This is a transcendental-institutionalist reasoning. From the viewpoint of many Chinese participant observers, 'transition' is in fact a process of 'realization-focused comparisons', meaning that the final state of the process is not exactly defined, and that current policies are shaped by currently prevailing costs and benefits of institutional change (according to Deng Xiaoping's dictum of 'mo shitou guo he' (摸石头过河), 'Crossing the river while touching the stones'). Indeed, one challenge for the transcendental institutionalist is exactly that the current process obviously does not generate cost structures that would drive the system in the direction which they posit from the transcendental vantage point. For example, capital controls actually protected China against the impact of the Asian crisis of 1997, and they continue to play a role in stabilizing the trajectory of financial reforms. What matters are not the costs that this system might generate relative to an imagined scenario of free flow of capital, but the disadvantages for China in direct comparison with other countries that appear to be closer to this transcendental state of institutions. Obviously, the current Chinese institutional set-up even provided a number of advantages to China in comparison with her direct competitors, namely other developing and emerging economies in the past 30 years.

So, I argue that what often appears to be a clash between 'principled' views of Western observers and Chinese 'pragmatism' is actually reflecting a foundational difference between two theoretical perspectives on institutional change in general. The problem is that the actual Chinese attitude is not undergirded by a corresponding theoretical foundation, even though one might argue that, to a certain extent in the context of international cooperation in policy design, the application of theories seems to approximate evolutionary methodologies. Yet, I hasten to add that one cannot simply construct a conflict between Chinese and Western views in the sense of illegitimately derogating Chinese practice for the sake of imposing Western concepts of institutions. The perspective of realization-focused comparisons has far-reaching consequences that I will explore in the final part of this chapter, namely that evaluating a process of institutional change would centre on the aforementioned issue of the degree of participation and inclusion of interests that are affected by it. This means that the relationship between political and economic reform obtains a principled status also in the empirical methodology of institutional analysis, since it is at least partly the political institutions that define this degree; and certainly, they would obtain a paramount role in normative judgement. At this stage of my reasoning, I concentrate on the methodology of analysing economic systems.

Notions such as 'state capitalism' are derived from a transcendental-institutionalist point of view, only grappling ineffectively with the large variety of real-world institutions. The notion simply takes one transcendental benchmark, capitalism, and adds reference to another major social phenomenon, the state, which is implicitly seen as being different from markets which stay at the heart of capitalism. All these notions do not primarily refer to real-world phenomena, although a term such as 'capitalism' may have originally been abstracted from empirical conditions in certain countries in the nineteenth century. But even at that time, Germany and England had very different institutional regimes, and until today the 'varieties of capitalism' approaches emphasize the continuing relevance of those differences across real-world institutional regimes. Yet, even this school of thought presupposes that there is one benchmark, 'capitalism', which is an abstract reference of the typology. That would compare with a biological taxonomist who would stop thinking in terms of phylogeny, but imagine an ideal-typical design of a 'mammal', and then classify all mammals in terms of differences relative to this abstract type of design.[7]

The approach of 'economic style' radically rejects references to ideal-typical notions of economic systems as a means of systems taxonomy, such as 'capitalism' or 'market economy'. The question of whether China is 'capitalist' or not is a meaningless question in this view; it is as if a biologist would use an abstract model of a 'mammal' and then ask whether certain existing animals match this model or not. An economic style may be compared to the notion of 'species' in biological taxonomy, referring to a pattern of institutional features that is reproduced through time in a certain spatial configuration, and therefore only having empirical meaning in terms of particular periods and territories. This means that an economic style is a singular phenomenon, in the same way as a species is singular, though being a set-theoretic term that includes a large number of various instantiations of the species in the shape of biological organisms. I do not wish to overdraw this comparison between biology and economics here, and there is no space to explore the theoretical issues further. But we can say accordingly that the economic style is represented by the flow of states of economic systems and their fractal representations in space, seen as the 'individuals' that relate with the style as a set theoretical term. So, for example, a 'Chinese economic style' would be represented by instantiations in certain villages, counties and provinces, and their related institutional features, but possibly also by Chinese economic institutions in other places, such as Chinese business systems in Southeast Asia; these instantiations are seen as points in trajectories through time which interlace in a complex fashion. The central point is that, as with the case of 'species', what counts empirically is a set of institutional features that vary across those individual instantiations, hence also allowing for varieties of the economic style.[8]

As I have amply shown in this book, an economic style has to be identified via the description and analysis of a set of single institutional mechanisms that establish causality linking institutions, behaviours and performance. So, for example, particular forms of economic organization such as the family firm are characterizations that count for the economic style. This is methodologically important in order to properly treat the question of the continuity of style through time. This continuity is manifest in the historicity of those individual institutional features. As I have argued, historicity does not imply that a certain institution in the past continues to exist in the same way in the present, or that there is a direct causal impact of past institutions upon present institutions. Take, for example, a core institution of the Imperial economy, the lineage. Certainly, we cannot assert that the lineage is a central element of China's modern economic institutions as far as their formal set-up is concerned. In contrast, the Imperial state recognized the lineage as an essential element of social order, and customary law recognized the related economic organizations, such as lineage estates. Indeed, the modern Chinese state even fought a battle against lineages. Yet, we have seen that, at least in some parts of China, lineages have resurged as an important element of economic phenomena. Partly the lineage was even implicitly recognized under the Maoist regime in adapting the collectivist institutions to the existing settlement structures, thus triggering path dependencies of institutional change. Further, today, under certain circumstances, the economic actors manifest interest in reconstituting lineages, such as the use of extended kinship relations in organizing business. These observations lead us to reconsider lineages as an element also of economic style in the present, without claiming that these phenomena are of similar quality to lineages in the past. What connects the two phenomena is the historicity of the lineage institution.

The important concomitant term is 'family resemblances'. Institutions with the property of historicity can be recognized via family resemblances between past and present. Certainly, Chinese lineages today bear resemblances to lineages in the past. Interestingly, we see the fractal principle again at work here. The lineage is an individual phenomenon in the larger patterns of economic style, and, in the same vein, certain aspects of the lineage are individual phenomena in the pattern of the lineage, which may also vary across different instantiations. For example, lineages even today may implicitly operate as land-holding units, as in Imperial China, but only in particular places, perhaps even as exceptions. Yet, remarkably, some of these instantiations are no longer rural, but urban phenomena, thus becoming part and parcel of the ongoing process of modernization.

In other words, in identifying the economic style we have to collect and analyse a large number of 'traits' on different levels of generality and aggregation. These traits are reproduced through time and therefore allow for establishing connections between past and present. However, the question is how we can select between different traits in being relevant for describing the economic style and fixing its conceptual and empirical borders in time and space. For example, the formal institution of a stock market may not be relevant for identifying an economic style, as this is shared by many different economic systems. Yet, historically, stock markets were an institutional innovation, and even today economic systems may differ in terms of the centrality of the stock market for certain economic processes, such as corporate governance. For example, as the 'varieties of capitalism' literature has emphasized, the stock market may be an integral part of the economic style of the USA, but less so for many European countries. On the other hand, empirical cases of stock markets, certainly in the Chinese case, may manifest distinct phenomena that result from other aspects of economic style, thus modifying the institution without it becoming an essential element in the decription of the economic style. So, Chinese stock markets are unique, but they may not be essential in identifying the economic style.

This example also shows that in identifying an economic style, we need not and should not necessarily refer to items that are particular to the societies we identify as the 'carriers' of the economic style, as in the previous example of lineage. Hence, we realize again the fundamental difference in analysing culture in the context of the economy. Economic styles can be shaped, for example, by the dominance of a particular institutional feature because this emerges from specific economic determinants prevailing at a certain time and place, without a strong role of cultural factors. Yet, the feature may appear to be distinctive, and may even remain so over a longer period. The major reasons for this are path dependencies and interdependencies with other institutions which impact upon the patterns of the diffusion of the institution across the borders between different economic systems. For example, venture capital finance emerged in the USA and is specific to high-tech industries; yet, in spite of many attempts to copy the 'Silicon Valley', the diffusion of the institution was relatively slow, so that one could argue that it is a distinctive feature of American financial capitalism as an economic style.[9]

In Chapter 1 I argued that ultimately the criterion of identifying an economic style is in the eye of the beholder, drawing the methodological consequences out of the analysis of the 'mirror of culture'. In order to establish the identity of the economic style, the observer has to propose a unifying idea. In principle, this idea is a creation by the observer, akin to an artistic act of imagination. However, as I have argued, the idea achieves empirical relevance mainly through two different ways. The first is that the idea is able to guide the identification of family resemblances across institutional phenomena, in particular also in the sense of referring to traits which are most widely shared across a variety of institutions, and therefore have a sufficiently high level of generality. The second is that this idea 'makes sense' also for participating observers, and can become an important part of narratives about institutions that shape the discourse both among participant observers and between them and the scientific observer. In the Introduction I mentioned the case of Germany. The idea of the 'social' can serve as a unifying idea to identify the German economic style as a 'social market economy'. For example, scientific observers may identify certain aspects of social policy that permeate many institutions, in comparison to other economic systems, and the term 'social' also plays a crucial role in German discourse about the economic system. Hence, even though it would be impossible to find a shared meaning of that term even among the participants in the German discourse, it 'makes sense' as a descriptor of the German economic style.[10]

Identifying an economic style is closely related to investigating the role of culture in economic processes; however, there is an important difference between the two notions. Since the meaning of 'culture' is extremely broad and disputed, this assertion depends of course on which definition of culture is used. I have adopted the meaning which relates culture to the identities of individuals and the groups to which they assign themselves. This is a narrower definition, as it is often used especially by economists, who tend to treat all phenomena as 'cultural' which are transmitted through time across generations of actors and which cannot be explained by economic causes working at present. In my sense, culture on the level of economic systems would be manifest in differences at the aggregate systems level which are expressed in corresponding distinctions of the identities of the respective societies at large. This means, for example, that the cultural aspect of the German economy would emerge in observations such as on different approaches to negotiations over a regional trading agreement, which are referred to as being constitutive about the identities of the different parties, representing society-level attitudes and value stances, and which cannot be directly explained as being expressions of contingent economic interests prevailing at the time of negotiations. In comparison, the notion of economic style also covers phenomena which do not establish differences of identity, and so includes traits that are shared across different economic systems, though being contextualized in different styles.[11]

That being said, this book has advanced the idea that 'ritual' is the unifying idea in identifying the Chinese economic style. The term 'ritual' has a generic meaning that is closely related to culture. I have defined ritual as a set of practices that reproduce culture in a given population of actors. This highlights the fact that identities are embedded in social status orders maintained by ritual actions, thus deconstructing the notion of 'culture' within a given population. Then, culture in the German economic style would no longer refer to German culture as compared to Chinese culture, but to culture in defining identities across different groups of German society, such as family entrepreneurs or government officials, who are actors in the economic system. This means that, in understanding economic style, culture does not mainly matter on the aggregate level, but may count in explaining the interactions between different segments of the economic system. In this sense, rituals matter for any economic style, as they may reproduce cultural elements that also have a constitutive significance for the style. For example, rituals certainly play a defining role for elite status in the French political economy, but whether these are also essential for defining the French economic style is an empirical issue that is contextualized in what is being proposed as a potential unifying idea for identification.

In the Chinese case, referring to ritual as a defining feature of economic style therefore raises intricate questions, because it implies that culture is also an important element in determining economic processes via social practices. In other words, we would argue that China is distinctive because culture plays a stronger and different role in the economy compared to other economic systems, and that this role is put into action by means of ritual. Hence, we would not say that 'China's economic culture' is different from 'Germany's economic culture', but that culture matters in the Chinese case because of its unique role in the economic process, and because this defines a difference between 'China's economic style' and 'Germany's economic style'. The specific functions of culture in China, or, more generally, the fact that culture has these functions, makes

Chinese economic style special, and warrants its characterization as 'ritual economy'. And, most importantly, referring to 'culture' here does not mean 'Chinese culture' *in toto*, but highlights the role of more specific cultural phenomena and mechanisms that may not even be directly related to what would define distinctions of 'Chinese culture' in comparison to 'German culture'. Against the background of the Aoki model, I argued in Chapter 1 that culture is a creative process that may imbue any kind of element with a cultural meaning. Thus, as I have shown, for instance, the organizational practices of the Chinese Communist Party may become an element in the cultural transformations which are enacted and reproduced by ritual.

This observation leads to surprising twists and turns of the intellectual effort in understanding the Chinese economic style. In Chapter 1 I noted that when talking about 'Chinese economic culture' this might also mean that Chinese culture is 'economic'. We can now understand this rhetorical point much better. Among many other observations, this means, for example, that markets are also a constituent element of culture, or market practices are part and parcel of ritual practices. We have met many instances that illustrate this insight, such as the following:

- In the Skinner model of the traditional economy, marketplaces are the arena in which many social relationships are mediated, such as marriages or popular religion.
- In the modernist view, markets are media of civilizational transformation of rural society into modern society, such as epitomized in the experience of migration.
- The Chinese family is perceived as a unit pursuing wealth and fortune, thus engendering a strong stance towards entrepreneurship.
- Managerial innovations in leading Chinese corporations in China today aim at expanding the reach of the market into their organization, and leaders frame this in Chinese philosophical traditions.

By implication, this means that markets cannot be separated analytically from cultural analysis, in the sense of first separating the economic domain, and only in the next step calculating the impact of culture upon the economic process. If markets are also part and parcel of culture, the economy turns out to be a cultural phenomenon *sui generis*.

As we have seen, characterizing the Chinese economy as a 'ritual economy' is probably not seen as problematic for the case of the Chinese Empire. In fact, the revisionist economic and social history explicitly builds on the recognition that institutions which formerly have largely been seen in the light of ritual are now being identified as functionally equivalent to 'economic' institutions in the West, with the latter apparently suggesting a mere economic functionality that can be separated from cultural frameworks. The paramount example is the lineage and the lineage trust, which evolved into functional equivalents to shareholding companies in the nineteenth century. The traditional Chinese family and its flexible handling of kin relations in the context of economic actions is another manifestation of the mutual conditioning of culture and economy. So, the entire previous narrative about Imperial China failing to create the institutions and practices of the modern capitalist market economy turns out to be fundamentally misguided, as it overlooked the symbiosis of culture and market in Chinese ritual. Indeed, this also shows that the Weberian narrative of the 'rationalization' of Western society and economy is actually a cultural phenomenon of its own, both in terms of the narrative proper and with regard to the phenomena that are its topic. In other words, Western capitalism builds on the cultural construction of markets as autonomous domains of social action, whereas in the Chinese ritual economy markets are part and parcel of ritual. This interaction between beliefs and ideologies that people maintain and the economic systems and economic practices in which they live is what I have called 'performativity' in Chapter 1.

It is certainly a much more difficult challenge to convince the reader that the modern Chinese economic system may also be qualified as a ritual economy. This includes the thesis that the modern and the traditional economy are connected via the historicity of many of their elements. Hence, the ritual economy as an economic style would encompass, roughly, conditions in late Imperial China, especially during the Qing dynasty, and China today. This book invites the reader at least to ponder whether this idea is worthwhile to be considered in more depth.

To repeat this central point, I have introduced the term 'ritual' in two senses. As I started to argue earlier, if we refer to the generic notion of ritual, we would have to ask in what sense the Chinese case shows a peculiar manifestation of ritual that allows for treating this as a distinctive feature of China's economic style. Ritual in the generic sense is a universal phenomenon. Take, for example, the British case, which was, after all, the object of a large number of contributions in 'cultural studies' as a specialized field in academia. In these views, the British economic system in the twentieth century certainly displayed a distinct role of cultural differences between the working class and the white-collar stratum, which were embodied in many societal rituals, such as in the highly stratified educational system. The question is whether this would suffice to denote the British economic style as a 'ritual economy'. I refrain from pursuing this extremely interesting question here for reasons of space, but take note of the fact that rituals matter in all economic systems, yet they have been largely overlooked by economists, even of the institutionalist tradition (presumably because they were satisfied with notions such as 'informal institutions', which, however, as we have seen in Chapter 1, are too broad and imprecise to catch the specific meaning and mechanisms of ritual).[12]

The generic meaning of ritual is important in the Chinese case because we can avoid getting caught in the analytical trap of cultural analysis in economics which sees culture only in the sense of an impact of the past on the present. This would also happen if we were approaching 'ritual' in the original Chinese meaning exclusively. In the case of Imperial China, both meanings seem to converge easily, and so the characterization as a 'ritual economy' appears less controversial. On the contrary, the generic meaning of ritual allows one to identify the ritual aspect of institutional innovations, and only in the second stage would we ask how these relate to the indigenous meaning of ritual, which tie up with the Imperial past, Confucian traditions or contemporary practices of popular religion, among other aspects. However, as we have seen, there is a difficult methodological issue here, as the indigenous meaning of modernization has been consistently defined as staying in contradiction with the traditional notion of ritual. Modernization deliberately and explicitly aimed at destroying the rituals on which traditional society was built, such as extended kinship organizations, Confucianism as an institution, or popular religion. As a result, the term 'ritual' in the indigenous sense is no longer used in the internal discourse for identifying the nature of social relations and social order, thus creating an obstacle against establishing connections between the ideas of an external observer and the observed communities of actors. However, even if we cannot identify an indigenous discourse which refers to ritual as a global and encompassing principle of Chinese social and economic order, we can establish an argument that builds on uses of ritual and related terms in the context of particular economic and social phenomena, hence on the level of 'traits'. The issue of *guanxi* is a prominent case in point where these cross-connections are immediately salient.

Beyond these cases, however, we saw that the generic notion of ritual applies to the notion of modernization as such. In other words, modernization as a societal battle against ritual has been implemented and is being implemented by ritual means. This almost paradoxical statement is the key to understanding the family resemblances between past and present and hence for identifying the unity of the Chinese economic style. Pertinent observations include the following:

- Modernization is seen as a process of civilizational transformation that is led by a political elite that has overturned the old power structures.
- Society is seen as being structured by differences in civilizational achievement that translate into a status order which is also materially embodied, such as in settlement patterns or standards of consumption.
- The status order of ownership rights assigns an elevated status to the modernizing avant-garde of leading SOEs.
- Economic growth is a means to achieve modernization, and performance is viewed in the context of a competition for relative status, such as between different territorial units.

All these ritual aspects of modernization boil down to a transformational stance that emerged in the late nineteenth century and became the mainstream view in Chinese intellectual circles after the May 4th movement. This is the belief that a cultural elite has the task of transforming Chinese society and culture fundamentally. Ideas of cultural leadership and 'socio-educational' effort are hallmarks of modernist ritual, which are enshrined in the many uses of the term 'civilization' in reform-era CCP ideology.

On the other hand, we can also diagnose a resurgence of ritual in the indigenous and traditional meaning. At first sight, this would indicate a failure of modernization as understood by the leading elites, such as the resurgence of popular religion after a decades-long struggle against 'superstition'. However, this simple juxtaposition would not acknowledge the insight that modernization itself has a ritual dimension, which also means that there are many ways in which the two aspects can mutually interfere. For example, in Maoist times, Maoist ideology was partly practised in similar ways to popular religion, such as ascribing almost magical effects to Mao Zedong's thought and Maoist paraphernalia, thus activating magical 'efficacy' via the ritual practices of ideology. Or, many traditional notions of gender were actually replicated in spite of the revolutionary agenda of pursuing women's liberation, such as when assuming that class status is inherited via patrilineality. This also applies to the deeper structures, such as in the previous list of ritual aspects of modernization, the fact that traditional *jiaohua* notions appear as a metamorphosis in the civilizational leadership by a political avant-garde. So, we can use the generic notion of ritual for identifying the resilience and path dependencies of traditional ritual. In doing this, family resemblances count more than do the explicit references to traditional concepts and terms. One example is the persistence of 'Legalist' practices in modern management, which stay in tension with the resurgence of explicit references to Confucianism and Daoism as important intellectual resources for Chinese management approaches to corporate culture. In constructing the economic style, therefore, the deep-seated duality of Legalist and Confucian thought may be seen as a defining element (and not Confucianism per se), even though Legalism is rarely invoked in modern contemporary discourses.

In this context, in understanding the economic style, the notion of governmentality is especially useful. The historical tension between Legalism and Confucianism is basically about forms of governmentality, since both schools of thought argue that governance necessarily has to build on individualized mechanisms of self-control and moral commitment. In the Confucian case, this was seen as reflecting the inherent morality of human beings; in the Legalist case, the idea of internalization of externally imposed and enforced laws loomed large. This duality has a far broader significance, however, as it also refers to different principles of designing the institutions of government. Overcoming this duality emerged as a major challenge for modernization in the twentieth century, and, I would dare to suggest, even in the twenty-first century.

The reason is that the Chinese process of modernization is not only state driven but is also a process of state building. In other words, the project of modernization has been facing a dilemma since its inception. The agent of modernization, namely the state, is endogenous to the process, and in fact the agent is also the object of the process. In other words, Chinese modernization is a bootstrapping exercise. This dilemma is expressed most succinctly in the duality of Party and government which is therefore certainly one defining element in the economic style. It was expressed in almost violent terms under Maoism, when Mao tried to mobilize the Party against the state, which of course also carried the conflict into the Party itself. However, the duality of Party and government is a core principle of Chinese political economy and is manifested in the duality of 'leadership' versus 'administration'. We have seen that on all levels of the economic system the leadership function is institutionally distinct. In practice, this is visible in the pervasive role of 'leading groups' or similar bodies which are 'informal' in relation to the formal structure of government administration, but achieve formal status because of the constitutional role of the CCP. The most important reflection of this fact is the particular nature of planning in China today, in spite of 30 years of 'transition to the market'. Economic plans in China today are essentially tools of leadership, and less of direct administrative intervention.

Take, for example, private business in relation to government. Even in market-oriented provinces such as Guangdong or Zhejiang, private entrepreneurs, once they have achieved a certain size of business, strive for political office, such as becoming representatives in People's Consultative Conferences. The motivation lies in the improved access to the internal leadership circles of the Communist Party; further, political recognition also means recognition as a leader in business. Economic plans matter also for private business, because, for example, they would deal with infrastructure issues and therefore may deeply affect the business environment and opportunities for business. In this way, leadership can be exerted via many indirect channels, and result in a 'soft coordination' of economic activities in the market domain. The plan becomes a medium of co-opting business for the purposes of the state. This interplay between Party and societal actors also emerges as a paradigm in the larger context of the budding civil society. This may be classified as a 'state corporatist' paradigm, but, on the one hand, this would not pay sufficient attention to the duality of Party and government, and on the other hand, it would not acknowledge the central importance of the duality of local states vs. central state.

As we have seen, the most salient aspect of governmentality and path dependencies connecting past and present is the duality of local state and central government, which also ties up with the leadership issue. To a large extent, economic planning in China today is in fact the coordination of local states by the central government. In other words, the central state is the domain of planning, the local states are the domain of the market. Although this is deliberately over-accentuating the differences, I think that this juxtaposition is helpful in applying the notion of governmentality in conceptually overcoming the simple dualism of plan and market. Plans in China today are cascading channels of exerting leadership in the economy. In the first place, following the severe fiscal crisis of the central state in the early 1990s, this means the coordination of local states. As we have seen, this is a cascading structure in turn, as the central state divides into the central and provincial governments, with the latter assuming a partly ambivalent role between the central government and the local states, and the local states from the bottom up, referring primarily to the counties in the rural areas, but also and increasingly to the municipalities of different sizes, including metropolitan agglomerations such as Chongqing or the Pearl River Delta. In this complex structure, market and plan are deeply enmeshed, with plans partly setting frameworks and guiding expectations of market actors, partly also directly intervening in particular processes; and markets generating information and even setting incentives for planners, and creating opportunities for political entrepreneurship which may rely on planning tools to pursue its goals, resulting in phenomena of both 'planning following the market' and 'plans leading the market'.

It goes without saying that we cannot identify direct equivalents of these phenomena in the Imperial past, although we do know many instances of government intervention deliberately activating and relying on markets even then.[13] What is more important is that the duality of local state versus central state has deep historical roots, and that therefore we observe strong path dependencies of institutional change, with the foremost case the series of fiscal reforms and the gradual extension of formal institutions of taxation below the county level. This is a most salient case of state building, for sure, and even manifested symptoms of government involution throughout the reform period, thus indicating continuities between past and present, especially with regard to the role of informal and irregular taxation at the grassroots level.

The duality of local states vs. central state is also that aspect of the Chinese economic system which is thus far widely recognized as a distinctive feature, enabling phenomena such as experimentalism at the local level and intense locational competition at every level of the territorial hierarchy, with townships competing against townships, counties against counties, municipalities against municipalities, and even provinces against provinces. I have argued that this complex phenomenon of 'government competition' is governed by ritual. As a matter of fact, there is no formal institutional framework for regulating government competition: the Chinese Constitution defines China as a centralized state. One can certainly say, however, that the institutions of planning offer such as framework, again in the sense of establishing leadership relations, or that the institutions of the tax system partly constitute a formal institutional setting, which, for example, sets the incentives for governments in pursuing certain competitive strategies. However, there is no systematic constitutional approach in regulating this process, which is manifest in many phenomena that appear to be unregulated or dysfunctional from the perspective of the central government, such as local protectionism.

So, I have proposed that government competition is partly ritual in nature, which does not imply that ritual is necessarily a remedy for dysfunctional phenomena. My point is that government competition is part and parcel of the ritual economy, and that therefore it appears to manifest distinct features as compared to locational competition in other countries. I have analysed different aspects in this regard, such as the ritual nature of statistics, which is a core performance indicator, or the pervasive impact of the status order of ownership upon the locational strategies being implemented. The status order of ownership and the corresponding allocation of rights of ownership to different parts of the government administration is a ritual phenomenon of its own, strongly imposing path dependencies upon the process of reforming the ownership regime in the past 30 years.

The notion of governmentality is also important in order to understand how state, economy and society relate in the Chinese economic style, thus tying in the institutional aspects of governmentality with the analysis of the individual behavioural phenomena. Governmentality emphasizes the emergence of mechanisms of individual self-control, partly embodied in social practices that focus on the individual. This introduces a notion of individualism that differs substantially from what I would largely see as 'naive individualism' in economics, which just emphasizes individual freedom of choice. Against the backdrop of governmentality, the individual also assumes an important role in reproducing the structures of power which actually constrain its freedom and subordinate it to the body politic. Quite naturally, this view separates economists from market critics, who are therefore much more sensitive to the issue of whether markets are part and parcel of power structures governing society. Indeed, if we look at China today, this aspect certainly looms large and is part of the solution of the riddle as to why Communist rule appears to cooperate with capitalist dynamics and practices. I have already pinpointed the role of markets as media of the civilizing process of modernization. More specifically, local states often collude with capitalist market actors in imposing social and political disciplines upon migrant workers. After all, the discrimination by the *hukou* system is an integral determinant of competitive advantages of firms and locations. Hence, the status order of the Chinese population certainly collaborates with market forces in creating distinct patterns of economic organization.

I have argued on several occasions that a most interesting aspect appears to be that government interventions may result in societal adaptations that eventually cause market forces to reproduce the results of those interventions, thus obviating the need for further intervention. This is one instance of what I have called 'market governmentality'. The *hukou* system is a case in point, as the resulting distribution of social capital plays together with the labour market and may therefore reproduce the existing stratification in Chinese society. The aggregate expression of this causal interdependence is the resilience and even growing significance of the dualism between the formal and informal labour market. Of course, we further need to observe the many attempts of the government in subduing those informal structures, but here the duality of local versus central states comes into play again, with local states often countervailing central policies. Another example of market forces actually substituting direct government intervention is the radical birth control policies. There are good reasons to expect that even the recent relaxation of the policies will not result in substantial increases in the growth rate of the population, because both urban and rural families have adapted to the economic circumstances, in particular the escalating costs of raising children. These adaptations may be observed over the life cycle. In particular, the marriage market manifests a complex interaction between economic modernization and traditional values, resulting in the reinforcement of current practices of status goods consumption, and ultimately even driving aggregate savings behaviour.

The latter example is interesting because it shows that one need not refer directly to 'Confucian thrift' in order to explain the extremely high savings rate in China. As we have seen, the high savings rate is a manifestation of various aspects of the ritual economy. On the one hand, the status order of ownership matters greatly, with SOEs retaining profits as savings; on the other hand, there are many incentives that maintain a strong savings motivation on the part of the private actors. The marriage market is one factor, especially against the backdrop of the one-child policy, as it triggers a 'Red Queen race', especially with reference to consumer durables, cars and housing. This mechanism fits individual behaviour into the mould of the modernist growth model. In other words, what was a forced industrialization model in Maoist times has emerged as a status-driven consumption-based model in the modern ritual economy under the aegis of modernization. Whether participation in this status goods competition is 'free to choose' is a question that is certainly treated differently from the viewpoint of governmentality than from the standard economist's viewpoint. I argue that China's modern consumer society is deeply shaped by the ritual economy, and hence is an important aspect of governmentality. This corresponds to the notion of 'ritual labour', as manifest in phenomena such as urban professionalism as a cultural phenomenon. Actively participating in the modernizing economy becomes an expression of the ritual obligations of modernity.

Ultimately, the relationship between the individual and the state is a core question in analysing governmentality. Hence, the notion of governmentality is also pertinent when, in conclusion, we consider the question of how to evaluate the performance of the Chinese economic style. There are many possible standards. Economics is in favour of individualistic standards of evaluation, thus looking at the results of economic development for individual welfare, though struggling until today with the question of how distributional issues can be properly weighed up. In comparison, environmentalists would highlight the consequences of economic growth for the natural environment, and thus diagnose a fundamental clash between individualistic notions of economic welfare and the broader concerns of future generations, and even life in general. Or, military strategists would emphasize the collective interests of the body politic in terms of future security, such as accessibility of natural resources.

This leads us back to the initial discussion about the two ways in which to evaluate institutional changes. The notion of economic style seems to suggest that there is no clear-cut approach to categorizing economic systems into theoretically grounded classes such as the 'capitalist' regime. This also applies to more detailed specifications such as 'state capitalism'. Therefore, we are also lacking unequivocal criteria for assessing the differences or the distances between a realized institutional structure and those theoretical benchmarks. This is exactly what observers have experienced in the past 30 years. We cannot explain the Chinese economic performance just by considering the distance between realized institutions and a theoretical benchmark, and would actually run into trouble in making sense of the factual success. So, the notion of economic style naturally comes together with the evaluative criterion of realization-focused comparisons. This method does not directly allow for deducing evaluative standards, since what count are the evaluations of the affected parties themselves. But, as we saw in the previous paragraph, it remains an open question how we define who are the affected parties. In principle, we could imagine alternative choices between individualistic criteria of how to define what a relevant 'realization' is, or more collectivistic ones.[14]

This would point towards the political mechanisms that allow for such endogenous evaluations, since we could argue that there is no external criterion of identifying the affected parties, but that these criteria emerge and have to emerge endogenously. Hence, the approach of economic style allows one to consider the role of the political system in establishing standards of evaluation, also from the viewpoint of the external observer. These standards are meta-criteria, as they do not directly refer to properties of the economic system and economic processes, such as 'efficiency' in the broadest sense, but refer to the process of institutional change under which those economic processes happen, and to which institutions govern the participation of different actors in designing and evaluating this process.

In a more general sense, realization-focused comparisons therefore refrain from setting direct standards of measurement and criteria for relevance of individuals and groups, and instead emphasize evaluative criteria which highlight notions of 'inclusiveness' as a central criterion of 'justice'. Again, there is no external criterion for assessing 'inclusiveness', since what counts is the way in which participating actors perceive themselves as being affected by institutional changes, and how they can in turn respond to these changes in a way which enables participation in the benefits of change. Now, considering the ritual economy as analysed in this book, there is obviously a fundamental tension between the modernist paradigm and the criterion of inclusiveness. Since the modernist paradigm establishes the leading role of a modernist elite, this necessarily also implies the exclusion of other actors from participating in designing institutional change. In other words, the elitist nature of the ritual economy calls into question whether the tremendous success of the Chinese growth model in the past meets the standards of procedural justice that inhere in the notion of realization-focused comparisons.

It is important to avoid a conceptual short cut here which would directly jump to the conclusion that this pinpoints the tension between market economy and authoritarian political system, and thus would conclude that in spite of great achievements in prosperity, the absence of democratic political institutions would relativize those achievements. The notion of inclusiveness in the general framework of economic style is much broader, abstract and more open to interpretation in terms of specific political institutions. Basically, it relates to the network structures and the distribution of social capital in a society, and the resulting mechanisms for being able to take part and influence processes of institutional change that affect an actor's opportunities for economic advancement. In many societies, in spite of formal democratic institutions, these structures can remain strongly elitist and may block the accessibility of political positions of power for the majority of the population, even in the most advanced industrial countries. Often this low permeability and openness of social networks of power is reflected in the distribution of wealth in society, which feeds back on the evolution of the network.[15]

This is not the place to discuss these issues further. I concentrate on the analysis of a few basic aspects of the Chinese economic style which are most salient. One observation is that the dualist nature of many economic institutions implies a low degree of inclusiveness of the processes that determine institutional changes, with the most glaring example being the weak position of farmers and migrants in taking part in shaping the institutions that affect their own economic fate. The phenomenon that stands at the centre is the system of land property rights. As we have seen, however, this diagnosis requires much more detailed exposition and also thorough empirical analysis, because conditions vary widely across the many local states in China. But, generally speaking, the fact that in the growing incidence of local political unrest issues of official abuse of land rights are by far the most important triggers clearly shows that the farmers also perceive the lack of participation and are willing to take the risks of expressing their dissatisfaction. Similarly, we note the fact that urbanization is a process that often excludes citizens from taking part in decisions that directly affect their economic well-being, such as large-scale urban restructuring.

So, we may say that the modernist framework of the ritual economy is itself a constraint upon achieving a high degree of inclusiveness in realization-focused comparisons, as it is a defining feature of the political status order. If we look at formal political institutions, the central expression of this fact is, of course, the constitutional role of the Chinese Communist Party. As I have argued, as an element of the ritual economy, the CCP is less conceived of as a particular politico-ideological movement today, but mainly as a formal organization of societal and political elites. This is strongly emphasized in contemporary views that highlight the 'meritocracy' of the Chinese political system, and which stay in stark contrast to the views that relate the CCP to abuses of power, corruption and violations of civil rights.[16] Again, I do not adopt a specific position here, but emphasize that the formal construct of one-Party rule would indicate low inclusiveness in the first place. That being said, however, the policy of the so-called 'Three Represents' grouped under the aegis of the Jiang Zemin leadership recognized this issue and aimed at increasing the scope of inclusiveness. However, this remained to be defined in elitist terms, focusing mainly on wealth and education as positive criteria for membership.

So, in the light of realization-focused comparisons, beyond the more specific issues of designing the political system, there is a principled tension between the elitist nature of the ritual economy and the normative requirement to expand the inclusiveness of evaluation. This observation certainly points to the central role of civil society in the future development of China, in particular in the context of the secular urbanization process. Enhancing the role and autonomy of China's civil society is a normative concern that could be pursued in many ways, especially in the context of the local states where the majority of political decisions regarding infrastructure, social services or education are being taken. Interestingly, this would mean taking up the strand of social movements in the final decades of the Chinese Empire, where civic groups in Chinese cities took many initiatives in urban self-government. Whether a strengthening of indigenous civil society will lead to particular forms of political governance so far prevailing in Western countries remains an open question; the answer certainly depends on the time horizon of the predictions. At this point, I only suggest that Chinese economic style, the ritual economy, may also go hand in hand with a strong role of civil society, as compared to formal political institutions and their reforms, in further developing the institutions of participation.[17] In other words, I do not believe that the ritual economy might also manifest the distinct combination of market economy and formal parliamentary democracy that has emerged in Western countries, but that there is much scope for civil society to become part and parcel of the ritual economy. In this case, I also surmise that civil society may turn out to become a stabilizing factor in the Chinese economic style.[18]

Thus far, my brief discussion of inclusiveness has only focused on the citizens of China. One important aspect of realization-focused comparisons is the inclusion of 'bystanders' in the process of institutional change and evaluation. In the context of economic systems, this refers to individuals and collective entities in other countries. In fact, there are many institutional arrangements in the world economy that actually enable this inclusion, in particular the institutions of international trade, such as the WTO. China underwent an arduous process of institutional evaluation by 'outsiders' when she negotiated the accession to WTO. It is important to note that this process directly matches the notion of realization-focused comparisons, as negotiations are driven by the interests of the different trading partners of China, and do not primarily refer to a transcendental institutional benchmark as a criterion for defining the conditions for accession. However, there are also elements in the WTO rules and practices that refer to such benchmarks, in particular with regard to the question of whether or not China may be classified as a 'market economy', with serious implications, for example, in the context of anti-dumping procedures. This question is actually relevant at the time of writing, as the accession protocol determined that China would not be recognized as a 'market economy' until the end of 2016; accordingly, important trading partners, foremost the EU and the USA, do not recognize China as such, and even appear determined to uphold this judgement after 2016.[19]

From the perspective of economic style, the term 'market economy' is not sufficient to characterize an economic system beyond some very broad and fundamental characteristics such as whether or not there are comprehensive economic plans based on material balances that define a centrally planned economy. Current tensions over the 'market economy status' are misplaced references to a transcendental benchmark, which differs from the situation of the accession negotiations, when China herself was claiming to be in a 'transitory status' from plan to market, thus even agreeing with the characterization as a 'non-market economy'. In other words, the characterization was not a judgement deduced from transcendental criteria, but expressed an inclusive mutual consent of all the affected parties. That would be different if the EU and the USA maintained their judgement unilaterally. Certainly, this would open the way for a WTO complaint, and hence would activate the dispute resolution process, which would restore inclusiveness. However, following the reasoning in this book, beyond the terms of accession protocol, reference to the 'market economy' as a justification for unilateral decisions would not be scientifically valid. This does not preclude pointing to government interventions as a source of market distortions in anti-dumping allegations, but the relevant WTO process would have to follow the rules that count for every WTO member.

So, the analysis of the ritual economy put forward in this book has also immediate practical relevance for international economic policies. As I have shown, the market is a fundamental element of the ritual economy, even culminating in forms of market governmentality. Approaching this system with crude conceptual dualisms prevalent in economics would fail to meet fundamental notions of fairness and inclusiveness in realization-focused comparisons as the only feasible and legitimate way of evaluating economic institutions.

Notes

1 The notion of 'state capitalism' largely appears to be a catchword in journalistic accounts (see e.g. *The Economist*, 21 January 2012 or 12 October 2013). There are attempts in political science at systematizing the notion (see e.g. Orenstein 2011), and it is increasingly used also in research on China (see e.g. McNally 2013). One problem is that it often refers to particular elements of government policies, such as sovereign wealth funds. Then, Singapore's or even Norway's sovereign wealth fund may be classified as 'state capitalist' without necessarily implying that the entire economic system is 'state capitalist' as is suggested for cases such as China or Russia. There are also alternative terms. As early as in 1993, I have used the term 'cadre capitalism' (Herrmann-Pillath 1993), thus highlighting the entrepreneurial role of political actors in distinction from the 'state', which matches with the network methodology of analysing economic styles.

2 The distinction between the two approaches to evaluating institutions is the cornerstone of Sen's (2009) theory of justice and goes back to his work (e.g. Sen 2002) on social choice, in particular the problem of aggregating over individual preferences in the context of the 'Arrow (im)possibility' theorem for establishing collective preference functions. Sen himself does not elaborate on the relationship with evolutionary approaches in general. In fact, the two literatures on social choice and evolutionary economics appear to be mostly disconnected thus far, which is evident from the fact that evolutionary economics struggles with the problem of how to define normative standards for policy evaluation (Witt 2003b). Interestingly, this also applies to the Aoki framework that I have adopted in this book. However, Aoki (2001: 228; cf. Aoki 1996) is explicit about the observation that phenomena such as path dependencies or complementarities of institutions imply that at least there are many cases in which it is not possible to rank institutional arrangements in terms of Pareto-improvements. In Herrmann-Pillath and Boldyrev (2014) I have introduced the Senian approach as a solution to these problems. Sen refers transcendental institutionalism to Kantian ethics, so that Hegel's Kant critique is also relevant here. Hegel argued that Kantian morality fails to apply in the real world because the problem of how to actually incentivize people to follow the 'rational norm' cannot be solved (for a modern economic version of this Kant critique, without reference to Hegel, see Binmore 2005). Therefore, Hegel claimed that general ethical norms can only be rooted in historically specific forms of 'ethical life' ('Sittlichkeit'). I have already pointed out (Chapter 1, n. 47) that this corresponds to the notion of 'ritual' in the generic meaning.

3 It is illuminating to refer to the substantial literature on endogenous trade policy which has demonstrated that welfare rankings of institutions can change if the interaction between policies and interest groups is made explicit and is introduced as a sole causal factor that drives institutional change; for example, the ranking of tariffs and subsidies as optimal policies might be reversed. The reason is that the costs of rent seeking are also determined by the policies which set the incentives for interest groups to invest in wasteful lobbying. If the role of political advisers is also made endogenous, rankings may turn out to be paradoxical in nature, thus ultimately reflecting the fact that any kind of ranking would have to build on aggregate welfare functions which must be known to the adviser, whose recommendations, however, would need to be implemented in an incentive-compatible way. I have collected a number of paradoxes in theorizing about trade policy in Herrmann-Pillath (2004); for a summary see Herrmann-Pillath and Boldyrev (2014: 194ff.). It is important to note that 'impartiality' is a central notion in Adam Smith's 'Theory of Moral Sentiments' which is also reviewed by Sen (2009). However, already in Smith, impartiality is seen as a position that can emerge endogenously from moral interactions, as being reflected in individual comparisons across different possible positions. This meaning of impartiality is also picked up by Sen (2009), hence relating the notion of realization-focused comparisons back to Smith.

4 The argument on the necessary complementarity of trade liberalization and the welfare state was seminally developed by Rodrik (1998); and on the necessity of partial restrictions to trade in order to stabilize trajectories of trade liberalization see the early work by Bagwell and Staiger (1990). For a full elaboration on this way of reasoning, see Herrmann-Pillath (2008b). This stands behind the many problems that economists have with the institutions of the WTO which apparently seem to allow for too much impact of special interests upon the process of trade liberalization. However, once one interprets the WTO as an institutional framework for realization-focused comparisons, these criticisms lose their bite.

5 This criterion explains why, for Sen, democracy, free media and civil rights are an essential element in judging economic institutions. This goes back to more fundamental arguments established in Sen (2002) of why 'freedom' is a core criterion for judging also the well-being of an individual. Sen's most famous example is comparing a person who starves because he imposes fasting upon himself voluntarily and a person in exactly the same physical status who also follows this personal rule, but actually would also have no opportunity to change his behaviour because the economic institutions of a country have caused a famine. In the first case the person has the freedom to change his behaviour, in the second he has not. In terms of mere physical status and consumption standards, the welfare status of the two people would be the same, but, according to Sen, the position of the second person would be much worse than the position of the first. Clearly, examples like this are highly relevant for the Chinese case, as in the context of criticisms of China's human rights record the Chinese government often argues that basic economic livelihood is also a human right, and that therefore different human rights may weigh differently in different stages of economic development. For Sen, civil rights matter on every level of development, for the principled reasons exposed.

6 This reasoning goes back to the foundational analysis of the opportunity cost principle by Buchanan (1969), which, however, is often ignored by economists. Buchanan argued that standard uses of opportunity costs implicitly assume that all information has been revealed in an equilibrium state, so that economic actors can choose the optimum while responding to price signals. However, if one considers real-world processes, only the competitive process reveals that

information, and actors need to take ongoing decisions out of the equilibrium. So, considering an actor who takes a decision based on her own private information, the true costs of this decision is not the costs that she actually perceives, but the costs that are imposed upon her by the actions taken by other actors who compete against her. This is the reason why accounting costs are not costs in the economic sense (which are only the opportunity costs). As a consequence, the true costs will only be revealed when the competitive process has achieved an equilibrium. In the actual decisions, however, it would be impossible to refer to this equilibrium in the sense of the distance from it and the imputed costs, because it is impossible to know these costs out of equilibrium.

7 In fact, the prevailing economic taxonomies adhere to a metaphysical standpoint that was prevalent in pre-Darwinian biology, as outlined in great depth by Mayr (1982) or Gould (2002). In these taxonomies, the existing animal species were seen in the light of a divine design that was eternally fixed. Only the early discoveries of fossils raised the question of whether and how change might happen in the realm of life. But even then, pre-Darwinian thinkers could only imagine clearly demarcated species as divine types, reflecting the ideas of the Creator. The breakthrough achieved by Darwin was to envisage the tree of life as reflecting a process of continuous gradual change, with species emerging as stable conjunctions of organismic properties, relative to certain environments, maintained by the dynamic forces of variation, selection and retention. Economic taxonomies similarly reflect a theoretical framework without taking constant historical change as the only relevant empirical condition. This problem was amply discussed in German-speaking economics at the times of the 'Methodenstreite', especially in the context of the Historical School. However, the Historical School mainly presented theories about stages of historical change. This led to a renewed and pronounced prevalence of theory-based taxonomies, such as in the work of Walter Eucken (1939), who introduced the 'ideal-typical' distinction between 'market economy' and 'centrally planned economy'. However, as I have discussed in Herrmann-Pillath (1990), Eucken did not claim that the ideal types are empirically relevant, but only 'real types' that are being constructed by means of the theoretical tools offered by the ideal type. This methodological stance was not fully pursued by Eucken himself (who passed away prematurely). Eucken's method explicitly built on Max Weber's thinking, though introducing some important distinctions. But with the exclusion of Max Weber from the internationally dominant disciplinary frame of economics, this entire methodological debate moved out of the scope of economic research. Although Weber himself was firmly opposed to biologistic metaphors and transfers in the social sciences, in fact he adopted basic evolutionary views in his emphasis on the individuality of social and economic systems and their dynamics of change. It is interesting to note that, in the recent debates about the 'varieties of capitalism' literature, Zhang and Peck (2014) propose the alternative approach of 'variegated capitalism' based on the case of China, emphasizing the complex and multi-scalar co-existence and interaction among different local systems in the larger spatial context, which certainly comes close to an 'ecological' perspective that matches biological approaches to taxonomy.

8 I have developed an evolutionary conceptual foundation for the notion of economic style in Herrmann-Pillath (2009d). In existing economic approaches to taxonomy, what comes closest is the literature on national innovation systems which is sometimes also explicitly related to evolutionary economics; for seminal contributions see Lundvall (1992) and for a related opinion see Ebner (1999). This literature is largely agnostic about generalizations over concepts such as 'market economy' and emphasizes the diversity of government–economy interactions, the embeddedness of institutions in the social and

cultural context, and the decisive role of global locational competition in selecting certain institutional arrangements. In the first place, national innovation systems are also seen as being unique configurations in time and space (see e.g. Zysman 1994).

9 In Aoki's (2001) 'Comparative Institutional Analysis' approach therefore, the notion of 'linkages' plays a central methodological role, with the two types of 'synchronic' and 'diachronic' linkages, as we have seen (Chapter 1, n. 58). Aoki does not assign a major causal force to culture in describing these patterns, which are largely explained by certain etic properties of the underlying economic processes, such as the distribution of information among partaking actors, or the complementarities between their skills, or the nature of the competitive field. Yet, the linkages imply that the resulting networks of institutions obtain a singular character which impedes the diffusion of certain individual elements. In case of intentional copying of individual elements, these may fail to perform in the same way as in the original system, because synergies with other institutions do not materialize.

10 See Chapter 1, n. 64, where I refer to Alfred Müller-Armack who explicitly alluded to Christiantity. Obviously, however, the term could also serve as a rallying point for German Social Democracy, which gave up the ideological ballast of traditional socialism after the Second World War, and later avidly embraced Keynesianism. Therefore, the specifically German canvas of debates over economic policy unfolded, with liberal interpretations of the social market economy closely attached to the Freiburg tradition of 'Ordo-Liberalism', and the Keynesian model that was established in the late 1960s and 1970s, to the chagrin of Müller-Armack, who tried to defend what he regarded as the 'original' idea of the social market economy (see Müller-Armack 1981).

11 For the example of conceptualizing 'profession' in the German and the US system, see Chapter 1, n. 67. This is interesting because it establishes a clear connection between certain collective narratives and even individual self-descriptions of identities in work contexts. Another example, which I discuss in Herrmann-Pillath and Boldyrev (2014), is the so-called 'precautionary principle' in environmental policy and consumer protection, which has achieved global significance in the context of WTO regulations and international treaties related to environmental issues. Whereas Germany (and many European countries) adopts the precautionary principle, the USA and other countries in the Anglo-Saxon tradition adopt a risk-based approach that emphasizes rational weighing of threats versus market opportunities and other possible benefits. These differences erupt recurrently, as recently in the context of the TTIP negotations. The strong reaction of German civil society towards the perceived erosion of the precautionary principle shows that these issues indeed express fundamentally different stances towards science and markets, which therefore are also interpreted as cultural differences between Americans and Germans or Europeans.

12 I would argue that the distinct intellectual history of the 'cultural studies' field is strong evidence for the centrality of ritual in British society (see Hartley 2003). Cultural studies emerged in Great Britain, and also remained a distinctively British research strand to a large degree. For example, the strong alternative tradition of German 'Kulturwissenschaften' impeded the establishment of a similar academic field in this country. So, we meet an interesting phenomenon of the endogeneity of scientific innovations in relation to the cultural context. I would argue that cultural studies indeed reflect the salience of ritual in defining the identities of different social strata in the British population, and even in the economy in particular, at least at the time when this academic field took off. In this sense, one could even argue that cultural studies became an

element in 'performing' ritual in the British context, although the critical stance of scientific research would also contribute to 'disenchantment' rituals, thus possibly contributing to their erosion. This may also explain the recent decline of cultural studies even in Britain.

13 See Chapter 2, n. 97.

14 It is important to note that Sen (2009: 246) does not commit himself clearly to an exclusively individualistic concept of evaluation. This relates to the open nature of his concept of 'capabilities' that is the ultimate anchor of his notion of welfare (see Chapter 1, n. 59). Then, the question is whether there are also collective capabilities, which may be rooted in the fact that individual capabilities may need to rely on public goods. For example, defending the country of which one is a citizen may be seen as a collective capability. This raises the possibility that an individual may have to subordinate its individualistic interests to the collective interests. As we will see, we will therefore need to distinguish clearly between individualistic measures of welfare and individualistic criteria in assessing the procedure of realization-focused comparisons.

15 This is a central point in John Rawls' (2001) theory of 'political liberalism'. Rawls argues that modern 'welfare capitalism' does not meet the criteria of political liberalism, since access to political elites remains restricted, and formal institutions of elections only create limited opportunities for citizens to influence the decisions of those elites. This is visible, among other observations, in the pervasive phenomenon of special interests in politics. He opposes 'welfare capitalism' with the notion of the 'property-owning democracy', in which the relatively equal distribution of wealth creates the conditions for universal participation of citizens in politics. However, Rawls also includes 'liberal socialism' in the scope of political liberalism, as he argues that collective ownership may also create the conditions for equal participation in politics. Rawls' approach matches models of political economy such as Acemoglu and Robinson (2009), in which political and economic elites engineer transitions from autocracy to democracy in order to stabilize their 'de facto political power'.

16 One of the most outspoken and visible protagonists of the alleged Chinese meritocracy in Western literature is Daniel Bell (2008), who combines this, in 'Chinese style', with a criticism of Western political conditions. Bell also puts this into the context of cultural revival in terms of a 'New Confucianism'. With regard to the constitutional dimension, the specific role of the CCP is elaborated in Jiang (2010) (see Chapter 4, n. 17). These strands of thought converge in the notion of 'Confucian constitutionalism' propagated by public intellectuals such as Jiang Qing, who questions one-Party rule but proposes an elitist system of representation that would also include Chambers of 'outstanding personalities'; see www.nytimes.com/2012/07/11/opinion/a-confucian-constitution-in-china.html?_r=0 (accessed 24 July 2014). His idea is, interestingly, that the principle of representation should not only refer to individuals but also to the collective of 'the nation'. These debates have to be seen against the backdrop of debates about constitutionalism also in other East Asian countries (for an overview see Ginsburg 2012).

17 This is certainly already visible in political practice. For example, Manion (2014) coined the term of 'authoritarian parochialism' in order to describe the phenomenon that delegates of local People's Congresses increasingly adopt an active role in taking up the citizens' concerns in their electoral district and representing their cases to higher level authorities, in particular also the CCP. They do not and cannot rally around general political programmes, but they design autonomous solutions and approaches to specific local political issues. This can combine with civil society initiatives, such as representations of local business interests.

18 I note that even libertarian approaches to economic policy can combine with an elitist approach to constitutional issues, as is most prominently illustrated by Hayek (1979); for a useful summary, see Boykin (2010). Hayek's views are similar to the aforementioned views championed by Jiang Qing in suggesting a bicameral system in which one Chamber is formed by individuals of merit who become lifelong members. The motivation for this is the deep libertarian mistrust in majoritarian democracy. Hence, even on the theoretical level we cannot clearly make the case that the ritual economy is politically unstable. This does not affect the general case for civil rights, such as the freedom of the press or freedoms of association, however, which are also essential in Amartya Sen's view. Interestingly, a leading 'Confucian liberal', Yao Yongqiu (pen-name Qiu Feng) (see Yao 2012a: 35ff.), argues that Hayek offers important theoretical perspectives for reconstructing a distinctively Chinese tradition of constitutionalism.

19 See www.borderlex.eu/understanding-china-market-economy-status-battle/ (accessed 21 November 2015).

References

Abelshauser, W. (2003) *Kulturkampf. Der deutsche Weg in die Neue Wirtschaft und die amerikanische Herausforderung*, Berlin: Kadmos.

Abramovitz, M. (1989) *Thinking About Growth and Other Essays on Economic Growth and Welfare*, Cambridge: Cambridge University Press.

Acemoglu, D. and Robinson, J.A. (2009) 'Persistence of Power, Elites, and Institutions', *American Economic Review*, 98(1): 276–293.

Acemoglu, D., Johnson, S. and Robinson, J.A. (2001) 'The Colonial Origins of Comparative Development: An Empirical Investigation', *American Economic Review*, 91(5): 1369–1401.

Acemoglu, D., Johnson, S. and Robinson, J.A. (2002) 'Reversal of Fortune: Geography and Institutions in the Making of the Modern World Income Distribution', *The Quarterly Journal of Economics*, 117: 1231–1294.

Ackermann, R. (2001) *Pfadabhängigkeit, Institutionen und Regelreform*, Tübingen: Mohr.

Ahlers, A.L. and Schubert, G. (2009) '"Building a New Socialist Countryside" – Only a Political Slogan?', *Journal of Current Chinese Affairs*, 38(4): 35–62.

Ahlers, A.L. and Schubert, G. (2013) 'Strategic Modelling: "Building a New Socialist Countryside" in Three Chinese Counties', *The China Quarterly*, 216: 831–849.

Akerlof, G.A. and Kranton, R.E. (2000) 'Economics and Identity', *Quarterly Journal of Economics*, 115(3): 715–753.

Akerlof, G.A. and Kranton, R.E. (2005) 'Identity and the Economics of Organizations', *Journal of Economic Perspectives*, 19(1): 9–32.

Aldrich, H. (1999) *Organizations Evolving*, London: Sage.

Allee, M.A. (2004) 'The Status of Contracts in Nineteenth-century Chinese Courts'. In Zelin, M., Ocko, J.K. and Gardella, R., eds, *Contract and Property in Early Modern China*, Stanford, CA: Stanford University Press, pp. 159–177.

Allen, Robert C. (2009), *The British Industrial Revolution in Global Perspective*, Cambridge: Cambridge University Press.

Alpermann, B. (2014) 'China's Cotton Market as a Strategic Action Field'. In Augustin-Jean, L. and Alpermann, B., eds, *The Political Economy of Agro-food Markets in China: The Social Construction of Markets in an Era of Globalization*, Basingstoke and New York: Palgrave Macmillan, pp. 183–209.

Anagnost, A. (1997) 'Constructing a Civilized Community'. In Huters, Th., Wong, R.B. and Yu, P., eds, *Culture and State in Chinese History. Conventions, Accomodations, and Critiques*, Stanford, CA: Stanford University Press, pp. 346–368.

Anagnost, A. (2004) 'The Corporeal Politics of Quality (*Suzhi*)', *Public Culture*, 16(2): 189–208.

Aoki, M. (1988) *Information, Incentives, and Bargaining in the Japanese Economy*, Cambridge: Cambridge University Press.

Aoki, M. (1996) 'An Evolutionary Parable of the Gains from International Organizational Diversity'. In Landau, R., Taylor, T. and Wright, G., eds, *The Mosaic of Economic Growth*, Stanford, CA: Stanford University Press, pp. 247–263.

Aoki, M. (2001) *Toward a Comparative Institutional Analysis*, Stanford, CA: Stanford University Press.

Aoki, M. (2007) 'Endogenizing Institutions and Institutional Change', *Journal of Institutional Economics*, 3(1): 1–31.

Aoki, M. (2010) *Corporations in Evolving Diversity: Cognition, Governance, and Institutions*, Oxford: Oxford University Press.

Aoki, M. (2011) 'Institutions as Cognitive Media between Strategic Interactions and Individual Beliefs', *Journal of Economic Behavior and Organization*, 79: 20–34.

Appelbaum, R.P. (2009) 'Big Suppliers in Greater China: A Growing Counterweight to the Power of Giant Retailers'. In Hung, H.-F., ed., *China and the Transformation of Global Capitalism*, Baltimore, MD: Johns Hopkins University Press, pp. 65–85.

Ariely, D. and Norton, M.I. (2007) 'How Actions Create – Not Just Reveal – Preferences', *Trends in Cognitive Science*, 12(1): 13–16.

Armbrüster, T. (2005) *Management and Organization in Germany*, Aldershot and Burlington, VA: Ashgate.

Arrighi, G. (2007) *Adam Smith in Beijing. Lineages of the Twenty-first Century*, London and New York: Verso.

Arthur, B. (1989) 'Competing Technologies, Increasing Returns and Lock-in by Historical Events', *Economic Journal*, 99: 116–131.

Augustin-Jean, L. (2010) 'The "Social Construction of a Market" in a Transitional Economy. The Sugar Industry in China in the Context of Globalization', *Economic Sociology. The European Electronic Newsletter*, 11(3): 33–42.

Baecker, D. (2000) *Wozu Kultur?*, Berlin: Kadmos.

Bagwell, K. and Staiger, R.W. (1990) 'A Theory of Managed Trade', *American Economic Review*, 80(4): 779–795.

Bai, C.-E., Tao, Z. and Tong, S.Y. (2004) 'Local Protectionism and Regional Specialization: Evidence From Chinese Industries', *Journal of International Economics*, 63: 397–417.

Baker, H.D.R. (1977) 'Extended Kinship in the Traditional City'. In Skinner, G.W., ed., *The City in Late Imperial China*, Stanford, CA: Stanford University Press, pp. 499–518.

Baker, H.D.R. (1979) *Chinese Family and Kinship*, London: Macmillan.

Barnes, B. (1995) *The Elements of Social Theory*, Princeton, NJ: Princeton University Press.

Barthélemy, J. and Poncet, S. (2008) 'China as an Integrated Area?', *Journal of Economic Integration*, 23: 896–926.

Baskerville, R.F. (2003) 'Hofstede Never Studied Culture', *Accounting, Organizations, and Society*, 28: 1–14.

Batisse, C. and Poncet, S. (2004) 'Protectionism and Industry Localization in Chinese Provinces', *Journal of Chinese Economic and Business Studies*, 2(2): 133–154.

Bauer, W. (1974) *China und die Hoffnung auf Glück. Paradiese, Utopien, Idealvorstellungen in der Geistesgeschichte Chinas*, Munich: dtv.

Bauer, W. (1990) *Das Antlitz Chinas. Die autobiographische Selbstdarstellung in der chinesischen Literatur von ihren Anfängen bis heute*, Munich: Hanser.

Baum, R. and Shevchenko, A. (1999) 'The State of the State'. In Goldman, M. and MacFarquhar, R., eds, *The Paradox of China's Post-Mao Reforms*, Cambridge: Cambridge University Press, pp. 333–360.

Bechtel, H. (1930) *Der Wirtschaftsstil des deutschen Spätmittelalters*, Munich and Leipzig: Duncker & Humblot.

Becker, G.S. (1996) *Accounting for Tastes*, Cambridge, MA: Harvard University Press.

Bednar, J. and Page, S. (2007) 'Can Game(s) Theory Explain Culture? The Emergence of Cultural Behavior Within Multiple Games', *Rationality and Society*, 19(1): 65–97.

Befu, H. and Kreiner, J., eds (1992) *Othernesses of Japan: Historical and Cultural Influences on Japanese Studies in Ten Countries*, Munich: Iudicium.

Behrens, L. (2007) *Konservierung von Stereotypen mit Hilfe der Statistik. Geert Hofstede und sein kulturvergleichendes Modell*, Arbeitspapier No. 51, Allgemeine Sprachwissenschaft, Institut für Linguistik, Universität zu Köln.

Bell, D.A. (2008) *China's New Confucianism. Politics and Everyday Life in a Changing Society*, Princeton, NJ: Princeton University Press.

Berger, S. and Dore, R., eds (1996) *National Diversity and Global Capitalism*, Ithaca, NY: Cornell University Press.

Bergère, M.-C. (1983) 'The Chinese Bourgeosie, 1911–37'. In Twitchett, D. and Fairbank, J.K., eds, *The Cambridge History of China, Volume 12: Republican China 1912–1949, Part 1*, Cambridge: Cambridge University Press, pp. 722–825.

Bergren, N., Elinder, M. and Johrdahl, H. (2008) 'Trust and Growth: A Shaky Relationship', *Empirical Economics*, 35, 251–274.

Beugelsdijk, S. (2006a) 'Social Capital and Growth in European Regions: An Empirical Test', *European Journal of Political Economy*, 21: 301–324.

Beugelsdijk, S. (2006b) 'A Note on the Theory and Measurement of Trust in Explaining Differences in Economic Growth', *Cambridge Journal of Economics*, 30: 371–387.

Beugelsdijk, S. and Maseland, R. (2010) *Culture in Economics. History, Methodological Reflections, and Contemporary Applications*, Cambridge: Cambridge University Press.

Bhaskar, R. (1989) *The Possibility of Naturalism: A Philosophical Critique of the Contemporary Human Sciences*, New York: Harvester Wheatsheaf.

Billioud, S. (2007) 'Confucianism, "Cultural Tradition," and Official Discourse in China at the Start of the New Century', *China Perspectives*, 2007(3): 50–64.

Billioud, S. (2011) 'Confucian Revival and the Emergence of "Jiaohua" Organizations: A Case Study of the Yidan Xuetang', *Modern China*, 37(3): 286–314.

Binmore, K. (1994) *Game Theory and the Social Contract, Volume I: Playing Fair*, Cambridge, MA, and London: MIT Press.

Binmore, K. (2005) *Natural Justice*, New York: Oxford University Press.

Bjørnskov, C. (2006) 'The Multiple Facets of Social Capital', *European Journal of Political Economy*, 22: 22–46.

Blake, C.F. (2011) *Burning Money. The Material Spirit of the Chinese Afterworld*, Honolulu: University of Hawai'i Press.

Blecher, M. and Shue, V. (2001) 'Into Leather: State-led Development and the Private Sector in Xinji', *The China Quarterly*, 166: 368–393.

Bloom, A.H. (1981) 'Language and Theoretical vs. Reality-centered Morality'. In Wilson, R.W., Greenblatt, S.L. and Wilson, A.A., eds, *Moral Behavior in Chinese Society*, New York: Praeger, pp. 21–38.

Bloom, I. (2004) 'The Moral Autonomy of the Individual in the Confucian Tradition'. In Kirby, W.C., ed., *Realms of Freedom in Modern China*, Stanford, CA: Stanford University Press, pp. 19–43.

Blyth, M. (2002) *Great Transformations: Economic Ideas and Institutional Change in the Twentieth Century*, Cambridge: Cambridge University Press.

Blyth, M. (2011) 'Ideas, Uncertainty, and Evolution'. In Béland, D. and Cox, R.H., eds, *Ideas and Politics in Social Science Research*, Oxford: Oxford University Press, pp. 83–103.

Bolt, J. and van Zanden, J.L. (2013) *The Maddison Project. The First Update of the Maddison Project – Restimating Growth Before 1820*, Groningen, www.ggdc.net/maddison/maddison-project/publications/wp4.pdf (accessed 23 February 2016).

Booz&Co (2009) *Shanzhai. A Chinese Phenomenon*, Bejing: Booz&Co.

Boretz, A. (2011) *Gods, Ghosts, and Gangsters. Ritual Violence, Martial Arts, and Masculinity on the Margins of Chinese Society*, Honululu: University of Hawaii Press.

Bosworth, B. and Collins, S.M. (2008) 'Accounting for Growth: Comparing China and India', *Journal of Economic Perspectives*, 22(1): 45–65.

Bouée, Ch.-E. (2011) *China's Management Revolution: Spirit, Land, Energy*, Basingstoke and New York: Palgrave Macmillan.

Bowen II, J.R. and Rose, D.C. (1998) 'On the Absence of Privately Owned, Publicly Traded Corporations in China: The Kirby Puzzle', *The Journal of Asian Studies*, 57(2): 442–452.

Bower, J.L., Dai, N.H. and Chen M.S.-T. (2012) *CNOOC: Building a World-class Energy Company*, HBS case 9–311–074.

Bowles, S. and Gintis, H. (2001) 'Cooperation and Exclusion in Networks'. In Nicita, A. and Pagano, U., eds, *The Evolution of Economic Diversity*, London and New York: Routledge, pp. 368–395.

Bowles, S. and Polanía-Reyes, S. (2012) 'Economic Incentives and Social Preferences: Substitutes or Complements?', *Journal of Economic Literature*, 50: 368–425.

Bowles, S., Choi, J.-K. and Hopfensitz, A. (2003) 'The Co-evolution of Individual Behaviors and Social Institutions', *Journal of Theoretical Biology*, 223: 135–147.

Boyd, R. and Richerson, P.J. (1985) *Culture and the Evolutionary Process*, Chicago, IL, and London: University of Chicago Press.

Boykin, S.A. (2010) 'Hayek on Spontaneous Order and Constitutional Design', *The Independent Review*, 15(1): 19–34.

Braczyk, H.-J., Cooke, P. and Heidenreich, M., eds (1998) *Regional Innovation Systems. The Role of Governances in a Globalized World*, London and Bristol: UCL Press.

Brandt, L., Ma, D. and Rawski, T.G. (2014) 'From Divergence to Convergence: Reevaluating the History Behind China's Economic Boom', *Journal of Economic Literature*, 52(1): 45–123.

Brandt, L., Huang, J., Guo, L. and Rozelle, S. (2002) 'Land Rights in China: Facts, Fictions, and Issues', *The China Journal*, 47: 67–100.

Bray, D. (2013) 'Urban Planning Goes Rural: Conceptualising the "New Village"', *China Perspectives*, 2013(3): 53–62.

Breton, A. (1996) *Competitive Governments. An Economic Theory of Politics and Public Finance*, Cambridge: Cambridge University Press.

Brewer, M.B. and Chen, Y.-R. (2007) 'Where (Who) Are Collectives in Collectivism? Toward Conceptual Clarification of Individualism and Collectivism', *Psychological Review*, 114(1): 133–151.

Broadberry, S. (2014) *Accounting for the Great Divergence*, mimeo, www2.warwick.ac.uk/fac/soc/economics/research/centres/cage/events/conferences/longrun-growth/broadberry.pdf (accessed 10 December 2015).

Broadberry, S., Guan, H. and Li, D.D. (2015) *China, Europe and the Great Divergence: A Study of National Accounting. 980–1850*, mimeo, www.nuffield.ox.ac.uk/users/broadberry/China8.pdf (accessed 10 December 2015).

Brockman, R.H. (1980/1996) 'Commercial Contract Law in Late Nineteenth-century Taiwan'. In Brown, R., ed., *Chinese Business Enterprise Vol. IV*, London and New York: Routledge, pp. 387–443.

Brødsgaard, K.E. (2012) 'Politics and Business Group Formation in China: The Party in Control?', *The China Quarterly*, 211: 624–648.

Brown, J.S. and Hagel III, J. (2005) 'Innovation Blowback: Disruptive Management Practices From Asia', *McKinsey Quarterly*, www.mckinsey.com/insights/innovation/innovation_blowback_disruptive_management_practices_from_asia.

Brown, M.J. (2007) 'Ethnic Identity, Cultural Variation, and Processes of Change. Rethinking the Insights of Standardization and Orthopraxy', *Modern China*, 33(1): 91–124.

Brown, M.J. and Feldman, M.W. (2009) 'Sociocultural Epistasis and Cultural Exaptation in Footbinding, Marriage Form, and Religious Practices in Early 20th-century Taiwan', *Proceedings of the National Academy of Sciences*, 106(52): 22139–22144.

Brown, P., Bulte, E. and Zhang Xiaobo (2010) *Positional Spending and Status Seeking in Rural China*, IFPRI Discussion Paper 00983.

Brumann, C. (1999) 'Writing for Culture: Why a Successful Concept Should not be Discarded', *Current Anthropology*, 40(Supplement): S1–S28.

Bryson, A., Forth, J. and Zhou, M. (2014) 'Same or Different? The CEO Labour Market in China's Public Listed Companies', *Economic Journal*, 124(574): F90–F108.

Buchanan, J. (1969) *Cost and Choice. An Inquiry in Economic Theory*, Chicago, IL: University of Chicago Press.

Buchwalter, A., ed. (2012) *Hegel and Global Justice*, Dordrecht, Heidelberg, New York and London: Springer.

Bünger, K. (1983) 'Das chinesische Rechtssystem und das Prinzip der Rechtsstaatlichkeit'. In Schluchter, W., ed., *Max Webers Studie über Konfuzianismus und Daoismus. Interpretation und Kritik*, Frankfurt am Main: Suhrkamp, pp. 134–173.

Buoye. T. (2004) 'Litigation, Legitimacy, and Lethal Violence: Why County Courts Failed to Prevent Violent Disputes over Property in Eighteenth-century China'. In Zelin, M., Ocko, J.K. and Gardella, R., eds, *Contract and Property in Early Modern China*, Stanford, CA: Stanford University Press, pp. 94–119.

Burt, R.S. (1992) *Structural Holes. The Social Structure of Competiton*, Cambridge, MA, and London: Harvard University Press.

Burt, R.S. (2000) *The Network Structure of Social Capital*, faculty.chicagogsb.edu/ronald.burt/research/NSSC.pdf.

Burt, R.S. (2002) 'The Social Capital of Structural Holes'. In Guillén, M.F., Collins, R., England, P. and Meyer, M., eds, *The New Economic Sociology. Developments in an Emerging Field*, New York: Russell Sage Foundation, pp. 148–192.

Butler, J. (2010) 'Performative Agency', *Journal of Cultural Economy*, 3(2): 147–161.

Byrd, W.A. (1987) 'The Impact of the Two-tier Plan/Market System in Chinese Industry', *Journal of Comparative Economics*, 11: 295–308.

Byrd, W.A. (1989) 'Plan and Market in the Chinese Economy: A Simple General Equilibrium Model', *Journal of Comparative Economics*, 13: 177–204.

Cai, Y. (2003) 'Collective Ownership or Cadres' Ownership? The Non-agricultural Use of Farmland in China', *The China Quarterly*, 175: 662–680.

Çalışkan, K. (2007) 'Price as a Market Device: Cotton Trading in Izmir Mercantile Exchange'. In Callon, M., Millo, Y. and Muniesa, F., eds, *Market Devices*, Malden, MA: Blackwell, pp. 241–261.

Çalışkan, K. and Callon, M. (2009) 'Economization, Part 1: Shifting Attention from the Economy Towards Processes of Economization', *Economy and Society*, 38(3): 369–398.

Çalışkan, K. and Callon, M. (2010) 'Economization, Part 2: A Research Programme for the Study of Markets', *Economy and Society*, 39(1): 1–32.

Callon, M. (2007) 'What Does It Mean to Say That Economics is Performative?' In MacKenzie, D., Muniesa, F. and Siu, L., eds, *Do Economists Make Markets? On the Performativity of Economics*, Princeton, NJ, and Oxford: Princeton University Press, pp. 344–357.

Callon, M. (2008) 'Economic Markets and the Rise of Interactive Agencements: From Prosthetic Agencies to Habilitated Agencies'. In Pinch, T. and Swedberg R., eds, *Living in a Material World: Economic Sociology Meets Science and Technology Studies*, Cambridge, MA: MIT Press, pp. 29–56.

Cameron, L., Erkal, N., Gangadharan, L. and Meng, X. (2013) 'Little Emperors: Behavioral Impacts of China's One-child Policy', *Science*, 339: 953–957.

Cao, N.L. (2008) 'Boss Christians: The Business of Religion in the Wenzhou Model of Christian Revival', *The China Journal*, 59: 63–88.

Cao, N.L. (2009) 'Raising the Quality of Belief. *Suzhi* and the Production of an Elite Protestantism', *China Perspectives*, 2009(4): 54–65.

Cao Chunfang (曹春方), Ma Lianfu (马连福) and Shen Xiaoxiu (沈小秀) (2014) 'Caizheng yali, jinsheng yali, guanyuan renqi yu difang quoqi guodu touzi' (财政压力，晋升压力，官员任期与地方国企过度投资), *China Economic Quarterly*, 13(4): 1415–1437.

Cao Yangfeng (曹仰锋) (2014) *Haier zhuanxing. Renren dou shi CEO* (海尔转型。人人都是CEO), Beijing: ChinaCITIC Press.

Carl, D., Gupta, V. and Javidan, M. (2004) 'Power Distance'. In House, R.J., Hanges, P.J., Javidan, M., Dorfman, P.W. and Gupta, V., eds, *Culture, Leadership, and Organizations. The Globe Study of 62 Societies*, Thousand Oaks, CA, London, and New Delhi: Sage, pp. 513–563.

Carrillo, B. (2011) *Small Town China. Rural Labour and Social Inclusion*, Abingdon and New York: Routledge.

Carroll, G.R. and Hannan, M.T. (2000) *The Demography of Corporations and Industries*, Princeton, NJ: Princeton University Press.

Carroll, W.K. and Sapinski, J.P. (2011) 'Corporate Elites and Intercorporate Networks'. In Scott, J. and Carrington, P.J., eds, *The Sage Handbook of Social Network Analysis*, London, Thousand Oaks, CA, New Delhi, and Singapore: Sage, pp. 180–195.

Cartier, C. (2002) 'Origins and Evolution of a Geographic Idea: The Macro-region in China', *Modern China*, 28(1): 79–142.

Casson, M. (1997) *Information and Organization. A New Perspective on the Theory of the Firm*, Oxford: Clarendon Press.

Chan, A. (2009) 'Unionizing Chinese Walmart Stores'. In Chan, A., ed., *Walmart in China*, Ithaca, NY, and London: Cornell University Press, pp. 199–217.

Chan, A. and Siu, K. (2009) 'Made in China: Work and Wages in Walmart Supplier Factories'. In Chan, A., ed., *Walmart in China*, Ithaca, NY, and London: Cornell University Press, pp. 71–96.

Chan, A. and Unger, J. (2009) 'A Chinese State Enterprise Under Reform: What Model of Capitalism?', *The China Journal*, 62: 1–28.

Chan, A., Madsen, R. and Unger, J. (2009) *Chen Village. Revolution to Globalization*, Berkeley, LA, and London: University of California Press.

Chan, C.K-C. and Hui, E.S-L. (2014) 'The Development of Collective Bargaining in China: From "Collective Bargaining by Riot" to "Party-State-led Wage Bargaining" ', *The China Quarterly*, 217: 221–242.

Chan, H.S. (2004) 'Cadre Personnel Management in China: The Nomenklatura System, 1990–1998', *The China Quarterly*, 179: 703–734.

Chan, W.K. (1991) *The Making of Hong Kong Society. Three Studies of Class Formation in Early Hong Kong*, Oxford: Oxford University Press.

Chang, C.-L. (1962) *The Income of the Chinese Gentry*, Seattle: University of Washington Press.

Chang, W.C. and Lee, L. (2012) 'The Concentric Circle Revisited: Allocentrism and Self in a Contemporary Chinese Community', *Psychology*, 3(4): 297–303.

Chang, X.Q. (2010) *Guanxi or Li shang wanglai? Reciprocity, Social Support Networks, and Social Creativity in a Chinese Village*, Taipei: Ariti Press.

Chao, K. (1986) *Man and Land in China: An Economic Analysis*, Stanford, CA: Stanford University Press.

Chau, A.Y. (2006) *Miraculous Response. Doing Popular Religion in Contemporary China*, Stanford, CA: Stanford University Press.

Chau, A.Y. (2011) 'Modalities of Doing Religion and Ritual Polytropy: Evaluating the Religious Market Model from the Perspective of Chinese Religious History', *Religion*, 14(4): 547–568.

Chau, A.Y. (2012) 'Efficacy, not Confessionality: On Ritual Polytropy in China'. In Bowman, G., ed., *Sharing the 'Sacra': The Politics and Pragmatics of Intercommunal Relations Around Holy Places*, Oxford: Berghahn Books, pp. 79–96.

Chau, A.Y. (2013) 'Actants Amassing (AA): Beyond Collective Effervescence and the Social'. In Hausner, S.L., ed., *Durkheim in Dialogue: A Centenary Celebration of The Elementary Forms of Religious Life*, London: Berghahn Books, pp. 206–230.

Chau, A.Y. (2014) 'Household Sovereignty and Religious Subjectification: China and the Christian West Compared', *Studies in Church History*, 50: 494–506.

Che, J. and Qian, Y. (1998a) 'Insecure Property Rights and Government Ownership of Firms', *Quarterly Journal of Economics*, 113(2): 467–496.

Che, J. and Qian, Y. (1998b) 'Institutional Environment, Community Government, and Corporate Governance: Understanding China's Township–Village Enterprises', *Journal of Law, Economics, and Organization*, 14(1): 1–23.

Chen An (2014) 'How Has the Abolition of the Agricultural Taxes Transformed Village Governance in China? Evidence from Agricultural Regions', *The China Quarterly*, 219: 715–732.

Chen, C.-C. and Farh, J.-L. (2010) 'Developments in Understanding Chinese Leadership: Paternalism and Its Elaborations, Moderations, and Alternatives'. In

Bond, M.H. ed., *The Oxford Handbook of Chinese Psychology*, Oxford: Oxford University Press, pp. 599–622.

Chen, C.-C. and Lee, Y.-T. (2008) 'Introduction: The Diversity and Dynamism of Chinese Philosophies on Leadership'. In Chen, C.-C. and Lee, Y.-T., eds, *Leadership and Management in China. Philosophies, Theories, and Practices*, Cambridge: Cambridge University Press, pp. 1–30.

Chen, C.-C., Chen, X.-P. and Huang, S. (2013) 'Chinese Guanxi: An Integrative Review and New Directions for Future Research', *Management and Organization Review*, 9(1): 167–207.

Chen, C.-J. (2004) *Transforming Rural China. How Local Institutions Shape Property Rights in China*, Abingdon and New York: Routledge.

Chen Chunhua (陈春花), Le Guolin (乐国林) and Cao Zhouchou (曹洲涛) (2014) *Zhongguo lingxian qiye guanli sixiang yanjiu* (中国领先企业管理思想研究), Beijing: China Machine Press.

Chen, F. and Xu, X. (2012) '"Active Judiciary": Judicial Dismantling of Workers' Collective Actions in China', *The China Journal*, 67: 87–107.

Chen, F.-M.C. and Myers, R. (1976) 'Customary Law and the Economic Growth of China During the Ch'ing Period, Parts I and II', *Modern China*, 3(4): 1–32, 3(5): 4–27.

Chen Feng (2003) 'Industrial Restructuring and Workers' Resistance in China', *Modern China*, 29(2): 237–262.

Chen Feng (2006) 'Privatization and Its Discontents in Chinese Factories', *The China Quarterly*, 185: 42–60.

Chen Feng (2010) 'Trade Unions and the Quadripartite Interactions in Strike Settlement in China', *The China Quarterly*, 201: 104–124.

Chen Jinguo (陈进国) (2013) 'Zhonghua xinyang bantu de jiegou yu minjian xinyang xingtai de fazhan' (中华信仰版图的结构与民间信仰形态的发展). In Jin Ze (金泽) and Qiu Yonghui (邱永辉), eds, *Zhongguo zongjiao baogao* (中国宗教报告), Beijing: Social Sciences Academic Press, pp. 201–243.

Chen Lai (陈来) (1994) 'Shisu rujia lunli yu houfa xiandaihua' (世俗儒家倫理與後發現代化), Ershiyi shijie (二十一世纪), 22: 112–120.

Chen Lai (陈来) (1995) *Die Kultur des Volkskonfuzianismus: Eine Untersuchung der Literatur zur kindlichen Erziehung (Meng xue)*, Duisburg Working Papers on East Asian Studies, No. 5.

Chen Ling (陈凌) and Dou Junsheng (窦军生) (2014) *2014 Zhongguo jiazu qiye jiankang zhishu baogao 2014* (中国家族企业健康指数报告), Hangzhou: Zhejiang daxue chubanshe.

Chen, M.K. (2013) 'The Effect of Language on Economic Behavior: Evidence From Savings Rates, Health Behaviors, and Retirement Assets', *American Economic Review*, 103(2): 690–731.

Chen, N.N. (2003) 'Healing Sects and Anti-cult Campaigns', *The China Quarterly*, 174: 505–520.

Chen, X.-P. and Chen, C.-C. (2004) 'On the Intricacies of the Chinese Guanxi: A Process Model of Guanxi Development', *Asia Pacific Journal of Management*, 21: 305–324.

Chen, X.-P., Wasti, S.A. and Triandis, H.C. (2007) 'When Does Group Norm or Group Identity Predict Cooperation in a Public Goods Dilemma? The Moderating Effects of Idiocentrism and Allocentrism', *International Journal of Intercultural Relations*, 31: 259–276.

Cheng, C., Lo, B.C.Y. and Chio, J.H.M. (2010) 'The Tao (Way) of Chinese Coping'. In Bond, M.H., ed., *The Oxford Handbook of Chinese Psychology*, Oxford: Oxford University Press, pp. 399–420.

Cheng, E.W. (2014) 'Managing Migrant Contestation. Land Appropriation, Intermediate Agency, and Regulated Space in Shenzhen', *China Perspectives*, 2014(2): 27–35.

Chin, G.T. (2011) 'Innovation and Preservation: Remaking China's National Leadership Training System', *The China Quarterly*, 205: 18–39.

Chow, I.H., Huang, J.-C. and Liu, S. (2008) 'Strategic HRM in China: Configurations and Competitive Advantage', *Human Resource Management*, 47(4): 687–706.

Ch'ü, T.-T. (1962) *Local Government in China under the Ch'ing*, Cambridge: Cambridge University Press.

Chua, R. (2012) 'Building Effective Business Relationships in China', *MIT Sloan Management Review*, 53(4): 27–33.

Chua, R.Y.J., Morris, M.W. and Ingram, P. (2009) '*Guanxi* vs. Networking: Distinctive Configurations of Affect- and Cognition-based Trust in the Networks of Chinese vs American Managers', *Journal of International Business Studies*, 40: 490–508.

Chung, H. and Unger, J. (2013) 'The Guangdong Model of Urbanisation: Collective Village Land and the Making of a New Middle Class', *China Perspectives*, 2013(3): 33–42.

Chung, J.H. (1999) 'Recipes for Development in Post-Mao Chinese Cities: Themes and Variations'. In Chung, J.H., ed., *Cities in China. Recipes for Economic Development in the Reform Era*, London and New York: Routledge, pp. 1–17.

Chung, J.H. (2016) 'China's Local Governance in Perspective: Instruments of Central Government Control', *The China Journal*, 75: 38–60.

Chwe, M.S.-Y. (2001) *Rational Ritual. Culture, Coordination, and Common Knowledge*, Princeton, NJ: Princeton University Press.

Clark, A. (2011) *Supersizing the Mind: Embodiment, Action, and Cognitive Extension*, Oxford: Oxford University Press.

Clark, A. and Chalmers, D.J. (1998) 'The Extended Mind', *Analysis*, 58: 10–23.

Clark, D.A. (2005) *The Capability Approach: Its Development, Critiques and Recent Advances*, GPRG-WPS-32, University of Manchester.

Clarke, D.C. (2010) 'Law without Order in Chinese Corporate Governance Institutions', *Northwestern Journal of International Law and Business*, 30(1): 131–199.

Clarke, D.C., Murrell, P. and Whiting, S. (2008) 'The Role of Law in China's Economic Development'. In Brandt, L. and Rawski, T., eds, *China's Great Economic Transformation*, Cambridge: Cambridge University Press, pp. 375–428.

Cliff, T. (2013) 'Peripheral Urbanism. Making History on China's Northwestern Frontier', *China Perspectives*, 2013(3): 13–23.

Clunas, C. (2004) *The Social Art of Wen Zhengming*, Honolulu: University of Hawaii Press.

Cohen, M.L. (1970) 'Developmental Process in the Chinese Domestic Group'. In Freedman, M., ed., *Family and Kinship in Chinese Society*, Stanford, CA: Stanford University Press, pp. 21–36.

Cohen, M.L. (1990) 'Lineage Organization in North China', *Journal of Asian Studies*, 49(3): 509–534.

Cohen, M.L. (1992) 'Family Management and Family Division in Contemporary Rural China', *The China Quarterly*, 130: 357–377.

Cohen, M.L. (1994) 'Being Chinese: The Peripheralization of Traditional Identity'. In Tu, W., ed., *The Living Tree. The Changing Meaning of Being Chinese Today*, Stanford, CA: Stanford University Press, pp. 88–108.

Cohen, M.L. (2004) 'Writs of Passage in Late Imperial China: The Documentation of Practical Understandings in Minong, Taiwan'. In Zelin, M., Ocko, J.K. and Gardella, R., eds, *Contract and Property in Early Modern China*, Stanford, CA: Stanford University Press, pp. 37–93.

Coleman, J. (1990) *Foundations of Social Theory*, Cambridge und London: Belknap Press.

Commission on Growth and Development (2008) *The Growth Report: Strategies for Sustained Growth and Inclusive Development*, Washington, DC: World Bank.

Conlé, M. (2015) *Architectural Innovation in China: The Concept and Its Implications for Institutional Analysis*, Duisburger Arbeitspapiere Ostasienwissenschaften, No. 104/2015.

Craver, C. (2007) *Explaining the Brain. Mechanisms and the Mosaic Unity of the Neurosciences*, New York: Oxford University Press.

Craver, C. and Tabery, J. (2015) 'Mechanisms in Science'. In Zalta, E.N., ed., *The Stanford Encyclopedia of Philosophy* (winter edn) (ed.), http://plato.stanford.edu/archives/win2015/entries/science-mechanisms/.

Cui, W. (2009) 'Women and Suicide in Rural China', *Bulletin of the World Health Organization*, 87(12), www.who.int/bulletin/volumes/87/12/09-011209/en/.

Cui, Z. (2011) 'Partial Intimations of the Coming Whole: The Chongqing Experiment in the Light of the Theories of Henry George, James Meade, and Antonio Gramsci', *Modern China*, 37(6): 646–661.

Curzio, A.Q. and Fortis, M., eds (2002) *Complexity and Industrial Clusters. Dynamics and Models in Theory and Practice*, Heidelberg: Springer.

Das, M. and N'Diaye, P. (2013) *Chronicle of a Decline Foretold: Has China Reached the Lewis Turning Point?* IMF Working Paper WP/13/26.

Dasgupta, P. (2005) 'Economics of Social Capital', *The Economic Record*, 81(255): 2–21.

Dasgupta, P. and Serageldin, I., eds (2000) *Social Capital. A Multifaceted Perspective*, Washington, DC: World Bank.

Davies, D.J. (2007) 'Wal-Mao: The Discipline of Corporate Culture and Studying Success at Wal-Mart China', *China Journal*, 58: 1–27.

Davis, D. (2010) 'Who Gets the House? Renegotiating Property Rights in Post-Socialist Urban China', *Modern China*, 36(5): 463–492.

Davis, J.B. (2003) *The Theory of the Individual in Economics. Identity and Value*, London and New York: Routledge.

Davis, J.B. (2007) 'Akerlof and Kranton on Identity in Economics: Inverting the Analysis', *Cambridge Journal of Economics*, 31(3): 349–362.

Davis, J.B. (2010) *Individuals and Identity in Economics*, Cambridge: Cambridge University Press.

De Glopper, D.R. (1972) 'Doing Business in Lukang'. In Wolf, A., ed., *Studies in Chinese Society*, Stanford, CA: Stanford University Press, pp. 209–226.

De Vries, J. (2008) *The Industrious Revolution. Consumer Behavior and the Household Economy, 1650 to the Present*, Cambridge: Cambridge University Press.

Dean, K. (2003) 'Local Communal Religion in Contemporary South-east China', *The China Quarterly*, 174: 338–358.

Debeir, J.-C., Deléage, J.-P. and Hémery, D. (2013) *Une histoire de l'energie*, Paris: Flammarion.

Delman, J. and Yin, X. (2010) 'Individualization and the Political Agency of Private Business People in China'. In Hansen, M.H. and Svarverud, R, eds, *iChina: The Rise of the Individual in Modern Chinese Society*, Copenhagen: NIAS Press, pp. 94–131.

Denzau, A.T. and North, D.C. (1994) 'Shared Mental Models: Ideologies and Institutions', *Kyklos*, 47: 3–32.

Dickson, B.J. (2007) 'Integrating Wealth and Power: The Communist Party's Embrace of the Private Sector', *The China Quarterly*, 192: 827–854.

Dickson, B.J. (2014) 'Who Wants to be Communist? Career Incentives and Mobilized Loyality in China', *The China Quarterly*, 217: 42–68.

DiMaggio, P. (1997) 'Culture and Cognition', *Annual Review of Sociology*, 23: 263–287.

DiMaggio, P. (2011) 'Cultural Networks'. In Scott, J. and Carrington, P., eds, *The Sage Handbook of Social Network Analysis*, Los Angeles, CA: Sage, pp. 286–301.

Dirlik, A. (1996) 'Critical Reflections on "Chinese Capitalism" as a Paradigm'. In Brown, R.A., ed., *Chinese Business Enterprise, Vol. I*, London and New York: Routledge, pp. 17–38.

Dixit, A.K. (2004) *Lawlessness and Economics. Alternative Modes of Governance*, Princeton, NJ, and Oxford: Princeton University Press.

Djankov, S., Glaeser, E., La Porta, R., Lopez-de-Silanes, E. and Shleifer, A. (2003) 'The New Comparative Economics', *Journal of Comparative Economics*, 31: 595–619.

Donaldson, J. (2010) 'Provinces: Paradoxical Politics, Problematic Partners'. In Chung, J.H. and Lam, T.-C., eds, *China's Local Administration. Traditions and Changes in the Sub-national Hierarchy*, Abingdon and New York: Routledge, pp. 14–61.

Dong Fangshi (东方史) (1999) *Xin guanxixue quanshu. Zhongguoren de chushi sheng jing* (新关系学全书。中国人的处世胜经), Beijing.

Donnithorne, A. (1972) 'China's Cellular Economy: Some Economic Trends Since the Cultural Revolution', *The China Quarterly*, 52: 605–619.

Du Yuping (2011) *Hebei Dawu Group: Building the First 'Family Business Constitution' in China*, China Managememt Case Sharing Center, Richard Ivey School of Business, W11100.

Duara, P. (1988) *Culture, Power, and the State. Rural North China, 1900–1942*, Stanford, CA: Stanford University Press.

DuBois, T.D. (2005) *The Sacred Village: Social Change and Religious Life in Rural North China*, Honolulu: University of Hawai'i Press.

Dynon, N. (2008) 'Four Civilizations and the Evolution of Post-Mao Chinese Socialist Ideology', *The China Journal*, 60: 83–110.

East Asia Analytical Unit (1995) *Overseas Chinese Business Networks in Asia*, Canberra.

Eastman, L.E. (1988) *Family, Fields, and Ancestors. Constancy and Change in China's Social and Economic History, 1550–1949*, New York and Oxford: Oxford University Press.

Eaton, S. and Kostka, G. (2014) 'Authoritarian Environmentalism Undermined? Local Leaders' Time Horizons and Environmental Policy Implementation in China', *The China Quarterly*, 218: 359–380.

Eberhard, W. (1971) *Moral and Social Values of the Chinese*, Taibei: Chinese Materials and Research Aids Service Center.

Eberstadt, N. (2011) 'The Global War Against Baby Girls', *The New Atlantis*, www.thenewatlantis.com/publications/the-global-war-against-baby-girls.

Ebner, A. (1999) 'Understanding Varieties in the Structure and Performance of National Innovation Systems: The Concept of Economic Style'. In Groenewegen, J. and Vromen, J., eds, *Institutions and the Evolution of Capitalism: Implications of Evolutionary Economics*, Cheltenham and Northampton: Edward Elgar, pp. 141–169.

Ebrey, P.B. (1985) 'The Chinese Family and the Spread of Confucian Values'. In Rozman, G., ed., *The East Asian Region. Confucian Heritage and Its Modern Adaptation*, Princeton, NJ: Princeton University Press, pp. 45–83.

Ebrey, P.B. (1986) 'The Early Stages in the Development of Descent Group Organization'. In Ebrey, P.B. and Watson, J.L., eds, *Kinship Organization in Late Imperial China, 1000–1949*, Berkeley, LA, and London: University of Califormia Press, pp. 16–61.

Ebrey, P.B. and Watson, J.L. (1986) 'Introduction'. In Ebrey, P.B. and Watson, J.L., eds, *Kinship Organization in Late Imperial China, 1000–1949*, Berkeley, LA, and London: University of Califormia Press, pp. 1–15.

Eckaus, R.S. (2014) 'Forced Savings in China', *The China Quarterly*, 217: 180–194.

Edin, M. (2003) 'State Capacity and Local Agent Control in China: CCP Cadre Management from a Township Perspective', *The China Quarterly*, 173: 35–52.

Egri, C.P. and Ralston, D.A. (2004) 'Generation Cohorts and Personal Values: A Comparison of China and the United States', *Organization Science*, 15(2): 210–220.

Elias, N. (1969a/1990) *Über den Prozeß der Zivilisation: Soziogenetische und psychogenetische Untersuchungen, Erster Band: Wandlungen des Verhaltens in den weltlichen Oberschichten des Abendlandes*, Frankfurt am Main: Suhrkamp.

Elias, N. (1969b/1989) *Die höfische Gesellschaft: Untersuchungen zur Soziologie des Königtums und der höfischen Aristokratie*, Frankfurt am Main: Suhrkamp.

Ellickson, R.C. (1991) *Order without Law. How Neighbours Settle Disputes*, Cambridge, MA: Harvard University Press.

Ellis, F. (1988) *Peasant Economics. Farm Households and Agrarian Development*, Cambridge: Cambridge University Press.

Elman, B. (1991) 'Political, Social, and Cultural Reproduction via Civil Service Examinations in Late Imperial China', *The Journal of Asian Studies*, 50(1): 7–28.

Elster, J. (1982) 'Sour Grapes – Utilitarianism and the Genesis of Wants'. In Sen, A. and Williams, B., eds, *Utilitarianism and Beyond*, Cambridge: Cambridge University Press, pp. 219–238.

Elster, J. (1989) *Nuts and Bolts for the Social Sciences*, Cambridge: Cambridge University Press.

Elvin, M. (1973) *The Pattern of the Chinese Past*, Stanford, CA: Stanford University Press.

Elvin, M. (1983) 'Warum hat das modern China keinen industriellen Kapitalismus entwickelt? Eine Auseinandersetzung mit Max Webers Ansatz'. In Schluchter, W., ed., *Max Webers Studie über Konfuzianismus und Daoismus. Interpretation und Kritik*, Frankfurt am Main: Suhrkamp, pp. 114–133.

Eucken, W. (1939) *Grundlagen der Nationalökonomie*, Berlin: Springer.

Evensky, J. (2005) 'Adam Smith's Theory of Moral Sentiments: On Morals and Why They Matter to a Liberal Society of Free People and Free Markets', *Journal of Economic Perspectives*, 19(3): 109–130.

Fairbank, J.K. (1978) 'Introduction: The Old Order'. In Twitchett, D. and Fairbank, J.K., eds, *The Cambridge History of China, Volume 10: Late Ch'ing, 1800–1911, Part 1*, Cambridge: Cambridge University Press, pp. 1–34.

Fairbank, J.K. (1992) *China. A New History*, Cambridge: Cambridge University Press.

Fan Gang (樊刚) (1989) 'Lun xiongdi jingzheng' (论兄弟竞争), Zhongguo: fazhan yu gaige (中国: 发展与改革), 1989(4): 26–37.

Fang Xiuwen (防秀文) and Lin Feng (林锋) (2011a) *Zhonghua shangye wenhua shilun, Vol. 1: Zhonghua shange wenhua tan yuan* (中国商业文化史论, 第一卷, 中华商业文化探源), Beijing: Zhongguo jingji chubanshe.

Fang Xiuwen (防秀文) and Lin Feng (林锋) (2011b) *Zhonghua shangye wenhua shilun, Vol. 2: bianyi de chuantong shangye wenhua* (中国商业文化史论, 第二卷, 变异的传统商业文化), Beijing: Zhongguo jingji chubanshe.

Fang Yuren (2013) *Ningbo FOTILE Kitchenware Co., Ltd.*, Tsinghua SEM, China Business Case Center, Case TU0049, 10/11/2013.

Farh, J.-L., Zhong, C.-B. and Organ, D.W. (2004) 'Organizational Citizenship Behavior in the People's Republic of China', *Organization Science*, 15(2): 241–253.

Farh, J.-L., Liang J., Chou L.-F. and Cheng, B.-S. (2008) 'Paternalistic Leadership in Chinese Organizations: Research Progress and Future Research Directions'. In Chen C.-C. and Lee, Y.-T., eds, *Leadership and Management in China*, Cambridge: Cambridge University Press, pp. 171–205.

Farrer, J. (2002) '"Idle Talk": Neighborhood Gossip as a Medium of Social Communication in Reform Era Shanghai'. In Gold, T., Guthrie, D. and Wank, D., eds, *Social Connections in China. Institutions, Culture, and the Changing Nature of Guanxi*, Cambridge: Cambridge University Press, pp. 197–220.

Faure, D. (1996a) 'Company Law and the Emergence of the Modern Firm'. In Brown, R.A., ed., *Chinese Business Enterprise, Vol. IV*, London und New York: Routledge, pp. 263–281.

Faure, D. (1996b) 'The Lineage as a Business Company: Patronage versus Law in the Development of Chinese Business'. In Brown, R.A., ed., *Chinese Business Enterprise, Vol. I*, London and New York: Routledge, pp. 82–106.

Faure, D. (2006) *China and Capitalism. A History of Business Enterprise in Modern China*, Hong Kong: Hong Kong University Press.

Faure, D. (2007) *Emperor and Ancestor: State and Lineage in South China*, Stanford, CA: Stanford University Press.

Feenstra, R.C., Yang, T.-H. and Hamilton, G.G. (1999) 'Business Groups and Product Variety in Trade: Evidence From South Korea, Taiwan and Japan', *Journal of International Economics*, 48: 71–100.

Feeny, D. (1983) 'The Moral or the Rational Peasant? Competing Hypotheses of Collective Action', *The Journal of Asian Studies*, 42(4): 769–789.

Fei Hsiao-tung (Xiaotong) (1939) *Peasant Life in China. A Field Study of Country Life in the Yangtze Valley*, London and Henley: Routledge & Kegan Paul.

Fei Hsiao-tung (Xiaotong) and Chang, C.-I. (1945) *Earthbound China. A Study of Rural Economy in Yunnan*, Chicago, IL: University of Chicago Press.

Fei Xiaotong (费孝通) (1947) *Xiangtu Zhongguo* (乡土中国), Shanghai.

Felden, B. and Hack, A. (2014) *Managememt von Familienunternehmen, Besonderheiten – Handlunsgfelder – Instrumente*, Wiesbaden: Springer FV.

Feleppa, R. (1986) 'Emics, Etics, and Social Objectivity', *Current Anthropology*, 27(5): 243–251.

Feng Junqi (冯军旗) (2010) *Zhong xian ganbu. Beijing daxue boshi yanjiusheng xuewei lunwen* (中县干部。北京大学博士研究生学位论文), Beijing.

Feng Xingyuan (2013) 'Local Government Debt and Municipal Bonds in China: Problems and a Framework for Rules', *Copenhagen Journal of Asian Studies*, 31(2): 23–53.

Feng, X. and Herrmann-Pillath, C. (2013) 'Wenzhou: Spearhead of Financial Sector Liberalization?', *Economic Freedom Network Asia*, www.efnasia.org/index.php?option=com_content&view=article&id=350:wenzhou-spearhead-of-financial-sector-liberalization-in-china&catid=1:latest-news&Itemid=4.

Fernandez, R. and Fogli, A. (2009) 'Culture: An Empirical Investigation of Beliefs, Work, and Fertility', *American Economic Journal Macroeconomics*, 1(1): 146–178.

Feuchtwang, S. (1992) *The Imperial Metaphor. Popular Religion in China*, London and New York: Routledge.

Feuerwerker, A. (1980) 'Economic Trends in the Late Ch'ing Empire, 1870–1911'. In Fairbank, J.K. and Liu, K.-C., eds, *The Cambridge History of China, Volume 11, Late Ch'ing, 1800–1911, Part 2*, Cambridge: Cambridge University Press, pp. 1–69.

Feuerwerker, A. (1983) 'Economic Trends, 1912–49'. In Fairbank, J.K., ed., *The Cambridge History of China, Volume 12, Republican China, 1912–1949, Part 1*, Cambridge: Cambridge University Press, pp. 28–127.

Fischer, D. (2014) 'Green Industrial Policies in China – The Example of Solar Energy'. In Pegels, A., ed., *Green Industrial Policies in Emerging Countries*, Abingdon and New York: Routledge, pp. 69–103.

Fitzgerald, J. (1995) 'The Nationless State: The Search for a Nation in Modern Chinese Nationalism', *The Australian Journal of Chinese Affairs*, 33: 75–106.

Fligstein, N. and McAdam, D. (2012) *A Theory of Fields*, Oxford: Oxford University Press.

Foster, K.W. (2002) 'Embedded within State Agencies: Business Associations in Yantai', *The China Journal*, 47: 41–65.

Foucault, M. (1997) *'Il faut defendre la société'. Cours au Collège de France, 1976*, Paris: Seuil.

Foucault, M. (2004a) *Sécurité, territoire, population. Cours au Collège de France, 1977–1978*, Paris: Seuil.

Foucault, M. (2004b) *Naissance de la biopolitique. Cours au Collège de France, 1978–1979*, Paris: Seuil.

Fouquet, R. and Broadberry, S. (2015) 'Seven Centuries of European Economic Growth and Decline', *Journal of Economic Perspectives*, 29(4): 227–244.

Fourcade, M., Ollion, E. and Algan, Y. (2015) 'The Superiority of Economists', *Journal of Economic Perspectives*, 29(1): 89–114.

Frank, R.H. (1985) *Choosing the Right Pond: Human Behavior and the Quest for Status*, New York and Oxford: Oxford University Press.

Feuerwerker, A. (1990) 'Chinese Economic History in Comparative Perspective'. In Ropp, P.S., ed., *Heritage of China: Contemporary Perspectives on Chinese Civilization*, Berkeley, LA and London: University of California Press, pp. 224–241.

Fujimoto, T. (2002) 'Thinking of the Chinese Manufacturing Sector in Architecture Context', *Keizai Sangyo Journal*, 2002(6), www.rieti.go.jp/en/papers/research-review/002.html (accessed 24 November 2015).

Fujimoto, T. (2007) 'Architecture-based Comparative Advantage – A Design Information View of Manufacturing', *Evolutionary and Institutional Economics Review*, 4(1): 55–112.

Fukuyama, F. (1992) *The End of History and the Last Man*, New York: Free Press.

Fukuyama, F. (2011) 'The Patterns of History', *Journal of Democracy*, 23(1): 14–26.

Gabrenya, W.K. and Hwang K.-K. (1996) 'Chinese Social Interaction: Harmony and Hierarchy on the Good Earth'. In Bond, M.H., ed., *The Handbook of Chinese Psychology*, Hong Kong: Oxford University Press, pp. 309–321.

Gao, G., Ting-Toomey, S. and Gudykunst, W.B. (1996) 'Chinese Communication Processes'. In Bond, M.H., ed., *The Handbook of Chinese Psychology*, Hong Kong: Oxford University Press, pp. 280–293.

Gardella, R. (1992) 'Squaring Accounts: Commercial Bookkeeping Methods and Capitalist Rationalism in Late Qing and Republican China', *The Journal of Asian Studies*, 51(2): 317–339.

Gardella, R. (2004) 'Contracting Business Partnerships in Late Qing and Republican China: Paradigms and Patterns'. In Zelin, M., Ocko, J.K. and Gardella, R., eds, *Contract and Property in Early Modern China*, Stanford, CA: Stanford University Press, pp. 298–326.

Gates, H. (1996) *China's Motor: A Thousand Years of Petty Capitalism*, Ithaca, NY, and London: Cornell University Press.

Gelfland, M.J., Bhawuk, D.P.S., Nishii, L.H. and Bechtold, D.J. (2004) 'Individualism and Collectivism'. In House, R.J., Hanges, P.J., Javidan, M., Dorfman, P.W. and Gupta, V., eds, *Culture, Leadership, and Organizations. The Globe Study of 62 Societies*, Thousand Oaks, CA, London, and New Delhi: Sage, pp. 437–512.

Gellner, E. (1983) *Nations and Nationalism*, Oxford: Oxford University Press.

Gereffi, G. (1996) 'Global Commodity Chains: New Forms of Coordination and Control Among Nations and Firms in International Industries'. *Competition and Change*, 1: 427–439.

Gerlach, C. (2005) *Wu-Wei in Europe: A Study of Eurasian Economic Thought*, LSE Department of Economic History Working Paper 12/05.

Gerth, K. (2003) *China Made. Consumer Culture and the Creation of the Nation*, Cambridge, MA, and London: Harvard University Press.

Gerth, K. (2010) *As China Goes, So Goes the World*, New York: Hill and Wang.

Gibbon, P., Blair, J. and Ponte, S. (2008) 'Governing Global Value Chains: An Introduction', *Economy and Society*, 37(3): 315–338.

Giddens, A. (1984) *The Constitution of Society*, Cambridge and Oxford: Polity Press.

Giles, J., Park, A. and Cai, F. (2006) 'How has Economic Restructuring Affected China's Urban Workers?', *The China Quarterly*, 185: 61–95.

Gilette, M. (2010) 'Copying, Counterfeiting, and Capitalism in Contemporary China: Jingdezhen's Porcelain Industry', *Modern China*, 36(4): 367–403.

Ginsburg, T. (2012) 'Constitutionalism: East Asian Antecedents', *Chicago Kent Law Review*, 88: 11–33.

Glaeser, E.L., Laibson, D.I. and Sacerdote, B. (2002) 'An Economic Approach to Social Capital', *The Economic Journal*, 112: F437–F458.

Glaeser, E.L., Laibson, D.I., Scheinkman, J.A. and Soutter, C.L. (2000) 'Measuring Trust', *The Quarterly Journal of Economics*, August(2000): 811–845.

Glahn, R. von (1991a) 'Municipal Reform and Urban Social Conflict in Late Ming Jiangnan' *The Journal of Asian Studies*, 50(2): 280–307.

Glahn, R. von (1991b) 'The Enchantment of Wealth: The God Wutong in the Social History of Jiangnan', *Harvard Journal of Asiatic Studies*, 51(2): 651–714.

Göbel, C. (2011a) 'Paving the Road to a Socialist New Countryside: China's Rural Tax and Fee Reform'. In Alpermann, B., ed., *Politics and Markets in Rural China*, Abingdon and New York: Routledge, pp. 155–171.

Göbel, C. (2011b) 'Uneven Policy Implementation in Rural China', *The China Journal*, 65: 53–76.

Goetzmann, W.N. and Köll, E. (2004) *The History of Corporate Ownership in China: State Patronage, Company Legislation, and the Issue of Control*, Yale ICF Working Paper No. 04–29.

Gold, T., Guthrie, D. and Wank, D., eds (2002) *Social Connections in China. Institutions, Culture, and the Changing Nature of Guanxi*, Cambridge: Cambridge University Press.

Goodman, D.S.G. (2000) 'Centre and Periphery after Twenty Years of Reform. Redefining the Chinese Polity', *China Perspectives*, 31: 4–18.

Goodman, D.S.G. and Segal, G., eds (1994) *China Deconstructs. Politics, Trade and Regionalism*, London and New York: Routledge.

Goody, J. (1983) *The Development of the Family and Marriage in Europe*, Cambridge: Cambridge University Press.

Goossaert, V. and Palmer, D.A. (2011) *The Religious Question in Modern China*, Chicago, IL: Chicago University Press.

Gottwald, J.-C. and Collins, N. (2012) *Market Creation by Leninist Means: The Party-State, Private Authority, and the Regulation of Financial Services in the People's Republic of China*, New Approaches to Building Markets in Asia Working Paper No. 23, National University of Singapore.

Gould, S.J. (2002) *The Structure of Evolutionary Theory*, Cambridge and London: Belknap Press.

Granick, D. (1990) *Chinese State Enterprises. A Regional Property Rights Analysis*, Chicago, IL: Chicago University Press.

Granovetter, M. (1985) 'Economic Action and Social Structure: The Problem of Embeddedness', *American Journal of Sociology*, 91(3): 481–510.

Granovetter, M. (2002) 'A Theoretical Agenda for Economic Sociology'. In Guillén, M.F., Collins, R., England, P. and Meyer, M., eds, *The New Economic Sociology. Developments in an Emerging Field*, New York: Russell Sage Foundation, pp. 35–60.

Granovetter, M. (2005) 'The Impact of Social Structure on Economic Outcomes', *Journal of Economic Perspectives*, 19(1): 33–50.

Greenhalgh, S. (1988) 'Families and Networks in Taiwan's Economic Development'. In Winckler, E.A. and Greenhalgh, S., eds, *Contending Approaches to the Political Economy of Taiwan*, Armonk, NY, and London: Sharpe, pp. 224–248.

Greenhalgh, S. (2012) 'Patriarchal Demographics? China's Sex Ratio Reconsidered', *Population and Development Review*, 38(Supplement): 130–149.

Greenhalgh, S. and Winckler, E.A. (2005) *Governing China's Population: From Leninist to Neoliberal Biopolitics*, Stanford, CA: Stanford University Press.

Gregory, A. (2003) 'Chinese Trademark Law and the TRIPS Agreement – Confucius Meets the WTO'. In Cass, D.Z., Williams, B.G. and Barker, G., eds, *China and the World Trading System. Entering the New Millennium*, Cambridge: Cambridge University Press, pp. 321–344.

Greif, A. (1994) 'Cultural Beliefs and the Organization of Society: A Historical and Theoretical Reflection on Collectivist and Individualist Societies', *Journal of Political Economy*, 102(5): 912–950.

Greif, A. and Tabellini, G. (2010) 'Cultural and Institutional Bifurcation: China and Europe Compared', *American Economic Review: Papers and Proceedings*, 100: 135–140.

Guala, F. (2007) 'How To Do Things with Experimental Economics'. In MacKenzie, D., Muniesa, F. and Siu, L., eds, *Do Economists Make Markets? On the Performativity of Economics*, Princeton, NJ, and Oxford: Princeton University Press, pp. 128–162.

Gui Hua (桂华) (2013) '"guo rize" yu yuanman rensheng – nongcun zongjiao shenghuo jiben xingtai' (过日子于圆满人生—农村宗教生活的基本形态), *Ershiyi shiji* (二十一世纪), 140: 40–54.

Gui Hua (桂华) (2014) *Li yu shengming jiazhi. Jiating shenghuo Zhong de daode, zongjiao yu fal* (礼与生命价值。家庭生活中的道德，宗教与法律), Beijing: Commercial Press.

Guiso, L., Sapienza, P. and Zingales, L. (2006) 'Does Culture Affect Economic Outcomes?', *Journal of Economic Perspectives*, 20(2): 23–48.

Guo, Y. (2008) 'Corruption in Transitional China: An Empirical Analysis', *The China Quarterly*, 194: 349–365.

Guo Yuhua (郭于华) (2015) 'Jiexi gongchanzhuyi wenming ji qi zhuanxing. Zhuanxing shehuixue lungang' (解析共产主义文明及其转型。转型社会学论纲), *Twenty-First Century*, 149: 4–22.

Guthrie, D. (1998) 'The Declining Significance of *Guanxi* in China's Economic Transition', *The China Quarterly*, 154: 254–282.

Hall, D.L. and Ames, R.T. (1998) *Thinking from the Han. Self, Truth, and Transcendence in Chinese and Western Culture*, New York: State University of New York Press.

Hall, E.T. (1976) *Beyond Culture*, New York: Anchor Books.

Hallpike, C.R. (1986) *The Principles of Social Evolution*, Oxford: Clarendon Press.

Hamilton, G.G. (1996a) 'The Organizational Foundations of Western and Chinese Commerce: A Historical and Comparative Analysis'. In Hamilton, G., ed., *Asian Business Networks*, Berlin: Springer, pp. 43–58.

Hamilton, G.G. (1996b) 'Competition and Organization: A Reexamination of Chinese Business Practices', *Journal of Asian Business*, 12(1): 7–20.

Hamilton, G.G. (2014) 'What Can Western Social Scientists Learn from the Writings of Fei Xiaotong?', *Journal of China in Comparative Perspective*, 1(2), www.journal.ccpn-global.org/cms.php?artid=489&catid=231.

Han, C. (2012) 'Satisfaction With the Standard of Living in Reform-Era China', *The China Quarterly*, 212: 919–940.

Hang, Z., Chen, C.C., Li, X. and Zhou, Y. (2013) 'From Personal Relationship to Psychological Ownership: The Importance of Manager–Owner Relationship Closeness in Family Business', *Management and Organization Review*, 9(2): 295–318.

Hannan, M.T., Pólos, L. and Carroll, G.R. (2007) *Logics of Organization Theory. Audiences, Codes, and Ecologies*, Princeton, NJ: Princeton University Press.

Hannerz, U. (1991) *Cultural Complexity. Studies in the Social Organization of Meaning*, New York: Columbia University Press.

Hannum, E., Wang, M. and Adams, J. (2010) 'Rural–Urban Disparities in Access to Primary and Secondary Education under Market Reforms'. In Whyte, M.K., ed., *One Country, Two Soceties: Rural–Urban Inequality in Contemporary China*, Cambridge: Cambridge University Press, pp. 125–146.

Hansen, M.H. (2013) 'Learning Individualism: Hesse, Confucius, and Pep-rallies in a Chinese Rural High School', *The China Quarterly*, 213: 60–77.

Hansen, M.H. and Svarverud, R., eds. (2010) *iChina: The Rise of the Individual in Modern Chinese Society*, Copenhagen: NIAS Press.

Hansen, V. (1995) *Negotiating Daily Life in Traditional China: How Ordinary People Used Contracts, 600–1400*, New Haven, CT: Yale University Press.

Hanson, G.H. (2012) 'The Rise of the Middle Kingdoms', *Journal of Economic Perspectives*, 26(2): 41–64.

Hao, Y.-P. (1986) *The Commercial Revolution in Nineteenth-century China. The Rise of Sino-Western Commercial Capitalism*, Berkeley, LA, and London: University of California Press.

Harbecke, J. (2014) 'The Role of Supervenience and Constitution in Neuroscientific Research', *Synthese*, 191(5): 725–743.

Harrell, S. (1990) 'Introduction'. In Lipman, J.N. and Harrell, S., eds, *Violence in China. Essays in Culture and Counterculture*, New York: State University of New York Press.

Harrell, S. (2011) 'Fei Xiaotong and the Vocabulary of Anthropology in China', *Journal of China in Comparative Perspective*, 1(1), www.journal.ccpn-global.org/cms.php?artid=804&catid=510.

Harris, M. (1979) *Cultural Materialism: The Struggle for a Science of Culture*, New York: Random House.

Hartley, J. (2003) *A Short History of Cultural Studies*, London: Sage.

Hartley, J. (2009) *The Uses of Digital Literacy*, St Lucia: Queensland University Press.

Hartley, J. and Potts, J. (2014) *A Natural History of Stories, Demes, Knowledge and Innovation*, London: Bloomsbury.

Harwitt, E. (2007) 'Building China's Telecommunications Network: Industrial Policy and the Role of Chinese State-owned, Foreign and Private Domestic Enterprise', *The China Quarterly*, 190: 311–332.

Hawes, C. (2008) 'Representing Corporate Culture in China: Official, Academic and Corporate Perspectives', *The China Journal*, 59: 33–61.

Hayek, F.A. von (1945) 'The Use of Knowledge in Society', *American Economic Review*, 35(4): 519–530.

Hayek, F.A. von (1973) *Law, Legislation and Liberty. A New Statement of the Liberal Principles of Justice and Political Economy. Volume 1: Rules and Order*, Chicago, IL: Chicago University Press.

Hayek, F.A. von (1979) *Law, Legislation and Liberty. A New Statement of the Liberal Principles of Justice and Political Economy, Volume 3: The Political Order of a Free People*, Chicago, IL: Chicago University Press.

Hayot, E. (2012) 'Chinese Modernism, Mimetic Desire, and European Time'. In Wollaeger, M. and Eatough, M., eds, *The Oxford Handbook of Global Modernisms*, Oxford: Oxford University Press, pp. 149–172.

Headland, T., Pike, K.L. and Harris, M., eds (1990) *Emics and Etics. The Insider/Outsider Debate*, Newbury Park, CA: Sage.

Heberer, T. and Schubert, G. (2012) 'County and Township Cadres as a Strategic Group. A New Approach to Political Agency in China's Local State', *Journal of Chinese Political Science*, 17: 221–249.

Hedström, P. and Ylikoski, P. (2010) 'Causal Mechanisms in the Social Sciences', *Annual Review of Sociology*, 36: 49–67.

Heilmann, S. (2005) 'Regulatory Innovation by Leninist Means: Communist Party Supervision in China's Financial Industry', *The China Quarterly*, 181: 1–21.

Heilmann, S. (2008) 'From Local Experiments to National Policy: The Origins of China's Distinctive Policy Process', *The China Journal*, 59: 1–32.

Heilmann, S. and Melton, O. (2013) 'The Reinvention of Development Planning in China, 1993–2012', *Modern China*, 39(6): 580–628.

Heilmann, S., Shih, L. and Hofem, A. (2013) 'National Planning and Local Technology Zones: Experimental Governance in China's Torch Programme', *The China Quarterly*, 216: 896–919.

Hendrischke, H. (1999) 'Provinces in Competition: Region, Identity and Cultural Construction'. In Hendrischke, H. and Feng, C., eds, *The Political Economy of China's Provinces*, London and New York: Routledge, pp. 1–30.

Henrich, J., Boyd, R., Bowles, S., Camerer, C., Fehr, E., Gintis, H., McElreath, R., Alvard, M., Barr, J., Ensminger, A., Hill, K., Gil-White, F., Gurven, M., Marlowe, F., Patton, J.Q., Smith, N. and Tracer, D. (2005) 'Economic Man in Cross-cultural Perspective: Behavioral Experiments in 15 Small-scale Societies', *Behavioral and Brain Sciences*, 28: 795–855.

Herrmann, B., Thöni, C. and Gächter, S. (2008) 'Antisocial Punishment across Societies', *Science*, 319: 1362–1367.

Herrmann-Pillath, C. (1986) *Die chinesische Wirtschaftsreform im Spiegel sowjetischer Darstellungen, 1979–1986*. Berichte des BIOst 42–1986, Köln: BIOst.

Herrmann-Pillath, C. (1990) 'Der Vergleich von Wirtschafts- und Gesellschaftssystemen: Wissenschaftsphilosophische und methodologische Überlegungen zur Zukunft eines ordnungstheoretischen Forschungsprogrammes', *ORDO*, 42: 15–68.

Herrmann-Pillath, C. (1991) *Institutioneller Wandel, Macht und Inflation in China: Ordnungstheoretische Analysen zur Politischen Ökonomie eines Transformationsprozesses*, Baden-Baden: Nomos.

Herrmann-Pillath, C. (1993) 'Schlüsselprobleme des chinesischen Kaderkapitalismus', *vierteljahresberichte – Problems of International Cooperation*, 131: 41–50.

Herrmann-Pillath, C. (1994a) 'China's Transition to the Market: A Paradox of Transformation and Its Institutionalist Solution'. In Wagener, H.-J., ed., *The Political Economy of Transformation*, Heidelberg: Springer, pp. 209–241.

Herrmann-Pillath, C. (1994b) *Wirtschaftsintegration durch Netzwerke: Die Beziehungen zwischen Taiwan und der Volksrepublik China*, Baden-Baden: Nomos.

Herrmann-Pillath, C. (2000a) 'Wirtschaftsordnung und Kultur aus evolutorischer Sicht'. In Leipold, H. and Pies, I., eds, *Ordnungstheorie und Ordnungspolitik. Konzeptionen und Entwicklungsperspektiven*, Stuttgart: G. Fischer, pp. 371–400.

Herrmann-Pillath, C. (2000b) 'Strange Notes on Modern Statistics and Traditional Popular Religion in China: Further Reflections on the Importance of Sinology for Social Science as Applied to China'. In Mende, E. von and Siebert, M., eds, *Ad Seres et Tungusos – Festschrift für Martin Gimm*, Wiesbaden: Harrassowitz, pp. 171–189.

Herrmann-Pillath, C. (2004) *Kritik der reinen Theorie des internationalen Handels, Band 2: Evolutionäre Politische Ökonomie*, Marburg: Metropolis.

Herrmann-Pillath, C. (2006) 'Cultural Species and Institutional Change in China', *Journal of Economic Issues*, 40(3): 539–574.

Herrmann-Pillath, C. (2008a) 'Automobile Industry'. In Leese, D., ed., *Brill's Encyclopedia of China*, Leiden: Brill.

Herrmann-Pillath, C. (2008b) 'International Market Access Rights and the Evolution of the International Trade System', *Journal of Theoretical and Institutional Economics*, 164(2): 302–326.

Herrmann-Pillath, C. (2009a) 'Brands'. In Pong, D., ed., *Encyclopedia of Modern China, Vol. 1,* Farmington Hills, pp. 148–152.

Herrmann-Pillath, C. (2009b) 'Ma Yin-chu'. In: Pong, D., ed., *Encyclopedia of Modern China, Vol. 3,* Farmington Hills, p. 164.

Herrmann-Pillath, C. (2009c) 'Social Capital, Chinese Style: Individualism, Relational Collectivism and the Cultural Embeddedness of the Institutions–Performance Link', *China Economic Journal,* 2(3): 325–350.

Herrmann-Pillath, C. (2009d) 'Time, Style and Institutions. An Evolutionary Approach to Institutional Diversity'. In Rieter, H. and Zweynert, J. eds, *Economic Styles in the Process of EU Eastern Enlargement,* HWWI, Schriften-reihe des Europa-Kollegs Hamburg zur Integrationsforschung Bd 58, Baden-Baden: Nomos, pp. 15–54.

Herrmann-Pillath, C. (2010) 'What Have We Learnt From Twenty Years of Economic Research Into Culture?', *International Journal of Cultural Studies,* 13(4): 317–335.

Herrmann-Pillath, C. (2011) *The Economics of Identity and Creativity. A Cultural Science Approach,* St Lucia: University of Queensland Press, and New Brunswick, NJ, and London: Transactions.

Herrmann-Pillath, C. (2012a) 'Institutions, Distributed Cognition and Agency: Rule-following as Performative Action', *Journal of Economic Methodology,* 19(1): 21–42.

Herrmann-Pillath, C. (2012b) 'Making Sense of Institutional Change in China: The Cultural Dimension of Economic Growth and Modernization'. In Aoki, M., Kuran, T. and Roland, G., eds, *Institutions and Comparative Economic Development,* IEA Conference Vol. 150/1, New York: Palgrave Macmillan, pp. 254–280.

Herrmann-Pillath, C. (2013a) *Foundations of Economic Evolution. A Treatise on the Natural Philosophy of Economics,* Cheltenham and Northampton: Edward Elgar.

Herrmann-Pillath, C. (2013b) 'Performativity of Economic Systems: Approaches and Implications for Taxonomy', *Journal of Economic Methodology,* 20(2): 139–163.

Herrmann-Pillath, C. (2015) 'A "Third Culture" in Economics? An Essay on Smith, Confucius and the Rise of China'. In *The Adam Smith Review,* Vol. 8, Abingdon and New York: Routledge, pp. 83–110.

Herrmann-Pillath, C. (2016) 'Performative Mechanisms'. In Boldyrev, I. and Svetlova, E., eds, *Enacting Dismal Science: New Perspectives on the Performativity of Economics,* New York: Palgrave Macmillan, forthcoming.

Herrmann-Pillath, C. and Boldyrev, I.A. (2014) *Hegel, Institutions and Economics. Performing the Social,* Abingdon and New York: Routledge.

Herrmann-Pillath, C. and Feng, X. (2004) 'Competitive Governments, Fiscal Arrangements, and the Provision of Local Public Infrastructure in China. A Theory-driven Study of Gujiao Municipality', *China Information,* 18(3): 373–428.

Herrmann-Pillath, C., Libman, A. and Yu, X. (2014) 'Economic Integration in China: Politics vs. Culture', *Journal of Comparative Economics,* 42: 470–492.

Hesse, G. (1982) *Die Entstehung industrialisierter Volkswirtschaften. Ein Beitrag zur theoretischen und empirischen Analyse der langfristigen wirtschaftlichen Entwicklung,* Tübingen: Mohr Siebeck.

Hesse, G. (1991) *Landnutzungssysteme und sozio-ökonomische Entwicklung: Zur theoretischen Begründung komparativer Wirtschafts- und Sozialgeschichte,* Sonderveröffentlichung des BIOst, Köln.

Hirshleifer, J. (2001) *The Dark Side of the Force. Economic Foundations of Conflict Theory,* Cambridge: Cambridge University Press.

Ho, P. (2001) 'Who Owns China's Land? Property Rights and Deliberate Institutional Ambiguity', *The China Quarterly*, 166: 394–423.

Hobson, J.M. (2004) *The Eastern Origins of Western Civilization*, Cambridge: Cambridge University Press.

Hodgson, G.M. and Knudsen, T. (2004) 'The Firm as an Interactor: Firms as Vehicles for Habits and Routines', *Journal of Evolutionary Economics*, 14(3): 281–309.

Hoffman, L.M. (2010) *Patriotic Professionalism in Urban China. Fostering Talent*, Philadelphia, PA: Temple University Press.

Hofman, P.S., Wu, B. and Liu, K. (2014) 'Collaborative Socially Responsible Practices for Improving the Position of Chinese Workers in Global Supply Chains', *Journal of Current Chinese Affairs*, 43(4): 111–141.

Hofstede, G., Hofstede, G.J. and Minkov, M. (2010) *Cultures and Organizations. Software of the Mind*, New York: McGraw Hill.

Holbig, H. (2014) 'China's Unwritten Constitution: Ideological Implications of a "Non-ideological" Approach', *Asien*, 132: 53–59.

Holmes, R. (2014) 'Pillars of Fat: The Corporeal Aesthetics of Civilization (Wenming) in Contemporary Art', *The China Journal*, 72: 121–138.

Holz, C. A. (2003) '"Fast, Clear and Accurate": How Reliable Are Chinese Output and Economic Growth Statistics?', *The China Quarterly*, 173: 122–163.

Holz, C.A. (2009) 'No Razor's Edge: Reexamining Alwyn Young's Evidence for Increasing Inter-Provincial Trade Barriers in China', *Review of Economics and Statistics*, 91(3): 599–616.

Honig, E. (1990) 'Invisible Inequalities: The Status of Subei People in Contemporary Shanghai', *The China Quarterly*, 122: 273–292.

Hooper, B. (2005) *The Consumer Citizen in Contemporary China*, Working Paper No. 12, Centre for East and South-East Asian Studies, Lund University.

Hopkins, E. and Kornienko, T. (2004) 'Running to Keep the Same Place: Consumer Choice as a Game of Status', *American Economic Review*, 94(4): 1085–1108.

House, R.J., Hanges, P.J., Javidan, M., Dorfman, P.W. and Gupta, V., eds (2004) *Culture, Leadership, and Organizations. The Globe Study of 62 Societies*, Thousand Oaks, CA, London, and New Delhi: Sage.

Hsing, Y-T. (2006) 'Land and Territorial Politics in Urban China', *The China Quarterly*, 187: 575–591.

Hsu, C.L. and Jiang, Y. (2015) 'An Institutional Approach to Chinese NGOs: State Alliance versus State Avoidance Resource Strategies', *The China Quarterly*, 221: 100–122.

Hsu, G. and Hannan, M.T. (2005) 'Identities, Genres, and Organizational Forms', *Organization Science*, 16(5): 474–490.

Hsu, R.C. (2005) *Economic Theories in China, 1978–1988*, Cambridge: Cambridge University Press.

Hu, B. (2007) *Informal Institutions and Rural Development in China*, Abingdon und New York: Routledge.

Hu, J. (2005) 在省部级主要领导干部提高构建社会主义和谐社会能力专题研讨班上的讲话, www.china.com.cn/chinese/news/899546.htm (accessed 19 November 2013).

Hu, X. (1998) 'Informal Property Rights and Their Formalization in 1997: A Political Economy Analysis'. In *China Review 1998*, Hong Kong: Hong University Press, pp. 313–338.

Huang, C. (2002) 'Mismatched Cultural Affinity: Industrial Relations in Overseas Chinese Enterprises in South China'. In Douw, L., Huang, C. and Ip, D., eds, *Rethinking Chinese Transnational Enterprises. Cultural Affinity and Business Strategies*, London: Curzon, pp. 16–37.

Huang Jing, Zhang Xiaofen and Xu Yushan (黄菁， 张晓芬 and 徐宇珊) (2013) 'Shenzhen shequ shehui zuzhi dengji bei'an zhengce de shenshi yu tantao' (深圳社区社会组织登记备案政策的审视与探讨). In Zhang Xiaoru (张骁儒), ed., *Shenzhen shehui fazhan baogao (2012–2013)* (深圳社会发展报告), Beijing: Shehui kexue wenxian chubanshe, pp. 197–210.

Huang, P.C.C. (1990) *The Peasant Family and Rural Development in the Yangzi Delta, 1350–1988*, Stanford, CA: Stanford University Press.

Huang, P.C.C. (1993) '"Public Sphere"/"Civil Society" in China? The Third Realm Between State and Society', *Modern China*, 19(2): 216–240.

Huang, P.C.C. (2006a) 'Civil Adjudication in China, Past and Present', *Modern China*, 32(2): 135–180.

Huang, P.C.C. (2006b) 'Court Mediation in China, Past and Present', *Modern China*, 32(3): 275–314.

Huang, P.C.C. (2008) 'Centralized Minimalism: Semiformal Governance by Quasi Officials and Dispute Resolution in China', *Modern China*, 34(1): 9–35.

Huang, P.C.C. (2009) 'China's Neglected Informal Economy: Reality and Theory', *Modern China*, 35(4): 405–438.

Huang, P.C.C. (2011a) 'Chongqing: Equitable Development Driven by a "Third Hand"?', *Modern China*, 37(6): 569–622.

Huang, P.C.C. (2011b) 'The Modern Chinese Family: In Light of Economic and Legal History', *Modern China*, 37(5): 459–497.

Huang, P.C.C. (2011c) 'China's New-age Small Farms and Their Vertical Integration: Agribusiness or Co-ops?', *Modern China*, 37(2): 107–134.

Huang, P.C.C. (2013) 'Misleading Chinese Legal and Statistical Categories: Labor, Individual Entities, and Private Enterprises', *Modern China*, 39(4): 347–379.

Huang, P.C.C. (2015) 'Morality and Law in China, Past and Present', *Modern China*, 41(1): 3–39.

Huang, R. (1988) *China: A Macro History*, Armonk, NY, and London: Sage.

Huang Yasheng (2003) *Selling China. Foreign Direct Investment in the Reform Period*, Cambridge: Cambridge University Press.

Huang Yasheng (2008) *Capitalism with Chinese Characteristics: Entrepreneurship and the State*, Cambridge: Cambridge University Press.

Huang Yasheng (2012) 'How Did China Take Off?', *Journal of Economic Perspectives*, 26(4): 147–170.

Huang Yasheng (2013) 'China's New Growth Model', *East Asia Forum*, 14 April 2013, www.eastasiaforum.org/2013/04/14/chinas-new-growth-model/.

Huckman, R.S. and Maccormack, A.D. (2009) *BYD Company, Ltd.*, Harvard Business School, Case 9–606–139.

Hui, C., Lee, C. and Rousseau, D.M. (2004) 'Employment Relationhips in China: Do Workers Relate to the Organization or to People?', *Organization Science*, 15(2): 232–240.

Hurst, W. and O'Brien, K. (2002) 'China's Contentious Pensioners', *The China Quarterly*, 170: 345–360.

Hutchins, E. (1995) *Cognition in the Wild*, Cambridge, MA, and London: MIT Press.

Hwang, K.-K. (2006a) 'Constructive Realism and Confucian Relationalism: An Epistemological Strategy for the Development of Indigenous Psychology'. In Kim, U., Yang, G.-S. and Hwang, K.-K., eds, *International and Cultural Psychology: Understanding People in Context*, New York: Springer, pp. 73–107.

Hwang, K.-K. (2006b) 'Moral Face and Social Face: Contingent Self-esteem in Confucian Society', *International Journal of Psychology*, 41(4): 276–281.

Hwang, K.-K. (2008) 'Leadership Theory of Legalism and Its Function in Confucian Society'. In Chen, C.-C. and Lee, Y.-T., eds, *Leadership and Management in China. Philosophies, Theories, and Practices*, Cambridge: Cambridge University Press, pp. 108–142.

Hwang, K.-K. and Han, K.-H. (2010) 'Face and Morality in Confucian Society'. In Bond, M.H., ed., *The Oxford Handbook of Chinese Psychology*, Oxford: Oxford University Press, pp. 479–498.

Imai, K. and Shiu, J. (2007) *A Divergent Path of Industrial Upgrading: Emergence and Evolution of the Mobile Handset Industry in China*, IDE Discussion Paper No. 125, Chiba: Institute of Developing Economies, JETRO.

Ingold, T. (1986) *Evolution and Social Life*, Cambridge: Cambridge University Press.

Ingold, T. (1993) 'The Art of Translation in a Continuous World'. In Pálsson, G., ed., *Beyond Boundaries. Understanding, Translation and Anthropological Discourse*, Oxford and Providence: Berg, pp. 211–230.

Inkeles, A., Broaded, C.M. and Cao, Z. (1997) 'Causes and Consequences of Individual Modernity in China', *The China Journal*, 37: 31–62.

Ip, I.-C. (2014) 'Urbanisation, the State, and Community Activism in the Pearl River Delta', *China Perspectives*, 2014(2): 53–60.

Ishihara, K. (1993) *China's Conversion to a Market Economy*, Tokyo: IDE.

Iwata, R. (1992) 'The Japanese Enterprise as a Unified Body of Employees: Origins and Development'. In Kumon, S. and Rosovsky, H., eds, *The Political Economy of Japan. Vol. 3: Cultural and Social Dynamics*, Stanford, CA: Stanford University Press, pp. 170–197.

Jackson, G. and Deeg, R. (2006) *How Many Varieties of Capitalism? Comparing the Comparative Institutional Analyses of Capitalist Diversity*, MPIfG Discussion Papers, 06/2, Köln: Max Planck Institute for the Study of Societies.

Jackson. M.O. (2014) 'Networks in the Understanding of Economic Behaviors', *Journal of Economic Perspectives*, 28(4): 3–22.

Jacobs, J.B. (1982) 'The Concept of *Guanxi* and Local Politics in a Rural Chinese Cultural Setting'. In Greenblatt, S., Wilson, R.W. and Wilson, A.A., eds, *Social Interaction in Chinese Society*, New York: Praeger, pp. 209–236.

Javidan, M., House, R.J., Dorfman, P.W., Hanges, P.J. and de Luque, M.S. (2006) 'Conceptualizing and Measuring Cultures and Their Consequences: a Comparative Review of GLOBE's and Hofstede's Approaches', *Journal of International Business Studies*, 37: 897–914.

Ji, L.-J., Lee, A. and Guo, T. (2010) 'The Thinking Styles of Chinese People'. In Bond, M.H., ed., *The Oxford Handbook of Chinese Psychology*, Oxford and New York: Oxford University Press, pp. 241–278.

Ji, L.-J., Nisbett, R.E. and Peng, K. (2000) 'Culture, Control, and Perception of Relationships in the Environment', *Journal of Personality and Social Psychology*, 78(5): 943–955.

Ji, L.-J., Nisbett, R.E. and Zhang, Z. (2004) 'Is It Culture or Is It Language? Examination of Language Effects in Cross-cultural Research on Categorization', *Journal of Personality and Social Psychology*, 87(1): 57–65.

Jiang, S. (2010) 'Written and Unwritten Constitutions: A New Approach to the Study of Constitutional Government in China', *Modern China*, 36(1): 12–46.

Jie Gao (2015) 'Pernicious Manipulation of Performance Measures in China's Cadre Evaluation System', *The China Quarterly*, 223: 618–638.

Jing, R. and Van de Ven, A.H. (2014) 'A Yin–Yang Model of Organizational Change: The Case of Chengdu Bus Group', *Management and Organization Review*, 10(1): 29–54.

Jones, E.L. (1988) *Growth Recurring: Economic Change in World History*, Oxford: Oxford University Press.

Jones, E.L. (2006) *Cultures Merging. A Historical and Economic Critique of Culture*, Princeton, NJ: Princeton University Press.

Judd, E.R. (1989) '*Niangjia*: Chinese Women and Their Natal Families', *The Journal of Asian Studies*, 48(3): 525–544.

Kang, X. (2009) 'Two Temples, Three Religions, and a Tourist Attraction: Contesting Sacred Space on China's Ethnic Frontier', *Modern China*, 35(3): 227–255.

Kang, X. and Han, H. (2008) 'Graduated Controls: The State–Society Relationship in Contemporary China', *Modern China*, 34(1): 36–55.

Karlan, D.S. (2005) 'Using Experimental Economics to Measure Social Capital and Predict Financial Decisions', *American Economic Review*, 95(5): 1688–1699.

Keister, L.A. (2000) *Chinese Business Groups. The Structure and Impact of Interfirm Relations During Economic Development*, Oxford: Oxford University Press.

Keller, W. and Shiue, C.H. (2007) 'Markets in China and Europe on the Eve of the Industrial Revolution', *American Economic Review*, 97(4): 1189–1216.

Kelly, D. (2013) 'Approaching Chinese Freedom: A Study in Absolute and Relative Values', *Journal of Current Chinese Affairs*, 2(2013): 141–166.

Keng, S. (2010) 'Developing into a Developmental State: Explaining the Changing Government–Business Relationships behind the Kunshan Miracle'. In Leng, T.-K. and Chu, Y.-H., eds, *Dynamics of Local Governance in China during the Reform Era*, Lanham, MD: Lexington, pp. 225–272.

Kennedy, D. (2013a) 'Law and Development Economics: A New Alliance'. In Kennedy, D. and Stiglitz, J.E., eds, *Law and Economics with Chinese Characteristics. Institutions for Promoting Development in the Twenty-first Century*, Oxford: Oxford University Press, pp. 19–70.

Kennedy, D. (2013b) 'Some Caution about Property Rights as a Recipe for Economic Development'. In Kennedy, D. and Stiglitz, J.E., eds, *Law and Economics with Chinese Characteristics. Institutions for Promoting Development in the Twenty-first Century*, Oxford: Oxford University Press, pp. 187–213.

Kennedy, J.J. (2007) 'From the Tax-for-fee Reform to the Abolition of the Agricultural Taxes: The Impact on Township Governments in North-west China', *The China Quarterly*, 189: 43–59.

Kennedy, J.J. and Shi, Y. (2011) 'Surveys and Learning about Village Elections and Rural China: An Analysis of a 2005 National Village Election Survey'. In Alpermann, B., ed., *Politics and Markets in Rural China*, Abingdon and New York: Routledge, pp. 202–217.

Kim, Y. and Gao, F.Y. (2010) 'An Empirical Study of Human Resource Management Practices in Family Firms in China', *International Journal of Human Resource Management*, 21(12): 2095–2119.

King, A.Y.-C. (1994) 'Kuan-hsi and Network Building: A Sociological Interpretation'. In Tu, W., ed., *The Living Tree. The Changing Meaning of Being Chinese Today*, Stanford, CA: Stanford University Press, pp. 109–126.

Kipnis, A. (1996) 'The Language of Gifts: Managing Guanxi in a North China Village', *Modern China*, 22(3): 285–314.

Kipnis, A. (2002) 'Practices of Guanxi Production and Ganqing Avoidance'. In Gold, T., Guthrie, D. and Wank, D., eds, *Social Connections in China. Institutions, Culture, and the Changing Nature of Guanxi*, Cambridge: Cambridge University Press, pp. 21–36.

Kipnis, A. (2006) '*Suzhi*: A Keyword Approach', *The China Quarterly*, 186: 295–313.

Kipnis, A. (2012) 'Constructing Commonality: Standardization and Modernization in Chinese Nation-building', *Journal of Asian Studies*, 71(3): 731–755.

Kipnis, A. (2016) 'Modernity and the Chinese Moral Crisis', *The China Journal*, 75: 121–127.

Kirby, W.C. (1995) 'China Unincorporated: Company Law and Business Enterprise in Twentieth-century China', *The Journal of Asian Studies*, 54(1): 43–63.

Kirby, W.C., Bynum, N., Manty, T.Y. and Zendell, E.M. (2013) *Kunshan, Incorporated: The Making of China's Richest Town*, Harvard Business School Case Study, 9–313–103.

Kirzner, I.M. (1997) 'Entrepreneurial Discovery and the Competitive Market Process: An Austrian Approach', *Journal of Economic Literature*, 35: 60–85.

Knoke, D. and Song, Y. (2008) *Social Network Analysis*, Los Angeles, CA: Sage.

Ko, K. and Weng, C. (2012) 'Structural Changes in Chinese Corruption', *The China Quarterly*, 211: 718–740.

Kostka, G. and Hobbs, W. (2012) 'Local Energy Efficiency Policy Implementation in China: Bridging the Gap between National Priorities and Local Interests', *The China Quarterly*, 211: 765–785.

Kostka, G. and Yu, X. (2015) 'Career Backgrounds of Municipal Party Secretaries: Why Do So Few Municipal Party Secretaries Rise From the County Level', *Modern China*, 41: 467–505.

KPMG (2013) *China 360: Innovated in China: New Frontier for Global R&D*, www.kpmg.com/DE/de/Documents/China-360-Issue11-201308-new-frontier-for-global-R-and-D-2013-KPMG.pdf.

KPMG (2014) *Hunhe suoyouzhi gaige zhi huo. Guoyou qiye gaizhi chuangxin xilie yanjiu baogao* (混合所有制改革之惑.《国有资本改制创新系列研究报告》之一), www.kpmg.com/CN/zh/IssuesAndInsights/ArticlesPublications/Documents/Issues-Facing-Chinese-SOE-Reforms-201412-c.pdf.

Kroker, E. (1959) 'The Concept of Property in Chinese Customary Law'. In Brown, R.A., ed., *Chinese Business Enterprise, Vol. IV*, London and New York: Routledge, pp. 370–386.

Kuah, K.E. (1999) 'The Singapore–Anxi Connection: Ancestor Worship as Moral-cultural Capital'. In Douw, L., Huang, C. and Godley, M.R., eds, *Qiaoxiang Ties. Interdisciplinary Approaches to 'Cultural Capitalism' in South China*, London, New York, Leiden and Amsterdam: Kegan Paul, pp. 143–157.

Kuhn, P.A. (1984) 'Chinese Views of Social Classification'. In Watson, J.L., ed., *Class and Social Stratification in Post-Revolution China*, Cambridge: Cambridge University Press, pp. 16–28.

Kuhn, P.A. (1990) *Soulstealers. The Chinese Sorcery Scare of 1768*, Cambridge: Cambridge University Press.

Kuhn, P.A. (2002) *Origins of the Modern Chinese State*, Stanford, CA: Stanford University Press.

Kulich, S.J. (2010) *Applying Cross-cultural Values Research to 'The Chinese': A Critical Integration of Etic and Emic Approaches*, Dissertation, Humboldt Universität Berlin.

Kulich, S.J. and Zhang, R. (2010) 'The Multiple Frames of Chinese "Values": From Tradition to Modernity and Beyond'. In Bond, M.H., ed., *The Oxford Handbook of Chinese Psychology*, Oxford and New York: Oxford University Press, pp. 241–278.

Kung, J.K. and Liu, S. (1997) 'Farmers' Preferences Regarding Ownership and Land Tenure in Post-Mao China: Unexpected Evidence from Eight Counties', *The China Journal*, 38: 33–64.

Kuran, T. (1995) *Private Truths, Public Lies. The Social Consequences of Preference Falsification*, Cambridge, MA, and London: Harvard University Press.

Kuran, T. (2009) 'Explaining the Economic Trajectories of Civilizations: The Systemic Approach', *Journal of Economic Behavior and Organization*, 71: 593–605.

Kuran, T. (2012) 'Political Consequences of Middle East's Islamic Economic Legacy'. In Aoki, M., Kuran, T. and Roland, G., eds, *Institutions and Comparative Economic Development*, IEA Conference Vol. 150/1, New York: Palgrave Macmillan, pp. 99–115.

La Porta, R., Lopez-de-Silvanes, F., Shleifer, A. and Vishny, R. (1997) 'Legal Determinants of External Finance', *Journal of Finance*, 52: 1131–1150.

La Porta, R., Lopez-de-Silanes, F., Shleifer, A. and Vishny, R. (1998) 'Law and Finance', *Journal of Political Economy*, 106: 1113–1155.

Lagerwey, J. (2010) *China. A Religious State*, Hong Kong: Chinese University Press.

Lai, J. (2015) '"Patrimonial Bureaucracy" and Chinese Law: Max Weber's Legacy and Its Limits', *Modern China*, 41(1): 40–59.

Lam, T.-C. (2010) 'The County System and County Governance'. In Chung, J.H. and Lam, T.-C., eds, *China's Local Administration. Traditions and Changes in the Subnational Hierarchy*, Abingdon and New York: Routledge, pp. 149–173.

Lan, P.-C. (2014) 'Segmented Incorporation: The Second Generation of Rural Migrants in Shanghai', *China Quarterly*, 217: 243–265.

Landa, J.T. (1994) *Trust, Ethnicity, and Identity. Beyond the New Institutional Economics of Ethnic Trading Networks, Contract Law, and Gift-exchange*, Ann Arbor: University of Michigan Press.

Landes, D.S. (2006) 'Why Europe and the West? Why Not China?', *Journal of Economic Perspectives*, 20(2): 3–22.

Landry, P.F. (2003) 'The Political Management of Mayors in Post-Deng China', *The Copenhagen Journal of Asian Studies*, 17: 31–58.

Latour, B. (2005) *Reassembling the Social: An Introduction to Actor–Network Theory*, Oxford: Oxford University Press.

Lau, K.L. and Young, A. (2013) 'Why China Shall Not Completely Transit from a Relation Based to a Rule Based Governance Regime: A Chinese Perspective', *Corporate Governance: An International Review*, 21(6): 577–585.

Lazaric, N. (2011) 'Organizational Routines and Cognition: An Introduction to Empirical and Analytical Contributions', *Journal of Institutional Economics*, 7(2): 147–156.

Ledderose, L. (2000) *Ten Thousand Things. Module and Mass Production in Chinese Art*, Princeton, NJ: Princeton University Press.

Lee, K.-P. (2007) 'Clans for Markets: The Social Organization of Inter-firm Trading Relations in China's Automobile Industry', *The China Quarterly*, 192: 876–898.

Lee, Y.-T., Han, A.-G., Byron, T.K. and Fan, H.-X. (2008) 'Daoist Leadership: Theory and Application'. In Chen, C.-C. and Lee, Y.-T., eds, *Leadership and Management in China. Philosophies, Theories, and Practices*, Cambridge: Cambridge University Press, pp. 83–107.

Lee, Z.-R. and Hsiao, H.-H.M. (2014) 'Taiwan. SME-oriented Capitalism in Transition'. In Witt, M.A. and Redding, G., eds, *The Oxford Handbook of Asian Business Systems*, Oxford: Oxford University Press, pp. 238–259.

Leibold, J. (2010) 'More Than a Category: Han Supremacism on the Chinese Internet', *The China Quarterly*, 203: 539–559.

Leung. K. (2010) 'Beliefs in Chinese Culture'. In Bond, M.H., ed., *The Oxford Handbook of Chinese Psychology*, Oxford: Oxford University Press, pp. 221–240.

Levenson, J.R. (1968) *Confucian China and Its Modern Fate. A Trilogy*, Berkeley: University of California Press.

Li, H. and Rozelle, S. (2003) 'Privatizing Rural China: Insider Privatization, Innovative Contracts and the Performance of Township Enterprises', *The China Quarterly*, 176: 981–1005.

Li, H., Loyalka, P., Rozelle, S., Wu, B. and Xie, J. (2015) 'Unequal Access to College in China: How Far Have Poor, Rural Students Been Left Behind?', *The China Quarterly*, 221: 185–207.

Li, J., Wang, L. and Fischer, K.W. (2004) 'The Organisation of Chinese Shame Concepts', *Cognition and Emotion*, 18(6): 767–797.

Li, L.C. (2006) 'Differentiated Actors: Central and Local Actors in China's Rural Tax Reforms', *Modern Asian Studies*, 40(1): 151–174.

Li, L.C. (2007) 'Working for the Peasants? Strategic Interactions and Un-intended Consequences in Chinese Rural Tax Reform', *The China Journal*, 57: 89–108.

Li, L. and Li, S. (2010) 'The Impact of Variations in Urban Registration within Cities'. In Whyte, M.K., ed., *One Country, Two Societies: Rural–Urban Inequality in Contemporary China*, Cambridge: Cambridge University Press, pp. 188–218.

Li, L., Liu, M. and O'Brien, K.J. (2012) 'Petitioning Beijing: The High Tide of 2003–2006', *The China Quarterly*, 210: 313–334.

Li, P.P. (2007) 'Guanxi as the Chinese Norm for Personalized Social Capital: Toward an Integrated Duality Framework of Informal Exchange'. In Yeung, H.W.-C., ed., *Handbook of Research on Asian Business*, Cheltenham and Northampton: Edward Elgar, pp. 62–83.

Li, P.P. (2014) 'The Unique Value of Yin–Yang Balancing: A Critical Response', *Management and Organization Review*, 10(2): 321–332.

Li Ruiquan (李瑞全) (2014) 'Rujia yingyong lunli zhi kaituo. Dangdai xinrujia lun keji yingyongyu xiandai shehui zhi daode wenti' (儒家应用伦理之开拓。当代新儒家论科技应用与现代社会之道德问题). In Jing Haifeng (景海峰), ed., *Ruxue de dangdai fazhan yu weilai qianzhan* (儒学的当代发展与未来前瞻), Beijing: Renmin chubanshe.

Li, S. and Sicular, T. (2014) 'The Distribution of Household Income in China: Inequality, Poverty and Politics', *The China Quarterly*, 217: 1–41.

Li, S. and Wu, J.J. (2007) 'Why China Thrives Despite Corruption', *Far Eastern Economic Review*, 170(3): 24–28.

Li Xin (2014) 'Can Yin–Yang Guide Chinese Indigenous Management Research?', *Management and Organization Review*, 10(1): 7–27.

Liang, X., Marler, J.H. and Cui, Z. (2012) 'Strategic Human Resource Management in China: East Meets West', *Academy of Management Perspectives*, 26(2): 55–70.

Licht, A., Goldschmidt, C. and Schwartz, S. (2007) 'Culture Rules: The Foundations of the Rule of Law and Other Norms of Governance', *Journal of Comparative Economics*, 35: 659–688.

Lieberthal, K.G. and Lampton, D.M., eds (1992) *Bureaucracy, Politics, and Decision-making in Post-Mao China*, Berkeley, LA and Oxford: University of California Press.

Liebman, B. and Wu, T. (2013) 'China's Network Justice'. In Kennedy, D. and Stiglitz, J.E., eds, *Law and Economics with Chinese Characteristics. Institutions for Promoting Development in the Twenty-first Century*, Oxford: Oxford University Press, pp. 510–567.

Liebman, B.L. and Milhaupt, C.J. (2007) 'Reputational Sanctions in China's Securities Market', http://ssrn.com/abstract=999698.

Lin, D.Q. (2010) 'Working to be Worthy: Shame and the Confucian Technology of Governing'. In Kipnis, A., ed., *Chinese Modernity and the Individual Psyche*, New York: Palgrave Macmillan, pp. 169–186.

Lin, K.-C. and Chen, S. (2013) 'The Local Government in Corporate Restructuring: Case Studies in Fractured Bargaining Relations', *Journal of Current Chinese Affairs*, 2013(4): 171–198.

Lin, N. (2001) *Social Capital. A Theory of Social Structure and Action*, Cambridge: Cambridge University Press.

Lin, T.W. (2005) 'OEC Management-control System Helps China Haier Group Achieve Competitive Advantage', *Management Accounting Quarterly*, 6(3): 1–11.

Lin, T.W. (2009) 'Haier is Higher: A Chinese Company's Roadmap to Success via Its Reengineering System', *Strategic Finance*, December: 41–49.

Lin, Y. (2011) 'Turning Rurality into Modernity: *Suzhi* Education in a Suburban Public School of Migrant Children in Xiamen', *The China Quarterly*, 206: 313–330.

Lingohr, S. (2007) 'Rural Households, Dragon Heads and Associations: A Case Study of Sweet Potato Processing in Sichuan Province', *The China Quarterly*, 192: 898–914.

Little, D. (1992) *Understanding Peasant China. Case Studies in the Philosophy of Social Science*, New Haven, CT, and London: Yale University Press.

Liu, J.H., Li M.-C. and Yue, X. (2010) 'Chinese Social Identity and Inter-group Relations: The Influence of Benevolent Authority'. In Bond, M.H., ed., *The Oxford Handbook of Chinese Psychology*, Oxford: Oxford University Press, pp. 579–598.

Liu, Y.-L. (2012) 'From Predator to Debtor: The Soft Budget Constraint and Semi-planned Administration in Rural China', *Modern China*, 38(3): 308–345.

Loh, C. and Remick, E.I. (2015) 'China's Skewed Sex Ratio and the One-child Policy', *The China Quarterly*, 222: 295–319.

Looney, K.E. (2015) 'China's Campaign to Build a New Socialist Countryside: Village Modernization, Peasant Councils, and the Ganzpou Model of Rural Development', *The China Quarterly*, 224: 909–933.

Lu, H. (2010) 'Small-town China: A Historical Perspective on Rural–Urban Relations'. In Whyte, M.K., ed., *One Country, Two Societies: Rural–Urban Inequality in Contemporary China*, Cambridge: Cambridge University Press, pp. 29–54.

Lu, J. (2012) 'Varieties of Electoral Institutions in China's Grassroots Democracy: Cross-sectional and Longitudinal Evidence from Rural China', *The China Quarterly*, 210: 482–493.

Lu, Y., Johnson, B. and Stark, R. (2008) 'Deregulation and Religious Market in Taiwan: A Research Note', *Sociological Quarterly*, 49: 139–153.

Lundvall, B.-Å., ed. (1992) *National Systems of Innovation. Towards a Theory of Innovation and Interactive Learning*, London and New York: Anthem Press.

Luo Danglun (罗党论), She Guoman (佘国满) and Chen Jie (陈杰) (2015) 'Jingji zengchang yeji yu defang guan jisheng de guanxing zai shenshi' (经济增长业绩与地方官晋升的关联再审视), *China Economic Quarterly*, 14(3): 1145–1172.

Lüthje, B. (2013) 'Diverging Trajectories: Economic Rebalancing and Labour Policies in China', *Journal of Current Chinese Affairs*, 2013(4): 105–138.

Lux, J.P. (1998) *Die ländlichen genossenschaftlichen Stiftungen (农村合作基金会 nongcun hezuo jijinhui) in der Provinz Sichuan*, Göttingen: Vandenhoek & Ruprecht.

Lyons, T.P. (1985) 'China's Cellular Economy: A Test of the Fragmentation Hypothesis', *Journal of Comparative Economics*, 9: 125–144.

Lyons, T.P. (1986) 'Explaining Economic Fragmentation in China: A Systems Approach', *Journal of Comparative Economics*, 10: 209–236.

Lyons, T.P. (1990) 'Planning and Inter-provincial Coordination in Maoist China', *The China Quarterly*, 121: 36–60.

Ma Hong (马宏), Luo Siying (罗思颖) and Guo Feng (郭峰) (2013) '2012 nian Shenzhen shehui zuzhi fazhan baogao' (年深圳社会组织发展报告). In Zhang Xiaoru (张骁儒), ed., *Shenzhen shehui fazhan baogao (2012–2013)* (深圳社会发展报告), Beijing: Shehui kexue wenxian chubanshe, pp. 187–196.

Ma Yinchu (马寅初) (1981) *Ma Yinchu jingji lunwen xuanji* (马寅初经济论文选集, 上, 下), Beijing: Beijing daxue chubanshe.

MacKenzie, D. (2006) *An Engine, Not a Camera: How Financial Models Shape Markets*, Cambridge and London: Cambridge University Press.

MacKenzie, D. (2007) 'Is Economics Performative? Option Theory and the Construction of Derivatives Markets'. In MacKenzie, D., Muniesa, F. and Siu, L., eds, *Do Economists Make Markets? On the Performativity of Economics*, Princeton, NJ, and Oxford: Princeton University Press, pp. 54–86.

Maddison, A. (2007) *Chinese Economic Performance in the Long Run. Second Edition, Revised and Updated, 960–2030 AD*, Paris: OECD.

Madsen, R. (1984) *Morality and Power in a Chinese Village*, Berkeley, LA and London: University of California Press.

Manion, M. (2014): 'Authoritarian Parochialism: Local Congressional Representation in China', *The China Quarterly*, 218: 311–338.

Mann, S. (1988) *Local Merchants and the Chinese Bureaucracy, 1750–1950*, Stanford, CA: Stanford University Press.

Maskin, E., Qian, Y. and Xu, C. (2000) 'Incentives, Information, and Organizational Form', *Review of Economic Studies*, 67(2): 359–378.

Matsumoto, D. and Hwang, H.S. (2011) 'Culture, Emotion, and Expression'. In Gelfland, M.J., Chiu, C.-Y. and Hong, Y.-Y., eds, *Advances in Culture and Psychology, Volume One,* Oxford and New York: Oxford University Press, pp. 53–98.

Mayhew, A. (1994) 'Culture'. in Hodgson, G., Samuels, W.J. and Tool, M.R., eds, *The Elgar Companion to Institutional and Evolutionary Economics,* Aldershot and Brookfield: Edward Elgar, pp. 115–119.

Mayr, E. (1982) *The Growth of Biological Thought. Diversity, Evolution, and Inheritance,* Cambridge and London: Belknap Press.

McCarthy, S.K. (2013) 'Serving Society, Repurposing the State: Religious Charity and Resistance in China', *The China Journal,* 70: 48–72.

McGregor, R. (2012) *The Party. The Secret World of China's Communist Rulers,* London: Penguin.

McNally, C.A. (2013) 'Refurbishing State Capitalism: A Policy Analysis of Efforts to Rebalance China's Political Economy', *Journal of Current Chinese Affairs,* 2013(4): 45–73.

Mehta, J. (2011) 'The Varied Roles of Ideas in Politics: From "Whether" to "How"'. In Béland, D. and Cox, R.H., eds, *Ideas and Politics in Social Science Research,* Oxford: Oxford University Press, pp. 23–46.

Menary, R. (2007) 'Writing as Thinking', *Language Sciences,* 29: 621–632.

Mertha, A.C. (2005) 'China's "Soft" Centralization: Shifting *Tiao/Kuai* Authority Relations', *The China Quarterly,* 184: 791–810.

Mertha, A.C. (2009) '"Fragmented Authoritarianism 2.0": Political Pluralization of the Chinese Policy Process', *China Quarterly,* 200: 995–1013.

Metzger, T.A. (1973) *The Internal Organization of Ch'ing Bureaucracy. Legal, Normative, and Communication Aspects,* Cambridge, MA: Harvard University Press.

Metzger, T.A. (1977) *Escape from Predicament. Neo-Confucianism and China's Evolving Political Culture,* New York: Columbia University Press.

Midler, P. (2008) 'Why Profit Zero Works in China', *Far Eastern Economic Review,* 171(2): 45–48.

Milgrom, P.R., North, D.C. and Weingast, B.R. (1990) 'The Role of Institutions in the Revival of Trade: The Law Merchant, Private Judges, and the Champagne Fairs', *Economics and Politics,* 2(1): 1–23.

Min, T.-K. (1989) *National Polity and Local Power. The Transformation of Late Imperial China,* Cambridge, MA, and London: Harvard University Press.

Minkov, M. and Hofstede, G. (2012) 'Hofstede's Fifth Dimension: New Evidence From the World Values Survey', *Journal of Cross-cultural Psychology,* 43(1): 3–14.

Moav, O. and Neeman, Z. (2012) 'Saving Rates and Poverty: The Role of Conspicuous Consumption and Human Capital', *Economic Journal,* 122: 933–956.

Mohr, J.W. and Rawlings, C. (2012) 'Four Ways to Measure Culture: Social Science, Hermeneutics, and the Cultural Turn'. In Alexander, J., Jacobs, R. and Smith. P., eds, *The Oxford Handbook of Cultural Sociology,* Oxford: Oxford University Press, pp. 70–113.

Mokyr, J. (2009) *The Enlightened Economy. Britain and the Industrial Revolution 1700–1850,* London: Penguin.

Moore, Ch., ed. (1967) *The Chinese Mind. Essentials of Chinese Philosophy and Culture,* Honululu: The University Press of Hawaii.

Müller-Armack, A. ([1940] 1971) 'Zur Geneaologie der Wirtschaftsstile'. In Schachtschabel, H.G., ed., *Wirtschaftsstufen und Wirtschaftsordnungen,* Darmstadt: Wissenschaftliche Buchgesellschaft, pp. 156–207.

Müller-Armack, A. (1981) *Genealogie der Sozialen Marktwirtschaft*, Bern: Haupt.

Mungello, D.E. (1999) *The Great Encounter of China and the West, 1500–1800*, Lanham, MD: Rowman & Littlefield.

Muniesa, F. and Callon, M. (2007) 'Economic Experiments and the Construction of Markets'. In MacKenzie, D., Muniesa, F. and Siu, L., eds, *Do Economists Make Markets? On the Performativity of Economics*, Princeton, NJ, and Oxford: Princeton University Press.

Munz, P. (1993) *Philosophical Darwinism. On the Origin of Knowledge by Means of Natural Selection*, London and New York: Routledge.

Murphy, R. (2004) 'Turning Peasants into Modern Chinese Citizens: "Population Quality" Discourse, Demographic Transition and Primary Education', *The China Quarterly*, 177: 1–21.

Myers, R.H. (1970) *The Chinese Peasant Economy. Agricultural Development in Hopei and Shantung, 1890–1949*, Cambridge: Cambridge University Press.

Naquin, S. and Rawski, E. (1987) *Chinese Society in the Eighteenth Century*, New Haven, CT, and London: Yale University Press.

Naughton, B. (1988) 'The Third Front: Defense Industrialization in the Chinese Industry', *The China Quarterly*, 115: 351–386.

Naughton, B. (2003) 'How Much Can Regional Integration Do to Unify China's Markets?' In Hope, N., Yang, D. and Li, M.Y., eds, *How Far Across the River? Chinese Policy Reform at the Millennium*, Stanford, CA: Stanford University Press, pp. 204–232.

Naughton, B. (2007) *The Chinese Economy. Transition and Growth*, Cambridge, MA, and London: MIT Press.

Naughton, B. (2009) 'Market Economy, Hierarchy and Single-Party Rule'. In Kornai, J. and Qian, Y., eds, *Market and Socialism in the Light of the Experiences of China and Vietnam*, International Economic Association Conference, Vol. 146, London: Palgrave Macmillan, pp. 135–161.

Nee, V. (2000) 'The Role of the State in Making a Market Economy', *Journal of Institutional and Theoretical Economics*, 156(1): 64–88.

Needham, J. (1977) *Wissenschaftlicher Universalismus. Über Ursprung und Bedeutung der chinesischen Wissenschaft*, Frankfurt am Main: Suhrkamp.

Nelson, R.R. and Winter, S.G. (1982) *An Evolutionary Theory of Economic Change*, Cambridge and London: Belknap Press.

Ng, I. (2010) 'Chinese Political Psychology: Political Participation in Chinese Societies'. In Bond, M.H., ed., *The Oxford Handbook of Chinese Psychology*, Oxford: Oxford University Press, pp. 563–578.

Ngai, P. (2003) 'Subsumption or Consumption? The Phantom of Consumer Revolution in "Globalizing" China', *Cultural Anthropology*, 18(4): 469–492.

Ngai, P. and Chan, J. (2012) 'Global Capital, Chinese State, and Chinese Workers: The Foxconn Experience', *Modern China*, 38(4): 383–410.

Ngok, K-l. (邱经纶) and Zhuang, W-J. (莊文嘉) (2013) 'Shehui gongmin quan yu shehui wending – "Xintang shijian" de ge'an yanjiu' (社会公民权与社会稳定—新塘事件的个案研究), *Ershiyi shiji* (二十一世纪), 135: 59–74.

Nisbett, R. (2003) *The Geography of Thought: How Asians and Westerners Think Differently … and Why*, New York: Free Press.

Nooteboom, B. (2002) *Trust. Forms, Foundations, Functions, Failures and Figures*, Cheltenham and Northampton: Edward Elgar.

Nooteboom, B., ed. (2006) 'Simmel's Treatise on the Triad (1908)', *Journal of Institutional Economics*, 2(3): 365–383.

Norman, J. (1988) *Chinese*, Cambridge: Cambridge University Press.

North, D.C. (1981) *Structure and Change in Economic History*, New York: Norton.

North, D.C. (1990) *Institutions, Institutional Change, and Economic Performance*, Cambridge: Cambridge University Press.

North, D.C. (2005) *Understanding the Process of Economic Change*, Princeton, NJ, and Oxford: Princeton University Press.

North, D.C., Wallis, J.J. and Weingast, B.R. (2009) *Violence and Social Orders. A Conceptual Framework for Interpreting Recorded Human History*, Cambridge: Cambridge University Press.

Numazaki, I. (1996) 'The Role of Personal Networks in the Making of Taiwan's Guanxiqiye (Related Enterprises)'. In Hamilton, G.G., ed., *Asian Business Networks*, Berlin and New York: Springer, pp. 71–86.

O'Brien, K. and Han, R. (2009) 'Path to Democracy? Assessing Village Elections in China', *Journal of Contemporary China*, 18(6): 359–378.

O'Brien, K.J. and Li, L. (2000) 'Accommodating Democracy in a One-Party State: Introducing Village Elections in China', *The China Quarterly*, 162: 465–489.

Ocko, J. (2004) 'The Missing Metaphor. Applying Western Legal Scholarship to the Study of Contract and Property in Early Modern China'. In Zelin, M., Ocko, J.K. and Gardella, R., eds, *Contract and Property in Early Modern China*, Stanford, CA: Stanford University Press, pp. 178–208.

OECD (2011) *Corporate Governance of Listed Companies in China: Self-assessment by the China Securities Regulatory Commission*, OECD Publishing, http://dx.doi.org/10.1787/9789264119208-en.

OECD (2013) *OECD Economic Surveys: China 2013*, Paris: OECD.

Oh, S.-Y. (2013) 'Fragmented Liberalization in the Chinese Automotive Industry: The Political Logic Behind Beijing Hyundai's Success in the Chinese Market', *China Quarterly*, 216: 920–945.

Oi, J.C. (1992) 'Fiscal Reform and the Economic Foundations of Local State Corporatism in China', *World Politics*, 45(1): 99–126.

Oi, J.C. (1996) 'The Role of the Local State in China's Transitional Economy', *The China Quarterly*, 144: 132–149.

Oi, J.C., Babiarz, K.S., Zhang, L., Luo, R. and Rozelle, S. (2012) 'Shifting Fiscal Control to Limit Cadre Power in China's Townships and Villages', *The China Quarterly*, 211: 624–648.

Ong, L.H. (2012) *Prosper or Perish: Credit and Fiscal Systems in Rural China*, Ithaca, NY: Cornell University Press.

Ong, L.H. (2014) 'State-led Urbanization in China: Skyscrapers, Land Revenue and "Concentrated Villages"', *The China Quarterly*, 217: 162–179.

Orenstein, M.A. (2011) 'Three Models of Contemporary Capitalism'. In Birdsall, N. and Fukuyama, F., eds, *New Ideas on Development after the Financial Crisis*, Baltimore, MD: Johns Hopkins University Press.

Orléans, A. (2011) *L'empire de la valeur. Refonder l'economie*, Paris: Seuil.

Osborne, A. (2004) 'Property, Taxes, and State Protection of Rights'. In Zelin, M., Ocko, J.K. and Gardella, R., eds, *Contract and Property in Early Modern China*, Stanford, CA: Stanford University Press, pp. 120–158.

Osnos, E. (2014) *Age of Ambition. Chasing Fortune, Truth and Faith in the New China*, London: The Bodley Head.

Ostrom, E. (1990) *Governing the Commons. The Evolution of Institutions for Collective Action*, Cambridge: Cambridge University Press.

Palmer, D. (2011a) 'Gift and Market in the Chinese Religious Economy', *Religion*, 41(4): 569–594.

Palmer, D. (2011b) 'The Body: Health, Nation, and Transcendence'. In Palmer, D., Shive, G. and Wickeri, P.L., eds, *Chinese Religious Life*, Oxford: Oxford University Press, pp. 87–106.

Parish, W. and Whyte, M. (1978) *Village and Family in Contemporary China*, Chicago, IL: Chicago University Press.

Parris, K. (1993) 'Local Initiative and National Reform: The Wenzhou Model of Development', *The China Quarterly*, 134: 242–263.

Pearson, M.M. (1997) *China's New Business Elite. The Political Consequences of Economic Reform*, Berkeley, LA and London: University of California Press.

Pei, X. (2002) 'The Contribution of Collective Landownership to China's Economic Transition and Rural Industrialization', *Modern China*, 28(3): 279–314.

Pelzel, J.C. (1970) 'Japanese Kinship: A Comparison'. In Freedman, M., ed., *Family and Kinship in Chinese Society*, Stanford, CA: Stanford University Press, pp. 227–248.

Peng Liqin (彭立勋), ed. (2013) *Shenzhen wenhua lanpishu 2013. Wenhua chuangzao huodong yu chengshi wenhua shili* (深圳文化蓝皮书2013。文化创造活动与城市文化实力), Beijing: Social Sciences Academic Press (China).

Pennarz, J. (1992) *Mazu, Macht und Marktwirtschaft. Die religiöse Organisation im sozialen und ökonomischen Wandlungsprozeß der ländlichen Gesellschaft Taiwans*, Munich: Anacon.

Perdue, P. (1987) *Exhausting the Earth. State and Peasant in Hunan, 1500–1850*, Cambridge, MA, and London: Harvard University Press.

Pesselhoy, K. (2006) 'Strukturelle Anpassungen in der chinesischen Automobilzulieferindustrie', *China aktuell*, 2006(5): 5–46.

Pieke, F.N. (2004) 'Contours of an Anthropology of the Chinese State: Political Structure, Agency and Economic Development in Rural China', *Journal of the Royal Anthropological Institute*, 10(3): 517–538.

Pieke, F.N. (2009) 'Marketization, Centralization and Globalization of Cadre Training in Contemporary China', *The China Quarterly*, 200: 953–972.

Pieke, F.N., Nyíri, P., Thunø, M. and Ceccagno, A. (2004) *Transnational Chinese. Fujianese Migrants in Europe*, Stanford, CA: Stanford University Press.

Pinker, S. (2011) *The Better Angels of Our Nature. The Decline of Violence in History and Its Causes*, London: Allen Lane.

Pippin, Robert B. (2008) *Hegel's Practical Philosophy. Rational Agency as Ethical Life*, Cambridge: Cambridge University Press.

Platteau, J-P. (1994) 'Behind the Market Stage Where Real Societies Exist – Part I: The Role of Public and Private Order Institutions, and Part II: The Role of Moral Norms', *Journal of Development Studies*, 30(3): 533–577, 30(4): 753–817.

Podolny, J.M. (2005) *Status Signals: A Sociological Study of Market Competition*, Princeton, NJ, and Oxford: Princeton University Press.

Pomeranz, K. (1996) 'Power, Gender, and Pluralism in the Cult of the Goddess of Taishan'. In Huters, Th., Wong, R.B. and Yu, P., eds, *Culture and State in Chinese History. Conventions, Accommodations, and Critiques*, Stanford, CA: Stanford University Press, pp. 182–204.

Pomeranz, K. (2000) *The Great Divergence. China, Europe, and the Making of the Modern World Economy*, Princeton, NJ, and Oxford: Princeton University Press.

Pomeranz, K. (2007) 'Orthopraxy, Orthodoxy and the Goddess(es) of Taishan', *Modern China*, 33(1): 22–46.

Poncet, S. (2005) 'A Fragmented China: Measure and Determinants of China's Domestic Market Disintegration', *Review of International Economics*, 13(3): 409–430.

Portes, A. and Sensenbrenner, J. (1993) 'Embeddedness and Immigration: Notes on the Social Determinants of Economic Action', *American Journal of Sociology*, 98: 1320–1350.

Potter, P.B. (2002) '*Guanxi* and the PRC Legal System: From Contradiction to Complementarity'. In Gold, T., Guthrie, D. and Wank, D., eds, *Social Connections in China. Institutions, Culture, and the Changing Nature of Guanxi*, Cambridge: Cambridge University Press, pp. 179–195.

Potter, S.H. and Potter, J. (1990) *China's Peasants: The Anthropology of a Revolution*, Cambridge and New York: Cambridge University Press.

Pricewaterhouse Coopers und VDA (2011) *Automobilindustrie und Mobilität in China: Plan, Wunsch und Realität*, Stuttgart.

Priddat, B.P. (1990) *Hegel als Ökonom*, Berlin: Duncker & Humblot.

Priddat, B.P. (2001) *Le concert universel: Die Physiokratie. Eine Transformationsphilosophie des 18. Jahrhunderts*, Marburg: Metropolis.

Prosterman, R. (2013) 'Rural Land Rights in China'. In Kennedy, D. and Stiglitz, J.E., eds, *Law and Economics with Chinese Characteristics. Institutions for Promoting Development in the Twenty-first Century*, Oxford: Oxford University Press, pp. 214–235.

Putnam, R. (2000) *Bowling Alone: The Collapse and Revival of American Community*, New York: Simon & Schuster.

Pye, L.W. (1981) *The Dynamics of Chinese Politics*, Cambridge: Oelgeschlager, Gunn & Hain.

Pye, L.W. (1988) *The Mandarin and the Cadre: China's Political Cultures*, Ann Arbor: University of Michigan Press.

Qi Hao (2014) 'The Labor Share Question in China', *Monthly Review*, 65(8), http://monthlyreview.org/2014/01/01/labor-share-question-china/.

Qian, Y.Y. and Weingast, B.M. (1996) 'China's Transition to Markets: Market-preserving Federalism, Chinese Style', *Policy Reform*, 1: 149–185.

Quine, W.V.O. (1969) *Ontological Relativity and Other Essays*, New York: Columbia University Press.

Rawls, J. (2001) *Justice as Fairness. A Restatement*, Cambridge and London: Belknap Press.

Rawski, T.G. (1989) *Economic Growth in Prewar China*, Berkeley, LA and Oxford: University of California Press.

Razo, A. (2013) 'Autocrats and Democrats'. In Reksulak, M., Razzaloni, L. and Shughart II, W.F., eds, *The Elgar Companion to Public Choice, Second Edition*, Cheltenham and Northampton: Edward Elgar, pp. 83–110.

Redding, S.G. (1990) *The Spirit of Chinese Capitalism*, Berlin and New York: DeGruyter.

Redding, S.G. (1996a) 'The Distinct Nature of Chinese Capitalism', *The Pacific Review*, 9(3): 426–440.

Redding, S.G. (1996b) 'Weak Organizations and Strong Linkages: Managerial Ideology and Chinese Family Business Networks'. In Hamilton, G.G., ed., *Asian Business Networks*, Berlin and New York: Springer, pp. 27–40.

Redding, S.G. and Witt, M.A. (2008) *The Future of Chinese Capitalism: Choices and Chances*, Oxford: Oxford University Press.

Richardson, P. (1999) *Economic Change in China, c.1800–1950*, Cambridge: Cambridge University Press.

Richerson, P.J.and Boyd, R. (2005) *Not By Genes Alone. How Culture Transformed Human Evolution*, Chicago, IL: University of Chicago Press.

Riskin, C. (1975) 'Surplus and Stagnation in Modern China'. In Perkins, D., ed., *China's Modern Economy in Historical Perspective*, Stanford, CA: Stanford University Press, pp. 49–84.

Rithmire, M. (2013) 'Land Politics and Local State Capacities: The Political Economy of Urban Change in China', *The China Quarterly*, 216: 872–895.

Robeyns, I. (2011) 'The Capability Approach'. In Zalta, E.N., ed., *The Stanford Encyclopedia of Philosophy* (summer edition), http://plato.stanford.edu/archives/sum2011/entries/capability-approach/.

Rodrik, D. (1998) 'Why Do More Open Economies Have Larger Governments?', *Journal of Political Economy*, 106: 997–1032.

Rodrik, D. (2007) *One Economics, Many Recipes. Globalization, Institutions, and Economic Growth*, Princeton, NJ, and Oxford: Princeton University Press.

Roetz, H. (1992) *Die chinesische Ethik der Achsenzeit. Eine Rekonstruktion unter dem Aspekt des Durchbruchs zu postkonventionellem Denken*, Frankfurt am Main: Suhrkamp.

Rogers, D.S. and Ehrlich, P.R. (2008) 'Natural Selection and Cultural Rates of Change', *Proceedings of the National Academy of Sciences*, 105(9): 3416–3420.

Roland, G. (2004) 'Understanding Institutional Change. Fast-moving and Slow-moving Institutions', *Studies in Comparative International Development*, 38(4): 109–131.

Ross, D. (2005) *Economic Theory and Cognitive Science: Microexplanations*, Cambridge, MA, and London: Harvard University Press.

Ross, D. (2007) 'H. sapiens as Ecologically Special: What Does Language Contribute?', *Language Studies*, 29: 710–731.

Ross, D. (2011) 'Hayek's Speculative Psychology, the Neuroscience of Value Estimation, and the Basis of Normative Individualism'. In Marsh, L., ed., *Hayek in Mind: Hayek's Philosophical Psychology*, Bingley: Emerald, pp. 51–72.

Ross, D., Spurrett, D., Kincaid, H. and Stephens, G.L., eds (2007) *Distributed Cognition and the Will. Individual Volition and Social Context*, Cambridge: Cambridge University Press.

Routledge, B.R. and von Amsberg, J. (2003) 'Social Capital and Growth', *Journal of Monetary Economics*, 50: 167–193.

Rowe, W.T. (1989) *Hankow. Conflict and Community in a Chinese City, 1796–1895*, Stanford, CA: Stanford University Press.

Rozelle, S., Huang, J. and Benziger, V. (2003) 'Continuity and Change in China's Rural Periodic Markets', *The China Journal*, 49: 89–118.

Rozman, G. (1991) 'The East Asian Region in Comparative Perspective'. In Rozman, G., ed., *The East Asian Region. Confucian Heritage and Its Modern Adaptation*, Princeton, NJ: Princeton University Press, pp. 3–42.

Ruan Rongping (阮荣平) and Zheng Fengtian (郑风田) (2012) 'Shichanghua jincheng zhong de jiazu wangluo yu xiangcun qiye' (市场化进程中的宗族网络与乡村企业), *China Economic Quarterly*, 12(1): 331–356.

Rühle, S. (2012) *Guanxi Capitalism in China. The Role of Private Enterprises and Networks for Economic Development*, Marburg: Metropolis.

Russell, J.A. and Yik, M.S.M. (1996) 'Emotion Among the Chinese'. In Bond, M.H., ed., *The Handbook of Chinese Psychology*, Hong Kong: Oxford University Press, pp. 166–188.

Saari, J.L. (1982) 'Breaking the Hold of Tradition: The Self-group Interface in Transitional China'. In Greenblatt, S.L., Wilson, R.W. and Wilson, A.A., eds, *Social Interaction in Chinese Society*, New York: Praeger, pp. 28–67.

Saich, T. and Hu, B. (2012) *Chinese Village, Global Market. New Collectives and Rural Development*, New York: Palgrave Macmillan.

Said, E. (1978) *Orientalism: Western Conceptions of the Orient*, London: Penguin.

Sanchez, R. and Mahoney, J.T. (2013) 'Modularity and Economic Organization: Concepts, Theory, Observations, and Predictions'. In Grandori, A., ed., *Handbook of Economic Organization: Integrating Economic and Organization Theory*, Cheltenham: Edward Elgar, pp. 383–399.

Sanchez-Burks, J., Lee, F., Choi, I., Nisbett, R. and Koo, J. (2003) 'Conversing Across Cultures: East–West Communication Styles in Work and Non-work Contexts', *Journal of Psychology and Social Psychology*, 85(2): 363–372.

Sangren, P.S. (1984) 'Traditional Chinese Corporations: Beyond Kinship', *The Journal of Asian Studies*, 43(3): 391–415.

Sapienza, P., Toldra-Simats, A. and Zingales, L. (2013) 'Understanding Trust', *The Economic Journal*, 123: 1313–1332.

Schak, D.C. (1991) 'Assistance to Poor Relatives: Chinese Kinship Reconsidered'. In Chen, E.K.Y., Williams, J.F. and Wong, J., eds, *Taiwan: Economy, Society and History*, Hong Kong: Hong Kong University Press, pp. 206–234.

Schak, D.C. (2002) 'Chineseness and Chinese Capitalism in East and Southeast Asia'. In Douw, L., Huang, C. and Ip, D., eds, *Rethinking Chinese Transnational Enterprises. Cultural Affinity and Business Strategies*, London: Curzon, pp. 83–101.

Schefold, B., ed. (2002) *Huan Kuan: Yan Tie Lun, Vademecum zu einem Klassiker der chinesischen Wirtschaftsdebatten*, Düsseldorf: Handelsblatt.

Schelling, T.C. (1978) *Micromotives and Macrobehavior*, New York and London: Norton.

Schlicht, E. (1998) *On Custom in the Economy*, Oxford: Oxford University Press.

Schluchter, W. (1983) 'Einleitung: Max Webers Konfuzianismusstudie – Versuch einer Einordnung'. In Schluchter, W., ed., *Max Webers Studie über Konfuzianismus und Daoismus. Interpretation und Kritik*, Frankfurt am Main: Suhrkamp, pp. 11–54.

Schmid, M. (2011) 'The Logic of Mechanistic Explanations in the Social Sciences'. In Demeulenaire, P., ed., *Analytical Sociology and Social Mechanisms*, Cambridge: Cambridge University Press, pp. 136–153.

Schmidt, V.A. (2008) 'Discursive Institutionalism: The Explanatory Power of Ideas and Discourse', *Annual Review of Political Science*, 11: 303–326.

Schmidt, V.A. (2011) 'Reconciling Ideas and Institutions Through Discursive Institutionalism'. In Béland, D. and Cox, R.H., eds, *Ideas and Politics in Social Science Research*, Oxford: Oxford University Press, pp. 47–65.

Schmidt-Dörr, T. (2015) 'Neue Strukturen für das Hochschulsystem in China: Akademikerarbeitslosigkeit versus Fachkräftemangel', *Forschung und Lehre*, 10(15): 838–840.

Schmidt-Glintzer, H. (1983) 'Viele Pfade oder ein Weg? Betrachtungen zur Durchsetzung der konfuzianischen Orthopraxie'. In Schluchter, W., ed., *Max Webers Studie über Konfuzianismus und Daoismus. Interpretation und Kritik*, Frankfurt am Main: Suhrkamp, pp. 298–341.

Schmidt-Trenz, H.-J. (1990) *Außenhandel und Territorialität des Rechts – Grundlegung einer Neuen Institutionenökonomik des Außenhandels*, Baden-Baden: Nomos.

Schneider, H.K. (1974) *Economic Man. The Anthropology of Economics*, New York: Free Press.

Schoppa, R.K. (1989) *Xiang Lake – Nine Centuries of Chinese Life*, New Haven, CT, and London: Yale University Press.

Schubert, G. (2008) 'One-Party Rule and the Question of Legitimacy in Contemporary China: Preliminary Thoughts on Setting up a New Research Agenda', *Journal of Contemporary China*, 17(54): 191–204.

Schubert, G. and Ahlers, A. (2012) 'County and Township Cadres as a Strategic Group: "Building a New Socialist Countryside" in Three Provinces', *The China Journal*, 67: 67–86.

Schüler-Zhou, Y., Schüller, M. and Clement, M. (2013) 'Internationalisierung chinesischer Unternehmen', *Die Betriebswirtschaft*, 73(5): 361–378.

Schumpeter, J.A. (1950) *Capitalism, Socialism, and Democracy, Third Edition*, New York: Harper.

Schurmann, F. (1966) *Ideology and Organization in Communist China*, Berkeley and LA: University of California Press.

Schützeichel, R. (2015) 'Mechanismen, Ereignisse. Zur gegenwärtigen Forschungslage in der Soziologie sozialer Prozesse'. In Schützeichel, R. and Jordan, S., eds, *Prozesse. Formen, Dynamiken, Erklärungen*, Wiesbaden: Springer VS, pp. 87–148.

Schwartz, B.I. (1987) 'The Primacy of the Political Order in East Asian Societies: Some Preliminary Generalizations'. In Schram, S., ed., *Foundations and Limits of State Power in China*, London and Hong Kong: Oxford University Press, pp. 1–11.

Searle, J.R. (1995) *The Construction of Social Reality*, New York: Free Press.

Searle, J.R. (2005) 'What is an Institution?', *Journal of Institutional Economics*, 1(1): 1–22.

Searle, J.R. (2010) *Making the Social World. The Structure of Human Civilization*, Oxford: Oxford University Press.

Sen, A. (1984) *Commodities and Capabilities*, reprinted 1999, New Delhi: Oxford University Press.

Sen, A. (2002) *Rationality and Freedom*, Cambridge and London: Belknap Press.

Sen, A. (2007) *Identity and Violence: The Illusion of Destiny*, London: Penguin.

Sen, A. (2009) *The Idea of Justice*, Cambridge: Cambridge University Press.

Senellart, M. (2004) 'Situation du cours'. In Foucault, M., *Sécurité, territoire, population. Cours au Collège de France, 1977–1978*, Paris: Seuil, pp. 381–411.

Shambaugh, D. (2008a) *China's Communist Party. Atrophy and Adaptation*, Berkeley, LA and London: University of California Press.

Shambaugh, D. (2008b) 'Training China's Political Elite: The Party School System', *The China Quarterly*, 196: 827–844.

Shavitt, S., Torelli, C.J. and Riemer, H. (2011) 'Horizontal and Vertical Individualism and Collectivism: Implications for Understanding Psychological Process'. In Gelfland, M.J., Chiu, C.-Y. and Hong, Y.-Y., eds, *Advances in Culture and Psychology, Volume One*, Oxford and New York: Oxford University Press, pp. 309–350.

Sheng Hong (盛洪) (2010) *Wei wan shi kai taiping* (为万世开天平) *Creating Peace Forever. Yi ge jingji xuejia dui wenming wenti de sikao* (一个经济学家对文明问题的思考), Beijing.

Sheng, H. and Zhao, N. (2013) *China's State-owned Enterprises: Nature, Performance and Reform*, Singapore: World Scientific.

Sheng, Y. (1993) 'The Capital Sources of China's Industrialization', *The Developing Economies,* 31(2): 173–206.

Shiba, Y. (1977) 'Ningbo and its Hinterland'. In Skinner, G.W., ed., *The City in Late Imperial China,* Stanford, CA: Stanford University Press, pp. 391–440.

Shih, V., Adolph, C. and Liu, M. (2012) 'Getting Ahead in the Communist Party: Explaining the Advancement of Central Committee Members in China', *America Political Science Review,* 106(1): 166–186.

Shih, W., Chie, C.-F. and Wang, J.-C. (2010) *Shanzhai! MediaTek and the 'White Box' Handset Market,* HBS Case Study 9–610–081.

Shirk, S.L. (1984) 'The Decline of Virtuocracy in China'. in Watson, J.L., ed., *Class and Social Stratification in Post-Revolution China,* Cambridge: Cambridge University Press, pp. 56–83.

Shue, V. (1988) *The Reach of the State. Sketches of the Chinese Body Politic,* Stanford, CA: Stanford University Press.

Siems, M. and Deakin, S. (2010) 'Comparative Law and Finance: Past, Present, and Future Research', *Journal of Institutional and Theoretical Economics,* 166(1): 120–140.

Sigley, G. (2006) 'Chinese Governmentalities: Government, Governance and the Socialist Market Economy', *Economy and Society,* 35(4): 487–508.

Silin, R.H. (1976) *Leadership and Values. The Organization of Large-scale Taiwanese Enterprises,* Cambridge, MA, and London: Harvard University Press.

Siu, H.F. (1989) *Agents and Victims in South China. Accomplices of Rural Revolution,* New Haven, CT, and London: Yale University Press.

Siu, H.F. (1995) 'Community Festivals in Post-Mao South China: Economic Transformation and Cultural Improvisation'. In *China Review 1995,* Hong Kong: Chinese University Press, ch. 16.

Skinner, G.W. (1964/1965) 'Marketing and Social Structure in Rural China, Parts I–III', *The Journal of Asian Studies,* 24(1): 3–43, 24(2): 195–228, 24(3): 363–399.

Skinner, G.W. (1977a) 'Introduction: Urban Development in Imperial China'. In Skinner, G.W., ed., *The City in Late Imperial China,* Stanford, CA: Stanford University Press, pp. 3–32.

Skinner, G.W. (1977b) 'Introduction: Urban and Rural in Chinese Society'. In Skinner, G.W., ed., *The City in Late Imperial China,* Stanford, CA: Stanford University Press, pp. 253–274.

Skinner, G.W. (1977c) 'Cities and the Hierarchy of Local Systems'. In Skinner, G.W., ed., *The City in Late Imperial China,* Stanford, CA: Stanford University Press, pp. 275–352.

Skinner, G.W. (1985a) 'The Structure of Chinese History', *The Journal of Asian Studies,* 44(2): 271–292.

Skinner, G.W. (1985b) 'Rural Marketing in China: Repression and Revival', *The China Quarterly,* 103: 393–413.

Skyrms, B. (2004) *The Stag Hunt and the Evolution of Social Structure,* Cambridge: Cambridge University Press.

Skyrms, B. (2010) *Signals. Evolution, Learning, and Information,* Oxford: Oxford University Press.

Smith, A. ([1759] 1976) *The Theory of Moral Sentiments,* Oxford: Oxford University Press.

Smith, D. (2012) 'Guanxi, Mianzi, and Business: The Impact of Culture on Corporate Governance in China', *Private Sector Opinion,* 26, Washington, DC: International Finance Corporation.

Smith, G. (2010) 'The Hollow State: Rural Governance in China', *The China Quarterly*, 203: 601–618.

Smyth, R. (1997) 'The Township and Village Enterprise Sector as a Specific Example of Regionalism – Some General Lessons for Socialist Transformation', *Economic Systems*, 21(3): 235–265.

Sobel, J. (2002) 'Can We Trust Social Capital?', *Journal of Economic Literature*, 40: 139–154.

Sobel, J. (2005) 'Interdependent Preferences and Reciprocity', *Journal of Economic Literature*, 43(2): 392–436.

Solinger, D.J. (1989) 'Urban Reform and Relational Contracting in Post-Mao China: An Interpretation of the Transition from Plan to Market', *Studies in Comparative Communism*, 22: 171–186.

Solomon, R.H. (1971) *Mao's Revolution and the Chinese Political Culture*, Berkeley, LA and London: University of California Press.

Sonobe, T., Hu, D. and Otsuka, K. (2006) 'Industrial Development in the Inland Region of China: A Case Study of the Motorcycle Industry', *Journal of Comparative Economics*, 34(4): 818–838.

Sperber, D. (2011) 'A Naturalistic Ontology for Mechanistic Explanations in the Social Sciences'. In Demeulenaere, P., ed., *Analytical Sociology and Social Mechanisms*, Cambridge: Cambridge University Press, pp. 64–77.

Spiethoff, A. ([1932] 1971) 'Die allgemeine Volkswirtschaftslehre als geschichtliche Theorie. Die Wirtschaftsstile'. In Schachtschabel, H.G., ed., *Wirtschaftsstufen und Wirtschaftsordnungen*, Darmstadt: Wissenschaftliche Buchgesellschaft, pp. 123–155.

Stacey, J. (1983) *Patriarchy and Socialist Revolution in China*, Berkeley, LA and London: University of California Press.

Stafford, Ch. (2000) 'Chinese Patriliny and the Cycles of Yang and Laiwang'. In Carsten, J., ed., *Cultures of Relatedness: New Approaches to the Study of Kinship*, Cambridge: Cambridge University Press, pp. 35–54.

Stafford, Ch. (2006) 'Deception, Corruption and the Chinese Ritual Economy'. In Latham, K., Thompson, S. and Klein, J., eds, *Consuming China: Approaches to Cultural Change in Contemporary China*, London: Routledge Curzon, pp. 42–55.

Stenner, K. (2005) *The Authoritarian Dynamic*, Cambridge: Cambridge University Press.

Storper, M. (1995) 'The Resurgence of Regional Economies, Ten Years Later: The Region as a Nexus of Untraded Interdependencies', *European Urban and Regional Studies*, 2(3): 91–221.

Stover, L.E. (1974) *The Cultural Ecology of Chinese Civilization. Peasants and Elites in the Last of the Agrarian States*, New York: Mentor Books.

Strauch, J. (1983) 'Community and Kinship in Southeastern China: The View from the Multilineage Villages of Hong Kong', *The Journal of Asian Studies*, 43(1): 21–50.

Sutton, D.S. (2007) 'Ritual, Cultural Standardization, and Orthopraxy in China: Reconsidering James L. Watson's Ideas', *Modern China*, 33(1): 3–21.

Tabellini, G. (2008a) 'Institutions and Culture', *Journal of the European Economic Association*, 6(2–3): 255–294.

Tabellini, G. (2008b) 'The Scope of Cooperation: Values and Incentives', *The Quarterly Journal of Economics*, 123(3): 905–950.

Talhelm, T., Zhang, X., Oishi, S., Shimin, C., Duan, D., Lan, X. and Kitayama. S. (2014) 'Large-scale Psychological Differences within China Explained by Rice versus Wheat Agriculture', *Science*, 344(6184): 603–608.

Tam, W.L. (2011) 'Communal Worship and Festivals in Chinese Villages'. In Palmer, D., Shive, G. and Wickeri, P.L., eds, *Chinese Religious Life*, Oxford: Oxford University Press, pp. 30–49.

Tan Tongxue (谭同学) (2010) *Qiao cun you dao. Zhuanxing xiangcun de daode quanli yu shehui jiegou* (桥村有道。转型乡村的道德权利与社会结构), Beijing: San lian shudian.

Tan Zhibo (谭之博), Zhou Li'an (周黎安) and Zhao Yue (赵岳) (2015) 'Sheng guan xian gaige, caizheng fenquan yu minsheng. Jiyu 'peichafa'de guji' (省管县改革，财政分权与民生。基于倍差法的估计), *China Economic Quarterly*, 14(3): 1093–1114.

Tang Beibei (2015) '"Not Rural but Not Urban": Community Governance in China's Urban Villages', *The China Quarterly*, 223: 724–744.

Taylor, C.M. (1989) *Sources of the Self. The Making of Modern Identity*, Cambridge, MA: Harvard University Press.

Teets, J.C. (2013) 'Let Many Civil Societies Bloom: The Rise of Consultative Authoritarianism in China', *The China Quarterly*, 213: 19–38.

Tenev, S. and Zhang, C. (2002) *Corporate Governance and Enterprise Reform in China. Building the Institutions of Modern Markets*, Washington, DC: World Bank and IFC.

Thaxton, R. (1983) *China Turned Rightside Up: Revolutionary Legitimacy in the Peasant World*, New Haven, CT: Yale University Press.

Thøgerson, S. (2011) 'Building a New Socialist Countryside. Model Villages in Hubei'. In Alpermann, B., ed., *Politics and Markets in Rural China*, Abingdon and New York: Routledge, pp. 172–186.

Thornton, P.M. (2013) 'The Advance of the Party: Transformation or Takeover of Urban Grassroots Society?', *The China Quarterly*, 213: 1–18.

Thun, E. (2006) *Changing Lanes in China: Foreign Direct Investment, Local Governments and Auto Sector Development*, Cambridge: Cambridge University Press.

Tian, K. and Dong, L. (2011) *Consumer-citizens of China. The Role of Foreign Brands in the Imagined Future China*, Abingdon and New York: Routledge.

Timmer, M.P., Erumban, A.A., Los, B., Stehrer, R. and de Vries, G.J. (2014) 'Slicing Up Global Value Chains', *Journal of Economic Perspectives*, 28(2): 99–118.

Ting, K.C. (1974) *Nord- und Südchina. Unterschiede der Wirtschafts- und Sozialstruktur aufgrund der natürlichen und kulturellen Voraussetzungen*, Nürnberg.

Tomba, L. (2004) 'Creating an Urban Middle Class: Social Engineering in Beijing', *The China Journal*, 51: 1–26.

Townsend, J. (1992) 'Chinese Nationalism', *The Australian Journal of Chinese Affairs*, 27: 97–130.

Trappel, R. (2011) 'Agrarian Change in China: The Commodification of Collective Land'. In Alpermann, B., ed., *Politics and Markets in Rural China*, Abingdon und New York: Routledge, pp. 15–29.

Triandis, H.C. (1995) *Individualism and Collectivism*, Boulder, CO: Sharpe.

Tsai, Chung-min (2014) 'Regulating China's Power Sector: Creating an Independent Regulator without Autonomy', *The China Quarterly*, 218: 452–473.

Tsai, J.L., Knutson, B. and Fung, H.F. (2006) 'Cultural Variation in Affect Valuation', *Journal of Personality and Social Psychology*, 90(2): 288–307.

Tsai, K.S. (2002) *Back-alley Banking. Private Entrepreneurs in China*, Ithaca, NY, und London: Cornell University Press.

Tsai, L.L. (2002) 'Cadres, Temple and Lineage Institutions, and Governance in Rural China', *The China Journal*, 48: 1–28.

Tsai, L.L. (2007) *Accountability without Democracy, Solidary Groups and Public Goods Provision in Rural China,* Cambridge: Cambridge University Press.

Tsai, L.L. (2008) 'Understanding the Falsification of Village Income Statistics', *The China Quarterly,* 196: 805–826.

Tsai, W.-H. and Dean, N. (2014) 'Experimentation under Hierarchy in Local Conditions: Cases of Political Reform in Guangdong and Sichuan', *The China Quarterly,* 218: 339–358.

Tsui, A.S. (2004) 'Contributing to Global Management Knowledge: A Case for High Quality Indigenous Research', *Asia Pacific Journal of Management,* 21(4): 491–513.

Tsui, A.S. and Jia, L. (2013) 'Editorial: Calling for Humanistic Scholarship in China', *Management and Organization Review,* 9(1): 1–15.

Tsui, A.S., Wang, H. and Xin, K.R. (2006) 'Organizational Culture in China: An Analysis of Culture Dimensions and Culture Types', *Management and Organization Review,* 2(3): 345–376.

Tsui, K.-Y. and Wang, Y. (2004) 'Between Separate Stoves and a Single Menu: Fiscal Decentralization in China', *The China Quarterly,* 177: 71–91.

Tung, J. (2007) *Eu Yan Sang: Reviving a Traditional Family Business with Modern Business Principles,* Stanford, CA: Graduate School of Business Case OB-65.

Tuomela, R. (1995) *The Importance of Us. A Philosophical Study of Basic Social Notions.* Stanford, CA: Stanford University Press.

Tuomela, R. (2007) *The Philosophy of Sociality,* Oxford: Oxford University Press.

Tuomela, R. (2011) 'Searle's New Construction of Social Reality', *Analysis Reviews,* 71(4): 707–719.

Twitchett, D. (1979) 'Introduction'. In Twitchett, D., ed., *The Cambridge History of China, Volume 3, Sui and T'ang China, 589–906, Part I,* Cambridge: Cambridge University Press, pp. 1–47.

Unirule Institute (2015) *Zhongguo minying qiye shengcun yu fazhan huanjing zhishu – Guangdong yu Zhejiang baogao* (中国民营企业生存与发展环境指数—广东与浙江省报告), Bejing, mimeo.

Vanberg, V. (1994) *Rules and Choice in Economics,* London: Routledge.

Vandermeersch, L. (1985) 'An Enquiry into the Chinese Conception of Law'. In Schram, S., ed., *The Scope of State Power in China,* London and Hong Kong: Chinese University Press, pp. 3–26.

Vanderschraaf, P. and Sillari, G. (2014) 'Common Knowledge'. In Zalta, E.N., ed., *The Stanford Encyclopedia of Philosophy* (spring edition) (ed.), http://plato.stanford.edu/archives/spr2014/entries/common-knowledge/.

Veblen, T. ([1899] 1965) *The Theory of the Leisure Class,* New York: Kelley.

Veblen, T. ([1914] 1990) *The Instinct of Workmanship and the State of Industrial Arts,* New Brunswick, NJ, and London: Transaction.

Voigtländer, N. and Voth, H.-J. (2013) 'Gifts of Mars: Warfare and Europe's Early Rise to Riches', *Journal of Economic Perspectives,* 27(4): 165–186.

Von Weizsäcker, C.C. (2011) *Homo Oeconomicus Adaptivus – Die Logik des Handelns bei veränderlichen Präferenzen,* Preprints of the Max Planck Institute for Research on Collective Goods 2011(10).

Vromen, J.J. (2011) 'Routines as Multilevel Mechanisms', *Journal of Institutional Economics,* 7(2): 175–196.

Wade, R. (1990) *Governing the Market: Economic Theory and the Role of the Government in East Asian Industrialization,* Princeton, NJ: Princeton University Press.

Walder, A.G. (1983) 'Organized Dependency and Cultures of Authority in Chinese Industry', *Journal of Asian Studies*, 43(1): 51–76.

Walder, A.G. (1986) *Communist Neo-traditionalism: Work and Authority in Chinese Industry*, Berkeley: University of California Press.

Wang, F. and Mason, A. (2008) 'The Demographic Factor in China's Transition'. In Brandt, L. and Rawski, T., eds, *China's Great Economic Transformation*, Cambridge: Cambridge University Press, pp. 136–166.

Wang Jiangyu (2010) 'The Political Logic of Securities Regulation in China'. In G.H. Yu, ed., *The Development of the Chinese Legal System: Changes and Challenges*, Abingdon and New York: Routledge, pp. 227–250.

Wang Jiangyu (2014) 'The Political Logic of Corporate Governance in China's State-owned Enterprises', *Cornell International Law Journal*, 47: 631–669.

Wang Jianhua (汪建华), Zheng Guanghuai (郑广怀), Meng Quan (孟泉) and Shen Yuan (沈原) (2015) 'Zai zhiduhua yu jijinhua zhi jian: Zhongguo xin shengdai nongmingong de zuzhihua qushi' (在制度化与激进化之间，中国新生代农民工的组织化趋势), *Twenty-First Century*, 150: 4–18.

Wang Jing (2008) *Brand New China. Advertising, Media, and Commercial Culture*, Cambridge, MA, and London: Harvard University Press.

Wang, J. (2012) 'Shifting Boundaries between the State and Society: Village Cadres as New Activists in Collective Petition', *The China Quarterly*, 211: 697–717.

Wang Shaoguang and Hu Angang (1995) 'Wang Shaoguang Proposal, Parts (I) and (II)', *Chinese Economic Studies*, 28(3), 28(4).

Wang, X. (2002) 'The Post-Communist Personality: The Spectre of China's Capitalist Market Reforms', *The China Journal*, 47: 1–18.

Wang Xiaoyi (王晓毅) and Zhu Chengbao (朱成堡) (1996) 'Zhongguo xiangcun de minying qiye yu jiazu jingji. Zhejiang sheng Cangnan xian Xiangdong cun diaocha' (中国乡村的民营企业与家族经济。浙江省苍南县项东村调查). In Chen Jiyuan (陈吉元) and Herrmann-Pillath, C. (He Mengbi) (何梦笔), eds, *Dangdai Zhongguo de cunzhuang yu cunluo wenhua congshu* (当代中国的村庄与村落文化丛书), Vol. 5, Taiyuan: Shanxi jingji chubanshe.

Wang, Y. and Minzner, C. (2015) 'The Rise of the Chinese Security State', *The China Quarterly*, 222: 339–359.

Wank, D. (1996) 'The Institutional Practice of Market Clientelism: Guanxi and Private Business in a South China City', *The China Quarterly*, 144: 820–838.

Wank, D. (2002) 'Business–State Clientelism in China: Decline or Evolution?' In Gold, T., Guthrie, D. and Wank, D., eds, *Social Connections in China. Institutions, Culture, and the Changing Nature of Guanxi*, Cambridge: Cambridge University Press, pp. 97–115.

Wasserman, S. and Faust, K. (1994) *Social Network Analysis. Methods and Applications*, Cambridge: Cambridge University Press.

Watanabe, M. (2014) *The Disintegration of Production: Firm Strategy and Industrial Development in China*, Cheltenham: Edward Elgar.

Watson, J.L. (1986) 'Anthropological Overview: The Development of Chinese Descent Groups'. In Ebrey, P.B. and Watson, J.L., eds, *Kinship Organization in Late Imperial China, 1000–1949*, Berkeley, LA and London: University of Califormia Press, pp. 274–292.

Watson, J. and Rawski, E., eds (1988) *Death Ritual in Late Imperial and Modern China*, Berkeley: University of California Press.

Watson, J.L. and Watson, R.S. (2004) *Village Life in Hong Kong. Politics, Gender, and Ritual in the New Territories*, Hong Kong: Chinese University Press.

Watt, J.R. (1972) *The District Magistrate in Late Imperial China*, New York and London: Columbia University Press.

Watt, J.R. (1977) 'The Yamen and Urban Administration'. In Skinner, G.W., ed., *The City in Late Imperial China*, Stanford, CA: Stanford University Press, pp. 353–390.

Weber, M. (1985) *Wirtschaft und Gesellschaft*, Studienausgabe 8, Auflage, Tübingen: Mohr Siebeck.

Weber, M. (1991) *Die Wirtschaftsethik der Weltreligionen: Konfuzianismus und Taoismus, Schriften 1915–1920*, Studienausgabe, Tübingen: Mohr.

Wedell-Wedellsborg, A. (2010) 'Between Self and Community: The Individual in Contemporary Chinese Literature'. In Hansen, M.H. and Svarverud, R., eds., *iChina: The Rise of the Individual in Modern Chinese Society*, Copenhagen: NIAS Press, pp. 164–192.

Wedeman, F. (2012) *Double Paradox: Rapid Growth and Rising Corruption in China*, Ithaca, NY: Cornell University Press.

Wegner, G. (2014) *Capitalist Transformation Without Political Participation – German Captalism in the First Half of the 19th Century*, Freiburg Discussion Papers on Constitutional Economics, 13/14.

Wei, S.-J. and Zhang, X. (2011) 'The Competitive Saving Motive: Evidence from Rising Sex Ratios and Savings Rates in China', *Journal of Political Economy*, 119(3): 511–564.

Wei Zhihua (魏志华), Lin Yaqing (林亚清), Wu Yuhui (吴育辉) and Li Changqing (李常青) (2013) 'Jiazuqiye yanji: yige wenxian jiliang fenxi' (家族企业研究。一个文献计量分析)，*China Economic Quarterly*, 13(1): 27–56.

Weller, R.P. (2004) 'Worship, Teachings, and State Power in China and Taiwan'. In Kirby, W.C., ed., *Realms of Freedom in Modern China*, Stanford, CA: Stanford University Press, pp. 285–316.

Weller, R.P. (2011) 'Chinese Cosmology and the Environment'. In Palmer, D., Shive, G. and Wickeri, P.L., eds, *Chinese Religious Life*, Oxford: Oxford University Press, pp. 124–138.

Wellman, B., Chen, W. and Dong, W. (2002) 'Networking Guanxi'. In Gold, T., Guthrie, D. and Wank, D., eds, *Social Connections in China. Institutions, Culture, and the Changing Nature of Guanxi*, Cambridge: Cambridge University Press, pp. 221–241.

White, D.R. (2011) 'Kinship, Class, and Community'. In Scott, J. and Carrington, P., eds, *The Sage Handbook of Social Network Analysis*, Los Angeles: Sage, pp. 129–147.

White, H.C. (2008) *Identity and Control: How Social Formations Emerge*, Princeton, NJ: Princeton University Press.

Whyte, M.K. (1997) 'The Fate of Filial Obligations in Urban China', *The China Journal*, 38: 1–32.

Whyte, M.K. (2010) *Myth of the Social Volcano. Perceptions of Inequality and Distributive Injustice in Contemporary China*, Stanford, CA: Stanford University Press.

Whyte, M.K., ed. (2010) *One Country, Two Societies: Rural–Urban Inequality in Contemporary China*, Cambridge: Cambridge University Press.

Whyte, M.K. (2016) 'China's Dormant and Active Social Volcanoes', *The China Journal*, 75: 9–37.

Whyte, M.K. and Parish, W.L. (1984) *Urban Life in Contemporary China,* Chicago, IL, and London: University of Chicago Press.

Wilhelm, R. (1930) *Chinesische Wirtschaftspsychologie,* Leipzig: Deutsche Wissenschaftliche Buchhandlung.

Will, P.-E. (1990) *Bureaucracy and Famine in Eighteenth-century China,* Stanford, CA: Stanford University Press.

Williamson, O. (1985) *The Economic Institutions of Capitalism,* New York: Free Press.

Wilson, R.W. (1981) 'Moral Behavior in Chinese Society: A Theoretical Perspective'. In Wilson, R.W., Greenblatt, S.L. and Wilson, A.A., eds, *Moral Behavior in Chinese Society,* New York: Praeger, pp. 1–20.

Wilson, S. (1997) 'The Cash Nexus and Social Networks: Mutual Aid and Gifts in Contemporary Shanghai Villages', *The China Journal,* 37: 91–115.

Wilson, S. (2002) 'Face, Norms, and Instrumentality'. In Gold, T., Guthrie, D. and Wank, D., eds, *Social Connections in China. Institutions, Culture, and the Changing Nature of Guanxi,* Cambridge: Cambridge University Press, pp. 163–177.

Witt, U. (2003a) *The Evolving Economy. Essays on the Evolutionary Approach to Economics,* Cheltenham and Northampton: Edward Elgar.

Witt, U. (2003b) 'Economic Policy Making in Evolutionary Perspective', *Journal of Evolutionary Economics,* 13(2): 77–94.

Wittgenstein, L. ([1971] 1958) *Philosophische Untersuchungen,* Frankfurt am Main: Suhrkamp.

Wohlgemuth, M. (2000) 'Political Entrepreneurship and Bidding for Political Monopoly', *Journal of Evolutionary Economics,* 10(3): 273–295.

Wohlgemuth, M. (2002) 'Evolutionary Approaches to Politics', *Kyklos,* 55(2): 223–247.

Wolf, M. (1972) *Women and the Family in Rural Taiwan,* Stanford, CA: Stanford University Press.

Wong, C.P.W. (2009) 'Rebuilding Government for the 21st Century: Can China Incrementally Reform the Public Sector?', *The China Quarterly,* 200: 929–952.

Wong, C.P.W. and Bird, R.M. (2008) 'China's Fiscal System: A Work in Progress'. In Brandt, L. and Rawski, T., eds, *China's Great Economic Transformation,* Cambridge: Cambridge University Press, pp. 429–466.

Wong, R.B. (1997) *China Transformed: Historical Change and the Limits of European Experience,* Ithaca, NY: Cornell University Press.

Wong, S.-L. (1985) 'The Chinese Family Firm: A Model', *British Journal of Sociology,* 36(1): 58–72.

Wong, S.W. (2015) 'Land Requisitions and State–Village Power Restructuring in Southern China', *The China Quarterly,* 224: 888–908.

Woolcock, M. (1998) 'Social Capital and Economic Development: Toward a Theoretical Synthesis and Policy Framework', *Theory and Society,* 27: 151–208.

Woon, Y.-F. (1989) 'Social Change and Continuity in South China: Overseas Chinese and the Guan Lineage of Kaiping County', *The China Quarterly,* 118: 322–344.

World Bank (2012) *China 2030: Building a Modern, Harmonious, and Creative High-income Society,* Washington, DC: World Bank.

World Bank (2014a) *Urban China. Toward Efficient, Inclusive, and Sustainable Urbanization,* Washington, DC: World Bank.

World Bank (2014b) *China Economic Update. Special Topic: An Update of China's Fiscal and Tax Reforms,* Beijing: World Bank.

World Trade Organization (2013) *World Trade Report 2013. Factors Shaping the Future of World Trade*, Geneva: WTO.

World Trade Organization (2014) *World Trade Report 2014. Trade and Development: Recent Trends and the Role of the WTO*, Geneva: WTO.

Wu Chongqing (吴重庆) (2014) *Sun cun de lu: hougeming shidai de ren gui shen* (孙村的路。后革命时代的人鬼神)， Beijing: Falü chubanshe.

Wu Chongqing (吴重庆) (2015) '"Beyond the Boundary": A Countermovement to the Hollowing-out of Rural China', *Modern China*, 41(4): 355–372.

Wu Jieh-min (2010) 'Rural Migrant Workers and China's Differential Citizenship: A Comparative Institutional Analysis'. In Whyte, M.K., ed., *One Country, Two Societies: Rural–Urban Inequality in Contemporary China*, Cambridge: Cambridge University Press, pp. 55–84.

Wu Jiyan (伍继延) (2014) *Zai shang yan shang? Xiang shang wenhua yu xiandai shanghui* (在商言商？湘商文化与现代商会)，Peking: Zhongguo shehui chubanshe.

Wu, J.C.H. (1967) 'Chinese Legal and Political Philosophy'. In Moore, Ch., ed., *The Chinese Mind. Essentials of Chinese Philosophy and Culture*, Honolulu: The University Press of Hawaii, pp. 213–237.

Wu, Y.-M. (2006) 'Hofstede's Cultural Dimensions 30 Years Later: A Study of Taiwan and the United States', *Intercultural Communication Studies*, 1: 33–42.

Xiao Lou (萧楼) (2010) *Xia cun shehui. Zhongguo 'jiangnan' nongcun richang shenghuo he shehui jiegou (1976–2006)* (夏村社会。中国《江南》农村的日常生活和社会结构, 1976–2006), Beijing: Sanlian shudian.

Xiao Tangbiao (肖唐镖), ed. (2001) *Cunzhi zhong de zongzu. Dui jiuge cun de diaocha yu yanjiu* (村治中的宗族。对九个村的调查与研究), Shanghai: Shanghai shudian chubanshe.

Xin, K. and Wang, H. (2011) 'Culture Clash in the Boardroom', *Harvard Business Review*, September, Reprint R1109L.

Xiong Yihan (2015) 'The Broken Ladder: Why Education Provides No Upward Mobility for Migrant Children in China', *The China Quarterly*, 221: 161–185.

Xu Chenggang (2011) 'The Fundamental Institutions of China's Reforms and Development', *Journal of Economic Literature*, 49(4): 1076–1151.

Xue, H. (2009) 'Oursourcing in China: Walmart and Chinese Manufacturers'. In Chan, A., ed., *Walmart in China*, Ithaca, NY, and London: Cornell University Press, pp. 34–53.

Yamagishi, T. (2012) 'Micro–Macro Dynamics of the Cultural Construction of Reality. A Niche Construction Approach to Culture'. In Gelfland, M.J., Chiu, C.-Y. and Hong Y.-Y., eds, *Advances in Culture and Psychology, Volume One*, Oxford and New York: Oxford University Press, pp. 251–308.

Yan Hairong (2003) 'Neoliberal Governmentality and Neohumanism: Organizing *Suzhi*/Value Flow through Labor Recruitment Networks', *Cultural Anthropology*, 18(4): 493–523.

Yan, X. (2012) '"To Get Rich Is Not Only Glorious": Economic Reform and the New Entrepreneurial Party Secretaries', *The China Quarterly*, 210: 335–354.

Yan Yunxiang (1996a) *The Flow of Gifts. Reciprocity and Social Networks in a Chinese Village*, Stanford, CA: Stanford University Press.

Yan Yunxiang (1996b) 'The Culture of Guanxi in a North China Village', *The China Journal*, 35: 1–26.

Yan Yunxiang (2010) 'The Chinese Path to Individualization', *British Journal of Sociology*, 61(3): 489–512.

Yan Yunxiang (2012) 'Food Safety and Social Risk in Contemporary China', *The Journal of Asian Studies*, 17(3): 705–729.

Yang, D.T. (2012) 'Aggregate Savings and External Imbalances in China', *Journal of Economic Perspectives*, 26(4): 125–146.

Yang Fenggang (2006) 'The Red, Black and Grey Markets for Religion in China', *Sociological Quarterly*, 47: 93–122.

Yang Fenggang (2011) 'Market Economy and the Revival of Religions'. In Palmer, D., Shive, G. and Wickeri, P.L., eds, *Chinese Religious Life*, Oxford: Oxford University Press, pp. 209–226.

Yang, G. (2013) 'Contesting Food Safety in the Chinese Media: Between Hegemony and Counter-hegemony', *The China Quarterly*, 214: 337–355.

Yang, K.-S. (杨国枢) (1989) *Zhongguo ren de tuobian* (中国人的脱变), Taibei: Guiguan tushu gongsi.

Yang, K.-S. (杨国枢) (1996) 'Psychological Transformation of the Chinese People as a Result of Societal Modernization'. In Bond, M.H., ed., *The Handbook of Chinese Psychology*, Hong Kong: Oxford University Press, pp. 479–498.

Yang, L.-S. (1957) 'The Concept of "Pao" as a Basis for Social Relations in China'. In Fairbank, J.K., ed., *Chinese Thought and Institutions*, Chicago, IL: Chicago University Press, pp. 291–309.

Yang, M.M.-H. (1994) *Gifts, Favours and Banquets: The Art of Social Relationships in China*, Ithaca, NY: Cornell University Press.

Yang, M.M.-H. (2002) 'The Resilience of *Guanxi* and Its New Deployments. A Critique of Some New *Guanxi* Scholarship', *The China Quarterly*, 170: 459–476.

Yang, M.M.-H. (2007) 'Ritual Economy and Rural Capitalism with Chinese Characteristics'. In Held, D. and Moore, H., eds, *Cultural Politics in a Global Age: Uncertainty, Solidarity and Innovation*, Oxford: Oneworld, pp. 216–223.

Yao, S. (2002) *Confucian Capitalism. Discourse, Practice, and the Myth of Chinese Enterprise*, London and New York: Routledge.

Yao, Y. (2013) 'Village Elections and Their Impact: An Investigative Report on a Northern Chinese Village', *Modern China*, 39(1): 2–36.

Yao Zhongqiu (姚中秋) (2012a) *Huaxia zhili zhixu shi, di yi juan, tianxia* (华夏治理秩序史, 第一卷, 天下), Hainan: Hainan Publishing House.

Yao Zhongqiu (姚中秋) (2012b) *Huaxia zhili zhixu shi, di er juan, fengjian* (华夏治理秩序史, 第二卷, 封建), Hainan: Hainan Publishing House.

Yazar, O.H. (2015) 'Regulation With Chinese Characteristics, Deciphering Banking Regulation in China', *Journal of Current Chinese Affairs*, 2015(2): 135–166.

Yeo, Y. (2009) 'Between Owner and Regulator: Governing the Business of China's Telecommunications Service Industry', *The China Quarterly*, 200: 1013–1033.

Yep, R. (2004) 'Can "Tax for Fee" Reform Reduce Rural Tension in China? The Process, Progress and Limitations', *The China Quarterly*, 177: 42–70.

Yeung, H.W.-C. (2002) 'Managing Traditional Chinese Family Firms Across Borders: Four Generations of Entrepreneurship in Eu Yan Sang'. In Douw, L., Huang, C. and Ip, D., eds, *Rethinking Chinese Transnational Enterprises. Cultural Affinity and Business Strategies*, London: Curzon, pp. 184–207.

Yik, M. (2010) 'How Unique is Chinese Emotion?' In Bond, M.H., ed., *The Oxford Handbook of Chinese Psychology*, Oxford: Oxford University Press, pp. 205–220.

Young, A. (2000) 'The Razor's Edge: Distortions and Incremental Reform in the People's Republic of China', *The Quarterly Journal of Economics*, 115(4): 1091–1135.

Yu, P.K. (2011) 'TRIPS Enforcement and Developing Countries', *American University International Law Review*, 26(3): 727–782.

Yu, X. and Pun, N. (2009) 'Walmartization, Corporate Social Responsibility, and the Labor Standards of Toy Factories in South China'. In Chan, A., ed., *Walmart in China*, Ithaca, NY, and London: Cornell University Press, pp. 54–70.

Zahavi, A. and Zahavi, A. (1997) *The Handicap Principle. A Missing Piece of Darwin's Puzzle*, New York and Oxford: Oxford University Press.

Zaloom, C. (2004) 'The Productive Life of Risk', *Current Anthropology*, 19(3): 365–391.

Zelin, M. (2004a) 'Economic Freedom in Late Imperial China'. In Kirby, W.C., ed., *Realms of Freedom in Modern China*, Stanford, CA: Stanford University Press, pp. 57–83.

Zelin, M. (2004b) 'A Critique of Rights of Property in Prewar China'. In Zelin, M., Ocko, J.K. and Gardella, R., eds, *Contract and Property in Early Modern China*, Stanford,CA: Stanford University Press, pp. 17–31.

Zelin, M. (2004c) 'Managing Multiple Ownership at the Zigong Saltyard'. In Zelin, M., Ocko, J.K. and Gardella, R., eds, *Contract and Property in Early Modern China*, Stanford, CA: Stanford University Press, pp. 230–268.

Zelin, M. (2009) 'The Firm in Early Modern China', *Journal of Economic Behavior and Organization*, 71: 623–637.

Zelizer, V.A. (1997) *The Social Meaning of Money*, Princeton, NJ: Princeton University Press.

Zhai Xuewei (翟学伟) (2011) *Zhongguo ren de guanxi yuanli. Shikong zhixu, shenghuo yunian ji qi liubian* (中国人的关系原理。时空秩序，生活欲念及其流变), Beijing: Peking University Press.

Zhai Xuewei (翟学伟) (2013) *Renqing, mianzi yu quanli zaishengchan* (人情，面子与权利的再生产)，Beijing: Peking University Press.

Zhan Shaohua (2011) 'What Determines Migrant Workers' Life Chances in Contemporary China? Hukou, Social Exclusion, and the Market', *Modern China*, 37(3): 243–295.

Zhang, H. (2012) *Qingdao TGOOD Electric Corporation*, Tsinghua SEM, China Business Case Center, Case TU0035, 2012–10–30.

Zhang, J. and Peck, J. (2014) 'Variegated Capitalism, Chinese Style: Regional Models, Multi-scalar Constructions', *Regional Studies*, DOI: 10.1080/00343404. 2013.856514.

Zhang, M., Nyland, C. and Zhu, C.J. (2010) 'Hukou-based HRM in Contemporary China: The Case of Jiangsu and Shanghai', *Asia Pacific Business Review*, 16(3): 377–393.

Zhang, Q.F. and Donaldson, J.A. (2008) 'The Rise of Agrarian Capitalism with Chinese Characteristics: Agricultural Modernization, Agribusiness and Collective Land Rights', *The China Journal*, 60: 25–48.

Zhang, X., Yang, J. and Wang, S. (2011) 'China has Reached the Lewis Turning Point', *China Economic Review*, 22: 542–554.

Zhang Yi (张翼) (2002) *Guoyou qiye the jiazuhua* (国有企业的家族化), Beijing: Shehui kexue wenxian chubanshe.

Zhang, Yin-Fang (2015) 'The Regulatory Framework and Sustainable Development in China's Electricity Sector', *The China Quarterly*, 222: 475–498.

Zhang, Z.-X., Zhen, X.C., Chen, Y.-R. and Ang, S. (2014) 'Business Leadership in the Chinese Context, Trends, Findings, and Implications', *Management and Organization Review*, 10(2): 199–221.

Zhao Fasheng (赵法生) (2013) Xingwang duanjie fanben kaixin. 2012 nian rujiao de fazhan yu shuyuan fuxing baogao (兴亡断绝，返本开新。2012年儒教的发展与书院复兴报告). In Jin Ze (金泽) and Qiu Yonghui (邱永辉), eds, *Zhongguo zongjiao baogao (2013)* (中国宗教报告2013), Beijing: Social Sciences Academic Press, pp. 180–200.

Zhong, Y. (2010) 'Chinese Township Government: Between a Rock and a Hard Place'. In Chung, J.H. and Lam, T.-C., eds, *China's Local Administration. Traditions and Changes in the Sub-national Hierarchy,* Abingdon and New York: Routledge, pp. 174–195.

Zhongguo guanli moshi jiechu jiang lishihui (中国管理模式杰出奖理事会), ed. (2011) *Jiema Zhongguo guanli moshi 3* (解码中国管理模式3), Beijing: China Machine Press.

Zhongguo guanli moshi jiechu jiang lishihui (中国管理模式杰出奖理事会), ed. (2012) *Zhongguo qiye zhuanxing zhi dao. Jiema Zhongguo guanli moshi 4* (中国企业转型之道。解码中国管理模式4), Beijing: China Machine Press.

Zhongguo guanli moshi jiechu jiang lishihui (中国管理模式杰出奖理事会), ed. (2014) *Yun guanli shidai. Jiema Zhongguo guanli moshi 4* (云管理时代。解码中国管理模式6), Beijing: China Machine Press.

Zhongguo shehui kexueyuan (中国社会科学院世界经济与政治所公司治理研究中心, 国家行政学院领导人员考试测评研究中心, 甫瀚咨询公司) (2009) 2009 nian Zhongguo shangshi gongsi 100 qiang gongsi zhili pingjia 2009 (年中国上市公司100强公司治理评价), http://wenku.baidu.com/link?url=bvMviEqp_8BFCvmh4AOlONj0D2qIQgzrtS8hk3X249rBDfQgOySKI-Qm_TcDstX_MDh97xMfl3DTYETNvr5n7S-lSMHFYw0SuCJaPUfBLy (accessed 17 September 2015).

Zhou Daming (周大鸣) (2003) *Dangdai Huanan de zongzu yu shehui* (当代华南的宗族与社会), Harbin.

Zhou Hua (周华) (2014) *Zongzu bian gongsi. Guangzhou zhangx cun cunmin zuzhi jiegou de bai nian yanbian* (宗族变公司。广州长X 村村民组织结构的百年演变), Beijing: Contemporary China Publishing House.

Zhou Li'an (周黎安) and Chen Yi (陈祎) (2015) 县级财政负担与公共服务农村税费改革的影响，经济学季刊, *China Economic Quarterly,* 14(2): 417–434.

Zhou Qingzhi (周庆智) (2014) *Xianzheng zhili. Quanwei, ziyuan, zhixu* (县政治理。权威，资源，秩序), Beijing: Zhongguo shehui kexue chubanshe.

Zhou Xibing (周锡冰) (2014) *Zhongguo jiazu qiye wei shenme jiaobuliao ban. Jiemi bu wei ren zhi de jiazu qiye jiaojie ban neimu* (中国家族企业为什么交不了班。解密不为人知的家族企业交接班内幕), Beijing: Dongfang chubanshe.

Zhou Xuegang (2010) 'The Institutional Logic of Collusion among Local Governments in China', *Modern China,* 36(1): 47–78.

Zhou Xuegang (2011) 'The Autumn Harvest: Peasants and Markets in Post-collective China', *The China Quarterly,* 208: 913–931.

Zhou Xuegang (2012) 'The Road to Collective Debt in Rural China: Bureaucracies, Social Institutions, and Public Goods Provision', *Modern China,* 38(3): 271–307.

Zhou Xuegang and Yun Ai (2014) 'Capitalism without Capital: Capital Conversion and Market Making in Rural China', *The China Quarterly,* 219: 693–714.

Zhou, X., Lian, H., Leonard, O. and Ye, Y. (2013) 'A Behavioural Model of "Muddling Through" in the Chinese Bureaucracy: The Case of Environmental Protection', *The China Journal,* 70: 120–147.

Zhu Jiangang (朱健刚) (2010) *Guo yu jia zhi jian. Shanghai linli de shimin tuanti yu shequ yundong de minzuzhi* (国与家之间。上海邻里的市民团体与社区运动的民族志), Beijing: Social Sciences Academic Press (China).

Zhu, X. (2012) 'Understanding China's Growth: Past, Present, and Future', *Journal of Economic Perspectives*, 26(4): 103–124.

Zhu, Y. and Warner, M. (2004) 'Changing Patterns of Human Resource Management in Contemporary China: WTO Accession and Enterprise Responses', *Industrial Relations Journal*, 35(4): 311–328.

Zhu, Y., Lin, M., Lin, L. and Chen, J. (2013) 'The Extent of In Situ Urbanisation in China's County Areas: The Case of Fujian Province', *China Perspectives*, 2013(3): 43–52.

Zhuang Wenjia and Feng Chen (2015) '"Mediate First": The Revival of Mediation in Labour Dispute Resolution in China', *The China Quarterly*, 222: 380–402.

Zilsel, E. (1976) *Die sozialen Ursprünge der neuzeitlichen Wissenschaft*, Frankfurt am Main: Suhrkamp.

Zweig, D. and Wang, H. (2013) 'Can China Bring Back the Best? The Communist Party Organizes China's Search for Talent', *The China Quarterly*, 215: 590–615.

Zysman, J. (1994) 'How Institutions Create Historically Rooted Trajectories of Growth', *Industrial and Corporate Change*, 3(1): 243–283.

Index

For Product Safety Concerns and Information please contact our EU representative GPSR@taylorandfrancis.com
Taylor & Francis Verlag GmbH, Kaufingerstraße 24, 80331 München, Germany

www.ingramcontent.com/pod-product-compliance
Lightning Source LLC
LaVergne TN
LVHW021002300926
849160LV00007B/224
* 9 7 8 1 1 3 8 5 8 8 0 8 0 *